Rome

DK **EYEWITNESS TRAVEL**

Rome

Project Editor Fiona Wild
Art Editor Annette Jacobs
Editors Ferdie McDonald, Mark Ronan,
Anna Streiffert
Designer Lisa Kosky
Design Assistant Marisa Renzullo
Picture Research Catherine O'Rourke
Research in Rome Sam Cole
DTP Editor Siri Lowe

Main Contributors
Olivia Ercoli, Ros Belford, Roberta Mitchell

Photographers
John Heseltine, Mike Dunning, Kim Sayer

Illustrators
Studio Illibill, Kevin Jones Associates, Martin
Woodward, Robbie Polley

This book was produced with the assistance of
Websters International Publishers.

Printed and bound in China.

First published in the UK in 1993 by
Dorling Kindersley Limited
80 Strand, London WC2R 0RL

17 18 19 20 10 9 8 7 6 5 4 3 2 1

Reprinted with revisions
2001, 2002, 2003, 2004, 2005, 2006,
2007, 2008, 2009,
2010, 2011, 2012, 2013, 2014, 2015,
2016, 2017

Copyright 1993, 2016 © Dorling Kindersley
Limited, London
A Penguin Random House Company

A CIP catalogue record is available from the
British Library.

ISBN: 978-0-2412-7734-8

Floors are referred to throughout in
accordance with European usage;
ie the "first floor" is the floor above
ground level.

MIX
Paper from
responsible sources
FSC™ C018179
www.fsc.org

Introducing Rome

The Fontana del Nettuno (Fountain of
Neptune) in the Piazza Navona

The famous spiral staircase of the Vatican Museums

◀ **Title page** The Colosseum by night.   **Front cover main image** Trevi Fountain.   **Back cover image** The Colosseum.

Contents

Bocca della Verità (the Mouth of Truth)

A section of the Gallery of Maps in the Vatican Museum

Trajan's Markets

HOW TO USE THIS GUIDE

This Eyewitness Travel Guide helps you get the most from your stay in Rome with the minimum of practical difficulty. The opening section, *Introducing Rome*, locates the city geographically, sets modern Rome in its historical context and explains how Roman life changes through the year. *Rome at a Glance* is an overview of the city's attractions. The main sightseeing section, *Rome Area by Area*, starts on page 64. It describes all the important sights with maps, photographs and detailed illustrations. In addition, nine planned walks take you to parts of Rome you might otherwise miss.

Carefully researched tips for hotels, shops and markets, restaurants and cafés, sports and entertainment are found in *Travellers' Needs*, and the *Survival Guide* has advice on everything from posting a letter to catching the Metro.

Finding Your Way Around the Sightseeing Section

Each of the 16 sightseeing areas in the city is colour-coded for easy reference. Every chapter opens with an introduction to the part of Rome it covers, describing its history and character, followed by a Street-by-Street map illustrating the heart of the area. Finding your way around each chapter is made simple by the numbering system used throughout. The most important sights are covered in detail in two or more full pages.

Each area has colour-coded thumb tabs.

A locator map shows where you are in relation to other areas in the city centre.

Locator map

1 Area map
For easy reference, the sights in each area are numbered and plotted on an area map. To help the visitor, this map also shows Metro stations. The area's key sights are listed by category, such as Churches and Temples, Museums and Galleries, and Ancient Sites.

A suggested route takes in some of the most interesting and attractive streets in the area.

2 Street-by-Street map
This gives a bird's-eye view of interesting and important parts of each sightseeing area. The numbering of the sights ties in with the area map and the fuller description of the entries on the pages that follow.

Stars indicate the sights that no visitor should miss.

Rome Area Map

The coloured areas shown on this map (see also inside front cover) are the 16 main sightseeing areas of Rome – each covered in a full chapter in *Rome Area by Area* (pp64–257). They are highlighted on other maps throughout the book. In *Rome at a Glance* (pp44–59), for example, they help locate the top sights. They are also used to help you find the position of the nine guided walks (p275).

Numbers refer to each sight's position on the area map and its place in the chapter.

Practical information provides everything you need to know to visit each sight. Map references pinpoint the sight's location on the *Street Finder* map (see pp388–411).

The façade of each major sight is shown to help you spot it quickly.

The visitors' checklist gives all the practical information needed to plan your visit.

3 Detailed information
All the important sights in Rome are described individually. They are listed in order following the numbering on the area map at the start of the section. Practical information includes a map reference, opening hours and telephone numbers. The key to the symbols is on the back flap.

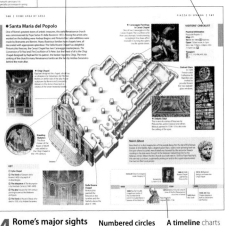

4 Rome's major sights
Historic buildings are dissected to reveal their interiors; museums and galleries have colour-coded floorplans to help you find the most important exhibits.

Numbered circles point out major features of the sight listed in the key.

A timeline charts the key events in the history of the building.

INTRODUCING ROME

GREAT DAYS IN ROME

Rome is a city packed with treasures and wonderful things to see and do. Its history can be traced in the crumbling columns of the ancient empire, the medieval alleys, Renaissance palaces, Baroque fountains and elegant piazzas. Whether here for several days or just wanting a flavour of this great city, you need to make the most of your time. Over the following pages, you'll find itineraries for some of the best of Rome's attractions, arranged first by theme and then by length of stay. Price guides on pages 10–11 include travel, food and admission for two adults, while family prices are for two adults and two children.

Theatre of Marcellus and the trio of standing columns

Ancient Rome

Two adults
allow at least €150

- **Explore the Republic**
- **Lunch in medieval ambience**
- **Absorb Imperial grandeur**
- **See how the Caesars lived**

Morning
Cram highlights of the 1,000-year history of ancient Rome's Republic and Empire into one very full day. Start at its heart, the **Roman Forum** *(see pp78–93)*, then spend an hour or so perusing some of its treasures inside the **Capitoline Museums** *(see pp70–3)*. Stroll over to Largo della Torre Argentina to gaze upon the remains of three Republican-era temples and the crumbling brick steps of the 55 BC Baths of Pompey, where Julius Caesar was murdered, ending the Republican era. The Baths of Pompey complex included a theatre that has now vanished but some of its vaults survive

in the foundations of the Campo de' Fiori area's medieval buildings – including the basement rooms of **Da Pancrazio** *(see p312)*, which serves excellent pasta.

Afternoon
Return to the core of ancient Rome past the Theatre of Marcellus – model for the Colosseum – and the two tiny **Temples of the Forum Boarium** *(see p205)* in Piazza della Bocca della Verità. Nip up Via del Velabro and skirt around the edge of the Forum. Head to the dank **Mamertine Prison** *(see p93)* to see where enemies of Rome were held and executed. Next, explore the ruins of Rome's Imperial era – the **Market and Forum of Trajan** *(see pp90–91)*, and look down on the **Forums of Caesar**, **Augustus** and **Nerva** *(see pp92–3)*. At the end, you can admire the **Colosseum** *(see pp94–7)*, built over Nero's former artificial lake. Stroll up the Via Sacra to roam the **Palatine Hill** *(see pp99–103;* entry for this and the Colosseum is included on the Forum ticket), peppered with original palatial homes.

Christian Rome

Two adults allow €140

- The Vatican Museums
- Picnic on the Piazza
- Works by Raphael, Bernini, Caravaggio, and Bramante
- Holy (dinner) orders

Morning
Exploring the **Vatican Museums** *(see pp232–45)* can easily occupy a full morning. When you're hungry, leave the museum and walk four streets up Via Tunisi to shop for goodies at the outdoor market on Via Andrea Doria. Take them back to picnic on Piazza San Pietro.

Afternoon
Pop into **St Peter's** *(see pp228–31)* to marvel at this capital of Christendom, then head to admire the glittering mosaics of **Santa Maria Maggiore** *(see pp174–5)*. Afterwards, visit **San Clemente** *(see pp188–9)*, a gorgeous 12th-century church built atop a 4th-century one, which stands on an ancient Mithraic temple. You will find important works by Raphael, Bernini, Caravaggio and Bramante in the church of **Santa Maria del Popolo** *(see pp140–41)*.

Detail of the mosaics in Santa Maria Maggiore

Dolce & Gabbana store window in Piazza di Spagna

Enjoy the evening *passeggiata* – Rome's see-and-be-seen stroll along the Via del Corso – with a drink at one of the busy cafés flanking the piazza. Round off by eating in hearty trattoria **Al Duello** (see p313), or the classic trattoria **Armando al Pantheon** (see p313).

Art and Shopping

Two adults
allow at least €30

- Fountains and piazzas
- National Gallery treasures
- Temples and boutiques
- Spanish Steps and the Trevi

Morning
Start at the fruit and flower market of **Campo de' Fiori** (see pp144–55), located around a statue of Giordano Bruno, who was burned at the stake in the Middle Ages. **Piazza Navona** (see pp118–29), with its Baroque fountains and excellent cafés, owes its oval shape to the ancient stadium beneath (a fragment is visible at its north end). Visit the collections of the National Gallery in the **Palazzo Altemps** (see p129). Peek into the church of **San Luigi dei Francesi** (see p124) for the early Caravaggios, then duck into Corso del Rinascimento 40 to

see the hidden fantasy façade on **Sant'Ivo alla Sapienza** (see p124). Do not miss Rome's **Pantheon** (see pp114–15), an ancient temple (now church), and **Santa Maria sopra Minerva** (see p112), for its art. Try the cappuccinos at **Caffè Sant'Eustachio** (see p322).

Afternoon
Cross the Via del Corso, and enjoy an afternoon's shopping in the chic boutiques of **Via Condotti** (see p135) and its tributaries fanning out from the base of the **Spanish Steps** (see pp136–7). To end the day treat yourself to one of Rome's best ice creams at **San Crispino** (see p322), and wander over to the nearby **Trevi Fountain** (see p161) before it melts.

A Family Day

Family of 4 allow at least €200

- Explore Villa Borghese park on two wheels
- See puppets, creatures and creepy crypts
- Cross the Tiber for medieval alleys and panoramic views

Morning
Rent bikes in **Villa Borghese** park (see pp260–61) where, as well as exploring, you can visit the Etruscan Museum in **Villa Giulia** (see pp264–5) or the excellent **Galleria Borghese** (see pp262–3; book ahead). If the kids need less art and more fun, take in Rome's zoo, the **Bioparco** (see p261). If it's a Sunday, stop at **Pincio Gardens** (see pp138–9) for an open-air carousel and the San Carlino, one of Rome's few remaining puppet theatres that puts on Pulcinella shows from 11am.

Afternoon
Return the bikes and stroll past the top of the **Spanish Steps** (see pp136–7) down Via Gregoriana, looking out for the Palazzetto Zuccari at number 28, whose windows and doors are shaped into hideous creatures. Below Via Veneto's **Santa Maria della Concezione** (see p256) lies the creepy Capuchin Crypt, which is covered in mosaics made from the bones of monks. (Cappuccino coffee was named after the colour of these friars' robes.)

At Piazza della Bocca della Verità, on the porch of **Santa Maria in Cosmedin** (see p204), sits the Mouth of Truth, an ancient drain cover carved as a monstrous face. The story goes that if you tell a lie with your fingers in the mouth, it will bite them off. Head across the river to **Trastevere** (see pp208–15), an area of twisting medieval alleys. Climb **Janiculum hill** (see pp217–19) to enjoy the sweeping views of the city. Descend to Trastevere for a pizza at **Pizzeria Ivo** (see p320).

Via Condotti, as seen from the top of the Spanish Steps

2 days in Rome

- Marvel at the treasures in the Vatican Museums
- See the sights of the ancient city, from the Colosseum to the Palatine
- Watch the world go by from the Spanish Steps

Day 1

Morning Book online to avoid the queues at the **Vatican Museums** (pp232–45), the largest art collection in the world. Admire Michelangelo's masterpieces in the **Sistine Chapel** (pp242–5), then head to the vast, ornate basilica, **St Peter's** (pp228–31).

Afternoon Cross the river via the Ponte Vittorio Emanuele II to the heart of the historic centre. A brisk walk takes in all the major sights, from the Baroque splendour of **Piazza Navona** (p122), to the architectural marvel of the ancient **Pantheon** (pp114–15). Be sure to also visit the **Trevi Fountain** (p161) and the **Spanish Steps** (pp136–7).

Day 2

Morning Take a trip to the **Colosseum** (pp94–7), Rome's spectacular amphitheatre, then take a stroll through the **Forum** (pp78–89), once the beating heart of the Empire. One ticket (buy at the entrance to the Forum) grants access to both sites, as well as the **Palatine**

(pp100–3), where Rome's emperors had their palaces. Don't miss the beautiful, 2,000-year-old frescoes in the **House of Livia** (p102).

Afternoon Take the glass elevator to the top of the **Victor Emmanuel Monument** (p76) for some of the best views in town. From here, an easy walk will lead you via the ancient **Portico of Octavia** (p154) to **Campo de' Fiori** (p148) for some people-watching. Cross **Ponte Sisto** (p212) to the picturesque neighbourhood of **Trastevere** (pp208–15) for dinner and a pleasant evening stroll.

3 days in Rome

- Be awed by the magificent interiors of the Pantheon
- Admire the art collection of the Borghese family
- Make a wish and throw a coin in the Trevi Fountain

Day 1

Morning A lifetime is not enough to see the whole of the **Vatican Museums** (pp232–45), so focus on highlights such as the awe-inspiring ancient sculpture *Laocoön* (p237), and the Renaissance treasures in the **Raphael Rooms** (pp240–41). Finish your visit with the magnificent **Sistine Chapel** (pp242–5) and the grand basilica of **St Peter's** (pp228–31).

Baroque Trevi Fountain, one of the most familiar sights of Rome

Afternoon A short walk from the Vatican is the imposing **Castel Sant'Angelo** (pp250–51). Cross Ponte Sant'Angelo to browse the antique shops lining **Via dei Coronari** (p128), then continue on to Rome's loveliest square, **Piazza Navona** (p122). Visit the **Pantheon** (pp114–15) for stunning architecture, before moving on to **Sant'Ignazio di Loyola** (p108) to see the *trompe l'oeil* paintings housed within.

Day 2

Morning Relive Rome's glorious past by roaming through the ancient paths, grandiose arches and solitary columns of the **Forum** (pp80–89). Explore the **Palatine** (pp100–3), and if you have time, climb the terraces of the **Colosseum** (pp94–7).

Afternoon See layers of history at **San Clemente** (pp188–9), then walk across the **Circus Maximus** (p207) to the beautifully simple church **Santa Maria in Cosmedin** (p204). Bustling **Campo de' Fiori** (p148) and lively **Trastevere** (pp208–15) are a pleasant stroll away.

Day 3

Morning Reserve in advance to visit the magnificent **Museo e Galleria Borghese** (pp262–3), with its masterpieces by Bernini. Afterwards, make your way to **Piazza del Popolo** (p139) with its towering obelisk and fantastic churches. Join the crowds on the **Spanish Steps** (pp136–7), then throw a coin in the **Trevi Fountain** (p161).

The Colosseum, where deadly gladiatorial combat and wild animal fights were once staged

Afternoon Stroll to the Capitol to visit the world's first public museum, **Palazzo Nuovo**, (pp70–71) for Greek and Roman sculpture, and the **Palazzo dei Conservatori** (pp72–3) for paintings by great artists such as Titian, Veronese, Rubens and Caravaggio. Stop off at the nearby **Victor Emmanuel Monument** (p76) for some truly magnificent views of the city.

5 days in Rome

- View Michelangelo's stunning *Pietà* in St Peter's
- Bike along the monument-lined Via Appia Antica
- Delight in Tivoli's ancient and Renaissance villas

Santa Maria in Trastevere, with its 12th-century apse mosaic of the Coronation of the Virgin

Day 1
Morning Walk in the footsteps of popes through the art-filled **Vatican Museums** (pp232–45) to the **Sistine Chapel** (pp242–5). Take in the wonders of **St Peter's** (pp228–31), with Michelangelo's famous sculpture *Pietà*, his soaring dome and Bernini's bronze masterpiece *baldacchino*. Book a tour of the Necropolis where St Peter is buried.

Afternoon Visit the ancient, medieval and Renaissance site of **Castel Sant'Angelo** (pp250–51), before crossing the river to the French national church **San Luigi dei Francesi** (p124), where three Caravaggio masterworks are on display.

Day 2
Morning Take the lift to the top of the **Victor Emmanuel Monument** (p76) for wonderful views, and to check out the layout of the ruins of the **Forum** (pp78–89), the **Palatine** (pp100–3) and the **Colosseum** (pp94–7). Then head down to see the ancient remains of these amazing historic sites close up.

Afternoon Marvel at the sheer enormity of the **Circus Maximus** (p207). Just around the corner, find the Bocca della Verità in **Santa Maria in**

Cosmedin (p204), and visit the well-preserved **Temples of the Forum Boarium** (p205). Explore the much-recycled **Theatre of Marcellus** (p153) and finish with a visit to the **Ghetto and Synagogue** (p154). Look out for a hidden gem, **Fontana delle Tartarughe** (p152), nearby.

Day 3
Morning Stroll through leafy **Villa Borghese** (p260–61) to work up an appetite for the glorious art at the **Museo e Galleria Borghese** (pp262–3). Check out the panoramic view from the **Pincio Gardens** (p138) before winding down to **Piazza del Popolo** (p139). Explore the square's famous church, **Santa Maria del Popolo** (pp140–41), with works by Caravaggio and Raphael. The elegant Rococo **Spanish Steps** (pp136–7) are just around the corner.

Afternoon Treat yourself to an ice cream en route to the iconic **Trevi Fountain** (p161). Continue your walk at a leisurely pace to the **Pantheon** (pp114–15) to explore its airy interiors. Next, visit the historic square **Campo de' Fiori** (p148) and walk over **Ponte Sisto** (p212) to gaze at medieval mosaics in **Santa Maria in Trastevere** (p214–15).

Day 4
Morning Visit the lowest level of **San Clemente** (pp188–9), where the ancient rites of Mithraism were practised. Not far away, the **Baths of Caracalla** (p199) give an idea of ancient Roman bathing facilities.

Afternoon Ride a bike or take a walk along the **Via Appia Antica** (p267), with sights along the way including the **Tomb of Cecilia Metella** (p268) and lots of spine-chilling catacombs.

Day 5
Morning Take a trip out of the city and explore the historic hilltown of **Tivoli** (p270) and the surrounding area. Be sure to visit Renaissance **Villa d'Este** (p270), with its world-famous gardens bursting with fountains and water features, sculptures and manicured hedges.

Afternoon Wander the sprawling ruins of **Hadrian's Villa** (p271), 6 km (4 miles) southwest of Tivoli, the emperor's 2nd-century AD summer retreat. It boasts pools, theatres, baths, libraries and gymnasiums. The grounds of the villa are great for a picnic.

Corinthian columns of the Temple of Castor and Pollux, rebuilt in AD 6, in the Forum

Putting Rome on the Map

Since its foundation over 2,760 years ago on seven hills near the banks of the River Tiber, Rome has grown into a city of three million people covering 1,500 sq km (580 sq miles) of central Italy. Within this area is the independent Vatican City State. Rome was made capital of the newly united Italy in 1870. It is about 28 km (17 miles) from the sea and has good rail and road links to nearby historic Italian towns and cities.

Key

≡≡ Motorway
≡≡ Major road
= = Road under construction
── Other road
---- Railway
▦▦ Regional border

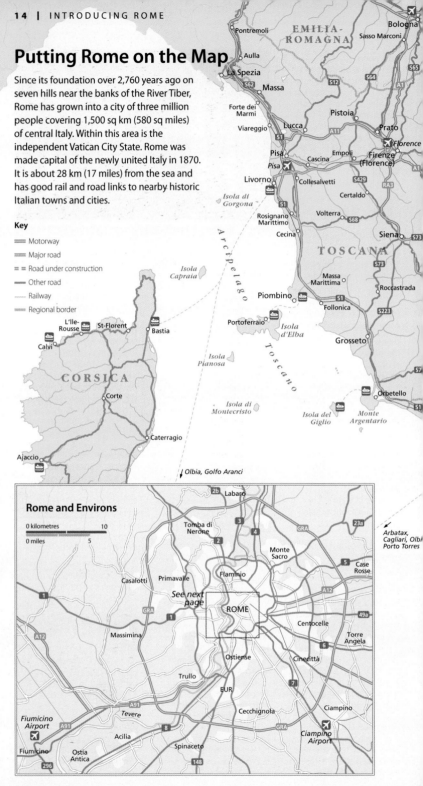

Rome and Environs

0 kilometres   10
0 miles   5

For keys to symbols see back flap

Europe

See inset map below

Central Rome

This book divides central Rome into 16 areas and has further sections for sights on the outskirts of the city, including some day trips, as well as some suggested walks. Each of the main areas has its own chapter and contains a selection of sights that convey some of its history and distinctive character. The Forum will give you a glimpse of ancient Rome, while the Capitol, Piazza della Rotonda and Piazza Navona represent the historic centre. If you are interested in Renaissance palaces, make a point of visiting the fine examples in Campo de' Fiori. In Piazza di Spagna, you can find designer shops and hints of the Grand Tour, with its array of Renaissance and Baroque art. A stop at the Vatican will reveal the impressive St Peter's at the heart of Roman Catholicism.

Pantheon
Fronted by lofty granite columns, the Pantheon was built as a Roman temple of "all the gods" (see pp114–15).

Vatican Museums
This vast complex of buildings holds one of the world's greatest collections of Classical and Renaissance art (see pp232–45).

For keys to symbols see back flap

Colosseum
One of Rome's most famous landmarks, the Colosseum *(see pp94–7)* was the venue for gladiatorial and animal fights. These provided a gory spectacle for Rome's citizens, up to 55,000 of whom would cram into the amphitheatre at one time.

Capitoline Museums
These fine collections *(see pp70–73)* include both Classical sculpture and Renaissance art, including this Greek statue of a discus thrower.

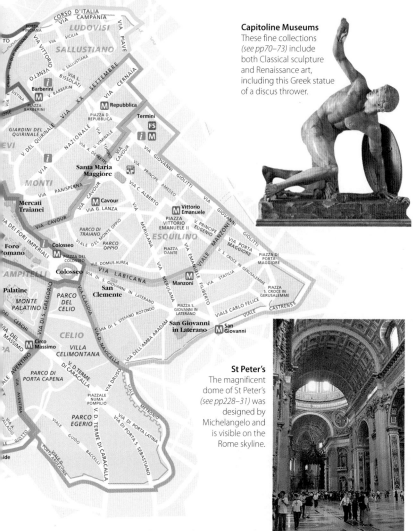

St Peter's
The magnificent dome of St Peter's *(see pp228–31)* was designed by Michelangelo and is visible on the Rome skyline.

THE HISTORY OF ROME

One of the most ancient cities in Europe, Rome was founded over 2,760 years ago. Since then it has been continuously inhabited, and, as the headquarters of the Roman Empire and then of the Catholic Church, it has had an immense impact on the world. Many European languages are based on Latin; many political and legal systems follow the ancient Roman model; and buildings all round the world utilize styles and techniques perfected in ancient Rome. The city itself retains layers of buildings spanning over two millennia. Not surprisingly, all this history can seem a little overwhelming.

Rome began as an Iron-Age hut-village, founded in the mid-8th century BC. In 616 BC, the Romans' sophisticated Etruscan neighbours seized power, but were ousted in 509 BC, when Rome became a Republic. It conquered most of the rest of Italy, then turned its attentions overseas, and by the 1st century BC ruled Spain, North Africa and Greece. The expansion of the Empire provided opportunities for power-hungry individuals, and the clashing of egos led to the collapse of democracy. Julius Caesar ruled for a time as dictator, and his nephew Octavian became Rome's first emperor, assuming the title Augustus. During the reign of Augustus, Christ was born, and though Christians were persecuted until the 4th century AD, the new religion took hold and Rome became its main centre.

Even though it was the seat of the papacy, during the Middle Ages Rome went into decline. The city recovered spectacularly in the mid-15th century, and for over 200 years was embellished by the greatest artists of the Renaissance and the Baroque. Finally, in 1870, Rome became the capital of the newly unified Italy.

15th-century map of Rome
from the north

◄ Detail from 2nd-century AD Roman mosaic from the Temple of Fortuna in Palestrina

Rome's Early Development

According to the historian Livy, Romulus founded Rome in 753 BC. Sometime later, realizing his tribe was short of females, he invited the neighbouring Sabines to a festival, and orchestrated the mass abduction of their women. Although Livy's account is pure legend, there is evidence that Rome was founded around the middle of the 8th century BC, and that the Romans and Sabines united shortly afterwards. Historical evidence also gives some support to Livy's claim that after Romulus's death Rome was ruled by a series of kings, and that in the 7th century BC it was conquered by the Etruscans and ruled by the Tarquin family. Last of the dynasty was Tarquinius Superbus (Tarquin The Proud). His despotic rule led to the Etruscans being expelled and the founding of a Republic run by two annually elected consuls. The uprising was led by Lucius Junius Brutus, the model of the stern, patriotic Roman Republican.

Extent of the City
☐ 750 BC   ▓ Today

Ceremonial trumpets

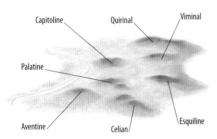

Capitoline   Quirinal   Viminal
Palatine
Aventine   Celian   Esquiline

The Seven Hills of Rome
By the 8th century BC, shepherds and farmers lived on four of Rome's seven hills. As the population grew, huts were built in the marshy valley later occupied by the Forum.

Augur, digging foundation

Iron Age Hut
Early settlers lived in wattle-and-daub huts. Traces of their foundations have been found on the Palatine.

Temple of Jupiter
This Renaissance painting by Perin del Vaga shows Tarquinius Superbus founding the Temple of Jupiter on the Capitol, the sacred citadel of Rome.

750 BC Tarpeia betrays city to the Sabines

700 BC Approximate beginning of Etruscan period

Etruscan jug (7th century BC)

750

700

650

753 BC Legendary founding of Rome by Romulus, first of seven kings

715–713 BC King Numa Pompilius establishes 12-month calendar

659 BC Romans destroy rival city, Alba Longa

Romulus and Remus

The Legend of the She-Wolf
The evil king of Alba threw his baby
nephews, Romulus and Remus, into
the Tiber but they were washed
ashore, and suckled by a she-wolf.

Apollo of Veio
Etruscan culture and
religion were influenced
by the Greeks. This 5th-
or 6th-century statue
of the Greek god Apollo
comes from Veio and
is in the Villa Giulia
museum (see pp264–5).

Raven, guardian
of the citadel

Tarquinius Superbus
(Tarquin The Proud)

The Legend of Aeneas
Some Roman legends make
the Trojan hero Aeneas
the grandfather of Romulus
and Remus.

Where to See Etruscan Rome

The Cloaca Maxima sewer
still functions, but there are
few other traces of Etruscan
Rome. Most finds come from
Etruscan sites outside Rome
like Tarquinia, with its tomb
paintings of sumptuous
banquets (see p273), but there
are major collections in the Villa
Giulia (pp264–5) and Vatican
Museums (p236). The most
famous object, however, is a
bronze statue of the legendary
she-wolf in the Capitoline
Museums (p73). The Anti-
quarium Forense (p89) displays
objects from the necropolis
which once occupied the site
of the Roman Forum.

Funeral urns shaped like huts
were used for cremation from
the mid-8th century BC.

Etruscan jewellery, like this
7th-century BC gold filigree
brooch, was lavish. Treasures
of this kind have given the
Etruscans a reputation
for luxurious living.

---

600 BC Possible date of
construction of Cloaca
Maxima sewer

565 BC Traditional date of the Servian
Wall around Rome's seven hills

534 BC King Servius
murdered

510 BC Temple of Jupiter
consecrated on the
Capitoline hill

Statue of Jupiter

600   **550**   **500**

578 BC Servius
Tullius Etruscan king

616 BC Tarquinius Priscus, first Etruscan
king. Forum and Circus Maximus established

509 BC Lucius Junios Brutus
expels Etruscans from Rome
and founds the Republic

L J Brutus

507 BC War against Etruscans. Horatius
defends wooden bridge across Tiber

Kings, Consuls, and Emperors

Rome had over 250 rulers in the 1,200 years between its foundation by Romulus and AD 476, when the last emperor was deposed by the German warrior Odoacer. Romulus was the first of seven kings, overthrown in 509 BC when Rome became a Republic. Authority was held by two annually elected consuls, but provision was made for the appointment of a dictator in times of crisis. In 494 BC, the office of Tribune was set up to protect the plebeians from injustice at the hands of their patrician rulers. Roman democracy, however, was always cosmetic. It was discarded completely in 27 BC, when absolute power was placed in the hands of the emperor.

205 BC Scipio Africanus

218 BC Quintus Fabius Maximus

Romulus, his twin Remus and the she-wolf who suckled them

456 BC Lucius Quintus Cincinnatus

c.753–715 BC Romulus

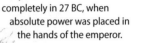

800 BC	700	600	500	400	300	20
SEVEN KINGS			REPUBLIC			
800 BC	700	600	500	400	300	20

c.715–673 BC Numa Pompilius

396 BC Marcus Furius Camillus

c.673–641 BC Tullus Hostilius

c.509 BC Lucius Junius Brutus and Horatius Pulvillus

c.534–509 BC Tarquinius Superbus

c.641–616 BC Ancus Marcius

c.579–534 BC Servius Tullius

616–579 BC Tarquinius Priscus

Tarquinius Priscus consulting an augur

Julius Caesar, whose rise to power marked the end of the Roman Republic

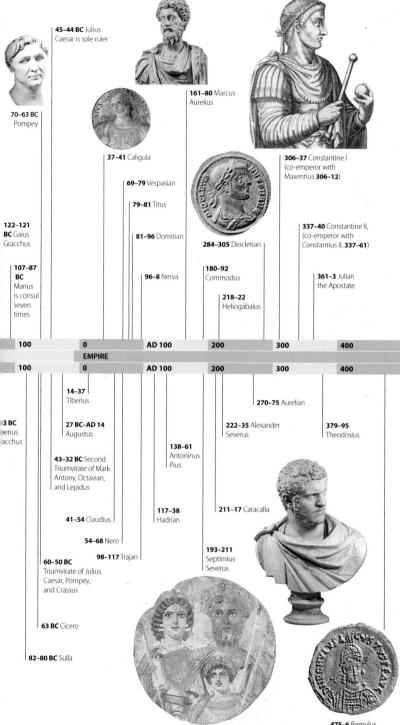

45–44 BC Julius Caesar is sole ruler

161–80 Marcus Aurelius

70–63 BC Pompey

306–37 Constantine I (co-emperor with Maxentius **306–12**)

37–41 Caligula

69–79 Vespasian

79–81 Titus

122–121 BC Gaius Gracchus

81–96 Domitian

337–40 Constantine II, (co-emperor with Constantius II, **337–61**)

284–305 Diocletian

107–87 BC Marius is consul seven times

96–8 Nerva

180–92 Commodus

218–22 Heliogabalus

361–3 Julian the Apostate

| 100 | 0 | AD 100 | 200 | 300 | 400 |

EMPIRE

| 100 | 0 | AD 100 | 200 | 300 | 400 |

14–37 Tiberius

270–75 Aurelian

27 BC–AD 14 Augustus

222–35 Alexander Severus

379–95 Theodosius

43–32 BC Second Triumvirate of Mark Antony, Octavian, and Lepidus

138–61 Antoninus Pius

.3 BC .erius .acchus

41–54 Claudius

117–38 Hadrian

211–17 Caracalla

54–68 Nero

98–117 Trajan

60–50 BC Triumvirate of Julius Caesar, Pompey, and Crassus

193–211 Septimius Severus

63 BC Cicero

82–80 BC Sulla

Septimius Severus and family

475–6 Romulus Augustulus

The Roman Republic

By the mid-2nd century BC, Rome controlled the western Mediterranean, policing and defending it with massive armies. The troops had more loyalty to the generals than to distant politicians, giving men like Marius, Sulla, Pompey and Caesar the muscle to seize political power. Meanwhile, peasants, whose land had been destroyed during the invasion of Hannibal in 219 BC, had flooded into Rome. They were followed by slaves and freedmen from conquered lands such as Greece, swelling the population to half a million. There was plenty of work for immigrants, constructing roads, aqueducts, markets and temples, financed by taxes on Rome's expanding trade.

Extent of the City

◻ 400 BC   ◻ Today

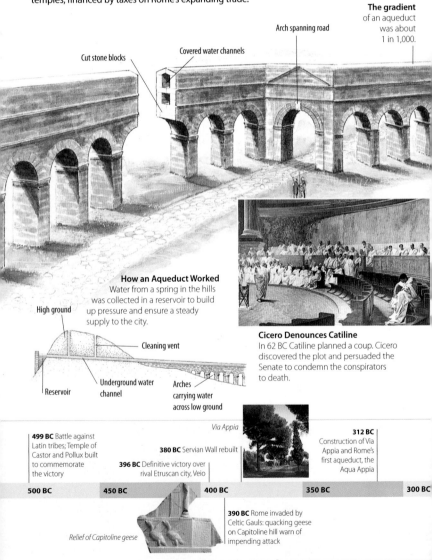

The gradient of an aqueduct was about 1 in 1,000.

Arch spanning road

Covered water channels

Cut stone blocks

How an Aqueduct Worked
Water from a spring in the hills was collected in a reservoir to build up pressure and ensure a steady supply to the city.

High ground

Cleaning vent

Reservoir

Underground water channel

Arches carrying water across low ground

Cicero Denounces Catiline
In 62 BC Catiline planned a coup. Cicero discovered the plot and persuaded the Senate to condemn the conspirators to death.

Via Appia

499 BC Battle against Latin tribes; Temple of Castor and Pollux built to commemorate the victory

380 BC Servian Wall rebuilt

396 BC Definitive victory over rival Etruscan city, Veio

312 BC Construction of Via Appia and Rome's first aqueduct, the Aqua Appia

| 500 BC | 450 BC | 400 BC | 350 BC | 300 BC |

Relief of Capitoline geese

390 BC Rome invaded by Celtic Gauls: quacking geese on Capitoline hill warn of impending attack

Roman Street
In the 1st century BC, most buildings in Rome were made from brick and concrete. Only a few public buildings used marble.

Aqueduct (2nd Century BC)

Rome owed much of her prosperity to her skilled civil engineers. When the city's wells were no longer sufficient, aqueducts were built to bring water from surrounding hills. Some were over 80 km (50 miles) long.

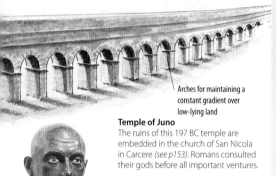

Arches for maintaining a constant gradient over low-lying land

This fresco depicting a gang of slaves building a wall can be seen at the Museo Nazionale Romano *(see p165)*.

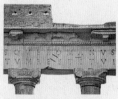

Temple of Juno
The ruins of this 197 BC temple are embedded in the church of San Nicola in Carcere *(see p153)*. Romans consulted their gods before all important ventures.

The Temple of Saturn, first built in 497 BC, now consists of eight majestic columns overlooking the Forum at the end of the Via Sacra *(see p85)*.

Rome's loveliest Republican buildings are the two Temples of the Forum Boarium *(see p205)*. Four more temples can be seen in the Area Sacra of Largo Argentina *(p152)*. Most monuments from this period, however, lie underground. Only a few, like the Tomb of the Scipios *(p197)*, have been excavated. One of the bridges leading to Tiber Island *(p155)*, the Ponte Fabricio, dates from the 1st century BC and is still used by pedestrians.

Scipio Africanus
In 202 BC the Roman general Scipio defeated Hannibal. Rome replaced Carthage as master of the Mediterranean.

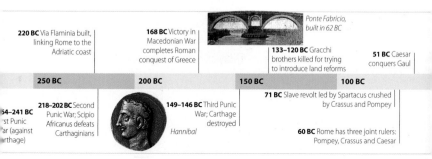

220 BC Via Flaminia built, linking Rome to the Adriatic coast

168 BC Victory in Macedonian War completes Roman conquest of Greece

Ponte Fabricio, built in 62 BC

133–120 BC Gracchi brothers killed for trying to introduce land reforms

51 BC Caesar conquers Gaul

250 BC	200 BC	150 BC	100 BC

264–241 BC 1st Punic War (against Carthage)

218–202 BC Second Punic War; Scipio Africanus defeats Carthaginians

Hannibal

149–146 BC Third Punic War; Carthage destroyed

71 BC Slave revolt led by Spartacus crushed by Crassus and Pompey

60 BC Rome has three joint rulers: Pompey, Crassus and Caesar

Imperial Rome

In 44 BC Caesar became dictator for life, only to be assassinated a month later. The result was 17 years of civil war, which ended only in 27 BC when Augustus became Rome's first emperor. The Empire expanded in fits and starts, but by the late 3rd century was so huge that Diocletian decided to share it between four emperors. Thanks to trade and taxes from its vast domains, Rome was the most magnificent city in the world, studded with the lavish buildings of emperors keen to advertise their civic munificence and military triumphs.

Extent of the City
☐ AD 250   ■ Today

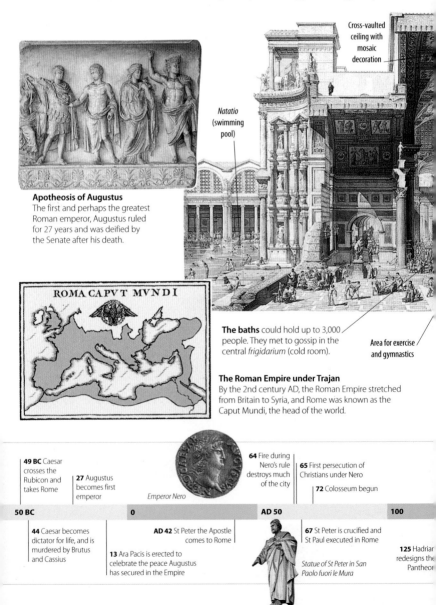

Cross-vaulted ceiling with mosaic decoration

Natatio (swimming pool)

Apotheosis of Augustus
The first and perhaps the greatest Roman emperor, Augustus ruled for 27 years and was deified by the Senate after his death.

ROMA CAPVT MVNDI

The baths could hold up to 3,000 people. They met to gossip in the central *frigidarium* (cold room).

Area for exercise and gymnastics

The Roman Empire under Trajan
By the 2nd century AD, the Roman Empire stretched from Britain to Syria, and Rome was known as the Caput Mundi, the head of the world.

49 BC Caesar crosses the Rubicon and takes Rome

27 Augustus becomes first emperor

Emperor Nero

64 Fire during Nero's rule destroys much of the city

65 First persecution of Christians under Nero

72 Colosseum begun

| 50 BC | 0 | AD 50 | 100 |

44 Caesar becomes dictator for life, and is murdered by Brutus and Cassius

AD 42 St Peter the Apostle comes to Rome

13 Ara Pacis is erected to celebrate the peace Augustus has secured in the Empire

67 St Peter is crucified and St Paul executed in Rome

Statue of St Peter in San Paolo fuori le Mura

125 Hadrian redesigns the Pantheon

Roman Revelry
Banquets could last for up to 10 hours, with numerous courses, between which guests would retire to a small room to relax.

Where to See Imperial Rome

There are relics of Imperial Rome throughout the city centre, some hidden below churches and palazzi, others like the Forum (see pp78–89), the Palatine (pp99–103), and the Imperial Fora (pp90–93), fully excavated. The magnificence of the era, however, is best conveyed by the Pantheon (pp114–15) and the Colosseum (pp94–7).

Baths of Diocletian (AD 298)

Rome's public baths were not just places to keep clean. They also had bars, libraries, barbers' shops, brothels and sports facilities.

The Arch of Titus (p89), erected in the Forum in AD 81, commemorates Emperor Titus's sack of Jerusalem in AD 70.

Tepidarium (warm room)

A relief of Mithras, a popular Persian god (3rd century AD), can be seen beneath the church of San Clemente (pp188–9).

Virgil (70–19 BC)
Virgil was Rome's greatest epic poet. His most famous work is the *Aeneid*, the story of the Trojan hero Aeneas's journey to the future site of Rome.

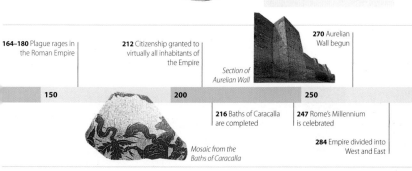

164–180 Plague rages in the Roman Empire

212 Citizenship granted to virtually all inhabitants of the Empire

Section of Aurelian Wall

270 Aurelian Wall begun

150

200

250

216 Baths of Caracalla are completed

247 Rome's Millennium is celebrated

284 Empire divided into West and East

Mosaic from the Baths of Caracalla

Early Christian Rome

In the 1st century AD, during the reign of Tiberius, a rebellious pacifist was crucified in a distant corner of the Empire. This was nothing unusual, but within a few years Jesus Christ and his teachings became notorious in Rome – his followers were perceived as a threat to public order and many were executed. This was no deterrent, and the new religion spread through all levels of Roman society. When the Apostles Peter and Paul arrived in Rome there was already a small Christian community, and in spite of continued persecution by the state, Christianity flourished. In AD 313 the Emperor Constantine issued an edict granting freedom of worship to Christians, and soon after founded a shrine on the site of St Peter's tomb. This secured Rome's position as a centre of Christianity, but in the 5th century the political importance of Rome declined and the city fell to Goths and other invaders.

Extent of the City
☐ AD 395   ▨ Today

St Paul

Youthful, beardless representation of Christ

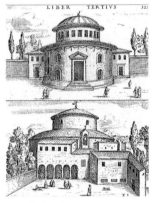

Santo Stefano Rotondo
This 17th-century engraving shows how a Roman temple *(top)* might have been transformed *(above)* into the 5th-century round church of Santo Stefano *(see p187)*.

Classical-style border decorated with fruit

The Good Shepherd
The pagan image of a shepherd sacrificing a lamb became a Christian symbol.

4th-Century Mosaic, Santa Costanza

Beautiful mosaics, often with palm trees and other oriental motifs suggesting Jerusalem, helped spread the message of early Christianity.

c.320 Building of first St Peter's	**356** Legendary founding of Santa Maria Maggiore	*Gold solidus of Theodosius*	**410** Rome sacked by Alaric's Goths	**455** Rome sacked again by Vandals
300	**350**		**400**	**450**
312 Control of Empire won by Constantine after battle at Milvian Bridge	**380** Emperor Theodosius makes Christianity the official religion of the Roman Empire	*Battle of the Milvian Bridge*	**395** Division of the Empire between Ravenna and Constantinople	**422** Founding of Santa Sabina

Epigraph of Peter and Paul
This is one of hundreds of early Christian graffiti housed in the Lapidary Gallery of the Vatican (see p238).

Crucifixion, Santa Sabina
This 5th-century panel on the door of Santa Sabina (see p206) is one of the earliest known representations of the Crucifixion. Interestingly, Christ's cross is not actually shown.

St Peter receiving peace from the Saviour

Lambs symbolizing the Christian flock

Constantine's Cross
Constantine's vision of the True Cross during the Battle of the Milvian Bridge made him convert to Christianity.

Where to See Early Christian Rome

There are traces of early Christianity all over Rome. Many ancient churches were built over early Christian meeting places and sites of martyrdoms: among them San Clemente (see pp188–9), Santa Pudenziana (p173) and Santa Cecilia (p213). Outside the walls of the old city are miles of underground catacombs (pp267–8), many decorated with Christian frescoes, while the Vatican's Pio-Christian Museum (p238) has the best collection of early Christian art.

This statuette, carved out of bone, is embedded in the rock of the Catacombs of San Panfilo, just off the Via Salaria (**map** 2 F4).

The Cross of Justin, in the Treasury of St Peter's (p230), was given to Rome by the Emperor Justin II in AD 578.

Illustration of Anastasius II

A Byzantine image of St Paul

609 Pantheon is consecrated as a Christian church

500　　**550**　　**600**

496 Anastasius II is first pope to assume title Pontifex Maximus

590–604 Pope Gregory the Great strengthens the papacy

630 Sant'Agnese fuori le Mura is built in Roman Byzantine style

475 Fall of Western Roman Empire; Byzantium becomes seat of Empire

The Papacy

The pope is considered Christ's representative on earth, claiming his authority from St Peter, the first Bishop of Rome. Though some popes have been great thinkers and reformers, the role has rarely been purely spiritual. In the Middle Ages, many popes were involved in power struggles with the Holy Roman Emperor. Renaissance popes like Julius II and Leo X, the patrons of Raphael and Michelangelo, lived as luxuriously as any secular prince. The popes listed here include all those who exercised significant political or religious influence, up as far as the end of the Counter-Reformation, when the power of the papacy began to wane.

St Ludovic Kneels before Boniface VIII *by Simone Martini*

314–35 St Sylvester I

590–604 St Gregory the Great

St. Gregory the Great leading a procession to end the plague

955–64 John XII

222–30 St Urban I

1227–41 Gregory IX

496–8 Anastasius II

931–5 John XI

1216–27 Honorius III Savelli

217–22 St Callixtus I

891–6 Formosus

0	200	400	600	800	1000	1200

PAPACY BASED IN ROME

0	200	400	600	800	1000	1200

336 Mark

579–90 Pelagius II

1032–44, 1047–8 Benedict IX

352–66 Liberius

c.88–97 St Clement

608–15 St Boniface IV

1073–85 St Gregory VII

731–41 St Gregory III

1099–1118 Paschal II

c.42–67 St Peter

772–95 Adrian I

1130–43 Innocent II

1154–9 Adrian IV

847–55 St Leo IV

817–24 St Paschal I

1198–1216 Innocent III

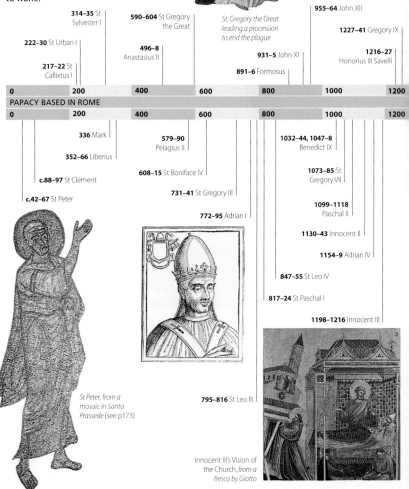

St Peter, from a mosaic in Santa Prassede (see p173)

795–816 St Leo III

Innocent III's Vision of the Church, from a fresco by Giotto

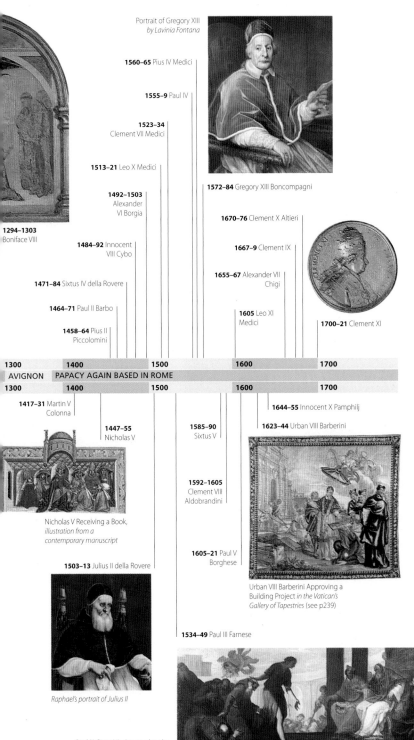

Portrait of Gregory XIII
by Lavinia Fontana

1560–65 Pius IV Medici

1555–9 Paul IV

1523–34
Clement VII Medici

1513–21 Leo X Medici

1572–84 Gregory XIII Boncompagni

1492–1503
Alexander
VI Borgia

1670–76 Clement X Altieri

1294–1303
Boniface VIII

1667–9 Clement IX

1484–92 Innocent
VIII Cybo

1655–67 Alexander VII
Chigi

1471–84 Sixtus IV della Rovere

1464–71 Paul II Barbo

1605 Leo XI
Medici

1458–64 Pius II
Piccolomini

1700–21 Clement XI

| 1300 | 1400 | 1500 | 1600 | 1700 |

AVIGNON   PAPACY AGAIN BASED IN ROME

| 1300 | 1400 | 1500 | 1600 | 1700 |

1417–31 Martin V
Colonna

1644–55 Innocent X Pamphilj

1447–55
Nicholas V

1585–90
Sixtus V

1623–44 Urban VIII Barberini

1592–1605
Clement VIII
Aldobrandini

Nicholas V Receiving a Book,
*illustration from a
contemporary manuscript*

1605–21 Paul V
Borghese

1503–13 Julius II della Rovere

Urban VIII Barberini Approving a
Building Project *in the Vatican's
Gallery of Tapestries* (see p239)

1534–49 Paul III Farnese

Raphael's portrait of Julius II

Paul III Gives His Approval to the
Capuchin Order *by Sebastiano Ricci*

Medieval Rome

Supplanted by Constantinople as capital of the Empire in the 4th century, Rome was reduced to a few thousand inhabitants by the early Middle Ages, its power just a memory. In the 8th and 9th centuries, the growing importance of the papacy revived the city and made it once more a centre of power. But continual conflicts between the pope and the Holy Roman Emperor soon weakened the papacy. The 10th, 11th and 12th centuries were among the bleakest in Roman history: violent invaders left Rome poverty-stricken and the constantly warring local barons tore apart what remained of the city. Despite this, the first Holy Year was declared in 1300 and thousands of pilgrims arrived in Rome. But by 1309 the papacy was forced to move to Avignon, leaving Rome to slide into further squalor and strife.

Extent of the City

☐ *1300*   ▨ *Today*

San Giovanni in Laterano

Aurelian Wall

Charlemagne Crowned in St Peter's
On Christmas Day in 800, Charlemagne was made "emperor of the Romans", ruler of a new Christian dominion to replace that of ancient Rome.

Trajan's Column

Column of Marcus Aurelius

Madonna and Child Mosaic
The Chapel of St Zeno (817–24) in the church of Santa Prassede *(see p173)* has some of the best examples of Byzantine mosaics in Rome.

Medieval Plan of Rome
Maps like this one, illustrating the principal features of the city, were produced for pilgrims, the tourists of the Middle Ages.

725 King Ine of Wessex founds the first hostel for pilgrims in the Borgo

852 The Vatican is fortified with walls following a raid by Saracens

Emperor Otto I

961 King Otto the Great of Germany becomes first Holy Roman Emperor

| 700 | 800 | 900 | 1000 |

778 Charlemagne, King of the Franks, conquers Italy

800 Charlemagne crowned emperor in St Peter's

880–932 Rome is ruled by two women, Theodora and then her daughter, Marozia

Stefaneschi Triptych (1315) Giotto and his pupils painted this triptych for Cardinal Stefaneschi as an altarpiece for St Peter's. It is now in the Vatican Museums *(see p238)*.

Where to see Medieval Rome

Among the most interesting churches of the period are San Clemente, with a fine apse mosaic and Cosmati floor *(see pp188–9)*, Santa Maria in Trastevere *(pp214–15)* and Santa Maria sopra Minerva, Rome's only Gothic church *(p112)*. Santa Cecilia in Trastevere *(p213)* has a Cavallini fresco, and there is fine Cosmati work in Santa Maria in Cosmedin *(p204)*.

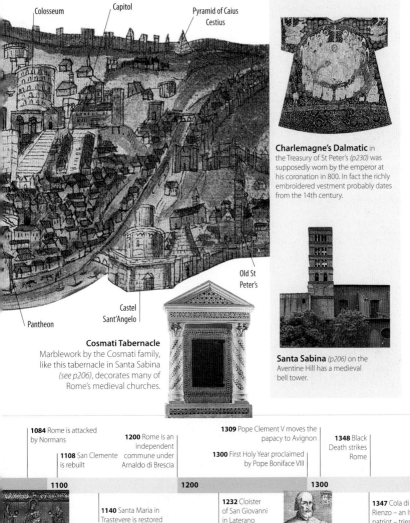

Colosseum Capitol Pyramid of Caius Cestius

Pantheon

Castel Sant'Angelo

Old St Peter's

Cosmati Tabernacle Marblework by the Cosmati family, like this tabernacle in Santa Sabina *(see p206)*, decorates many of Rome's medieval churches.

Charlemagne's Dalmatic in the Treasury of St Peter's *(p230)* was supposedly worn by the emperor at his coronation in 800. In fact the richly embroidered vestment probably dates from the 14th century.

Santa Sabina *(p206)* on the Aventine Hill has a medieval bell tower.

1084 Rome is attacked by Normans

1108 San Clemente is rebuilt

1200 Rome is an independent commune under Arnaldo di Brescia

1309 Pope Clement V moves the papacy to Avignon

1300 First Holy Year proclaimed by Pope Boniface VIII

1348 Black Death strikes Rome

1100　　　**1200**　　　**1300**

1140 Santa Maria in Trastevere is restored

Mosaic façade, Santa Maria in Trastevere (pp214–15)

1232 Cloister of San Giovanni in Laterano completed

Cola di Rienzo

1347 Cola di Rienzo – an Italian patriot – tries to restore the Roman Republic

Renaissance Rome

Pope Nicholas V came to the throne in 1447 determined to make Rome a city fit for the papacy. Among his successors, men like Julius II and Leo X eagerly followed his lead, and the city's appearance was transformed. The Classical ideals of the Renaissance inspired artists, architects and craftsmen, such as Michelangelo, Bramante, Raphael and Cellini, to build and decorate the churches and palaces of a newly confident Rome.

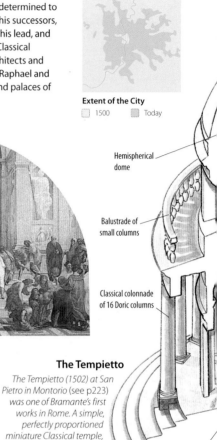

Extent of the City
☐ 1500   ▨ Today

Hemispherical dome

Balustrade of small columns

Classical colonnade of 16 Doric columns

School of Athens by Raphael
In this fresco *(see p241)*, Raphael complimented many of his peers by representing them as ancient Greek philosophers. The building shown is based on a design by Bramante.

The Tempietto

The Tempietto (1502) at San Pietro in Montorio (see p223) was one of Bramante's first works in Rome. A simple, perfectly proportioned miniature Classical temple, it is a model of High Renaissance architecture.

Cosmati-style mosaic floor

Palazzo Caprini
Bramante's design had a strong influence on later Renaissance palazzi. Parts of the building survive in Palazzo dei Convertendi *(see p247)*.

1377 Papacy returns to Rome from Avignon under Pope Gregory XI

1409–15 Papacy moves to Pisa

1444 Birth of Bramante

1417 Pope Martin V ends the Great Schism in the papacy

1452 Demolition of old St Peter's basilica begins

1350

1400

1450

1378–1417 The Great Schism, a division in the papacy in Avignon

Pope Martin V, reigned 1417–31

Sack of Rome
In 1527, the unruly troops of Charles V of Spain pillaged the city, destroying countless works of art. Pope Clement VII took refuge in Castel Sant'Angelo.

Pope Nicholas V
Nicholas ordered the demolition of the old St Peter's.

Statue of St Peter, believed to have been crucified on this site

Underground chapel

Where to See Renaissance Rome

The Campo de' Fiori area *(see pp144–55)* is full of grand Renaissance palazzi, especially along Via Giulia *(pp278–9)*. Across the river stands the delightful Villa Farnesina *(pp220–21)*. The most typical church of the period is Santa Maria del Popolo *(pp140–41)*, and the best collection of Renaissance art is in the Vatican Museums *(pp232–45)*. These include the Sistine Chapel *(pp242–5)* and the Raphael Rooms *(pp240–41)*.

The Madonna di Foligno by Raphael (1511–12) is one of the fine Renaissance paintings in the Vatican Pinacoteca *(p239)*.

The Pietà, commissioned for St Peter's in 1501, was one of Michelangelo's first sculptures executed in Rome *(p231)*.

1483 Birth of Raphael

1486 Building of Palazzo della Cancelleria

1519 Frescoes completed in Villa Farnesina

1527 Troops of Emperor Charles V sack Rome

Emperor Charles V

1500

1550

75 Birth of ...chelangelo

1508 Michelangelo begins painting the Sistine Chapel ceiling

1506 Pope Julius II orders start of work on new St Peter's

1547 Pope Paul III appoints Michelangelo architect of St Peter's

Cumaean Sibyl, Sistine Chapel

Baroque Rome

By the 16th century, the Catholic Church had become immensely rich – one of the chief criticisms of the Protestant reformers. The display of grandeur and extravagance by the papal court contrasted sharply with the poverty of the people, and wealthy Roman society was characterized by sumptuous luxury and a ceaseless round of entertainment. To make the Catholic faith more appealing than Protestantism, scores of churches were built and monuments and fountains were erected to glorify the Holy See. The finest architects in the ornate, dramatic style of the Baroque were Bernini and Borromini.

Extent of the City
☐ 1645　　■ Today

Ceiling portraying
heavenly scenes

Gian Lorenzo Bernini (1598–1680)
The favourite artist of the papacy, Bernini transformed Rome with his churches, palaces, statues and fountains.

Monument to Pope Alexander VII
This Bernini tomb in St Peter's *(pp228–31)* includes a skeleton brandishing an hour-glass.

Tapestry of Pope Urban VIII
Bernini's most devoted patron, Pope Urban VIII Barberini (1623–44), is shown here receiving the homage of the nations.

Holy Family fresco

Pozzo Corridor
The use of perspective to create an illusion of depth and space was a favourite Baroque device. Andrea Pozzo painted this illusionistic corridor in the 1680s in the Rooms of St Ignatius near the Gesù (see pp110–11).

1568 The Jesuits build the Gesù, prototypical church of the early Baroque

Altar carving from the Gesù

1595 Annibale Carracci begins to fresco Palazzo Farnese

1624 Bernini's sculpture of *Apollo and Daphne*

1626 Work on St Peter's is completed

1550　　　　**1575**　　　　**1600**　　　　**1625**

1585 Pope Sixtus V plans new streets

1600 Philosopher Giordano Bruno is burned at the stake for heresy

1571 Birth of Caravaggio

Galileo

1633 Galileo condemned to house arrest for heresy

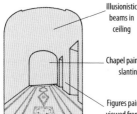

Illusionistic beams in ceiling

Chapel painted on flat slanting wall

Figures painted to be viewed from an angle

Queen Christina of Sweden
In a coup for Catholicism, Christina renounced Protestantism and abdicated her throne. In 1655 she moved to Rome, where she became the centre of a lively literary and scientific circle.

St Ignatius, founder of the Jesuits

Francesco Borromini (1599–1667)
In the many churches he built in Rome, Borromini made use of revolutionary geometric forms.

San Carlo alle Quattro Fontane
One of Borromini's most influential designs was this tiny oval church *(see p163)* on the Quirinal hill.

A marble rose marks the best place to stand to appreciate the illusion of space created by the artist.

1651 Bernini redesigns much of Piazza Navona

Bernini's Fontana dei Quattro Fiumi in Piazza Navona

1694 Palazzo di Montecitorio is completed

1735 Spanish Steps are designed

1732 Work starts on the Trevi Fountain

1650 **1675** **1700** **1725**

1657 Borromini completes Sant'Agnese in Agone

1656 Work starts on Bernini's colonnade for St Peter's Square

Bonnie Prince Charlie, pretender to the throne of England

1721 Bonnie Prince Charlie is born in Rome

1734 Clement XII makes Palazzo Nuovo world's first public museum

Understanding Rome's Architecture

The architecture of Imperial Rome kept alive the Classical styles of ancient Greece, at the same time developing new, uniquely Roman forms based on the arch, the vault and the dome. The next important period was the 12th century, when many Romanesque churches were built. The Renaissance saw a return to Classical ideals, inspired by the example of Florence, but in the 17th century Rome found a style of its own again in the flamboyance of the Baroque.

The entablature above these columns has both straight and arched sections (Hadrian's Villa).

Classical Rome

Most Roman buildings were of concrete faced with brick, but from the 1st century BC, the Romans started to imitate earlier Greek models, using marble to decorate temples and other public buildings.

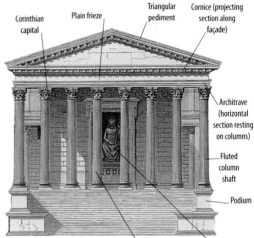

Corinthian capital — Plain frieze — Triangular pediment — Cornice (projecting section along façade)

Architrave (horizontal section resting on columns)

Fluted column shaft

Podium

Cella (inner sanctuary)

Colonnade enclosing portico

Roman temples were usually built on a raised dais or podium, to make them prominent. Many were fronted by a portico, a roofed porch with columns.

Caryatids were sculpted columns, usually in the form of a female figure. Roman caryatids, like this one in the Forum of Augustus, were often copied in detail from earlier Greek examples.

The orders of Classical architecture were building styles, each based on a different column design. The three major orders were borrowed by the Romans from the Greeks.

Doric order   Ionic order   Corinthian order

Aedicules were small shrines, framed by two pillars, usually containing a statue of a god.

Coffers were decorative sunken panels that reduced the weight of domed and vaulted ceilings.

Early Christian and Medieval Rome

The first Christian churches in Rome were based on the basilica: oblong, with three naves, each usually ending in an apse. From the 10th to the 13th centuries, most churches were built in the Romanesque style, which used the rounded arches of ancient Rome.

Basilicas in Rome have, in most cases, kept their original rectangular shape. The nave of San Giovanni in Laterano retains its 4th-century floorplan.

The triumphal arch divides the nave of a church from the apse. Here, in San Paolo fuori le Mura, it is decorated with mosaics.

A tabernacle is used to house the Sacrament for the mass. This 13th-century Gothic wall tabernacle is in San Clemente.

Renaissance and Baroque Rome

Renaissance architecture (15th–16th centuries) drew its inspiration directly from Classical models. It revived the use of strict geometric proportions. The Baroque age (late 16th–17th centuries) broke many established rules, favouring grandiose decoration over pure Classical forms.

A baldacchino is a canopy, supported on columns, rising over the main altar. This Baroque example is in St Peter's.

Putti were a popular decorative feature in the Baroque. A putto is a painting or a sculpture of a child like a Cupid or cherub.

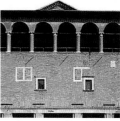

A loggia is an open-sided gallery or arcade. It may be a separate structure or part of a building, as here at San Saba.

Rusticated masonry decorates the exterior of many Renaissance palazzi. It consists of massive blocks divided by deep joints.

Cosmatesque Sculpture and Mosaics

The Cosmati family, active in Rome during the 12th and 13th centuries, have given their name to a particularly Roman style of decoration. They worked in marble, producing all kinds of fittings for churches, including cloisters, episcopal thrones, tombs, pulpits, fonts and candlesticks. These were often

Cosmatesque floor, Santa Maria in Cosmedin

decorated with bands of colourful mosaic. They also left many fine floor mosaics, usually of white marble with an inlay of red and green porphyry. Ancient Roman columns were cut up to provide the materials. Several other families of stonemasons used a similar style, and their work is also described as Cosmatesque.

Rome During Unification

Under the French Emperor Napoleon, Italy had a brief taste of unity, but by 1815 it was once more divided into many small states and papal rule was restored in Rome. Over the next 50 years, patriots, led by Mazzini, Garibaldi, and others, struggled to create an independent, unified Italy. In 1848 Rome was briefly declared a Republic, but Garibaldi's forces were driven out by French troops. The French continued to protect the pope, while the rest of Italy was united as a kingdom under Vittorio Emanuele of Savoy. In 1870, troops stormed the city, and Rome became capital of Italy.

Extent of the City
- 1870
- Today

Allegory of Italy's Liberty
This patriotic poster from 1890 shows the king, his chief minister Cavour, Garibaldi, and Mazzini. The woman in red represents Italy.

Porta Pia

Tricoloured flag of the new Italian kingdom

Plumed hat of the Bersaglieri, crack troops from Savoy

Vittorio Emanuele II
Vittorio Emanuele of Savoy became the first King of Italy in 1861.

Royalists Storm Porta Pia
On 20 September 1870, troops of the kingdom of Italy put an end to papal domination of Rome. They breached the city walls near Porta Pia; the pope retreated and Rome was made the Italian capital.

1751 Piranesi's *Views of Rome* revive interest in Classical ruins

1762 Trevi Fountain is completed

Napoleon Bonaparte

1799 Napoleon expelled from Italy by Austrians and Russians

1797 Napoleon captures Rome

1807 Birth of Garibaldi

1750

1775

1800

1792 Canova creates the Tomb of Pope Clement XIII, St Peter's

1800–1 Napoleon takes Italy again

Piranesi etching of Trajan's Forum

Garibaldi and Rome
The charismatic leader Giuseppe Garibaldi had taken much of Italy from foreign rule by 1860. Rome still remained a crucial problem. Here he declares "O Roma o morte" (Rome or Death).

Villa Paolina

Giuseppe Verdi (1813–1901)
Verdi, the opera composer, supported unification and in 1861 became a member of Italy's first national parliament.

Breach in Aurelian Wall

Victor Emmanuel Monument
A vast monument to Italy's first king (see p76) stands in Piazza Venezia.

S · P · Q · R ·
VRBE · ITALIAE · VINDICATA
INCOLIS · FELICITER · AVCTIS
GEMINOS · FORNICES · CONDIDIT

A Freed City
This marble plaque was set up at Porta Pia to commemorate the liberation of Rome.

Fountain in Piazza del Popolo

1848 Nationalist uprising in Rome. Pope flees and a Republic is formed

1849 Pope is restored to power, protected by a French garrison

1870 Royalist troops take Rome, completing the unification of Italy

1816 Work begins on Piazza del Popolo

1825

1850

1821 English poet Keats dies in Piazza di Spagna

1820 Revolts throughout Italy

Pope Pius IX

1860 Garibaldi and his 1,000 followers take Sicily and Naples

1861 Kingdom of Italy founded with capital in Turin

Modern Rome

The Fascist dictator Mussolini dreamed of recreating the immensity, order and power of the old Roman Empire: "Rome", he said, "must appear wonderful to the whole world". He began to build a grandiose new complex, EUR, in the suburbs, and razed 15 churches and many medieval houses to create space for wide new roads. Fortunately most of the old centre has survived, leaving the city with one of Europe's most picturesque historic cores. To mark the Holy Year and the new millennium, many crumbling churches, buildings and monuments were given a thorough facelift.

Extent of the City
☐ 1960s   ☐ Today

Mussolini's Plans for Rome
This propaganda poster reflects Mussolini's grandiose projects such as Via dei Fori Imperiali in the Forum area (see p79), and EUR (p268).

Pope Francis
After the abdication of Pope Benedict XVI in 2013, the Argentinian cardinal Jorge Mario Bergoglio was elected Pope Francis. The Pope exerts a huge influence on the lives of the world's Catholics.

Jubilee Celebrations
Jubilee Years are usually celebrated every quarter of a century. Millions of Catholics visited Rome to celebrate the year 2000.

1911 Victor Emmanuel Monument is completed

1929 Lateran Treaty creates a separate Vatican state

1926 Opposition parties banned

1944 Allies liberate Rome from Germans

1960 Olympic Games are held in Rome

1946 National referendum establishes Italy as a Republic; King Umberto II exiled

1900	1915	1930	1945	1960

1915 Italy enters World War I

1922 Fascists march on Rome. Mussolini becomes prime minister

Poster for EUR

1940 Italy enters World War II; work begins on EUR zone

1957 Treaty of Rome initiates European Common Market

1962 Second Vatican Council brings about Church reforms

Three Tenors Concert (1990)
Combining Italy's love for music and football, this opera recital at the Baths of Caracalla was broadcast live during the World Cup.

Poster for La Dolce Vita
In the 1950s and 1960s Rome was Europe's Hollywood. *Ben-Hur*, *Quo Vadis?* and *Cleopatra* were made at the Cinecittà studios, as well as Italian films like Fellini's *La Dolce Vita*.

Valentino Model
While not as important as Milan for fashion, Rome is still home to some of the industry's leading designers.

City-Centre Traffic
Rome's streets are congested, and many buildings have been damaged by pollution. There are plans to close the historic centre to cars. The former Mayor, Ignazio Marino, began closing stretches of Via dei Fori Imperiali to cars and scooters in 2013.

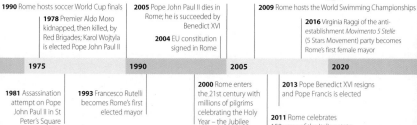

1990 Rome hosts soccer World Cup finals

1978 Premier Aldo Moro kidnapped, then killed, by Red Brigades; Karol Wojtyla is elected Pope John Paul II

2005 Pope John Paul II dies in Rome; he is succeeded by Benedict XVI

2004 EU constitution signed in Rome

2009 Rome hosts the World Swimming Championships

2016 Virginia Raggi of the anti-establishment *Movimento 5 Stelle* (5 Stars Movement) party becomes Rome's first female mayor

1975 — **1990** — **2005** — **2020**

1981 Assassination attempt on Pope John Paul II in St Peter's Square

1993 Francesco Rutelli becomes Rome's first elected mayor

2000 Rome enters the 21st century with millions of pilgrims celebrating the Holy Year – the Jubilee

2013 Pope Benedict XVI resigns and Pope Francis is elected

2011 Rome celebrates 150 years of the Italian state

ROME AT A GLANCE

From its early days as a settlement of shepherds on the Palatine hill, Rome grew to rule a vast empire stretching from northern England to North Africa. Later, after the empire had collapsed, Rome became the centre of the Christian world and artists and architects flocked to work for the popes. The legacy of this history can be seen all over the city. The following pages are a time-saving summary of some of the best Rome has to offer. There are sections on churches, museums and galleries, fountains and obelisks, and celebrated artists and writers in Rome. Listed below are the top attractions that no visitor should miss.

Rome's Top Tourist Attractions

Capitoline Museums
See pp70–73.

Colosseum
See pp94–7.

Sistine Chapel
See pp242–5.

Spanish Steps
See p136.

Raphael Rooms
See pp240–41.

Trevi Fountain
See p161.

Castel Sant'Angelo
See pp250–51.

Pantheon
See pp114–15.

St Peter's
See pp228–31.

Roman Forum
See pp80–89.

Piazza Navona
See p122.

◀ *The Last Judgment* by Michelangelo on the altar wall of the Sistine Chapel, Vatican

Rome's Best: Churches and Temples

As the centre of Christianity, Rome has a vast wealth of beautiful and interesting churches. These range from magnificent great basilicas, built to assert the importance of the medieval and Renaissance Catholic church, to smaller, humbler buildings where the first Christians gathered, often in secret. Among the most fascinating early churches are those converted from ancient Roman temples. Additions to these over the years have resulted in some intriguing, many-layered buildings. A more detailed historical overview of Rome's churches is on pages 48–9.

Pantheon
This monumental 2,000-year-old building is one of the largest surviving temples of ancient Rome.

St Peter's
At 136 m (450 ft) high, Michelangelo's dome is the tallest in the world. Sadly, the artist died before seeing his work completed.

Santa Maria in Trastevere
Built over a very early Christian foundation, this church is famous for its ornate mosaics.

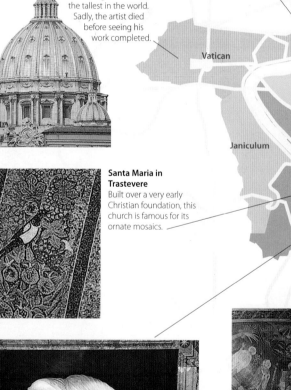

Piazza di Spagna

Vatican

Piazza della Rotonda

Piazza Navona

Campo de' Fiori

Janiculum

Cap

Trastevere

Aventine

Santa Maria in Cosmedin
The decorations in this 6th-century church are 12th-century and earlier. A restored painting in the apse shows the Virgin, Child and saints.

Santa Cecilia in Trastevere
This statue of Cecilia, showing her as she lay when her tomb was uncovered, was sculpted in 1599 by Stefano Maderno.

Sant'Andrea al Quirinale
Bernini made maximum use of strong, dynamic curves in this oval interior (1658–70), creating a small masterpiece of the Roman Baroque.

Santa Maria Maggiore
Rich mosaics and relics contrast with the sober interior form of Santa Maria Maggiore. Among its treasures are vestments bearing the Borghese coat of arms.

Santa Prassede
Magnificent Byzantine mosaics cover the walls and ceilings of this 9th-century church. This Christ with Angels is in the Chapel of St Zeno.

Via Veneto

Quirinal

Esquiline

Lateran

Caracalla

orum

atine

0 metres   500
0 yards   500

Santa Croce in Gerusalemme
Saints adorn the façade of Santa Croce. Inside are relics of the Cross, brought from Jerusalem by St Helena.

San Clemente
Different archaeological layers lie beneath the 12th-century church. This sarcophagus dates from the 4th century.

San Giovanni in Laterano
The original church was built by Constantine, the first Christian emperor. The Chapel of St Venantius mosaics include the figure of St Venantius himself.

Exploring Churches and Temples

There are more churches in Rome than there are days of the year, so you will have to be selective. Catholic pilgrims have always been drawn to the seven major basilicas: **St Peter's**, the heart of the Roman Catholic church, **San Giovanni in Laterano**, **San Paolo fuori le Mura**, **Santa Maria Maggiore**, **Santa Croce in Gerusalemme**, **San Lorenzo fuori le Mura** and **San Sebastiano**. These have a wealth of relics, tombs and magnificent works of art from many different periods. Smaller churches can be equally fascinating, especially those where the original character is preserved.

13th-century fresco by Pietro Cavallini in Santa Cecilia

Ancient Temples

One pagan temple survives virtually unaltered since it was erected in the 2nd century AD. The **Pantheon**, "Temple of all the Gods", has a domed interior quite different in structure from any other church in Rome. It was reconsecrated as a Christian church in the 7th century.

Other Roman temples have been incorporated into Christian churches at various times. Two of these are in the Forum; **Santi Cosma e Damiano** was established in the Temple of Romulus in 526, while San Lorenzo in Miranda was built on to the ruins of the

Temple of Antoninus and Faustina in the 11th century. The Baroque façade, built in 1602, looms behind the columns of the temple.

Another church that clearly shows its ancient Roman origins is **Santa Costanza**, built as a mausoleum for Constantine's daughter. It is a round church with some splendid 4th-century mosaics.

Early Christian and Medieval Churches

Some early basilicas – the 5th-century **Santa Maria Maggiore** and **Santa Sabina**, for example – retain much of their original structure. Other, even earlier, churches such as the 4th-century **San Paolo fuori le Mura** and **San Giovanni in Laterano** still preserve their original basilica shape. San Paolo was rebuilt after a fire in 1823 destroyed the original building, and the San Giovanni of today dates from a 1646 reconstruction by Borromini. Both these churches still have their medieval cloisters.

Santa Maria in Trastevere and **Santa Cecilia in Trastevere**

were built over houses where the earliest Christian communities met and worshipped in secret to avoid persecution. One church where the different layers of earlier structures can clearly be seen is **San Clemente**. At its lowest level, it has a Mithraic temple of the 3rd century AD. Other early churches include **Santa Maria in Cosmedin**, with its impressive Romanesque bell tower, and the fortified convent of **Santi Quattro Coronati**. Many Roman churches, most notably **Santa Prassede**, contain fine early Christian and medieval mosaics.

The impressive domed interior of the Pantheon, which became a church in 609

Cloister of San Giovanni in Laterano

Unusual Floorplans

The design of Rome's first churches was based on the ancient basilica, a rectangular building divided into three naves. Since then there have been many bold departures from this plan, including round churches, square churches based on the shape of the Greek cross, as in Bramante's plan for St Peter's, and, in the Baroque period, even oval and hexagonal ones.

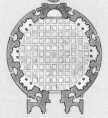

Pantheon (2nd century)

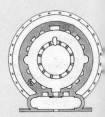

Santa Costanza (4th century)

Renaissance

The greatest undertaking of the Renaissance popes was the rebuilding of **St Peter's**. Disagreements on the form it should take meant that, although work started in 1506, it was not completed until well into the 17th century. Fortunately, this did not prevent the building of Michelangelo's great dome. As well as working on St Peter's, Michelangelo also provided the **Sistine Chapel** with its magnificent frescoes.

On a completely different scale, another key work of Renaissance architecture is Bramante's tiny **Tempietto** (1499) on the Janiculum. **Santa Maria della Pace** has a Bramante cloister, some frescoes by Raphael, and a charming portico by Pietro da Cortona. Also of interest is Michelangelo's imaginative use of the great vaults of the Roman Baths of Diocletian in the church of **Santa Maria degli Angeli**.

There are other churches worth visiting for the sake of their outstanding paintings and sculptures. **Santa Maria del**

Michelangelo's dramatic dome crowning the interior of St Peter's

Popolo, for example, has two great paintings by Caravaggio, the Chigi Chapel designed by Raphael, and a series of 15th-century frescoes by Pinturicchio. **San Pietro in Vincoli**, besides having the chains with which St Peter was bound in prison, also has Michelangelo's awe-inspiring statue of Moses, while **San Luigi dei Francesi** has three Caravaggios depicting St Matthew and frescoes by Domenichino.

Interior of Rosati's dome in San Carlo ai Catinari (1620)

Baroque

The Counter-Reformation inspired the exuberant, lavish style of churches such as the **Gesù** and **Sant'Ignazio di Loyola**. The best-loved examples of Roman Baroque are the later works associated with Bernini, such as the great colonnade and baldacchino he built for **St Peter's**. Of the smaller churches he designed, perhaps the finest is **Sant'Andrea al Quirinale**, while **Santa Maria della Vittoria** houses his truly astonishing Cornaro Chapel with its sculpture of the *Ecstasy of St Teresa*. The late Baroque was not all Bernini, however. You should also look out for churches such as **San Carlo ai Catinari** with its beautiful dome

by Rosato Rosati and the many churches by Bernini's rival, Borromini. **Sant'Agnese in Agone** and **San Carlo alle Quattro Fontane** are famed for the dramatic concave surfaces of their façades, while the complex structure of **Sant'Ivo alla Sapienza** makes it one of the miniature masterpieces of the Baroque.

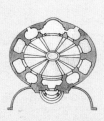

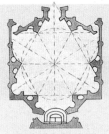

Bramante's St Peter's (1503)

Sant'Andrea al Quirinale (1658)

Sant'Ivo alla Sapienza (1642)

Rome's Best: Museums and Galleries

The museums of Rome are among the richest in the world; the Vatican alone contains incomparable collections of Egyptian, Etruscan, Greek, Roman and Early Christian artifacts, as well as frescoes by Michelangelo and Raphael, priceless manuscripts and jewels. Excavations in the 19th century added treasures from ancient Rome which are now on show in museums throughout the city. The finest Etruscan collections in the world can be enjoyed in the Villa Giulia. More details of Rome's museums and galleries are given on pages 52–3.

Villa Giulia
Etruscan treasures from Rome's early history are displayed in this beautiful Renaissance villa.

0 metres 500
0 yards 500

Vatican Museums
The galleries and long corridors hold priceless artifacts such as this 9th-century mosaic showing scenes from the life of Christ.

Vatican

Piazz
Spac

Piaz
dell
Piazza Roto
Navona

Campo
de' Fiori

Janiculum

Trastevere

Ave

Galleria Spada
This collection's strength lies in its 17th- and 18th-century paintings. Earlier works include a *Visitation* by Andrea del Sarto (1486–1530).

Palazzo Corsini
Included here are works by Caravaggio, Rubens and Van Dyck, as well as a painting of the Baroque sculptor Bernini – a rare portrait by Il Baciccia (1639–1709).

Galleria Doria Pamphilj
Most of the great names of the Renaissance are represented on this gallery's crowded walls. Titian (1485–1576) painted *Salome* early in his career.

Museo e Galleria Borghese
The ground-floor museum houses ancient Greek and Roman sculpture as well as early Bernini masterpieces such as his *David* (1619). Upstairs are paintings by Titian, Rubens and other masters.

Palazzo Barberini
The works of art here date mainly from the 13th to the 16th centuries. This figure of Providence comes from Pietro da Cortona's *The Triumph of Divine Providence* (1633–9).

Museo Nazionale Romano
This fresco, from Livia's Villa (1st century AD) outside Rome, is one of a huge collection of finds from archaeological sites throughout the city.

Palazzo Venezia
The highlights of Rome's most significant museum of decorative arts are its Byzantine and medieval collections, including this Byzantine enamel of Christ dating from the 13th century.

Capitoline Museums: Palazzo dei Conservatori
Pietro da Cortona's *Rape of the Sabine Women* (1629) is one of many Baroque paintings in the picture gallery.

Capitoline Museums: Palazzo Nuovo
Among the sculptures is this head of Giulia Domna (wife of Septimius Severus) from the 2nd century AD.

Exploring Museums and Galleries

Rome's museums and galleries have two major strengths: Greek and Roman archaeological treasures, and paintings and sculptures of the Renaissance and the Baroque periods. The Vatican Museums have superb collections of both, as do, on a smaller scale, the Capitoline Museums. Fine paintings can also be found scattered throughout Rome in museums, galleries and churches (see pp48–9).

Centurion's breast-plate, Museo della Civiltà Romana

statuettes and artifacts are relics of the Faliscans, Latins and other tribes who inhabited central Italy before the Romans.

The Gregorian Etruscan Museum in the **Vatican Museums** was opened in 1837 to house Etruscan finds from tombs on Church-owned land. The Museo Barracco in the **Piccola Farnesina** has statues from the much older civilizations of ancient Egypt and Assyria.

Ancient Roman Art

The archaeological zone in Rome forms a huge open-air museum of evidence of ancient Roman life, while the porticoes and cloisters of the city's churches are filled with ancient sarcophagi and fragments of statuary. The largest important collection can be seen in the **Museo Nazionale Romano** at the Baths of Diocletian and the Palazzo Massimo. The museum's many ancient artifacts include, most notably, a sarcophagus from Livia's Villa at Prima Porta just north of Rome. Also on display are some wonderfully well-preserved mosaics. The museum's great collection of Roman statues is now housed in the **Palazzo Altemps**. The most venerated statues are in the **Vatican Museums**, which also have the best of the great Greek works, such as the *Laocoön and His Sons*, brought to Rome around the 1st century AD. It had tremendous influence on the subsequent development of Roman art. Splendid copies of Greek originals can be seen in the **Capitoline Museums**. In the Forum, occupying two floors

of the church of Santa Francesca Romana, is the **Antiquarium Forense** with restored finds from the excavations. For those who enjoy history, the large-scale model at the **Museo della Civiltà Romana** in EUR gives an excellent idea of what ancient Rome looked like in the 4th century AD.

5th-century BC Etruscan gold plate with inscription, Villa Giulia

Etruscan Artifacts

The Etruscans inhabited an area stretching from Florence to Rome from the 8th century BC, and ruled Rome from the late 7th century BC (see pp20–21). It was the Etruscan custom to bury the dead along with their possessions, and as a result Etruscan artifacts have been excavated from tombs all over central Italy. Three main collections can be seen in Rome. The **Villa Giulia** has been the home of the Museo Nazionale Etrusco since 1889. The villa, designed by Vignola for Pope Julius III for summer outings, is one of Rome's prettiest Renaissance buildings. Its gardens contain a reconstructed Etruscan temple. Not all objects here are Etruscan, however; some of the pottery,

Muses in Raphael's *Parnassus* (1508–11), Vatican Museums

Art Galleries

In the past, many of Rome's great aristocratic families owned magnificent private collections of paintings and sculpture. Some of these are still housed in ancestral palazzi, which are open to the public. One is the **Galleria Doria Pamphilj**, which has the greatest concentration of paintings of any palazzo in Rome. It is well worth searching through the various rooms to find the pearls of the collection, which include works by Raphael, Filippo Lippi, Caravaggio, Titian and Claude

Victory banner, Museo della Civiltà Romana

Lorrain, and a portrait of Pope Innocent X Pamphilj by the Spanish artist Velázquez. The **Galleria Spada** collection, begun by Bernardino Spada in 1632, is still housed in the fine original gallery built for it.

Hellenistic faun, Museo Borghese

The paintings demonstrate 17th-century Roman taste and include works by Rubens, Guido Reni, Guercino and Jan Brueghel the Elder. The **Galleria Colonna** contains a collection of art dating from the same period.

Other old family residences are now showcases for state art collections. The Galleria Nazionale d'Arte Antica is divided between **Palazzo Barberini** and **Palazzo Corsini**. Palazzo Barberini, built between 1625 and 1633 by Bernini and others for the Barberini family, houses paintings from the 13th to the 16th centuries. Pietro da Cortona painted the stunning *Triumph of Divine Providence* on the ceiling of the Grand Salon. Palazzo Corsini, on the south side of the Tiber, is famed for its collection of 16th–17th-century art. Another wonderful private collection was that of the

Borghese family, also now managed by the state. The sculpture collection of the **Museo e Galleria Borghese** includes the amazing *Apollo and Daphne* by Bernini and the famous statue of Pauline Borghese by Canova. On the first floor is the picture collection with paintings by Titian, Correggio and others.

The **Capitoline Museums** hold collections that were gifts of the popes to the people of Rome. The Pinacoteca (art gallery) in the **Palazzo dei Conservatori** contains works by Titian, Guercino and Van Dyck. There is an art gallery at the **Vatican Museums**, but lovers of Renaissance art will head straight for the Sistine Chapel and the Raphael Rooms. Rome's main modern art collection is in the **Galleria Nazionale d'Arte Moderna**, though modern art aficionados should not miss the Zaha Hadid-designed **MAXXI** museum of 21st-century art.

Smaller Museums

The most significant of the smaller collections is the beautifully laid-out medieval museum in **Palazzo Venezia**, with exhibits ranging from ceramics to sculpture. Rome has a wealth of specialist museums like the **Museum of Musical Instruments**, the **Museo di Roma in Trastevere**, with tableaux showing life in Rome during the last century, and the **Burcardo Theatre Museum**. For those with an interest in the English Romantic poets who lived in Rome in the 19th century, there is the **Keats-Shelley Memorial House**, a museum in the house where John Keats died. Focusing on the French Empire, the **Museo Napoleonico** has relics and paintings

Laocoön and His Sons (1st century AD) in the Vatican's Pio-Clementine Museum

of Napoleon and members of his family, many of whom came to live in Rome.

Portrait of Napoleon's sister Pauline Borghese, painted by Kinson (c.1805), in the Museo Napoleonico

The Deposition (1604) by Caravaggio, Vatican Museums

Rome's Best: Fountains and Obelisks

Rome has some of the loveliest fountains in the world. Many of them are the work of the greatest Renaissance and Baroque sculptors. Some fountains are flamboyant displays, others restful trickles of water. Many are simply drinking fountains, while a few cascade from the sides of buildings. Obelisks date from far earlier in the city's history. Although some of them were commissioned by Roman emperors, many are even older and were brought to Rome by conquering armies. A more detailed overview of Rome's fountains and obelisks is on pages 56–7.

Piazza San Pietro
Twin fountains give life to the splendid monumental piazza of St Peter's. Maderno designed the one on the Vatican side in 1614; the other was later built to match.

Piazza del Popolo
Nineteenth-century marble lions and fountains surround an ancient obelisk in the centre of the piazza.

Piazza Spagna

Vatican

Piazza Navona

Piazza di Roma

Campo de' Fiori

Janiculum

Fontana dei Quattro Fiumi
The fountain of the four rivers is the work of Bernini. The four figures represent the Ganges, the Plate, the Danube and the Nile.

Trastevere

Obelisk of Santa Maria sopra Minerva
The Egyptian obelisk, held up by Bernini's marble elephant, dates from the 6th century BC.

Fontana delle Tartarughe
One of Rome's more secret fountains, this jewel of Renaissance sculpture shows youths helping tortoises into a basin.

Fontana della Barcaccia
This elegant fountain of 1627 is probably the work of Pietro Bernini, father of the more famous Gian Lorenzo.

Trevi Fountain
The Trevi, inspired by Roman triumphal arches, was designed by Nicola Salvi in 1732. Tradition has it that a coin thrown into the water guarantees a visitor's return to Rome.

| 0 metres | 500 |
| 0 yards | 500 |

Via Veneto

Quirinal

Esquiline

ıtol

Forum

Palatine

Lateran

ıntine

Caracalla

Fontana delle Naiadi
When this fountain was unveiled in 1901, the realistically sensual bronze nymphs caused a storm of protest.

Piazza della Bocca della Verità Fountain
In this 18th-century fountain, built by Carlo Bizzaccheri for Pope Clement XI, water spills over a craggy rock formation where two Tritons hold aloft a large shell.

Obelisk of Piazza San Giovanni in Laterano
The oldest obelisk in Rome dates from the 14th century BC. It came to Rome in AD 357, brought here on the orders of Constantine II.

Exploring Fountains and Obelisks

The popes who restored the ancient Roman aqueducts used to build fountains to commemorate their deeds of munificence. As a result, fountains of all sizes and shapes punctuate the city, drawing grateful crowds on hot summer days. Ancient obelisks provide powerful reminders of the debt Roman civilization owed to the Egyptians. Architects have learnt to incorporate them into Roman piazzas in fascinating ways.

The Pantheon Fountain

Fountains

The Trevi Fountain is one of the most famous of all. It is a *mostra*, a monumental fountain built to mark the end of an aqueduct – in this case the Acqua Vergine, built by Marcus Agrippa in 19 BC, although the Trevi itself was only completed in 1762. Other *mostre* are the **Fontana dell'Acqua Paola**, built for Pope Paul V in 1612 on the Janiculum, and the **Moses Fountain**, commemorating the opening of the Acqua Felice by Pope Sixtus V in 1587.

Almost all Rome's famous piazzas have fountains. In **Piazza San Pietro** there is a matching pair of powerful fountains. Piazza Navona has Bernini's wonderful Baroque **Fontana dei Quattro Fiumi** (fountain of the four rivers) as its main attraction. The fountain's four figures each represent one of the principal rivers of the four continents then known. To the south of this is the smaller **Fontana del Moro** (the Moor), also by Bernini, showing an Ethiopian struggling with a dolphin. At the north end, Neptune wrestles with an octopus on a

19th-century fountain. In Piazza Barberini is the magnificent Bernini creation of 1642–3: the **Fontana del Tritone** with its sea god blowing through a shell.

More recently, large piazzas have been redesigned around fountains. Valadier's great design for **Piazza del Popolo** (1816–20) has marble lions and fountains surrounding the central obelisk plus two more fountains on the

Fountain of the four tiaras located behind St Peter's

east and west sides of the square. The early 20th century saw the opening of the **Fontana delle Naiadi** (nymphs) in Piazza della Repubblica; its earthy figures caused great scandal at the time. The highly original **Fountain of the Amphorae** (**map** 8 D2) was erected in Piazza dell'Emporio during the 1920s. The same designer, Pietro Lombardi, also created the **Fountain of the Four Tiaras** (**map** 3 C3) behind the colonnade of St Peter's.

The city also has a number of smaller, and often very charming, fountains. At the foot of the Spanish Steps is the **Fontana della Barcaccia** (the leaking boat) of 1627; the **Fontana delle Tartarughe** (the tortoise fountain) has

Fontana dei Cavalli Marini

The Trevi Fountain

Appropriately for a fountain resembling a stage set, the theatrical Trevi has been the star of many films set in Rome, including romantic films like *Three Coins in a Fountain* and *Roman Holiday*, but also *La Dolce Vita*, Fellini's satirical portrait of Rome in the 1950s. Whatever liberties Anita Ekberg took then, paddling in the fountains of Rome is now forbidden, however tempting it could be in the summer heat.

Anita Ekberg in *La Dolce Vita* (1960)

been in the tiny Piazza Mattei since 1581, and by Santa Maria in Domnica is the **Fontana della Navicella** (little boat), created out of an ancient Roman sculpture in the 16th century. In the forecourt of **Santa Sabina** (**map** 8 D2) water gushes from a huge mask set in an ancient basin. The **Pantheon Fountain** (**map** 4 F4), from 1575, is by Jacopo della Porta. **Le Quattro Fontane** (four fountains) have stood at the Quirinal hill crossroads since 1593.

Fountains in parks and gardens include the **Galleon Fountain** (1620–21) at the Vatican, and the **Fontana dei Cavalli Marini** (seahorses), of 1791, at Villa Borghese. The somewhat decayed 16th-century terraced gardens of the **Villa d'Este**, with their display of over 500 fountains, are still worth the journey.

Piazza Navona with Fontana dei Quattro Fiumi, by Pannini (1691–1765)

The Ovato fountain at Villa d'Este

Obelisks

The most ancient and tallest of Rome's obelisks is the **Obelisk of Piazza di San Giovanni in Laterano**. Built of red granite, 31 m (100 ft) high, it came from the Temple of Amon at Thebes, erected in the 14th century BC. Brought to Rome in AD 357 by the order of Constantine II, it was put up in the Circus Maximus. In 1587 it was rediscovered, broken into three pieces, and was re-erected in the following year. Next in age is the obelisk in **Piazza del Popolo**, from the 13th or 12th century BC. It was brought to Rome in the time of Augustus and also erected in the Circus

Maximus. The slightly smaller **Obelisk of Piazza Montecitorio** was another of Augustus's trophies. The bronze ball and spike at the top recall its past use as a gnomon for a sundial of vast proportions. Other obelisks, such as the one at the top of the Spanish Steps, are Roman imitations of Egyptian originals. The **Obelisk of Piazza dell' Esquilino** and the one in **Piazza del Quirinale** (**map** 5 B4) first stood at the entrance to the Mausoleum of Augustus. When re-erected, most obelisks were mounted on decorative bases, often with statues and fountains at their foot. Others became parts of sculptures. Bernini was the creator of the marble

Obelisk in Piazza del Popolo

elephant balancing the Egyptian **Obelisk of Santa Maria sopra Minerva** on its back, and the **Fontana dei Fiumi**, with an obelisk from the Circus of Maxentius. Another obelisk was added to the remodelled Pantheon Fountain in 1711. The obelisk in **Piazza San Pietro** is Egyptian but does not have the usual hieroglyphics.

Wall fountain at Villa d'Este

Where to Find the Fountains and Obelisks

Artists and Writers Inspired by Rome

Artists and writers have been attracted to Rome since Classical times. Many came to work for the emperors; the poets Horace, Virgil and Ovid, for example, all enjoyed the patronage of Emperor Augustus. Later on, especially in the Renaissance and Baroque periods, the greatest artists and architects came to Rome to compete for commissions from the popes. However, patronage was not the only magnet. Since the Renaissance, Rome's Classical past and its picturesque ruins have drawn artists, architects, and writers from all over Italy and abroad.

Self-portrait by the 18th-century artist Angelica Kauffmann, c.1770

Diego Velázquez, one of many great 17th-century artists to visit Rome

Painters, Sculptors and Architects

In the early 16th century, artists and architects were summoned from all parts of Italy to realize the grandiose building projects of the popes. From Urbino came Bramante (1444–1514) and Raphael (1483–1520); from Perugia Perugino (1450–1523); from Florence Michelangelo (1475–1564) and many others. They worked in the Vatican, on the new St Peter's and the decoration of the Sistine Chapel. Artists were often well rewarded, but they also lived in dangerous times. Florentine sculptor and goldsmith Benvenuto Cellini (1500–71) helped defend Castel Sant'Angelo *(see pp250–51)* during the Sack of Rome (1527), but was later imprisoned there and made a dramatic escape. His memoirs tell the story.

Towards the end of the 16th century Church patronage was generous to the Milanese-born Caravaggio (1571–1610) despite his violent character

and unruly life. The Carracci family from Bologna also flourished – especially brothers Annibale (1560–1609) and Agostino (1557–1602).

The work of Gian Lorenzo Bernini (1598–1680) can be seen all over Rome. He succeeded Carlo Maderno (1556–1629) as architect of St Peter's, and created its great bronze baldacchino, the splendid colonnade *(see pp228–9)* and numerous fountains, churches and sculptures. His rival for the title of leading architect of the Roman Baroque was Francesco Borromini (1599–1667), whose highly original genius can be appreciated in many Roman churches and palazzi.

In the 17th century it became more common for artists from outside Italy to come and work in Rome. Diego Velázquez (1599–1660), King Philip IV of Spain's court painter, came in 1628 to study the art treasures of the Vatican. Rubens

(1577–1640) came from Antwerp to study, and carried out various commissions. The French artists Nicolas Poussin (1594–1665) and Claude Lorrain (1600–82) lived here for many years.

The Classical revival of the 18th century attracted artists to Rome in unprecedented numbers. From Britain came the Scottish architect Robert Adam (1728–92) and the Swiss artist Angelica Kauffmann (1741–1807), who settled here and was buried with great honour in Sant'Andrea delle Fratte. After the excesses of the Baroque, sculpture also turned to the simplicity of Neo-Classicism. A leading exponent of this movement was Antonio Canova (1757–1821). Sculptors from all over Europe were influenced by him, including the Dane Bertel Thorvaldsen (1770–1844) who lived in Rome for many years.

Claude Lorrain's view of the Forum, painted in Rome in 1632

Writers

Dante (1262–1321) visited Rome during his exile from Florence and in the *Inferno* describes the great influx of pilgrims for the first Holy Year (1300). The poet Petrarch (1304–74), born in Arezzo, was crowned with laurels on the Capitol in 1341. The poet Torquato Tasso (1544–95), from Sorrento, was invited to receive a similar honour, but died soon after his arrival. He is buried in Sant'Onofrio *(see p223)* on the Janiculum. Two of the first writers from abroad to visit Rome were the French essayist Montaigne (1533–92) and English poet John Milton (1608–74). Then, by the early 18th century, writers seemed to flock to Rome. Edward Gibbon (1737–94) was inspired to write *Decline and Fall of the Roman Empire* when he heard the monks singing the Angelus outside Santa Maria in Aracoeli *(see p75)*. German visitors included J J Winckelmann (1717–68), who wrote studies of ancient art, and poet J W von Goethe (1749–1832).

Portrait of the poet John Keats painted by his friend Joseph Severn in 1819

In the Romantic period Rome teemed with English writers: Keats, Shelley and Byron, followed by the Brownings and Charles Dickens. Travel writers in the 19th century included Augustus Hare (1834–1903) and the German historian Ferdinand Gregorovius (1821–91). Much of *The Portrait of a Lady* by American Henry James (1843–1916) is set in Rome.

Modern life in Rome is brilliantly captured by the Roman writer Alberto Moravia (1907–90), whose residence is sometimes open to visitors (www.fondo albertomoravia.it).

Musicians

Giovanni Pierluigi da Palestrina (1525–94), from the town of that name, became choirmaster and organist to the Vatican and composed some of the greatest unaccompanied choral music ever written. In 1770 the 14-year-old Mozart heard Gregorio Allegri's unpublished *Miserere* in the Sistine Chapel and wrote it down from memory. Arcangelo Corelli (1653–1713), the great violinist and composer of the Baroque age, worked in Rome under the patronage of Cardinal Ottoboni. One of his first commissions was to provide a festival of music for Queen Christina of Sweden.

During the 19th century the Prix de Rome brought many French musicians to study here at the Villa Medici *(see p137)*. Hector Berlioz (1803–69) owed the inspiration for his popular *Roman Carnival*, the overture to his opera *Benvenuto Cellini*, to his two-year stay in Rome. Georges Bizet (1838–75) and Claude Debussy (1862–1918) were also Prix de Rome winners. Franz Liszt (1811–86), after his 50th year, settled in Rome, took minor orders and became known as Abbé Liszt. He wrote *Fountains of the Villa d'Este* while staying at the villa in Tivoli.

Twentieth-century musical associations with Rome include the popular works by Ottorino Respighi (1870–1936): *The Fountains of Rome* and *The Pines of Rome*, while Giacomo Puccini (1858–1924) used Roman settings when creating his dramatic, tragic opera *Tosca*.

Giacomo Puccini

Torquato Tasso

Roman Cinema

The Cinecittà studios, built in 1937 just outside Rome, are most famous for the films made here in the 1940s – classics of Italian Neo-Realism such as Roberto Rossellini's *Roma Città Aperta* and Vittorio De Sica's *Sciuscià* and *Ladri di Biciclette*. The director most often linked with Roman cinema is Federico Fellini, through films like *La Dolce Vita* (1960) and *Roma* (1972). However, perhaps the most famous artist associated with Rome is the controversial writer-turned-film-maker Pier Paolo Pasolini (1922–75), widely known for his films *Teorema* (1968) and *Il Decamerone* (1971).

Since the 1950s, Rome and Cinecittà have also been much used for foreign films: from *Ben-Hur* and *Spartacus* in the 1950s through to *Gladiator* and Woody Allen's *To Rome with Love*.

Pier Paolo Pasolini

ROME THROUGH THE YEAR

The best times to visit Rome are spring and autumn when the weather is usually warm, and sometimes even hot enough to sunbathe and swim at the beaches and lakes outside the city. In the winter months, the weather tends to be grey and wet, while in high summer, most people (including Romans, who leave the city in their droves) find the heat unbearable. Easter and Christmas are obviously very special in Rome, but there are other religious festivals worth seeing at other times in the year, as well as some enjoyable secular events like the Festa de' Noantri in Trastevere and the Flower Festival in Genzano. In villages outside Rome, local celebrations are held to welcome new crops such as strawberries and beans in the spring, and grapes and truffles in the autumn.

Spring

Easter, falling in March or April, marks the official beginning of the tourist season in Rome. Catholics from all over the world flock into the city to make their pilgrimages to the main basilicas and to hear the Pope's Easter Sunday address outside St Peter's, while the less devout come simply to take advantage of the mild weather. Meanwhile, Romans pile into their cars and head for the coast and countryside, so you can expect the roads, beaches and restaurants of the Castelli Romani and Lake Bracciano to be busy.

Temperatures tend to be around 18° C (66° F), but can hit 28° C (82° F), so by mid-May it is usually possible to lunch and dine outside. However, there can still be sudden downpours and temperature swings, so do bring warm clothes and an umbrella. In April tubs full of colourful azaleas are ranged on the Spanish Steps and along Via Veneto, and once the roses start to flower in

Participants of the Rome Marathon make their way through the streets

the city's rose garden overlooking the Circus Maximus, it is opened to the public.

For a fortnight from mid-May Via dei Coronari is lit by candles, lined with plants and hung with banners for the street's antiques fair, while Via Margutta hosts an outdoor art show. In the first week of May the International Horse Show is held in the Villa Borghese. Also usually in May, many world-class tennis players flock to Rome to compete in the International Tennis Championships held annually at the Foro Italico.

Events

Festa di Santa Francesca Romana *(9 March)*, Santa Francesca Romana. Blessing of the city's vehicles *(see p89)*.
Festa di San Giuseppe *(19 March)*, in the Trionfale area. St Joseph's (and Father's) Day celebrated in the streets.
Rome Marathon *(late March)*, through the city *(see p359)*.
Festa della Primavera *(March/April)*, Spanish Steps and Trinità dei Monti. Azaleas in the street and concerts.
Good Friday *(March/April)*, Colosseum. Procession of the Cross at 9pm led by the Pope.
Easter Sunday *(March/April)*, St Peter's Square. Address made by the Pope *(see p229)*.
Rome's Birthday *(21 April)*, Piazza del Campidoglio and elsewhere.
Beni Culturali Week *(April)*. Free entry to most galleries.
Art exhibition *(April/May)*, Via Margutta *(see p345)*.
International Horse Show *(early May)*, Villa Borghese *(see p358)*.
International Tennis Championships *(usually May)*, Foro Italico *(see p358)*.

International Horse Show in Villa Borghese in May

Average Daily Hours of Sunshine

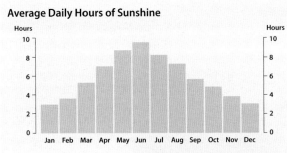

Hours

Jan Feb Mar Apr May Jun Jul Aug Sep Oct Nov Dec

Hours

Sunshine Chart
Rome is famous for its light. June is the sunniest month but it is also very dry, and without the odd shower the bright heat can feel intense. In autumn, Rome's southerly position means that the sun can still be enjoyably warm at midday.

Summer

In June a season of concerts begins, with performances in some of the city's most beautiful palaces, churches and courtyards. In July and August opera and drama are staged at Ostia Antica (see pp272–3) and in various outdoor locations. During the summer there are also contemporary cultural events – film, music of all kinds, dance and theatre. On midsummer evenings there are stalls and amusements on the Tiber embankments by Castel Sant'Angelo, while in the last two weeks of July Trastevere becomes an open-air party as the Noantri festival is celebrated with trinket stalls, dining in the street and fireworks. The sales (saldi) begin in mid-July, and the Alta Moda Fashion Show is usually held mid- to late July at the Spanish Steps.

Many Romans leave the city at the end of June, when schools close, but as June and July are peak tourist months, hotels, cafés, restaurants and all the main places of interest and

Flower-carpeted streets in Genzano

other attractions are packed out. In August, when the temperature often soars to over 40° C (104° F), virtually all Romans flee the city for the seaside, meaning that many cafés, shops and restaurants close for the entire month.

Events

Flower Festival (June, the Sunday after Corpus Domini), Genzano, Castelli Romani, south of Rome. Streets are carpeted with flowers.
Festa di San Giovanni (23–24 June), Piazza di Porta San Giovanni. Celebrated with meals of snails in tomato sauce, suckling pig, a fair and fireworks.
Festa dei Santi Pietro e Paolo (29 June), many churches. Celebrations mark the feast of Saints Peter and Paul.

Lungo il Tevere (end June–mid-July), along the Tiber. Crafts, food and wine, music and fireworks.
Festa de' Noantri (last two weeks in July), the streets of Trastevere. Food and entertainment (see p345 and p347).
Alta Roma Fashion Show (usually mid- to late July), Spanish Steps (see p345).
Estate Romana (July/August), Villa Ada, Ostia Antica, in parks, by the Tiber. Opera, concerts, drama, dance and film.
Festa della Madonna della Neve (5 August), Santa Maria Maggiore (see pp174–5). Fourth-century snowfall re-enacted with white flower petals.
Ferragosto (15 August), Santa Maria in Trastevere. Midsummer holiday; almost everything closes down. Celebrations are held for the Feast of the Assumption.

The heat of an August afternoon in front of St Peter's

Display of Roberto Cavalli's fashion collection on the Spanish Steps

Average Monthly Rainfall

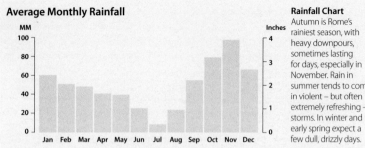

Rainfall Chart
Autumn is Rome's rainiest season, with heavy downpours, sometimes lasting for days, especially in November. Rain in summer tends to come in violent – but often extremely refreshing – storms. In winter and early spring expect a few dull, drizzly days.

Autumn

September and October are the best – and among the most popular – months to visit Rome. The fiery heat of July and August will have cooled a little, but midday can be very hot, and you can still eat and drink outside without feeling chilly until late at night. Visiting Rome in November is not recommended: it is the wettest month of the year and Roman rainstorms are often very strong and heavy.

At the beginning of October an artisans' fair is held on Via dell'Orso and adjacent streets, while nearby the antiques galleries of Via dei Coronari hold open house. There are also October antiques fairs in Orvieto and Perugia, two of the loveliest Umbrian hill towns, which are about an hour's drive north of Rome. In November, there is yet another prestigious antiques fair at the papal palace of Viterbo, 65 km (40 m) north of Rome (see p273). Autumn is the season of harvest festivals, so head out to the small towns around Rome to sample delicacies such as local cheeses, sausages, chestnuts and mushrooms. Another reason for taking a trip out of Rome is the wine festival in Marino, in the Castelli Romani, south of the city. There are many opportunities to sample the wines of this region that was once the home to luxurious 16th- and 17th-century country residences but now is renowned particularly for its spectacular white wines.

Throughout the autumn and winter in Rome freshly roasted chestnuts can be bought from vendors on street corners, and occasionally there is a stand on Campo de' Fiori where you can sample *vino novello*, the new season's wine.

A roast-chestnut stall in autumn

On All Saints' and All Souls' Days, which fall on 1 and 2 November respectively, the Romans make pilgrimages to place chrysanthemums on the tombs of relatives who are buried in the two main cemeteries of Prima Porta and Verano. On a happier note, the classical concert and opera seasons begin again in October and November. Details of performances can be found in listings magazines such as *Where Rome*, in supplements from daily newspapers, such as *La Repubblica's TrovaRoma (see p346)*, and on posters around the city.

Events

RomaEuropa *(autumn)*. Films, dance, theatre and concerts around Rome.

Crafts fair *(last week September/ first week October)*, Via dell'Orso.
International Festival of Cinema *(October)*. New screenings and stars aplenty *(see p352)*.
Marino Wine Festival *(first Sunday in October)*, Marino. Celebrations include tastings and street entertainment.
Antiques Fair *(mid-October)*, Via dei Coronari.
Festival di Musica e Arte Sacra *(October & November)*. Concerts by the world's leading choirs and orchestras take place in Rome's most important churches.
All Saints' and All Souls' Days *(1, 2 November)*, Prima Porta and Verano cemeteries. The Pope usually celebrates Mass in the Verano cemetery.
Festa di Santa Cecilia *(22 November)*, Santa Cecilia in Trastevere and Catacombs of San Callisto.

Autumn in the Villa Doria Pamphilj park

Average Monthly Temperature

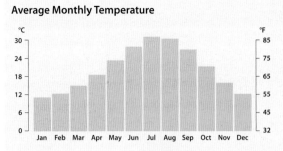

Temperature Chart
The chart shows the average minimum and maximum monthly temperatures. July and August can be unbearably hot, making sightseeing a chore. The fresher days of spring and autumn are ideal to visit Rome, but there are some dull and rainy spells.

Winter

During the winter Rome is bracingly chilly but the temperature rarely drops below freezing. Not all buildings are centrally heated so if you are staying in a small hotel bring warm clothes and request extra blankets as soon as you arrive, as they can be in short supply. Warm up in cafés with hot chocolate and cappuccino.

The run-up to Christmas is great fun in Rome, especially if you have children. Manger scenes, *presepi*, are set up in many churches, piazzas and public places and from mid-December to Twelfth Night Piazza Navona hosts a market where you can buy manger scenes, decorations and toys. Unless you have friends in Rome, Christmas itself can be rather lonely, as it is very much a family event. On New Year's Eve, however, everyone is out on the street to drink sparkling wine and let off fireworks.

La Befana, on 6 January, is a traditional holiday when a witch, called La Befana, delivers sweets to children.

The Carnival season runs from late January through to February, celebrated largely by children with fancy-dress parties and parades along Via Nazionale,

Rome during one of its rare snowfalls

Via Cola di Rienzo and the Pincio. Keep out of the way of teenagers with shaving-cream spray cans and water-filled balloons.

Events

Festa della Madonna Immacolata *(8 December)*, Piazza di Spagna. In the pope's presence, firemen climb up a ladder to place a wreath on the statue of the Virgin Mary.
Christmas Market *(mid-December–6 January)*, Piazza Navona. Christmas and children's market.
Nativity scenes *(mid-December–mid-January)*, many churches. Life-size scene in St Peter's Square, collection at Santi Cosma e Damiano.
Midnight Mass *(24 December)*, at most churches.
Christmas Day *(25 December)*, St Peter's Square. Blessing by the pope.
New Year's Eve *(31 December)*, all over city. Firework displays, furniture thrown out.
La Befana *(6 January)*, all over city. Parties for children.

Public Holidays

New Year's Day (1 Jan)
Epiphany (6 Jan)
Easter Monday
Liberation Day (25 Apr)
Labour Day (1 May)
Republic Day (2 Jun)
SS Peter & Paul (29 Jun)
Ferragosto (15 Aug)
All Saints' Day (1 Nov)
Immaculate Conception (8 Dec)
Christmas Day (25 Dec)
Santo Stefano (26 Dec)

Market on Piazza Navona

Via Condotti at Christmas

View of St Peter's Basilica, Vatican ▶

ROME
AREA BY AREA

CAPITOL

The temple of Jupiter on the Capitol, the southern summit of the Capitoline hill, was the centre of the Roman world. Reached by a zig-zag path up from the Forum, the temple was the scene of all the most sacred religious and political ceremonies. The hill and its temple came to symbolize Rome's authority as *caput mundi*, head of the world, and the Capitol gave its name to the seat of the US Congress. Throughout the city's history, the Capitol (Campidoglio), has remained the seat of municipal government. Today's city council, the Comune di Roma,

meets in the Renaissance splendour of Palazzo Senatorio. The Capitol also serves as Rome's Registry Office. Rome's position as a modern capital is forcefully expressed in the enormous Victor Emmanuel Monument, which unfortunately blots out the view of the Capitol from Piazza Venezia. The present arrangement on the hill dates from the 16th century, when Michelangelo created a beautiful piazza reached by a flight of steps, the Cordonata. Two of the buildings around the piazza now house the Capitoline Museums.

Sights at a Glance

Churches and Temples
7 Santa Maria in Aracoeli
8 Temple of Jupiter
12 San Marco

Museums and Galleries
1 *Capitoline Museums: Palazzo Nuovo pp70–71*
2 *Capitoline Museums: Palazzo dei Conservatori pp72–3*
11 Palazzo Venezia and Museum

Historic Buildings
5 Roman *Insula*

Historic Streets and Piazzas
3 Piazza del Campidoglio
4 Cordonata
6 Aracoeli Staircase

Ancient Sites
9 Tarpeian Rock

Monuments
10 Victor Emmanuel Monument

0 metres 100
0 yards 100

See also Street Finder maps 5, 12

◀ The God of the River Nile in front of the Roman City Hall, Piazza del Campidoglio

Street-by-Street: The Capitol and Piazza Venezia

The Capitol, citadel of ancient Rome, is a must for every visitor. A broad flight of steps (the Cordonata) leads up to Michelangelo's spectacular Piazza del Campidoglio. This is flanked by the Palazzo Nuovo and Palazzo dei Conservatori, housing the Capitoline Museums with their fine collections of sculptures and paintings. The absence of cars makes the hill a welcome retreat from the squeal of brakes below, but you should brave the traffic to visit Palazzo Venezia and its museum.

⑩ Victor Emmanuel Monument
This huge white marble monument to Italy's first king was completed in 1911.

PIAZZA VENEZIA

PIAZZA VENEZIA

⑫ San Marco
The church of the Venetians in Rome has a fine 9th-century apse mosaic.

⑪ Palazzo Venezia
The museum's finest exhibits, such as this 13th-century gilded angel decorated with enamel, date from the late Middle Ages.

VIA DEL TEATRO DI MARCELLO

⑤ Roman *Insula*
This is a ruined apartment block dating from Imperial Rome.

⑥ Aracoeli Staircase
When it was built in 1348, the staircase became a centre for political debate.

④ Cordonata
Michelangelo's great staircase changed the orientation of the Capitol towards the west.

⑦ Santa Maria in Aracoeli
The treasures hidden behind the church's brick façade include this 15th-century fresco of the Funeral of St Bernardino by Pinturicchio.

Key

— Suggested route

| 0 metres | | 75 |
| 0 yards | | 75 |

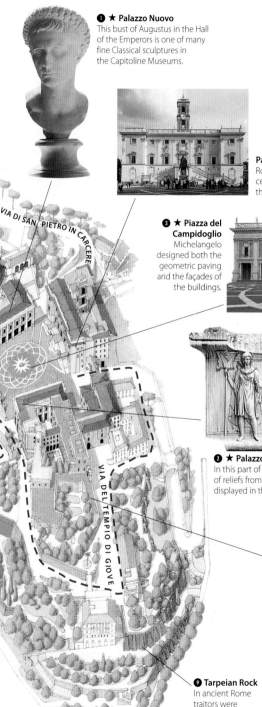

① ★ Palazzo Nuovo
This bust of Augustus in the Hall of the Emperors is one of many fine Classical sculptures in the Capitoline Museums.

Locator Map
See Central Rome Map pp16–17

Palazzo Senatorio was used by the Roman Senate from about the 12th century. It now houses the offices of the mayor.

③ ★ Piazza del Campidoglio
Michelangelo designed both the geometric paving and the façades of the buildings.

② ★ Palazzo dei Conservatori
In this part of the Capitoline Museums a fine series of reliefs from the Temple of Hadrian *(see p108)* is displayed in the courtyard.

⑨ Tarpeian Rock
In ancient Rome traitors were thrown to their death from this cliff on the Capitol.

⑧ Temple of Jupiter
This artist's impression shows the gold and ivory statue of Jupiter that stood in the temple.

VIA DI SAN PIETRO IN CARCERE

VIA DEL TEMPIO DI GIOVE

❶ Capitoline Museums: Palazzo Nuovo

A collection of Classical statues has been kept on the Capitoline hill since the Renaissance. The first group of bronze sculptures was given to the city by Pope Sixtus IV in 1471 and more additions were made by Pope Pius V in 1566. The Palazzo Nuovo was designed by Michelangelo as part of the renovation of the Piazza del Campidoglio, and after its completion in 1655, a number of the statues were transferred here. In 1734 Pope Clement XII Corsini decreed that the building be turned into the world's first public museum.

★ Capitoline Venus
This marble statue of Venus dating from around AD 100–150 is a Roman copy of the original carved in the 4th century BC by the Greek sculptor Praxiteles. The statue is prized for its striking beauty.

Museum Guide

The Palazzo Nuovo is devoted chiefly to sculpture, and most of its finest works, such as the Capitoline Venus, are Roman copies of Greek masterpieces. For visitors keen to identify the philosophers and poets of ancient Greece and the rulers of ancient Rome, there are collections of busts assembled in the 18th century. Admission price also includes entry to the Palazzo dei Conservatori opposite. A gallery below Piazza del Campidoglio links the two buildings.

Portrait of a Flavian Lady
The woman wears the fanciful and elaborate hairstyle popular among the female aristocracy of the 1st century AD.

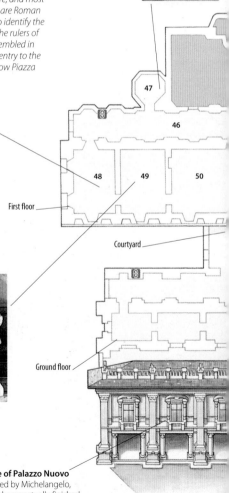

First floor

47

46

48   49   50

Courtyard

Ground floor

Hall of the Philosophers
The hall contains a rich mix of portraits of Greek politicians, scientists and literary figures.

The façade of Palazzo Nuovo was designed by Michelangelo, but the work was actually finished in 1655 by the brothers Carlo and Girolamo Rainaldi.

Key to Floorplan

▢ Non-exhibition space
▢ Exhibition space

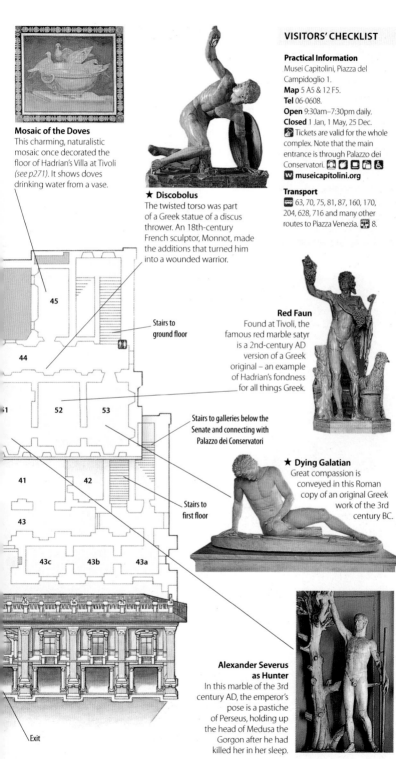

Mosaic of the Doves
This charming, naturalistic mosaic once decorated the floor of Hadrian's Villa at Tivoli (*see p271*). It shows doves drinking water from a vase.

★ **Discobolus**
The twisted torso was part of a Greek statue of a discus thrower. An 18th-century French sculptor, Monnot, made the additions that turned him into a wounded warrior.

VISITORS' CHECKLIST

Practical Information
Musei Capitolini, Piazza del Campidoglio 1.
Map 5 A5 & 12 F5.
Tel 06-0608.
Open 9:30am–7:30pm daily.
Closed 1 Jan, 1 May, 25 Dec.
Tickets are valid for the whole complex. Note that the main entrance is through Palazzo dei Conservatori.
W museicapitolini.org

Transport
63, 70, 75, 81, 87, 160, 170, 204, 628, 716 and many other routes to Piazza Venezia. 8.

45

44

Stairs to ground floor

Red Faun
Found at Tivoli, the famous red marble satyr is a 2nd-century AD version of a Greek original – an example of Hadrian's fondness for all things Greek.

51   52   53

Stairs to galleries below the Senate and connecting with Palazzo dei Conservatori

★ **Dying Galatian**
Great compassion is conveyed in this Roman copy of an original Greek work of the 3rd century BC.

41   42

43

Stairs to first floor

43c   43b   43a

Alexander Severus as Hunter
In this marble of the 3rd century AD, the emperor's pose is a pastiche of Perseus, holding up the head of Medusa the Gorgon after he had killed her in her sleep.

Exit

❷ Capitoline Museums: Palazzo dei Conservatori

The Palazzo dei Conservatori was the seat of the city's magistrates during the late Middle Ages. Its frescoed halls are still used occasionally for political meetings and the ground floor houses the municipal registry office. The palazzo was built by Giacomo della Porta who carried out Michelangelo's designs for the Piazza del Campidoglio in the mid-16th century. While much of the palazzo is given over to sculpture, the art galleries on the second floor hold works by Veronese, Guercino, Tintoretto, Rubens, Caravaggio, Van Dyck and Titian.

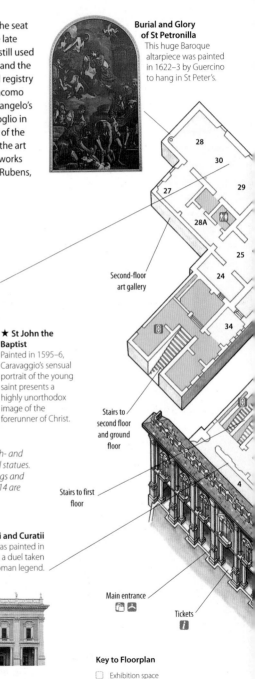

Burial and Glory of St Petronilla
This huge Baroque altarpiece was painted in 1622–3 by Guercino to hang in St Peter's.

Second-floor art gallery

Stairs to second floor and ground floor

Stairs to first floor

Main entrance

Tickets

★ St John the Baptist
Painted in 1595–6, Caravaggio's sensual portrait of the young saint presents a highly unorthodox image of the forerunner of Christ.

Museum Guide

The first-floor rooms have original 16th- and 17th-century decoration and Classical statues. The second-floor gallery holds paintings and a porcelain collection. Rooms 13 and 14 are used as temporary exhibition space.

The Horatii and Curatii
D'Arpino's fresco was painted in 1613 and depicts a duel taken from early Roman legend.

Façade of Palazzo dei Conservatori
Work began on this Michelangelo design in 1563, the year before his death.

Key to Floorplan
☐ Exhibition space
▨ Non-exhibition space

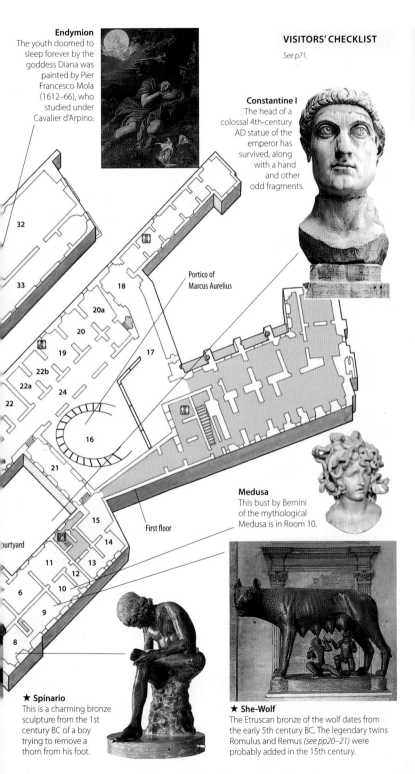

Endymion
The youth doomed to sleep forever by the goddess Diana was painted by Pier Francesco Mola (1612–66), who studied under Cavalier d'Arpino.

VISITORS' CHECKLIST
See p71.

Constantine I
The head of a colossal 4th-century AD statue of the emperor has survived, along with a hand and other odd fragments.

Portico of Marcus Aurelius

Medusa
This bust by Bernini of the mythological Medusa is in Room 10.

First floor

32
33
18
20a
20
19
17
22b
22a
24
22
16
21
15
14
11   13
12
10
6
9
8

urtyard

★ **Spinario**
This is a charming bronze sculpture from the 1st century BC of a boy trying to remove a thorn from his foot.

★ **She-Wolf**
The Etruscan bronze of the wolf dates from the early 5th century BC. The legendary twins Romulus and Remus *(see pp20–21)* were probably added in the 15th century.

❸ Piazza del Campidoglio

Map 5 A5 & 12 F5. 🚌 40, 62, 63, 64, 110, 170. 🚋 8.

When the Holy Roman Emperor Charles V visited Rome in 1536, Pope Paul III Farnese was so embarrassed by the muddy state of the Capitol that he asked Michelangelo to draw up plans for repaving the piazza, and for renovating the façades of the Palazzo dei Conservatori and Palazzo Senatorio.

Michelangelo proposed adding the Palazzo Nuovo to form a piazza in the shape of a trapezium, embellished with Classical sculptures chosen for their relevance to Rome. Building started in 1546 but progressed so slowly that Michelangelo only lived to oversee the double flight of steps at the entrance of Palazzo Senatorio. The piazza was completed in the 17th century, the design remaining largely faithful to the original. Pilasters two storeys high and balustrades interspersed with statues link the buildings thematically. The piazza faces west towards St Peter's, the Christian equivalent of the Capitol. At its centre stands a replica of a statue of Marcus Aurelius. The original is in the Palazzo dei Conservatori (see pp72–3).

Statue of Marcus Aurelius on Piazza del Campidoglio

❹ Cordonata

Map 5 A5 & 12 F5. 🚌 40, 62, 63, 64, 110, 170. 🚋 8.

From Piazza Venezia, the Capitol is approached by a gently rising, subtly widening ramp – the Cordonata. At the foot is a pair of granite Egyptian lions, and on the left a 19th-century monument to Cola di Rienzo, close to where the dashing 14th-century tyrant was executed. The top of the ramp is guarded by Classical statues of the Dioscuri – Castor and Pollux.

❺ Roman *Insula*

Piazza d'Aracoeli. **Map** 5 A5 & 12 F4. **Tel** 06-0608. 🚌 40, 62, 63, 64, 110, 170. 🚋 8. **Open** by appt only: call first.

Two thousand years ago the urban poor of Rome used to make their homes in *insulae* – apartment blocks. These were often badly maintained by landlords, and expensive to rent in a city where land costs were high. This 2nd-century AD tenement block, of barrel-vault construction, is the only survivor in Rome from that era. The fourth, fifth and part of the sixth storey remain above current ground level.

In the Middle Ages, a section of these upper storeys was converted into a church; its bell tower and 14th-century Madonna in a niche are visible from the street.

During the Fascist years, the area was cleared, and three lower floors emerged. Some 380 people may have lived in the tenement, in the squalid conditions described by the 1st-century AD satirical writers Martial and Juvenal. The latter mentions that he had to climb 200 steps to reach his garret.

This *insula* may once have had more storeys. The higher you lived, the more dismal the conditions, as the poky spaces of the building's upper levels testify.

The Dioscuri twins looking onto the Cordonata leading up to the Piazza del Campidoglio

❻ Aracoeli Staircase

Piazza d'Aracoeli. **Map** 5 A5 & 12 F4.
🚌 40, 62, 63, 64, 110, 170. 🚋 8.

The Aracoeli Staircase numbers 124 marble steps (122 if you start from the right) and was completed in 1348, some say in thanks for the passing of the Black Death, but probably in view of the Holy Year of 1350.

The 14th-century tribune-turned-tyrant Cola di Rienzo used to harangue the masses from the Aracoeli Staircase; in the 17th century foreigners used to sleep on the steps, until Prince Caffarelli, who lived on the hill, scared them off by rolling barrels filled with stones down them.

Popular belief has it that by climbing the steps on your knees you can win the Italian national lottery. From the top there is a good view of Rome, with the domes of Sant'Andrea della Valle and St Peter's slightly to the right.

Aracoeli Staircase

❼ Santa Maria in Aracoeli

Piazza d'Aracoeli (entrances via Aracoeli Staircase and door behind Palazzo Nuovo). **Map** 5 A5 & 12 F4. **Tel** 06-6976 3839. 🚌 40, 62, 63, 64, 110, 170. 🚋 8. **Open** summer: 9am–6:30pm daily; winter: 9am–5:30pm daily.

Dating from at least the 6th century, the church of Santa Maria in Aracoeli, or St Mary of the Altar in the Sky, stands on the northern summit of the Capitoline, on the site of the ancient temple to Juno. Its 22 columns were taken from various ancient buildings; the inscription on the third column to the left tells us that it comes *"a cubiculo Augustorum"* – from the bedroom of the emperors.

Ceiling commemorating the Battle of Lepanto in Santa Maria in Aracoeli

The church of the Roman senators and people, Santa Maria in Aracoeli, has been used to celebrate many triumphs over adversity. Its ceiling, with naval motifs, commemorates the Battle of Lepanto (1571), and was built under Pope Gregory XIII Boncompagni, whose family crest, the dragon, can be seen towards the altar end.

Many other Roman families and individuals are honoured by memorials in the church. To the right of the entrance door, the tombstone of archdeacon Giovanni Crivelli, rather than being set into the floor of the church, stands eternally to attention, partly so that the signature "Donatelli" (by Donatello) can be read at eye-level.

The frescoes in the first chapel on the right, painted by Pinturicchio in the 1480s in the beautifully clear style of the early Renaissance, depict St Bernardino of Siena. On the left wall, the perspective of *The Burial of the Saint* slants to the right, taking into account the position of the viewer just outside the chapel.

The church is most famous, however, for an icon with apparently miraculous powers, the *Santo Bambino*, a 15th-century olive-wood figure of the Christ Child which was carved out of a tree from the garden of Gethsemane. Its powers are said to include resurrecting the dead, and it is sometimes summoned to the bedsides of the gravely ill. The original figure was stolen in 1994 but has been replaced by a replica.

At Christmas the Christ Child takes its place in the centre of a picturesque crib (second chapel to the left) but is usually to be found in the sacristy, as is the panel of the *Holy Family* from the workshop of Giulio Romano.

The miraculous olive-wood Christ Child at Santa Maria in Aracoeli

❽ Temple of Jupiter

Via del Tempio di Giove. **Map** 5 A5 &
12 F5. 40, 62, 63, 64, 110, 170.
Open 9:30am–7:30pm daily.

The temple of Jupiter, the most
important in ancient Rome,
was founded in honour of the
arch-god around 509 BC on
the southern summit of the
Capitoline hill. From the few
traces that remain, archaeologists have been able to
reconstruct the rectangular,
Greek appearance of the temple
as it once stood. In places
you can see remnants of its
particularly Roman feature,
the podium. Most of this lies
beneath the Museo Nuovo
wing of the Palazzo dei
Conservatori (see pp72–3).

By walking around the site,
from the podium's southwestern
corner in Via del Tempio di Giove
to its southeastern corner in
Piazzale Caffarelli, you can see
that the temple was about the
same size as the Pantheon.

Ancient coin showing the
Temple of Jupiter

❾ Tarpeian Rock

Via di Monte Caprino and Via del
Tempio di Giove. **Map** 5 A5 & 12 F5.
40, 62, 63, 64, 110, 170. 8.

The southern tip of the
Capitoline is called the Tarpeian
Rock (Rupe Tarpea), after
Tarpeia, the young daughter
of Spurius Tarpeius, defender
of the Capitol in the 8th-century
BC Sabine War.

The Sabines, bent on
vengeance for the rape of their

Sabine soldiers crushing the treacherous Tarpeia with their shields

women by Romulus and his
men, bribed Tarpeia to let
them up on to the Capitol.
As the Augustan historian
Livy records, the Sabines used
to wear heavy gold bracelets
and jewelled rings on their left
hands, and Tarpeia's reward for
her treachery was to be "what
they wore on their shield-arms".

The Sabines kept to the letter
of the bargain if not to its spirit
– they repaid Tarpeia not with
their jewellery but by crushing
her to death between their
shields. Tarpeia was possibly
the only casualty of her
act of treachery – as the
invading warriors met
the Roman defenders,
the Sabine women
leapt between the two
opposing armies, forcing
a reconciliation. Traitors and
other condemned criminals
were subsequently executed
by being thrown over the
sheer face of the rock.

The place was considered
dangerous, but restoration work
has since been carried out to
ensure the safety of visitors.

❿ Victor Emmanuel Monument

Piazza Venezia. **Map** 5 A5 & 12 F4.
Tel 06-678 3587. 40, 62, 63, 64,
110, 170. 8. **Open** 9:30am–
7:30pm (last adm: 45 mins before
closing).

Known as Il Vittoriano, this
monument was begun in
1885 and inaugurated in 1911
in honour of Victor Emmanuel II
of Savoy, the first king of a
unified Italy. The king is
depicted here in a gilt bronze
equestrian statue, oversized
like the monument itself –
the statue is 12 m (39 ft) long.

The edifice also contains a
museum of the Risorgimento, the
events that led to unification (see
pp40–41). Built in white Brescian
marble, the "wedding cake" (one
of its many nicknames) will never
mellow into the ochre tones
of surrounding buildings. It is
widely held to be the epitome
of self-important, insensitive
architecture, though the views
it offers are spectacular. A glass
lift at the back of the building
takes visitors to the very top.

Victor Emmanuel Monument in Piazza Venezia

⓫ Palazzo Venezia and Museum

Via del Plebiscito 118. **Map** 5 A4 & 12 E4. **Tel** 06-6999 4388. ▨ 40, 62, 63, 64, 110, 170. ▨ 8. **Open** 8:30am–7:30pm Tue–Sun (last adm: 30 mins before closing). **Closed** 1 Jan, 1 May, 25 Dec. ▨ ▨ Temporary exhibitions.

The arched windows and doors of this Renaissance civic building are so harmonious that the façade was once attributed to the great Humanist architect Leon Battista Alberti (1404–72). It was more probably built by Giuliano da Maiano, who is known to have carved the fine doorway on to the piazza. Palazzo Venezia was built in 1455–64 for the Venetian cardinal Pietro Barbo, who later became Pope Paul II. It was at times a papal residence, but it also served as the Venetian Embassy to Rome before passing into French hands in 1797. Since 1916 it has belonged to the state; in the Fascist era, Mussolini used Palazzo Venezia as his headquarters and addressed crowds from the central balcony.

Palazzo Venezia with Mussolini's balcony in the centre

The interior is best seen by visiting the Museo del Palazzo Venezia, Rome's most underrated museum. It holds first-class collections of early Renaissance painting; painted wood sculptures and Renaissance chests from Italy; tapestries from all of Europe; majolica; silver; Neapolitan ceramic figurines; Renaissance bronzes; arms and armour; Baroque terracotta sculptures by Bernini, Algardi and others; and 17th- and 18th-century Italian painting. There is a marble screen from the Aracoeli convent, destroyed to make way for the Victor Emmanuel Monument, and a bust of Paul II, showing him to rank with Martin V and Leo X among the fattest-ever popes. The building also hosts major temporary exhibitions.

Pope Paul II

⓬ San Marco

Piazza San Marco 48. **Map** 5 A4 & 12 F4. **Tel** 06-679 5205. ▨ 40, 62, 63, 64, 110, 170. ▨ 8. **Open** 4–7pm Mon, 7:30am–12:30pm & 4–7pm Tue–Sat, 7:30am–12:30pm & 4–7:30pm Sun. ✝

The church of San Marco was founded in 336 by Pope Mark, in honour of St Mark the Evangelist. The Pope's relics lie under the altar. The church was restored by Pope Gregory IV in the 9th century – the magnificent apse mosaics date from this period.

Further major rebuilding took place in 1455–71, when Pope Paul II Barbo made San Marco the church of the Venetian community in Rome.

Coat of arms of Pope Paul II

The blue and gold coffered ceiling is decorated with Pope Paul's heraldic crest, the lion rampant, recalling the lion of St Mark, the patron saint of Venice. The appearance of the rest of the interior, with its colonnades of Sicilian jasper, was largely the creation of Filippo Barigioni in the 1740s. Complemented by an interesting array of funerary monuments in the aisles, the style is typical of the late Roman Baroque.

Leon Battista Alberti, whose name is also mentioned tentatively in connection with Palazzo Venezia, may have been the architect of the elegant travertine arcade and loggia of the façade.

San Marco's apse mosaic of Christ, with Gregory IV on the far left

FORUM

The Forum was the centre of political, commercial and judicial life in ancient Rome. The largest buildings were the basilicas, where legal cases were heard. According to the playwright Plautus, the area teemed with "lawyers and litigants, bankers and brokers, shopkeepers and strumpets, good-for-nothings waiting for a tip from the rich".

As Rome's population boomed, the Forum became too small. In 46 BC Julius Caesar built a new one, setting a precedent that was followed by emperors from Augustus to Trajan. Emperors also erected triumphal arches to themselves, and just to the east Vespasian built the Colosseum – the centre of entertainment after the business of the day was done.

See also Street Finder maps 5, 8, 9, 12

Sights at a Glance

Churches and Temples
- ⑤ Temple of Saturn
- ⑧ Temple of Castor and Pollux
- ⑨ Temple of Vesta
- ⑪ Temple of Antoninus and Faustina
- ⑫ Temple of Romulus and Santi Cosma e Damiano
- ⑭ Santa Francesca Romana
- ⑰ Temple of Venus and Rome

Historic Buildings
- ① Basilica Aemilia
- ② Curia
- ⑦ Basilica Julia
- ⑩ House of the Vestal Virgins
- ⑬ Basilica of Constantine and Maxentius
- ⑱ *Trajan's Markets pp90–91*
- ⑳ Torre delle Milizie

- ㉑ Casa dei Cavalieri di Rodi
- ㉔ Mamertine Prison
- ㉗ *Colosseum pp94–7*

Museums
- ⑮ Antiquarium Forense

Arches and Columns
- ④ Arch of Septimius Severus
- ⑥ Column of Phocas
- ⑯ Arch of Titus
- ⑲ Trajan's Column
- ㉖ Arch of Constantine

Ancient Sites
- ③ Rostra
- ㉒ Forum of Augustus
- ㉓ Forum of Caesar
- ㉕ Forum of Nerva

◀ Ancient ruins at the Roman Forum

For keys to symbols *see back flap*

A Tour of the Roman Forum: West

To appreciate the layout of the Forum before visiting its confusing patchwork of ruined temples and basilicas, it is best to view the whole area from above, from the back of the Capitol. From there you can make out the Via Sacra (the Sacred Way), the route followed through the Forum by religious and triumphal processions towards the Capitol. Up until the 18th century when archaeological excavations began, the Arch of Septimius Severus and the columns of the Temple of Saturn lay half-buried underground. Excavation of the Forum continues, and the ruins uncovered date from many different periods of Roman history.

The Temple of Vespasian was the point from where Piranesi made this 18th-century engraving of the Forum. Its three columns were then almost completely buried.

Temple of Concord

Portico of the Dii Consentes

❺ Temple of Saturn
The eight surviving columns of this temple stand close by the three columns of the Temple of Vespasian.

Arch of Septimius Severus

❸ Rostra
These are the ruins of the platform used for public oratory in the Forum.

❼ Basilica Julia
Named after Julius Caesar, who ordered its construction, the basilica housed important law courts.

❻ Column of Phocas
One of the very last monuments erected in the Forum, this single column dates from AD 608.

❹ ★ Arch of Septimius Severus
A 19th-century engraving shows the arch after the Forum was first excavated.

Locator Map
See Central Rome Map pp16–17

Key
— Suggested route

Santi Luca e Martina was an early medieval church, but was rebuilt in 1635–64 by Pietro da Cortona.

The Forum included the area under Via dei Fori Imperiali. More parts have now been made public.

❷ Curia
This 3rd-century rebuilding of the Curia was greatly restored in 1937.

❶ Basilica Aemilia
This large meeting hall was razed to the ground in the 5th century AD.

| 0 metres | 75 |
| 0 yards | 75 |

VIA DEI FORI IMPERIALI

VIA DELLA CURIA

VIA DELLA SALARA VECCHIA

A SACRA

Entrance to Forum

The Temple of Julius Caesar was erected in his memory by Augustus on the spot where Caesar's body was cremated after his assassination in 44 BC.

Julius Caesar

To Roman Forum: East
See pp82–3

❽ Temple of Castor and Pollux
A temple to the twin brothers (of whom only Pollux was fathered by Jupiter) stood on this spot from the 5th century BC. This section of cornice and its supporting columns date from its rebuilding in AD 6.

A Tour of the Roman Forum: East

The eastern end of the Roman Forum is dominated by the massive barrel-vaulted ruins of the Basilica of Constantine. To picture the building as it was in the 4th century AD, you must imagine marble columns, floors and statues, and glittering tiles of gilt bronze. The remains of the other important buildings are scanty, though the garden and ponds in the centre of the House of the Vestal Virgins make it a very attractive spot. The two churches in this part of the Forum cannot be reached from within the archaeological area, but are accessible from the road outside.

The Regia was the office of the Pontifex Maximus, the chief priest of ancient Rome.

To Forum entrance

VIA SACRA

⓫ Temple of Antoninus and Faustina
The portico of this temple, built in AD 141, has been incorporated in the church of San Lorenzo in Miranda.

An early Iron Age necropolis was found here in 1902. Finds from it, such as this burial urn, are on view in the Antiquarium.

❾ Temple of Vesta
Partly reconstructed, this tiny temple to the goddess of the hearth was one of ancient Rome's most sacred shrines.

❿ ★ House of the Vestal Virgins
The priestesses who tended the sacred flame in the Temple of Vesta lived here. The house was a large rectangular building around a central garden.

⓬ Temple of Romulus
This domed building from the 4th century AD has survived as part of the church of Santi Cosma e Damiano.

⑬ ★ Basilica of Constantine and Maxentius
The stark remains of the basilica's huge arches and ceilings give some idea of the original scale and grandeur of the Forum's public buildings.

Locator Map
See Central Rome Map pp16–17

⑭ Santa Francesca Romana
The church takes its name from a saint who cared for the Roman poor in the 15th century.

⑮ Antiquarium Forense
A small museum houses archaeological finds made in the Forum. They include this frieze of *Aeneas and the Founding of Rome* from the Basilica Aemilia.

VIA DEI FORI IMPERIALI

Colonnade surrounding Temple of Venus and Rome

VIA SACRA

⑰ Temple of Venus and Rome
These extensive ruins are of a magnificent temple, built here in AD 121 by the Emperor Hadrian, largely to his own design.

Ruined Baths

To the Palatine

⑯ Arch of Titus
This 19th-century reconstruction shows how the arch may have looked when it spanned the flagstoned roadway of the Via Sacra.

Key

— Suggested route

| 0 metres | | 75 |
| 0 yards | | 75 |

● Basilica Aemilia

See Visitors' Checklist.

Originally this building was a rectangular colonnaded hall, with a multicoloured marble floor and a bronze-tiled roof. It was built by the consuls Marcus Aemilius Lepidus and Marcus Fulvius Nobilor in 179 BC. The two consuls, who were elected annually, exercised supreme power over the Republic.

Basilicas in ancient Rome served no religious purpose; they were meeting halls for politicians, moneylenders and *publicani* (businessmen contracted by the state to collect taxes). A consortium agreed to hand over a specified sum to the state, but its members were allowed to collect as much as they could and keep the difference. This is why tax-collectors in the Bible were so loathed.

The basilica was rebuilt many times; it was finally burned down when the Visigoths sacked Rome in AD 410. Business seems to have carried on until the last moment, for the pavement is splashed with tiny lumps of coins that melted in the fire.

Melted coins embedded in the floor of the Basilica Aemilia

The Curia, or the Court of Rome, rebuilt by Diocletian in the 3rd century

● Curia

See Visitors' Checklist.

A modern restoration now stands over the ruins of the hall where Rome's Senate (chief council of state) used to meet. The first Curia stood on the site now occupied by the church of Santi Luca e Martina, but after the building was destroyed by fire in 52 BC, Julius Caesar built a new Curia at the edge of the Forum. This was restored by Domitian in AD 94 and, after another fire, rebuilt by Diocletian in the 3rd century. The current building is a 1937 restoration of Diocletian's Curia. Inside are two relief panels commissioned by Trajan to decorate the Rostra. One shows Trajan destroying records of unpaid taxes to free citizens from debt; in the other he sits on a throne receiving a mother and child.

● Rostra

See Visitors' Checklist.

Speeches were delivered from this dais, the most famous – thanks to Shakespeare – being Mark Antony's "Friends, Romans, Countrymen" oration after the assassination of Julius Caesar in 44 BC. Caesar himself had just reorganized the Forum and this speech was made from the newly sited Rostra, where the ruins now stand. In the following year the head and hands of Cicero were put on show here after he had been put to death by the second Triumvirate (Augustus, Mark Antony and Marcus Lepidus). Fulvia, Mark Antony's wife, stabbed the great orator's tongue with a hairpin. It was also here that Julia, Augustus's daughter, was said to have played the prostitute – one of many scandalous acts that led to her banishment.

The dais took its name from the ships' prows *(rostra)* with which it was decorated. Sheathed in iron (for ramming enemy vessels), these came from ships captured at the Battle of Antium in 338 BC.

● Arch of Septimius Severus

See Visitors' Checklist.

This triumphal arch, one of the most striking and best preserved monuments of the Forum, was erected in AD 203 to celebrate the tenth anniversary of the accession of

Honorary statue

Relief panel in balustrade, showing Trajan's acts of charity

Prows of ships *(rostra)*

Rostra
This reconstruction shows the platform for public speaking in the Forum, as it looked in Imperial times.

Septimius Severus. The relief panels – largely eroded – celebrate the emperor's victories in Parthia (modern-day Iraq and Iran) and Arabia. Originally, the inscription along the top of the arch was to Septimius and his two sons, Caracalla and Geta, but after Septimius died Caracalla murdered Geta, and had his brother's name removed. Even so the holes into which the letters of his name were pegged are still visible.

During the Middle Ages the central arch, half buried in earth and debris, was used to shelter a barber's shop.

Ionic capitals on the surviving columns of the Temple of Saturn

Triumphal arch celebrating the accession of Emperor Septimius Severus

❺ Temple of Saturn

See Visitors' Checklist.

The most prominent of the ruins in the fenced-off area between the Forum and the Capitoline Hill is the Temple of Saturn. It consists of a high platform, eight columns and a section of entablature. There was a temple dedicated to Saturn here as early as 497 BC, but it had to be rebuilt many times and the current remains date only from 42 BC.

Saturn was the mythical god-king of Italy, said to have presided over a prosperous and peaceful Golden Age from which slavery, private property, crime and war were absent. As such, he appealed particularly to the lower and slave classes. Every year, between 17 December and 23 December, Saturn's reign was remembered in a week of sacrifices and feasting, known as the Saturnalia.

As long as the revels lasted, the normal social order was turned upside down. Slaves were permitted to drink and dine with (and sometimes even be served by) their masters. Senators and other high-ranking Romans would abandon the aristocratic togas that they usually wore to distinguish themselves from the lower classes and wear more democratic, loose-fitting gowns. During the holidays, all the courts of law and schools in the city were closed. No prisoner could be punished, and no war could be declared.

People also celebrated the Saturnalia in their own homes: they exchanged gifts, in particular special wax dolls and wax tapers, and played light-hearted gambling games, the stakes usually being nuts, a symbol of fruitfulness. Much of the spirit and many of the rituals of the festival have been preserved in the Christian celebration of Christmas.

❻ Column of Phocas

See Visitors' Checklist.

This column, 13.5 m (44 ft) high, is one of the few to have remained upright since the day it was put up. Until 1816, when an inquisitive Englishwoman, Lady Elizabeth Foster, widow of the fifth Duke of Devonshire, decided to excavate its pedestal, nobody knew what it was. It turned out to be the youngest of the Forum's monuments, erected in AD 608 in honour of the Byzantine emperor, Phocas, who had just paid a visit to Rome. The column may have been placed here as a mark of gratitude to Phocas for giving the Pantheon to the pope *(see pp114–15).*

VISITORS' CHECKLIST

Practical Information
Entrance: Via della Salara Vecchia 5/6. **Map** 5 B5 & 8 F1. **Tel** 06-3996 7700. **Open** 8:30am–approx 1 hour before sunset daily. **Closed** 1 Jan, 25 Dec. 🖼 (includes entry to Colosseum and Palatine). Tickets can be bought in advance at www.coopculture.it

Transport
Ⓜ Colosseo. 🚌 75, 85, 87, 117, 186, 810. 🚋 3.

Slender, fluted Column of Phocas

Remains of the Basilica Julia, a Roman court of civil law

❼ Basilica Julia

See Visitors' Checklist, p85.

This immense basilica, which occupied the area between the temple of Saturn and the temple of Castor and Pollux, was begun by Julius Caesar in 54 BC and completed after his death by his great-nephew Augustus. It was damaged by fire almost immediately afterwards in 9 BC, but was subsequently repaired and dedicated to the emperor's grandsons, Gaius and Lucius.

After numerous sackings and pilferings, only the steps, pavement and column stumps remain. Nevertheless the ground plan is fairly clear.

The basilica had a central hall, measuring 80 m by 18 m (260 ft by 59 ft), surrounded by a double portico. The hall was on three floors, while the outer portico had only two.

The Basilica Julia was the seat of the *centumviri*, a body of 180 magistrates who tried civil law cases. They were split into four chambers of 45 men, and unless a case was particularly complicated they would all sit separately.

The four courts were, however, divided only by screens or curtains, and the voices of lawyers and cheers and boos of spectators in the upper galleries echoed through the building. Lawyers used to hire crowds of spectators, who would applaud every time the lawyer who was paying them made a point and jeer at his opponents. The clappers and booers must have had a good deal of time on their hands: scratched into the steps are chequerboards where they played dice and other gambling games to while away the time between cases.

Corinthian columns of the Temple of Castor and Pollux

❽ Temple of Castor and Pollux

See Visitors' Checklist, p85.

The three slender fluted columns of this temple form one of the Forum's most beautiful ruins. The first temple here was probably dedicated in 484 BC in honour of the mythical twins and patrons of horsemanship, Castor and Pollux. During the battle of Lake Regillus (499 BC) against the ousted Tarquin kings, the Roman dictator Postumius promised to build a temple to the twins if the Romans were victorious. Some said the twins appeared on the battlefield, helped the Romans to victory and then materialized in the Forum – the temple marks the spot – to announce the news.

The temple, like most buildings in the Forum, was rebuilt many times. The three surviving columns date from the last occasion on which it was rebuilt – by the future Emperor Tiberius after a fire in AD 6. For a long period the temple housed the city's office of weights and measures, and it was also used at times by a number of bankers.

❾ Temple of Vesta

See Visitors' Checklist, p85.

The Forum's most elegant temple, a circular building originally surrounded by a ring of 20 fine fluted columns, dates from the 4th century AD, though there had been a temple on the site for far longer. It was partially reconstructed in 1930.

The cult of the Vestals was one of the oldest in Rome, and centred on six Vestal Virgins, who were required to keep alight the sacred flame of Vesta, the goddess of the hearth.

Temple of Vesta

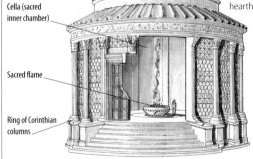

Cella (sacred inner chamber)

Sacred flame

Ring of Corinthian columns

The temple preserved the shape of an original primitive structure made of wooden posts with a thatched roof.

This responsibility was originally entrusted to the daughters of the king, but it then passed to the Vestals, the only group of women priests in Rome. It was no easy task, as the flame was easily blown out. Any Vestal who allowed the flame to die was whipped by the high priest (Pontifex Maximus) and dismissed.

The girls, who had to belong to noble families, were selected when they were between 6 and 10 years old. They served for 30 years: the first ten were spent learning their duties, the next ten performing them and the final ten teaching novices. They enjoyed high status and financial security, but had to remain virgins. The penalty for transgressing was to be buried alive, although only ten Vestals are recorded as ever having suffered this fate. The men concerned were whipped to death. When Vestals retired, they were free to live the rest of their lives as ordinary citizens. If they wished they could marry, but few ever did.

Another of the Vestals' duties was to guard the Palladium, a sacred statue of the goddess Pallas Athenae. The irreverent Emperor Heliogabalus burgled the temple in the 3rd century AD. He thought he had succeeded in stealing the Palladium, but the Vestals had been warned of his intention and had replaced it with a replica.

Central courtyard of the House of the Vestal Virgins

⑩ House of the Vestal Virgins

See Visitors' Checklist, p85.

Honorary statue of a Vestal Virgin

As soon as a girl became a Vestal she came to live in the House of the Vestal Virgins. This was once an enormous complex with about 50 rooms on three storeys. The only remains today are some of the rooms around the central courtyard. This space is perhaps the most evocative part of the Forum. Overlooking ponds of water lilies and goldfish is a row of eroded, and mostly headless, statues of senior Vestals, dating from the 3rd and 4th centuries AD. The better-preserved examples are in the Museo Nazionale Romano *(see p165)*. On one of the pedestals the inscription has been removed because the disgraced Vestal in question may have been a certain Claudia, known to have betrayed the cult by converting to Christianity.

Though many of the rooms surrounding the courtyard are well preserved – some even retain flights of steps – entry is not allowed. If you peep into the series of rooms along the south side, however, you might be able to see the remains of a mill, used for grinding the grain with which the Vestals made a special sacrificial cake. The bakery was next door.

Restored section of Temple of Vesta

⑪ Temple of Antoninus and Faustina

See Visitors' Checklist, p85.

One of the Forum's oddest sights is the Baroque façade of the church of San Lorenzo in Miranda rising above the porch of a Roman temple. First dedicated in AD 141 by Emperor Antoninus Pius to his late wife Faustina, the temple was rededicated to them both on the death of the emperor. In the 11th century it was converted into a church because it was believed that San Lorenzo (St Lawrence) had been condemned to death there. The current church dates from 1601.

Temple of Antoninus and Faustina

⓬ Temple of Romulus and Santi Cosma e Damiano

See Visitors' Checklist, p85. Santi Cosma e Damiano: **Tel** 06-692 0441. **Open** 9am–1pm, 3–7pm daily. Donation for crib. 🏛 ♿

No one is sure to whom the Temple of Romulus was dedicated, but it was probably to the son of Emperor Maxentius, and not to Rome's founder.

The temple is a circular brick building, topped by a cupola, with two rectangular side rooms and a concave porch. The heavy, dull bronze doors are original.

Since the 6th century the temple has acted as a vestibule to the church of Santi Cosma e Damiano, which itself occupies an ancient building – a hall in Vespasian's Forum of Peace. The entrance to the church is on Via dei Fori Imperiali. The beautiful carved figures of its 18th-century Neapolitan *presepio* (crib or Nativity scene) are on view, and the church has a vivid Byzantine apse mosaic with Christ pictured against orange clouds.

Roof of the Temple of Romulus

⓭ Basilica of Constantine and Maxentius

See Visitors' Checklist, p85.

The basilica's three vast, coffered barrel vaults are powerful relics of what was the largest building in the Forum. Work began in AD 308 under Emperor Maxentius. When he was deposed by Constantine after the Battle of the Milvian Bridge in AD 312, work on the massive project continued under the new regime. The building, which, like other Roman basilicas, was used for the administration of justice and for carrying on business, is often referred to simply as the Basilica of Constantine.

The area covered by the basilica was roughly 100 m by 65 m (330 ft by 215 ft). It was originally designed to have a long nave and aisles running from east to west, but Constantine switched the axis around to create three short broad aisles with the main entrance in the centre of the long south wall. The height of the building was 35 m (115 ft). In the apse at the western end, where it could be seen from all over the building, stood a 12 m (39 ft) statue of the emperor, made partly of wood and partly of marble. The giant head, hand and foot are on display in the courtyard of the Palazzo dei Conservatori (*see pp72–3*). The roof of the basilica glittered with gilded tiles until the 7th century when they were stripped off to cover the roof of the old St Peter's.

The octagonal coffers in the vaulted ceiling were originally faced with marble.

The three barrel-vaulted aisles of the basilica were used as law courts.

The main entrance was added by Constantine in AD 313.

The roof was supported by eight massive Corinthian columns. One now stands in Piazza Santa Maria Maggiore (*see p175*).

⓮ Santa Francesca Romana

Piazza di Santa Francesca Romana 4.
Map 5 B5. **Tel** 06-679 5528. 🚌 85,
87, 117, 810. 🚋 3. Ⓜ Colosseo.
Open 10am–noon, 3–5pm daily.
🔒 📷

Dedication to Titus and Vespasian on the Arch of Titus

Every year on 9 March devout Roman drivers try to park as close as possible to this Baroque church with a Romanesque bell tower. The aim of their pilgrimage is to have their vehicles blessed by Santa Francesca Romana, the patron saint of motorists. During the 15th century, Francesca of Trastevere founded a society of pious women devoted to helping the less fortunate. After her canonization in 1608 the church, originally named Santa Maria Nova, was rededicated to Francesca.

The most curious sight inside the church is a flagstone with what are said to be the imprints of the knees of St Peter and St Paul. A magician, Simon Magus, decided to prove that his powers were superior to those of the Apostles by levitating above the Forum. As Simon was in mid-air, Peter and Paul fell to their knees and prayed fervently for God to humble him, and Simon immediately plummeted to his death.

Bell tower of Santa Francesca

⓯ Antiquarium Forense

See Visitors' Checklist, p85.

The former convent of Santa Francesca Romana is now occupied by the offices in charge of the excavations of the Forum and a small museum. The latter is currently being reorganized and the rooms are being restored. They contain Iron Age burial urns, graves and their skeletal occupants along with some ancient bric-a-brac

exhumed from the Forum's drains. When the reorganization is complete, fragments of statues, capitals, friezes and other architectural decoration taken from the Forum's buildings will be on show.

⓰ Arch of Titus

See Visitors' Checklist, p85.

This triumphal arch was erected in AD 81 by the Emperor Domitian in honour of the victories of his brother, Titus, and his father, Vespasian, in Judaea. In AD 66 the Jews, weary of being exploited by unscrupulous Roman officials, rebelled. A bitter war broke out which ended four years later in the fall of Jerusalem and the Jewish Diaspora.

Although the reliefs inside the arch are badly eroded, you can

Frieze of Aeneas in the Antiquarium Forense

make out a triumphant procession of Roman soldiers carrying off spoils from the Temple of Jerusalem. The booty includes the altar, silver trumpets and a golden seven-branched candelabrum.

⓱ Temple of Venus and Rome

See Visitors' Checklist, p85.

The emperor Hadrian designed this temple to occupy what had been the vestibule to Nero's Domus Aurea (see p177). Many of the columns have been re-erected, and though there is no access, there is a good view as you leave the Forum and from the upper tiers of the Colosseum. The temple, the largest in Rome, was dedicated to Roma, the personification of the city, and to Venus because she was the mother of Aeneas, father of Romulus and Remus. Each goddess had her own cella (shrine). When the architect Apollodorus pointed out that the seated statues in the niches were too big (had they tried to "stand" their heads would have hit the vaults), Hadrian had him put to death.

⑱ Trajan's Markets

Originally considered among the wonders of the Classical world, Trajan's Markets now show only a hint of their former splendour. Emperor Trajan and his architect, Apollodorus of Damascus, built this visionary new complex of 150 shops and offices (probably used for administering the corn dole) in the early 2nd century AD. It was the ancient Roman equivalent of the modern shopping centre, selling everything from silks and spices imported from the Middle East to fresh fish, fruit and flowers.

The Markets Today
Above the façade stands the 13th-century Torre delle Milizie, built for defensive purposes.

Main Hall
Twelve shops were built on two floors, and the corn dole was shared out on the upper storey. This was a free corn ration given to Roman men to prevent hunger.

KEY

① **Staircase**

② **Small semicircle of shops**

③ **Cross vaulting**

④ **Market Shops** were built with arched entrances, with jambs and lintels creating rectangular portals and windows. A wooden mezzanine was used for storage.

⑤ **The terrace** over the archway spanning Via Biberatica has a good view of the Forum of Trajan below.

⑥ **Large hall with semidomed ceiling**

⑦ **Forum of Trajan**, built in front of the markets in AD 107–113, was flanked by the Basilica Ulpia. The basilica, measuring 170 m (558 ft) by 60 m (197 ft), was the largest in Rome. A small portion of the Forum has been excavated; unfortunately, however, the rest of it remains buried beneath modern Rome's busy city streets.

⑧ **Wall dividing market area from Forum of Trajan**

Trajan
The emperor was a benevolent ruler and a successful general.

Via Biberatica
The main street which runs through the market is named after the drinking inns which once lined it.

The Markets in the 16th Century
This fanciful fresco depicts a gladiatorial combat taking place in front of the partly buried remains of Trajan's Markets.

VISITORS' CHECKLIST

Practical Information
Mercati Traianei,
Via IV Novembre 94.
Map 5 B4. **Tel** 06-0608.
Open 9:30am–7:30pm daily;
(last adm: 1 hour before closing).
Closed 1 Jan, 25 Dec.

Transport
64, 70, 170 and many routes
to Piazza Venezia.

Upper Corridor
Shops on this upper level were thought to have sold wine and oil, since a number of storage jars were discovered here.

Market Shopping

Shops opened early and closed about noon. The best ones were decorated with mosaics of the goods they sold. Almost all the shopping was done by men, though women visited the dressmaker and cobbler. The tradesmen were almost all male. In employment records for the period AD 117–193, the only female shopkeepers mentioned are three wool-sellers, two jewellers, a greengrocer and a fishwife.

Fish mosaic

AD 100–112 Building of Trajan's Markets

472 Invasion by Ricimer the Suevian. Some of his Germanic troops stationed here

1200s Torre delle Milizie built on top of the markets

1572 Convent of Santa Caterina da Siena built over part of markets

1924 Many medieval houses demolished

1911–14 Convent demolished

AD 0	AD 390	780	1170	1560

AD 117 Death of Trajan

AD 98 Trajan succeeds Nerva as emperor

552 Byzantine takeover of Rome. Markets occupied and fortified by the army

1300s Annibaldi and Caetani families vie for control of the area

1828 First tentative excavations, but value of site not recognized

1930–33 Markets finally excavated

Detail of Trajan's Column

⓳ Trajan's Column

Via dei Fori Imperiali. **Map** 5 A4 & 12 F4. *See Visitors' Checklist for Trajan's Markets, p91.*

This elegant marble column was inaugurated by Trajan in AD 113, and celebrates his two campaigns in Dacia (Romania) in AD 101–3 and AD 107–8. The column, base and pedestal are 40 m (131 ft) tall – precisely the same height as the spur of Quirinal Hill which was excavated to make room for Trajan's Forum.

Spiralling up the column are minutely detailed scenes from the campaigns, beginning with the Romans preparing for war and ending with the Dacians being ousted from their homeland. The column is pierced with small windows to illuminate its internal spiral staircase (closed to the public). To see the reliefs in detail there is a complete set of casts in the Museo della Civiltà Romana at EUR *(see p268).*

When Trajan died in AD 117 his ashes, along with those of his wife Plotina, were placed in a golden urn in the column's hollow base. The column's survival was largely thanks to the intervention of Pope Gregory the Great (reigned 590–604). He was so moved by a relief showing Trajan helping a woman whose son had been killed that he begged God to release the emperor's soul from hell. God duly appeared to the pope to say that Trajan had been rescued,

but asked him not to pray for the souls of any more pagans.

According to legend, when Trajan's ashes were exhumed his skull and tongue were not only intact, but his tongue told of his release from hell. The land around the column was then declared sacred and the column itself was spared. The statue of Trajan remained on top of the column until 1587, when it was replaced with one of St Peter.

⓴ Torre delle Milizie

Mercati Traianei, Via IV Novembre. **Map** 5 B4. **Tel** 06-679 0048. **Closed** to the public.

For centuries this massive brick tower was thought to have been the one in which Nero stood watching Rome burn, after he had set it alight to clear the city's slums. It is uncertain whether arson was among Nero's crimes, but it is certain that he did not watch the fire from this tower – it was built in the 13th century.

㉑ Casa dei Cavalieri di Rodi

Piazza del Grillo 1. **Map** 5 B5. **Tel** 06-0608. 85, 87, 117, 186, 810. **Open** Tue am, Thu am (by appt only, well in advance).

Since the 12th century the crusading order, the Knights of St John, also known as the Knights of Rhodes (Rodi) or Malta, have had their priorate in this medieval house above the Forum of Augustus. If you are lucky enough to get inside, ask to see the beautiful Cappella di San Giovanni (Chapel of St John).

㉒ Forum of Augustus

Piazza del Grillo 1. **Map** 5 B5. *See Trajan's Markets' Visitors' Checklist, p91.* **Tel** 06-0608. **Closed** to the public, but viewable from above.

The Forum of Augustus was built to celebrate Augustus's victory over Julius Caesar's assassins, Brutus and Cassius, at the Battle of Philippi in 41 BC. The temple in its centre was dedicated to Mars the Avenger. The forum stretched from a high wall at the foot of the sleazy Suburra quarter to the edge of the Forum of Caesar. At least half of it is now concealed below Mussolini's Via dei Fori Imperiali. The temple is easily identified, with its cracked steps and four Corinthian columns. Originally it had a statue of Mars which looked very like Augustus. In case anyone failed to notice the resemblance, a giant statue of Augustus himself was placed against the Suburra wall.

㉓ Forum of Caesar

Via del Carcere Tulliano. **Map** 5 A5 & 12 F5. **Tel** 06-0608. 85, 87, 186, 810, 850. **Open** by appointment only.

The first of Rome's Imperial fora was built by Julius Caesar. He spent a fortune – most of it booty from his conquest of Gaul – buying up and demolishing houses on the site. Pride of place went to a temple dedicated in 46 BC to the goddess Venus Genetrix, from whom Caesar claimed descent. The temple contained statues of Caesar and Cleopatra as well as of Venus. All that remains of this temple to vanity is a platform and three

Forum of Augustus, as seen from the Temple of Mars

Corinthian columns. The forum was enclosed by a double colonnade which sheltered a row of shops, but this burned down in AD 80 and was rebuilt by Domitian and Trajan. Trajan also added the Basilica Argentaria and a heated public lavatory.

The forum is open by appointment only, but parts are visible from above in Via dei Fori Imperiali.

17th-century view of the ruined Forum of Nerva

㉕ Forum of Nerva

Piazza del Grillo 1 (reached through Forum of Augustus). **Map** 5 B5. **Tel** 06-0608. 85, 87, 186, 810. **Closed** to the public but viewable from above.

The Forum of Nerva was begun by his predecessor, Domitian, and completed in AD 97. Little more than a long corridor with a colonnade along the sides and a Temple of Minerva at one end, it was also known as the Forum Transitorium because it lay between the Forum of Peace built by the Emperor Vespasian in AD 70 and the Forum of Augustus. Vespasian's forum is almost completely covered by Via dei Fori Imperiali,

as is much of the Forum of Nerva itself. Excavations have unearthed Renaissance shops and taverns, but only part of the forum can be seen, including the base of the temple and two columns that were part of the original colonnade. These support a relief of Minerva above a frieze of young girls learning to sew and weave.

㉖ Arch of Constantine

Between Via di San Gregorio and Piazza del Colosseo. **Map** 8 F1. 75, 85, 87, 673, 810. 3. Colosseo.

This triumphal arch was dedicated in AD 315 to celebrate Constantine's victory three years before over his co-emperor, Maxentius. Constantine claimed he owed his victory to a vision of Christ, but there is nothing Christian about the arch – in fact, most of the medallions, reliefs and statues were scavenged from earlier monuments. There are statues of Dacian prisoners taken from Trajan's Forum and reliefs of Marcus Aurelius, including one where he distributes bread to the poor. Inside the arch are reliefs of Trajan's victory over the Dacians. These were probably by the artist who worked on Trajan's Column.

Medallion on the Arch of Constantine

19th-century engraving of guards visiting prisoners in the Mamertine

㉔ Mamertine Prison

Clivo Argentario 1. **Map** 5 A5 & 12 F5. **Tel** 06-698 961. 85, 87, 186, 810. **Open** 9am–4pm daily (guided tours by appt only; call in advance for details).

Below the 16th-century church of San Giuseppe dei Falegnami (St Joseph of the Carpenters) is a dank dungeon in which, according to Christian legend, St Peter was imprisoned. He is said to have caused a spring to bubble up into the cell, and used the water to baptize his guards.

The prison, also known as Tullianum, was in an old cistern with access to the city's main sewer (the Cloaca Maxima). The lower cell was used for executions and bodies were thrown into the sewer. Among the enemies of Rome to be executed here was the Gaulish leader Vercingetorix, defeated by Julius Caesar in 52 BC.

North side of the Arch of Constantine, facing the Colosseum

㉗ Colosseum

Rome's greatest amphitheatre was commissioned by the Emperor Vespasian in AD 72 on the marshy site of a lake in the grounds of Nero's palace, the Domus Aurea (*see p177*). Deadly gladiatorial combats and wild animal fights were staged by the emperor and wealthy citizens for public viewing, free of charge. The Colosseum was built to a practical design, with its 80 arched entrances allowing easy access to 55,000 spectators, but it is also a building of great beauty. The drawing here shows how it looked at the time of its opening in AD 80. It was one of several similar amphitheatres built in the Roman Empire, and some survive at El Djem in North Africa, Nîmes and Arles in France, and Verona in northern Italy. Despite being damaged over the years by neglect and theft, it remains a majestic sight.

KEY

① **The bollards** anchored the velarium.

② **The outer walls** are made of travertine. Stone plundered from the façade during the Renaissance was used to build several palaces, bridges and parts of St Peter's.

③ **The vomitorium** was the exit used from each numbered section.

④ **Brick** formed the inner walls.

⑤ **Entry routes** to take the spectators to their seats were reached by means of staircases to the various levels of the amphitheatre.

⑥ **The podium** was a large terrace where the emperor and the wealthy upper classes had their seats.

⑦ **The velarium** was a huge awning which shaded spectators from the sun. Supported on poles fixed to the upper storey of the building, it was then hoisted into position with ropes anchored to bollards outside the stadium.

⑧ **Corinthian columns**

⑨ **Ionic columns**

⑩ **Doric columns**

⑪ **Arched entrances**, 80 in total, were all numbered to speed up the entry of the vast crowds.

0		400		800		1200

72 Emperor Vespasian begins work on the Colosseum

230 Colosseum restored by Alexander Severus

248 Thousandth anniversary celebration of founding of Rome by Romulus and Remus

442 Building damaged in an earthquake

A gladiator's shield

1312 Emperor Henry VII gives Colosseum to the Senate and people of Rome

81–96 Amphitheatre completed in reign of Domitian

523 Wild animal fights banned

1200s Frangipane family turns Colosseum into a fortress

404 Gladiatorial combats banned

80 Vespasian's son, Titus, stages inaugural festival in the amphitheatre. It lasts 100 days

15th–16th centuries Ruins used as quarry. Travertine blocks recycled by popes

Internal Corridors
These were designed to allow the large and often unruly crowd to move freely and to be seated within ten minutes of arriving at the Colosseum.

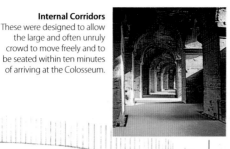

VISITORS' CHECKLIST

Practical Information
Piazza del Colosseo 1.
Map 9 A1. **Tel** 06-3996 7700.
Open 8:30am–approx 1 hour before sunset daily (last adm: 1 hour before closing).
Closed 1 Jan, 25 Dec. (includes Palatine & Forum). Additional fees for upper tier and guided tours of underground areas. Tickets can be bought in advance at www.coopculture.it limited. **Beware** of "gladiators" who charge for photos.

Transport
75, 81, 85, 87, 117, 673, 810.
3 to Piazza del Colosseo.
Colosseo.

Colossus of Nero
The Colosseum may have acquired its name from this huge gilt bronze statue that stood near the amphitheatre.

The Founder of the Colosseum
Vespasian was a professional soldier who became emperor in AD 69, founding the Flavian dynasty.

1870 All vegetation removed

1600

9 Colosseum dedicated to sion of Jesus

1893–6 Structure below arena revealed

Flora of the Colosseum
By the 19th century the Colosseum was heavily overgrown. Different microclimates in various parts of the ruin had created an impressive variety of herbs, grasses and wild flowers. Several botanists were inspired to study and catalogue them and two books were published, one listing 420 different species.

Borage, a herb

How Fights were Staged in the Arena

The emperors held shows here which often began with animals performing circus tricks. Then on came the gladiators, who fought each other to the death. When one was killed, attendants dressed as Charon, the mythical ferryman of the dead, carried his body off on a stretcher, and sand was raked over the blood ready for the next bout. A badly wounded gladiator would surrender his fate to the crowd. The "thumbs up" sign from the emperor meant he could live, "thumbs down" that he die, and the victor became an instant hero. Animals were brought here from as far away as North Africa and the Middle East. The games held in AD 248 to mark the 1,000th anniversary of Rome's founding saw the death of a host of lions, elephants, hippos, zebras and elks.

Beneath the Arena
Late 19th-century excavations exposed the network of underground rooms where the animals were kept.

Interior of the Colosseum
The amphitheatre was built in the form of an ellipse, with tiers of seats around a vast central arena.

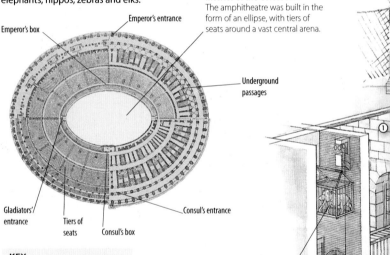

Emperor's entrance

Emperor's box

Underground passages

Gladiators' entrance

Tiers of seats

Consul's box

Consul's entrance

KEY

① **A complex** of rooms, passages and lifts lies underneath the arena.

② **Metal fencing** kept animals penned in, while archers stood by just in case any escaped.

③ **Seating** was tiered, and different social classes were segregated.

④ **A winch** brought the animal cages up to arena level when they were due to fight.

⑤ **A ramp and trap door** enabled the animal to reach the arena after walking along a corridor.

⑥ **Cages** were like three-sided lifts which went up to the next level where the animals were released.

Dramatic Entrances
Below the sand was a wooden floor through which animals, men and scenery appeared in the arena.

Roman Gladiators
These were usually slaves, prisoners of war or condemned criminals. Most were men, but there were a few female gladiators.

The Colosseum by Antonio Canaletto
This 18th-century view of the Colosseum shows the Meta Sudans fountain (now demolished). Water "sweated" from a metal ball on top of its brick cone.

Sea Battles in the Arena

The historian Dion Cassius, writing in the 4th century AD, relates how, 150 years earlier, the Colosseum's arena was flooded to stage a mock sea battle. Scholars now believe that he was mistaken. The spectacle probably took place in the Naumachia of Augustus, a water-filled arena situated across the Tiber in Trastevere.

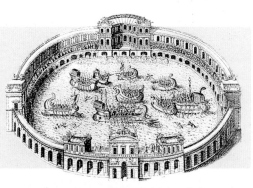

PALATINE

According to legend, Romulus and Remus were brought up here by a wolf in a cave. Traces of Iron-Age huts, dating from the 9th century BC, have been found on the Palatine hill, providing archaeological support for the area's legendary links with the founding of Rome. The Palatine was a very desirable place to live, becoming home to some of the city's most famous inhabitants. The great orator Cicero had a house here, as did the lyric poet Catullus. Augustus was born on the hill and continued to live here in very modest circumstances even when he became emperor. The two buildings identified as the House of Augustus and the House of Livia, his wife, are among the best preserved. The first emperor's example of frugality was ignored by his successors, Tiberius, Caligula and Domitian, who all built extravagant palaces here. The ruins of Tiberius's palace lie beneath the 16th-century Farnese Gardens. The most extensive ruins are those of the Domus Augustana and Domus Flavia, the two wings of Domitian's palace, and the later extension built by Septimius Severus.

Sights at a Glance

Temples
❼ Temple of Cybele

Historic Buildings
❶ Domus Flavia
❸ Domus Augustana
❺ House of Livia
❻ House of Augustus

Ancient Sites
❷ Cryptoporticus
❹ Stadium
❽ Huts of Romulus

Parks and Gardens
❾ Farnese Gardens

See also Street Finder map 8

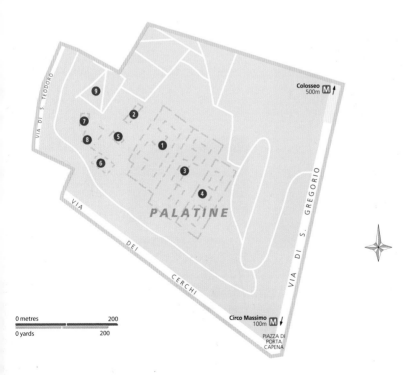

0 metres 200
0 yards 200

◀ Scenic view of umbrella pine trees on the Palatine Hill

For keys to symbols *see back flap*

A Tour of the Palatine

Shaded on its lower slopes with pines, and scattered in spring with wild flowers, the Palatine is the most pleasant and relaxing of the city's ancient sites. You can reach the hill by walking up from the Roman Forum *(see p83)*. The area is dominated by the ruins of the Domus Flavia and the Domus Augustana, two parts of Domitian's huge palace built at the end of the 1st century AD. What you are able to see depends on where excavations are taking place at the time.

To Farnese Gardens *(see p103)*

❼ Temple of Cybele
Also known as the Temple of the Magna Mater, this was the centre of an important fertility cult.

❽ Huts of Romulus
These are traces of a 9th-century BC village on the Palatine.

❻ ★ House of Augustus
Splendid frescoes, painted in about 30 BC, can be seen in four rooms here.

❺ ★ House of Livia
Many of the wall paintings have survived in the house where Augustus lived with his wife Livia.

| 0 metres | | 75 |
| 0 yards | | 75 |

Key

— Suggested route

❶ ★ Domus Flavia
This oval fountain was designed to be seen from the dining hall of the palace.

❸ Domus Augustana
The Roman emperors lived in this part of the palace, while the Domus Flavia was used for public functions.

2 Cryptoporticus
In this long underground tunnel, built by Nero, the stuccoes that decorated the walls and vault have been replaced with copies.

Locator Map
See Central Rome Map pp16–17

Octagonal fountain of the Domus Flavia

The Palatine Museum is inside a former convent, and houses artifacts from ancient Rome.

4 Stadium
Part of the Imperial palace, this enclosure may have been used by the emperors as a private garden.

Via San Gregorio entrance

The exedra of the Stadium may have housed a balcony for emperors to view races.

Baths of Septimius Severus

The Palace of Septimius Severus (reigned AD 193–211) was an extension of the Domus Augustana. It projected beyond the hillside, requiring enormous arched supports.

Substructure of palace

Marble pavement in the courtyard of the Domus Flavia

❶ Domus Flavia

See Visitors' Checklist.

In AD 81 Domitian, the third of the Flavian dynasty of emperors, decided to build a splendid new palace on the Palatine hill. But the western peak, the Germalus, was covered with houses and temples, while the eastern peak, the Palatium, was very steep. So the emperor's architect, Rabirius, flattened the Palatium and used the soil to fill in the cleft between the two peaks, burying (and preserving) a number of Republican-era houses.

The palace had two wings – one official (the Domus Flavia), the other private (the Domus Augustana). It was the main Imperial palace for 300 years. At the front of the Domus Flavia, the surviving stubs of columns and fragments of walls trace the shapes of three adjoining rooms. In the first of these, the Basilica, Domitian dispensed his personal brand of justice.

The central Aula Regia was a throne room decorated with 12 black basalt statues. The third room (now covered with corrugated plastic) was the Lararium, a shrine for the household gods known as Lares (usually the owner's ancestors). It may have been used for official ceremonies or by the palace guards.

Fearing assassination, Domitian had the walls of the courtyard covered with shiny marble slabs designed to act as mirrors so that he could see anyone lurking behind him. In the event, he was assassinated in his bedroom, possibly on the orders of his wife, Domitia. The courtyard is now a pleasant place to pause;

the flower beds in the centre follow the maze pattern of a sunken fountain pool.

❷ Cryptoporticus

See Visitors' Checklist.

The Cryptoporticus, a series of underground corridors, was built by Nero to connect his Domus Aurea (see p177) with the palaces of earlier emperors on the Palatine. A further branch leading to the Palace of Domitian was added later. Its vaults are decorated with delicate stucco reliefs – copies of originals now kept in the Palatine's museum.

❸ Domus Augustana

See Visitors' Checklist.

This part of Domitian's palace was called the Domus Augustana because it was the private resi-dence of the "august" emperors. On the upper level a high brick wall remains, and you can make out the shape of its two court-yards. The far better-preserved lower level is closed to the public, though you can look down on its sunken courtyard with the geometric foundations of a fountain in its centre. Sadly, you cannot see the stairs linking the two levels (once lit by sunlight falling on a mirror-paved pool), nor the surrounding rooms, paved with coloured marble.

❹ Stadium

See Visitors' Checklist.

The Stadium on the Palatine was laid out at the same time as the Palace of Domitian. It is not

clear whether it was a public stadium, a private track for exercising horses, or simply a large garden. The alcove in the eastern wall looks as though it may have held a box from which the emperor could have watched races. It is, however, known that the Stadium was used for foot races by the Ostrogothic king, Theodoric, in the 6th century – he added the small oval-shaped enclosure at the southern end of the site.

Stadium viewed from the south

❺ House of Livia

See Visitors' Checklist. If closed, apply to custodian.

This house dating from the 1st century BC is one of the best preserved on the Palatine. It was probably part of the house in which the Emperor Augustus and his wife Livia lived. Compared with later Imperial palaces, it is a relatively modest home. According to Suetonius, the biographer of Rome's early emperors, Augustus slept in

Remains of the Domus Augustana and the Palace of Septimius Severus

the same small bedroom for 40 years on a low bed which had "a very ordinary coverlet".

A flight of steps leads down to a mosaic-paved corridor into a courtyard. Its imitation-marble wall frescoes have been detached in order to preserve them, but they still hang in situ. They are faded, but you can make out the veining patterns nonetheless. Off the courtyard are three small reception rooms. The frescoes in the central one include a faded scene of Hermes coming to the rescue of Zeus's beloved Io, who is guarded by the 100-eyed Argos. In the left-hand room are frescoed figures of griffins and other beasts, while the decor in the right-hand room includes both landscapes and cityscapes.

❻ House of Augustus

See Visitors' Checklist.

Painted in about 30 BC, the frescoes in the House of Augustus are among the most impressive existing examples of Roman wall paintings, similar in quality to those found in Pompeii and Herculaneum. In vivid shades of red, blue and ochre, they include various *trompe l'oeil* effects, including a room with walls painted to resemble a stage with side doors, and a garden vista.

Although the frescoes are impressive, the house itself is modest. This is where Augustus (or Octavian, as he was then known) lived before assuming supreme power as Rome's first emperor. Only a few visitors are allowed in at any one time.

❼ Temple of Cybele

See Visitors' Checklist.

Other than a platform with a few column stumps and capitals, there is little to see

Vaulted ceiling painting in the House of Augustus

Statue of the goddess Cybele

of the Temple of Cybele, a popular fertility goddess imported to Rome from Asia. The priests of the cult castrated themselves in the belief that if they sacrificed their own fertility it would guarantee that of the natural world. The annual festival of Cybele, in early spring, culminated with frenzied eunuch-priests slashing their bodies to offer up their blood to the goddess, and the ceremonial castration of novice priests.

❽ Huts of Romulus

See Visitors' Checklist.

According to legend, after killing his brother Remus, Romulus founded a village on the Palatine. In the 1940s a series of holes was found, and archaeologists deduced that these must originally have held the supporting poles of three Iron-Age huts – the first foundations of Rome *(see pp20–21).*

❾ Farnese Gardens

See Visitors' Checklist.

In the mid-1500s Cardinal Alessandro Farnese, grandson of Pope Paul III, bought the ruins of Tiberius's palace on the Palatine. He filled in the ruined building and had the architect Vignola design a garden. The result was one of the first botanical gardens in Europe, its terraces linked by steps stretching from the House of Vestal Virgins in the Forum to the Palatine's Germalus peak. The gardeners introduced a number of plants to Italy and Europe, among them *Acacia farnesiana*. Farnese was at the centre of a glittering set that included a number of courtesans, so the parties here are likely to have been somewhat unholy.

The area was dug up during the excavation of the Palatine and re-landscaped. The tree-lined avenues, rose gardens and glorious views make it an ideal place to unwind.

VISITORS' CHECKLIST

Practical Information
Entrances & ticket kiosks: Via di San Gregorio 30. **Map** 8 E1–8 F1.
Tel 06-3996 7700.
Open 8:30am–approx 1 hour before sunset daily; (last adm: 1 hour before closing).
Closed 1 Jan, 25 Dec.
🎫 (includes entry to the Palatine Museum, the Forum & the Colosseum). 🖼️ 📷 🏛️

Transport
🚌 75, 85, 87, 117, 186, 810, 850 to Via dei Fori Imperiali.
🚃 3. Ⓜ Colosseo.

Farnese pavilions, relics of the age when the Palatine was a private garden

PIAZZA DELLA ROTONDA

The Pantheon, one of the great buildings in the history of European architecture, has stood at the heart of Rome for nearly 2,000 years. The historic area around it has seen uninterrupted economic and political activity throughout that time. Palazzo di Montecitorio, built for Pope Innocent XII as a papal tribunal in 1694, is now the Italian parliament and many nearby buildings are government offices. This is also the main financial district of Rome with banking headquarters and the stock exchange. Not many people live here, but in the evenings, Romans stroll in the narrow streets and fill the lively restaurants and cafés that make this a focus for the city's social life.

Sights at a Glance

Churches and Temples
1 Temple of Hadrian
3 Sant'Ignazio di Loyola
9 *Gesù pp110–11*
11 Santa Maria sopra Minerva
13 *Pantheon pp114–15*
14 Sant'Eustachio
15 La Maddalena
18 Santa Maria in Campo Marzio
20 San Lorenzo in Lucina

Historic Streets and Piazzas
2 Piazza di Sant'Ignazio
7 Via della Gatta

Historic Buildings
4 Palazzo del Collegio Romano
6 Palazzo Doria Pamphilj
8 Palazzo Altieri
17 Palazzo Baldassini
19 Palazzo Borghese
21 Palazzo di Montecitorio
24 Palazzo Capranica

Columns, Obelisks and Statues
10 Pie' di Marmo
12 Obelisk of Santa Maria sopra Minerva
22 Obelisk of Montecitorio
23 Column of Marcus Aurelius

Fountains
5 Fontanella del Facchino

Historic Cafés
16 Caffè Giolitti

Restaurants
see pp311–15
1 Al Duello
2 Armando al Pantheon
3 Il Bacaro
4 Clemente alla Maddalena
5 Enoteca Capranica
6 Nest Osteria in Roma
7 Maccheroni
8 Osteria del Sostegno
9 Pantha Rei
10 La Rosetta
11 Vitti

See also Street Finder maps 4, 5, 12

0 metres   200
0 yards   200

◀ Fountain outside the Pantheon at dusk   For keys to symbols *see back flap*

Street-by-Street: Piazza della Rotonda

If you wander through this area, sooner or later you will emerge into Piazza della Rotonda with its jumble of open-air café tables in front of the Pantheon. The refreshing splash of the fountain makes it a welcome resting place. In this warren of narrow streets, it can be hard to realize just how close you are to some of Rome's finest sights. The magnificent art collection of Palazzo Doria Pamphilj and the Baroque splendour of the Gesù are just a few minutes' walk from the Pantheon. At night there is always a lively buzz of activity, as people dine in style or enjoy the coffee and ice cream for which the area is famous.

❷ Piazza di Sant'Ignazio
The square is a rare example of stylish domestic architecture from the early 18th century.

❶ Temple of Hadrian
The columns of this Roman temple now form the façade of the stock exchange.

La Tazza d'Oro enjoys a reputation for the potent coffee consumed on its premises as well as for its freshly ground coffee to take away *(see p322)*.

❸ ★ Pantheon
The awe-inspiring interior of Rome's best-preserved ancient temple is only hinted at from the outside.

❶ Santa Maria sopra Minerva
The rich decoration of Rome's only Gothic church was added in the 19th century.

❷ Obelisk of Santa Maria sopra Minerva
In 1667 Bernini dreamed up the idea of mounting a recently discovered obelisk on the back of a marble elephant.

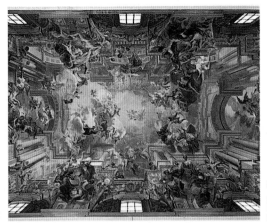

Locator Map
See Central Rome Map pp16–17

❸ ★ Sant'Ignazio di Loyola
Andrea Pozzo painted this glorious
Baroque ceiling (1685) to celebrate
St Ignatius and the Jesuit order.

❺ Fontanella del Facchino
The water in this small
16th-century fountain spurts
from a barrel held by a porter.

**❹ Palazzo del
Collegio Romano**
Up until 1870, the
college educated
many leading figures
in the Catholic Church.

❻ ★ Palazzo Doria Pamphilj
Among the masterpieces
in the art gallery of this magnificent
family palazzo is this portrait of Pope
Innocent X by Velázquez (1650).

❼ Via della Gatta
The street is named
after the statue of a cat.

❽ Palazzo Altieri
This enormous 17th-century
palazzo is decorated with the
arms of Pope Clement X.

Key

— Suggested route

0 metres	75
0 yards	75

❿ Pie' di Marmo
This marble foot is a stray
fragment from a gigantic
Roman statue.

❾ ★ Gesù
The design of the first-ever Jesuit
church had a great impact on
religious architecture.

❶ Temple of Hadrian

La Borsa, Piazza di Pietra. **Map** 4 F3 & 12 E2. ■ 117, 119, 492 and routes along Via del Corso or stopping at Piazza S. Silvestro. **Open** for exhibitions.

This temple honours the emperor Hadrian as a god and was dedicated by his son and successor, Antoninus Pius in AD 145. The remains of the temple are visible on the southern side of Piazza di Pietra, incorporated in a 17th-century building. This was originally a papal customs house, completed by Carlo Fontana and his son in the 1690s. Today the building houses the Roman stock exchange (La Borsa).

Eleven marble Corinthian columns 15 m (49 ft) high stand on a base of *peperino*, a volcanic rock quarried from the Alban hills to the south of Rome. The columns decorated the northern flank of the temple enclosing its inner shrine, the *cella*. The *peperino* wall of the *cella* is still visible behind the columns, as is part of the coffered portico ceiling.

A number of reliefs from the temple, representing conquered Roman provinces, are now in the courtyard of the Palazzo dei Conservatori *(see pp72–3)*. They reflect the mostly peaceful foreign policy of Hadrian's reign.

Illusionistic ceiling in the crossing of Sant'Ignazio

Remains of Hadrian's Temple

❷ Piazza di Sant'Ignazio

Map 4 F4 & 12 E3. ■ 117, 119, 492 and routes along Via del Corso or stopping at Piazza San Silvestro.

One of the major works of the Roman Rococo, the piazza (1727–8) is Filippo Raguzzini's masterpiece. It offsets the imposing façade of the church of Sant'Ignazio with the intimacy of the houses belonging to the bourgeoisie. The theatrical setting, the curvilinear design and the playful forms of its windows, balconies and balusters mark the piazza as one of a highly distinct group of structures. Along with Palazzo Doria Pamphilj (1731), the façade of La Maddalena (1735) and the aristocratic Spanish Steps (1723), it belongs to the moment when Rome's opulent Rococo triumphed over conservative Classicism.

❸ Sant'Ignazio di Loyola

Piazza di Sant'Ignazio. **Map** 4 F4 & 12 E3. **Tel** 06-679 4406. ■ 117, 119, 492 and along Via del Corso. **Open** 7:30am–7pm Mon–Sat, 9am–7pm Sun. ⛪ ♿

The church was built by Pope Gregory XV in 1626 in honour of St Ignatius of Loyola, founder of the Society of Jesus and the man who most embodied the zeal of the Counter-Reformation.

Together with the Gesù *(see pp110–11)*, Sant'Ignazio forms the centre of the Jesuit area in Rome. Built in Baroque style, its vast interior, lined with precious stones, marble, stucco and gilt, creates a sense of theatre. The church has a Latin-cross plan, with an apse and many side chapels. A cupola was planned but never built, so the space it would have filled was covered by a fake perspective painting. The piers built to uphold the cupola support the observatory of the Collegio Romano.

❹ Palazzo del Collegio Romano

Piazza del Collegio Romano. **Map** 5 A4 & 12 E3. ■ 117, 119, 492 and along Via del Corso or stopping at Piazza Venezia. **Closed** to the public.

On the same block as the church of Sant'Ignazio is the palazzo used by Jesuits as a college where many future bishops, cardinals and popes studied. The college was con-fiscated in 1870 and turned into an ordinary school. The portals bear the coat of arms of its founder, Pope Gregory XIII of Boncompagni (reigned 1572–85). The façade is also adorned with a bell, a clock, and two sundials. On the right is a tower built in 1787 as a meteorological observatory. Until 1925 its time signal regulated all the clocks within the city.

❺ Fontanella del Facchino

Via Lata. **Map** 5 A4 & 12 E3. 🚌 64, 81, 85, 117, 119, 492 and many other routes.

Il Facchino (the Porter), once in the Corso, now set in the wall of the Banco di Roma, was one of Rome's "talking statues" like Pasquino (*see p126*). Created around 1590, the fountain may have been based on a drawing by painter Jacopino del Conte. The statue of a man holding a barrel most likely represents a member of the Università degli Acquaroli (Fraternity of Water-carriers), though it is also said to be of Martin Luther, or of the porter Abbondio Rizzio, who died carrying a barrel.

The Facchino drinking fountain

❻ Palazzo Doria Pamphilj

Via del Corso 305. **Map** 5 A4 & 12 E3. **Tel** 06-679 7323. 🚌 64, 81, 85, 117, 119, 492 and many other routes. **Open** 9am–7pm daily. **Closed** 1 Jan, Easter Sun, 25 Dec. 🚭 ♿ 📷 for private apartments. 🔲 📷 🖥 Concerts. 🌐 **doriapamphilj.it**

Palazzo Doria Pamphilj is a great island of stone in the heart of Rome, the oldest parts dating from 1435. Through the Corso entrance you can see the 16th-century porticoed courtyard with the coat of arms of the della Rovere family. The Aldobrandini were the next owners. Between 1601 and 1647 the mansion acquired a second courtyard and flanking wings at the expense of a public bath that stood nearby.
    When the Pamphilj family took over, they completed the Piazza del Collegio Romano façade and the Via della Gatta

The façade of the Rococo palace building, Palazzo Doria Pamphilj

wing, a splendid chapel and a theatre inaugurated by Queen Christina of Sweden in 1684.
    In the first half of the 1700s, Gabriele Valvassori created the gallery above the courtyard and a new façade along the Corso, using the highly decorative style of the period, Rococo, which now dominates the building. The stairways and salons, the Mirror Gallery and the picture gallery all radiate a sense of light and space.
    The family collection in the Doria Pamphilj gallery has over 400 paintings dating from the 15th to the 18th century, including the famous portrait of Pope Innocent X Pamphilj by Velázquez. There are also works by Titian, Caravaggio, Lorenzo Lotto and Guercino. The rooms in the private apartment have many of their original furnishings, including splendid Brussels and Gobelin tapestries.

Occasionally, the gallery hosts concerts and evening visits of the collection.

❼ Via della Gatta

Map 5 A4 & 12 E3. 🚌 62, 63, 64, 70, 81, 87, 186, 492 & routes along Via del Plebiscito & Corso Vittorio Emanuele II.

This narrow street runs between the Palazzo Doria Pamphilj and the smaller Palazzo Grazioli. The ancient marble sculpture of a cat (*gatta*) that gives the street its name is on the first cornice on the corner of Palazzo Grazioli.

❽ Palazzo Altieri

Via del Gesù 49. **Map** 4 F4 & 12 E3. 🚌 46, 62, 63, 64, 70, 81, 87, 186, 492 and routes along Via del Plebiscito and Corso Vittorio Emanuele II. 🚋 8. **Closed** to the public.

The Altieri family is first mentioned in Rome's history in the 9th century. This palazzo was built by the last male heirs, the brothers Cardinal Giambattista di Lorenzo Altieri and Cardinal Emilio Altieri, who later became Pope Clement X (reigned 1670–76). Many surrounding houses had to be demolished, but an old woman called Berta refused to leave, so her hovel was incorporated in the palazzo. Its windows are still visible on the west end of the building.

Caravaggio's *Rest during the Flight into Egypt* in Palazzo Doria Pamphilj

⑨ Gesù

Dating from between 1568 and 1584, the Gesù was the first Jesuit church to be built in Rome. Its design epitomizes Counter-Reformation Baroque architecture and has been much imitated throughout the Catholic world. The layout proclaims the church's two major functions: a large nave with side pulpits for preaching to great crowds, and a main altar as the centrepiece for the celebration of the Mass. The illusionistic decoration in the nave and dome was added a century later. Its message is clear and confident: faithful Catholic worshippers will be joyfully uplifted into the heavens while Protestants and other heretics are flung into hell's fires.

★ Chapel of Sant'Ignazio
Above its altar is a statue of the saint, framed by gilded lapis lazuli columns. The chapel was built in 1696–1700 by Andrea Pozzo, a Jesuit artist.

Triumph of Faith Over Idolatry
This vivid Baroque allegory sculpted by Théudon illustrates the great ambition of Jesuit theology.

St Ignatius and the Jesuit Order

Spanish soldier Ignatius of Loyola (1491–1556) joined the Church after being wounded in battle in 1521. He came to Rome in 1537 and founded the Jesuits, sending missionaries and teachers all over the world to win souls for Catholicism.

Main entrance

KEY

① **The Chapel of St Francis Xavier** is a memorial to the great missionary who died alone on an island off China in 1552.

Allegorical Figures
Antonio Raggi made these stuccoes, which were designed by Il Baciccia to complement the figures on his own nave frescoes.

Madonna della Strada
This 15th-century image, the Madonna of the Road, was originally displayed on the façade of Santa Maria della Strada which once stood on this site.

★ **Monument to San Roberto Bellarmino**
Bernini captured the forceful personality of this anti-Protestant theologian, who died in 1621.

★ **Nave Ceiling Decorations**
The figures in Il Baciccia's astonishing fresco of the *Triumph of the Name of Jesus* spill out on to the coffered vaulting of the nave.

Cupola Frescoes
The cupola was completed by della Porta to Vignola's design. The frescoes, by Il Baciccia, feature Old Testament figures.

1540 Founding of the Society of Jesus (the Jesuits)

1571 Giacomo della Porta's design chosen for the façade

1584 Church's consecration

1696–1700 The Chapel of Sant'Ignazio is designed by Andrea Pozzo, a Jesuit artist

1622 Ignatius of Loyola is canonized

1773 Pope Clement XIV orders the suppression of the Jesuit order

1500 **1600** **1700**

1545–63 Council of Trent defines the new Catholic orthodoxy
1556 Ignatius of Loyola dies

1568–71 Vignola builds the church up to the crossing, under the patronage of Cardinal Alessandro Farnese

1670–83 Giovanni Battista Gaulli (Il Baciccia) paints the nave vault, dome and apse

Marble foot from a Roman statue

⓿ Pie' di Marmo

Via Santo Stefano del Cacco. **Map** 4 F4
& 12 E3. 🚌 62, 63, 64, 70, 81, 87, 116,
186, 492 and other routes along Via
del Corso, Via del Plebiscito and Corso
Vittorio Emanuele II.

It was popularly believed in
the Middle Ages that half the
population of ancient Rome was
made up of bronze and marble
statues. Fragments of these
giants, usually gods or emperors,
are scattered over the city. This
piece, a marble foot *(pie' di
marmo)*, comes from an area
dedicated to the Egyptian gods
Isis and Serapis and was probably
part of a temple statue. Statues
were painted and covered with
jewels and clothes given by the
faithful – a great fire risk with
unattended burning tapers.

⓫ Santa Maria sopra Minerva

Piazza della Minerva 42. **Map** 4 F4 &
12 E3. **Tel** 06-679 3926. 🚌 116 and
along Via del Corso, Via del Plebiscito
and Corso Vittorio Emanuele II.
Open 7:30am–7pm Mon–Fri, 7:30am
–12:30pm & 3:30–7pm Sat, 8am–noon
& 3:30–7pm Sun. Cloister: **Open** call in
advance for details. 🕇 🏛 Concerts.

Few other churches display
such a complete and impressive
record of Italian art. Dating from
the 13th century, the Minerva
is one of the few examples of
Gothic architecture in Rome.
It was the traditional stronghold
of the Dominicans, whose
anti-heretical zeal earned them
the nickname of *Domini Canes*
(the hounds of the Lord).
    Built on ancient ruins,
supposed to have been the
Temple of Minerva, the simple
T-shaped vaulted building
acquired rich chapels and works
of art by which its many patrons

wished to be remembered.
Note the Cosmatesque
13th-century tombs and the
exquisite works of 15th-century
Tuscan and Venetian artists.
Local talent of the period can
be admired in Antoniazzo
Romano's *Annunciation*,
featuring Cardinal Juan de
Torquemada, uncle of the
infamous Spanish Inquisitor.
    The more monumental style
of the Roman Renaissance is
well represented in the tombs
of the 16th-century Medici
popes, Leo X and his cousin
Clement VII, and in the richly
decorated Aldobrandini
Chapel. Near the steps of
the choir is the celebrated
sculpture of the *Risen Christ*,
started by Michelangelo but
completed by Raffaello da
Montelupo in 1521. There are
also splendid works of art from
the Baroque period, including
a tomb and a bust by Bernini.
    The church is also visited
because it contains the
tombs of many famous
Italians: St Catherine of
Siena, who died here
in 1380; the Venetian
sculptor Andrea Bregno
(died 1506); the
Humanist Cardinal
Pietro Bembo (died
1547); and Fra Angelico,
the Dominican friar
and painter, who died
in Rome in 1455.

⓬ Obelisk of Santa Maria sopra Minerva

Piazza della Minerva. **Map** 4 F4 & 12
D3. 🚌 116 and routes along Via del
Corso and Corso Vittorio Emanuele II.

Originally meant to decorate
Palazzo Barberini as a joke, this
exotic elephant and obelisk
sculpture is typical of Bernini's
inexhaustible imagination (the
elephant was actually sculpted
by Ercole Ferrata to Bernini's
design). When the ancient
obelisk was found in the
garden of the monastery of
Santa Maria sopra Minerva,
the friars wanted the
monument erected in their
piazza. The elephant was
provided with its enormous
saddle-cloth because of a
friar's insistence that the gap
under the animal's abdomen
would undermine its
stability. Bernini knew
better: you need only look
at the Fontana dei
Quattro Fiumi *(see
p122)* to appreciate
his use of empty
space. The elephant,
an ancient symbol of
intelligence and piety,
was chosen as the
embodiment of the
virtues on which
Christians should
build true wisdom.

Bernini's marble elephant
and Egyptian obelisk

Nave of Santa Maria sopra Minerva

⑬ Pantheon

See pp114–15.

⑭ Sant'Eustachio

Piazza Sant'Eustachio. **Map** 4 F4 & 12 D3. **Tel** 06-686 5334. 116 and routes along Corso Vittorio Emanuele II. **Open** 9am–noon, 4–7:30pm daily.

The origins of this church date to early Christian times, when it offered relief to the poor. In medieval times, many charitable brotherhoods elected St Eustachio as their patron and had chapels here.

The Romanesque bell tower is one of the few surviving remains of the medieval church, which was completely redecorated in the 17th and 18th centuries.

Nearby is the excellent Caffè Sant'Eustachio *(see p322).*

Bell tower of Sant'Eustachio

⑮ La Maddalena

Piazza della Maddalena. **Map** 4 F3 & 12 D2. **Tel** 06-899 281. 116 and many routes along Via del Corso and Corso Vittorio Emanuele II. **Open** 8:30–11:30am, 5–6:30pm daily (9–11:30am Sat).

Situated in a small piazza near the Pantheon, the Maddalena's Rococo façade, built in 1735, epitomizes the love of light and movement of the late Baroque. Its curves are reminiscent of Borromini's San Carlo alle Quattro Fontane *(see p163).* The façade has been lovingly restored, although die-hard Neo-Classicists dismiss its painted stucco as icing sugar.

The small size of the Maddalena did not deter

The old-fashioned *salone* of the Caffè Giolitti

the 17th- and 18th-century decorators who filled the interior with ornaments from the floor to the top of the elegant cupola. The organ loft and choir are particularly powerful examples of the Baroque's desire to fire the imagination of the faithful.

Many of the paintings and sculptures adopt the Christian imagery of the Counter-Reformation. In the niches of the nave, the statues are personifications of virtues such as Humility and Simplicity. There are also scenes from the life of St Camillus de Lellis, who died in the adjacent convent in 1614. The church belonged to his followers, the Camillians, a preaching order active in Rome's hospitals. Like the Jesuits, they commissioned powerful works of art to convey the force of their religious message.

La Maddalena's stuccoed façade

⑯ Caffè Giolitti

Via degli Uffici del Vicario 40. **Map** 4 F3 & 12 D2. **Tel** 06-699 1243. 116 and many routes along Via del Corso and Corso Rinascimento. **Open** 7am–1am daily.

Founded in 1900, the Caffè Giolitti is the heir to the Belle Époque cafés that lined the nearby Via del Corso in Rome's first days as capital of the new Italian state. Its *salone* holds tourists in summer and Roman families at weekends, and on weekdays is frequented by local workers. Its ice creams are especially good.

⑰ Palazzo Baldassini

Via delle Coppelle 35. **Map** 4 F3 & 12 D2. **Tel** 06-684 0421. 116 and many routes along Via del Corso and Corso Rinascimento. **Open** 9:30am–noon Sat by reservation only, call 06-684 0421.

Melchiorre Baldassini commissioned Antonio da Sangallo the Younger to build his home in Florentine Renaissance style in 1514–20. With its cornices marking the different floors and wrought-iron window grilles, this is one of the best examples of an early 16th-century Roman palazzo. It stands in the part of Rome still known as the Renaissance Quarter, which flourished around the long straight streets such as Via di Ripetta and Via della Scrofa built at the time of Pope Leo X (reigned 1513–21).

⑬ Pantheon

In the Middle Ages the Pantheon, the Roman temple of "all the gods", became a church; in time this magnificent building with its awe-inspiring domed interior became a symbol of Rome itself. The rectangular portico screens the vast hemispherical dome: only from inside can its true scale and beauty be appreciated. The rotunda's height and diameter are equal: 43.3 m (142 ft). The hole at the top of the dome, the *oculus*, provides the only light. We owe this marvel of Roman engineering to the emperor Hadrian, who designed it (AD 118–125) to replace an earlier temple built by Marcus Agrippa, son-in-law of Augustus. The shrines that now line the wall of the Pantheon range from the Tomb of Raphael to those of the kings of modern Italy.

★ Interior of the Dome
The dome was cast by pouring concrete mixed with tufa and pumice over a temporary wooden framework.

Floor Patterning
The marble floor, restored in 1873, preserves the original Roman design.

The portico, enclosed by granite columns

KEY

① **The immense portico** is built on the foundations of Agrippa's temple.

② **The walls** of the drum supporting the dome are 6 m (19 ft) thick.

③ **Oculus**

④ **Constructing the dome** from hollow decorative coffers reduced its weight.

Bell Towers
This 18th-century view by Bernardo Bellotto shows Bernini's much-ridiculed turrets, which were removed in 1883.

Raphael and La Fornarina

Raphael, at his own request, was buried here when he died in 1520. He had lived for years with his model, La Fornarina (*see p212*), seen here in a painting by Giulio Romano, but she was excluded from the ceremony of his burial. On the right of his tomb is a memorial to his fiancée, Maria Bibbiena, niece of the artist's patron, Cardinal Dovizi di Bibbiena.

VISITORS' CHECKLIST

Practical Information
Piazza della Rotonda.
Map 4 F4 & 12 D3.
Tel 06-6830 0230.
Open 9am–7:30pm Mon–Sat,
9am–6pm Sun, 9am–1pm public
hols. **Closed** 1 Jan, 1 May, 25 Dec.
🔲 pantheonroma.com

Transport
🚌 116 and routes along Via del
Corso, Corso Vittorio Emanuele II
& Corso del Rinascimento.

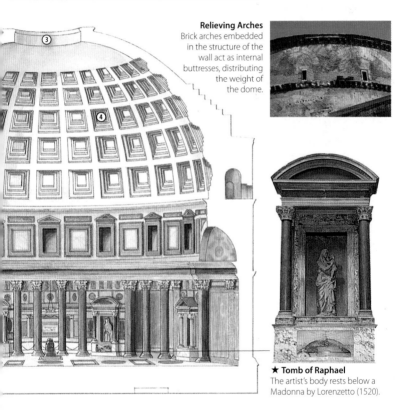

Relieving Arches
Brick arches embedded in the structure of the wall act as internal buttresses, distributing the weight of the dome.

★ **Tomb of Raphael**
The artist's body rests below a Madonna by Lorenzetto (1520).

27–25 BC Marcus Agrippa builds first Pantheon

Inscription on pediment

735 Gregory III roofs the Pantheon in lead

1309–77 While papal seat is in Avignon, Pantheon is used as a fortress and poultry market

50 BC | **0** | **AD 600** | **1200** | **1800**

118–25 Hadrian builds new Pantheon

609 Pope Boniface IV consecrates Pantheon as church of Santa Maria ad Martyres

1632 Urban VIII melts down bronze from portico for Bernini's baldacchino in St Peter's

663 Byzantine Emperor Constans II strips gilded tiles from the roof

1888 Tomb of King Vittorio Emanuele II completed

Bernini's curving southern façade of Palazzo di Montecitorio

⓲ Santa Maria in Campo Marzio

Piazza di Campo Marzio 45. **Map** 4 F3 & 12 D2. 🚌 116 and many routes on Via del Corso and Corso Rinascimento. **Closed** to the public.

The church's interior cannot be accessed, but it is worth a visit to see the courtyard by Baroque architect Giovanni Antonio de Rossi, who used an architectural illusion to make it look wider than it actually is. Around the courtyard, there are fascinating remnants of medieval houses. The church itself was rebuilt in 1685 by De Rossi, using a square Greek-cross plan with a cupola.

⓳ Palazzo Borghese

Largo della Fontanella di Borghese. **Map** 4 F3 & 12 D1. 🚌 81, 117, 492, 628. **Closed** to the public.

The palazzo was acquired in about 1605 by Cardinal Camillo Borghese, just before he became Pope Paul V. Flaminio Ponzio was hired to enlarge the building and give it the grandeur appropriate to the residence of the pope's family. He added a wing overlooking Piazza Borghese and the delightful porticoed courtyard inside. Subsequent enlargements included the building and decoration of a great *nymphaeum* known as the Bath of Venus. For more than two centuries this palazzo housed the Borghese family's renowned collection of paintings, which was bought by the Italian

state in 1902 and transferred to the Galleria Borghese (*see pp262–3*).

Pope Paul V, who commissioned Palazzo Borghese for his family

⓴ San Lorenzo in Lucina

Via in Lucina 16A. **Map** 4 F3 & 12 E1. **Tel** 06-687 1494. 🚌 81, 117, 492, 628. **Open** 8am–8pm daily. 🚻

The church is one of Rome's oldest Christian places of worship, and was probably built on a well sacred to Juno, protectress of women. It was rebuilt during the 12th century, and today's external appearance is quite typical of the period featuring a portico with reused Roman columns crowned by medieval capitals, a plain triangular pediment and a Romanesque bell tower with coloured marble inlay.

The interior was totally rebuilt in 1856–8. The old basilical plan was destroyed and the two side naves were replaced by Baroque chapels.

Do not miss the fine busts in the Fonseca Chapel, designed by Bernini, or the *Crucifixion* by Guido Reni above the main altar. There is also a 19th-century monument honouring French painter Nicolas Poussin, who died in Rome in 1655 and was buried in the church.

㉑ Palazzo di Montecitorio

Piazza di Monte Citorio. **Map** 4 F3 & 12 E2. **Tel** 06-676 01. 🚌 116 and all routes along Via del Corso or stopping at Piazza S. Silvestro. **Open** usually 1st Sun each month (except Jul & Aug). Times vary (see website), pick up tickets in advance from info point on Via Uffici del Vicario. 🆆 **camera.it**

The palazzo's first architect, Bernini, got the job after he presented a silver model of his design to the wife of his patron, Prince Ludovisi. The building was completed in 1694 by Carlo Fontana and became the Papal Tribunal of Justice. In 1871 it was chosen to be Italy's new Chamber of Deputies and by 1927 it had doubled in size with a second grand façade. The 630 members of parliament are elected by a majority system with proportional representation.

The church of San Lorenzo in Lucina

Emperor Augustus's obelisk

㉒ Obelisk of Montecitorio

Piazza di Monte Citorio 33. **Map** 4 F3 & 12 E2. 🚌 116 and routes along Via del Corso or to Piazza S. Silvestro.

The measurement of time in ancient Rome was always a rather hit-and-miss affair: for many years the Romans relied on an imported (and therefore inaccurate) sundial, a trophy from the conquest of Sicily. In 10 BC the Emperor Augustus laid out an enormous sundial in the Campus Martius. Its centre was roughly in today's Piazza di San Lorenzo in Lucina. The shadow was cast by a huge granite obelisk that he had brought back from Heliopolis in Egypt. Unfortunately this sundial too became inaccurate after only 50 years, possibly due to subsidence.

The obelisk was still in the piazza in the 9th century, but then disappeared until it was rediscovered lying under medieval houses in the reign of Pope Julius II (1503–13). The pope was intrigued, because Egyptian hieroglyphs were thought to hold the key to the wisdom of Adam before the Fall, but it was only under Pope Benedict XIV (reigned 1740–58) that the obelisk was finally unearthed. It was erected in its present location in 1792 by Pope Pius VI.

㉓ Column of Marcus Aurelius

Piazza Colonna. **Map** 5 A3 & 12 E2. 🚌 116 and routes along Via del Corso or to Piazza S. Silvestro.

Clearly an imitation of the column of Trajan *(see p92)*, this monument was erected after the death of Marcus Aurelius in AD 180 to commemorate his victories over the barbarian tribes of the Danube. The 80-year lapse between the two works produced a great artistic change: the wars of Marcus Aurelius are rendered with simplified pictures in stronger relief, sacrificing Classical proportions for the sake of clarity and immediacy. The spirit of the work is more akin to the 4th-century Arch of Constantine *(see p93)* than to Trajan's monument. Gone are the heroic qualities of the Roman soldiers, by now mostly barbarian mercenaries, and a sense of respect for the vanquished. A new emphasis on the supernatural points to the end of the Hellenistic tradition and the beginning of Christianity.

Composed of 28 drums of marble, the column was restored in 1588 by Domenico Fontana on the orders of Pope Sixtus V. The emperor's statue on the summit was replaced by a bronze of St Paul. The 20 spirals of the low relief chronicle the German war of AD 172–3, and (above) the Sarmatic war of AD 174–5. The column is almost 30 m (100 ft) high and 3.7 m (12 ft) in diameter. An internal

spiral staircase leads to the top. The easiest way to appreciate the sculptural work, however, is to visit the Museo della Civiltà Romana at EUR *(see p268)* and study the casts of the reliefs.

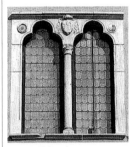

Windows of Palazzo Capranica

㉔ Palazzo Capranica

Piazza Capranica 101. **Map** 4 F3 & 12 D2. 🚌 116 and routes along Via del Corso or to Piazza S. Silvestro. **Closed** to the public.

One of Rome's small number of surviving 15th-century buildings, the palazzo was commissioned by Cardinal Domenico Capranica both as his family residence and as a college for higher education. Its fortress-like appearance is a patchwork of subsequent additions, not unusual in the late 15th century, when Rome was still hovering between medieval and Renaissance taste. The Gothic-looking windows on the right of the building show the cardinal's coat of arms and the date 1451 is inscribed on the doorway underneath. The palazzo now houses a conference centre.

Relief of the emperor's campaigns on the Column of Marcus Aurelius

PIAZZA NAVONA

The foundations of the buildings surrounding the elongated oval of Piazza Navona were the ruined grandstands of the vast Stadium of Domitian. The piazza still provides a dramatic spectacle today with the obelisk of the Fontana dei Quattro Fiumi in front of the church of Sant'Agnese in Agone as its focal point.

The predominant style of the area is Baroque, many of its finest buildings dating from the reign of Innocent X Pamphilj (1644–55), patron of Bernini and Borromini. Of special interest is the complex of the Chiesa Nuova, headquarters of the Filippini, the order founded by San Filippo Neri, the 16th-century "Apostle of Rome".

Sights at a Glance

Churches and Temples
4 Sant'Agnese in Agone
5 Santa Maria dell'Anima
6 Santa Maria della Pace
7 San Luigi dei Francesi
9 Sant'Ivo alla Sapienza
10 Sant'Andrea della Valle
15 Chiesa Nuova
16 Oratorio dei Filippini
20 San Salvatore in Lauro

Museums
12 Palazzo Braschi
21 Museo Napoleonico

Historic Buildings
3 Palazzo Pamphilj
8 Palazzo Madama
11 Palazzo Massimo
   alle Colonne
17 Torre dell'Orologio
18 Palazzo del Banco
   di Santo Spirito
23 Palazzo Altemps

Fountains and Statues
1 Fontana dei Quattro Fiumi
13 Pasquino

Historic Streets and Piazzas
2 Piazza Navona
14 Via del Governo Vecchio
19 Via dei Coronari

Historic Restaurants
22 Hostaria dell'Orso

Restaurants
see pp311–15

1 Baffetto
2 CamBio Vita
3 La Campana
4 Cantina e Cucina
5 Casa Bleve
6 Il Convivio-Troiani
7 Il Corallo
8 Cul de Sac
9 Hostaria dell'Orso
10 The Library

11 Mimí e Cocó
12 Montevecchio
13 Osteria del Gallo
14 Osteria del Pegno
15 Sangallo ai Coronari
16 Terra di Siena

See also Street Finder maps
4, 11, 12

0 metres   200
0 yards   200

◀ Detail from the Fontana dei Quattro Fiumi, Piazza Navona

For keys to symbols see back flap

Street-by-Street: Piazza Navona

No other piazza in Rome can rival the theatricality of Piazza Navona. Day and night there is always something going on in the pedestrian area around its three flamboyant fountains. The Baroque is also represented in many of the area's churches. To discover an older Rome, walk along Via del Governo Vecchio to admire the façades of its Renaissance buildings and browse in the fascinating antiques shops.

⑯ Oratorio dei Filippini
The musical term oratorio comes from this place of informal worship.

⑰ Torre dell'Orologio
This clock tower by Borromini (1648) is part of the Convent of the Filippini.

⑮ Chiesa Nuova
This church was rebuilt in the late 16th century for the order founded by San Filippo Neri.

VIA DEL CORALLO

VIA DEL GOVERNO VECCHIO

VIA DI PARIONE

To Corso Vittorio Emanuele II

⑭ Via del Governo Vecchio
This street preserves a large number of fine Renaissance houses.

CORSO VITTORIO EMANUELE II

⑬ Pasquino
Romans hung satirical verses and dialogues on this weather-beaten statue.

PIAZZA DI PASQU

⑥ Santa Maria della Pace
This medallion shows Pope Sixtus IV who reigned 1471–84 and under whose orders the church was built.

❸ Palazzo Pamphilj
This grand town house was built for Pope Innocent X and his family in the mid-17th century.

PIAZZA DI SAN PANTALEO

⑪ Palazzo Massimo alle Colonne
The magnificent curving colonnade (1536) is by Baldassarre Peruzzi.

⑫ Palazzo Braschi
A late 18th-century building with a splendid balcony, the palazzo houses the Museo di Roma.

Key

 — Suggested route

0 metres	75
0 yards	75

5 Santa Maria dell'Anima
For four centuries this has been the German church in Rome.

Santa Maria della Pace

4 Sant'Agnese in Agone
Borromini's startling concave façade (1657) dominates one side of Piazza Navona.

2 ★ Piazza Navona
This unique piazza owes its shape to a Roman race-track and its stunning decor to the genius of the Roman Baroque.

Locator Map
See Central Rome Map pp16–17

7 ★ San Luigi dei Francesi
An 18th-century statue of St Louis stands in a niche in the façade.

8 Palazzo Madama
A spread-eagled stone lion skin decorates the central doorway of the palazzo, now the Italian Senate.

1 Fontana dei Quattro Fiumi
This fountain supporting an Egyptian obelisk was designed by Bernini.

Fontana del Moro was remodelled in 1653 by Bernini, who designed the central sea god.

9 Sant'Ivo alla Sapienza
This tiny domed church is one of Borromini's most original creations. He worked on it between 1642 and 1650.

10 ★ Sant'Andrea della Valle
The church, with its grandiose façade by Carlo Rainaldi (1665), has gained fame outside Rome as the setting of the first act of Puccini's *Tosca*.

To Campo de' Fiori

❶ Fontana dei Quattro Fiumi

Piazza Navona. **Map** 4 E4 & 11 C3.
🚌 46, 62, 64, 70, 81, 87, 116, 492, 628.

Built for Pope Innocent X Pamphilj, this magnificent fountain in the centre of Piazza Navona was unveiled in 1651. The pope's coat of arms, the dove and the olive branch decorate the pyramid rock formation supporting the Roman obelisk, which once stood in the Circus of Maxentius on the Appian Way. Bernini designed the fountain, which was paid for by means of taxes on bread and other staples. The great rivers – the Ganges, the Danube, the Nile and the River Plate – are represented by four giants. The Nile's veiled head symbolizes the river's unknown source, but there is also a legend that the veil conveys Bernini's dislike for the nearby Sant'Agnese in Agone, designed by his rival Borromini. Similarly, the athletic figure of the River Plate, cringing with arm upraised, is supposed to express Bernini's fear that the church will collapse. Sadly, these widely believed stories can have no basis in fact: Bernini had completed the fountain before Borromini started work on the church.

Palazzo Pamphilj, the largest building in Piazza Navona

❷ Piazza Navona

Map 4 E3 & 11 C2. 🚌 46, 62, 64, 70, 81, 87, 116, 492, 628.

Rome's most beautiful Baroque piazza follows the shape of Domitian's Stadium which once stood on this site – some of its arches are still visible below the church of Sant' Agnese in Agone. The *agones* were athletic contests held in the 1st-century stadium, which could seat 33,000 people. The word "Navona" is thought to be a corruption of *in agone*. The piazza's unique appearance and atmosphere were created in the 17th century with the

addition of the Fontana dei Quattro Fiumi. The other fountains date from the previous century but have been altered several times since. The basin of the Fontana di Nettuno, at the northern end, was built by Giacomo della Porta in 1576, while the statues of Neptune and the Nereids date from the 19th century. The Fontana del Moro, at the southern end, was also designed by della Porta, though Bernini altered it later, adding a statue of a Moor fighting a dolphin.

Up until the 19th century, Piazza Navona was flooded during August by stopping the fountain outlets. The rich would splash around in carriages, while street urchins paddled after them. Today, with its numerous shops and cafés, the piazza is a favourite in all seasons. In summer it is busy with street entertainers, while in winter it fills with colourful stalls selling toys and sweets for the feast of the Befana.

Coat of arms with dove and olive branch on the façade of Palazzo Pamphilj

❸ Palazzo Pamphilj

Piazza Navona. **Map** 4 E4 & 11 C3.
🚌 46, 62, 64, 70, 81, 87, 116, 492, 628.
Closed to the public.

In 1644 Giovanni Battista Pamphilj became Pope Innocent X. During his 10-year reign, he heaped riches on his own family, especially his domineering sister-in-law, Olimpia Maidalchini. The "talking statue" Pasquino *(see p126)* gave her the nickname "Olim-Pia", Latin for "formerly virtuous". She lived in the grand Palazzo Pamphilj, which has frescoes by Pietro da Cortona and a gallery by Borromini. The building is now the Brazilian embassy and cultural centre.

Bernini's Fontana dei Quattro Fiumi in Piazza Navona

❹ Sant'Agnese in Agone

Piazza Navona. **Map** 4 E4 & 11 C3. **Tel** 06-6819 2134. 46, 62, 64, 70, 81, 87, 116, 492, 628. **Open** 9:30am–12:30pm, 3:30–7pm Tue–Fri, 9am–1pm & 4–8pm Sun.

This church is believed to have been founded on the site of the brothel where, in AD 304, the young St Agnes was exposed naked to force her to renounce her faith. A marble relief in the crypt shows the miraculous growth of her hair, which fell around her body to protect her modesty. She was martyred on this site and is buried in the catacombs that bear her name along the Via Nomentana (see p266).

Today's church was commissioned by Pope Innocent X in 1652. The first architects were father and son, Girolamo and Carlo Rainaldi, but they were replaced by Borromini in 1653. He stuck more or less to the Rainaldi scheme except for the concave façade designed to emphasize the dome. A statue of St Agnes on the façade is said to be reassuring the Fontana dei Quattro Fiumi's statue of the River Plate that the church is stable.

Statue of St Agnes on façade of Sant' Agnese in Agone

Carlo Saraceni's *Miracle of St Benno and the Keys of Meissen Cathedral*

❺ Santa Maria dell'Anima

Via Santa Maria dell'Anima 66. **Map** 4 E4 & 11 C2. **Tel** 06-682 8181. 46, 62, 64, 70, 81, 87, 116, 492, 628. **Open** 9am–12:45pm, 3–7pm daily.

Pope Adrian VI (reigned 1522–3), son of a ship-builder from Utrecht, was the last non-Italian pope before John Paul II. He would have disapproved of his superb tomb by Baldassarre Peruzzi in Santa Maria dell'Anima. It stands to the right of Giulio Romano's damaged altarpiece and is redolent of the pagan Renaissance spirit the pope had so condemned during his brief, rather gloomy reign, when patronage of the arts ground to a halt. Santa Maria dell'Anima is the German church in Rome and some of its paintings, such as the *Miracle of St Benno* by Carlo Saraceni (1618), illustrate events connected with the history of Germany.

❻ Santa Maria della Pace

Vicolo dell'Arco della Pace 5. **Map** 4 E3 & 11 C2. 46, 62, 64, 70, 81, 87, 116, 492, 628. **Open** 9–11:45am Mon, Wed & Sat. 2 steps. Exhibitions, concerts.

A drunken soldier allegedly pierced the breast of a painted Madonna on this site, causing it to bleed. Pope Sixtus IV della Rovere (reigned 1471–84) placated the Virgin by ordering Baccio Pontelli to build her a church if she would bring the war with Turkey to an end. Peace was restored and the church was named Santa Maria della Pace (St Mary of Peace).

The cloister was added by Bramante in 1504. As in his famous Tempietto (see p223), he scrupulously followed Classical rules of proportion and achieved a monumental effect in a relatively small space. Pietro da Cortona may have had Bramante's Tempietto in mind when he added the church's charming semi-circular portico in 1656. The interior, a short nave ending under an octagonal cupola, houses Raphael's famous frescoes of four *Sybils*, and four *Prophets* by his pupil Timoteo Viti, painted for the banker Agostino Chigi in 1514. Baldassarre Peruzzi also did some work in the church (fresco in the first chapel on the left), as did the architect Antonio da Sangallo the Younger, who designed the second chapel on the right.

❼ San Luigi dei Francesi

Piazza di San Luigi dei Francesi 5.
Map 4 F4 & 12 D2. **Tel** 06-688 271.
🚌 70, 81, 87, 116, 186, 492, 628.
Open 10am–12:30pm, 3–7pm daily.
Closed Thu pm. 🕎 📷 ✉ ♿

The French national church was founded in 1518, but it took until 1589 to complete, with contributions by Giacomo della Porta and Domenico Fontana. The church serves as a last resting place for many illustrious French people, including Chateaubriand's lover Pauline de Beaumont.

Three Caravaggios hang in the fifth chapel on the left, all dedicated to St Matthew. Painted between 1597 and 1602, these were Caravaggio's first great religious works: the *Calling of St Matthew*, the *Martyrdom of St Matthew* and *St Matthew and the Angel*. The first version of this last painting was rejected because of its vivid realism; never before had a saint been shown as a tired old man with dirty feet. All three works display very disquieting realism and a highly dramatic use of light.

St Matthew and the Angel by Caravaggio, San Luigi dei Francesi

Shield linking symbols of France and Rome on façade of San Luigi

❽ Palazzo Madama

Corso del Rinascimento. **Map** 4 F4 & 12 D3. **Tel** 06-67061. 🚌 70, 81, 87, 116, 186, 492, 628. **Open** 10am–6pm generally first Sat of month (exc Aug). Tickets available from 8:30am on day of visit. 🖥 **senato.it**

This 16th-century palazzo was built for the Medici family. It was the residence of Medici cousins Giovanni and Giuliano, both of whom became popes: Giovanni as Leo X and Giuliano as Clement VII. Caterina de' Medici, Clement VII's niece, also lived here before she was married to Henri, son of King François I of France, in 1533.

The palazzo takes its name from Madama Margherita of Austria, illegitimate daughter of Emperor Charles V, who married Alessandro de' Medici and, after his death, Ottavio Farnese. Thus part of the art collection of the Florentine Medici family was inherited by the Roman Farnese family.

The spectacular façade was built in the 17th century by Paolo Maruccelli. He gave it an ornate cornice and whimsical decorative details on the roof.

Cornice of Palazzo Madama

Since 1871 the palazzo has been the seat of the upper house of the Italian parliament.

❾ Sant'Ivo alla Sapienza

Corso del Rinascimento 40.
Map 4 F4 & 12 D3. **Tel** 06-0608. 🚌 40, 46, 64, 70, 81, 87, 116, 186, 492, 628.
Open 9am–noon Sun. 🕎

The church's lantern is crowned with a cross on top of a dramatic twisted spiral – a highly distinctive landmark from Rome's roof terraces. No other Baroque church is quite like this one, made by Borromini. Based on a ground design of astonishing geometrical complexity, the walls are a breathtaking combination of concave and convex surfaces. The church stands in the small courtyard of the Palazzo della Sapienza, seat of the old University of Rome from the 15th century until 1935.

Dome of Sant'Andrea della Valle

❿ Sant'Andrea della Valle

Piazza Sant'Andrea della Valle. **Map** 4 E4 & 12 D4. **Tel** 06-686 1339. 🚌 H, 40, 46, 62, 64, 70, 81, 87, 116, 186, 492, 628. 🚋 8. **Open** 7:30am–12:30pm, 4:30–7:30pm daily. 🕆

The church is the scene of the first act of Puccini's opera *Tosca*, though opera fans will not find the Attavanti chapel a poetic invention. The real church has much to recommend it – the impressive façade shows the flamboyant Baroque style at its best. Inside, a golden light filters through high windows, showing off the gilded interior. Here lie the two popes of the Sienese Piccolomini family: on the left of the central nave is the tomb of Pius II, the first Humanist pope (reigned 1458–64); Pope Pius III lies opposite – he reigned for less than a month in 1503.

The church is famous for its beautiful dome, the largest in Rome after St Peter's. It was built by Carlo Maderno in 1622–5 and was painted with splendid frescoes by Domenichino and Giovanni Lanfranco. The latter's extravagant style, to be seen in the dome fresco *Glory of Paradise*, won him most of the commission, and the jealous Domenichino is said to have tried to kill his colleague. He failed, but Domenichino's jealousy was unnecessary, as shown by his two beautiful paintings of scenes from the life of St Andrew around

the apse and altar. In the Strozzi Chapel, built in the style of Michelangelo, the altar has copies of the *Leah* and *Rachel* by Michelangelo in San Pietro in Vincoli (*see p172*).

Roman column, Palazzo Massimo

⓫ Palazzo Massimo alle Colonne

Corso Vittorio Emanuele II 141. **Map** 4 F4 & 11 C3. 🚌 40, 46, 62, 64, 70, 81, 87, 116, 186, 492, 628. Chapel: **Open** 7am–1pm 16 Mar.

During the last two years of his life, Baldassarre Peruzzi built this palazzo for the Massimo family, whose home had been destroyed in the 1527 Sack of Rome. Peruzzi displayed great ingenuity in dealing with an awkwardly shaped site. The previous building had stood on the ruined Theatre of Domitian, which created a curve in the great processional Via Papalis. Peruzzi's convex colonnaded façade follows the line of the street. His originality is also evident in the small square upper windows, the courtyard and the stuccoed vestibule. The Piazza de' Massimi entrance has a Renaissance-style, frescoed façade. A single column from the theatre has been set up in the piazza.

The Massimo family traced its origins to Quintus Fabius Maximus, conqueror of Hannibal in the

3rd century BC, and their coat of arms is borne by an infant Hercules. Over the years the family produced many great Humanists, and in the 19th century, it was a Massimo who negotiated peace with Napoleon. On 16 March each year the family chapel opens to the public to commemorate young Paolo Massimo's resurrection from the dead by San Filippo Neri in 1538.

⓬ Palazzo Braschi

Piazza San Pantaleo 10. **Map** 4 E4 & 11 C3. **Tel** 06-6710 8303. 🚌 40, 46, 62, 64, 70, 81, 87, 116, 186, 492, 628. **Open** 10am–7pm Tue–Sun (ticket office closes at 6pm). ♿ 🎫 📷 📱 🛍️

On one side of Piazza San Pantaleo is the last Roman palazzo to be built for the family of a pope. Palazzo Braschi was built in the late 18th century for Pope Pius VI Braschi's nephews by the architect Cosimo Morelli. He gave the building its imposing façade which looks out on to the piazza.

The palazzo now houses the municipal Museo di Roma. It holds collections of pictures, drawings and everyday objects illustrating life in Rome from medieval times to the 19th century.

Angel with raised wing by Ercole Ferrata, flanking the façade of Sant'Andrea della Valle

Pasquino, the most famous of Rome's satirical "talking statues"

⑬ Pasquino

Piazza di Pasquino. **Map** 4 E4 & 11 C3.
🚌 40, 46, 62, 64, 70, 81, 87, 116, 492, 628.

This rough chunk of marble is all that remains of a Hellenistic group, probably representing the incident in Homer's *Iliad* in which Menelaus shields the body of the slain Patroclus. For years it lay as a stepping stone in a muddy medieval street until it was erected on this corner in 1501, near the shop of an outspoken cobbler named Pasquino. Freedom of speech was not encouraged in papal Rome, so the cobbler wrote out his satirical comments on current events and attached them to the statue.

Other Romans followed suit, hanging their maxims and verses on the statue by night to escape punishment. Despite the wrath of the authorities,

the sayings of the "talking statue" (renamed Pasquino) were part of popular culture up until the 19th century. Other statues started to "talk" in the same vein; Pasquino used to conduct dialogues with the statue Marforio in Via del Campidoglio (now in the courtyard of Palazzo Nuovo, *see pp70–71*) and with the Babuino in Via del Babuino (*see p137*). Pasquino still "speaks" on occasion.

⑭ Via del Governo Vecchio

Map 4 E4 & 11 B3. 🚌 40, 46, 62, 64.

The street takes its name from Palazzo del Governo Vecchio, the seat of papal government in the 17th and 18th centuries. Once part of the Via Papalis, which led from the Lateran to St Peter's, the street is lined with 15th- and 16th-century houses and small workshops. Particularly interesting are those at No. 104 and No. 106. The small palazzo at No. 123 was once thought to have been the home of the architect Bramante.

Opposite is Palazzo del Governo Vecchio. It is also known as Palazzo Nardini, from the name of its founder, which is inscribed on the first-floor windows along with the date 1477.

Via del Governo Vecchio

Façade of the Chiesa Nuova

⑮ Chiesa Nuova

Piazza della Chiesa Nuova. **Map** 4 E4 & 11 B3. **Tel** 06-687 5289. 🚌 40, 46, 62, 64. **Open** 7:30am–noon, 4:30–7pm daily. 🛕

San Filippo Neri (St Philip Neri) is the most appealing of the Counter-Reformation saints. A highly unconventional reformer, he required his noble Roman followers to humble themselves in public. He made aristocratic young men parade through the streets of Rome in rags or even with a fox's tail tied behind them, and set noblemen to work as labourers building his church. With the help of Pope Gregory XIII, his church was built in place of an old medieval church, Santa Maria in Vallicella, and it has been known ever since as the Chiesa Nuova (new church).

Begun in 1575 by Matteo da Città di Castello and continued by Martino Longhi the Elder, it was consecrated in 1599 (although the façade, by Fausto Rughesi, was only finished in 1606). Against San Filippo's wishes, the interior was decorated after his death; Pietro da Cortona frescoed the nave, dome and apse, taking nearly 20 years. There are also three paintings by Rubens: *Madonna and Angels* above the altar, *Saints Domitilla, Nereus and Achilleus* on the right of the altar, and *Saints Gregory, Maurus and Papias* on the left. San Filippo is buried in his own chapel, to the left of the altar.

Borromini's façade of the Oratorio

🕚 Oratorio dei Filippini

Piazza della Chiesa Nuova. **Map** 4 E4 & 11 B3. **Tel** 06-6710 8100. 🚌 46, 62, 64. **Closed** to the public.

With the adjoining church and convent, the oratory formed the centre of Filippo Neri's religious order, which was founded in 1575. Its members are commonly known as Filippini. The musical term "oratorio" (a religious text sung by solo voices and chorus) derives from the services that were held here.

Filippo Neri came to Rome aged 18 to work as a tutor. The city was undergoing a period of religious strife and an economic slump after the Sack of Rome in 1527. There was also an outbreak of the plague. It was left to newcomers like Neri and Ignazio di Loyola to revive the spiritual life of the city.

Neri formed a brotherhood of laymen who worshipped together and helped pilgrims and the sick (see Santissima Trinità dei Pellegrini p149). He founded the Oratory as a centre for religious discourse. Its conspicuous curving brick façade was built by Borromini in 1637–43.

🕛 Torre dell'Orologio

Piazza dell'Orologio. **Map** 4 E4 & 11 B3. 🚌 40, 46, 62, 64.

Borromini built this clock tower to decorate one corner of the Convent of the Oratorians of San Filippo Neri in 1647–9. It is typical of Borromini in that the front and rear are concave and the sides convex. The mosaic of the Madonna beneath the clock is by Pietro da Cortona, while on the corner of the building is a small tabernacle to the Madonna flanked by angels in the style of Bernini.

Pietro da Cortona (1596–1669)

🕓 Palazzo del Banco di Santo Spirito

Via del Banco di Santo Spirito. **Map** 4 D4 & 11 A2. 🚌 40, 46, 62, 64. **Open** normal banking hours.

Formerly the mint of papal Rome, this palazzo is often referred to as the Antica Zecca (old mint). The upper storeys of the façade, built by Antonio da Sangallo the Younger in the 1520s, are in the shape of a Roman triumphal arch. Above it stand two Baroque statues symbolizing Charity and Thrift, and in the centre of the arch above the main entrance an inscription records the founding of the Banco di Santo Spirito by Pope Paul V Borghese in 1605.

Pope Paul was a very shrewd financier and he encouraged Romans to deposit their money at the bank by offering the vast estates of the Hospital of Santo Spirito (see p246) as security. The system catered only for the rudimentary banking requirements of the population, but business was brisk as people deposited money here safe in the knowledge that they could get it out simply by presenting a chit. The hospital coffers also gained from the system. The Banco di Santo Spirito still exists, but is now part of the Banca di Roma.

Façade of the Banco di Santo Spirito, built to resemble a Roman arch

Cloister, San Salvatore in Lauro

⑲ Via dei Coronari

Map 4 D3 & 11 B2. 🚌 40, 46, 62, 64, 70, 81, 87, 116, 186, 280, 492.

Large numbers of medieval pilgrims making their way to St Peter's walked along this street to cross over the Tiber at Ponte Sant'Angelo. Of the businesses that sprang up to try to part the pilgrims from their money, the most enduring was the selling of rosaries, and the street is still named after the rosary sellers (coronari). The street followed the course of the ancient Roman Via Recta (straight street), which originally ran from today's Piazza Colonna to the Tiber.

Making one's way through the vast throng of people in Via dei Coronari could be extremely hazardous. In the Holy Year of 1450, some 200 pilgrims died, crushed by the crowds or drowned in the Tiber. Following the tragedy, Pope Nicholas V demolished the Roman triumphal arch that stood at the entrance to Ponte Sant'Angelo. In the late 15th century, Pope Sixtus IV encouraged the building of private houses and palaces along the street.

Although the rosary sellers have been replaced by antiques dealers, the street still has many original buildings from the 15th and 16th centuries. One of the earliest, at Nos. 156–7, is known as the House of Fiammetta, the mistress of Cesare Borgia.

⑳ San Salvatore in Lauro

Piazza San Salvatore in Lauro 15. **Map** 4 E3 & 11 B2. **Tel** 06-687 5187. 🚌 70, 81, 87, 116, 186, 280, 492. **Open** 9am–noon & 3–7pm daily. 🕇

Named "in Lauro" after the laurel grove that grew here in ancient times, this church was built at the end of the 16th century by Ottaviano Mascherino. The bell tower and sacristy were 18th-century additions by Nicola Salvi, famous for the Trevi Fountain (see p161).

The church contains the first great altarpiece by the 17th-century artist Pietro da Cortona, *The Birth of Jesus*, in the first chapel to the right.

The adjacent convent of San Giorgio, to the left, has

Façade of San Salvatore in Lauro

a pretty Renaissance cloister, a frescoed refectory and the monument to Pope Eugenius IV (reigned 1431–47), moved here when the old St Peter's was pulled down. An extravagant Venetian, Eugenius would willingly spend thousands of ducats on his gold tiara, but requested a "simple, lowly burial place" near his predecessor Pope Eugenius III. His portrait, painted by Salviati, hangs in the refectory.

In 1669 San Salvatore in Lauro became the seat of a pious association, the Confraternity of the Piceni, who were inhabitants of the Marche region. Fanatically loyal to the pope, the Piceni were traditionally employed as papal soldiers and tax collectors.

㉑ Museo Napoleonico

Piazza di Ponte Umberto 1. **Map** 4 E3 & 11 C1. **Tel** 06-0608. 🚌 70, 81, 87, 116, 186, 280, 492. **Open** 10am–6pm Tue–Sun. **Closed** 1 Jan, 1 May, 25 Dec. 📷 ✉ 🚫 ♿ 🌐 **museonapoleonico.it**

This museum contains memorabilia and portraits of Napoleon Bonaparte and his family. Personal relics of Napoleon himself include an Indian shawl he wore during his exile on St Helena.

After his death in 1821, the pope allowed many of the Bonaparte family to settle in Rome, including his mother Letizia, who lived in Palazzo Misciattelli on Via del Corso, and his sister Pauline who married the Roman Prince Camillo Borghese. The museum has a cast of her right breast, made by Canova in 1805 as a study for his statue of her as a reclining Venus, now in the Museo Borghese (see p263). Portraits and personal effects of other members of the family are on display, including uniforms, court dresses, and a penny-farthing bicycle that belonged to Prince Eugène, the son of Emperor Napoleon III.

The last male of the Roman branch of the family was Napoleon Charles, portrayed in a late 19th-century painting by Guglielmo de Sanctis. The collection was assembled in 1927 by the Counts Primoli, the sons of Charles's sister, Carlotta Bonaparte.

The palace next door, in Via Zanardelli, houses the Racolta Praz, an impressive selection of over one thousand *objets d'art*, paintings and pieces of furniture. Dating from the 17th and 18th centuries, they were collected by the art historian and literary critic Mario Praz.

Side relief of the Ludovisi Throne, Palazzo Altemps

Entrance to Museo Napoleonico

㉒ Hostaria dell'Orso

Via dei Soldati 25. **Map** 4 E3 & 11 C2. **Tel** 06-6830 1192. 70, 81, 87, 116, 186, 204, 280, 492, 628. **Open** 8pm–2am Mon–Sat.

This ancient inn *(see p314)* has a 15th-century portico and loggia built with columns from Roman ruins. Visitors included the 16th-century French writers Rabelais and Montaigne.

㉓ Palazzo Altemps

Via di Sant'Apollinare 46. **Map** 4 E3 & 11 C2. **Tel** 06-3996 7700. 70, 81, 87, 116, 280, 492, 628. **Open** 9am–7:45pm Tue–Sun (last adm: 1 hour before closing). **Closed** 1 Jan, 25 Dec.

An extraordinary collection of Classical sculpture is housed in this branch of the Museo Nazionale Romano. Restored as a museum during the 1990s, the palazzo was originally built for Girolamo Riario, nephew of Pope Sixtus IV in 1480. The Riario coat of arms can still be seen in the janitor's room. In the popular uprising that followed the pope's death in 1484, the building was sacked and Girolamo fled the city.

In 1568 the palazzo was bought by Cardinal Marco Sittico Altemps. His family was of German origin – the name is an Italianization of Hohenems – and influential in the church. The palazzo was renovated by Martino Longhi the Elder in the 1570s. He added the great belvedere, crowned with obelisks and a marble unicorn.

The Altemps family were ostentatious collectors; the courtyard and its staircase are lined with ancient sculptures. These form part of the museum's collection, together with the Ludovisi collection of ancient sculptures, which was previously housed in the Museo Nazionale Romano in the Baths of Diocletian *(see p165)*. Located on the ground floor is the Greek statue of Athena Parthenos and the Dionysius group, a Roman copy of the Greek original. On the first floor, at the far end of the courtyard, visitors can admire the Painted Loggia, dating from 1595. The Ludovisi throne, a Greek original carved in the 5th century BC, is on the same floor. It is decorated with reliefs, one of which shows a young woman rising from the sea, who is thought to represent Aphrodite. In the room which is known as the Salone del Camino is the powerful statue *Galatian's Suicide*, a marble copy of a group originally made in bronze. Nearby is the Ludovisi Sarcophagus, dating from the 3rd century AD.

Galatian's Suicide in the Palazzo Altemps

PIAZZA DI SPAGNA

By the 16th century, the increase in numbers of visiting pilgrims and ecclesiastics was making life in Rome's already congested medieval centre unbearable. A new triangle of roads was built, still in place today, to help channel pilgrims as quickly as possible from the city's north gate, the Porta del Popolo, to the Vatican. By the 18th century, hotels had sprung up all over the district. Today this attractive area offers much more: the superb works of Renaissance and Baroque art in Santa Maria del Popolo and Sant'Andrea delle Fratte, the magnificent reliefs of the restored Ara Pacis, art exhibitions in the Villa Medici, fine views of the city from the Spanish Steps and the Pincio Gardens, and Rome's most famous shopping streets, centred on Via Condotti.

Sights at a Glance

Churches
1. Sant'Andrea delle Fratte
10. Trinità dei Monti
12. All Saints
14. Santa Maria dei Miracoli and Santa Maria in Montesanto
17. *Santa Maria del Popolo pp140–41*
21. San Rocco
22. Santi Ambrogio e Carlo al Corso

Museums and Galleries
7. Keats-Shelley Memorial House
13. Casa di Goethe

Historic Buildings
2. Palazzo di Propaganda Fide
11. Villa Medici

Arches, Gates and Columns
3. Colonna dell'Immacolata
18. Porta del Popolo

Historic Streets and Piazzas
4. Via Condotti
6. Piazza di Spagna
9. Spanish Steps
16. Piazza del Popolo

Monuments and Tombs
19. Ara Pacis
20. Mausoleum of Augustus

Parks and Gardens
15. Pincio Gardens

Historic Cafés and Restaurants
5. Antico Caffè Greco
8. Babington's Tea Rooms

Restaurants
see pp315–17
1. Babette
2. Canova-Tadolini Museum Atelier
3. 'Gusto
4. Gusto Rotisserie
5. Hamasei
6. Imàgo
7. Le Jardin de Russie
8. Osteria Margutta
9. Il Palazzetto Wine Bar
10. Rhome

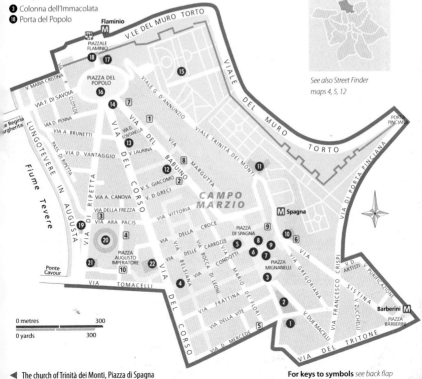

See also Street Finder maps 4, 5, 12

◀ The church of Trinità dei Monti, Piazza di Spagna

For keys to symbols *see back flap*

Street-by-Street: Piazza di Spagna

The network of narrow streets between Piazza di Spagna and Via del Corso is one of the liveliest areas in Rome, drawing throngs of tourists and Romans to its discreet and elegant shops. In the 18th century the area was full of hotels for frivolous English aristocrats doing the Grand Tour, but there were also artists, writers and composers, who took the city's history and culture more seriously.

Spagna station

❽ **Babington's Tea Rooms**
English tourists are catered for in the style of the 1890s.

❻ ★ **Piazza di Spagna**
For almost three centuries the square with its curious Barcaccia fountain in the centre has been the chief meeting place for visitors to Rome.

PIAZZA DI SPAGNA

VIA VITTORIA

VIA DELLA CROCE

VIA BOCCA

VIA DELLA CARROZZE

DI LEONE

❺ **Antico Caffè Greco**
Busts and portraits recall the café's former artistic patrons.

VIA DEL CORSO

Via delle Carrozze
took its name from the carriages of wealthy tourists that used to queue up here for repairs.

VIA CONDOTTI

VIA BORGONONA

VIA FRAT

❹ **Via Condotti**
This shadowy, narrow street has the smartest shops in one of the smartest shopping areas in the world.

| 0 metres | | 75 |
| 0 yards | | 75 |

Bulgari sells very expensive jewellery behind an austere shopfront in Via Condotti.

Key

— Suggested route

Ⓜ Metro station

9 ★ Spanish Steps
Even when obscured by crowds, the steps are one of the glories of late Baroque Rome.

Locator Map
See Central Rome Map pp16–17

3 Colonna dell'Immacolata
A Roman column supports a statue of the Virgin Mary.

10 Trinità dei Monti
This 16th-century church has a spectacular setting and some of the finest views in Rome.

1 Sant'Andrea delle Fratte
Pasquale Marini painted *The Redemption* to decorate the interior of Borromini's high dome in 1691.

VIA DI PROPAGANDA

ELLA VITE

2 Palazzo di Propaganda Fide
This façade (1665) was one of the last works of the great Francesco Borromini.

7 ★ Keats-Shelley Memorial House
The library is part of the small museum established in the house where the English poet Keats died in 1821.

❶ Sant'Andrea delle Fratte

Via Sant'Andrea delle Fratte 1.
Map 5 A3 & 12 F1. **Tel** 06-679
3191. 116, 117. Ⓜ Spagna.
Open 6:30am–12:30pm, 4–7pm
daily (to 8pm Sat & Sun). ✝

When Sant'Andrea delle Fratte
was built in the 12th century,
this was the northernmost edge
of Rome. Though the church is
now firmly embedded in the city,
its name (*fratte* means thickets)
recalls its original setting.

The church was completely
rebuilt in the 17th century, partly
by Borromini. His bell tower and
dome, best viewed from the
higher ground further up Via
Capo le Case, are remarkable
for the complex arrangement
of concave and convex surfaces.
The bell tower is particularly fanciful, with angel caryatids, flaming torches, and exaggerated

scrolls like semi-folded hearts
supporting a spiky crown.

In 1842, the Virgin Mary
appeared in the church to a
Jewish banker, who promptly
converted to Christianity and
became a missionary. Inside,
the chapel of the Miraculous
Madonna is the first thing you
notice. The church is better
known, however, for the angels
that Borromini's rival, Bernini,
carved for the Ponte Sant'Angelo.
Pope Clement IX declared they
were too lovely to be exposed
to the weather, so they remained
with Bernini's family until 1729,
when they were moved to
the church.

❷ Palazzo di Propaganda Fide

Via di Propaganda 1. **Map** 5 A2 &
12 F1. **Tel** 06-6988 0266. 116,
117. Ⓜ Spagna. Museum:
Closed for restoration.

The powerful Jesuit Congregation
for the Propagation
of the Faith was
founded in 1622.
Although Bernini
had originally
been commis-
sioned to
create their
headquarters,
Innocent X, who
became pope in
1644, preferred the
style of Borromini
who was asked
to continue. His
extraordinary west
façade, completed
in 1662, is striped
with broad
pilasters,
between which the first-
floor windows bend in, and
the central bay bulges.
A rigid band divides its
floors, and the cornice
above the convex
central bay swerves
inwards. The more
you look at it, the
more restless it seems; a
sign perhaps of the increasing
unhappiness of the architect
who committed suicide in
1667. The building houses the
Vatican's missionary museum.

Entrance to the Palazzo di Propaganda Fide

❸ Colonna dell'Immacolata

Piazza Mignanelli. **Map** 5 A2.
116, 117. Ⓜ Spagna.

Inaugurated in 1857, the
column commemorates Pope
Pius IX's proclamation of the
doctrine of the Immaculate
Conception, holding that the
Virgin Mary was the only human
being ever to have been born
"without the stain of original
sin". The column itself dates
from ancient, pagan Rome but
is crowned with a statue of the
Virgin Mary.

On 8 December the pope,
assisted by the fire brigade,
places a wreath around the
head of the statue *(see p63)*.

Portrait of Pope Pius IX (reigned 1846–78)

Angel by Bernini,
Sant'Andrea delle Fratte

❹ Via Condotti

Map 5 A2. 🚌 81, 116, 117, 119, 492 and many routes along via del Corso or stopping at Piazza S. Silvestro. Ⓜ Spagna. *See Shops and Markets pp326–33.*

Named after the conduits that carried water to the Baths of Agrippa near the Pantheon, Via Condotti is now home to the most traditional of Rome's designer clothes shops. Stores selling shoes and other leather goods are also well represented. The street is extremely popular for early evening strolls, when elegant Italians mingle with casually dressed tourists.

Laura Biagiotti and the Fendi sisters have shops on the parallel Via Borgognona, while Valentino and Giorgio Armani both have shops on Via Condotti itself. Valentino has a second branch on Via Bocca di Leone, which crosses Via Condotti just below Piazza di Spagna, and Versace also has a shop here. Giorgio Armani has a second store on nearby Via del Babuino, among the discreet art galleries, exclusive antique shops and furnishing stores.

Crowds strolling along the chic Via Condotti, lined with designer clothes shops

❺ Antico Caffè Greco

Via Condotti 86. **Map** 5 A2. **Tel** 06-679 1700. 🚌 81, 116, 117, 119, 492. Ⓜ Spagna. **Open** 9am–9pm daily. **Closed** 1 Jan, 15 Aug. ♿

This café was opened by a Greek (hence *greco*) in 1760, and throughout the 18th century it was a favourite

Antico Caffè Greco, over 250 years old

meeting place for foreign artists. Writers such as Keats, Byron and Goethe and composers like Liszt, Wagner and Bizet all breakfasted and drank here. So too did Casanova, and mad King Ludwig of Bavaria. Today, Italians stand in the crowded foyer to sip a quick espresso coffee, and foreigners sit in a cosy back room, whose walls are studded with portraits of the café's illustrious customers.

❻ Piazza di Spagna

Map 5 A2. 🚌 116, 117, 119. Ⓜ Spagna.

Shaped like a crooked bow tie and surrounded by tall, shuttered houses painted in muted shades of ochre, cream and russet, Piazza di Spagna (Spanish square) is crowded all day and (in summer) most of the night. It is the most famous square in Rome, and has long been the haunt of foreign visitors and expatriates.

In the 17th century Spain's ambassador to the Holy See had his headquarters on the square, and the area around it was deemed to be Spanish territory. Foreigners who unwittingly trespassed were liable to be dragooned into the Spanish army. In the 18th and 19th centuries Rome was almost as popular with visitors as it is

today, and the square stood at the heart of the city's main hotel district. Some of the travellers came in search of knowledge and artistic inspiration, but most were more interested in gambling, collecting ancient statues and conducting love affairs with Italian women.

Not surprisingly, the wealthy travellers attracted hordes of beggars, who were usually supplied with tear-jerking letters by scribes who worked in the square.

The Fontana della Barcaccia in the square is the least showy of Rome's Baroque fountains, and it is often completely

Pope Urban VIII's arms, with the Barberini bees

screened from view by people resting on its rim. It was designed either by the famous Gian Lorenzo Bernini or by his father Pietro. Because the pressure from the aqueduct that feeds the fountain is extremely low there are no spectacular cascades or spurts of water. Instead, Bernini constructed a leaking boat – *barcaccia* means useless, old boat – which lies half submerged in a shallow pool.

The bees and suns that decorate the Fontana della Barcaccia are taken from the family coat of arms of Pope Urban VIII Barberini, who commissioned the fountain.

Fontana della Barcaccia at the foot of the Spanish Steps

Bust of Shelley by Moses Ezekiel

❼ Keats-Shelley Memorial House

Piazza di Spagna 26. **Map** 5 A2.
Tel 06-678 4235. 🚌 116, 117, 119.
Ⓜ Spagna. **Open** 10am–1pm,
2–6pm Mon–Sat. **Closed** 8 Dec, 23
Dec–1 Jan. 🚫 📷 book in advance.
📷 🌐 keats-shelley-house.org

In November 1820 the English
poet John Keats came to stay
with his friend, the painter
Joseph Severn, in a dusty pink
house, the Casina Rossa, on the
corner of the Spanish Steps.
Suffering from consumption,
Keats had been sent to Rome
by his doctor, in the hope
that the mild, dry climate
would help the young man's
recovery. Depressed because
of scathing criticism of his
work and tormented by his
love for a young girl named
Fanny Brawne, Keats died the
following February, aged 25.

His death inspired fellow
poet Percy Bysshe Shelley to
write the poem *Mourn not for
Adonais*. In July 1822 Shelley
himself was drowned in a
boating accident in the Gulf
of La Spezia off the coast of
Liguria. Keats, Shelley and
Severn are all buried in Rome's
Protestant Cemetery *(see p207)*.

In 1906 the house was
bought by an Anglo-American
association and preserved as
a memorial and library in
honour of English Romantic
poets. The relics include a

lock of Keats's hair, some
fragments of Shelley's bones
in a tiny urn and a garish
carnival mask picked up by
Lord Byron as a souvenir of
a trip to Venice. You can visit
the room where Keats died,
though all the original furniture
was burnt after his death, on
papal orders.

❽ Babington's Tea Rooms

Piazza di Spagna 23. **Map** 5 A2.
Tel 06-678 6027. 🚌 116, 117, 119.
Ⓜ Spagna. **Open** 9am–9:30pm daily.
Closed 25 Dec. ♿

These august, old-fashioned
tea rooms were opened in
1896 by two Englishwomen,
Anna Maria and Isabel Cargill
Babington, to serve homesick
British tourists with scones,
jam and pots of Earl Grey tea.
The food remains homely –
shepherd's pie for a winter
lunch, muffins and cinnamon
toast for tea – although these
days the menu offers pancakes
with maple syrup for breakfast
as well as eggs Benedict and
the traditional bacon and egg.

Purveyors of English breakfasts to homesick
exiles since 1896

❾ Spanish Steps

Scalinata della Trinità dei Monti,
Piazza di Spagna. **Map** 5 A2.
🚌 116, 117, 119. Ⓜ Spagna.

In the 17th century the French
owners of Trinità dei Monti
decided to link the church with
Piazza di Spagna by building a
magnificent new flight of steps.
They also planned to place an
equestrian statue of King Louis
XIV at the top. Pope Alexander
VII Chigi was not too happy at
the prospect of erecting a

Barcaccia Fountain at the foot of the magnificent Spanish Steps

statue of a French monarch in the papal city, and the arguments continued until the 1720s when an Italian architect, Francesco de Sanctis, produced a design that satisfied both parties. The steps, completed in 1726, combine straight sections, curves and terraces to create one of the city's most dramatic and distinctive landmarks.

When the Victorian novelist Charles Dickens visited Rome, he reported that the Spanish Steps were the meeting place for artists' models, who would dress in colourful traditional costumes, hoping to catch the attention of a wealthy artist. The steps are now a popular place to sit, write postcards, take photos, flirt, busk or watch the passers-by, but eating here is not allowed.

Trinità dei Monti's bell towers

⑩ Trinità dei Monti

Piazza della Trinità dei Monti. **Map** 5 A2. **Tel** 06-679 4179. 🚌 116, 117, 119. Ⓜ Spagna. **Open** 6:30am–8pm Tue–Sun (to midnight Thu). 🛐

The views of Rome from the platform in front of the twin bell-towered façade of Trinità dei Monti are so beautiful that the church itself is often ignored. It is, however, unusual for Rome, because it was founded by the French in 1495, and although it was later badly damaged, there are still traces of attractive late Gothic latticework in the vaults of the transept. The interconnecting side chapels are decorated with Mannerist paintings, including two fine works by Daniele da Volterra.

19th-century engraving of the inner façade of the Villa Medici

A pupil of Michelangelo, Volterra had to paint clothes on the nudes in the *Last Judgment* in the Sistine Chapel, in response to the objections of Pope Pius IV.

Michelangelo's influence is obvious in the powerfully muscled bodies shown in the *Deposition* (second chapel on the left). The circles of gesturing figures and dancing angels surrounding the Virgin Mary in the *Assumption* (third chapel on the right) have more in common with the graceful style of Raphael.

⑪ Villa Medici

Accademia di Francia a Roma, Viale Trinità dei Monti 1. **Map** 5 A2. **Tel** 06-67611. 🚌 117, 119. Ⓜ Spagna. **Open** for exhibitions and concerts. Villa and gardens: **Open** Tue–Sun (four to six guided visits daily, times vary – call ahead; in English at noon). 🎟 📷 🖥 🌐 villamedici.it

Superbly positioned on the Pincio hill above Piazza di Spagna, this 16th-century villa has kept the name it assumed when Cardinal Ferdinando de' Medici bought it in 1576. From the terrace you can look across the city to Castel Sant'Angelo, from where Queen Christina of Sweden is said to have fired the large cannon ball which now sits in the basin of the fountain.

The villa is home to the French Academy. This was founded by Louis XIV in 1666 to give a few select painters the

chance to study in Rome. Nicolas Poussin was one of the first advisers to the Academy, Ingres was a director and former students include Jean-Honoré Fragonard and François Boucher.

After 1803 when the French Academy moved to the Villa Medici, musicians were also admitted; both Berlioz and Debussy came to Rome as students of the Academy.

⑫ All Saints

Via del Babuino 153B. **Map** 4 F2. **Tel** 06-3600 1881. 🚌 117, 119. **Open** 8:30am–7pm daily. 🛐

In 1816 the pope gave English residents and visitors the right to hold Anglican services in Rome, but it was not until the early 1880s that they acquired a site to build their own church. The architect was G E Street, best known in Britain for his Neo-Gothic churches and the London Law Courts. All Saints is also built in Victorian Neo-Gothic, and the interior, though splendidly decorated with different coloured Italian marbles, has a very English air. Street also designed St-Paul's-within-the-Walls in Via Nazionale, whose interior is a jewel of British Pre-Raphaelite art.

The street on which All Saints stands got its name from the Fontana del Sileno, known as Babuino (baboon) due to the sad condition in which it was found.

Fontana del Sileno, on Via del Babuino since 1957

⓭ Casa di Goethe

Via del Corso 18. **Map** 4 F1.
Tel 06-3265 0412. ▣ 117, 119, 490,
495, 628, 926. ▣ 2. Ⓜ Flaminio.
Open 10am–6pm Tue–Sun. ▨ ▧
▨ ▨ ▥ casadigoethe.it

The German poet, dramatist
and novelist Johann Wolfgang
von Goethe (1749–1832) lived
in this house from 1786 until
1788 and worked on a journal
that eventually formed part of
his travel book *The Italian
Journey*. Rome's noisy street life
irritated him, especially during
Carnival time. He was a little
perturbed by the number of
murders in his neighbourhood,
but Rome energized him and
his book became one of the
most influential ever written
about Italy.

⓮ Santa Maria dei Miracoli and Santa Maria in Montesanto

Piazza del Popolo. **Map** 4 F1.
▣ 117, 119, 490, 495, 628, 926.
▣ 2. Ⓜ Flaminio. Santa Maria dei
Miracoli: **Tel** 06-361 0250. **Open**
7am–12:30pm, 4–7:30pm daily.
▨ ▧ Santa Maria in Montesanto:
Tel 06-361 0594. **Open** 5:30–8pm
Mon–Fri, 11am–1:30pm Sun.

The two churches at the south
end of Piazza del Popolo were
designed by the architect
Carlo Rainaldi (1611–91), the
plans were revised by Bernini
and it was Carlo Fontana
who eventually completed the
project. To provide a focal point
for the piazza, the churches had
to appear symmetrical, but the
site on the left

Portrait of Goethe in the Roman countryside by Tischbein (1751–1821)

was narrower. So, Rainaldi gave
Santa Maria dei Miracoli (on the
right) a circular dome and Santa
Maria in Montesanto an oval
one to squeeze it into the
narrower site, while keeping the
sides of the supporting drums
that face the piazza identical.

⓯ Pincio Gardens

Il Pincio. **Map** 4 F1. ▣ 117, 119, 490,
495, 628, 926. ▣ 2. Ⓜ Flaminio.

The Pincio Gardens lie above
Piazza del Popolo on a hillside
that has been so skilfully
terraced and richly planted with
trees that, from below, the zig-
zagging road climbing to the
gardens is virtually invisible.
In ancient Roman times, there
were magnificent gardens on
the Pincio hill, but the present
gardens were designed in
the early 19th century by
Giuseppe Valadier (who also
redesigned the Piazza del
Popolo). The broad avenues,
lined with umbrella pines,
palm trees and
evergreen oaks

The Pincio Gardens water clock

soon became a fashionable
place to stroll, and even in
the 20th century such diverse
characters as Gandhi and
Mussolini, Richard Strauss
and King Farouk of Egypt
patronized the Casina Valadier,
an exclusive café and restaurant
in the grounds.

From the Pincio's main
square, Piazzale Napoleone I,
the panoramic views of Rome
stretch from the Monte Mario
to the Janiculum. For full effect,
approach the gardens from the
grounds of Villa Borghese (see
pp260–61) above the Pincio,
or along Viale della Trinità
dei Monti. The panorama is
particularly beautiful at sunset,

The twin churches of Santa Maria in Montesanto (left) and Santa Maria dei Miracoli in a
19th-century view of Piazza del Popolo

the traditional time for tourists to take a stroll in the gardens.

One of the most striking features of the park itself is an Egyptian-style obelisk which Emperor Hadrian erected on the tomb of his favourite, the beautiful male slave Antinous. After the slave's premature death (according to some accounts he died saving the emperor's life), Hadrian deified him.

The 19th-century water clock on Via dell'Orologio was designed by a Dominican monk. It was displayed at the Paris Exhibition of 1889.

Traditional carnival band in Piazza del Popolo

The Casina Valadier restaurant in the Pincio Gardens

⓰ Piazza del Popolo

Map 4 F1. 🚌 117, 119, 490, 495, 926. 🚃 2. Ⓜ Flaminio.

A vast cobbled oval standing at the apex of the triangle of roads known as the Trident, Piazza del Popolo forms a grand symmetrical antechamber to the heart of Rome. Twin Neo-Classical façades stand on either side of the Porta del Popolo; an Egyptian obelisk rises in the centre; and the matching domes and porticoes of Santa Maria dei Miracoli and Santa Maria in Montesanto flank the beginning of Via del Corso.

Although it is now one of the most unified squares in Rome, Piazza del Popolo evolved gradually over the centuries. In 1589 the great town-planning pope, Sixtus V, had the obelisk erected in the

centre by Domenico Fontana. Over 3,000 years old, the obelisk was originally brought to Rome by Augustus to adorn the Circus Maximus after the conquest of Egypt. Almost a century later Pope Alexander VII commissioned Carlo Rainaldi to build the twin Santa Marias.

In the 19th century the piazza was turned into a grandiose oval by Giuseppe Valadier, the designer of the Pincio Gardens. He also encased Santa Maria del Popolo in a Neo-Classical shell to make its south façade fit in better with the overall appearance of the piazza.

In contrast to the piazza's air of ordered rationalism, many of the events staged here were barbaric. In the 18th and 19th centuries, public executions were held in Piazza del Popolo, often as part of the celebration of Carnival. Condemned men were sometimes hammered to death by repeated blows to the temples. The last time a criminal was executed in this way was in 1826, even though the guillotine had by then been adopted as a more scientific means of execution.

The riderless horse races from the piazza down Via del Corso were scarcely more humane: the performance of the runners was enhanced by feeding the horses stimulants, wrapping them in nail-studded ropes, and letting off fireworks at their heels.

⓱ Santa Maria del Popolo

See pp140–41.

⓲ Porta del Popolo

Between Piazzale Flaminio and Piazza del Popolo. **Map** 4 F1. 🚌 117, 119, 490, 495, 926. 🚃 2. Ⓜ Flaminio.

The Via Flaminia, built in 220 BC to connect Rome with Italy's Adriatic coast, enters the city at Porta del Popolo, a grand 16th-century gate built on the orders of Pope Pius IV de' Medici. The architect, Nanni di Baccio Bigio, modelled it on a Roman triumphal arch. The outer face has statues of St Peter and St Paul on either side and a huge Medici coat of arms above.

A century later, Pope Alexander VII commissioned Bernini to decorate the inner face to celebrate the arrival in Rome of Queen Christina of Sweden. Lesser visitors were often delayed while customs officers rifled their luggage. The only way to speed things up was with a bribe.

Porta del Popolo's central arch

⑰ Santa Maria del Popolo

One of Rome's greatest stores of artistic treasures, this early Renaissance church was commissioned by Pope Sixtus IV della Rovere in 1472. Among the artists who worked on the building were Andrea Bregno and Pinturicchio. Later additions were made by Bramante and Bernini. Many illustrious families have chapels here, all decorated with appropriate splendour. The Della Rovere Chapel has delightful Pinturicchio frescoes, the Cerasi Chapel has two Caravaggio masterpieces, *The Conversion of St Paul* and *The Crucifixion of St Peter*, but the finest of all is the Chigi Chapel designed by Raphael for his patron, the banker Agostino Chigi. The most striking of the church's many Renaissance tombs are the two by Andrea Sansovino behind the main altar.

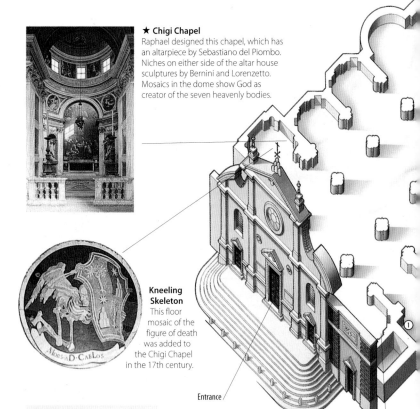

★ **Chigi Chapel**
Raphael designed this chapel, which has an altarpiece by Sebastiano del Piombo. Niches on either side of the altar house sculptures by Bernini and Lorenzetto. Mosaics in the dome show God as creator of the seven heavenly bodies.

Kneeling Skeleton
This floor mosaic of the figure of death was added to the Chigi Chapel in the 17th century.

Entrance

KEY

① **Cybo Chapel**

② **The tomb** of Giovanni della Rovere (1483) is by pupils of Andrea Bregno.

③ **The altarpiece** of *The Assumption* is by Annibale Carracci (1540–1609).

④ **The altar** houses the 13th-century painting known as the *Madonna del Popolo*.

⑤ **The tomb** of Ascanio Sforza, who died in 1505, is by Andrea Sansovino.

Della Rovere Chapel
Pinturicchio painted the frescoes in the lunettes and the Nativity above the altar in 1490.

★ Caravaggio Paintings in Cerasi Chapel

One of two Caravaggios in the Cerasi Chapel, *The Crucifixion of St Peter* uses dramatic foreshortening to highlight the sheer effort involved in turning the saint's crucifix upside down.

VISITORS' CHECKLIST

Practical Information
Piazza del Popolo 12.
Map 4 F1.
Tel 06-361 0836.
Open 7:30am–12:30pm, 4–7pm Mon–Thu; 7:30am–7pm Fri & Sat.

Transport
117, 119, 490, 495, 926.
2. M Flaminio.

Stained Glass
In 1509 French artist Guillaume de Marcillat was invited to provide Rome's first two stained-glass windows.

★ Delphic Sibyl

This is one of a series of frescoes by Pinturicchio, some Classical and others Biblical, painted in 1508–10 to decorate the ceiling of the apse.

Nero's Ghost

Nero lived on in the imagination of the people long after the fall of the Roman Empire. In the Middle Ages a legend arose that a walnut tree growing here on the spot where his ashes were buried was haunted by the emperor. Ravens roosting in the tree were thought to be demons tormenting him for his hideous crimes. When the first church was built here in 1099 by Pope Paschal II, the tree was cut down, supposedly putting an end to the supernatural events that had terrified local people.

1213–27 Church enlarged under Gregory IX

1485–9 Della Rovere Chapel painted by Pinturicchio

1513–16 Raphael designs and executes Chigi Chapel

Pinturicchio (c.1454–1513)

1050   **1200**   **1350**   **1500**

1099 Paschal II builds chapel over tombs of the Domitia family (which included Nero) in honour of the Madonna

Pope Paschal II (reigned 1099–1118)

1472–8 Sixtus IV builds church (one of the first Renaissance churches in Rome)

1473 Main altar built

1530–34 Chigi Chapel altarpiece built by Sebastiano del Piombo

⓳ Ara Pacis

Lungotevere in Augusta. **Map** 4 F2.
Tel 06-0608. 🚌 70, 81, 117, 119, 186,
628. **Open** 9:30am–7:30pm daily (last
adm: 6:30pm). **Closed** 1 Jan, 1 May, 25
Dec. 🔲 ♿ 📷 📺 **W** arapacis.it

Reconstructed at considerable
expense over many years, the
Ara Pacis (Altar of Peace) is one
of the most significant monuments of ancient Rome. It
celebrates the peace created
throughout the Mediterranean
area by Emperor Augustus after
his victorious campaigns in Gaul
and Spain. The monument was
commissioned by the Senate in
13 BC and completed four years
later. It was positioned so that
the shadow of the huge obelisk
sundial on Campus Martius
(see p117) would fall upon it
on Augustus's birthday. It is a

Frieze on south wall showing procession with the family of Augustus

square enclosure on a low
platform with the altar in
the centre. All surfaces are
decorated with magnificent
friezes and reliefs carved in
Carrara marble. The reliefs
on the north and south walls
depict a procession that took
place on 4 July 13 BC, in which
the members of the emperor's
family can be identified, ranked
by their position in the succes-
sion. At the time the heir
apparent was Marcus Agrippa,
husband of Augustus's daughter
Julia. All the portraits in the
relief are carved with extraordinary realism, even the

innocent toddler clinging
to his mother's skirts.

The tale of the rediscovery
of the Ara Pacis dates back to
the 16th century, when the first
panels were unearthed. One
section ended up in Paris,
another in Florence. Further
discoveries were made in
the late 19th century, when
archaeologists finally realized
just what they had found.
What we see today has all been
pieced together since 1938, in
part original, in part facsimile.
In 1999 the architect Richard
Meier designed a building to
house the monument.

Marcus Agrippa (on the right)

The altar was used once
a year for a sacrifice on
the anniversary of the
monument's
inauguration.

East wall

South wall

West wall

North wall

Augustus's young
grandson, Lucius

An acanthus frieze
runs around the
lower half of the
outside wall.

⓴ Mausoleum of Augustus

Piazza Augusto Imperatore. **Map** 4 F2.
Tel 06-0608. 81, 117, 492, 628, 926.
Open on special occasions only
(call for details).

Now just a weedy mound ringed with cypresses, this was once the most prestigious burial place in Rome. Augustus had the mausoleum built in 28 BC, the year he became sole ruler, as a tomb for himself and his descendants. The circular building was 87 m (285 ft) in diameter.

Inside were four concentric passageways linked by corridors where the urns containing the ashes of the Imperial family were placed. The first to be buried here was Augustus's favourite nephew, Marcellus, who had married Julia, the emperor's daughter. He died in 23 BC, possibly poisoned by Augustus's second wife Livia, who felt that her son, Tiberius, would make a more reliable emperor. When Augustus died in AD 14, his ashes were placed in the mausoleum, Tiberius duly became emperor, and dynastic poisonings continued to fill the family vault with urns.

This sinister monument was later used as a medieval fortress, a vineyard, a private garden, and even, in the 18th century, as an auditorium and theatre.

While the mausoleum is now only open for special occasions, the impressive structure can still be admired from the outside.

Augustus, the first Roman emperor

Madonna, San Rocco and Sant'Antonio with Victims of the Plague by Il Baciccia (1639–1709)

⓴ San Rocco

Largo San Rocco 1. **Map** 4 F2.
Tel 06-689 6416. 81, 117, 492, 628, 926. **Open** 7–9am, 4:30–8pm Mon–Sat, 8:30am–1pm, 4:30–8pm Sun. **Closed** 17–31 Aug.

This church, with a restrained Neo-Classical façade by Giuseppe Valadier, the designer of Piazza del Popolo, began life as the chapel of a 16th-century hospital with beds for 50 men – San Rocco was a healer of the plague-stricken. A maternity wing was added for the wives of Tiber bargees to save them from having to give birth in the insanitary conditions of a boat. The hospital came to be used by unmarried mothers, and one section was set aside for women who wished to be unknown. They were even permitted to wear a veil for the duration of their stay. Unwanted children were sent to an orphanage, and if any mothers or children died they were buried in anonymous graves. The hospital was abandoned in the early 20th century, and demolished in the 1930s during the excavation of the Mausoleum of Augustus.

The church sacristy contains an interesting Baroque altarpiece (c.1660) by Il Baciccia, the artist who decorated the ceiling of the Gesù (see pp110–11).

⓶ Santi Ambrogio e Carlo al Corso

Via del Corso 437. **Map** 4 F2.
Tel 06-682 8101. 81, 117, 492, 628, 926. **Open** 7am–7pm daily.

This church belonged to the Lombard community in Rome, and is dedicated to two canonized bishops of Milan, Lombardy's capital. In 1471, Pope Sixtus IV gave the Lombards a church which they dedicated to Sant'Ambrogio, who died in 397. Then in 1610, when Carlo Borromeo was canonized, the church was rebuilt in his honour. Most of the new church was the work of father and son, Onorio and Martino Longhi, but the fine dome is by Pietro da Cortona. The altarpiece by Carlo Maratta (1625–1713) is the *Gloria dei Santi Ambrogio e Carlo*. An ambulatory leads behind the altar to a chapel housing the heart of San Carlo in a richly decorated reliquary.

Statue of San Carlo by Attilio Selva (1888–1970) behind the apse of Santi Ambrogio e Carlo

CAMPO DE' FIORI

Between Corso Vittorio Emanuele II and the Tiber, the city displays many distinct personalities. The open-air market of Campo de' Fiori preserves the lively, bohemian atmosphere of the medieval inns that once flourished here, while the area also contains Renaissance palazzi, such as Palazzo Farnese and Palazzo Spada, where powerful Roman families built their fortress-like houses near the route of papal processions. Close by, overlooking the picturesque Tiber Island, lies the former Jewish Ghetto, where many traces of daily life from past centuries can still be seen. The Portico of Octavia and the Theatre of Marcellus are spectacular examples of the city's many-layered history, built up over the half-ruined remains of ancient Rome.

Sights at a Glance

Churches and Temples
5 Santissima Trinità dei Pellegrini
7 Santa Maria dell'Orazione e Morte
9 San Girolamo della Carità
10 Sant'Eligio degli Orefici
11 Santa Maria in Monserrato
18 San Carlo ai Catinari
20 Santa Maria in Campitelli
21 San Nicola in Carcere
29 San Giovanni dei Fiorentini

Museums and Galleries
6 Palazzo Spada
14 Piccola Farnesina
15 Burcardo Theatre Museum

Historic Buildings
2 Palazzo Pio Righetti
3 Palazzo del Monte di Pietà
8 Palazzo Farnese
12 Palazzo Ricci
13 Palazzo della Cancelleria
25 Casa di Lorenzo Manilio
26 Palazzo Cenci

Fountains
19 Fontana delle Tartarughe

Historic Streets and Piazzas
1 Campo de' Fiori
24 Ghetto and Synagogue
27 Tiber Island
28 Via Giulia

Famous Theatres
16 Teatro Argentina

Ancient Sites
4 Sotterranei di San Paolo alla Regola
17 Area Sacra dell'Argentina
22 Theatre of Marcellus
23 Portico of Octavia

Restaurants
see pp311–14
1 Acchiappafantasmi
2 Angolo Divino
3 Ba'Ghetto Milky
4 Camponeschi
5 Da Giggetto
6 Da Pancrazio
7 Enoteca il Goccetto
8 Nonna Betta
9 Open Baladin
10 Il Pagliaccio
11 Pierluigi
12 Piperno
13 Polese
14 La Pollarola
15 Roscioli
16 Il Sanlorenzo
17 Settimio al Pellegrino
18 Sora Lella
19 Sora Margherita
20 Vinando
21 Vino e Camino

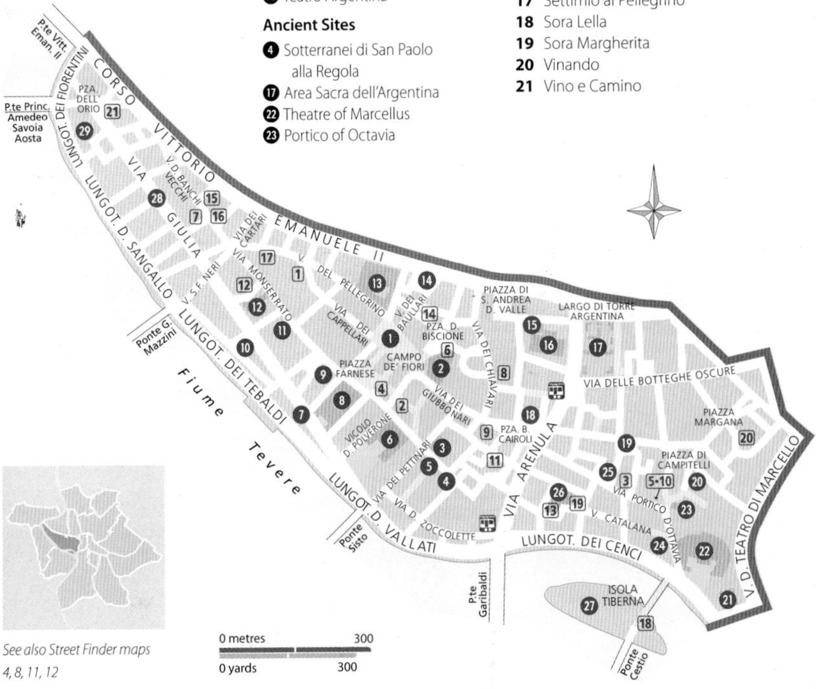

See also Street Finder maps 4, 8, 11, 12

0 metres 300
0 yards 300

◀ Theatre of Marcellus

For keys to symbols see back flap

Street-by-Street: Campo de' Fiori

This fascinating part of Renaissance Rome is also an exciting area for shopping and nightlife, centred on the market square of Campo de' Fiori. Its stalls supply many nearby restaurants, and young people shop for clothes in Via dei Giubbonari. Popular restaurants keep the area alive late into the night, when overcrowding and drunks can become a problem. By day there are great buildings to admire, though few are open to the public. Two exceptions are the Piccola Farnesina, with its collection of Classical statues, and Palazzo Spada, home to many significant paintings.

⑩ Sant'Eligio degli Orefici
A small Renaissance church designed by Raphael is concealed behind a later façade.

⑫ Palazzo Ricci
Painted Classical scenes were a favourite form of decoration for the façades of Renaissance houses.

⑪ Santa Maria in Monserrato
This church, which has strong connections with Spain, houses a Bernini bust of Cardinal Pedro Foix de Montoya.

⑨ San Girolamo della Carità
The chief attraction of this church is Borromini's fabulous Spada Chapel.

⑧ Palazzo Farnese
Michelangelo and other great artists helped create this monumental Renaissance palazzo.

Key

— Suggested route

0 metres   75
0 yards   75

⑦ Santa Maria dell'Orazione e Morte
A pair of dramatic winged skulls flank the doorway to this church dedicated to the burial of the dead.

❶ ★ Campo de' Fiori
This colourful market makes Piazza Campo de' Fiori one of Rome's most entertaining squares.

Locator Map
See Central Rome Map pp16–17

❸ Palazzo della Cancelleria
The papal administration ran the affairs of the Church from this vast building.

❹ Piccola Farnesina
This plaque honours Giovanni Barracco. His sculpture collection is housed in the palazzo.

❷ Palazzo Pio Righetti
Heraldic eagles stare down from the pediments of the palazzo's windows.

❺ Santissima Trinità dei Pellegrini
The principal role of this church was one of charity, looking after poor pilgrims arriving in Rome.

❹ Sotterranei di San Paolo alla Regola
Remains of a Roman house have survived in the basement of an old palace.

❸ Palazzo del Monte di Pietà
This was a papal institution, where the poor pawned their possessions in order to borrow small sums of money.

❻ ★ Palazzo Spada
The picture gallery houses a collection started by two wonderfully eccentric 17th-century cardinals.

❶ Campo de' Fiori

Piazza Campo de' Fiori. **Map** 4 E4 & 11 C4. 🚌 116 and routes to Largo di Torre Argentina or Corso Vittorio Emanuele II. *See Markets p344.*

The Campo de' Fiori (field of flowers), once a meadow, occupies the site of the open space facing the Theatre of Pompey. Cardinals and noblemen used to rub shoulders with fishmongers and foreigners in the piazza's market, making it one of the liveliest areas of medieval and Renaissance Rome. Today's market retains much of the traditional lively atmosphere.

In the centre of the square is a statue of the philosopher Giordano Bruno, burnt at the stake for heresy here in 1600. The hooded figure is a grim reminder of the executions that were held here.

The piazza was surrounded by inns for pilgrims and other travellers. Many of these were once owned by the successful 15th-century courtesan, Vannozza Catanei, mistress of Pope Alexander VI Borgia. On the corner between the piazza and Via del Pellegrino you can see Catanei's shield, which she had decorated with her own coat of arms, those of her husband and those of her lover, the Borgia pope.

❷ Palazzo Pio Righetti

Piazza del Biscione 95–99. **Map** 4 E5 & 11 C4. 🚌 116 and routes to Largo Torre Argentina or Corso Vittorio Emanuele II. **Closed** to the public.

The vast 17th-century Palazzo Pio Righetti was built over the ruined Theatre of Pompey.

The windows of the palazzo are decorated with lions and pine cones from the coat of arms of the Pio da Carpi family who lived here.

The curve of the Theatre of Pompey, completed in 55 BC, is followed by Via di Grotta Pinta. Rome's first permanent theatre was built of stone and concrete and in the basement of the Pancrazio restaurant you can see early examples of *opus*

Window pediment with heraldic lion and pine cones, Palazzo Pio Righetti

reticulatum – small square blocks of tufa (porous rock) set diagonally as a facing for a concrete wall.

❸ Palazzo del Monte di Pietà

Piazza del Monte di Pietà 33. **Map** 4 E5 & 11 C4. **Tel** 06-622 7252. 🚌 116 and routes to Largo di Torre Argentina or Corso Vittorio Emanuele II. 🚊 8. Chapel: **Open** by appt for accredited groups. Ring in advance.

The Monte, as it is known, is a public institution, founded in 1539 by Pope Paul III Farnese as a pawnshop to staunch the usury then rampant in the city. The building still has offices and auction rooms for the sale of unredeemed goods.

The stars with diagonal bands on the huge central plaque decorating the façade are the coat of arms of Pope Clement VIII Aldobrandini, added when Carlo Maderno enlarged the palace in the 17th

century. The clock on the left was added later.

Within, the chapel is a jewel of Baroque architecture, adorned with gilded stucco, marble panelling and reliefs. It is a perfect setting for the sculptures by Domenico Guidi – a bust of San Carlo Borromeo and a relief of the *Pietà*. There are also splendid reliefs by Giovanni Battista Théudon and Pierre Legros of biblical scenes illustrating the charitable nature of the institution.

❹ Sotterranei di San Paolo alla Regola

Via di San Paolo alla Regola. **Map** 11 C5. **Tel** 06-0608. 🚌 23, 116, 280 and routes to Largo di Torre Argentina. 🚊 8. **Open** by appt only, with permit.

An old palace hides the perfectly conserved remains of an ancient Roman house, dating from the 2nd–3rd centuries. Restoration works

Relief by Théudon of *Joseph Distributing Grain to the Egyptians* in Palazzo del Monte di Pietà

are being carried out in order to open this site to the public, but at present it is only possible to visit by special arrangement.

A ramp leads down well below today's street level, to reveal the locations of shops of the time. One level above is the Stanza della Colonna, at one time an open courtyard, with traces of frescoes and mosaics on its walls.

Guido Reni's *Holy Trinity*, in Santissima Trinità dei Pellegrini

❺ Santissima Trinità dei Pellegrini

Via dei Pettinari 36A. **Map** 4 E5 & 11 C5. **Tel** 06-686 8451. ⊞ 23, 116, 280 and routes to Largo di Torre Argentina. ⊞ 8. **Open** 4–8pm Mon–Sat; 8am–1pm, 4–8pm Sun.

The church was donated in the 16th century to a charitable organization founded by San Filippo Neri to care for the poor and sick, in particular the thousands of paupers who flocked in pilgrimage to Rome during the special holy years known as Jubilees. The 18th-century façade has niches with statues of the Evangelists by Bernardino Ludovisi. The interior, with Corinthian columns, ends in a horseshoe vault and apse, dominated by Guido Reni's striking altarpiece of the Holy Trinity (1625). The frescoes in the lantern are also by Reni. Other interesting paintings include *St Gregory the Great Freeing Souls from Purgatory*, by Baldassarre Croce (third chapel to the left); Cavalier

d'Arpino's *Virgin and Saints* (second chapel to the left); and a painting by Borgognone (1677) of the Virgin and recently canonized saints. In the sacristy are depictions of the nobility washing the feet of pilgrims, a custom started by San Filippo.

❻ Palazzo Spada

Piazza Capo di Ferro 13. **Map** 2 F5. **Tel** 06-6821 2743 (Palazzo) or 06-683 2409 (Galleria). ⊞ 23, 116, 280 and routes to Largo di Torre Argentina. ⊞ 8. Galleria Spada: **Open** 8:30am–7:30pm daily (last adm: 7pm). **Closed** 1 Jan, 25 Dec. 🎫 🎫 ♿ 🎫 📷

This majestic palazzo, built around 1550 for Cardinal Capo di Ferro, has an elegant stuccoed courtyard and façade decorated with reliefs evoking Rome's glorious past.

Cardinal Bernardino Spada, who lived here in the 17th century with his brother Virginio (also a cardinal), hired architects Bernini and Borromini to work on the building. The brothers' whimsical delight in false perspectives resulted in a colonnaded gallery by Borromini that appears four times longer than it really is.

The cardinals also amassed a superb private collection of paintings, which is now on display in the Galleria Spada. The collection features a wide range of artists, including Rubens, Dürer and Guido Reni. The most important works on display include *The Visitation* by Andrea del Sarto (1486–1530), *Cain and Abel* by Giovanni Lanfranco (1582–1647) and *The Death of Dido* by Guercino (1591–1666).

❼ Santa Maria dell'Orazione e Morte

Via Giulia 262. **Map** 4 E5 & 11 B4. **Tel** 06-6880 6862. ⊞ 23, 116, 280. **Closed** for restoration. Crypt: **Open** 4–6pm Sat & Sun.

A pious confraternity was formed here in the 16th century to collect the bodies of the unknown dead and give them a Christian burial. The theme

Offertory box in Santa Maria dell'Orazione e Morte

of death is stressed in this church, dedicated to St Mary of Prayer and Death. The doors and windows of Ferdinando Fuga's dramatic Baroque façade are decorated with winged skulls. Above the central entrance there is a *clepsydra* (an ancient hour-glass) – symbolic of death.

❽ Palazzo Farnese

Piazza Farnese. **Map** 4 E5 & 11 B4. **Tel** 06-686 011. ⊞ 23, 116, 280 and routes to Corso Vittorio Emanuele II. **Open** for guided tours only (Mon, Wed & Fri in English). Times vary. Book at least one week ahead at www.inventerrome.com 🎫

The prototype for numerous princely palaces, the imposing Palazzo Farnese was originally built for Cardinal Alessandro Farnese (who became Pope Paul III in 1534). He commissioned the greatest artists to work on it, starting with Antonio da Sangallo the Younger as architect in 1517. Michelangelo, who took over after him, contributed the great cornice and central window of the main façade, and the third level of the courtyard.

Michelangelo had a plan for the Farnese gardens to be connected by a bridge to the Farnese home in Trastevere, Villa Farnesina (see pp220–21). The elegant arch spanning Via Giulia belongs to this sadly unrealized scheme. The palazzo was completed in 1589, on a less ambitious scale, by Giacomo della Porta. It is now the home of the French Embassy, which moved in as early as 1635.

Spada Chapel in San Girolamo

9 San Girolamo della Carità

Via di Monserrato 62A. **Map** 4 E5 & 11 B4. **Tel** 06-687 9786. 🚌 23, 40, 46, 62, 64, 116, 280. **Open** Oct–Jun: 10:30am–12:30pm Sun & public hols. 🔝

The church was built on a site incorporating the home of San Filippo Neri, the 16th-century saint from Tuscany who renewed Rome's spiritual and cultural life by his friendly, open approach to religion. He would have loved the frolicking putti shown around his statue, in his chapel, reminding him of the Roman urchins he had cared for during his lifetime.

The breathtaking Spada Chapel was designed by Borromini, and is unique both as a work of art and as an illustration of the spirit of the Baroque age. All architectural elements are concealed so that the space of the chapel's interior is defined solely by decorative marblework and statues. Veined jasper and precious multicoloured marbles are sculpted to imitate flowery damask and velvet hangings. Even the altar rail is a long swag of jasper drapery held up by a pair of kneeling angels with wooden wings.

Although there are memorials to former members of the Spada family, oddly there is no indication as to which of the Spadas was responsible for endowing the chapel. It was probably art-lover Virgilio Spada, a follower of San Filippo Neri.

10 Sant'Eligio degli Orefici

Via di Sant'Eligio 8A. **Map** 4 D4 & 11 B4. **Tel** 06-686 8260. 🚌 23, 40, 46, 62, 64, 116, 280. **Open** 9:30am–1pm Mon–Fri (call first at Via di Sant'Eligio 7). **Closed** Aug. 🔝

The name of the church still records the fact that it was commissioned by a rich corporation of goldsmiths *(orefici)* in the early 16th century. The original design was by Raphael, who, like his master Bramante, had acquired a sense of the grandiose from the remains of Roman antiquity. The influence of some of Bramante's works, such as the choir of Santa Maria del Popolo *(see pp140–41)*, is evident in the simple way the arches and pilasters define the structure of the walls.

The cupola of Sant' Eligio is attributed to Baldassarre Peruzzi, while the façade was added in the early 17th century by Flaminio Ponzio. Among the various 16th-century painters who decorated the interior was Taddeo Zuccari, who worked on Palazzo Farnese *(see p149)*.

Statue of San Filippo Neri by Pierre Legros

An early bust by Bernini of Cardinal Pedro Foix de Montoya

11 Santa Maria in Monserrato

Via di Monserrato 115. **Map** 4 E4 & 11 B3. **Tel** 06-686 5865. 🚌 23, 40, 46, 62, 64, 116, 280. **Open** 5–7pm Sat; 10am–1pm, 5–7pm Sun. To arrange a visit Mon–Fri, call 06-688 9651. 🔝

The origins of the Spanish national church in Rome go back to 1506, when a hospice for Spanish pilgrims was begun by a brotherhood of the Virgin of Montserrat in Catalonia. Inside is Annibale Carracci's painting *San Diego de Alcalà* and, in the third chapel on the left, a copy of a Sansovino statue of St James. Some beautiful 15th-century tombs by Andrea Bregno and Luigi Capponi are in the courtyard and side chapels. Do not miss Bernini's bust of Pedro Foix de Montoya, the church's benefactor, in the annexe.

San Diego by Annibale Carracci

⑫ Palazzo Ricci

Piazza de' Ricci. **Map** 4 D4 & 11 B4.
🚌 23, 40, 46, 62, 64, 116, 280, 870.
Closed to the public.

Palazzo Ricci was famous for its frescoed façade – now rather faded – originally painted in the 16th century by Polidoro da Caravaggio, a follower of Raphael.

In Renaissance Rome it was common to commission artists to decorate the outsides of houses with heroes of Classical antiquity. A fresco by a leading artist such as Polidoro, reputedly the inventor of this style of painting, was a conspicuous status symbol, in the nobility's attempts to outshine each other with their palazzi.

⑬ Palazzo della Cancelleria

Piazza della Cancelleria. **Map** 4 E4 & 11 C3. **Tel** 06-6988 7566. 🚌 40, 46, 62, 64, 70, 81, 87, 116, 492. Courtyard: **Open** 7:30am–8pm Mon–Sat, 9:30am–7pm Sun. Sala Riaria: **Open** Tue pm & Sat am (call 06-6989 3405 at least a month in advance).

The palazzo, a supreme example of the confident architecture of the Early Renaissance, was begun in 1485. It was financed partly with the gambling winnings of Cardinal Raffaele Riario. Roses, the emblem of the Riario family, adorn the vaults and capitals of the beautiful Doric courtyard. The palazzo's interior was decorated after the Sack of Rome in 1527. Giorgio Vasari boasted that he had completed work on one enormous room in just 100 days; Michelangelo allegedly retorted: "It looks like it." Other Mannerist artists, Perin del Vaga and Francesco Salviati, frescoed the rooms of the cardinal in charge of the Papal Chancellery, the office that gave the palazzo its name when it was installed here by Pope Leo X.

On the right of the main entrance is the unobtrusive and rather quaint church of San Lorenzo in Damaso, founded by Pope Damasus (reigned 366–84). It was reconstructed in 1495 and although Bernini made alterations

Courtyard of Palazzo della Cancelleria

to the transept and apse in 1638, it was later restored to its 15th-century lines. Its porticoes housed libraries for the first Papal Archives.

⑭ Piccola Farnesina

Corso Vittorio Emanuele II 168. **Map** 4 E4 & 11 C3. **Tel** 06-0608. 🚌 40, 46, 62, 64, 70, 81, 87, 116, 492. **Open** Oct–May: 10am–4pm Tue–Sun; Jun–Sep: 1–7pm Tue–Sun. 🅦 **museobarracco.it**

This delightful miniature palazzo acquired its name from the lilies decorating its cornices. These were mistakenly identified as part of the Farnese family crest. In fact they were part of the coat of arms of a French clergyman, Thomas Le Roy, for whom the palazzo was built in 1523.

The entrance is in a façade built to overlook Corso Vittorio Emanuele II when the road was

Inner courtyard, Piccola Farnesina

constructed at the start of the 20th century. The original façade on the left of today's entrance is attributed to Antonio da Sangallo the Younger. Note the asymmetrical arrangement of its windows and ledges. The elegant central courtyard also retains its original appearance.

The Piccola Farnesina now houses the Museo Barracco, a collection of ancient sculpture assembled during the 19th century by the politician Baron Giovanni Barracco. A bust of the baron can be seen in the courtyard. The collection includes an ancient Egyptian relief of the scribe Nofer, some Assyrian artifacts and, among the Etruscan exhibits, a delicate ceramic female head. On the first floor is the Greek collection with a head of Apollo.

⑮ Burcardo Theatre Museum

Via del Sudario 44. **Map** 4 F4 & 12 D4. **Tel** 06-6819 471. 🚌 40, 46, 62, 64, 70, 81, 186, 492. 🚃 8. Museum: **Open** 9:15am–4:30pm Tue & Thu. **Closed** Aug. 🅦 **burcardo.org**

This late 15th-century house once belonged to Johannes Burckhardt, chamberlain to Pope Alexander VI Borgia and author of a diary of Rome under the Borgias. His house now holds Rome's most complete collection of theatre literature, plus Chinese puppets and comic masks from the various regions of Italy.

Detail of façade, Teatro Argentina

⑯ Teatro Argentina

Largo di Torre Argentina 52. **Map** 4 F4 & 12 D4. **Tel** 06-684 0001. 🚌 40, 46, 62, 64, 70, 81, 87, 186, 492, 810. 🚋 8. **Open** Museum by appt only (call 06-0608). 🎭 Plays performed Oct–Jun. *See Entertainment pp352–3.* 🔲 teatrodiroma.net

One of the city's most influential theatres was founded by the Sforza Cesarini family in 1732, though the façade dates from a century later. Many famous operas, including those of Verdi, were first performed here. In 1816, the theatre saw the ill-fated début of Rossini's *Barber of Seville*, during which the composer insulted the unappreciative audience, who then pursued him through the streets.

⑰ Area Sacra dell'Argentina

Largo di Torre Argentina. **Map** 4 F4 & 12 D4. 🚌 40, 46, 62, 64, 70, 81, 87, 186, 492, 810. 🚋 8. **Closed** to the public, but ruins clearly visible from street.

The remains of four temples were discovered here in the 1920s. Dating from the Republican era, they are among the oldest in Rome. They are known as A, B, C and D. The oldest (temple C) dates from the early 3rd century BC. It was placed on a high platform preceded by an altar and is typical of Italic plans. Temple A is from later in the 3rd century BC. In medieval times the church of San Nicola de' Cesarini was built over its podium: remains of its two apses are still visible. The north column stumps belonged to a great portico, the Hecatostylum (portico of 100 columns).

In Imperial times two marble lavatories were built here – the remains of one is visible behind temple A. Behind temples B and C are remains of a great platform of tufa blocks identified as part of the Curia of Pompey – a rectangular building with a statue of Pompey. It was here that the Senate met and Julius Caesar was murdered on 15 March 44 BC. At the southwest corner of the site is a cat sanctuary, home to Rome's abandoned felines. The ruins are closed to the public, however they can be admired from the street.

⑱ San Carlo ai Catinari

Piazza B. Cairoli. **Map** 4 F5 & 12 D4. **Tel** 06-6830 7070. 🚌 40, 46, 62, 64, 70, 81, 87, 186, 492, 810. 🚋 8. **Open** 7:30am–noon, 4–7pm daily. 🚫 No visits during services.

In 1620, Rome's Milanese congregation decided to honour Cardinal Carlo Borromeo with this great church. It was called "ai Catinari" on account

San Carlo at Prayer by Guido Reni

of the bowl-makers' *(catinari)* shops in the area. The solemn travertine façade was completed in 1638 by the Roman architect Soria. The 16th-century basilican plan is flanked by chapels. The St Cecilia chapel was designed and decorated by Antonio Gherardi, who added a family portrait. The church's paintings and frescoes by Pietro da Cortona and Guido Reni are mature works of the Counter-Reformation, depicting the life and acts of the recently canonized San Carlo.

The ornate crucifix on the sacristy altar is inlaid with marble and mother-of-pearl and is by the 16th-century sculptor Algardi.

Sacristy altar, San Carlo ai Catinari

⑲ Fontana delle Tartarughe

Piazza Mattei. **Map** 4 F5 & 12 D4. 🚌 46, 62, 63, 64, 70, 87, 186, 492, 810. 🚋 8.

The delightful Fontana delle Tartarughe (*tartarughe* are tortoises) was commissioned by the Mattei family between 1581 and 1588 to decorate "their" piazza. The design was by Giacomo della Porta, but the fountain owes much of its charm to the four bronze youths each resting one foot on the head of a dolphin, sculpted by Taddeo Landini. Nearly a

Della Porta's graceful Fontana delle Tartarughe

century after the fountain was built an unknown sculptor added the struggling tortoises to complete the composition.

⑳ Santa Maria in Campitelli

Piazza di Campitelli 9. **Map** 4 F5 & 12 E5. **Tel** 06-6880 3978. 🚌 40, 46, 62, 63, 64, 70, 87, 186, 780, 810. **Open** 7am–7pm daily. 🚻 ♿

In 17th-century Rome the plague could still strike fiercely and there were no reliable, effective remedies. Many Romans simply prayed for a cure to a sacred medieval icon of the Virgin, the Madonna del Portico. When a particularly lethal outbreak of plague abated in 1656, popular gratitude was so strong that a new church was built to house the icon.

Lavish altar tabernacle in Santa Maria in Campitelli

The church, designed by a pupil of Bernini, Carlo Rainaldi, was completed in 1667. The main elements of the lively Baroque façade are the graceful columns, symbolizing the supporters of the true faith.

Inside the church stands a fabulously ornate, gilded altar tabernacle with spiral columns which was designed by Giovanni Antonio de Rossi to contain the image of the Virgin. The side chapels are decorated by some of Rome's finest Baroque painters: Sebastiano Conca, Giovanni Battista Gaulli (known as Il Baciccia) and Luca Giordano.

Façade and medieval bell tower of San Nicola in Carcere

㉑ San Nicola in Carcere

Via del Teatro di Marcello 46. **Map** 5 A5 & 12 E5. **Tel** 06-6830 7198. 🚌 44, 63, 81, 160, 170, 628, 780, 781. **Open** 10am–5pm daily. Excavations: call 347-381 1874 to book. 📷 📷 for tours. 🚻

The medieval church of San Nicola in Carcere stands on the site of three Roman temples of the Republican era which were converted into a prison (carcere) in the Middle Ages. The temples of Juno, Spes and Janus faced a city gate leading from the Forum Holitorium, the city's vegetable and oil market, to the road down to the port on the Tiber. The columns embedded in the walls of the church belonged to two flanking temples whose platforms are

now marked by lawns. The church was rebuilt in 1599 and restored during the 19th century, but the bell tower and Roman columns are part of the original design.

The Theatre of Marcellus by Thomas Hartley Cromek (1809–73)

㉒ Theatre of Marcellus

Via del Teatro di Marcello. **Map** 4 A5 & 12 E5. **Tel** 06-0608. 🚌 44, 63, 81, 160, 170, 628, 780, 781. **Open** 9am–6pm daily (to 7pm in summer).

The curved outer wall of this vast amphitheatre has supported generations of Roman buildings. It was built by Emperor Augustus (27 BC–AD 14), who dedicated it to Marcellus, his nephew and son-in-law, who had died aged 19 in 23 BC.

The Middle Ages were a turbulent time of invasions and local conflicts (see p32) and by the 13th century the theatre had been converted into the fortress of the Savelli family. In the 16th century Baldassarre Peruzzi built a great palace on the theatre ruins for the Orsini family. This included a garden that faced the Tiber. The lower arches were later occupied by humble dwellings and workshops.

Close to the theatre stand three beautiful Corinthian columns and a section of frieze. These are from the Temple of Apollo, which once housed many great works of art that the Romans had plundered from Greece in the 2nd century BC.

㉓ Portico of Octavia

Via del Portico d'Ottavia. **Map** 4 F5 & 12 E5. 46, 62, 63, 64, 70, 87, 186, 780, 810.

Built in honour of Octavia (the sister of Augustus and the abandoned wife of Mark Antony), this is the only surviving portico of what used to be the monumental piazza of Circus Flaminius. The rectangular portico enclosed temples dedicated to Jupiter and Juno, decorated with bronze statues. The part we see today is the great central atrium originally covered by marble facings.

In the Middle Ages a great fish market and a church, Sant'Angelo in Pescheria, were built in the ruins of the portico. As the church was associated with the fishing activities of the nearby river port, aquatic flora and fauna feature in many of its inlays. Links with the Tiber are also apparent in the stucco façade on the adjacent Fishmonger's Oratory, built in 1689. The church has a fresco of the Madonna and angels by the school of Benozzo Gozzoli.

㉔ Ghetto and Synagogue

Synagogue: Lungotevere dei Cenci. **Map** 4 F5 & 12 E5. **Tel** 06-6840 0661. 23, 63, 280, 780 and routes to Largo di Torre Argentina. 8. Museum: **Open** Apr–mid-Sep: 10am–6pm Sun–Thu, 10am–4pm Fri; mid-Sep–Mar: 10am–5pm Sun–Thu, 9am–2pm Fri. Last adm: 45 mins before closing. **Closed** on Jewish public hols.
W museoebraico.roma.it

The first Jews came to Rome as traders in the 2nd century BC and there has been a Jewish community in Rome ever since. Jews were much appreciated for their financial and medical skills during the time of the Roman Empire.

Systematic persecution began in the 16th century. From 25 July 1556 all Rome's Jews were forced to live inside a high-walled enclosure erected on the orders of Pope Paul IV. The Ghetto was in a damp, unhealthy part of Rome. Inhabitants were only allowed out during the day, and on Sundays they were driven into the Church of Sant'Angelo in Pescheria to listen to Christian sermons – a practice that was only abolished in 1848.

Persecution started again in 1943 with the German occupation. Although many Jews were helped to escape or hidden by Roman citizens, thousands were deported to German concentration camps.

Today many Jews still live in the former Ghetto around Via del Portico d'Ottavia and the medieval streets retain much of their old character. The Synagogue on Lungotevere was completed in 1904 and houses a Jewish museum that describes the history of the community through plans, Torahs and other artifacts.

㉕ Casa di Lorenzo Manilio

Via del Portico d'Ottavia 1D. **Map** 4 F5 & 12 D5. 46, 62, 63, 64, 70, 87, 186, 780, 810. **Closed** to the public.

Before the Renaissance, most Romans had only vague ideas of their city's past, but the 15th-century revival of interest in the philosophy and arts of antiquity inspired some to build houses recalling the splendour of ancient Rome. In 1468 a certain Lorenzo Manilio built a great house for his family, decorating it with an elegant Classical plaque. The Latin inscription dates the building according to the ancient Roman method – 2,221 years after the foundation of the city – and gives the owner's name. Original reliefs are embedded in the façades as well as a fragment of an ancient sarcophagus. The Piazza Costaguti façade's windows are inscribed *Ave Roma* (Hail Rome).

Balcony of Palazzo Cenci

㉖ Palazzo Cenci

Vicolo dei Cenci. **Map** 4 F5 & 12 D5. 23, 63, 280, 780 and routes to Largo di Torre Argentina. **Closed** to the public.

Palazzo Cenci belonged to the family of Beatrice Cenci, who was accused, together with her brothers and stepmother, of witchcraft and the murder of her tyrannical father. She was condemned to death and beheaded at Ponte Sant'Angelo in 1599.

Most of the original medieval palazzo has been demolished, and the building you see today

Row of Roman busts decorating the Casa di Lorenzo Manilio

Tiber Island, with Ponte Cestio linking it to Trastevere

dates back to the 1570s, though its rather forbidding appearance seems medieval. Heraldic half-moons decorate the main façade on Via del Progresso while pretty balconies open on the opposite side where a medieval arch joins the palace to Palazzetto Cenci, designed by Martino Longhi the Elder. Inside is a traditional courtyard with an Ionic-style loggia; many of the rooms retain the decoration that the unfortunate Beatrice would have known as a child.

㉗ Tiber Island

Isola Tiberina. **Map** 8 D1 & 12 D5.
23, 63, 280, 780. 8.

In ancient times the island, which lay opposite the city's port, had large structures of white travertine at either end, built to resemble the stern and prow of a ship.

Since 293 BC, when a temple was dedicated here to Aesculapius, the god of healing and protector against the plague, the island has been associated with the sick and there is still a hospital here.

San Bartolomeo all'Isola, the church in the island's central piazza, was built on the ruins of the Temple of Aesculapius in the 10th century. Its omanesque bell tower is clearly visible from across the river.

From the Ghetto area you can reach the island by a footbridge, the Ponte Fabricio. The oldest original bridge over the Tiber still in use, it was built in 62 BC. In medieval times the Pierleoni and then the Caetani, two powerful families, controlled this strategic point by means

of a tower, still *in situ*. The other bridge to the island, the Ponte Cestio, is inscribed with the names of the Byzantine emperors associated with its restoration in AD 370.

Mask fountain in Via Giulia

㉘ Via Giulia

Map 4 D4 & 11 A3. 23, 116, 280, 870.

This picturesque street was laid out by Bramante for Pope Julius II della Rovere. Lined with 16th- to 18th- century aristocratic palazzi, as well as fine churches and antique shops, Via Giulia makes a fascinating walk (*see pp278–9*).

㉙ San Giovanni dei Fiorentini

Via Acciaioli 2. **Map** 4 D4 & 11 A2.
Tel 06-6889 2059. 23, 40, 46, 62, 64, 116, 280, 870. **Open** 7:25am–noon, 5–7pm daily.

The church of St John of the Florentines was built for the large Florentine community living in this area. Pope Leo X wanted it to be an expression of the cultural superiority of Florence over Rome. Started in the early 16th century, the church took over a century to build. The principal architect was Antonio da Sangallo the Younger, but many others contributed before Carlo Maderno's elongated cupola was finally completed in 1620. The present façade was added in the 18th century.

The church was decorated mainly by Tuscan artists. One interesting exception is the 15th-century statue of San Giovannino by the Sicilian Mino del Reame in a niche above the sacristy. The spectacular high altar houses a marble group by Antonio Raggi, the *Baptism of Christ*. The altar itself is by Borromini, who is buried in the church along with fellow architect Carlo Maderno.

This and San Lorenzo in Lucina (*see p116*) are the only churches in Rome which admit animals: the faithful can bring their pets, and an Easter lamb-blessing takes place.

Antonio Raggi's *Baptism of Christ* in San Giovanni dei Fiorentini

QUIRINAL

One of the original seven hills of Rome, the Quirinal was a largely residential area in Imperial times. To the east of the hill were the vast Baths of Diocletian, still standing in front of what is now the main rail station. Abandoned in the Middle Ages, the district returned to favour in the late 16th century. The prime site was taken by the popes for Palazzo del Quirinale. Great families such as the Colonna and the Aldobrandini had their palazzi lower down the hill. With the end of papal rule in 1870, the surrounding area, especially Via Nazionale, was redeveloped as the Quirinal became the residence of the kings of Italy, then of the Italian president.

Sights at a Glance

Churches
- ④ Santi Apostoli
- ⑤ San Marcello al Corso
- ⑦ Santa Maria in Trivio
- ⑨ Santi Vincenzo e Anastasio
- ⑪ Sant'Andrea al Quirinale
- ⑫ San Carlo alle Quattro Fontane
- ⑮ Santa Maria degli Angeli e dei Martiri
- ⑳ Santa Maria dei Monti
- ㉑ Sant'Agata dei Goti
- ㉓ Santi Domenico e Sisto

Museums and Galleries
- ⑧ Accademia Nazionale di San Luca
- ⑩ Scuderie del Quirinale
- ⑯ Museo Nazionale Romano (Palazzo Massimo)
- ⑲ Palazzo delle Esposizioni

Historic Piazzas
- ⑱ Piazza della Repubblica

Historic Buildings
- ② Palazzo del Quirinale
- ③ Palazzo Colonna
- ⑰ Baths of Diocletian

Fountains and Statues
- ① Castor and Pollux
- ⑥ Trevi Fountain
- ⑬ Le Quattro Fontane
- ⑭ Moses Fountain

Parks and Gardens
- ㉒ Villa Aldobrandini

Restaurants
see pp315–17
1. Abruzzi ai SS Apostoli
2. Ai Tre Scalini
3. Antica Birreria Peroni
4. L'Asino d'Oro
5. Asmara
6. Baccano
7. La Carbonara
8. Cavour 313
9. Colline Emiliane
10. Doozo
11. Eataly
12. Open Colonna
13. Piccolo Buco
14. Pipero al Rex
15. Taverna dei Fori Imperiali
16. Trimani il Wine Bar
17. Urbana 47
18. Vineria Il Chianti
19. Vivendo il Mediterraneo

See also Street Finder maps
5, 6, 12

0 metres   300
0 yards   300

◀ Baroque statuary of the Trevi Fountain

For keys to symbols *see back flap*

Street-by-Street: The Quirinal Hill

Even though Palazzo del Quirinale is usually closed to the public, it is well worth walking up the hill to the palace to see the giant Roman statues of Castor and Pollux in the piazza and enjoy fine views of the city. Come down the hill by way of the narrow streets and stairways that lead to one of Rome's unforgettable sights, the Trevi Fountain. Many small churches lie hidden away in the back streets. Towards Piazza Venezia there are grand palazzi, including that of the Colonna, one of Rome's most ancient and powerful families.

Santa Maria in Via is famous for its medieval well and miraculous 13th-century icon of the Madonna.

7 Santa Maria in Trivio
The attractive façade of this tiny church conceals a rich Baroque interior.

8 Accademia Nazionale di San Luca
The art academy has works by famous former members, such as Canova and Angelica Kauffmann.

6 ★ Trevi Fountain
Rome's grandest and best-known fountain almost fills the tiny Piazza di Trevi.

9 Santi Vincenzo e Anastasio
The grand façade of this small Baroque church is on a corner facing the Trevi Fountain.

5 San Marcello al Corso
This stark *Crucifixion* by Van Dyck hangs in the sacristy of the church.

Palazzo Odescalchi has a Bernini façade from 1664, with a balustrade and richly decorated cornice. The building faces Santi Apostoli.

To Piazza Venezia

The magnificent gardens of the presidential palace Giardini del Quirinale are open to visitors just once a year, on 2 June.

Locator Map
See Central Rome Map pp16–17

❷ **Palazzo del Quirinale**
The old papal palace is now the home of the president of Italy. Palace guards in uniform can often be seen outside.

❶ **Castor and Pollux**
The statues are grouped with an obelisk and a fountain.

Piazza della Pilotta is dominated by the imposing façade of the Gregorian University.

PIAZZA DEL QUIRINALE

A DELLA DATARIA

IAZZA DELLA PILOTTA

❸ **Palazzo Colonna**
One of the art gallery's finest old masters is Annibale Carracci's *The Bean Eater*.

❹ **Santi Apostoli**
The figures of Christ and the Apostles on the balustrade were added by Carlo Rainaldi in 1681.

Museo delle Cere, a wax museum that opened in 1953, places its emphasis on horror.

Key

— Suggested route

| 0 metres | 75 |
| 0 yards | 75 |

Quirinal fountain and obelisk with Roman statues of Castor and Pollux

❶ Castor and Pollux

Piazza del Quirinale. **Map** 5 B4.
🚌 H, 40, 64, 70, 170 and many routes along Via del Tritone.

Castor and Pollux – the patrons of horsemanship – and their prancing horses stand in splendour in the Piazza del Quirinale. Over 5.5 m (18 ft) high, these statues are huge Roman copies of 5th-century BC Greek originals. They once stood at the entrance to the nearby Baths of Constantine. Pope Sixtus V had them restored and placed here in 1588. Formerly known as the "horse tamers", they gave the square its familiar name of Monte Cavallo (horse hill).

The obelisk which stands between them was brought here in 1786 from the Mausoleum of Augustus. In 1818 the composition was completed by the addition of a massive granite basin, once a cattle trough in the Forum.

❷ Palazzo del Quirinale

Piazza del Quirinale. **Map** 5 B3.
Tel 06-46991. 🚌 H, 40, 64, 70, 170 and many routes along Via del Tritone.
Open 9:30am–4pm Tue, Wed, Fri–Sun. **Closed** pub hols & late Jun–mid-Sep.
🚹 🖥 quirinale.it

By the 1500s, the Vatican had a reputation as an unhealthy location because of the high incidence of malaria, so Pope Gregory XIII chose this site on the highest of Rome's seven hills as a papal summer residence. Work began in 1573. Piazza del Quirinale has buildings on three sides while the fourth is open, with a splendid view of the city. Many great architects worked on the palace before it assumed its present form in the 1730s. Domenico Fontana designed the main façade, Carlo Maderno the huge chapel and Bernini the narrow wing on Via del Quirinale.

After Rome became the capital city of the new united Italy in 1870, the palace became the official residence of the king, then, in 1947, of the president of the republic.

The immaculately manicured palace gardens are open to the public only once a year, on Republic Day (2 June).

❸ Palazzo Colonna

Via della Pilotta 17. **Map** 5 A4 & 12 F3. **Tel** 06-678 4350. 🚌 H, 40, 64, 70, 170 and many routes to Piazza Venezia. **Open** 9am–1:15pm Sat only (guided tour in English at noon) or by appt (call 06-679 4350 to book). 🚹 🖥 📷
🖥 galleriacolonna.it

Pope Martin V Colonna (reigned 1417–31) began building the palazzo, but most of the structure dates from the 18th century. The art gallery, built by Antonio del Grande between 1654 and 1665, is the only part open to the public. The pictures are numbered but unlabelled, so pick up a guide first. Go up the stairs and through the antechamber leading to a series of three

Palazzo del Quirinale, official residence of the president of Italy

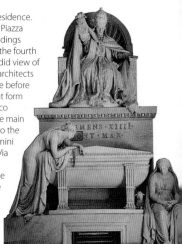

Canova's monument to Pope Clement XIV in Santi Apostoli, with figures of Humility and Modesty

gleaming marble rooms with prominent yellow columns, the Colonna family emblem (colonna means column).

The ceiling frescoes celebrate Marcantonio Colonna's victory over the Turks at the Battle of Lepanto (1571). On the walls are 16th- to 18th-century paintings, including Annibale Carracci's The Bean Eater (see p159). The room of landscape paintings, many by Poussin's brother-in-law Gaspare Dughet, reflects the 18th-century taste of Cardinal Girolamo Colonna. Beyond is a room with a ceiling fresco of The Apotheosis of Martin V. The throne room has a chair reserved for visiting popes and a copy of Pisanello's portrait of Martin V. The gallery also offers a fine view of the private palace garden, site of the ruined Temple of Serapis.

❹ Santi Apostoli

Piazza dei Santi Apostoli. **Map** 5 A4 & 12 F3. **Tel** 06-699 571. 🚌 H, 40, 64, 70, 170 and many other routes to Piazza Venezia. **Open** 7am–noon, 4–7pm daily. 🚹

The original 6th-century church on this site was rebuilt in the 15th century by popes Martin V Colonna and Sixtus IV della Rovere, whose oak-tree crest decorates the capitals of the late 15th-century portico. Inside the portico on the left is Canova's 1807 memorial to the engraver Giovanni Volpato. The church itself contains a much larger monument by Canova, his Tomb of Clement XIV (1789).

The Baroque interior by Francesco and Carlo Fontana was completed in 1714. Note the 3-D effect of Giovanni Odazzi's painted *Rebel Angels*, who really look as though they are falling from the sky. A huge 18th-century altarpiece by Domenico Muratori shows the martyrdom of the Apostles James and Philip, whose tombs are in the crypt.

Detail of Triton and *hippocampo* (sea-horse) at Rome's grandest fountain, the Trevi

❺ San Marcello al Corso

Piazza San Marcello 5. **Map** 5 A4 & 12 F3. **Tel** 06-679 3910. 🚌 62, 63, 81, 85, 117, 119, 160, 492, 628. **Open** 7:30am–11pm Mon–Sat, 9:30am–11pm Sun. ✝

This church was originally one of the first places of Christian worship in Rome, which were known as *tituli*. A later Romanesque building burned down in 1519, and was rebuilt by Jacopo Sansovino with a single nave and many richly decorated private chapels on either side. The imposing travertine façade was designed by Fontana in late Baroque style.

The third chapel on the right has fine frescoes of the Virgin Mary by Francesco Salviati. The decoration of the next chapel was interrupted by the Sack of Rome in 1527. Raphael's follower Perin del Vaga fled, leaving the ceiling frescoes to be completed by Daniele da Volterra and Pellegrino Tibaldi when peace returned to the city. In the nave stands a splendid Venetian-style double tomb by Sansovino, a memorial to Cardinal Giovanni Michiel (victim of a Borgia poisoning in 1503) and his nephew, Bishop Antonio Orso.

❻ Trevi Fountain

Fontana di Trevi. **Map** 5 A3 & 12 F2. 🚌 52, 53, 61, 62, 63, 71, 80, 116, 119 and many other routes along Via del Corso and Via del Tritone.

Most visitors gathering around the coin-filled fountain assume that it has always been here, but by the standards of the Eternal City, the Trevi is a fairly recent creation. Nicola Salvi's theatrical design for Rome's largest and most famous fountain *(see p56)* was completed only in 1762. The central figures are Neptune, flanked by two Tritons. One struggles to master a very unruly "sea-horse", the other leads a far more docile animal. These symbolize the two contrasting moods of the sea.

The site originally marked the terminal of the Aqua Virgo aqueduct built in 19 BC. One of the first-storey reliefs shows a young girl (the legendary virgin after whom the aqueduct was named) pointing to the spring from which the water flows.

Chapel in San Marcello al Corso, decorated by Francesco Salviati

Façade of Santa Maria in Trivio

❼ Santa Maria in Trivio

Piazza dei Crociferi 49. **Map** 5 A3 & 12 F2. **Tel** 06-678 9645. 🚌 52, 53, 61, 62, 63, 71, 80, 116, 119. **Open** 8am– noon, 4–8pm daily. ✝

It has been said that Italian architecture is one of façades, and nowhere is this clearer than in the 1570s façade of Santa Maria in Trivio, delightfully stuck on to the building behind it. Note the false windows. There is illusion inside too, particularly in the ceiling frescoes, which show scenes from the New Testament by Antonio Gherardi (1644–1702).

The name of the tiny church probably means "St Mary-at- the-meeting-of-three-roads".

❽ Accademia Nazionale di San Luca

Piazza dell'Accademia di San Luca 77. **Map** 5 A3 & 12 F2. **Tel** 06-679 8850. 🚌 52, 53, 61, 62, 63, 71, 80, 116, 119 and many routes along Via del Corso and Via del Tritone. **Open** 10am– 12:30pm Mon–Sat. 🌐 accademiasanluca.it

St Luke is supposed to have been a painter, hence the name of Rome's academy of fine arts. Appropriately, the gallery contains a painting of *St Luke Painting a Portrait of the Virgin* by Raphael and his followers. The academy's heyday was in the 17th and 18th centuries, when many members gave their work to the collection.

Canova donated a model for his famous marble group, *The Three Graces*.

Of particular interest are three fascinating self-portraits painted by women: the 17th-century Italian Lavinia Fontana; the 18th-century Swiss Angelica Kauffmann, whose painting is copied from a portrait of her by Joshua Reynolds; and Elisabeth Vigée-Lebrun, the French painter of the years before the 1789 Revolution.

❾ Santi Vincenzo e Anastasio

Vicolo dei Modelli 73. **Map** 5 A3 & 12 F2. 🚌 52, 53, 61, 62, 63, 71, 80, 116, 119. **Open** 9am–8pm daily. ✝ (Bulgarian Orthodox services).

Overlooking the Trevi Fountain is one of the most over-the-top Baroque façades in Rome. Its thickets of columns are crowned by the huge coat of arms of Cardinal Raimondo Mazzarino, better known as Cardinal Mazarin, chief minister of France, who commissioned Martino Longhi the Younger to build the church in 1650. The female bust above the door is

of one of the cardinal's famous nieces, either Louis XIV's first love, Maria Mancini (1639–1715), or her younger sister, Ortensia. In the apse, memorial plaques record the popes whose *praecordia* (a part of the heart) are enshrined behind the wall. This gruesome tradition was started at the end of the 16th century by Pope Sixtus V and continued until Pius X stopped it in the early 20th century.

❿ Scuderie del Quirinale

Via 24 Maggio 16. **Map** 5 B4. **Tel** 06-3996 7500. 🚌 H, 40, 60, 64, 70, 170. **Open** for exhibitions 10am–8pm Mon–Thu, 10am–10:30pm Fri & Sat, 10am–9pm Sun. 🌐 scuderiequirinale.it

The Scuderie started life as stables for the nearby Palazzo del Quirinale. Built in the early 1700s by Ferdinando Fuga over the remains of the ancient Temple of Serapis, the stables were remodelled by Gae Aulenti at the end of the 20th century and now house some of the best temporary art exhibitions in the country.

Self-portrait by Lavinia Fontana in the Accademia Nazionale di San Luca

The magnificent altar at Sant'Andrea al Quirinale

⓫ Sant'Andrea al Quirinale

Via del Quirinale 29. **Map** 5 B3.
Tel 06-487 4565. 🚌 116, 117 and routes to Via del Tritone. **Open** 8:30am–noon, 2:30–6pm Tue–Sat, 9am–noon, 2:30–6pm Sun. ✝ ♿

Known as the "Pearl of the Baroque" because of its beautiful roseate marble interior, Sant'Andrea was designed by Bernini and executed by his assistants between 1658 and 1670. It was built for the Jesuits, hence the many IHS emblems (*Iesus Hominum Salvator* – Jesus Saviour of Mankind).

The site for the church was wide but shallow, so Bernini pointed the long axis of his oval plan not towards the altar, but towards the sides; he then leads the eye round to the altar end. Here Bernini ordered works of art in various media which function not in isolation, but together. The crucified St Andrew (Sant'Andrea) of the altarpiece looks up at a stucco version of himself, who in turn ascends towards the lantern and the Holy Spirit.

The rooms of St Stanislas Kostka in the adjacent convent should not be missed. The quarters of the Jesuit novice, who died in 1568 at the age of 19, reflect not his own spartan taste, but the richer style of the 17th-century Jesuits. The Polish saint has been brilliantly immortalized in marble by Pierre Legros (1666–1719).

⓬ San Carlo alle Quattro Fontane

Via del Quirinale 23. **Map** 5 B3.
Tel 06-488 3261. 🚌 116, 117 & routes to Piazza Barberini. Ⓜ Barberini.
Open 10am–1pm, 3–6pm Mon–Fri (mornings only Jul & Aug); 10am–1pm Sat, 10am–1pm Sun. ✝

In 1634, the Trinitarians, a Spanish order whose role was to pay the ransom of Christian hostages to the Arabs, commissioned Borromini to design a church and convent at the Quattro Fontane crossroads. The church, so small it would fit inside one of the piers of St Peter's, is also known as "San Carlino".

Although dedicated to Carlo Borromeo, the 16th-century Milanese cardinal canonized in 1620, San Carlo is as much a monument to Borromini. Both the façade and interior employ bold curves that give light and life to a small, cramped site. The oval dome and tiny lantern are particularly ingenious. The undulating lines of the façade are decorated with angels and a statue of San Carlo. Finished in 1667, the façade is one of Borromini's very last works.

There are further delights in the playful inverted shapes in the cloister and the stucco work in the refectory (now the sacristy), which houses a painting of San Carlo by Orazio Borgianni (1611).

In a small room off the sacristy hangs a portrait of Borromini himself wearing the Trinitarian cross. Borromini committed suicide in 1667, and in the crypt (which is now open to the public) a small curved chapel reserved for him remains empty.

Dome of San Carlo alle Quattro Fontane, lit by concealed windows

Fountain of Strength (or Juno)

⓭ Le Quattro Fontane

Intersection of Via delle Quattro Fontane and Via del Quirinale. **Map** 5 B3. 🚌 Routes to Piazza Barberini or Via Nazionale. Ⓜ Barberini.

These four small fountains are attached to the corners of the buildings at the intersection of two narrow, busy streets. They date from the great redevelopment of Rome in the reign of Sixtus V (1585–90). Each fountain has a statue of a reclining deity. The river god accompanied by the she-wolf is clearly the Tiber; the other male figure may be the Arno. The female figures represent Strength and Fidelity or the goddesses Juno and Diana.

The crossroads is at the highest point of the Quirinal hill and commands splendid views of three distant landmark obelisks: those placed by Sixtus V in front of Santa Maria Maggiore and Trinità dei Monti, and the one that stands in Piazza del Quirinale.

⓮ Moses Fountain

Fontana dell'Acqua Felice, Piazza San Bernardo. **Map** 5 C2. 🚌 36, 60, 61, 62, 492. Ⓜ Repubblica.

Officially known as the Fontana dell'Acqua Felice, this fountain owes its popular name to the grotesque statue of Moses in the central niche. The massive structure with its three elegant arches was designed by Domenico Fontana to mark the terminal of the Acqua Felice aqueduct, so called because it was one of the many great improvements commissioned by Felice Peretti, Pope Sixtus V. Completed in 1587, it brought clean piped water to this quarter of Rome for the first time.

The notorious statue of Moses striking water from the rock is larger than life and the proportions of the body are obviously wrong. Sculpted either by Prospero Bresciano or Leonardo Sormani, it is a clumsy attempt at recreating the awesome appearance of Michelangelo's *Moses* in the church of San Pietro in Vincoli *(see p172)*. As soon as it was unveiled, it was said to be frowning at having been brought into the world by such an inept sculptor. The side reliefs also illustrate water

Fontana's Moses Fountain

stories from the Old Testament: Aaron leading the Israelites to water and Joshua pointing the army towards the Red Sea. The fountain's four lions are copies of Egyptian originals (now in the Vatican Museums), which Sixtus V had put there for the public's "convenience" and "delight".

Gold coin with head of the Emperor Diocletian (AD 285–305)

⓯ Santa Maria degli Angeli e dei Martiri

Piazza della Repubblica. **Map** 5 C3. **Tel** 06-488 0812. 🚌 36, 60, 61, 62, 64, 90, 116, 170, 492, 910. Ⓜ Repubblica, Termini. **Open** 7am–6:30pm Mon–Sat, 7am–7:30pm Sun. 🕆 ♿ 📷

Parts of the ruined Baths of Diocletian *(right)* provided building material and setting for this church, constructed by Michelangelo in 1563. The church was so altered in the 18th century that it has lost most of its original character.

An exhibition in the sacristy gives a detailed account of Michelangelo's original design.

Fidelity (or Diana) with her attendant dog, one of the Quattro Fontane

Part of the Museo Nazionale Romano in the Baths of Diocletian

ⓖ Museo Nazionale Romano (Palazzo Massimo)

Palazzo Massimo, Largo di Villa Peretti 1. **Map** 6 D3. **Tel** 06-3996 7700. 36, 38, 40, 64, 170, H and other routes to Piazza dei Cinquecento. M Repubblica, Termini. **Open** 9am–7:45pm Tue–Sun (last adm: 6:45pm). **Closed** 1 Jan, 25 Dec. (the biglietto cumulativo gives entry to the museum's five branches).

Founded in 1889, the Museo Nazionale Romano holds most of the antiquities found in Rome since 1870 as well as pre-existing collections, and is one of the world's leading museums of Classical art. It now has five branches: its original site, occupying part of the Baths of Diocletian; the Palazzo Massimo; the Palazzo Altemps (see p129); the Aula Ottagona (near the Baths of Diocletian); and Crypta Balbi at Via delle Botteghe Oscure 31, excavated from the foyer of the theatre of Balbus (1st century BC) and housing findings from medieval Rome.

The Palazzo Massimo, built in 1883–7 on the site of a villa

which belonged to Sixtus V, used to be a Jesuit college. In 1981–97 it was restored to house a significant proportion of the museum's collections. The exhibits, contained on four floors, are originals dating from the 2nd century BC to the end of the 4th century AD.

The basement contains an excellent display of ancient coins, precious artifacts and the only mummified child to be found in the ancient city. The ground floor is devoted to Roman statuary, with funeral monuments in Room 2 and Emperor Augustus in Pontifex Maximus guise in Room 5. Upstairs there are statues from Nero's summer villa in Anzio and Roman copies of famous Greek originals, such as the *Discobolos Ex-Lancellotti*.

The real joy of the museum, however, is on the second floor, where entire rooms of wall paintings have been brought from various villas excavated in and around Rome. The most incredible frescoes are from Livia's Villa at Prima Porta. Her *triclinium* (dining room) was decorated with an abundance of trees, plants and fruit, painted in a totally naturalistic style to fool guests that they were eating alfresco, rather than indoors. Oaks, pine trees

and cypresses, oleanders, roses, poppies and irises are all clearly distinguishable. Other marvels include rooms brought from the first Villa Farnesina: the children's room has a mainly white design, while the adults' bedroom is red, complete with erotic paintings. Equally impressive is the display of mosaics on the same floor.

ⓗ Baths of Diocletian

Terme di Diocleziano, Viale E de Nicola 79. **Map** 6 D3. **Tel** 06-3996 7700. 36, 60, 61, 62, 90. M Repubblica, Termini. **Open** 9am–7:30pm Tue–Sun (last adm: 6:45pm). **Closed** 1 Jan, 25 Dec. (the biglietto cumulativo gives entry to the museum's five branches).

Built in AD 298–306 under the infamous Emperor Diocletian, who murdered thousands of Christians, the baths (see pp26–7) were the most extensive in Rome and could accommodate up to 3,000 bathers at a time.

Part of the Museo Nazionale Romano, the complex houses a vast collection of Roman statues and inscriptions and incorporates the former Carthusian monastery of Santa Maria degli Angeli, which has a beautiful cloister designed by Michelangelo.

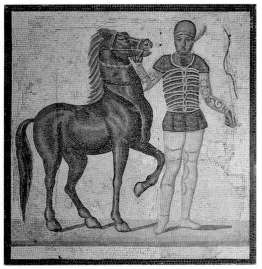

One of the Quattro Aurighe mosaics, Museo Nazionale Romano

⓲ Piazza della Repubblica

Map 5 C3. 🚌 36, 60, 61, 62, 64, 90, 170, 492, 646, 910. Ⓜ Repubblica.

Romans often refer to the piazza by its old name, Piazza Esedra, so called because it follows the shape of an *exedra* (a semicircular recess) that was part of the Baths of Diocletian. The piazza was included in the great redevelopment undertaken when Rome became capital of a unified Italy. Under its sweeping 19th-century colonnades there were once elegant shops, but they have been ousted by banks, travel agencies and cafés.

In the middle of the piazza stands the Fontana delle Naiadi. Mario Rutelli's four naked bronze nymphs caused something of a scandal when they were unveiled in 1901. Each reclines on an aquatic creature symbolizing water in its various forms: a sea-horse for the oceans, a water snake for rivers, a swan for lakes, and a curious frilled lizard for subterranean streams. The figure in the middle, added in 1911, is

Piazza della Repubblica and the Fontana delle Naiadi

of the sea god Glaucus, who represents man victorious over the hostile forces of nature.

⓳ Palazzo delle Esposizioni

Via Nazionale 194. **Map** 5 B4. **Tel** 06-3996 7500. 🚌 40, 60, 64, 70, 116T, 170. **Open** 10am–8pm Tue–Thu, 10am–10:30pm Fri & Sat, 10am–8pm Sun. 🎫 ♿ from Via Piacenza or Via Milano 13 entrance. ✏ 🖥 📷 W **palazzoesposizioni.it**

Façade of the Palazzo delle Esposizioni

This grandiose building, with wide steps, Corinthian columns and statues, was designed as an exhibition centre by the architect Pio Piacentini and built by the city of Rome in 1882 during the reign of Umberto I.

The main entrance looks like a triumphal arch.

The restored palazzo is still used to house high-profile exhibitions of contemporary art. The exhibitions are changed every three to six months and include a variety of sculpture and paintings. Live performances, films and lectures also take place here (*see p352*). Foreign films are usually shown in the original language.

⓴ Santa Maria dei Monti

Via Madonna dei Monti 41. **Map** 5 B4. **Tel** 06-485 531. 🚌 75, 117. Ⓜ Cavour. **Open** 7am–noon, 4:30–7:30pm daily. 🚻 ♿

Designed by Giacomo della Porta, this church, dating from 1580, has a particularly splendid dome. Over the high altar is a stunning medieval painting of the Madonna dei Monti, patroness of this quarter of Rome. The altar in the left transept houses the tomb and effigy of the unworldly French saint Benoît-Joseph Labre, who died here in 1783, having spent his life as a solitary pilgrim. He slept rough in the ruins of the Colosseum, gave away any charitable gifts he received, and came regularly to worship. His faith could not sustain his body: still in his mid-thirties, he collapsed and died outside the church. The foul rags he wore are preserved.

One of the bronze nymphs of the fountain in Piazza della Repubblica

㉑ Sant'Agata dei Goti

Via Mazzarino 16 and Via Panisperna 29. **Map** 5 B4. **Tel** 06-4893 0456. 🚌 40, 60, 64, 70, 71, 117, 170. **Open** 7am–1pm & 4–7pm daily. 🏠 ♿

The Goths (*Goti*) who gave their name to this church occupied Rome in the 6th century AD. They were Aryan heretics who denied the divinity of Christ. The church was founded between AD 462 and 470, shortly before the main Gothic invasions, and the beautiful granite columns date from this period. The main altar has a well-preserved 12th-century Cosmatesque tabernacle, but the most delightful part of the church is the charming 18th-century courtyard built around an ivy-draped well.

㉒ Villa Aldobrandini

Via Panisperna. Entrance to gardens: Via Mazzarino 1. **Map** 5 B4. 🚌 40, 60, 64, 70, 71, 117, 170. Gardens: **Open** dawn–dusk daily. Villa: **Closed** to the public.

Built in the 16th century for the Dukes of Urbino and acquired for his family by Pope Clement VIII Aldobrandini (reigned 1592–1605), the villa is now government property and houses an international law library.

The villa itself, decorated with the family's six-starred coat of arms, is closed to the public, but the gardens and terraces, hidden behind a high wall that runs along Via Nazionale, can be reached through an iron

18th-century courtyard of Sant'Agata dei Goti

gate in Via Mazzarino. Steps lead up past 2nd-century AD ruins into the gardens, highly recommended as an oasis of tranquillity in the centre of the city. Gravel paths lead between formal lawns and clearly marked specimen trees, and benches are provided for the weary. Since the garden is raised some 10 m (30 ft) above street level, the views are excellent.

㉓ Santi Domenico e Sisto

Largo Angelicum 1. **Map** 5 B4. **Tel** 06-670 2201. 🚌 40, 60, 64, 70, 71 117, 170. **Open** 3–6pm Sat.

The church has a tall, slender Baroque façade rising above a steep flight of steps. This divides into two curving flights that sweep up to the terrace in front of the entrance. The pediment of the façade is crowned by eight flaming candlesticks.

The interior has a vaulted ceiling with a large fresco of *The Apotheosis of St Dominic* by Domenico Canuti (1620–84). The first chapel on the right was decorated by Bernini, who

may also have designed the sculpture of Mary Magdalene meeting the risen Christ in the Garden of Gethsemane. This fine marble group was executed by Antonio Raggi (1649). Above the altar is a 15th-century terracotta plaque of the Virgin and Child. On the left, over a side altar, is a large painting of the Madonna from the same period, attributed to Benozzo Gozzoli (1420–97), a pupil of Fra Angelico.

Chapel in Santi Domenico e Sisto

The imposing façade of Villa Aldobrandini

S. PP. IIII·

ESQUILINE

The Esquiline is the largest and highest of Rome's seven hills. In Imperial Rome the western slopes overlooking the Forum housed the crowded slums of the Suburra. On the eastern side there were a few villas belonging to wealthy citizens like Maecenas, patron of the arts and adviser to Augustus. The essential character of the place has persisted through two millennia; it is still one of the poorer quarters of the city.

The area is now heavily built up, except for a rather seedy park on the Colle Oppio, a smaller hill to the south of the Esquiline, where you can see the remains of the Baths of Titus, the Baths of Trajan and Nero's Domus Aurea. The area's main interest, however, lies in its churches. Many of these were founded on the sites of private houses where Christians met to worship secretly in the days when their religion was banned.

Sights at a Glance

Churches
1 San Martino ai Monti
2 San Pietro in Vincoli
3 Santa Pudenziana
4 *Santa Maria Maggiore pp174–5*
5 Santa Prassede
7 Santa Bibiana

Museums
9 Museo Nazionale d'Arte Orientale

Historic Piazzas
8 Piazza Vittorio Emanuele II

Ancient Sites
10 Auditorium of Maecenas
11 Sette Sale
12 Domus Aurea

Arches
6 Arch of Gallienus

See also Street Finder maps 5, 6, 9

Restaurants
see pp310–11
1 Agata e Romeo
2 Cuoco e Camicia
3 Da Danilo
4 La Gallina Bianca
5 Hang Zhou
6 Tempio di Iside
7 Trattoria Monti

| 0 metres | 300 |
| 0 yards | 300 |

◀ Detail from the apse mosaic at Santa Maria Maggiore

For keys to symbols *see back flap*

Street-by-Street: The Esquiline Hill

The sight that draws most people to this rather scruffy part of Rome is the great basilica of Santa Maria Maggiore. But it is also well worth searching out some of the smaller churches on the Esquiline: Santa Pudenziana and Santa Prassede with their celebrated mosaics, and San Pietro in Vincoli, home to one of Michelangelo's most famous sculptures. To the south, in the Colle Oppio park, are the scattered remains of the Baths of Trajan.

❸ Santa Pudenziana
The apse of this ancient church has a magnificent 4th-century mosaic of Christ surrounded by the Apostles.

Piazza dell'Esquilino was furnished with an obelisk in 1587 by Pope Sixtus V. This helped to guide pilgrims coming from the north to the important church of Santa Maria Maggiore.

❷ ★ San Pietro in Vincoli
The church's treasures include Michelangelo's *Moses* and the chains that bound St Peter.

To the Colosseum

The Baths of Trajan (AD 109) were the first to be built on the massive scale later used in the Baths of Diocletian and of Caracalla.

The Torre dei Capocci, a restored medieval tower, is one of the area's most distinctive landmarks.

PIAZZA ESO

VIA CAVOUR

VIA DEI QUATTRO CANTONI

VIA SFORZA

VIA GIOVANNI LANZA

PIAZZA SAN MARTINO AI MON

VIA IN SELCI

PIAZZA DI SAN PIETRO IN VINCOLI

VIALE DEL MONTE OPPIO

❹ ★ Santa Maria Maggiore
This imposing rear façade was added by Baroque architect Carlo Rainaldi in 1673. Santa Maria's interior is one of the most richly decorated in Rome.

Locator Map
See Central Rome Map pp16–17

The Tomb of Pius V
(died 1572) by Domenico Fontana stands in this less well-known Sistine Chapel, under the northeast dome of Santa Maria Maggiore.

VIA DELL' ESQUILINO

PIAZZA DI SANTA MARIA MAGGIORE

VIA CARLO ALBERTO

VIA MERULANA

To Vittorio
Emanuele Metro

❻ Arch of Gallienus
This was built in the 3rd century AD to replace an entrance in the old Servian Wall.

❺ ★ Santa Prassede
The 9th-century mosaics in the Chapel of San Zeno are among the finest in Rome.

❶ San Martino ai Monti
The frescoes include 17th-century Roman landscapes and scenes from the life of Elijah by Gaspare Dughet.

Key
— Suggested route

| 0 metres | | 75 |
| 0 yards | | 75 |

Fresco of old San Giovanni in Laterano in San Martino ai Monti

❶ San Martino ai Monti

Viale del Monte Oppio 28. **Map** 6 D5.
Tel 06-478 4701. ▦ 16, 714.
Ⓜ Cavour, Vittorio Emanuele.
Open 7.30am–noon, 4–7pm daily.
🚹 ♿

Christians have been worshipping on the site of this church since the 3rd century, when they used to meet in the house of a man named Equitius. In the 4th century, after Constantine had legalized Christianity, Pope Sylvester I built a church, one of the very few things he did during his pontificate. In fact he was so insignificant that in the 5th century a more exciting life was fabricated for him – which included tales of him converting Constantine, curing him of leprosy and forcing him to close all pagan temples. Pope Sylvester's fictional life was further enhanced in the 8th century, with the forgery of a document in which Constantine offered him the Imperial crown.

Pope Sylvester's church was replaced in about AD 500 by St Symmachus, rebuilt in the 9th century and then transformed completely in the 1630s. The only immediate signs of its age are the ancient Corinthian columns dividing the nave and aisles. The most interesting interior features are a series of frescoed landscapes of the countryside around Rome (*campagna*

romana) by the 17th-century French artist Gaspare Dughet, Poussin's brother-in-law, in the right aisle. The frescoes by Filippo Gagliardi, at either end of the left aisle, show old St Peter's and the interior of San Giovanni in Laterano before Borromini's redesign. If you can find the sacristan, you can go beneath the church to see the remains of Equitius's house.

❷ San Pietro in Vincoli

Piazza di San Pietro in Vincoli 4A.
Map 5 C5. **Tel** 06-9784 4950.
▦ 75, 117. Ⓜ Cavour, Colosseo.
Open 8am–12.30pm, 3–7pm (Oct–Mar: until 6pm) daily. 🚹 ♿ 📷

According to tradition, the two chains (*vincoli*) used to shackle St Peter while he was being held in the depths of

Reliquary with St Peter's chains

the Mamertine Prison (*see p93*) were subsequently taken to Constantinople. In the 5th century, Empress Eudoxia deposited one in a church in Constantinople and sent the other to her daughter Eudoxia in Rome. She in turn gave hers to Pope Leo I, who had this church built to house it. Some years later the second chain was brought to Rome, where it linked miraculously with its partner.

The chains are still here, displayed below the high altar, but the church is now best known for Michelangelo's *Tomb of Pope Julius II*. When it was commissioned in 1505, Michelangelo spent eight months searching for perfect blocks of marble at Carrara in Tuscany, but Pope Julius became more interested in the building of a new St Peter's and the project was laid aside. After the pope's death in 1513, Michelangelo resumed work on the tomb, but had only finished the statues of *Moses* and *The Dying Slaves* when Pope Paul III persuaded him to start work on the Sistine Chapel's *Last Judgment*. Michelangelo had planned a vast monument with over 40 statues, but the tomb that was built – mainly by his pupils – is simply a façade with six niches for statues. *The Dying Slaves* are in Paris and Florence, but the tremendous bearded *Moses* is here. The horns on Moses's head should really be beams of light – they are the result of the original Hebrew from the Old Testament being wrongly translated.

Michelangelo's *Moses* in San Pietro in Vincoli

❸ Santa Pudenziana

Via Urbana 160. **Map** 5 C4.
Tel 06-481 4622. 🚌 16, 75, 105, 714.
Ⓜ Cavour. **Open** 8:30am–noon,
3–6pm daily. 🛉

Churches tend to be dedicated to existing saints, but in this case, the church, through a linguistic accident, created a brand new saint. In the 1st century AD a Roman senator called Pudens lived here, and, according to legend, allowed St Peter to lodge with him. In the 2nd century a bath house was built on this site and in the 4th century a church was established inside the baths, known as the *Ecclesia Pudentiana* (the church of Pudens). In time it was assumed that "Pudentiana" was a woman's name and a life was created for her – she became the sister of Prassede and was credited with caring for Christian victims of persecution. In 1969 both saints were declared invalid, though their churches both kept their names.

The 19th-century façade of the church retains an 11th-century frieze depicting both Prassede and Pudenziana dressed as crowned Byzantine empresses. The apse has a remarkable 4th-century mosaic, clearly influenced by Classical pagan art in its use of subtle colours. The Apostles are

Apse mosaics in Santa Prassede, showing the saint with St Paul

represented as Roman senators in togas but a clumsy attempt at restoration in the 16th century destroyed two of the Apostles and left other figures without legs.

❹ Santa Maria Maggiore

See pp174–5.

❺ Santa Prassede

Via Santa Prassede 9A. **Map** 6 D4.
Tel 06-488 2456. 🚌 16, 70, 71, 75, 714. Ⓜ Vittorio Emanuele.
Open 7am–noon, 4–6:30pm daily (from 7:30am Sun; Aug: pm only). 🛉 ♿

The church was founded by Pope Paschal II in the 9th century, on the site of a 2nd-century oratory. Although the interior has been altered and rebuilt, the structure of the original design of the 9th-century church is clearly visible. Its three aisles are separated by rows of granite

Nineteenth-century façade of the ancient church of Santa Pudenziana

columns. In the central nave, there is a round stone slab covering the well where, according to legend, Santa Prassede is said to have buried the remains of 2,000 martyrs.

Artists from Byzantium decorated the church with glittering, jewel-coloured mosaics. Those in the apse and choir depict stylized white-robed elders, the haloed elect looking down from the gold and blue walls of heaven, spindly legged lambs, feather-mop palm trees and bright red poppies.

In the apse, Santa Prassede and Santa Pudenziana stand on either side of Christ, with the fatherly arms of St Paul and St Peter on their shoulders. Beautiful mosaics of saints, the Virgin and Christ, and the Apostles also cover the walls and vault of the Chapel of St Zeno, built as a mausoleum for Pope Paschal's mother, Theodora. Part of a column brought back from Jerusalem, allegedly the one to which Christ was bound and flogged, also stands here.

❹ Santa Maria Maggiore

Of all the great Roman basilicas, Santa Maria has the most successful blend of different architectural styles. Its colonnaded nave is part of the original 5th-century building. The Cosmatesque marble floor and delightful Romanesque bell tower, with its blue ceramic roundels, are medieval. The Renaissance saw a new coffered ceiling, and the Baroque gave the church twin domes and its imposing front and rear façades. The mosaics are Santa Maria's most famous feature. From the 5th century come the biblical scenes in the aisle and the spectacular mosaics on the triumphal arch. Medieval highlights include a 13th-century enthroned Christ in the loggia.

Obelisk in Piazza dell'Esquilino
The Egyptian obelisk was erected by Pope Sixtus V in 1587 as a landmark for pilgrims.

★ **Cappella Paolina**
Flaminio Ponzio designed this richly decorated chapel (1611) for Pope Paul V Borghese.

Coffered Ceiling
The gilded ceiling, possibly by Giuliano da Sangallo, was a gift of Alexander VI Borgia at the end of the 15th century. The gold is said to be the first brought from America by Columbus.

356 Virgin appears to Pope Liberius

Pope Gregory VII

1347 Cola di Rienzo crowned Tribune of Rome in Santa Maria Maggiore

1673 Carlo Rainaldi rebuilds apse

300 AD	600	900	1200	1500

432–40 Sixtus III completes church

420 Probable founding date

1075 Pope Gregory VII kidnapped by opponents while saying Christmas mass in Santa Maria

Coat of arms of Gregory VII

1288–92 Nicholas IV adds apse and transepts

1743 Ferdinando Fuga adds main façade on orders of Benedict XIV

★ Coronation of the Virgin Mosaic
This is the central image of a series of wonderful apse mosaics of the Virgin by Jacopo Torriti (1295).

Baldacchino (1740s)
Its columns of red porphyry and bronze were the work of Ferdinando Fuga.

★ Tomb of Cardinal Rodriguez
The Gothic tomb (1299) contains magnificent Cosmatesque marblework.

★ Cappella Sistina
This Sistine Chapel was built for Pope Sixtus V (1584–7) by Domenico Fontana and houses his tomb.

Column in Piazza Santa Maria Maggiore
A bronze of the Virgin and Child was added to this ancient marble column in 1615. The column came from the Basilica of Constantine in the Forum.

Legend of the Snow

In 356, Pope Liberius had a dream in which the Virgin told him to build a church on the spot where he found snow. When it fell on the Esquiline, on the morning of 5 August in the middle of a baking Roman summer, he naturally obeyed. The miracle of the snow is commemorated each year by a service during which thousands of white petals float down from the ceiling of Santa Maria. Originally roses were used, but nowadays the petals are more usually taken from dahlias.

❻ Arch of Gallienus

Via Carlo Alberto. **Map** 6 D4.
🚌 16, 71, 714. Ⓜ Vittorio Emanuele.

Squashed between two
buildings just off Via Carlo
Alberto is the central arch of
an originally three-arched
gate erected in memory of
Emperor Gallienus, who was
assassinated by his Illyrian
officers in AD 262. It was built
on the site of the old Esquiline
Gate in the Servian Wall, parts
of which are visible nearby.

Roman ruins at the centre of Piazza Vittoria Emanuele II

Arch erected in memory of
Emperor Gallienus

❼ Santa Bibiana

Via Giovanni Giolitti 154. **Map** 6
F4. **Tel** 06-446 5235. 🚌 71.
🚊 5, 14. Ⓜ Vittorio Emanuele.
Open 7:30–10am, 4:30–7:30pm
Mon–Sat; 7:30am–12:30pm,
4:30–7:30pm Sun. 🕇 ♿

The deceptively simple
façade of Santa Bibiana
was Bernini's first foray into
architecture. It is a clean,
economic design with
superimposed pilasters and
deeply shadowed archways.
The church itself was built
on the site of the palace
belonging to Bibiana's
family. This is where the
saint was buried after being
flogged to death with
leaded cords during
the brief persecution
of the Christians in
the reign of Julian the
Apostate (361–3). Just

inside the church is a small
column against which Bibiana
is said to have been whipped.
Her remains, along with those
of her mother Dafrosa and her
sister Demetria, who also suffered
martyrdom, are preserved in an
alabaster urn below the altar.
In a niche above the altar stands
a statue of Santa Bibiana by
Bernini – the first fully clothed
figure he ever sculpted. He depicts
her standing beside a column,
holding the cords with which
she was whipped, apparently
on the verge of a deadly swoon.

Early sculpture by Bernini of the martyr
Santa Bibiana (1626)

❽ Piazza Vittorio Emanuele II

Map 6 E5. 🚌 4, 9, 71. 🚊 5, 14.
Ⓜ Vittorio Emanuele.

Piazza Vittorio, as it is called for
short, was once one of the city's
main open-air food markets.
The market has moved around
the corner to new, covered
premises and is now called Nuovo
Mercato Esquilino *(see p344)*.
The arcaded square was built
in the urban development
undertaken after the unification
of Italy in 1861. It was named after
Italy's first king, but there is nothing
regal about its appearance today.
However, the garden area in the
centre of the square has been
restored. It contains a number of
mysterious ruins, including a large
mound, part of a Roman fountain
from the 3rd century AD and the
Porta Magica, a curious 17th-
century doorway inscribed with
alchemical signs and formulae.

❾ Museo Nazionale d'Arte Orientale

Via Merulana 248. **Map** 6 D5.
Tel 06-4697 4832. 🚌 16, 70, 71,
714. Ⓜ Vittorio Emanuele.
Open 9am–2pm Tue, Wed & Fri;
9am–7:30pm Thu, Sat & Sun. 🖼 ♿
🌐 **museoorientale.beniculturali.it**

The museum occupies part of
the late 19th-century Palazzo
Brancaccio, home of the Italian
Institute of the Middle and Far
East since 1957. The collection
ranges from prehistoric Iranian
ceramics, sculpture from
Afghanistan, Nepal, Kashmir
and India to 18th-century
Tibetan paintings on vellum.

From the Far East there are collections of Japanese screen paintings and Chinese jade.

The most unusual exhibits are the finds from the Italian excavation of the ancient civilization of Swat in northeast Pakistan. This fascinating Gandhara culture lasted from the 3rd century BC to about the 10th century AD. Its wonderfully exotic, sensual reliefs show an unusual combination of Hellenistic, Buddhist and Hindu influences.

Nepalese Bodhisattva in the Museo Nazionale d'Arte Orientale

⑩ Auditorium of Maecenas

Largo Leopardi 2. **Map** 6 D5.
Tel 06-0608. 16, 714. Vittorio Emanuele. **Open** by appt; phone in advance.

Maecenas, a fop, gourmet and patron of the arts, was also an astute adviser and colleague of the Emperor Augustus. Fabulously rich, he created a fantastic villa and gardens on the Esquiline hill, most of which has long disappeared beneath the modern city. The partially reconstructed auditorium, isolated on a traffic island, is all that remains.

Inside, a semicircle of tiered seats suggests that it may have been a place for readings and performances. If it was, then Maecenas would have been entertained here by his protégés, the lyric poet Horace and Virgil, author of the *Aeneid*, reading their latest works.

However, water ducts have also been discovered and it may well have been a *nympheum* – a kind of summerhouse – with fountains. Traces of frescoes remain on the walls: you can make out garden scenes and a procession of miniature figures – including one of a characteristically drunken Dionysus (the Greek god of wine) being propped upright by a satyr.

⑪ Sette Sale

Via delle Terme di Traiano. **Map** 5 C5.
Tel 06-0608. 85, 87, 117, 186, 810, 850. 3. Colosseo. **Open** by appt; phone in advance.

Not far from Nero's Domus Aurea is the cistern of the Sette Sale. It was built here to supply the enormous quantities of water needed for the Baths of Trajan. These were built for Emperor Trajan in AD 104 on parts of the Domus Aurea that had been damaged by a fire.

A set of stairs leads down into the cistern, well below street level. There is not much to see here now, but a walk through the huge, echoing cistern where light rays illuminate the watery surfaces is still an evocative experience. The nine sections, 30 m (98 ft) long and 5 m (16 ft) wide, had a capacity of eight million litres.

⑫ Domus Aurea

Viale della Domus Aurea. **Map** 5 C5.
Tel 06-3996 7700. 85, 87, 117, 186, 810, 850. 3. Colosseo. **Open** for guided tours on weekends only; phone in advance.

After allegedly setting fire to Rome in AD 64, Nero decided to build himself an outrageous new palace. The Domus Aurea (sometimes called Nero's Golden House) occupied part of the Palatine and most of the Celian and Esquiline hills – an area approximately 25 times the size of the Colosseum. The vestibule on the Palatine side of the complex contained a colossal gilded statue of Nero. There was an artificial lake, with

gardens and woods where imported wild beasts were allowed to roam free. According to Suetonius in his *Life of Nero*, the palace walls were adorned with gold and mother-of-pearl, rooms had ceilings that showered guests with flowers or perfumes, the dining hall rotated and the baths were fed with both sulphurous water and sea water.

Tacitus described Nero's debauched garden parties, with banquets served on barges and lakeside brothels serviced by aristocratic women. Since Nero killed himself in AD 68, however, he did not have long to enjoy his new home.

Nero's successors, anxious to distance themselves from the monster-emperor, did their utmost to erase all traces of the palace. Vespasian drained the lake and built the Colosseum (*see pp94–7*) in its place, Titus and Trajan each erected a complex of baths over the palace, and Hadrian placed the Temple of Venus and Rome (*see p89*) over the vestibule.

Rooms from one wing of the palace have survived, buried beneath the ruins of the Baths of Trajan on the Oppian hill. Excavations have revealed large frescoes and mosaics which are thought to be a panorama of Rome from a bird's-eye perspective.

Visitors are advised to bring a jacket as the temperature inside the building is around 10°C (50°F).

Frescoed room in the ruins of the Domus Aurea

LATERAN

In the Middle Ages the Lateran Palace was the residence of the popes, and the Basilica of San Giovanni beside it rivalled St Peter's in splendour. After the return of the popes from Avignon at the end of the 14th century, the area declined in importance. Pilgrims still continued to visit San Giovanni and Santa Croce in Gerusalemme, but the area remained sparsely inhabited. Ancient convents were situated amid gardens and vineyards until Rome became capital of Italy in 1870 and a network of residential streets was laid out here to house the influx of newcomers. Archaeological interest lies chiefly in the Aurelian Wall and the ruins of the Aqueduct of Nero.

Sights at a Glance

Churches
1 San Giovanni in Laterano pp182–3
5 Santa Croce in Gerusalemme
11 Santi Quattro Coronati
12 San Clemente pp188–9
13 Santo Stefano Rotondo

Shrines
2 Scala Santa and Sancta Sanctorum

Arches and Gates
3 Porta Asinaria
7 Porta Maggiore

Ancient Sites
4 Amphiteatrum Castrense
8 Baker's Tomb
9 Aqueduct of Nero and the Freedmen's Tombs

Museums
6 Museum of Musical Instruments
10 Museo Storico della Liberazione di Roma

See also Street Finder maps 6, 9, 10

Restaurants
see pp310–11
1 Aroma
2 Bibenda
3 Charly's Saucière
4 I Clementini
5 Il Pentagrappolo
6 La Tavena dei Quaranta

0 metres 300
0 yards 300

◀ The impressive interior of the Basilica of San Clemente

For keys to symbols see back flap

Street-by-Street: Piazza di San Giovanni

Both the Basilica of San Giovanni and the Lateran Palace look out over a huge open area, the Piazza di San Giovanni, laid out at the end of the 16th century with an Egyptian obelisk, the oldest in Rome, in the centre. Sadly the traffic streaming in and out of the city through Porta San Giovanni tends to detract from its grandeur. Across the square is the building housing the Scala Santa (the Holy Staircase), one of the most revered relics in Rome and the goal for many pilgrims. The area is also a venue for political rallies, and the feast of St John on 24 June is celebrated with a fair at which Romans consume roast *porchetta (see p61)*.

The Chapel of Santa Rufina, originally the portico of the baptistry, has a 5th-century mosaic of spiralling foliage in the apse.

VIA DI SAN STEFANO ROTO

VIA DELL'AMBA ARADAM

VIA DEI LATERANI

The Cloister of San Giovanni fortunately survived the two fires that destroyed the early basilica. A 13th-century masterpiece of mosaic work, the cloister now houses fragments from the medieval basilica.

Key

— Suggested route

0 metres   75
0 yards   75

The Chapel of San Venanzio is decorated with a series of 7th-century mosaics on a gold background. This detail from the apse shows one of the angels flanking the central figure of Christ. San Venanzio was an accomplished 6th-century Latin poet.

Piazza di San Giovanni in Laterano boasts an ancient obelisk and parts of Nero's Aqueduct. This 18th-century painting by Canaletto shows how the piazza once looked.

Locator Map
See Central Rome Map pp16–17

The Lateran Palace, residence of the popes until 1309, was rebuilt by Domenico Fontana in 1586.

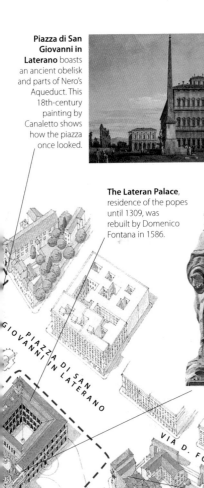

PIAZZA DI SAN GIOVANNI IN LATERANO

VIA D. FONTANA

PIAZZA DI PORTA SAN GIOVANNI

❶ ★ San Giovanni in Laterano
Borromini's interior dates from the 17th century, but the grand façade by Alessandro Galilei, with its giant statues of Christ and the Apostles, was added in 1735.

❷ Scala Santa
This door at the top of the Holy Staircase leads to the Sancta Sanctorum.

❸ Porta Asinaria
This minor gateway, no longer in use, is as old as the Aurelian Wall, dating back to the 3rd century AD.

The Triclinio Leoniano is a piece of wall and a mosaic from the dining hall of the 8th-century Pope Leo III.

❶ San Giovanni in Laterano

Early in the 4th century, the Laterani family were disgraced and their land taken by Emperor Constantine to build Rome's first Christian basilica. Today's church retains the original shape, but has been destroyed by fire twice and rebuilt several times. Borromini undertook the last major rebuild of the interior in 1646, and the main façade is an 18th-century addition. Before the pope's move to Avignon in 1309, the adjoining Lateran Palace was the official papal residence, and until 1870 all popes were crowned in the church. This is the city's main cathedral, and the seat of the Bishop of Rome, the pope, who celebrates Maundy Thursday Mass here and attends the annual blessing of the people.

★ **Baptistry**
Though much restored, the domed baptistry dates back to Constantine's time. It assumed its present octagonal shape in AD 432 and the design has served as the model for baptistries throughout the Christian world.

Entrance to museum

KEY

① **Apse**

② **The Chapel of San Venanzio** is attached to the baptistry and is decorated with 7th-century mosaics.

③ **The original Lateran Palace** was almost destroyed by the fire of 1308, which devastated San Giovanni. Pope Sixtus V commissioned Fontana to replace it in 1586.

④ **Statues of Christ and the Apostles** crown the façade.

⑤ **A side door** is opened only on Holy Years.

⑥ **The main entrance's** bronze doors originally came from the Curia (see p84).

Papal Altar
Only the pope can celebrate mass at this altar. The Gothic baldacchino, decorated with frescoes, dates from the 14th century.

★ **Cloisters**
Built by the Vassalletto family in about 1220, the cloisters are remarkable for their twisted twin columns and inlaid marble mosaics.

North Façade
This was added by Domenico Fontana in 1586. The pope gives his blessing from the upper loggia.

Boniface VIII Fresco
This fragment showing the pope proclaiming the Holy Year of 1300 is attributed to Giotto.

VISITORS' CHECKLIST

Practical Information
Piazza di San Giovanni in Laterano 4. **Map** 9 C2. **Tel** 06-6988 6433. Cathedral: **Open** 7am–6:30pm daily. Cloister: **Open** 9am–6pm daily. Museum: **Open** 10am–5:30pm daily. Baptistry: **Open** 7am–12:30pm, 4–7pm daily. 🎟 for museum and cloister. 🚻 📷

Transport
🚌 16, 81, 85, 87, 186, 650, 850 and other routes to Piazza San Giovanni. Ⓜ San Giovanni. 🚊 3.

Corsini Chapel
This chapel was built in the 1730s for Pope Clement XII. The altarpiece is a mosaic copy of Guido Reni's painting of Sant'Andrea Corsini.

Trial of a Corpse

Fear of rival factions led the early popes to extraordinary lengths. An absurd case took place at the Lateran Palace in 897 when Pope Stephen VI tried the corpse of his predecessor, Formosus, for disloyalty to the Church. The corpse was found guilty, its right hand was mutilated and it was thrown in to the Tiber.

Pope Formosus

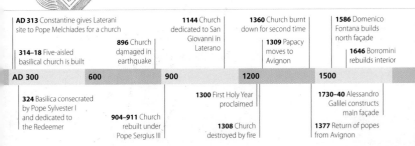

Devout Christians climbing the Scala Santa on their knees

❷ Scala Santa and Sancta Sanctorum

Piazza di San Giovanni in Laterano 14. **Map** 9 C1. **Tel** 06-772 6641. 16, 81, 85, 87, 186 and other routes to Piazza di San Giovanni in Laterano. 3. San Giovanni. **Open** 6:30am–6:30pm Mon–Sat, 7am–7pm Sun & hols.

On the east side of Piazza di San Giovanni in Laterano, a building designed by Domenico Fontana (1589) houses two surviving parts of the old Lateran Palace. One is the Sancta Sanctorum, the other the holy staircase, the Scala Santa. The 28 steps, said to be those that Christ ascended in Pontius Pilate's house during his trial, are supposed to have been brought from Jerusalem by St Helena, mother of the Emperor Constantine. This belief, however, cannot be traced back any earlier than the 7th century.

The steps were moved to their present site by Pope Sixtus V (reigned 1585–90) when the old Lateran Palace was destroyed. No foot may touch the holy steps, so they are covered by wooden boards. They may only be climbed by the faithful on their knees, a penance that is performed especially on Good Friday. In the vestibule there are various 19th-century sculptures including an *Ecce Homo* by Giosuè Meli (1874).

The Scala Santa and two side stairways lead to the Chapel of St Lawrence or Sancta

Sanctorum (Holy of Holies), built by Pope Nicholas III in 1278. Decorated with fine Cosmatesque marble-work, the chapel contains many important relics, the most precious being an image of Jesus – the *Acheiropoeton* or "picture painted without hands", said to be the work of St Luke, with the help of an angel. It was taken on procession in medieval times to ward off plagues.

On the walls and in the vault, restoration work has revealed 13th-century frescoes which for 500 years had been covered by later paintings. The frescoes, representing the legends of St Nicholas, St Lawrence, St Agnes and St Paul, show signs of the style that would characterize the frescoes of Giotto in Assisi, made a few years later.

❸ Porta Asinaria

Between Piazza di Porta San Giovanni and Piazzale Appio. **Map** 10 D2. 16, 81, 85, 87. 3. San Giovanni. *See Markets p345.*

The Porta Asinaria (Gate of the Donkeys) is one of the minor gateways in the Aurelian Wall *(see p198)*. Twin circular towers were added and a small enclosure built around the entrance; the remains are still visible. From outside the walls you can see the gate's

Porta Asinaria from inside the wall

white travertine façade and two rows of small windows, giving light to two corridors built into the wall above the gateway. In AD 546 treacherous barbarian soldiers serving in the Roman army opened this gate to the hordes of the Goth Totila, who mercilessly looted the city. In 1084 the Holy Roman Emperor Henry IV entered Rome via Porta Asinaria with the antipope Guibert to oust Pope Gregory VII. The gate was badly damaged in the conflicts that followed.

The area close to the gate, especially in the Via Sannio, is the home of a popular flea market *(see p345)*.

Bargain for clothes at the Via Sannio flea market near Porta Asinaria

❹ Amphiteatrum Castrense

Between Piazza di Santa Croce in Gerusalemme and Viale Castrense. **Map** 10 E1. 649. 3. **Open** first and third Sat of month by appt (call 06-3996 7700).

This small 3rd-century amphitheatre was used for games and baiting animals. It owes its preservation to the fact that it was incorporated in the Aurelian Wall *(see p198)*, which included several existing high buildings in its fortifications. The graceful arches framed by brick semi-columns were blocked up. The amphitheatre is best seen from outside the walls, from where there is also a good view of the bell tower of Santa Croce in Gerusalemme.

Discovery and Triumph of the Cross, attributed to Antoniazzo Romano, in Santa Croce in Gerusalemme

❺ Santa Croce in Gerusalemme

Piazza di Santa Croce in Gerusalemme 12. **Map** 10 E1. **Tel** 06-7061 3053. 🚌 16, 81, 649, 810. 🚊 3. **Open** 7am–12:45pm, 3:30–7:30pm daily. 🚻 📷

Emperor Constantine's mother St Helena founded this church in AD 320 in the grounds of her private palace. Although the church stood at the edge of the city, the relics of the Crucifixion that St Helena had brought back from Jerusalem made it a centre of pilgrimage. Most important were the pieces of Christ's Cross (*croce* means cross) and part of Pontius Pilate's

18th-century statue of St Helena on the façade of Santa Croce

inscription in Latin, Hebrew and Greek: "Jesus of Nazareth King of the Jews".

In the crypt is a Roman statue of Juno, found at Ostia (*see pp272–3*), transformed into a statue of St Helena by replacing the head and arms and adding a cross.

The 15th-century apse fresco shows the medieval legends that arose around the Cross. Helena is shown holding it over a dead youth and restoring him to life. Another episode shows its recovery from the Persians by the Byzantine Emperor Heraclitus after a bloody battle. In the centre of the apse is a magnificent tomb by Jacopo Sansovino made for Cardinal Quiñones, Emperor Charles V's confessor (died 1540).

❻ Museum of Musical Instruments

Museo degli Strumenti Musicali, Piazza di Santa Croce in Gerusalemme 9a. **Map** 10 E1. **Tel** 06-701 4796. 🚌 16, 81, 649, 810. 🚊 3. **Open** 9am–7pm Tue–Sun. **Closed** 1 Jan, 25 Dec. 🚻 ♿ 🅦 **museostrumentimusicali.it**

One of Rome's lesser-known museums, the building stands on the site of the Sessorianum, the great Imperial villa belonging to Empress St Helena, later included in the Aurelian Wall. Opened in 1974, the museum

has a collection of more than 3,000 outstanding musical instruments from all over the world, including instruments typical of the various regions of Italy, and wind, string and percussion instruments of all ages (including ancient Egyptian, Greek and Roman).

There are also sections dedicated to church and military music. The greater part of the collection is composed of Baroque instruments: be sure to see the gorgeous Barberini harp, remarkably well-preserved, on the first floor in Room 13. There are spinets, harpsichords and clavichords, and one of the first pianos ever made, dating from 1722.

Art Nouveau entrance to the Museum of Musical Instruments

❼ Porta Maggiore

Piazza di Porta Maggiore. **Map** 6 F5.
🚌 105. 🚋 3, 5, 14, 19.

Originally the two arches of
Porta Maggiore were not part
of the city wall, but part of an
aqueduct built by the Emperor
Claudius in AD 52. They carried
the water of the Aqua Claudia
over the Via Labicana and
Via Prenestina, two of ancient
Rome's main south-bound roads.
You can still see the original
roadway beneath the gate. In
the large slabs of basalt – a hard
volcanic rock used in all old
Roman roads – note the great
ruts created by centuries of
cartwheel traffic. On top of the
arches separate conduits carried
the water of two aqueducts: the
Aqua Claudia, and its offshoot,
the Aqueduct of Nero. They
bear inscriptions from the time
of the Emperor Claudius and
also from the reigns of Vespasian
and Titus, who restored them in
AD 71 and AD 81 respectively.
In all, six aqueducts from
different water sources entered
the city at Porta Maggiore.
    The Aqua Claudia was 68 km
(43 miles) long, with over
15 km (9 miles) above ground.
Its majestic arches are a
notable feature of the Roman
countryside, and a popular
mineral water bears its name.
One stretch of the Aqua Claudia
had its arches bricked up
when it was incorporated
into the 3rd-century Aurelian
Wall (see p198).

Relief showing breadmaking on the tomb of the baker Eurysaces

❽ Baker's Tomb

Piazzale Labicano. **Map** 6 F5. 🚌 105.
🚋 3, 5, 14, 19.

In the middle of the tram
junction near Porta Maggiore
stands the tomb of the rich
baker Eurysaces and his wife
Atistia, built in 30 BC.
Roman custom forbade
burials within city walls,
and the roads leading
out of cities became
lined with tombs and
monuments for the
middle and upper
classes. This tomb is
shaped like a baking
oven: a low-relief
frieze at the top
shows Eurysaces
presiding over his
slaves in the various phases
of breadmaking. The inscription
proudly asserts his origins
and reveals him as a freed slave,
probably of Greek origin. Many
men like him saved money
from their meagre slave salaries
to earn their freedom and set
up businesses, becoming the
backbone of Rome's economy.

Relief on the Tomb of
the Statilii freedmen

❾ Aqueduct of Nero and the Freedmen's Tombs

Intersection of Via Statilia and
Via di Santa Croce in Gerusalemme.
Map 10 D1. 🚌 105, 649. 🚋 3, 5, 14, 19.
Open by appt only (call 06-0608).

The aqueduct was built by Nero
in the 1st century AD as an
extension of the Aqua Claudia
to supply Nero's Golden House
(see p177). It was later extended
to the Imperial residences on
the Palatine. Partly incorporated
into later buildings, the imposing arches make their way via
the Lateran to the Celian hill.
Along the first section of the
aqueduct, in Via Statilia, is a
small tomb in the
shape of a house,
dating from the
1st century BC,
bearing the names
and likenesses of a
group of freed slaves.
Their name, Statilii,
indicates that they
had been freed by the
Statilii, the family of
Claudius's notorious
wife Messalina.
Servants of families
often pooled funds in this way
to pay for a dignified burial in
a common resting place.

Porta Maggiore, a city gate formed by the
arches of an aqueduct

Well-preserved section of Nero's Aqueduct
near San Giovanni

❿ Museo Storico della Liberazione di Roma

Via Tasso 145. **Map** 9 C1. **Tel** 06-700 3866. Ⓜ Manzoni, San Giovanni. 🚋 3. **Open** 3:30–7:30pm Tue, Thu & Fri, 9:30am–12:30pm Tue–Sun. **Closed** Aug.

This museum, dedicated to the resistance to the Nazi occupation of Rome, is housed in the ex-prison of the Gestapo. The makeshift cells with bloodstained walls make a strong impact *(see also Fosse Ardeatine p268)*.

⓫ Santi Quattro Coronati

Via Santi Quattro Coronati 20. **Map** 9 B1. **Tel** 06-7047 5427. 🚌 85, 117. 🚋 3. Cloister and church: **Open** 10–11:45am & 4–5:45pm Mon–Sat, 4–5:45pm Sun. 🔲 🔲 ♿

The name of this fortified convent (Four Crowned Saints) refers to four Christian soldiers martyred after refusing to worship a pagan god. For centuries it was the bastion of the pope's residence, the Lateran Palace. Its high apse looms over the houses below, while a Carolingian tower dominates the entrance. Erected in the 4th century AD, it was rebuilt after the invading Normans set fire to the neighbourhood in 1084. Hidden within is the garden of the delightful inner cloister (admission on request), one of the earliest of its kind, built c.1220.

The remains of medieval frescoes can be seen in the Chapel of St Barbara, but the convent's main feature is the Chapel of St Sylvester – its remarkable frescoes (1246) recount the legend of the conversion to Christianity of the Emperor Constantine by Pope Sylvester I (reigned 314–35), then living as a hermit on Monte Soratte, north of Rome.

Stricken by the plague, Constantine is prescribed a bath in children's blood, to the horror of the matrons of Rome. Unable to bring himself to obey, Constantine is visited in a dream

Distinctive circular outline of Santo Stefano Rotondo

by St Peter and St Paul. They advise him to find Sylvester, who cures him and baptizes him. The final scene shows the emperor kneeling before the pope. The implied idea of the pope as heir to the Roman Empire would affect the whole course of medieval European history.

⓬ San Clemente

See pp188–9.

⓭ Santo Stefano Rotondo

Via di Santo Stefano Rotondo 7. **Map** 9 B2. **Tel** 06-421 199. 🚌 81, 117, 673. **Open** 9:30am–12:30pm, 3–6pm (2–5pm winter) daily. **Closed** three weeks in Aug. ✉

One of Rome's earliest Christian churches, Santo Stefano Rotondo was constructed between 468 and 483. It has an unusual circular

plan with four chapels in the shape of a cross. The round inner area was surrounded by concentric corridors with 22 Ionic supporting columns. The high drum in the centre is 22 m (72 ft) high and just as wide. It is lit by 22 high windows, a few of them restored or blocked by restorations carried out under Pope Nicholas V (reigned 1447–55), who consulted the Florentine architect Leon Battista Alberti. The archway in the centre may have been added during this period.

In the 16th century the church walls were frescoed by Niccolò Pomarancio, with particularly gruesome illustrations of the martyrdom of innumerable saints. Some of the medieval decor remains: in the first chapel to the left of the entrance is a 7th-century mosaic of Christ with San Primo and San Feliciano.

Fresco of St Sylvester and Constantine in Santi Quattro Coronati

⑫ San Clemente

San Clemente provides an opportunity to travel back through three layers of history. At street level, there is a 12th-century church; underneath this lies a 4th-century church; and below that are ancient Roman buildings, including a Temple of Mithras. Mithraism, an all-male cult imported from Persia in the 1st century BC, was a rival to Christianity in Imperial Rome.

The upper levels are dedicated to St Clement, the fourth pope, who was exiled to the Crimea and martyred by being tied to an anchor and drowned. His life is illustrated in some of the frescoes in the 4th-century church. The site was taken over in the 17th century by Irish Dominicans, who still continue the excavation work begun by Father Mullooly in 1857.

★ Cappella di Santa Caterina
The restored frescoes by the 15th-century Florentine artist, Masolino da Panicale, show scenes from the life of the martyred St Catherine of Alexandria.

18th-century Façade
Twelfth-century columns were used in the arcade.

Piscina
This deep pit was discovered in 1967. It could have been used as a font or fountain.

★ 11th-century Frescoes
Commissioned by the de Rapiza family, one shows the story of a boy found alive in St Clement's tomb beneath the Black Sea.

KEY

① **1st–3rd-century temple and buildings**

② **4th-century church**

③ **12th-century church**

④ **Entrance** to the church is through a door in Via di San Giovanni in Laterano.

⑤ **Temple of Mithras**

Catacomb
Discovered in 1938 and dating from the 5th or 6th century, it contains 16 wall tombs known as *loculi.*

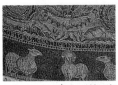

★ Apse Mosaic
The 12th-century *Triumph of the Cross* includes beautifully detailed animals and acanthus leaves.

VISITORS' CHECKLIST

Practical Information
Via di San Giovanni in Laterano.
Map 9 B1.
Tel 06-774 0021.
Open 9am–12:30pm, 3–6pm
Mon–Sat; noon–6pm Sun (last adm: 20 mins before closing).
to excavations.
basilicasanclemente.com

Transport
85, 87, 117, 186, 810, 850.
3. Colosseo.

Schola Cantorum
The 6th-century enclosure for the choir was retained for the new church, built in 1108.

Paschal Candlestick
This 12th-century spiralling candlestick, striped with glittering mosaic, is a magnificent example of Cosmati work.

★ Triclinium and Altar of Mithras
The altar, with a relief of Mithras slaying the bull, stands in the *triclinium*, a room used for ritual banquets.

d century Site possibly used in secret Christian worship	**867** Reputed transfer of remains of St Clemente to Rome	**1108** New church built over 4th-century church	**1857** Original 4th-century church rediscovered by Father Mullooly
Late 2nd century Temple of Mithras built			

500	1000	1500	2000

7 Papacy **lement**	**4th century** First church built over courtyard of earlier Roman building	**1667** Church and convent given to Irish Dominicans	
Jero's fire s area	**1084** Church destroyed during Norman invasion led by Robert Guiscard	**1861** Church is excavated. Roman ruins discovered	

CARACALLA

The Celian Hill overlooks the Colosseum, and takes its name from Caelius Vibenna, the legendary hero of Rome's struggle against the Tarquins (see pp20–21). In Imperial Rome this was a fashionable place to live, and some of its vanished splendour is still apparent in the vast ruins of the Baths of Caracalla. Today, thanks to the Archaeological Zone established at the beginning of the 20th century, it is a peaceful area, a green wedge from the Aurelian Wall to the heart of the city. Through it runs the cobbled Via di Porta San Sebastiano, part of the old Via Appia. This road leads to Porta San Sebastiano, one of the best-preserved gates in the ancient city wall.

Sights at a Glance

Churches
1 Santi Giovanni e Paolo
2 San Gregorio Magno
4 Santa Maria in Domnica
6 San Sisto Vecchio
7 Santi Nereo e Achilleo
8 San Cesareo
9 San Giovanni a Porta Latina
10 San Giovanni in Oleo
16 Santa Balbina

Arches and Gates
3 Arch of Dolabella
13 Arch of Drusus
14 Aurelian Wall and Porta San Sebastiano
15 Sangallo Bastion

Historic Buildings
17 Baths of Caracalla

Tombs
11 Columbarium of Pomponius Hylas
12 Tomb of the Scipios

Parks and Gardens
5 Villa Celimontana

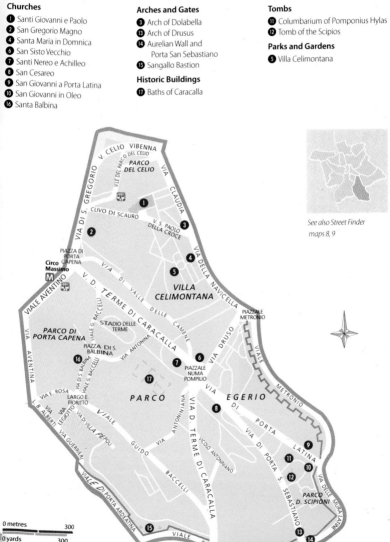

See also Street Finder maps 8, 9

◀ The Baths of Caracalla

Street-by-Street: The Celian Hill

In the course of a morning exploring the green slopes of the Celian hill, you will see a fascinating assortment of archaeological remains and beautiful churches. A good starting point is the church of San Gregorio Magno, from where the Clivo di Scauro leads up to the top of the hill. The steep narrow street passes the ancient porticoed church of Santi Giovanni e Paolo with its beautiful Romanesque bell tower soaring above the surrounding medieval monastery buildings. Of the parks on the hill, the best kept and most peaceful is the Villa Celimontana with its formal walks and avenues. There are few bars or restaurants in the area but the green spaces are great for a picnic.

Clivo di Scauro, the Roman Clivus Scauri, leads up to Santi Giovanni e Paolo, passing under the flying buttresses that support the church.

VIA DI SAN GREGORIO

CLIVO DI SCAURO

La Vignola is a delightful Renaissance pavilion, reconstructed here in 1911 after it had been demolished during the creation of the Archaeological Zone around the Baths of Caracalla.

To Circo Massimo Metro

❷ San Gregorio Magno
A monastery and chapel were founded here by Pope Gregory the Great at the end of the 6th century.

❶ ★ Santi Giovanni e Paolo
The nave of the church, lit by a blaze of chandeliers, has been restored many times, assuming its present appearance in the 18th century.

❺ ★ Villa Celimontana
The beautiful 16th-century villa built for the Mattei family is now the centre of a public park.

Trams passing over the Celian hill from the Colosseum rumble up a picturesque narrow track through the Parco del Celio.

Locator Map
See Central Rome Map pp16–17

Ruins of the Temple of Claudius are visible over a large area of the Celian hill. These travertine blocks have been incorporated in the base of the bell tower of Santi Giovanni e Paolo.

❸ **Arch of Dolabella**
Built in the 1st century AD, probably as an entrance to the city, this archway was later incorporated in Nero's aqueduct to the Palatine.

The gateway of San Tommaso in Formis is decorated with a wonderful 13th-century mosaic showing Christ with two freed slaves, one white, one black.

❹ ★ **Santa Maria in Domnica**
This church is famed for its 9th-century mosaics. These Apostles appear on the triumphal arch above the apse, flanking a medallion containing the figure of Christ.

Key
— Suggested route

0 metres   75
0 yards   75

❶ Santi Giovanni e Paolo

Piazza Santi Giovanni e Paolo 13.
Map 9 A1. **Tel** 06-772 711. 🚌 75, 81,
117, 673. 🚋 3. Ⓜ Colosseo or Circo
Massimo. Church: **Open** 8:30am–
noon, 3:30–6pm daily. Roman houses:
Clivo di Scauro. **Tel** 06-7045 4544.
Open 10am–1pm, 3–6pm Thu–Mon.
🔲 ♿ church only. 🆆 **caseromane.it**

Santi Giovanni e Paolo is
dedicated to two martyred
Roman officers whose house
originally stood on this site.
Giovanni (John) and Paolo (Paul)
had served the first Christian
emperor, Constantine. When
they were later called to arms
by the pagan emperor Julian
the Apostate, they refused and
were beheaded and buried in
secret in their own house
in AD 362.

Built towards the end of
the 4th century, the church
retains many elements of its
original structure. The Ionic
portico dates from the 12th
century, and the apse and
bell tower were added by
Nicholas Breakspeare, the
only English pope, who reigned
as Adrian IV (1154–9). The base
of the superb 13th-century
Romanesque bell tower was
part of the Temple of Claudius
that stood on this site. The
interior, which was remodelled
in 1718, has granite piers and
columns. A tomb slab in the
nave marks the burial place
of the martyrs, whose relics
are preserved in an urn under
the high altar. In a tiny room

near the altar, a magnificent
13th-century fresco depicts the
figure of Christ flanked by his
Apostles (ask the sacristan who
will be able to unlock the door).

Excavations beneath the
church have revealed two 2nd-
and 3rd-century Roman houses
used as a Christian burial place.
These are well worth a visit.
The two-storey construction,
with 20 rooms and a labyrinth
of corridors, has well-preserved
pagan and Christian paintings.
The arches to the left of the
church were part of a 3rd-
century street of shops.

Façade of San Gregorio Magno

❷ San Gregorio Magno

Piazza di San Gregorio 1. **Map** 8 F2.
Tel 06-700 8227. 🚌 75, 81, 117, 673.
🚋 3. Ⓜ Circo Massimo. **Open** 9am
–1pm, 3:30–7pm daily. 🔲

To the English, this is one of the
most important churches in
Rome, for it was from here that
St Augustine was sent on his
mission to convert England to

Marble throne of Gregory the Great from
the 1st century BC

Christianity. The church was
founded in AD 575 by San
Gregorio Magno (St Gregory
the Great), who turned his
family home on this site into
a monastery. It was rebuilt in
medieval times and restored
in 1629–33 by Giovanni Battista
Soria. The church is reached via
a flight of steps from the street.

The forecourt contains some
interesting tombs. To the left is
that of Sir Edward Carne, who
came to Rome several times
between 1529 and 1533 as
King Henry VIII's envoy to gain
the pope's consent to the
annulment of Henry's marriage
to Catherine of Aragon.

The interior, remodelled by
Francesco Ferrari in the mid-
18th century, is Baroque, apart
from the fine mosaic floor and
some ancient columns. At the
end of the right aisle is the
chapel of St Gregory. Leading
off it, another small chapel,
believed to have been the
saint's own cell, houses his
episcopal throne – a Roman
chair of sculpted marble.
The Salviati Chapel on
the left contains a picture
of the Virgin said to have
spoken to St Gregory.

Outside, amid the cypresses
to the left of the church, stand
three small chapels, dedicated
to St Andrew, St Barbara and
St Sylvia (Gregory the Great's
mother). The chapels contain
frescoes by Domenichino and
Guido Reni.

Fresco of Christ and the Apostles in Santi Giovanni e Paolo

❸ Arch of Dolabella

Via di San Paolo della Croce.
Map 9 A2. 🚌 81, 117, 673. 🚃 3.
Ⓜ Colosseo.

The arch was built in AD 10 by consuls Caius Junius Silanus and Cornelius Dolabella, possibly on the site of one of the old Servian Wall's gateways. It was made of travertine blocks and later used to support Nero's extension of the Claudian aqueduct, built to supply the Imperial Palace on the Palatine Hill.

The restored Arch of Dolabella

❹ Santa Maria in Domnica

Piazza della Navicella 12. **Map** 9 A2. **Tel** 06-7720 2685. 🚌 81,117, 673. 🚃 3.
Ⓜ Colosseo. **Open** 9am–noon, 3:30–6pm daily (to 7pm in summer). 🚻 ♿

The church overlooks the Piazza della Navicella (little boat) and takes its name from the 16th-century fountain. Dating from the 7th century, the church was probably built on the site of an ancient Roman firemen's barracks, which later became a meeting place for Christians. In the 16th century Pope Leo X added the portico and the coffered ceiling.

In the apse behind the modern altar is a superb 9th-century mosaic commissioned by Pope Paschal I. Wearing the square halo of the living, the pope appears at the feet of the Virgin and Child. The Virgin, surrounded by a throng of angels, holds a handkerchief like a fashionable lady at the Byzantine court.

❺ Villa Celimontana

Piazza della Navicella. **Map** 9 A2.
🚌 81, 117, 673. Park: **Open** 7am–dusk daily.

The Dukes of Mattei bought this land in 1553 and transformed the vineyards that covered the hillside into a formal garden. As well as palms and other exotic trees, the garden has its own Egyptian obelisk. Villa Mattei, built in the 1580s and now known as Villa Celimontana, houses the Italian Geographical Society.

The Mattei family used to open the park to the public on the day of the Visit of the Seven Churches, an annual event instituted by San Filippo Neri in 1552. Starting from the Chiesa Nuova (see p126), Romans went on foot to the city's seven major churches and, on reaching Villa Mattei, were given bread, wine, salami, cheese, an egg and two apples. The garden, now owned by the city of Rome, still makes an ideal place for a picnic. In summer it hosts an excellent jazz festival.

Park of Villa Celimontana

❻ San Sisto Vecchio

Piazzale Numa Pompilio 8. **Map** 9 A3.
Tel 06-7720 5174. 🚌 160, 628, 671, 714. **Open** 9–11am, 3–5:30pm daily. ✉

This small church is of great historical interest as it was granted to St Dominic in 1219 by Pope Honorius III. The founder of the Dominican order soon moved his own headquarters to Santa Sabina (see p206), San Sisto becoming the first home of the order of Dominican nuns who still occupy the monastery. The church, with its 13th-century bell tower and frescoes, is also a popular place for weddings.

Apse mosaic of the Virgin and Child in Santa Maria in Domnica

Fresco by Niccolò Pomarancio of the *Martyrdom of St Simon* in Santi Nereo e Achilleo

❼ Santi Nereo e Achilleo

Via delle Terme di Caracalla 28. **Map** 9 A3. **Tel** 06-687 3124. 160, 628, 671, 714. **Open** noon–12:30pm Sun (for half an hour only). 🚹

According to legend, St Peter, after escaping from prison, was fleeing the city when he lost a bandage from his wounds. The original church was founded here in the 4th century on the spot where the bandage fell, but it was later re-dedicated to the 1st-century AD martyrs St Nereus and St Achilleus.

Restored at the end of the 16th century, the church has retained many medieval features, including some fine 9th-century mosaics on the triumphal arch. A magnificent pulpit rests on an enormous porphyry pedestal which was found nearby in the Baths of Caracalla. The walls of the side aisles are decorated with grisly 16th-century frescoes by Niccolò Pomarancio, showing in clinical detail how each of the Apostles was martyred.

Detail of mosaic, Santi Nereo e Achilleo

❽ San Cesareo

Via di Porta San Sebastiano. **Map** 9 A3. **Tel** 338-491 6838. 218, 628. **Open** 10am–4pm Sat, 10am–noon Sun. **Closed** Aug.

This splendid old church was built over Roman ruins of the 2nd century AD. You can still admire Giacomo della Porta's fine Renaissance façade, but by phoning ahead to book a visit, you can also see Cosmatesque mosaic work and carving to rival that of any church in Rome. The episcopal throne, altar and pulpit are decorated with delightful animals The church was restored in the 16th century by Pope Clement VIII, whose coat of arms decorates the ceiling.

❾ San Giovanni a Porta Latina

Via di San Giovanni a Porta Latina. **Map** 9 B3. **Tel** 06-7047 5938. 218, 360, 628. **Open** 7:30am–12:30pm, 3–7pm daily. 🚹 🚹

The church of "St John at the Latin Gate" was founded in the 5th century, rebuilt in 720 and restored in 1191. This is one of the most picturesque of the old Roman churches. Classical columns support the medieval portico, and the 12th-century bell tower is superb. A tall cedar tree shades an ancient well standing in the forecourt. The interior has been restored, but it preserves the rare simplicity of its early origins with ancient columns of varying styles lining the aisles. Traces of early medieval frescoes can still be seen within the church. The 12th-century frescoes show 46 different biblical scenes, from both the Old and New Testaments and are among the finest of their kind in Rome.

❿ San Giovanni in Oleo

Via di Porta Latina. **Map** 9 C4. **Tel** 06-7740 0032. 628. ask at San Giovanni a Porta Latina.

The name of this charming octagonal Renaissance chapel means "St John in Oil". The tiny building marks the spot where, according to legend, St John was boiled in oil – and came out unscathed, or even refreshed. An earlier chapel is said to have existed on the site; the present one was built in the early 16th century. The design has been attributed to Baldassare Peruzzi or Antonio da Sangallo the Younger. It was restored by Borromini, who altered the roof, crowning it with a cross supported by a sphere decorated with roses. He also added a terracotta frieze of roses and palm leaves. The wall paintings inside the chapel include one of St John in a cauldron of boiling oil.

Fresco, San Giovanni a Porta Latina

Niches for funerary urns in the Columbarium of Pomponius Hylas

⓫ Columbarium of Pomponius Hylas

Via di Porta Latina 10. **Map** 9 B4. **Tel** 06-0608. 🚌 218, 360, 628. **Open** for guided tours only; phone ahead.

Known as a columbarium because it resembles a dovecote (*columba* is the Latin word for dove), this kind of vaulted tomb was usually built by rich Romans to house the cremated remains of their freedmen. Many similar tombs have been uncovered in this part of Rome, which up until the 3rd century AD lay outside the city wall. This one, excavated in 1831, dates from the 1st century AD. An inscription informs us that it is the tomb of Pomponius Hylas and his wife,

Mosaic inscription in the Columbarium of Pomponius Hylas

Pomponia Vitalinis. Above her name is a "V" which indicates that she was still living when the inscription was made. The tomb was probably a commercial venture. Niches in the interior walls of the columbarium were sold to people who could not afford to build vaults of their own.

⓬ Tomb of the Scipios

Via di Porta San Sebastiano 9. **Map** 9 B4. **Tel** 06-0608. 🚌 218, 360, 628. **Open** for guided tours only; phone ahead.

The Scipios were a family of conquering generals. Southern Italy, Corsica, Algeria, Spain and Asia Minor all fell to their victorious Roman armies. The most famous of these generals was Publius Cornelius Scipio Africanus, who defeated the great Carthaginian general Hannibal at the Battle of Zama in 202 BC (*see p25*). Scipio Africanus himself was not buried here in the family tomb, but at Liternum near Naples, where he owned a favourite villa.

The Tomb of the Scipios was discovered in 1780. It contained various sarcophagi, statues and niches with terracotta burial urns. Many of the originals have now been moved to the Vatican Museums and copies stand in their place.

The earliest sarcophagus was that of Cornelius Scipio Barbatus, consul in 298 BC, for whom the tomb was built. Members of his illustrious family continued to be buried here up to the middle of the 2nd century BC. Excavations in the area have revealed a columbarium similar to that of Pomponius Hylas, a Christian catacomb and a three-storey house dating from the 3rd century AD, which was built over the Tomb of the Scipios.

⓭ Arch of Drusus

Via di Porta San Sebastiano. **Map** 9 B4. 🚌 218, 360.

Once mistakenly identified as a triumphal arch, the so-called Arch of Drusus merely supported the branch aqueduct that supplied the Baths of Caracalla. It was built in the 3rd century AD, so had no connection with Drusus, a stepson of the Emperor Augustus. Its monumental appearance was due to the fact that it carried the aqueduct across the important route, Via Appia. The arch still spans the old cobbled road, just 50 m (160 ft) short of the gateway Porta San Sebastiano.

Arch of Drusus, part of the Aqua Antoniniana aqueduct

⑭ Aurelian Wall and Porta San Sebastiano

Museo delle Mura, Via di Porta San Sebastiano 18. **Map** 9 B4. 218, 360. **Tel** 06-0608. **Open** 9am–2pm Tue–Sun (last adm: 30 mins before closing). **Closed** 1 Jan, 1 May, 25 Dec.
W museodellemuraroma.it

Most of the Aurelian Wall, begun by the emperor Aurelian (AD 270–75) and completed by his successor Probus (AD 276–82), has survived. Aurelian ordered its construction as a defence against Germanic tribes, whose raids were penetrating deeper and deeper into Italy. Some 18 km (11 miles) round, with 18 gates and 381 towers, the wall took in all the seven hills of Rome. It was raised to almost twice its original height by Maxentius (AD 306–12).

The wall was Rome's main defence until 1870, when it was breached by Italian artillery just by Porta Pia, close to today's British Embassy. Many of the gates are still in use, and although the city has spread, most of its noteworthy historical and cultural sights still lie within the wall.

Porta San Sebastiano, the gate leading to the Via Appia Antica (see p286), is the largest and best-preserved gateway in the Aurelian Wall. It was rebuilt by Emperor Honorius in the 5th century AD. Originally the Porta Appia, in Christian times it gradually became known as the Porta San Sebastiano, because the Via Appia led to the basilica and catacombs of San Sebastiano, which were popular places of pilgrimage.

It was at this gate that the last triumphal procession to enter the city by the Appian Way was received in state – that of Marcantonio Colonna after the victory of Lepanto over the Turkish fleet in 1571. Today the gate's towers house a museum with prints and models showing the wall's history. From here you can take a short walk along the restored wall. The views are spectacular.

Pope Paul III Farnese

⑮ Sangallo Bastion

Viale di Porta Ardeatina. **Map** 9 A4. 160. **Closed** for restoration.

Haunted by the memory of the Sack of Rome in 1527 and fearing attack by the Turks, Pope Paul III asked Antonio da Sangallo the Younger to reinforce the Aurelian Wall. Work on the huge projecting bastion began in 1537. For the moment its massive bulk can only be admired from outside.

The high altar of Santa Balbina

⑯ Santa Balbina

Piazza di Santa Balbina 8. **Map** 8 F3. **Tel** 06-578 0207. 160. 3. **M** Circo Massimo. **Open** 10:30–11:30am Sun.

Overlooking the Baths of Caracalla, this isolated church is dedicated to Santa Balbina, a 2nd-century virgin martyr. It is one of the oldest in Rome, dating back to the 5th century, and was built on the remains of a Roman villa. Consecrated by Pope Gregory the Great, in the Middle Ages Santa Balbina was a fortified monastery and over time has changed in appearance several times, regaining its Romanesque aspect in the 1920s.

From the piazza in front of the church, a staircase leads up to a three-arched portico. Inside, light streams in from a series of high windows along the length of the nave. The remains of St Balbina and her father, St Quirinus, are in an urn at the high altar, though the church's real treasure is situated in the far right-hand corner: the magnificent sculpted and inlaid tomb of Cardinal Stefanis de Surdis by Giovanni di Cosma (1303).

Other features worth noting are a 13th-century episcopal throne and various fragments of frescoes. These include a lovely Madonna and Child, an example of the school of Pietro Cavallini, in the second chapel on the left. Fragments of first-century Roman mosaics were also dis-covered in the 1930s. Depicting birds and signs of the zodiac, these are now set into the church floor.

Fortified gateway of Porta San Sebastiano

⓱ Baths of Caracalla

Viale delle Terme di Caracalla 52.
Map 9 A3. **Tel** 06-3996 7700.
🚌 160, 628. 🚃 3. Ⓜ Circo Massimo.
Open 9am–2pm Mon, 9am–approx
1 hour before sunset Tue–Sun (last
adm: 1 hour before closing).
Closed 1 Jan, 25 Dec. 🅿 🅰 🅰 🅰 ♿

Part of one of the gymnasia in the Baths of Caracalla

Completed by Emperor
Caracalla in AD 217, the
baths functioned for about
300 years, until the plumbing
was destroyed by invading
Goths. Over 1,600 bathers at a
time could enjoy the facilities.
A Roman bath was a serious
business, beginning with a sort
of Turkish bath, followed by a
spell in the *caldarium*, a large
hot room with pools
of water to provide
humidity. Then came
the lukewarm
tepidarium, a visit to
the large central
meeting place,
known as the
frigidarium, and
finally a plunge into

**Fragment of mosaic
pavement**

the *natatio*, an open-air swimming pool. For the rich, this was
followed by a rub-down with a
scented woollen cloth. As well
as the baths, there were
spaces for exercise,
libraries, art galleries
and gardens – a true
leisure centre. Most of
the rich marble deco-
rations of the baths
were removed by the
Farnese family in the
16th century to adorn

the interior of Palazzo Farnese
(see p149). Open-air operas,
mostly Verdi or Puccini, are
performed in these spectacular
settings in the summer months
and are very well attended.

Key

▨ *Caldarium* (very hot)
▨ *Tepidarium* (lukewarm)
▨ *Frigidarium* (cold)
▢ *Natatio* (pool)
▢ Garden

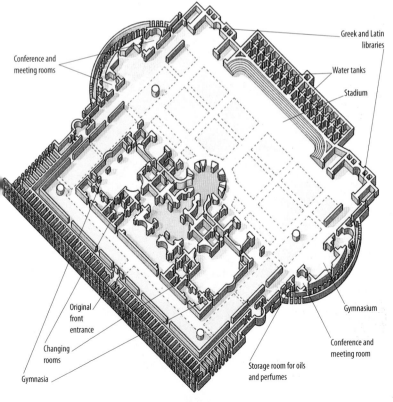

Greek and Latin
libraries

Conference and
meeting rooms

Water tanks

Stadium

Original
front
entrance

Changing
rooms

Gymnasia

Storage room for oils
and perfumes

Gymnasium

Conference and
meeting room

AVENTINE

This is one of the most peaceful areas within the walls of the city. Although it is largely residential, there are some unique historic sights. From the top of the Aventine Hill, crowned by the magnificent basilica of Santa Sabina, there are fine views across the river to Trastevere and St Peter's.

At the foot of the hill, ancient Rome is preserved in the two tiny Temples of the Forum Boarium and the Circus Maximus. The liveliest streets are in Testaccio, which has shops, restaurants and clubs, while to the south, beside Rome's solitary pyramid, the Protestant Cemetery is another oasis of calm.

Sights at a Glance

Churches and Temples
1 Santa Maria in Cosmedin
3 San Giorgio in Velabro
4 San Teodoro
5 Santa Maria della Consolazione
7 San Giovanni Decollato
9 Temples of the Forum Boarium
10 Santa Sabina
11 Santi Bonifacio e Alessio
16 San Saba

Historic Buildings
8 Casa dei Crescenzi

Arches
2 Arch of Janus

Historic Streets and Piazzas
12 Piazza dei Cavalieri di Malta

Ancient Sites
6 Area Archeologica di Sant'Omobono
13 Monte Testaccio
17 Circus Maximus

Monuments and Tombs
14 Protestant Cemetery
15 Pyramid of Caius Cestius

Restaurants
see pp310–11
1 0,75
2 Angelina a Testaccio
3 Checchino dal 1887
4 Da Oio a Casa Mia
5 Da Remo
6 Felice a Testaccio
7 Flavio al Velavevodetto
8 Il Nuovo Mondo
9 Oasi della Birra
10 Pecorino
11 Perilli
12 Queen Makeda

See also Street Finder
maps 7, 8, 12

For keys to symbols see back flap

◀ Mask fountain in courtyard of Santa Sabina

Street-by-Street: Piazza della Bocca della Verità

The area attracts visitors eager to place their hands inside the Bocca della Verità (the Mouth of Truth) in the portico of Santa Maria in Cosmedin. There are many other sights to see in this quiet corner of the city beside the Tiber, which was the site of ancient Rome's first port and its busy cattle market. Substantial Classical remains include two small temples from the Republican age and the Arch of Janus from the later Empire. In the 6th century the area became home to a Greek community from Byzantium, who founded the churches of San Giorgio in Velabro and Santa Maria in Cosmedin.

⑧ Casa dei Crescenzi
This 11th-century building used columns and capitals from ancient Roman temples.

Key

— Suggested route

0 metres
0 yards   75

⑥ Sant'Omobono
This 16th-century church stands in isolation in the middle of an important archaeological site. The remains of sacrificial altars and two temples from the 6th century BC have been discovered.

Ponte Rotto, as this forlorn ruined arch in the Tiber is called, means simply "broken bridge". Built in the 2nd century BC, its original name was Pons Aemilius.

LUNGOTEVERE DEI PIERLEONI

Tevere

PONTE PALATINO

⑨ ★ Temples of the Forum Boarium
The tiny round Temple of Hercules and its neighbour, the Temple of Portunus, are the best preserved of Rome's Republican temples.

The Fontana dei Tritoni by Carlo Bizzaccheri was built here in 1715. The style shows the powerful influence of Bernini.

5 Santa Maria della Consolazione
This 16th-century church used to serve a hospital nearby.

4 San Teodoro
The 15th-century portal of this ancient round church is decorated with the insignia of Pope Nicholas V.

Locator Map
See Central Rome Map pp16–17

7 San Giovanni Decollato
The plain Renaissance façade was completed in about 1504.

VIA DEI FIENILI

VIA DI SAN TEODORO

3 San Giorgio in Velabro
The simple 12th-century portico of Ionic columns was destroyed by a bomb in 1993 but has been restored.

The Arco degli Argentari, dedicated to Emperor Septimius Severus in AD 204, is decorated with scenes of religion and war.

2 Arch of Janus
This square structure with arches on each side dates from the 4th century AD.

VIA DEI CERCHI

DELLA GRECA

1 ★ Santa Maria in Cosmedin
This medieval church has a fine marble mosaic floor and a Gothic baldacchino.

❶ Santa Maria in Cosmedin

Piazza della Bocca della Verità 18.
Map 8 E1. **Tel** 06-678 7759. 🚌 23, 44, 81, 160, 170, 280, 628, 715, 716.
Open 9:30am–6pm daily (in winter: to 5pm. Gates close: 10 mins before closing). 🚻 ♿ 📷

This beautiful unadorned church was built in the 6th century on the site of the ancient city's food market. The elegant Romanesque bell tower and portico were added during the 12th century. In the 19th century a Baroque façade was removed and the church restored to its original simplicity. It contains many fine examples of Cosmati work, in particular the mosaic pavement, the raised choir, the bishop's throne and the canopy over the main altar.

Set into the wall of the portico is the Bocca della Verità (Mouth of Truth). This may have been a drain cover, dating back to before the 4th century BC. Medieval tradition had it that the formidable jaws would snap shut over the hand of those who told lies – a useful trick for testing the faithfulness of spouses.

Bocca della Verità at Santa Maria in Cosmedin

❷ Arch of Janus

Via del Velabro. **Map** 8 E1. 🚌 23, 44, 63, 81, 160, 170, 280, 628, 715, 716, 780.

Probably dating from the reign of Constantine, this imposing four-faced marble arch stood at the crossroads on the edge of the Forum Boarium, near the ancient docks. Merchants did business in its shade. On the

keystones above the four arches you can see small figures of the goddesses Roma, Juno, Ceres and Minerva. In medieval times the arch formed the base of a tower fortress. It was restored to its original shape in 1827.

San Giorgio in Velabro after its restoration in 1999

❸ San Giorgio in Velabro

Via del Velabro 19. **Map** 8 E1. **Tel** 06-6979 7536. 🚌 23, 44, 81, 160, 170, 280, 628, 715, 716, 780. **Open** 10am–12:30pm, 4–6:30pm Tue, Fri & Sat.

In the hollow of the street named after the Velabrum, the swamp where Romulus and Remus are said to have been found by the she-wolf, is a small church dedicated to St George, whose bones lie under the altar.

The 7th-century basilica has suffered over time from periodic floods, and in 1993 a bomb damaged the front of the church. Careful restoration has, however, returned it to its original appearance.

A double row of granite and marble columns (taken from ancient Roman temples) divides the triple nave. The austerity of the grey interior is relieved by golden frescoes in the apse (attributed to Pietro Cavallini, 1295). The façade and the bell tower date from the 12th century.

❹ San Teodoro

Via di San Teodoro 7. **Map** 8 E1.
Tel 06-678 6624. 🚌 23, 44, 81, 160, 170, 280, 628, 715, 716.
Open 9:30am–12:30pm Sun–Fri.

This small, round 6th-century church at the foot of the Palatine features breathtaking 6th-century mosaics in the apse, and a Florentine cupola dating from 1454. The fetching outer courtyard was designed by Carlo Fontana in 1705. Greek Orthodox services are held here on Sunday mornings.

❺ Santa Maria della Consolazione

Piazza della Consolazione 94.
Map 5 A5, 12 F5. **Tel** 06-678 4654.
🚌 23, 44, 63, 81, 160, 170, 280, 628, 715, 716, 780. **Open** 6:30am–6:30pm Mon–Sat; 10am–6:30pm Sun. 🚻 ♿

The church stands near the foot of the Tarpeian Rock, the site of public execution of traitors since the time of the Sabine War (see p76).

In 1385, Giordanello degli Alberini, a condemned

The Arch of Janus, where cattle dealers sheltered from the midday sun

Façade of Santa Maria della Consolazione

nobleman, paid two gold florins for an image of the Virgin Mary to be placed here, to provide consolation to prisoners in their final moments before execution. Hence the name of the church that was built here in 1470. It was reconstructed between 1583 and 1600 by Martino Longhi, who provided the early Baroque façade at the same time.

The church's 11 side-chapels are owned by noble families and local crafts guild members. Taddeo Zuccari was responsible for the 1556 frescoes depicting scenes from the Passion (first chapel on the right), while the Mannerist artist Niccolò Circignani painted the scenes from the life of Mary and Jesus housed in the fifth chapel. In the presbytery is the image of Mary, attributed to Antoniazzo Romano.

❻ Area Archeologica di Sant'Omobono

Vico Jugario 4. **Map** 8 E2. **Tel** 06-0608. 🚌 23, 44, 63, 81, 160, 170, 280, 628, 715, 716, 780.

Unearthed in 1937, this important archaeological area opened to the public in 2013. The remains of the temple Mater Matuta, dating from the 6th century BC, have been attributed to the time of King Tullius. The excavations have also revealed traces of a pre-Roman cult.

❼ San Giovanni Decollato

Via di San Giovanni Decollato 22. **Map** 8 E1. **Tel** 06-679 1890. 🚌 23, 44, 63, 81, 160, 170, 280, 628, 715, 716, 780. **Open** only for the feast of St John (9:30 am–12:30pm, 24 Jun).

Giorgio Vasari's *The Beheading of St John* (1553), from which the church takes its name, dominates the main altar. In 1490 Pope Innocent VIII gave this site to build a church for a Florentine confraternity. Clad in black robes and hoods, they would encourage prisoners to repent and give them a decent burial after they had been hanged. In the cloisters there are seven manholes, which received the bodies. The confraternity still exists, with church funds assisting prisoners' families.

The oratory holds a cycle of frescoes by Florentine Mannerists Francesco Salviati and Jacopino del Conte depicting events in the life of St John the Baptist.

❽ Casa dei Crescenzi

Via Luigi Petroselli. **Map** 8 E1. 🚌 23, 44, 63, 81, 160, 170, 280, 628, 715, 716, 780.

Studded with archaeological fragments, the house is what remains of an 11th-century tower fortress. The powerful Crescenzi family built it to keep an eye on the docks and on the bridge where they collected a toll.

❾ Temples of the Forum Boarium

Piazza della Bocca della Verità. **Map** 8 E1. 🚌 23, 44, 81, 160, 170, 280, 628, 715, 716. Temple of Hercules: **Open** for guided tours: first and third Sun of month by appt. Call 06-3996 7700). 🅦 **coopculture.it**

These incredibly well-preserved Republican temples date from the 2nd century BC and were saved for posterity when they were reconsecrated as Christian churches in the Middle Ages. They offer rare examples of combined elements from Greek and Roman architecture.

The rectangular temple (formerly known as the Temple of Fortuna Virilis) was dedicated to Portunus, god of rivers and ports. Set on a podium, it has four Ionic travertine columns and 12 half-columns, embedded in the tufa wall of the *cella* – the room that housed the image of the god.

Nearby is the small circular Temple of Hercules, its slender Corinthian columns surrounding the central *cella*. Built around 120 BC, the temple is thought to be the earliest Roman marble edifice to have survived to the present day. It is often referred to as the Temple of Vesta due to its similarity to the one in the Forum.

Ancient Roman fragments in the Casa dei Crescenzi

Luminous interior of Santa Sabina

⑩ Santa Sabina

Piazza Pietro d'Illiria 1. **Map** 8 E2.
Tel 06-579 401. 🚌 23, 280, 716.
Ⓜ Circo Massimo. **Open** 8:15am–
12:30pm, 3:30–6pm daily. ♿

High on the Aventine stands
an early Christian basilica,
founded by Peter of Illyria
in AD 425 and restored to
its original simplicity in the
early 20th century. Light filters
through 9th-century windows
upon a wide nave framed
by white Corinthian columns
supporting an arcade decorated
with a marble frieze. Over the
main door is a 5th-century blue
and gold mosaic dedicatory
inscription. The pulpit, carved
choir and bishop's throne
date from the 9th century.

The church was given to
the Dominicans in the 13th
century and in the nave is the
magnificent mosaic tombstone
of one of the first leaders of the
order, Muñoz de Zamora
(died 1300).

The side portico has
5th-century panelled doors
carved from cypress wood,
representing scenes from
-the Bible, including one of the
earliest Crucifixions in existence.

⑪ Santi Bonifacio e Alessio

Piazza di Sant'Alessio 23. **Map** 8 D2.
Tel 06-574 3446. 🚌 23, 280, 716.
Ⓜ Circo Massimo. **Open** for special
events only. ♿

The church is dedicated to
two early Christian martyrs,
whose remains lie under the

main altar. Legend has it that
Alessio, son of a rich senator
living on the site, fled east to
avoid an impending marriage
and became a pilgrim. Returning
home after many years, he
died as a servant, unrecognized,
under the stairs of the family
entrance hall, clutching
the manuscript of his story
for posterity.

The original 5th-century
church has undergone many
changes over time. Noteworthy
are the 18th-century façade
with its five arches, the
restored Cosmati doorway
and pavement, and the
magnificent Romanesque
five-storey bell tower (1217).

An 18th-century Baroque
chapel by Andrea Bergondi
houses part of the famous
staircase. Other relics include
the well from Alessio's family
home and the glowing
Byzantine Madonna of the
Intercession brought from
Damascus to Rome at the
end of the 10th century.

⑫ Piazza dei Cavalieri di Malta

Map 8 D2. 🚌 23, 280, 716.
Ⓜ Circo Massimo.

Surrounded by cypress trees,
this ornate walled piazza
decorated with obelisks and
military trophies was designed
by Piranesi in 1765.
It is named after the
Order of the Knights
of Malta (Cavalieri di
Malta), whose priory
(at No. 3) is famous
for the bronze
keyhole through
which there is a
miniature view of
St Peter's, framed by
a tree-lined avenue.
The priory church,
Santa Maria del
Priorato, was restored
in Neo-Classical style
by Piranesi in the
18th century. To
visit the church,
ask permission in
person at the Order's
building at Via
Condotti 48. At the

southwest corner of the square
is Sant'Anselmo, the international
Benedictine church, where
Gregorian chant may be heard
on Sundays (see p348).

Doorway of the Priory of the Knights of Malta

⑬ Monte Testaccio

Via Galvani. **Map** 8 D4. Ⓜ Piramide.
🚌 23, 83, 719. 🚋 3. **Open** by appt
only; call 06-0608.

From about 140 BC to AD
250 this hill was created by
dumping millions of testae
(hence Testaccio) – pieces
of the amphorae used to
carry goods to nearby
warehouses. The full archaeological significance of this
36 m (118 ft) high artificial
hill was not realized until
the late 18th century.

Façade of Santi Bonifacio e Alessio

⓮ Protestant Cemetery

Cimitero Acattolico, Via Caio Cestio 6. **Map** 8 D4. **Tel** 06-574 1900. 🚌 23, 280, 716. 🚊 3. Ⓜ Piramide.
Open 9am–5pm Mon–Sat, 9am–1pm Sun (last adm: 30 mins before closing). Donation expected. 📷

The peace of this well-tended cemetery beneath the Aurelian Wall is profoundly moving. Non-Catholics, mainly English and German, have been buried here since 1738. In the oldest part are the graves of John Keats (died 1821), whose epitaph reads "Here lies One Whose Name was writ in Water", and his friend Joseph Severn (died 1879); not far away are the ashes of Percy Bysshe Shelley (died 1822). Goethe's son Julius is also buried here.

Tombstone of John Keats

Memorial pyramid of Caius Cestius

⓯ Pyramid of Caius Cestius

Piazzale Ostiense. **Map** 8 E4. 🚌 23, 280, 716. 🚊 3. Ⓜ Piramide.
Open 10:30am first and third Sun of the month by appt (call 06-574 3193).
🌐 coopculture.it

Caius Cestius, a wealthy *praetor* (senior Roman magistrate), died in 12 BC. His main claim to fame is his tomb, an imposing pyramid faced in white marble, set in the Aurelian Wall near Porta San Paolo. It stands 36 m (118 ft) high and, according to an inscription, took 330 days to build. Unmistakable as a landmark, it must have looked almost as incongruous when it was built as it does today.

Detail of carving on sarcophagus in the portico of San Saba

⓰ San Saba

Via di San Saba. **Map** 8 F3. **Tel** 06-6458 0140. 🚌 75, 673. 🚊 3.
Open 8am–noon, 4–7:10pm Mon–Sat, 9:30am–1pm, 4–7:30pm Sun. 🚹

Tucked away in a residential street on the Little Aventine hill, San Saba began life as an oratory for Palestinian monks fleeing from Arab invasions in the 7th century. The existing church dates from the 10th century and has undergone much restoration. The portico houses a fascinating collection of archaeological remains and a fresco depicting St Sabas.
 The church has three naves in the Greek style and a short fourth 11th-century nave to the left with vestiges of 13th-century frescoes of the life of St Nicholas of Bari. Particularly intriguing is a scene of three naked young ladies lying in bed, who are saved from penury by the gift of a bag of gold from St Nicholas, the future Santa Claus. The beautiful marble inlay in the main door, the floor and the remains of the choir are all 13th-century Cosmati work.

⓱ Circus Maximus

Via del Circo Massimo. **Map** 8 F2.
🚌 81, 160, 628, 715. 🚊 3.
Ⓜ Circo Massimo.

What was once ancient Rome's largest stadium is today little more than a long grassy esplanade. Set in the valley between the Palatine and Aventine hills, the Circus Maximus was continually embellished and expanded from the 4th century BC until AD 549 when the last races were held. The grandstands held some 300,000 spectators, cheering wildly at the horse and chariot races, athletic contests and wild animal fights, betting furiously throughout.
 The Circus had a central dividing barrier (*spina*) with seven large egg-shaped objects on it used for counting the laps of a race. These were joined in 33 BC by seven bronze dolphins that served a similar purpose. In 10 BC Augustus built the Imperial box under the Palatine and decorated the *spina* with the obelisk that now stands in the centre of Piazza del Popolo (*see p139*). A second obelisk, which was added in the 4th century by Constantine II, is now in Piazza di San Giovanni in Laterano (*see pp180–81*).

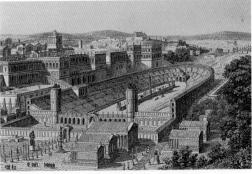

Reconstruction of the Circus Maximus in its heyday

TRASTEVERE

The proud and aggressively independent inhabitants of Trastevere, the area "across the Tiber", consider themselves the most authentic of Romans. In one of the most picturesque old quarters of the city, it is still possible to glimpse scenes of everyday life that seem to belong to bygone centuries. There are, however, signs that much of the earthy, proletarian character of the place may soon be destroyed by the proliferation of fashionable clubs, restaurants and boutiques.

Some of Rome's most fascinating medieval churches lie hidden away in the patchwork of narrow, cobbled back-streets, the only clue to their location an occasional glimpse of a Romanesque bell tower. Of these, Santa Cecilia was built on the site of the martyrdom of the patron saint of music, San Francesco a Ripa commemorates St Francis of Assisi's visit to Rome, and Santa Maria in Trastevere is the traditional centre of the spiritual and social life of the area.

Sights at a Glance

Churches

3 Santa Maria della Scala
5 *Santa Maria in Trastevere pp214–15*
6 San Crisogono
8 Santa Cecilia in Trastevere
10 San Francesco a Ripa

Museums and Galleries

4 Sant'Egidio and Museo di Roma in Trastevere

Historic Buildings

1 Casa della Fornarina
7 Caserma dei Vigili della VII Coorte
9 San Michele a Ripa Grande

Bridges

2 Ponte Sisto

Parks and Gardens

11 Villa Sciarra

See also Street Finder maps 4, 7, 8, 11

▢ Restaurants

see pp317–19

1 Bir & Fud
2 Da Gildo
3 Da I Sandri
4 Dar Poeta
5 Da Teo
6 Fish Market
7 La Gensola
8 Glass
9 In Vino Veritas
10 Ivo a Trastevere
11 Meridionale
12 Pizzeria Panattoni (L'Obitorio)
13 Roma Sparita
14 Spirito Divino
15 Taverna Trilussa

◀ Vintage FIAT parked in a cobbled street in Trastevere district

For keys to symbols *see back flap*

Street-by-Street: Trastevere

All year round Trastevere is a major attraction both for its restaurants, clubs and cinemas, and for its picturesque maze of narrow cobbled alleyways. On summer evenings the streets are packed with jostling groups of pleasure-seekers, especially during the noisy local festival, the Festa de' Noantri *(see p61)*. Everywhere café and restaurant tables spill out over pavements, especially around Piazza di Santa Maria in Trastevere and outside the pizzerias along Viale di Trastevere. There are also kiosks selling slices of watermelon and *grattachecca*, a mixture of syrup and grated ice. It is usually easier to appreciate the antique charm of Trastevere's narrow streets in the more tranquil atmosphere of the early morning.

❶ Casa della Fornarina
Raphael's beautiful mistress is said to have lived here. There is now a flourishing restaurant in the back garden.

The church of Santa Maria dei Sette Dolori (1643) is a minor work by Borromini.

❸ Santa Maria della Scala
The church's unassuming façade conceals a rich Baroque interior.

❹ Sant'Egidio and Museo di Roma in Trastevere
This 17th-century fresco of Sant'Egidio by Pomarancio decorates the left-hand chapel in the church. The convent next door is a museum of Roman life and customs.

Vicolo del Piede is one of the picturesque narrow streets lined with restaurant tables leading off Piazza di Santa Maria in Trastevere.

❺ ★ Santa Maria in Trastevere
The church is famous for its mosaics by Pietro Cavallini but it also has earlier works such as this mosaic of the prophet Isaiah to the left of the apse.

Key

— Suggested route

0 metres	150
0 yards	150

The fountain of Piazza di Santa Maria in Trastevere by Carlo Fontana (1692) is a popular meeting place. At night it is floodlit and dozens of young people sit on the steps around its octagonal base.

Locator Map
See Central Rome Map pp16–17

❷ Ponte Sisto
This bridge was built on the orders
of Sixtus IV in 1474 to link
Trastevere to central Rome.

**The Torre degli
Anguillara** (13th century)
is the only survivor of the
many medieval towers
that once dominated
the Trastevere skyline.

Piazza Belli is named after Giuseppe Gioacchino
Belli (1791–1863), who wrote satirical sonnets
in Roman dialect rather than academic Italian.
At the centre of the piazza stands a statue of
the poet (1913).

**❼ Caserma dei
Vigili della VII
Coorte**
The courtyard of this
antique Roman fire
station still stands.

❻ San Crisogono
The Romanesque bell tower
datés from the early 12th century.
The plain portico is a later addition
(1626), but is in keeping with the spirit
of this ancient church.

❶ Casa della Fornarina

Via di Santa Dorotea 20. **Map** 4 D5 & 11 B5. 🚌 23, 280.

Not much is known about Raphael's model and lover, La Fornarina, yet over the centuries she has acquired a name, Margherita, and even a biography. Her father was a Sienese baker (*la fornarina* means the baker's girl) and his shop was here in Trastevere near Raphael's frescoes in the Villa Farnesina (*see pp220–21*).

Margherita earned a reputation as a "fallen woman" and Raphael, wishing to be absolved before dying, turned her away from his deathbed. After his death she took refuge in the convent of Santa Apollonia in Trastevere.

She is assumed to have been the model for Raphael's famous portrait *La Donna Velata* in the Palazzo Pitti in Florence.

❷ Ponte Sisto

Map 4 E5 & 11 B5. 🚌 23, 280.

Named after Pope Sixtus IV della Rovere (reigned 1471–84), who commissioned it, this bridge was built by Baccio Pontelli to replace an ancient Roman bridge. The enterprising pope also built the Sistine Chapel (*see pp242–5*), the Hospital of Santo Spirito (*see p246*) and restored many churches and monuments. This put him in great financial difficulties and he had to sell personal collections in order to finance his projects.

Another method of financing projects was to levy a tax on the city's prostitutes. Several popes are known to have resorted to this unpopular form of taxation.

Pope Sixtus IV

Gilded Baroque altar of Santa Maria della Scala

❸ Santa Maria della Scala

Piazza della Scala 23. **Map** 4 D5 & 11 B5. **Tel** 06-580 6233. 🚌 23, 280. **Open** 10am–1pm, 4–5:30pm daily. 🚻

This church belongs to a time of great building activity that lasted about 30 years from the end of the 16th to the early 17th century. Its simple façade contrasts with a rich interior decorated with multicoloured marbles and a number of spirited Baroque altars and reliefs. In 1849, the church was used as a hospital to treat the soldiers of Garibaldi's army (*see pp40–41*).

❹ Sant'Egidio and Museo di Roma in Trastevere

Piazza Sant'Egidio 1. **Map** 7 C1. 🚌 H, 23, 280. 🚋 8. Church: **Tel** 06-589 5945. **Closed** for restoration. Museo di Roma in Trastevere: **Tel** 06-0608. **Open** 10am–8pm Tue–Sun (last adm: 7pm). 🚻 🅆 **museodiromaintrastevere.it**

Built in 1630, Sant'Egidio was the church of the adjoining Carmelite convent, one of many founded in the area to shelter the poor and destitute. The convent is now a museum, containing a wealth of material relating to the festivals, pastimes, superstitions and customs of the Romans when they lived under papal rule.

There are old paintings and prints of the city and tableaux showing scenes of everyday life in 18th- and 19th-century Rome, including reconstructions of shops and a tavern.

The museum also has manuscripts by the much-loved poets Belli (*see p211*) and Trilussa who wrote in local dialect.

Watercolour of public scribe (1880) in the Museo di Roma in Trastevere

❺ Santa Maria in Trastevere

See pp214–15.

❻ San Crisogono

Piazza Sonnino 44. **Map** 7 C1. **Tel** 06-5810 0076. 🚌 H, 23, 280, 780. 🚋 8. **Open** 7–11:30am, 4–7:30pm Mon–Sat; 8am–1pm, 4–7:30pm Sun. 🗝 for excavations. 🚻 🅃

This church was built on the site of one of the city's oldest *tituli* (private houses used for Christian worship). An 8th-century church with 11th-century frescoes can still be seen beneath the present church. This dates from the early 12th century, a period of intense building activity in Rome. San Crisogono was decorated by Pietro Cavallini – the apse mosaic remains. Most of the church's columns

Apse mosaic in San Crisogono

were taken from previous buildings, including the great porphyry ones of a triumphal arch. The mosaic floor is the result of recycling precious marble from various Roman ruins.

❼ Caserma dei Vigili della VII Coorte

Via della VII Coorte 9. **Map** 7 C1. **Tel** 06-0608. H, 23, 280, 780. 8. **Closed** for restoration work; call for details.

Not all Roman ruins are Imperial villas or grand temples; one that illustrates the daily life of a busy city is the barracks of the guards of the VII Coorte (7th Cohort), the Roman fire brigade. It was built in Augustus's reign, in the 1st century AD, and the excavated courtyard is where the men would rest while waiting for a call out.

❽ Santa Cecilia in Trastevere

Piazza di Santa Cecilia. **Map** 8 D1. **Tel** 06-589 9289. H, 23, 44, 280. 8. **Open** 10am–1pm, 4–7pm daily. Excavations: **Open** 10am–1pm, 4–7pm daily. Cavallini fresco: **Open** 10am–12:30 daily.

St Cecilia, aristocrat and patron saint of music, was martyred here in AD 230. After an attempt at scalding her to death, she was beheaded. A church was founded – perhaps in the 4th century – on the site of her house. (The house, beneath the church with the remains of a Roman tannery, is well worth a visit.) Her body turned up in the Catacombs of San Callisto (*see p267*) and was buried here in the 9th century by Pope Paschal I, who rebuilt the church. A fine apse mosaic survives from this period.

The altar canopy by Arnolfo di Cambio and the fresco of *The Last Judgment* by Pietro Cavallini, reached through the adjoining convent, date from the 13th century, one of the few periods when Rome had a distinctive artistic style of its own. In front of the altar is a

Detail of 13th-century fresco by Pietro Cavallini in Santa Cecilia

statue of St Cecilia by Stefano Maderno, who used her miraculously preserved remains as a model when she was briefly disinterred in 1599.

❾ San Michele a Ripa Grande

Via di San Michele 25. **Map** 8 D2. **Tel** 06-6723 1440. 23, 44, 75, 280. **Open** for special exhibitions only.

This huge, imposing complex, now housing the Ministry of Culture, stretches 300 m (985 ft) along the river Tiber. It was built on the initiative of Pope Innocent XII and contained a home for abandoned elderly, a boys' reform school, a woollen mill and various

chapels. Today contemporary exhibitions are occasionally held here.

❿ San Francesco a Ripa

Piazza San Francesco d'Assisi 88. **Map** 7 C2. **Tel** 06-581 9020. H, 23, 44, 75, 280. 8. **Open** 7:30am–1pm, 2–7:30pm daily.

St Francis of Assisi lived here in a hospice when he visited Rome in 1219 and his stone pillow and crucifix are preserved in his cell. The church was rebuilt by his follower, the nobleman Rodolfo Anguillara, who is portrayed on his tombstone wearing the Franciscan habit.

Entirely rebuilt in the 1680s by Cardinal Pallavicini, the church is rich in sculptures. Particularly flamboyant are the 18th-century Rospigliosi and Pallavicini monuments in the transept chapel.

The Paluzzi-Albertoni chapel (fourth on the left, along the nave) contains Bernini's breathtaking *Ecstasy of Beata Ludovica Albertoni*.

⓫ Villa Sciarra

Via Calandrelli 35. **Map** 7 B2. 44, 75. Park: **Open** 9am–sunset daily.

In Roman times the site of this small, attractive public park was a nymph's sanctuary. It is especially picturesque in spring when its wisterias are in full bloom. The paths through the park are decorated with Romantic follies, fountains and statues, and there are splendid views over the bastions of the Janiculum.

Bernini's *Ecstasy of Beata Ludovica Albertoni* (1674) in San Francesco a Ripa

❺ Santa Maria in Trastevere

Probably the first official Christian place of worship to be built in Rome, this basilica became the focus of devotion to the Virgin Mary. According to legend, the church was founded by Pope Callixtus I in the 3rd century, when Christianity was still a minority cult. Today's church is largely a 12th-century building, remarkable for its mosaics, in particular those by Pietro Cavallini. The 22 granite columns in the nave were taken from the ruins of ancient Roman buildings. Despite some 18th-century Baroque additions, Santa Maria has retained its medieval character. This friendly church has strong links with the local community.

Piazza Santa Maria in Trastevere
The piazza in front of the church is the traditional heart of Trastevere. Today it is surrounded by lively bars and restaurants. Carlo Fontana built the octagonal fountain in the late 17th century.

★ Façade Mosaics
The 12th-century mosaic shows Mary feeding the baby Jesus and ten women holding lamps. Eight of the lamps are lit, symbolizing virginity; the veiled women whose lamps have gone out are probably widows.

Modest Donors

Many of Rome's mosaics include a portrait of the pope or cardinal responsible for the building of the church. Often the portrait is dwarfed by the rest of the picture, which glorifies the saint to whom the church is dedicated. On the façade of Santa Maria, two tiny unidentified figures kneel at the Virgin's feet. Were they to stand up, the men would barely reach her knees.

Façade mosaic, detail

KEY

① **The portico** was remodelled in 1702 by Carlo Fontana. Statues of four popes decorate the balustrade above.

② **The bell tower** was built in the 12th century. At the top is a small mosaic of the Virgin.

③ **The floor**, relaid in the 1870s, is a re-creation of the Cosmatesque mosaic floor of the 13th century.

④ **15th-century wall tabernacle** by Mino del Reame

Front entrance

Apse Mosaic
The 12th-century mosaic in the basin of the apse shows the Coronation of the Virgin. She sits on Christ's right hand, surrounded by saints.

VISITORS' CHECKLIST

Practical Information
Via della Paglia 14c,
Piazza Santa Maria in Trastevere.
Map 7 C1. **Tel** 06-581 4802.
Open 7:30am–9pm daily
(8am–12:30pm, 4–9pm Aug).
🕇 9am & 5:30pm daily. ⚐ 📷

Transport
🚌 H & 780 to Piazza S. Sonnino,
23 & 280 along Lungotevere
Sanzio. 🚋 8 from Piazza Venezia.

Madonna della Clemenza
The life-size icon probably dates from the 7th century. A replica is displayed above the altar of the Cappella Altemps.

★ Cavallini Mosaics
The details in the six mosaics of the Life of the Virgin (1291) display a touching realism.

Tomb of Cardinal Pietro Stefaneschi
The last of his line, Pietro Stefaneschi died in 1417. His tomb is by an otherwise unknown sculptor called Paolo.

AD 217–22
Church founded by Pope Callixtus I

Pope Innocent II

1291 Pietro Cavallini adds mosaics of scenes from the life of the Virgin for his patron, Bertoldo Stefaneschi

1866–77 Church restored by Virginio Vespignani

50 BC	0	600	1200	1800

38 BC Jet of mineral oil spouts from the ground on this site. Later interpreted as a portent of the coming of Christ

c.1138 Pope Innocent II starts rebuilding the church

1580 Martino Longhi the Elder restores church and builds family chapel for Cardinal Marco Sittico Altemps

1702 Pope Clement XI has portico rebuilt

1617 Domenichino designs coffered ceiling with octagonal panel of the Assumption of the Virgin

JANICULUM

Overlooking the Tiber on the Trastevere side of the river, the Janiculum hill has often played its part in the defence of the city. The last occasion was in 1849 when Garibaldi held off the attacking French troops. The park at the top of the hill is filled with monuments to Garibaldi and his men. A popular place for walks, the park provides a welcome escape from the densely packed streets of Trastevere. You will often come across puppet shows and other children's amusements. In medieval times most of the hill was occupied by monasteries and convents. Bramante built his miniature masterpiece, the Tempietto, in the convent of San Pietro in Montorio. The Renaissance also saw the development of the riverside area along Via della Lungara, where the rich and powerful built beautiful houses such as the Villa Farnesina.

Sights at a Glance

Churches and Temples
6 Sant'Onofrio
7 San Pietro in Montorio
8 Tempietto

Museums and Galleries
2 Palazzo Corsini and Galleria Nazionale d'Arte Antica

Historic Buildings
1 Villa Farnesina pp220–21

Fountains
9 Fontana dell'Acqua Paola

Monuments
5 Garibaldi Monument

Arches and Gates
3 Porta Settimiana

Parks and Gardens
4 Botanical Gardens

See also Street Finder maps 3, 4, 7, 11

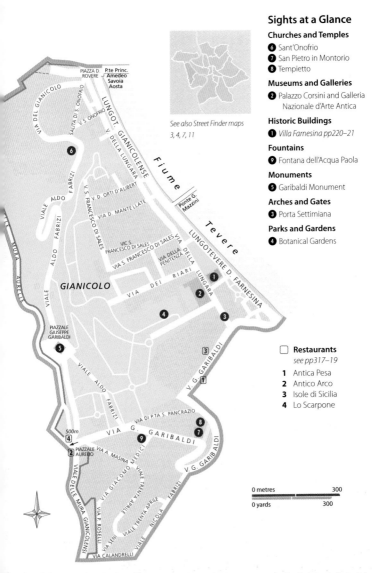

Restaurants
see pp317–19
1 Antica Pesa
2 Antico Arco
3 Isole di Sicilia
4 Lo Scarpone

0 metres 300
0 yards 300

◀ The Garibaldi Monument on Janiculum Hill

For keys to symbols *see back flap*

A Tour of the Janiculum

The long hike to the top of the Janiculum is rewarded by wonderful views over the city. The park's monuments include a lighthouse and statues of Garibaldi and his wife Anita. There is also a cannon which is fired at noon each day. In Via della Lungara, between the Janiculum and the Tiber, stand Palazzo Corsini, with its national art collection and the Villa Farnesina, decorated by Raphael for his friend and patron, the fabulously wealthy banker Agostino Chigi.

Tasso's Oak is a memorial to the poet Torquato Tasso, who liked to sit here in the days before he died in 1595. The tree was struck by lightning in 1843.

The Manfredi Lighthouse, built in 1911, was a gift to the city of Rome from Italians in Argentina.

The Monument to Anita Garibaldi by Mario Rutelli was erected in 1932. The great patriot's Brazilian wife lies buried beneath the statue.

The view from Villa Lante, a beautiful Renaissance summer residence, gives a magnificent panorama of the whole city.

⑤ Garibaldi Monument
The inscription on the base of the equestrian statue says "Rome or Death".

VIALE AL DI FABRIZI

PIAZZALE GIUSEPPE GARIBALDI

4 Botanical Gardens
These were established in 1883 when part of the grounds of Palazzo Corsini was given to the University of Rome.

1 ★ Villa Farnesina
The suburban villa of the banker Agostino Chigi is celebrated for its frescoes by Raphael, Baldassarre Peruzzi and other Renaissance masters.

Locator Map
See Central Rome Map pp16–17

2 ★ Palazzo Corsini
This 15th-century triptych by Fra Angelico hangs in the Galleria Nazionale d'Arte Antica.

VICOLO DELLA PENITENZA

VIA DELLA PENITENZA

VIA DEI RIARI

VIA DELLA LUNGARA

VIA CORSINI

VIA G. GARIBALDI

Key

— Suggested route

0 metres   75
0 yards   75

3 Porta Settimiana
Looking through this Renaissance gateway from Via della Lungara, you catch a glimpse of Trastevere's warren of narrow streets.

❶ Villa Farnesina

The wealthy Sienese banker Agostino Chigi, who had established the headquarters of his far-flung financial empire in Rome, commissioned the villa in 1508 from his compatriot Baldassare Peruzzi. The simple, harmonious design, with a central block and projecting wings, made this one of the earliest true Renaissance villas. The decoration was carried out between 1510 and 1519 and this has been restored. Peruzzi frescoed some of the interiors himself. Later, Sebastiano del Piombo, Raphael and his pupils added more elaborate works. The frescoes illustrate Classical myths, and the vault of the main hall, the Sala di Galatea, is adorned with astrological scenes showing the position of the stars at the time of Chigi's birth. Artists, poets, cardinals, princes and the pope himself were entertained here in magnificent style by their wealthy and influential host. In 1577 the villa was bought by Cardinal Alessandro Farnese. Since then, it has been known as the Villa Farnesina.

North Façade
The Loggia of Cupid and Psyche looks out on formal gardens that were used for parties and putting on plays.

The Wedding of Alexander and Roxanne by Sodoma
Cherubs are shown helping the bride Roxanne to prepare for her marriage.

Entrance

★ **Triumph of Galatea by Raphael**
The beautiful sea nymph Galatea was one of the 50 daughters of the god Nereus.

The Architect

Baldassare Peruzzi, painter and architect, arrived in Rome from Siena in 1503 aged 20 and became Bramante's chief assistant. Although his architectural designs were typical of Classicism, his painting owes more to Gothic influences, as his figurework is very highly stylized. On Raphael's death, he became Head of Works at St Peter's, but was captured in the Sack of Rome (*see p35*), exiled to Siena until 1535, and died in 1536.

Baldassare Peruzzi

Frescoes in the Room of Galatea
Perseus beheads Medusa in a scene from one of Peruzzi's series of mythological frescoes.

★ **Salone delle Prospettive**
Peruzzi's frescoes create the illusion of looking out at views of 16th-century Rome through a marble colonnade.

VISITORS' CHECKLIST

Practical Information
Via della Lungara 230. **Map** 4 D5 & 11 A5. **Tel** 06-6802 7268.
Open 9am–2pm Mon–Sat and second Sun of every month.
Closed Aug. ♿ ✉ 🏠 ♿ 🚫
W villafarnesina.it

Transport
🚌 23, 280 to Lungotevere Farnesina.

Fresco from the Salone delle Prospettive
This scene shows the Torre delle Milizie (see p92) as it looked in the 1500s.

★ **Loggia of Cupid and Psyche**
The model for the figure on the left in Raphael's painting of *The Three Graces* was Agostino Chigi's mistress, the courtesan Imperia.

Lunette in the Room of Galatea
This giant monochrome head by Peruzzi was once attributed to Michelangelo.

Queen Christina's bedroom in the Palazzo Corsini

❷ Palazzo Corsini and Galleria Nazionale d'Arte Antica

Via della Lungara 10. **Map** 4 D5 & 11 A5. **Tel** 06-6880 2323. 🚌 23, 280. **Open** 8:30am–7:30pm Mon, Wed–Sun. **Closed** 1 Jan, 25 Dec. 🚻 📷 📹 ♿ 🖼 🌐 **galleriacorsini. beniculturali.it**

The history of Palazzo Corsini is intimately entwined with that of Rome. Built for Cardinal Domenico Riario in 1510–12, it has boasted among its many distinguished guests Bramante, the young Michelangelo, Erasmus and Queen Christina of Sweden, who died here in 1689. The old palazzo was completely rebuilt for Cardinal Neri Corsini by Ferdinando Fuga in 1736. As Via della Lungara is too narrow for a good frontal view, Fuga designed the façade so it could be seen from an angle.

Palazzo Corsini houses the Galleria Nazionale d'Arte Antica, also known as Galleria Corsini. This outstanding collection includes paintings by Rubens, Van Dyck, Murillo, Caravaggio and Guido Reni, together with 17th- and 18th-century Italian regional art. The palazzo is also home to the Accademia dei Lincei, a learned society founded in 1603, which once included Galileo among its members.

In 1797 Palazzo Corsini was the backdrop to momentous events: French General Duphot (the fiancé of Napoleon's sister Pauline) was killed here in a skirmish between papal troops and Republicans. The consequent French occupation of the city and the deportation of Pope Pius VI led to the proclamation of a short-lived Roman Republic (1798–9).

❸ Porta Settimiana

Between Via della Scala and Via della Lungara. **Map** 4 D5 & 11 B5. 🚌 23, 280.

This gate was built in 1498 by Pope Alexander VI Borgia to replace a minor passageway in the Aurelian Wall. The Porta Settimiana marks the start of Via della Lungara, a long straight road built in the early 16th century.

❹ Botanical Gardens

Largo Cristina di Svezia 24, off Via Corsini. **Map** 4 D5. **Tel** 06-4991 7108. 🚌 23, 280. **Open** Apr–Sep: 9:30am–6:30pm Mon–Sat; Oct–Mar: 9:30am–5:30pm. **Closed** public hols. 📷 📹 (phone to book).

Sequoias, palm trees and splendid collections of orchids and bromeliads are cultivated in Rome's Botanical Gardens (Orto Botanico). These tranquil gardens contain more than 7,000 plant species from all over the world. Indigenous and exotic species are grouped to illustrate their botanical families and their adaptation to different climates and ecosystems.

There are also plants such as the ginkgo that have survived virtually unchanged from prehistoric eras. The gardens were originally part of the Palazzo Corsini, but since 1983 have belonged to the University of Rome.

Base of the Garibaldi Monument

❺ Garibaldi Monument

Piazzale Giuseppe Garibaldi. **Map** 3 C5. 🚌 870.

This huge equestrian statue is part of a commemorative park, recalling the heroic events witnessed on the Janiculum when the French army attacked the city in 1849. Garibaldi's Republicans fended off the greatly superior French forces for weeks, until the Italians were overwhelmed. Garibaldi and his men escaped. The monument, erected in 1895, was the work of Emilio Gallori. Around the pedestal are four smaller sculptures in bronze showing battle scenes and allegorical figures.

Steps and tiered fountains at the Botanical Gardens

Courtyard of Sant'Onofrio

❻ Sant'Onofrio

Piazza di Sant'Onofrio 2. **Map** 3 C4.
Tel 06-686 4498. 870. **Open** 9am–
1pm Sun–Fri. **Closed** Aug.
Museum: **Open** by appt only.
(call 06-686 9040).

Beato Nicola da Forca Palena, whose tombstone guards the entrance, founded this church in 1419 in honour of the hermit St Onofrio. It retains the flavour of the 15th century in the simple shapes of the portico and the cloister. In the early 17th century the portico was decorated with frescoes by Domenichino.

The monastery next to the church houses a small museum that is dedicated to the 16th-century Italian poet Torquato Tasso, who died there.

❼ San Pietro in Montorio

Piazza San Pietro in Montorio 2.
Map 7 B1. **Tel** 06-581 3940. 44,
75. **Open** 8am–noon, 3–4pm daily
(times may vary in summer).

San Pietro in Montorio – the church of St Peter on the Golden Hill – was founded in the Middle Ages near the spot where St Peter was presumed to have been crucified. It was rebuilt by order of Ferdinand and Isabella of Spain at the end of the 15th century, and decorated by outstanding artists of the Renaissance.

The façade is typical of a time when clean, geometric shapes derived from Classical architecture were in vogue. The single nave ends in a deep apse that once contained Raphael's *Transfiguration*, now in

the Vatican. Two wide chapels, one on either side of the nave, were decorated by some of Michelangelo's most famous pupils. The left-hand chapel was designed by one of the few artists Michelangelo openly admired, Daniele da Volterra, also responsible for the altar painting, *The Baptism of Christ*. The chapel on the right was the work of Giorgio Vasari, who included a self-portrait (in black, on the left) in his altar painting, *The Conversion of St Paul*.

The first chapel to the right of the entrance contains a powerful *Flagellation*, by the Venetian artist Sebastiano del Piombo (1518); Michelangelo is said to have provided the original drawings. Work by Bernini and his followers can be seen in the second chapel on the left and in the flanking De Raymondi tombs.

❽ Tempietto

Piazza San Pietro in Montorio (in courtyard). **Map** 7 B1. **Tel** 06-581 2806. 44, 75. **Open** 10am–6pm Tue–Sun. *See The History of Rome pp34–5.*

Around 1502 Bramante completed what many consider to be the first true Renaissance building in Rome – the Tempietto. The name means simply "little temple". Its circular shape echoes early Christian *martyria*, chapels built on the site of a saint's martyrdom. This was believed to be the place where St Peter was crucified.

Bramante chose the Doric order for the 16 columns surrounding the domed chapel. Above the columns is a Classical frieze and a delicate balustrade. Though the scale of the Tempietto is tiny, Bramante's masterly use of Classical proportions creates a satisfyingly harmonious whole. The Tempietto illustrates the great

Renaissance dream that the city of Rome would once again relive its ancient glory.

Fontana dell'Acqua Paola

❾ Fontana dell'Acqua Paola

Via Garibaldi. **Map** 7 B1.
44, 75.

This monumental fountain commemorates the reopening in 1612 of an aqueduct originally built by Emperor Trajan in AD 109. The aqueduct was renamed the "Acqua Paola" after Paul V, the Borghese pope who ordered its restoration. When it was first built, the fountain had five small basins, but in 1690 Carlo Fontana altered the design, adding the huge basin you can see today. Despite many laws intended to deter them, generations of Romans used this convenient pool of fresh water for bathing and washing their vegetables.

Bramante's round chapel, the Tempietto

VATICAN

As the site where St Peter was martyred and buried, the Vatican became the residence of the popes who succeeded him. Decisions taken here have shaped the destiny of Europe, and the great basilica of St Peter's draws pilgrims from all over the Christian world. The papal palaces beside St Peter's house the Vatican Museums. With the added attractions of Michelangelo's Sistine Chapel and the Raphael Rooms, their wonderful collections of Classical sculpture make them the finest museums in Rome. The Vatican's position as a state within a state was guaranteed by the Lateran Treaty of 1929, marked by the building of a new road, the Via della Conciliazione. This leads from St Peter's to Castel Sant'Angelo, a monument to a far grimmer past. Built originally as the Emperor Hadrian's mausoleum, this papal fortress and prison has witnessed many fierce battles for control of the city.

Sights at a Glance

Churches and Temples
1 St Peter's pp228–31
4 Santo Spirito in Sassia
9 Santa Maria in Traspontina

Museums and Galleries
2 Vatican Museums pp232–45

Historic Buildings
5 Hospital of Santo Spirito
6 Palazzo del Commendatore
7 Palazzo dei Convertendi
8 Palazzo dei Penitenzieri
12 Palazzo Torlonia
13 Castel Sant'Angelo pp250–51
14 Palazzo di Giustizia

Gates
3 Porta Santo Spirito

Historic Streets and Piazzas
10 The Borgo
11 Vatican Corridor

☐ Restaurants
see pp317–19

1 Arlù
2 Da Benito e Gilberto
3 Da Cesare
4 Taverna Angelica
5 Velando
6 Veranda

See also Street Finder
maps 3, 4, 11

◀ The statue of St Peter, St Peter's Sqaure

For keys to symbols see back flap

A Tour of the Vatican

The Vatican, a centre of power for Catholics all over the world and a sovereign state since February 1929, is ruled by the pope. About 1,000 people live here, staffing the Vatican's facilities. These include a post office and shops; Vatican radio, broadcasting to the world in over 20 languages; a daily newspaper (*L'Osservatore Romano*); Vatican offices and a publishing house.

The Madonna of Guadalupe shows the miraculous image of the Madonna which appeared on the cloak of an indigenous Mexican in 1531.

Papal heliport

The Grotto of Lourdes is a replica of the grotto in the southwest of France, where in 1858 the Virgin appeared to St Bernadette.

Radio Vatican is broadcast from this tower, part of the Leonine Wall built in 847.

The Vatican Railway Station, opened in 1930, connects with the line from Rome to Viterbo, but is now used only for freight.

The Papal Audience Chamber, by Pier Luigi Nervi, was opened in 1971. It seats up to 12,000.

The information office gives details of tours of the Vatican Gardens.

❶ ★ **St Peter's**
The Chapel of St Peter is in the Grottoes under the basilica. The rich marble decoration was added by Clement VIII at the end of the 16th century.

Piazza San Pietro was laid out by Bernini between 1656 and 1667. The narrow space in front of the church opens out into an enormous ellipse flanked by colonnades.

PIAZZA DEL SANT'UFFIZIO

Key

— Suggested route

| 0 metres | 150 |
| 0 yards | 150 |

The Eagle Fountain was built to celebrate the arrival of water from the Acqua Paola aqueduct at the Vatican. The eagle is the Borghese crest.

Locator Map
See Central Rome Map pp16–17

The Casina of Pius IV is a delightful summerhouse in the Vatican Gardens built by Pirro Ligorio in the mid-16th century.

Entrance to Vatican Museums

❷ ★ **Vatican Museums**
Raphael's *Madonna of Foligno* (1513) is just one of the Vatican's many Renaissance masterpieces.

The Galleon Fountain is a perfect scale model of a 17th-century ship in lead, brass and copper. It was made by a Flemish artist for Pope Paul V.

VIA DI PORTA ANGELICA

PIAZZA SAN PIETRO

PIAZZA PIO XII

The obelisk was erected here in 1586 with the help of 150 horses and 47 winches.

To Via della Conciliazione

The Cortile della Pigna is mostly the work of Bramante. The niche for the pine cone, once a Roman fountain, was added by Pirro Ligorio in 1562.

❶ St Peter's

The centre of the Roman Catholic faith, St Peter's draws pilgrims from all over the world. Few are disappointed when they enter the sumptuously decorated basilica beneath Michelangelo's vast dome.

A shrine was erected on the site of St Peter's tomb in the 2nd century and the first great basilica, ordered by the Emperor Constantine, was completed around AD 349. By the 15th century it was falling down, so in 1506 Pope Julius II laid the first stone of a new church. It took more than a century to build and all the great architects of the Roman Renaissance and Baroque had a hand in its design.

★ **Dome of St Peter's**
Designed by Michelangelo, though not finished in his lifetime, the spectacular cupola, 136.5 m (448 ft) high, gives unity to the majestic interior of the basilica.

Papal Altar
The present altar dates from the reign of Clement VIII (1592–1605). The plain slab of marble found in the Forum of Nerva stands under Bernini's baldacchino, overlooking the well of the *confessio*, the crypt where St Peter's body is reputedly buried.

Baldacchino
This magnificent canopy of gilded bronze, supported on spiral columns 20 m (66 ft) high, was designed by Bernini in the 17th century.

KEY

① **The nave's** total length is 218 m (715 ft).

② **The two minor cupolas** at the corners of the transept are by Vignola.

③ **Façade by Carlo Maderno** (1614)

④ **Stairs to the dome**

Pope Urban VIII's Keys
At the base of the columns of the baldacchino, the coat of arms of Pope Urban VIII features the keys to the Kingdom of Heaven.

★ **St Peter's square as seen from the Dome**
The superb symmetry of Bernini's colonnade can be appreciated from the dome.

Piazza San Pietro
On Sundays and religious occasions the pope blesses the crowds from his balcony above the square.

③

④

Entrance

Filarete Door
Finished in 1445, Antonio Averulino's bronze door came from the original basilica.

AD 61 Burial of St Peter						**1626** New basilica of St Peter's consecrated
	324 Constantine builds basilica	**1452** Nicholas V plans restoration	**1506** Julius II lays first stone	**1547** Michelangelo named as chief architect of St Peter's	**1593** Dome completed	
AD 60	**800**	**1500**		**1550**	**1600**	
	200 Altar built marking grave of St Peter	**1503** Pope Julius II chooses Bramante as architect for new basilica	**1538** Antonio da Sangallo the Younger made director of works	**1606** Carlo Maderno extends basilica		**1614** Maderno finishes the façade
	800 Charlemagne crowned Emperor of the Romans in St Peter's		**1514** Raphael named director of works	**1564** Death of Michelangelo		

A Guided Tour of St Peter's

The vast basilica's 187 m- (615 ft-) long, marble-encrusted interior contains 11 chapels, 45 altars, and a wealth of precious works of art. Some were salvaged from the original basilica and others commissioned from late Renaissance and Baroque artists, but much of the elaborate decoration is owed to Bernini's mid-17th-century work. The two side aisles are 76-m- (250-ft-) long and converge under Michelangelo's enormous dome. The building's central focus is the Papal Altar beneath Bernini's great baldacchino, filling the space between the four piers which support the dome. From the basilica you can visit the Grottoes – where the late Pope John Paul II is buried, the Treasury and St Peter's Sacristy, or the terrace for panoramic views.

⑤ **Baldacchino by Bernini**
Commissioned by Pope Urban VIII in 1624, the extravagant Baroque canopy dominates the nave and crowns the Papal Altar, at which only the pope may celebrate mass.

Bernini's Monument to Urban VIII

④ **Throne of St Peter in Glory**
In the domed apse, look up to the window above Bernini's Baroque sculpture of 1656–65. It lights the image of the Holy Spirit, shown as a dove amid clouds, rays of sunlight and flights of angels.

Entrance to Treasury and Sacristy

Entrance to Necropolis

Historical Plan of the Basilica of St Peter's

St Peter was buried c. AD 64 in a necropolis near his crucifixion site at the Circus of Nero. Constantine built a basilica on the burial site in AD 324. In the 15th century the old church was found to be unsafe and had to be demolished. It was rebuilt in the 16th and 17th centuries. By 1614 the façade was ready, and in 1626 the new church was consecrated.

Key

Circus of Nero
Constantinian
Renaissance
Baroque

③ **Monument to Pope Alexander VII**
Bernini's last work was finished in 1678 and is in an alcove on the left of the transept. The pope sits among the figures of Truth, Justice, Charity and Prudence.

② **Monument to Leo XI**
On the left beneath the aisle arch is Alessandro Algardi's white marble 1650 monument to Leo XI, whose reign as pope lasted only 27 days.

Key

— Tour route

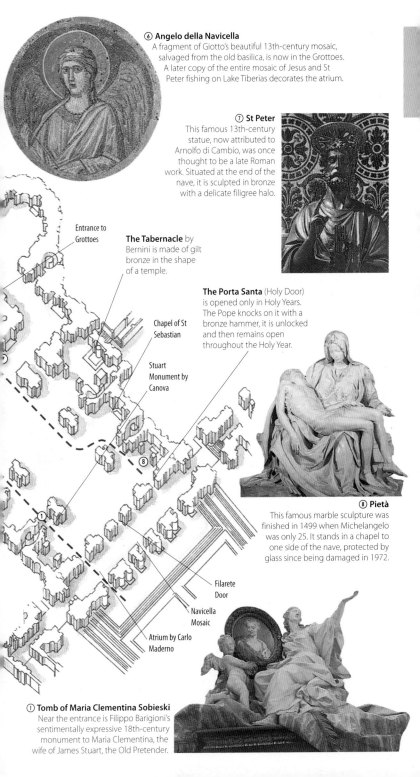

⑥ Angelo della Navicella
A fragment of Giotto's beautiful 13th-century mosaic, salvaged from the old basilica, is now in the Grottoes. A later copy of the entire mosaic of Jesus and St Peter fishing on Lake Tiberias decorates the atrium.

⑦ St Peter
This famous 13th-century statue, now attributed to Arnolfo di Cambio, was once thought to be a late Roman work. Situated at the end of the nave, it is sculpted in bronze with a delicate filigree halo.

Entrance to Grottoes

The Tabernacle by Bernini is made of gilt bronze in the shape of a temple.

Chapel of St Sebastian

Stuart Monument by Canova

The Porta Santa (Holy Door) is opened only in Holy Years. The Pope knocks on it with a bronze hammer, it is unlocked and then remains open throughout the Holy Year.

⑧ Pietà
This famous marble sculpture was finished in 1499 when Michelangelo was only 25. It stands in a chapel to one side of the nave, protected by glass since being damaged in 1972.

Filarete Door

Navicella Mosaic

Atrium by Carlo Maderno

① Tomb of Maria Clementina Sobieski
Near the entrance is Filippo Barigioni's sentimentally expressive 18th-century monument to Maria Clementina, the wife of James Stuart, the Old Pretender.

❷ Vatican Museums

The buildings that house one of the world's finest art collections were once papal palaces built for Renaissance popes such as Sixtus IV, Innocent VIII and Julius II. The long courtyards and galleries, linking Innocent VIII's Belvedere Palace to the other buildings, are by Donato Bramante and were commissioned for Julius II in 1503. Most of the later additions to the buildings were made in the 18th century, when priceless works of art were first put on show. This complex of museums also houses the Sistine Chapel and the Raphael Rooms, and should not be missed. Note that no bare knees or shoulders are allowed.

KEY

① Cortile di San Damaso

② Raphael Loggia

③ Borgia Apartment

④ Borgia Tower

⑤ Sistine Chapel

⑥ Apartment of Pius V

⑦ Cortile del Belvedere

⑧ Cortile della Biblioteca

⑨ Braccio Nuovo

⑩ **The Belvedere Palace** was commissioned in the late 15th century by Pope Innocent VIII.

⑪ **The Spiral Ramp**, a spectacular stairway leading down from the museums to the street, was designed by Giuseppe Momo in 1932.

★ **Atrium of the Four Gates**
Built by Camporese in 1792–3, this vast domed edifice was the original entrance to the Vatican Museums.

Simonetti Stairway
Built in the 1780s with a vaulted ceiling, the stairs were part of the conversion of the Belvedere Palace into the Pio-Clementine Museum.

★ Cortile della Pigna
This huge bronze pine cone, part of an ancient Roman fountain, once stood in the courtyard of old St Peter's. Its niche was designed by Pirro Ligorio.

Entrance

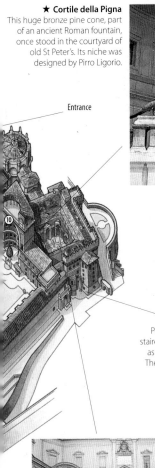

VISITORS' CHECKLIST

Practical Information
Città del Vaticano. Entrance in Viale Vaticano. **Map** 3 B2. **Tel** 06-6988 3145. **Open** 9am–6pm (last adm: 4pm) Mon–Sat, 9am–2pm (last adm: 12:30pm) last Sun of each month. Also occasionally 7–11pm Fri (book in adv). **Closed** public & religious hols. Special permit needed for Bramante Staircase, Raphael Loggia, Vatican Library, Lapidary Gallery & Vatican Archives. 🅿 (free last Sun of month). ♿ special routes. 📷 Temp exhibitions, lectures. 🚻 🖥 📅 📷 Book visits to gardens and guided tours in advance online. W **mv.vatican.va**

Transport
🚌 49 to entrance, 23, 81, 492, 990 to Piazza del Risorgimento or 40 or 62 to St Peter's. Ⓜ Cipro Musei Vaticani, Ottaviano S. Pietro.

★ Bramante Stairway
Pope Julius II built the spiral staircase within a square tower as an entrance to the palace. The staircase could be ridden up on horseback in case of emergency.

Octagonal Courtyard
The inner court of the Belvedere Palace was given its octagonal shape in 1773.

1198 Innocent III creates papal palace

1506 Bramante lays out Belvedere Courtyard

1508 Raphael begins work on Rooms

1756 Foundation of Christian Museum

1655 Bernini designs Royal Staircase

1806 Chiaramonti Museum founded

1837 Etruscan Museum founded

1000	1500	1600	1700	1800	1900

1473 Pope Sixtus IV builds Sistine Chapel

1503–13 Pope Julius II starts Classical sculpture collection

Bramante (1444–1514)

1758 Museum of Pagan Antiquities founded

1776–84 Pius VI enlarges museum

1822 Braccio Nuovo is opened

1970 Pope Paul VI opens Gregorian Museum of Pagan Antiquities

Exploring the Vatican Museums

Four centuries of papal patronage and connoisseurship have resulted in one of the world's great collections of Classical and Renaissance art. The Vatican houses many of the great archaeological finds of central Italy including the *Laocoön* group, discovered in 1506 on the Esquiline, the *Apollo del Belvedere* and the Etruscan bronze known as the *Mars of Todi*. During the Renaissance, parts of the museums were decorated with wonderful frescoes commissioned for the Sistine Chapel, the Raphael Rooms and the Borgia Apartment.

Gallery of the Candelabra
Once an open loggia, this gallery of mostly Roman copies of Greek sculptures has a view of the Vatican Gardens.

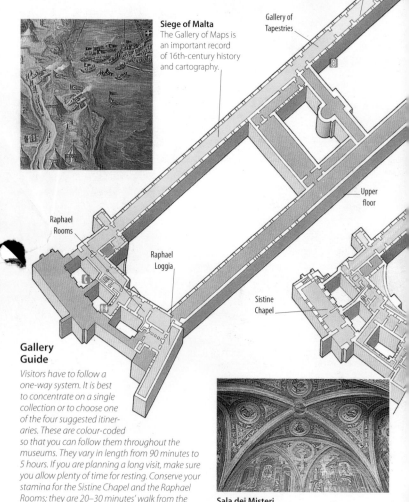

Siege of Malta
The Gallery of Maps is an important record of 16th-century history and cartography.

Gallery of Tapestries

Chariot Room

Upper floor

Raphael Rooms

Raphael Loggia

Sistine Chapel

Gallery Guide

Visitors have to follow a one-way system. It is best to concentrate on a single collection or to choose one of the four suggested itineraries. These are colour-coded so that you can follow them throughout the museums. They vary in length from 90 minutes to 5 hours. If you are planning a long visit, make sure you allow plenty of time for resting. Conserve your stamina for the Sistine Chapel and the Raphael Rooms; they are 20–30 minutes' walk from the entrance, without allowing for any viewing time along the way.

Sala dei Misteri
This is one of the rooms of the Borgia Apartment, richly decorated with Pinturicchio frescoes.

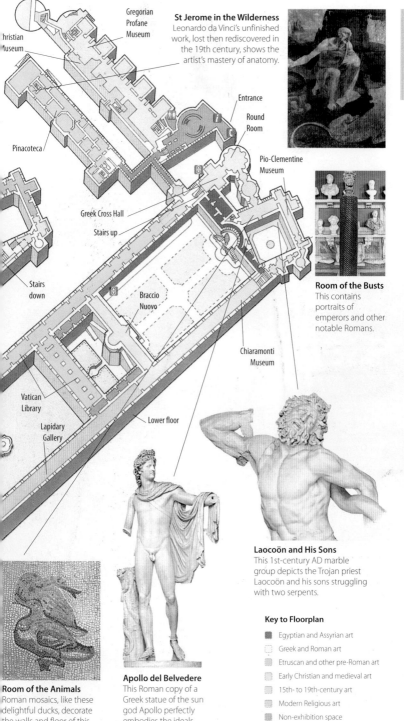

Gregorian
Profane
Museum

Christian
Museum

St Jerome in the Wilderness
Leonardo da Vinci's unfinished
work, lost then rediscovered in
the 19th century, shows the
artist's mastery of anatomy.

Entrance

Round
Room

Pinacoteca

Pio-Clementine
Museum

Greek Cross Hall

Stairs up

Room of the Busts
This contains
portraits of
emperors and other
notable Romans.

Stairs
down

Braccio
Nuovo

Chiaramonti
Museum

Vatican
Library

Lapidary
Gallery

Lower floor

Laocoön and His Sons
This 1st-century AD marble
group depicts the Trojan priest
Laocoön and his sons struggling
with two serpents.

Key to Floorplan

- Egyptian and Assyrian art
- Greek and Roman art
- Etruscan and other pre-Roman art
- Early Christian and medieval art
- 15th- to 19th-century art
- Modern Religious art
- Non-exhibition space
- Open by special permit only

Room of the Animals
Roman mosaics, like these
delightful ducks, decorate
the walls and floor of this
room of animal sculptures.

Apollo del Belvedere
This Roman copy of a
Greek statue of the sun
god Apollo perfectly
embodies the ideals
of Classical beauty.

Exploring the Vatican's Collections

The Vatican's greatest treasures are its Greek and Roman antiquities. These have been on display since the 18th century. The 19th century saw the addition of exciting discoveries from Etruscan tombs and excavations in Egypt. In the Pinacoteca (art gallery) there is a small, choice collection of paintings, including works by Raphael, Titian and Leonardo. Works by great painters and sculptors are also on view throughout the older parts of the museums in the form of sumptuous decorations commissioned by the Renaissance popes.

Coloured bas-relief from an Egyptian tomb (c.2400 BC)

Egyptian and Assyrian Art

The Egyptian collection contains finds from 19th- and 20th-century excavations in Egypt and statues which were brought to Rome in Imperial times. There are also Roman imitations of Egyptian art from Hadrian's Villa (see p271) and from the Campus Martius district of ancient Rome. Egyptian-style statuary from Hadrian's Villa was used to decorate the Greek Cross Hall, the entrance to the new wing built in 1780 by Michelangelo Simonetti.

The genuine Egyptian works, exhibited on the lower floor of the Belvedere Palace, include statues, mummies, mummy cases and funerary artifacts. There is also a large collection of documents written on papyrus, the paper the ancient Egyptians made from reeds. Among the main treasures is a colossal granite statue of Queen Tuya, the mother of Rameses II, found on the site of the Horti Sallustiani gardens (see p253) in 1714. The statue, which dates

from the 13th century BC, may have been brought to Rome by the Emperor Caligula (reigned AD 37–41), who had an unhealthy interest in pharaohs and in his own mother, Agrippina.

Also noteworthy are the head of a statue of Mentuhotep IV (21st century BC), the beautiful mummy case of Queen Hetepheres, and the funerary stela of Iry, administrator of the Necropolis of Giza (26th century BC).

The Assyrian Stairway is decorated with fragments of reliefs from the palaces of the kings of Nineveh (8th century BC). These depict the military exploits of King Sennacherib and his son Sargon II, and show scenes from Assyrian and Chaldean mythology.

Etruscan and Other Pre-Roman Art

This collection comprises artifacts from pre-Roman civilizations in Etruria and Latium, from Neolithic times to the 1st century BC, when these ancient populations were assimilated into the Roman state. Pride of place in the Gregorian Etruscan Museum goes to the objects found in the Regolini-Galassi tomb, excavated in 1836 at the necropolis of Cerveteri (see p273). The tomb was found intact and yielded numerous everyday household objects, plus a throne, a bed and a funeral cart, all cast in bronze, dating from the 7th century BC. Beautiful black vases, delightful terracotta figurines and bronze statues such as the famous Mars of Todi, displayed in the Room of the Bronzes, show the Etruscans to have been a highly civilized, sophisticated people.

A number of Greek vases that were found in Etruscan tombs are on display in the Vase Collection. The Room of the Italiot Vases contains only vases produced locally in the Greek cities of Southern Italy and in Etruria itself. These date from the 5th to the 4th century BC.

Etruscan gold clasp (fibula) from the 7th century BC

Head of an athlete in mosaic from the Baths of Caracalla

Greek and Roman Art

The greater part of the Vatican Museums is dedicated to Greek and Roman art. Exhibits line connecting corridors and vestibules; walls and floors display fine mosaics; and famous sculptures decorate the main courtyards.

The first serious organization of the collection took place in the reign of Julius II (1503–13) around Bramante's Belvedere Courtyard. The prize pieces form the nucleus of the 18th-century Pio-Clementine Museum. In the pavilions of the Octagonal Courtyard and in the surrounding rooms are sculptures considered among the greatest achievements of Western art. The *Apoxyomenos* (an athlete wiping his body after a race) and the *Apollo del Belvedere* are high-quality Roman copies of Greek originals of about 320 BC. The magnificent *Laocoön and His Sons*, sculpted by three artists from Rhodes, had long been known to exist from a description by Pliny the Elder. It was rediscovered near the ruins of the Domus Aurea (*see p177*) in 1506. Classical works such as these had a profound influence on Michelangelo and other Renaissance artists.

The much smaller Chiaramonti Museum, named after Pope Pius VII Chiaramonti, was laid out by Canova in the early 19th century. It includes a striking colossal head of the goddess Athena. The Braccio Nuovo, an extension of the Chiaramonti, decorated with Roman floor mosaics, contains a statue of Augustus from the villa of his wife Livia at Prima Porta. Its pose is based on the famous *Doryphoros* by the Greek sculptor Polyclitus, of which there is a Roman copy on display opposite.

Exhibits in the Vase Rooms range from the Greek geometric style (8th century BC) to black-figure vases from Corinth, such as the famous vase by Exekias, with Achilles and Ajax playing a game similar to draughts (530 BC), and the later red-figure type, such as the *kylix* (a wide shallow cup) with Oedipus and the Sphinx from the 5th century BC. A stairway links this section to the Gallery of the Candelabra and the Chariot Room (containing a marble horse-drawn chariot dating from the 1st Century BC).

The Gregorian Profane Museum charts the evolution of Roman art from dependence

The *Doryphoros* or spear-carrier, a Roman copy in marble of an original Greek bronze

upon Greek models to a recognizably Roman style. Original Greek works include large marble fragments from the Parthenon in Athens. There is also a Roman copy of *Athena and Marsyas* by Myron, which was part of the decoration of the Parthenon. Totally Roman in character are two reliefs known as the *Rilievi della Cancelleria*, because they were discovered beneath the Palazzo della Cancelleria (*see p151*) in the 1930s. They show military parades of the Emperor Vespasian and his son Domitian. This section also has fine Roman floor mosaics. There are two from the Baths of Caracalla (*see p199*), depicting athletes and referees. They date from the 3rd century AD. Most striking of all is a mosaic that creates the impression of an unswept floor, covered with debris after a meal.

Away from the main Classical collections, in one of the rooms of the Vatican Library, is the *Aldobrandini Wedding*, a beautiful Roman fresco of a bride being prepared for her marriage, dating from the 1st century AD.

Floor mosaic from the Baths of Otricoli in Umbria, in the Chiaramonti Museum

Detail from Giotto's *Stefaneschi Triptych*

Early Christian and Medieval Art

The main collection of early Christian antiquities is in the Pio-Christian Museum, founded in the 19th century by Pope Pius IX and formerly housed in the Lateran Palace. It contains inscriptions and sculpture from catacombs and early Christian basilicas. The sculpture consists chiefly of reliefs decorating sarcophagi, though the most striking work is a free-standing 4th-century statue of the *Good Shepherd*. The sculpture's chief interest lies in the way it blends Biblical episodes with pagan mythology. Christianity adopted Classical images so that its doctrines could be understood in clear visual terms. The idealized pastoral figure of the shepherd, for example, became Christ himself, while bearded philosophers turned into the Apostles. At the same time, Christianity laid claim to be the spiritual and cultural heir of the Roman Empire.

The first two rooms of the Pinacoteca are dedicated to late medieval art, mostly tempera-painted wooden panels which served as altarpieces.

The outstanding work is Giotto's altarpiece dating from about 1300, known as the *Stefaneschi Triptych*. It expresses much the same theme as the early Christian works: the continuity between the Classical world of the Roman Empire and the new order of Christian Europe. The crucifixion of St Peter takes place between two landmarks of ancient Rome, the Pyramid of Caius Cestius (*see p207*), and the pyramid known in the Middle Ages as the Tomb of Romulus, which stood near the Vatican (*see p248*). The triptych, which decorated the main altar of old St Peter's, includes portraits of Pope St Celestine I (reigned 422–432), and of the donor, Cardinal Jacopo Stefaneschi, shown offering the triptych to St Peter.

The Vatican Library has a number of medieval treasures exhibited rather haphazardly in showcases; these include woven and embroidered cloths, reliquaries, enamels and icons. One of the aims of the 18th-century reorganization of the Vatican collections was to glorify Christian works by contrasting them with earlier pagan creations. In the long Lapidary Gallery over 3,000 stone tablets with Christian and pagan inscriptions are displayed on opposite walls. The world's greatest collection of its kind, it may be visited only with special permission.

15th- to 19th-Century Art

The Renaissance popes, many of whom were cultured connoisseurs of the arts, considered it their duty to sponsor the leading painters, sculptors and goldsmiths of the age.

Lament over the Dead Christ by the Venetian artist Giovanni Bellini (1430–1516)

Raphael's Last Painting

When Raphael died in 1520, the *Transfiguration* was found in his studio, almost complete. The wonderful luminous work was placed at the head of the bier where the great artist's body lay. It depicts the episode in the Gospels in which Christ took three of the Apostles to the top of a mountain, where He appeared to them in divine glory. In the detail shown here Christ floats above the ground in a halo of ethereal light.

The galleries around the Cortile del Belvedere were all decorated by great artists between the 16th and the 19th centuries. The Gallery of Tapestries is hung with tapestries woven in Brussels to designs by students of Raphael; the Apartment of Pope Pius V has beautiful 15th-century Flemish tapestries; and the Gallery of Maps is frescoed with 16th-century maps of ancient and contemporary Italy. When you go to visit the Raphael Rooms *(see pp240–41)*, you should not overlook the nearby Room of the Chiaroscuri and Pope Nicholas V's tiny private chapel, frescoed by Fra Angelico between 1447 and 1451. Similarly, before reaching the Sistine Chapel *(see pp242–5)*, visit the Borgia Apartment, frescoed in a decorative, flowery style by Pinturicchio and his students in the 1490s. The contrast with Michelangelo's Sistine Chapel ceiling, begun in 1508, could hardly be greater. Another set of fascinating frescoes decorates the Loggia of Raphael, but this requires special permission to visit.

Many important works by Renaissance masters are on show in the Pinacoteca (art gallery). Highlights among the works by 15th-century painters are the *Lament over the Dead Christ* by the Venetian Giovanni Bellini and Leonardo da Vinci's unfinished *St Jerome in the Wilderness*. Of the great 16th-century works, do not miss the fine altarpiece by Titian, the *Crucifixion of St Peter* by Guido Reni, the *Deposition* by Caravaggio and the *Communion of St Jerome* by Domenichino. Raphael has a whole room dedicated to his work. It contains the beautiful *Madonna of Foligno* and the *Transfiguration* as well as eight tapestries made to his designs.

Lunette of the *Adoration of the Magi* by Pinturicchio in the Room of the Mysteries in the Borgia Apartment

Modern Religious Art

Modern artists exhibited in the Vatican Museums face daunting competition from the great works of the past. Few modern works are displayed conspicuously, the exceptions being Momo's spiral staircase of 1932, which greets visitors as they enter the museums, and Arnaldo Pomodoro's abstract sculpture in the centre of the Cortile della Pigna.

In 1973 a contemporary art collection was inaugurated by Pope Paul VI. Housed in the Borgia Apartment, it includes over 800 exhibits by modern artists from all over the world, donated by collectors or the artists themselves. Works in a great variety of media show many contrasting approaches to religious subjects. There are paintings, drawings, engravings and sculpture by 19th- and 20th-century artists, as well as mosaics, stained glass, ceramics and tapestries. Well-known modern painters such as Georges Braque, Paul Klee, Edvard Munch and Graham Sutherland are all represented. There are also drawings by Henry Moore, ceramics by Picasso and stained glass by Fernand Léger. Projects for modern church ornaments include Matisse's decorations for the church of St Paul de Vence, Luigi Fontana's models for the bronze doors of Milan cathedral, and Emilio Greco's panels for the doors of Orvieto cathedral.

City with Gothic Cathedral by Paul Klee (1879–1940)

Raphael Rooms

Pope Julius II's private apartments were built above those of his hated predecessor, Alexander VI, one of the Borgias, who died in 1503. Julius was impressed with Raphael's work and chose him to redecorate the four rooms *(stanze)*. Raphael and his pupils began the task in 1508, replacing existing

Cortile del Belvedere

works by several better-known artists, including Raphael's own teacher, Perugino. The work took over 16 years and Raphael himself died before its completion. The frescoes express the religious and philosophical ideals of the Renaissance. They quickly established Raphael's reputation as an artist in Rome, putting him on a par with Michelangelo, then working on the ceiling of the Sistine Chapel.

Detail from *The Expulsion of Heliodorus from the Temple*, showing Pope Julius II watching the scene from his litter

Key to Floorplan

① Hall of Constantine
② Room of Heliodorus
③ Room of the Segnatura
④ Room of *The Fire in the Borgo*

① Hall of Constantine

The frescoes in this room were started in 1517, three years before Raphael's death, but Raphael himself probably had little hand in their execution. As a result they are not held in the same high regard as those in the other rooms. The work was completed in 1525 in the reign of Pope Clement VII by Giulio Romano and two other former pupils of Raphael, Giovanni Francesco Penni and Raffaellino del Colle.

The theme of the decoration is the triumph of Christianity over paganism. The four major frescoes show scenes from the life of Constantine and include his *Vision of the Cross* and his victory over his rival Maxentius at *The Battle of the Milvian Bridge*, for which Raphael had provided a preparatory sketch. In both *The Baptism of Constantine* and *The Donation of Constantine*, the figure of Pope Sylvester *(see p172)* was given the features of Clement VII.

② Room of Heliodorus

This private antechamber was decorated by Raphael between 1512 and 1514. The main frescoes show the miraculous protection granted to all the Church's ministers, doctrines and property. The room's name refers to the fresco on the right, *The Expulsion of Heliodorus from the Temple*. This shows a story from Jewish history, in which a thief called Heliodorus is felled by a horseman as

Swiss guards waiting with papal chair in *The Mass at Bolsena*

he tries to make off with the treasure from the Temple of Jerusalem. The scene is witnessed by the pope, borne on a litter by courtiers. The incident is also a thinly veiled reference to Julius II's success in driving foreign armies out of Italy. In *The Meeting of Leo I and Attila* Raphael pays a similar compliment to the pope's political skill. Pope Leo was originally given the face of Julius II, but after his death, Raphael substituted the features of Julius's successor, Leo X.

The Mass at Bolsena depicts a miracle that occurred in 1263. A priest who doubted that the bread and

The Battle of the Milvian Bridge, completed by one of Raphael's assistants

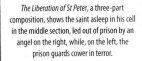

The Liberation of St Peter, a three-part composition, shows the saint asleep in his cell in the middle section, led out of prison by an angel on the right, while, on the left, the prison guards cower in terror.

The most famous, *The Fire in the Borgo*, was painted from Raphael's designs and reflects his maturity as an artist. It celebrates the miracle that took place in 847, when Pope Leo IV extinguished a fire raging in the Borgo *(see p248)* by making the sign of the cross. The incident is likened to the flight of Aeneas from Troy described by Virgil. The figure of Aeneas appears in the foreground carrying his father on his back. This borrowing of an event from Classical legend shows a new willingness to experiment on the part of Raphael. Sadly, his pupils did not always follow his designs faithfully and this, combined with some poor restoration, has spoilt the work.

wine really were the body and blood of Christ suddenly saw the host bleed while he was celebrating mass. Julius II appears in this fresco, accompanied by a colourful group of Swiss guards.

Julius appears yet again as St Peter in *The Liberation of St Peter*. This fresco is remarkable for its dramatic lighting effects, achieved despite the painting's awkward shape and its position above a window.

③ Room of the Segnatura

The name is derived from a special council which met in this room to sign official documents. The frescoes here were completed between 1508 and 1511. The scheme Raphael followed was dictated by Pope Julius II. It reflects the Humanist belief that there could be perfect harmony between Classical culture and Christianity in their mutual search for truth.

The Dispute over the Holy Sacrament, the first fresco completed by Raphael for Pope Julius, represents the triumph of religion and spiritual truth. The consecrated host is shown at the centre of the painting. This links the group of learned scholars, who discuss its significance, to the Holy Trinity and the saints floating on clouds up above.

On the opposite wall, *The School of Athens (see p34)* is a bustling scene centred around the debate on the search for truth between Greek philosophers Plato and Aristotle. It also features portraits of many of Raphael's contemporaries, including Leonardo da Vinci, Bramante and Michelangelo. The other works include a portrait of the bearded Pope Julius II, who in 1511 vowed not to shave until he managed to rid Italy of all usurpers.

④ Room of *The Fire in the Borgo*

This was originally the dining room, but when the decoration was completed under Pope Leo X, it became a music room. All the frescoes exalt the reigning pope by depicting events in the lives of his namesakes, the 9th-century popes Leo III and IV. The main frescoes were finished by two of Raphael's assistants between 1514 and 1517, following their master's own plans.

Detail from *The Fire in the Borgo*, showing Aeneas, the Trojan hero, with his father on his back, fleeing from the fire

The Dispute over the Holy Sacrament, the first fresco completed in the Raphael Rooms

Sistine Chapel: The Walls

The massive walls of the Sistine Chapel, the main chapel in the Vatican Palace, were frescoed by some of the finest artists of the 15th and 16th centuries. The 12 paintings on the side walls, by artists including Perugino, Ghirlandaio, Botticelli and Signorelli, show parallel episodes from the lives of Moses and Christ. The decoration of the chapel walls was completed between 1534 and 1541 by Michelangelo, who added the great altar wall fresco, *The Last Judgment*.

Key to the Frescoes: Artists and Subjects

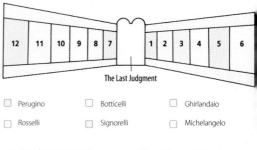

The Last Judgment

☐ Perugino   ☐ Botticelli   ☐ Ghirlandaio
☐ Rosselli   ☐ Signorelli   ☐ Michelangelo

1 Baptism of Christ in the Jordan
2 Temptations of Christ
3 Calling of St Peter and St Andrew
4 Sermon on the Mount
5 Handing over the Keys to St Peter
6 Last Supper
7 Moses's Journey into Egypt
8 Moses Receiving the Call
9 Crossing of the Red Sea
10 Adoration of the Golden Calf
11 Punishment of the Rebels
12 Last Days of Moses

The Last Judgment by Michelangelo

Revealed in 1993 after a year's restoration, *The Last Judgment* is considered to be the masterpiece of Michelangelo's mature years. It was commissioned by Pope Paul III Farnese, and required the removal of some earlier frescoes and two windows over the altar. A new wall was erected which slanted inwards to stop dust settling on it. Michelangelo worked alone on the fresco for seven years, until its completion in 1541.

The painting depicts the souls of the dead rising up to face the wrath of God, a subject that is rarely used for an altar decoration. The pope chose it as a warning to Catholics to adhere to their faith in the turmoil of the Reformation. In fact the work conveys the artist's own tormented attitude to his faith. It offers neither the certainties of Christian orthodoxy, nor the ordered view of Classicism.

In a dynamic, emotional composition, the figures are caught in a vortex of motion. The dead are torn from their graves and hauled up to face Christ the Judge, whose athletic, muscular figure is the focus of all the painting's movement. Christ shows little sympathy for the agitated saints around him, clutching the instruments of their martyrdom. Neither is any pity shown for the damned, hurled down to the demons in hell. Here Charon, pushing people off his boat into the depths of Hades, and the infernal judge Minos, are taken from Dante's *Inferno*. Minos has ass's ears, and is a portrait of courtier Biagio da Cesena, who had objected to the nude figures in the fresco. Michelangelo's self-portrait is on the skin held by the martyr St Bartholomew.

Souls meeting the wrath of Christ in Michelangelo's *Last Judgment*

Wall Frescoes

Detail from Botticelli's fresco
Temptations of Christ

When the Sistine Chapel was built, the papacy was a strong political power with vast accumulated wealth. In 1475 Pope Sixtus IV was able to summon some of the greatest painters of his day to decorate the chapel. Among the artists employed were Perugino, who was Raphael's master and is often credited with overseeing the project, Sandro Botticelli, Domenico Ghirlandaio, Cosimo Rosselli and Luca Signorelli. Their work on the chapel's frescoes took from 1481 to 1483.

Although frequently overlooked by visitors who concentrate on Michelangelo's work, the frescoes along the side walls of the chapel include some of the finest works of 15th-century Italian art. The two cycles of frescoes represent scenes from the lives of Moses and Christ. Above them in the spaces between the windows are portraits of the earliest popes, painted by various artists, including Botticelli.

The fresco cycles start at the altar end of the chapel, with the story of Christ on the right-hand wall and that of Moses on the left. Originally there were two paintings, *The Birth of Christ* and *The Finding of Moses*, on the wall behind the altar, but these were both destroyed to make way for Michelangelo's *Last Judgment*. The final paintings of the two

cycles are also lost. They were on the entrance wall, which collapsed during the 16th century. When the wall was restored, they were replaced with poor substitutes.

As was customary at the time, each fresco contains a series of scenes, linked thematically to the central episode. Hidden meanings and symbols connect each painting with its counterpart on the opposite wall, and there are also many allusions to contemporary events.

The elaborate architectural details in the frescoes include familiar Roman monuments. The Arch of Constantine *(see p93)* provides the backdrop for the *Punishment of the Rebels* by Botticelli, the fifth panel in the cycle of Moses, in which the artist himself appears as the last figure but one on the right. Two similar arches appear in the painting opposite, Perugino's *Handing over the Keys to St Peter*.

Moses was both spiritual and temporal leader of his people. He called down the wrath of God on those who challenged his decisions, thus setting a precedent for the power

The crowd of onlookers in the *Calling of St Peter and St Andrew* by Ghirlandaio

exercised by the pope. In *Handing over the Keys to St Peter*, Christ confers spiritual and

temporal authority on St Peter by giving him the keys to the Kingdoms of Heaven and Earth. The golden-domed building in the centre of the vast piazza represents both the Temple of Jerusalem and the Church, as founded by Peter, the first pope. The fifth figure on the right is thought to be a self-portrait by Perugino.

The central episode in Botticelli's
Punishment of the Rebels

Botticelli's *Temptations of Christ* includes a view of the Hospital of Santo Spirito, rebuilt in 1475 by Sixtus IV *(see p246)*. Here the devil is disguised in the habit of a Franciscan monk. Portraits of both Botticelli and Filippino Lippi are visible in the left hand corner. A portrait of the pope's nephew, Girolamo Riario, appears in the painting of the *Crossing of the Red Sea* by Rosselli, in which the sea is literally red. This painting also commemorates the papal victory at Campomorto in 1482.

Perugino's *Handing over the Keys to St Peter*

Sistine Chapel: The Ceiling

Michelangelo frescoed the ceiling for Pope Julius II between 1508 and 1512, working on specially designed scaffolding. The main panels, which chart the Creation of the World and Fall of Man, are surrounded by subjects from the Old and New Testaments – except for the Classical Sibyls who are said to have foreseen the birth of Christ. In the 1980s the ceiling was restored revealing colours of an unsuspected vibrancy.

Libyan Sibyl
The pagan prophetess reaches for the Book of Knowledge. Like most female figures Michelangelo painted, the beautiful Libyan Sibyl was probably modelled on a man.

Creation of the Sun and Moon
Michelangelo depicts God as a dynamic but terrifying figure commanding the sun to shed light on the earth.

KEY

① **Illusionistic architecture**

② **The lunettes** are devoted to frescoes of the ancestors of Christ, like Hezekiah.

③ **The Ignudi** are athletic male nudes whose significance is uncertain.

Key to Ceiling Panels

☐ **Genesis: 1** God Dividing Light from Darkness; **2** Creation of the Sun and Moon; **3** Separating Waters from Land; **4** Creation of Adam; **5** Creation of Eve; **6** Original Sin; **7** Sacrifice of Noah; **8** The Deluge; **9** Drunkenness of Noah.

☐ **Ancestors of Christ: 10** Solomon with his Mother; **11** Parents of Jesse; **12** Rehoboam with Mother; **13** Asa with Parents; **14** Uzziah with Parents; **15** Hezekiah with Parents; **16** Zerubbabel with Parents; **17** Josiah with Parents.

☐ **Prophets: 18** Jonah; **19** Jeremiah; **20** Daniel; **21** Ezekiel; **22** Isaiah; **23** Joel; **24** Zechariah.

☐ **Sibyls: 25** Libyan Sibyl; **26** Persian Sibyl; **27** Cumaean Sibyl; **28** Erythrean Sibyl; **29** Delphic Sibyl.

☐ **Old Testament Scenes of Salvat...** **30** Punishment of Haman; **31** Mos... and the Brazen Serpent; **32** David... Goliath; **33** Judith and Holofernes.

Original Sin
This shows Adam and Eve tasting the forbidden fruit from the Tree of Knowledge, and their expulsion from Paradise. Michelangelo represents Satan as a snake with the body of a woman.

Restoration of the Sistine Ceiling

Restorers used computers, photography and spectrum analysis to inspect the fresco before cleaning began. They were therefore able to detect and remove the changes previous restorers had made to Michelangelo's original work. Analysis showed that the ceiling had been cleaned with materials ranging from bread to retsina wine. The restoration then revealed the familiarly dusky, eggshell-cracked figures to have creamy skins, lustrous hair and to be dressed in brightly coloured, luscious robes: "a Benetton Michelangelo" mocked one critic, claiming that a layer of varnish which the artist had added to darken the colours had been removed. However, after examining the work, most experts agreed that the new colours probably matched those painted by Michelangelo.

A restorer cleaning the Libyan Sibyl

❸ Porta Santo Spirito

Via dei Penitenzieri. **Map** 3 C3. 🚌 23, 34, 46, 62, 64, 98, 870, 881, 982.

This gate is situated at what was the southern limit of the "Leonine City", the area enclosed within walls by Pope Leo IV as a defence against the Saracens who had sacked Rome in AD 845. The walls measure 3 km (2 miles) in circumference.

Work on the walls started in AD 846. Pope Leo supervised the huge army of labourers personally, and thanks to his encouragement, the job was completed in 4 years. He then consecrated his massive feat of construction.

Since the time of Pope Leo the walls have needed much reinforcement and repair. The gateway visible today at Porta Santo Spirito was built by the architect Antonio da Sangallo the Younger in 1543–4. It is framed by two huge bastions that were added in 1564 by Pope Pius IV Medici. Sadly, Sangallo's design for a monumental entrance to the Vatican was never completed; the principal columns come to an end somewhat abruptly in a modern covering of cement.

Nave of Santo Spirito in Sassia

❹ Santo Spirito in Sassia

Via dei Penitenzieri 12. **Map** 3 C3. **Tel** 06-687 9310. 🚌 23, 34, 46, 62, 64, 98, 870, 881, 982. **Open** 7:30am–noon, 3–6:30pm Mon–Sat, 9:30am–1pm, 3–6:30pm Sun. 🕐 ♿

Sixtus V's arms over door of Santo Spirito

Built on the site of a church erected by King Ine of Wessex, who died in Rome in the 8th century, the church is the work of Antonio da Sangallo the Younger. It was rebuilt (1538–44) after the Sack of Rome left it in ruins in 1527. The façade was added under Pope Sixtus V (1585–90). The nave and side chapels are decorated with a series of light, lively frescoes. The pretty bell tower is earlier, dating from the reign of Sixtus IV (1471–84). It was probably the work of the pope's architect, Baccio Pontelli, who also built the Hospital of Santo Spirito, and the Ponte Sisto *(see p212)* further down the River Tiber.

❺ Hospital of Santo Spirito

Borgo Santo Spirito 2. **Map** 3 C3. 🚌 23, 34, 46, 62, 64. Complex & chapel: **Open** for events only (call 06-6835 2433). ♿

The oldest hospital in Rome, this is said to have been founded as a result of a nightmare experienced by Pope Innocent III (1198–1216). In the dream, an angel showed him the bodies of Rome's unwanted babies dredged up from the River Tiber in fishing nets. As a result, the pope hastened to build a hospice for sick paupers. In 1475 the hospital was reorganized by

Fresco of an angel in the octagonal chapel of the Hospital of Santo Spirito

Pope Sixtus IV to care for the poor pilgrims expected for the Holy Year. Sixtus's hospital was a radical building. Cloisters divided the different types of patients; one area is still reserved for orphans and their nurses.

Unwanted infants were passed through a revolving barrel-like contraption called the *rota*, still visible to the left of the central entrance in Borgo Santo Spirito, to guarantee anonymity. Martin Luther, who visited in 1511, was shocked by the number of abandoned children he saw, believing them to be "the sons of the pope himself".

In the centre, under the hospital's conspicuous drum, is an octagonal chapel, where mass was said for patients. This room can be visited while the rest of the building still functions as a hospital.

Rusticated doorway of the Palazzo dei Convertendi

The *rota* of Santo Spirito, where mothers left unwanted babies

❻ Palazzo del Commendatore

Borgo Santo Spirito 3. **Map** 3 C3. 23, 34, 46, 62, 64. **Open** courtyard is open to the public.

As director of the Hospital of Santo Spirito, the Commendatore not only oversaw the running of the hospital, he was also responsible for its estates and revenues. This important post was originally given to members of the pope's family.

The palazzo, built next door to the hospital, has a spacious 16th-century frescoed loggia appropriate to the dignity and sobriety of its owners. The frescoes represent the story of the founding of the Hospital

of Santo Spirito. To the left of the entrance is the Spezieria, or Pharmacy. This still has the wheel used for grinding the bark of the cinchona tree to produce the drug quinine, first introduced here in 1632 by Jesuits from Peru as a cure for malaria.

Above the courtyard is a splendid clock (1827). The dial is divided into six; it was not until 1846 that the familiar division of the day into two periods of 12 hours was introduced in Rome by Pope Pius IX.

❼ Palazzo dei Convertendi

Via della Conciliazione 43. **Map** 3 C3. 23, 34, 62, 64. **Closed** to the public.

With the building of Via della Conciliazione in the 1930s, Palazzo dei Convertendi was taken down and later moved to this new site nearby. The house, partly attributed to the architect Bramante, is where the artist Raphael died in 1520.

❽ Palazzo dei Penitenzieri

Via della Conciliazione 33. **Map** 3 C3. **Tel/Fax** 06-6989 2930. 23, 34, 62, 64. **Open** 2:30–5pm Mon–Fri, appt only (by fax) for groups.

Della Rovere arms

The palazzo owes its name to the fact that the place was once home to the confessors *(penitenzieri)* of St Peter's. Now partly housing the Hotel Columbus, it was originally built by Cardinal Domenico della Rovere in 1480. The palazzo still bears the family's coat of arms, the oak tree *(rovere* means oak), on its graceful courtyard well-head. On the cardinal's death, the palazzo was acquired by Cardinal Francesco Alidosi, Pope Julius II della Rovere's favourite. Suspected of treason, the cardinal was murdered in 1511 by the pope's nephew, the Duke of Urbino, who took over the palazzo. A few of the rooms of the palazzo still contain beautiful frescoes.

View of the Tiber and the Borgo between Castel Sant'Angelo and St Peter's by Gaspare Vanvitelli (1653–1736)

❾ Santa Maria in Traspontina

Via della Conciliazione 14. **Map** 3 C3. **Tel** 06-6880 6451. 🚌 23, 34, 62, 64. **Open** 6:30am–noon, 4–7:15pm Mon–Sat; 7:30am–1pm Sun. ⛪ ♿

The church occupies the site of an ancient Roman pyramid, believed in the Middle Ages to have been the Tomb of Romulus. The pyramid was destroyed by Pope Alexander VI Borgia, but representations of it survive in the bronze doors at the entrance to St Peter's and in a Giotto triptych housed in the Vatican Pinacoteca *(see p238)*.

The present church was begun in 1566 to replace an earlier one which had been in the line of fire of the cannons defending Castel Sant'Angelo during the Sack of Rome in 1527. The papal artillery officers insisted that the dome of the new church should be as low as possible, so it was built without a supporting drum. The first chapel to the right is dedicated to the gunners' patron saint, Santa Barbara, and is decorated with warlike motifs. In the third chapel on the left are two columns, popularly thought to be the ones which SS Peter and Paul were bound to before going to their martyrdom nearby.

❿ The Borgo

Map 3 C3. 🚌 23, 34, 40, 62.

The Borgo's name derives from the German *burg*, meaning town. Rome's Borgo is where the first pilgrims to St Peter's were housed in hostels and hospices, often for quite lengthy periods. The first of these foreign colonies, called "schools", was founded in AD 725 by a Saxon, King Ine of Wessex, who wished to live a life of penance and to be buried near the Tomb of St Peter. These days hotels and hostels have made the Borgo a colony of international pilgrims once again. Much of the area's

character was lost after redevelopment in the 1930s, but it is still enjoyable to stroll the old narrow streets on either side of Via della Conciliazione.

Clement VII, who used the Vatican Corridor to evade capture in 1527

⓫ Vatican Corridor

Castel Sant'Angelo to the Vatican. **Map** 3 C3. 🚌 23, 34, 40, 62. **Closed** to the public except for special summer evening events; call 06-0608 for info.

Locally known as the Passetto (small corridor), this long passageway was built into the fortifications during medieval

The façade of the Carmelite church of Santa Maria in Traspontina

times. Intended as a link between the Vatican and Castel Sant'Angelo, it constituted a fortified escape route which could also be used to control the strategic Borgo area. Arrows and other missiles could be fired from its bastions onto the streets and houses below. The corridor was used in 1494 by Pope Alexander VI Borgia when Rome was invaded by King Charles VIII of France. In 1527 it enabled Pope Clement VII to take refuge in Castel Sant'Angelo, as the troops commanded by the Constable of Bourbon began the Sack of Rome.

Palazzo Torlonia (1496), unaffected by changes to the surrounding area

⓬ Palazzo Torlonia

Via della Conciliazione 30. **Map** 3 C3. 🚌 23, 34, 40, 62, 64. **Closed** to the public.

The palazzo was built in the late 15th century by the wealthy Cardinal Adriano Castellesi, in a style closely resembling Palazzo della Cancelleria (see p151). The cardinal was a much-travelled rogue, who collected vast revenues from the bishopric of Bath and Wells which he was given by his friend King Henry VII of England. In return he gave Henry his palazzo for use as the seat of the English ambassador to the Holy See. Castellesi was finally stripped of his cardinalate by Pope Leo X Medici and disappeared from history.

Pope Leo X

Since then the palazzo has had many owners and tenants. In the 17th century it was rented for a time by Queen Christina of Sweden. The Torlonia family, who acquired the building in 1820, owed its fortune to the financial genius of shopkeeper-turned-banker Giovanni Torlonia. He lent money to the impoverished Roman nobility and bought up their property during the Napoleonic Wars.

⓭ Castel Sant'Angelo

See pp250–51.

⓮ Palazzo di Giustizia

Piazza Cavour. **Map** 4 E3. 🚌 34, 49, 70, 87, 186, 280, 492, 913, 926, 990. **Closed** to the public.

The monumental Palazzo di Giustizia (Palace of Justice) was built between 1889 and 1910 to house the national law courts.

Its riverside façade is crowned with a bronze chariot and fronted by giant statues of the great men of Italian law.

The building was supposed to embody the new order replacing the injustices of papal rule, but it has never endeared itself to the Romans. It was soon dubbed the Palazzaccio (roughly, "the ugly old palazzo") both for its appearance and for the nature of its business. By the 1970s the building was collapsing under its own weight, but it has now been restored.

The ornate travertine façade of the Palazzo di Giustizia

⑬ Castel Sant'Angelo

The massive fortress of Castel Sant'Angelo takes its name from the vision that Pope Gregory the Great had of the Archangel Michael on this site. It began life in AD 139 as Emperor Hadrian's mausoleum. Since then it has had many roles: as part of Emperor Aurelian's city wall, as a medieval citadel and prison, and as the residence of the popes in times of political unrest. From the dank cells in the lower levels to the fine apartments of the Renaissance popes above, a 58-room museum covers all aspects of the castle's history.

Mausoleum of Hadrian
This artist's impression shows the tomb before Aurelian fortified its walls in AD 270–75.

Courtyard of Honour
Heaps of stone cannonballs decorate the courtyard, once the castle's ammunition store.

KEY

① **The spiral ramp** was the entrance to the mausoleum.

② **The Rooms of Clement VIII** are inscribed with the family crest of the Aldobrandini pope (1592–1605).

③ **Loggia of Paul III**

④ **Hall of the Library**

⑤ **Hall of the Columns**

⑥ **The Treasury** was probably the original site of Hadrian's burial chamber.

⑦ **The Round Hall** houses the original model from which Verschaffelt's angel was cast.

⑧ **The Hall of Justice** is decorated with a fresco of *The Angel of Justice* by Domenico Zaga (1545).

⑨ **Hall of Apollo** The room is frescoed with scenes from mythology attributed to the pupils of Perin del Vaga (1548).

⑩ **Ventilation shaft**

⑪ **Bridge**

⑫ **The Chamber of the Urns** housed the ashes of members of Hadrian's family.

★ **View from Terrace**
The castle's terrace, scene of the last act of Puccini's opera *Tosca*, offers splendid views in every direction.

Protecting the Pope

The Vatican Corridor leads from the Vatican Palace to Castel Sant'Angelo. It was built in 1277 to provide an escape route when the pope was in danger. The pentagonal ramparts built around the castle during the 17th century improved its defences in times of siege.

■ Walls and fortifications
☐ Vatican Corridor

Bronze Angel
The gigantic statue of the Archangel Michael is by the 18th-century Flemish sculptor Pieter Verschaffelt.

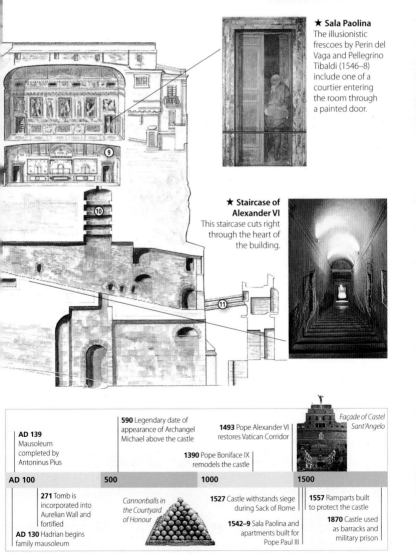

★ **Sala Paolina**
The illusionistic frescoes by Perin del Vaga and Pellegrino Tibaldi (1546–8) include one of a courtier entering the room through a painted door.

★ **Staircase of Alexander VI**
This staircase cuts right through the heart of the building.

AD 139 Mausoleum completed by Antoninus Pius

590 Legendary date of appearance of Archangel Michael above the castle

1493 Pope Alexander VI restores Vatican Corridor

1390 Pope Boniface IX remodels the castle

Façade of Castel Sant'Angelo

| AD 100 | 500 | 1000 | 1500 |

271 Tomb is incorporated into Aurelian Wall and fortified
AD 130 Hadrian begins family mausoleum

Cannonballs in the Courtyard of Honour

1527 Castle withstands siege during Sack of Rome

1542–9 Sala Paolina and apartments built for Pope Paul III

1557 Ramparts built to protect the castle

1870 Castle used as barracks and military prison

VIA VENETO

In Imperial Rome, this was a suburb where rich families owned luxurious villas and gardens. Ruins from this era can be seen in the excavations in Piazza Sallustio, named after the most extensive gardens in the area, the Horti Sallustiani. After the Sack of Rome in the 5th century (see p28), the area reverted to open countryside. Not until the 17th century did it recover its lost splendour, with the building of Palazzo Barberini and the now-vanished Villa Ludovisi. When Rome became capital of Italy in 1870, the Ludovisi sold their land for development. They kept a plot for a new house, but tax on the profits from the sale was so high, they had to sell that too. By 1900, Via Veneto had become a street of smart modern hotels and cafés. It featured prominently in Fellini's 1960 film *La Dolce Vita*, a scathing satire on the lives of film stars and idle rich, but since then has lost its position as the meeting place of the famous.

Sights at a Glance

Churches and Temples
3 Santa Maria della Concezione and Capuchin Crypt
7 Santa Susanna
8 Santa Maria della Vittoria

Historic Buildings
2 Casino dell'Aurora Ludovisi
6 Palazzo Barberini

Famous Streets
1 Via Veneto

Fountains
4 Fontana delle Api
5 Fontana del Tritone

See also Street Finder map 5, 6

Restaurants
see pp315–17
1 Edoardo
2 Brunello Lounge & Restaurant
3 Harry's Bar
4 Mirabelle
5 San Marco
6 La Terrazza dell'Eden

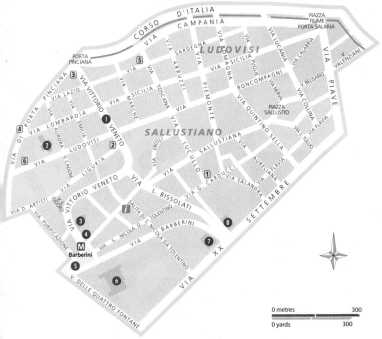

| 0 metres | 300 |
| 0 yards | 300 |

◀ The magnificent interior of Santa Maria della Vittoria

For keys to symbols *see back flap*

Street-by-Street: Via Veneto

The streets around Via Veneto, though within the walls of ancient Rome, contain little dating from before the unification of Italy in 1861. With its hotels, restaurants, bars and travel agencies, the area is the centre of 21st-century tourism in the way that Piazza di Spagna was the hub of the tourist trade in the Rome of the 18th-century Grand Tour. However, glimpses of the old city can be seen among the modern streets. These include Santa Maria della Concezione, the church of the Capuchin friars, whose convent once stood in its own gardens. In the 17th century Palazzo Barberini was built here for the powerful papal family. Bernini's Fontana del Tritone and Fontana delle Api have stood in Piazza Barberini since it was the meeting place of cart tracks entering the city from surrounding vineyards.

❸ Santa Maria della Concezione and Capuchin Crypt
This church is best known for the macabre collection of bones in its crypt.

❹ Fontana delle Api
Bernini's drinking fountain is decorated with bees, emblem of his Barberini patrons.

Barberini station

PIAZZA BARBERINI

VIA VENETO

VIA DI SAN BA

VIA DI SAN NICOLA DA TOLENTINO

VIA BARBERINI

❺ Fontana del Tritone
Bernini's muscular sea god has been spouting water skywards for over 350 years.

❻ ★ Palazzo Barberini
Pietro da Cortona worked on his spectacular ceiling fresco *The Triumph of Divine Providence* between 1633 and 1639.

VIA XX SETTEMBRE

The Porta Pinciana was built in AD 403. Only the central arch of white travertine is original.

Locator Map
See Central Rome Map pp16–17

② **Casino dell'Aurora Ludovisi**
A pavilion is all that remains of the great Ludovisi estate that once occupied most of this quarter of Rome.

① **Via Veneto**
Built during the redevelopment of Rome at the end of the 19th century, this street of smart hotels and spacious pavement cafés enjoyed its heyday during the 1950s and 1960s.

Key

— Suggested route

| 0 metres | 75 |
| 0 yards | 75 |

⑦ **Santa Susanna**
This church is dedicated to a martyr executed during Diocletian's persecution of Christians in the 3rd century AD.

⑧ ★ Santa Maria della Vittoria
The highlight of this Baroque church is the Cornaro Chapel, designed to resemble a theatre. The centre of the stage is occupied by Bernini's thrilling sculpture of *The Ecstasy of St Teresa*.

Pavement café in Via Veneto

❶ Via Veneto

Map 5 B1. 52, 53, 63, 80, 116, 119, 160 and many routes to Piazza Barberini. Barberini.

Via Veneto descends in a lazy curve from the Porta Pinciana to Piazza Barberini, lined in its upper reaches with exuberant late 19th-century hotels and canopied pavement cafés. It was laid out in 1879 over a large estate sold by the Ludovisi family in the great building boom of Rome's first years as capital of Italy. Palazzo Margherita, intended to be the new Ludovisi family palazzo, was completed in 1890. It now houses the American embassy.

In the 1960s this was the most glamorous street in Rome, its cafés patronized by film stars and plagued by paparazzi. Most of the people drinking in the cafés today are tourists, as film stars now seem to prefer the bohemian atmosphere of Trastevere or the luxury of the Parioli neighbourhood.

❷ Casino dell'Aurora Ludovisi

Via Lombardia 46. **Map** 5 B2. **Tel** 06-483 942. 52, 53, 63, 80, 116, 119. Barberini. **Open** for private groups by appt only; ring well in advance.

The Casino (a stately country residence) was a summer-house on the grounds of the Ludovisi Palace. It was built by Cardinal Ludovisi in the 17th century, and frescoed by Caravaggio and Guercino. Guercino's ceiling fresco makes it seem as if the Casino has no roof, but lies open to a cloudy sky, across which horses pull the carriage of Aurora, the goddess of dawn, from darkness towards light.

❸ Santa Maria della Concezione and Capuchin Crypt

Via Veneto 27. **Map** 5 B2. **Tel** 06-8880 3695. 52, 53, 61, 62, 63, 80, 116, 119. Barberini. Capuchin Crypt: **Open** 7am–1pm, 3–6pm daily. Museum: **Open** 7am–7pm daily. **Closed** some religious holidays. **cappucciniviaveneto.it**

Pope Urban VIII's brother, Antonio Barberini was a cardinal and a Capuchin friar. In 1626 he founded this plain church at what is now the foot of the Via Veneto. When he died he was buried not, like most cardinals, in a grand marble sarcophagus, but below a simple flag-stone near the altar, with the bleak epitaph in Latin: "Here lies dust, ashes, nothing".

The grim reality of death is illustrated even more graphically in the crypt beneath the church, where generations of Capuchin friars decorated the walls of the five vaulted chapels with the bones and skulls of their departed brethren. In all, some 4,000 skeletons were used over about 100 years to create this macabre *memento mori* started in the late 17th century. Some of the bones are wired together to form Christian symbols such as crowns of thorns, crucifixes and sacred hearts. There are also some complete skeletons, including one of a Barberini princess who died as a child. At the exit, an inscription in Latin reads: "What you are, we used to be. What we are, you will be."

❹ Fontana delle Api

Piazza Barberini. **Map** 5 B2. 52, 53, 61, 62, 63, 80, 116, 119. Barberini.

The fountain of the bees – *api* are bees, symbol of the Barberini family – is one of Bernini's more modest works. Tucked away in a corner of Piazza Barberini, it is quite easy to miss. Dating from 1644, it pays homage to Pope Urban VIII Barberini, and features rather crab-like bees which appear to be sipping the water as it dribbles down into the basin. A Latin inscription informs us that the water is for the use of the public and their animals.

Bernini's Fontana delle Api

❺ Fontana del Tritone

Piazza Barberini. **Map** 5 B3. 52, 53, 61, 62, 63, 80, 116, 119. Barberini.

In the centre of busy Piazza Barberini is one of Bernini's liveliest creations, the Triton Fountain. It was created for Pope Urban VIII Barberini in 1642, shortly after the completion of his palace on the ridge above. Acrobatic dolphins stand on their heads, twisting

Pope Urban VIII

The Triton and his conch shell in Bernini's Fontana del Tritone

their tails together to support a huge scallop shell on which the sea god Triton kneels, blowing a spindly column of water up into the air through a conch shell. Entwined artistically among the dolphins' tails are the papal tiara, the keys of St Peter and the Barberini coat of arms.

❻ Palazzo Barberini

Via delle Quattro Fontane 13. **Map** 5 B3. **Tel** 06-482 4184. ☎ 52, 53, 61, 62, 63, 80, 116, 492, 590. Ⓜ Barberini. **Open** 8:30am–7pm Tue–Sun (last adm: 6pm). **Closed** 1 Jan, 25 Dec. ▦▦▦▦▦▦▦
🆆 galleriabarberini.beniculturali.it

When Maffeo Barberini became Pope Urban VIII in 1623 he decided to build a grand palace for his family on the fringes of the city, overlooking a ruined temple. The architect, Carlo Maderno, designed it as a typical rural villa, with wings extending into the surrounding gardens. Maderno died in 1629 and Bernini took over, assisted by Borromini. The peculiar pediments on some of the top floor windows, and the oval staircase inside, are almost certainly by Borromini.

Of the many sumptuously decorated rooms, the most striking is the Gran Salone, with a dazzling illusionistic ceiling fresco by Pietro da Cortona. The palazzo also

houses paintings from the 13th to the 16th centuries, part of the Galleria Nazionale d'Arte Antica, with notable works by Filippo Lippi, El Greco and Caravaggio. There is also a Holbein portrait of King Henry VIII of England dressed for his wedding to Anne of Cleves. Of greater local significance are Guido Reni's *Beatrice Cenci*, the young woman accused of and executed for planning her father's murder (*see p154*), and *La Fornarina*, traditionally identified as a portrait of Raphael's mistress (*see p212*), although not necessarily painted by him.

Façade of Santa Susanna

❼ Santa Susanna

Via XX Settembre 14. **Map** 5 C2. **Tel** 06-4201 4554. ☎ 60, 61, 62, 492, 910. Ⓜ Repubblica. **Closed** for restoration. 🕇 🆆 santasusanna.it

Santa Susanna's most striking feature is its vigorous Baroque façade by Carlo Maderno, finished in 1603. Christians have worshipped on the site since at least the 4th century. In the nave, there are four huge frescoes by Baldassarre Croce (1558–1628), painted to resemble tapestries. These depict scenes from the life of Susanna, an obscure Roman saint who was martyred here, and the rather better-known life of the Old Testament Susanna, who was spotted bathing in her husband's garden by two lecherous judges.

Santa Susanna is the Catholic church for Americans in Rome. It is closed for restoration; see website for latest information and alternative services.

❽ Santa Maria della Vittoria

Via XX Settembre 17. **Map** 5 C2. **Tel** 06-4274 0571. ☎ 60, 61, 62, 492, 910. Ⓜ Repubblica. **Open** 8:30am–noon, 3:30–6pm daily. 🕇 🖂

This intimate Baroque church has a lavishly decorated candlelit interior. It contains one of Bernini's most ambitious sculptural works, *Ecstasy of St Teresa* (1646), the centrepiece of the Cornaro Chapel, built to resemble a miniature theatre. It even has an audience: sculptures of the chapel's benefactor, Cardinal Federico Cornaro, and his ancestors sit in boxes, as if watching and discussing the scene occurring in front of them.

Visitors may be shocked or thrilled by the apparently physical nature of St Teresa's ecstasy. She lies on a cloud, her mouth half open and her eyelids closed, with rippling drapery covering her body. Looking over her with a smile, which from different angles can appear either tender or cruel, is a curly-haired angel holding an arrow with which he is about to pierce the saint's body for a second time. The marble figures are framed and illuminated by rays of divine light materialized in bronze.

Bernini's astonishing *Ecstasy of St Teresa*

FURTHER AFIELD

The more inquisitive visitor to Rome may wish to try a few excursions to the large parks and some of the more isolated churches on the outskirts of the city. With a day to spare, you can explore the villas of Tivoli and the ruins of the ancient Roman port of Ostia. Traditional haunts of the Grand Tour *(see p132)*, such as the catacombs and the ruined aqueducts of Parco Appio Claudio, still offer glimpses of the rapidly vanishing Campagna, the countryside around Rome. More modern sights include the suburb of EUR, built in the Fascist era, and the Resistance memorial at the Fosse Ardeatine.

Sights at a Glance

Towns and Areas
⑮ EUR
⑲ Tivoli

Historic Roads
⑨ Via Appia Antica

Churches
⑥ Santa Costanza
⑦ Sant'Agnese fuori le Mura
⑧ San Lorenzo fuori le Mura
⑯ San Paolo fuori le Mura

Museums and Galleries
② *Museo e Galleria Borghese pp262–3*

③ *Villa Giulia pp264–5*
④ MAXXI
⑤ Museo d'Arte Contemporanea di Roma (MACRO)
⑰ Centrale Montemartini

Ancient Sites
㉒ Hadrian's Villa
㉓ Ostia Antica

Parks and Gardens
① Villa Borghese
⑱ Villa Doria Pamphilj

⑳ Villa d'Este
㉑ Villa Gregoriana

Tombs and Catacombs
⑩ Catacombs of San Callisto
⑪ Catacombs of San Sebastiano
⑫ Catacombs of Domitilla
⑬ Fosse Ardeatine
⑭ Tomb of Cecilia Metella

Key
▇ Main sightseeing areas
═ Motorway
▬ Main road
— Railway

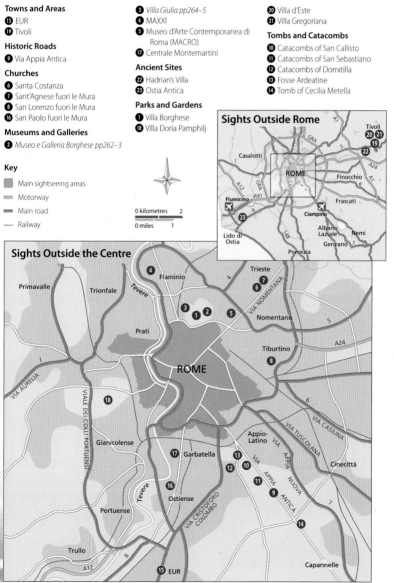

Sights Outside Rome

Casalotti
ROME
Tivoli
⑳ ㉑
⑲
㉒
Finocchio
Frascati
Fiumicino
㉓
Ciampino
Lido di Ostia
Albano Laziale
Nemi
Pomezia
Genzano

0 kilometres   2
0 miles   1

Sights Outside the Centre

Primavalle
Trionfale
Flaminio
④
Trieste
⑦
⑥
③ ① ②
⑤
VIA NOMENTANA
Nomentano
Prati
Tiburtino
⑧
ROME
A24
⑱
Gianicolense
⑰ Garbatella
Appio-Latino
⑬
⑩
Cinecittà
⑫
⑯
Ostiense
⑪
⑨
Portuense
⑭
Trullo
⑮ EUR
Capannelle

◀ One of the many fountains in the gardens of Villa d'Este

For keys to symbols *see back flap*

❶ Villa Borghese

Map 2 E5. 🚌 52, 53, 88, 116, 490, 495.
🚋 3, 19. Park: **Open** dawn to dusk.
Bioparco: Viale del Giardino Zoologico
20. **Map** 2 E4. **Tel** 06-360 8211. 🚌 52.
🚋 3, 19. **Open** 9:30am–sunset daily.
Closed 25 Dec. ♿ 🔲 🏪 🏨
🌐 **bioparco.it**. Galleria Nazionale
d'Arte Moderna: Viale delle Belle Arti
131. **Map** 2 D4. **Tel** 06-3229 8221. 🚋
3, 19. **Open** 8:30am–7:30pm Tue–Sun
(last adm: 6:45pm). **Closed** 1 Jan,
1 May, 25 Dec. ♿ 🔲 🏪 🏨
Museo Carlo Bilotti: Viale F. La Guardia.
Map 2 D5. **Open** Oct–May: 10am–4pm
Tue–Fri, 10am–7pm Sat–Sun; Jun–Sep:
1–7pm Mon–Fri, 10am–7pm Sat–Sun.
Closed 1 Jan, 1 May, 25 Dec. 🏨 🔲

British School at Rome, designed by Edwin Lutyens in 1911

The villa and its park were designed in 1605 for Cardinal Scipione Borghese, nephew of Pope Paul V. The park was the first of its kind in Rome. It contained 400 newly planted pine trees, garden sculpture by Bernini's father, Pietro, and dramatic waterworks built by Giovanni Fontana. The layout of the formal gardens was imitated by other prominent Roman families at Villa Ludovisi and Villa Doria Pamphilj.

In the early 19th century Prince Camillo Borghese assembled the family's magnificent art collection in the Casino Borghese, now the home of the Galleria and Museo Borghese.

In 1901 the park became the property of the Italian state. Within its 6 km (4 mile) circumference there are now museums and galleries, foreign academies and schools of archaeology, a zoo, a riding school, a grassy amphitheatre, an artificial lake, an aviary and an array of summerhouses, fountains, Neo-Classical statuary and exotic follies.

There are several ways into the park, including a monumental entrance on Piazzale Flaminio, built for Prince Camillo Borghese in 1825 by Luigi Canina. Other conveniently-sited entrances are at Porta Pinciana at the end of Via Veneto and from the Pincio Gardens (see p138). Piazza di Siena, a pleasantly open, grass-covered amphitheatre surrounded by tall umbrella pines, was the inspiration for Ottorino Respighi's famous symphonic poem *The Pines of Rome*, written in 1924. Near Piazza di Siena are the so-called Casina di Raffaello, said to have been owned by Raphael, and the 18th-century Palazzetto dell'Orologio. These were summer-houses from which people enjoyed the beautiful vistas across the park. Many buildings in

Statue of the English poet Byron by Thorvaldsen

the park were originally surrounded by formal gardens: the Casino Borghese and the nearby 17th-century Casino della Meridiana and its aviary *(uccelliera)* have both kept their geometrical flower-beds. Throughout the park the inter-sections of paths and avenues are marked by fountains and statues. West of Piazza di Siena is the Fontana dei Cavalli Marini (the Fountain of the Seahorses), added during the villa's 18th-century remodelling. Walking through the park you will encounter statues of Byron, Goethe and Victor Hugo, and a gloomy equestrian King Umberto I.

Dotted about the park are picturesque temples made to look like ruins, including a circular Temple of Diana between Piazza di Siena and Porta Pinciana, and a Temple of Faustina, wife of Emperor Antoninus Pius, on the hill north of Piazza di Siena. The nearby medieval-looking Fortezzuola by Canina contains the works of the sculptor Pietro Canonica, who lived in the building and died there in 1959. In the garden stands Canonica's *Monument to the Alpino and his Mule*, which honours the humblest protagonists in Italy's alpine battles against Austria in World War I.

Neo-Classical Temple of Diana

onic temple dedicated to Aesculapius, built on the lake island

In the centre of the park is the Giardino del Lago, its main entrance marked by an 18th-century copy of the Arch of Septimius Severus. The garden has an artificial lake complete with an Ionic temple to Aesculapius, the god of healing, by the 18th-century architect Antonio Asprucci. Rowing boats and ducks make the lake a favourite with children, banana trees and bamboo grow around the shore, and clearings are studded with sculptures.

Surrounded by flowerbeds south of the lake is the Art Nouveau Fontana dei Fauni, one of the garden's prettiest sculptures. In a clearing close to the entrance on Viale Pietro Canonica are the original Tritons of the Fontana del Moro in Piazza Navona (see p122) – they were moved here and replaced by copies in the 19th century.

From the northwest the park is entered by the Viale delle Belle Arti, where the **Galleria Nazionale d'Arte Moderna** houses a good collection of 19th- and 20th-century paintings. The Art Nouveau character of the area dates from the International Exhibition held here in 1911, for which pavilions were built by many nations, the most impressive being Edwin Lutyens' the British School at Rome, with a façade adapted from the upper west portico of St Paul's Cathedral in London. It is now a research institute for classical studies, history and the visual arts. Nearby statues include one of Simon Bolivar and other liberators of Latin America.

In the northeastern corner of the park lie the Museo Zoologico and a small zoo, the **Bioparco**, where the emphasis is on conservation. Nearby, the pretty 16th-century Villa Giulia houses a world-famous collection of Etruscan and other pre-Roman remains. Another Renaissance building of importance is the Palazzina of Pius IV, designed by the architect Vignola in 1552. It now houses the Italian embassy to the Holy See.

Named after its principal benefactor, the **Museo Carlo Bilotti** is situated in the centre of the Villa Borghese. This former orangery has been transformed into a modern art gallery boasting works by Giorgio de Chirico, Andy Warhol and Gino Severini.

❷ Museo e Galleria Borghese

See pp262–3.

❸ Villa Giulia

See pp264–5.

❹ MAXXI (National Museum of 21st Century Arts)

Via Guido Reni 4A. **Map** 1 A2. **Tel** 06-320 1954. 🚌 53, 217, 225, 910. 🚋 2. **Open** 11am–7pm Tue–Sun (to 10pm Sat). **Closed** 1 May, 25 Dec. ♿ 🅿️💻📷 (free up to age 14). 🏛 w fondazionemaxxi.it

Along with the nearby Parco della Musica (see p350), MAXXI, the National Museum of 21st Century Arts, has put Rome on the contemporary arts map. Located in a stunning building designed by architect Zaha Hadid, it showcases emerging Italian and international artists. An impressive amount of space is also given over to architecture.

MAXXI, the National Museum of 21st Century Arts, designed by Zaha Hadid

❽ Museo e Galleria Borghese

The villa and park were laid out by Cardinal Scipione Borghese, favourite nephew of Paul V, who had the house designed for pleasure and entertainment. The hedonistic cardinal was also an extravagant patron of the arts and he commissioned sculptures from the young Bernini which now rank among the artist's most famous works. Scipione also opened his pleasure park to the public. Today the villa houses the superb private Borghese collection of sculptures and paintings in the Museo and Galleria Borghese.

Façade of the Villa Borghese
This painting (1613) by the villa's Flemish architect Jan van Santen shows the highly ornate façade of the original design.

Rear entrance

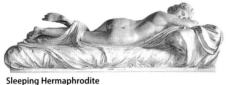

Sleeping Hermaphrodite
This is a marble Roman copy of the Greek original by Polycles, dated around 150 BC. The head and mattress were added by Andrea Bergondi in the 17th century.

The Egyptian Room
Frescoes show episodes in Egyptian history and Egyptian motifs.

★ **Rape of Proserpine**
One of Bernini's finest works shows Pluto (Hades) abducting his bride. The sculptor's amazing skill with marble can be seen clearly in the twisting figures.

Gladiator Mosaic
The floor is decorated with the fragments of a 4th-century AD mosaic from a villa in Torrenova.

1610	1710	1810

1613 15-year-old Bernini sculpts *Aeneas and Anchises*

1622–5 Bernini sculpts *The Rape of Proserpine*

Early 1800s Statues and reliefs are considered too ornate and stripped from the villa's façade

1902 Villa, grounds and collection bought by the state

1809 Much of the collection is sold by Prince Camillo Borghese to France and goes to the Louvre

1622–5 Bernini sculpts *Apollo and Daphne*

1613–15 The Flemish architect Jan van Santen designs and builds Villa Borghese

1805 Canova sculpts the semi-nude, reclining Pauline Borghese

Daphne's fingers turning into leaves

Early 1900s Balustrade round the forecourt is bought by Lord Astor for the Cliveden estate in England

★ Apollo and Daphne

Bernini's most famous masterpiece depicts the nymph Daphne fleeing the sun god Apollo at the moment of Daphne's dramatic transformation into a tree.

VISITORS' CHECKLIST

Practical Information
Villa Borghese, Piazzale del Museo Borghese 5.
Map 2 F5.
Tel 06-32810 (reservations).
Open 9am–7pm Tue–Sun.
Closed 1 Jan, 25 Dec.
🎫 Advance booking (by phone or online). Free on first Sun of month. 🖊 🏛 ♿ 🚫 📷 🎧
W galleriaborghese.
beniculturali.it

Transport
🚌 52, 53, 116, 910 to Via Pinciana. 🚊 3, 19 to Viale delle Belle Arti.

★ Galleria Borghese

The gallery has old master paintings, such as Titian's *Sacred and Profane Love* (detail) dating from 1514.

★ Pauline Borghese

Napoleon's sister Pauline posed as Venus for this sculpture. Once the statue was finished, her husband Prince Camillo locked it away, even from its sculptor Canova.

Front entrance

Key to Floorplan

⬜ Exhibition space

▨ Non-exhibition space

Museum Guide

The museum is divided into two sections: the sculpture collection (Museo Borghese) occupies the entire ground floor and the picture gallery (Galleria Borghese) is on the upper floor. The museum also hosts splendid temporary exhibitions.

David

This sculpture, by Bernini (1624), captures the moment just before David attacks Goliath with a rock. Bernini modelled David's face on his own.

❸ Villa Giulia

Built as a country retreat for Pope Julius III, this villa was designed for entertaining rather than as a permanent home. It once housed an impressive collection of statues – 160 boatloads were sent to the Vatican after the pope died in 1555. The villa, gardens, pavilions and fountains were designed by exceptional architects: Vignola (designer of the Gesù), Vasari and the sculptor Ammannati. Michelangelo also contributed. The villa's main features are its façade, the courtyard and garden and the *nymphaeum*. Since 1889 Villa Giulia has housed the Museo Nazionale Etrusco, with its outstanding collection of pre-Roman antiquities from central Italy.

★ Ficoroni Cist
Engraved and beautifully illustrated, this fine bronze marriage coffer dates from the 4th century BC.

★ Sarcophagus of the Spouses
This 6th-century BC masterpiece, from Cerveteri, shows a dead couple at the eternal banquet.

Votive Offering
The religious Etruscans made artifacts, such as this model of a boy feeding a bird, in their gods' honour.

Museum Guide

This is the most important Etruscan museum in Italy, housing artifacts from most of the major excavations in Tuscany and Lazio. Rooms 1–13b and 30–40 are arranged by site and include Vulci, Todi, Veio and Cerveteri, while private collections are in rooms 14–24.

1550 Work begins on Villa Giulia under Pope Julius III

1655 Queen Christina of Sweden stays in villa as Vatican guest

Late 1700s First large-scale studies of Etruscan artifacts

1889 Etruscan museum founded

1919 Castellani private collection donated to museum

1550	1650	1750	1850	1950	2050

Late 1500s First chance finds of Etruscan artifacts raise some scholastic interest

1908 Barberini private collection bought by the state

2012 Museum expands with opening of nearby Villa Poniatowski

Corner decoration of bronze chariot used to burn incense

1972 Pesciotti private collection bought by the state

1555 Villa completed

Façade
The villa's façade dates from 1551. The entrance is designed in the form of a triumphal arch.

Chigi Vase
Battle and hunting scenes adorn this Corinthian vase from the 6th century BC.

Faliscan Crater of the Dawn
This ornate vase, painted in the free style of the 4th century BC, shows Dawn rising in a chariot.

★ Reconstruction of an Etruscan Temple
Count Adolfo Cozza built the Temple of Alatri here in 1891. He based his design on the accounts of Vitruvius and 19th-century excavations.

Main entrance

Nymphaeum
Literally, the "area dedicated to the nymphs", this is a sunken courtyard decorated with Classical mosaics, statues and fountains.

Key to Floorplan
- Lower ground floor
- Ground floor
- First floor
- Non-exhibition space

❺ Museo d'Arte Contemporanea di Roma (MACRO)

Via Nizza 138. **Map** 6 E1. **Tel** 06-671 070 400. 🚌 36, 60, 90. **Open** 10:30am–7:30pm Tue–Sun (to 10pm Sat). Also at: Piazza Giustiniani 4 (Testaccio). **Map** 7 C4. 🚌 23, 280, 719. **Open** 10:30am–7:30pm Tue–Sun. 🏛 🏛 🖥 🖥 museomacro.org

The historic Peroni beer factory is now home to the MACRO gallery of contemporary art. Apart from a permanent collection of late 20th-century art, featuring artists such as Carla Accardi and Mario Schifano, there are interesting exhibitions – both here and at the Testaccio outpost – showcasing the latest on the local and national scene.

Interior of Santa Costanza

❻ Santa Costanza

Via Nomentana 349. **Tel** 06-8620 5456. 🚌 36, 60, 84, 90. Ⓜ S. Agnese Annibaliano. **Open** 9am–noon, 3–6pm Mon–Sat, 3–6pm Sun. 🏛 ♿ 📷

The round church of Santa Costanza was first built as a mausoleum for Emperor Constantine's daughters, Constantia and Helena, in the early 4th century. The dome and its drum are supported by a circular arcade resting on 12 magnificent pairs of granite columns. The ambulatory that runs around the outside of the

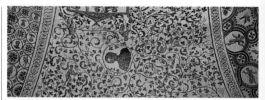

Part of the 4th-century mosaic in the ambulatory of Santa Costanza

central arcade has a barrel-vaulted ceiling decorated with wonderful 4th-century mosaics of flora and fauna and charming scenes of a Roman grape harvest. In a niche on the far side of the church from the entrance is a replica of Constantia's ornately carved porphyry sarcophagus. The original was moved to the Vatican Museums in 1790.

Constantia's sanctity is debatable – she was described by the historian Marcellinus as a fury incarnate, goading her equally unpleasant husband Hannibalianus to violence. Her canonization was probably the result of some confusion with a saintly nun of the same name.

❼ Sant'Agnese fuori le Mura

Via Nomentana 349. **Tel** 06-8620 5456. 🚌 36, 60, 84, 90. Ⓜ S. Agnese Annibaliano. Church: **Open** 8am–7pm daily. Catacombs: **Open** 9am–noon, 3–5pm (4–6pm in summer) daily. **Closed** Nov. 🏛 ♿ 📷

The church of Sant'Agnese stands among a group of early Christian buildings which includes the ruins of a covered cemetery, some extensive catacombs and the crypt where the 13-year-old martyr St Agnes was buried in AD 304. Agnes was exposed naked by order of Emperor Diocletian, furious that she should have rejected the advances of a young man at his court, but her hair miraculously grew to protect her modesty (see p123).

The church is said to have been built at the request of the Emperor Constantine's daughter, Constantia, after she had prayed at the Tomb of St Agnes for delivery from leprosy.

Though much altered over the centuries, the form and much of the structure of the 4th-century basilica remain intact. In the 7th-century apse mosaic St Agnes appears as a bejewelled Byzantine empress. According to tradition she appeared like this eight days after her death, holding a white lamb. Every year on 21 January two lambs are blessed on the church altar and a vestment called the *pallium* is woven from their wool. Every newly appointed archbishop is sent a *pallium* by the pope.

Apse mosaic in Sant'Agnese, showing the saint flanked by two popes

Cloister, San Lorenzo fuori le Mura

❽ San Lorenzo fuori le Mura

Piazzale del Verano 3. **Tel** 06-446 6184.
🚌 71, 492. 🚋 3, 19. **Open** 7:30am–
12:30pm, 3:30–7pm (4–8pm in
summer) daily. ♿

Just outside the eastern wall
of the city stands the church
of San Lorenzo. Roasted slowly
to death in AD 258, San Lorenzo
was one of the most revered of
Rome's early Christian martyrs.
The first basilica erected over
his burial place by Constantine
was largely rebuilt in 576 by
Pope Pelagius II. Close by
stood a 5th-century church
dedicated to the Virgin Mary.
The intriguing two-level church
we see today is the result of
these two churches being
knocked into one. This process,
started in the 8th century, was
completed in the 13th century
by Pope Honorius III, when the
nave, the portico
and much of the
decoration were
added. The
remains of San
Lorenzo are in
the choir of the
6th-century
church (beneath
the 13th-century
high altar).

**Romanesque
bell tower of
San Lorenzo**

❾ Via Appia Antica

🚌 118, 218. 🌐 **parcoappiaantica.it**
See Walks pp286–7. Villa dei Quintili: Via
Appia Nuova 1092. **Tel** 06-3996 7700

The first part of the Via Appia
was built in 312 BC by the Censor
Appius Claudius Caecus. When
it was extended to the ports
of Benevento, Taranto and
Brindisi in 190 BC, the road
became Rome's link with its
expanding empire in the East.
It was the route taken by
the funeral processions of
the dictator Sulla (78 BC) and
Emperor Augustus (AD 14) and
it was along this road that St Paul
was led as a prisoner to Rome
in AD 56. Gradually abandoned
during the Middle Ages, the
road was restored by Pope Pius
IV in the mid-16th century. It
is lined with ruined family
tombs and collective burial
places known as columbaria.
Beneath the fields on either side
lies a vast maze of catacombs.
Today the road starts at Porta
San Sebastiano *(see p198).* Major
Christian sights include the
church of Domine Quo Vadis,
built where St Peter is said to
have met Christ while fleeing
from Rome, and the Catacombs
of San Callisto and San
Sebastiano. The tombs lining
the road include those of Cecilia
Metella *(see p268)* and Romulus
(son of Emperor Maxentius)
who died in 309. The ancient
Villa dei Quintili is nearby.

❿ Catacombs of San Callisto

Via Appia Antica 126. **Tel** 06-513 0151.
🚌 118, 218. **Open** 9am–noon,
2–5pm Thu–Tue. **Closed** 1 Jan, late
Jan–late Feb, Easter Sun & 25 Dec.
🚌🚻♿📷🎧
🌐 **catacombe.roma.it**

In burying their dead in
underground cemeteries
outside the city walls, the early
Christians were obeying the
laws of the time: it was not
because of persecution. So
many saints were buried that
the catacombs became shrines
and places of pilgrimage.
The vast Catacombs of San
Callisto are on four different

levels and only partly explored.
The rooms and connecting
passageways are hewn out of
volcanic tufa. The dead were
placed in niches, known as *loculi,*
which held two or three bodies.
The most important rooms were
decorated with stucco and
frescoes. The area that can be
visited includes the Crypt of the
Popes, where many of the early
popes were buried, and the
Crypt of Santa Cecilia, where the
saint's body was discovered in
820 before being moved to her
church in Trastevere *(see p213).*

⓫ Catacombs of San Sebastiano

Via Appia Antica 136. **Tel** 06-785 0350.
🚌 118, 218. **Open** 10am–4:30pm
Mon–Sat. **Closed** 1 Jan, mid-Nov–
mid-Dec, 25 Dec. 🚌🚻♿📷
🌐 **catacombe.org**

The 17th-century church of
San Sebastiano, above the
catacombs, occupies the site
of a basilica. Preserved at the
entrance to the catacombs is
the *triclia,* a building that once
stood above ground and was
used by mourners for taking
funeral refreshments. Its walls
are covered with graffiti
invoking St Peter and St Paul,
whose remains may have been
moved here during one of the
periods of persecution.

Cypresses lining part of the Roman Via
Appia Antica

⑫ Catacombs of Domitilla

Via delle Sette Chiese 282. **Tel** 06-511 0342. 🚌 218, 716. **Open** 9am–noon, 2–5pm Wed–Mon (summer: 5:30pm). **Closed** mid-Dec–mid-Jan, Easter Sun. 🅿️ ♿ 🎥 📷 🌐 domitilla.info

This network of catacombs is the largest in Rome. Many of the tombs from the 1st and 2nd centuries AD have no Christian connection. In the burial chambers there are frescoes of both Classical and Christian scenes, including one of the earliest depictions of Christ as the *Good Shepherd*. Above the catacombs stands the basilica of Santi Nereo e Achilleo. After plenty of rebuilding and restoration, little remains of the original 4th-century church.

Bronze entrance gates to the Fosse Ardeatine by Mirko Basaldella

⑬ Fosse Ardeatine

Via Ardeatina 174. **Tel** 06-513 6742. 🚌 218, 716. **Open** 8:15am–3:15pm Mon–Fri, 8:15am–4:45pm Sat & Sun. **Closed** public hols.

On the evening of 24 March 1944, Nazi forces took 335 prisoners to this abandoned quarry south of Rome and shot them at point blank range. The execution was in reprisal for a bomb attack that had killed 32 German soldiers. The victims included various political prisoners, 73 Jews and ten other civilians, among them a priest and a 14-year-old boy. The Germans blew up the tunnels where the massacre had taken place, but a local peasant had witnessed the scene and later

helped find the corpses. The site is now a memorial to the values of the Resistance against the Nazi occupation, which gave birth to the modern Italian Republic *(see also p187)*. A forbidding bunker-like monument houses the rows of identical tombs containing the victims.

Beside it is a museum of the Resistance. Interesting works of modern sculpture include *The Martyrs*, by Francesco Coccia, and the gates shaped like a wall of thorns by Mirko Basaldella.

⑭ Tomb of Cecilia Metella

Via Appia Antica, km 3. **Tel** 06-3996 7700. 🚌 118, 660. **Open** 9am–approx 1 hr before sunset Tue–Sun.

One of the most famous landmarks on the Via Appia Antica is the huge tomb built for the noblewoman Cecilia Metella. Her father and husband were rich patricians and successful generals of late Republican Rome, but hardly anything is known about the woman herself. Byron muses over her unknown destiny in his poem *Childe Harold*.

In 1302 Pope Boniface VIII donated the tomb to his family, the Caetani. They incorporated it in a fortified castle that blocked the Via Appia, allowing them to control the traffic on the road and exact high tolls. The marble facing of the tomb was pillaged by another pope, Sixtus V, at the end of the 16th century.

On the opposite side of the road stands what remains of the early 14th-century church of San Nicola.

Fragments of marble relief on the Tomb of Cecilia Metella

EUR's Palazzo della Civiltà del Lavoro, the "Square Colosseum"

⑮ EUR

🚌 170, 671, 714 and other routes. Ⓜ️ EUR Fermi, EUR Palasport. Museo della Civiltà Romana: Piazza G. Agnelli 10. **Tel** 06-0608. **Open** 9am–2pm Tue–Sun (last adm: 1pm). Undergoing restoration; call ahead. **Closed** 1 Jan, 1 May, 25 Dec. 🅿️

The Esposizione Universale di Roma (EUR), a suburb south of the city, was built for an international exhibition, a kind of "Work Olympics", that was planned for 1942, but never took place because of the war. The architecture was intended to glorify Fascism and the style of the buildings is very over-blown and rhetorical. The eerie shape of the Palazzo della Civiltà del Lavoro (The Palace of the Civilization of Work) is an unmistakable landmark for people arriving from Fiumicino airport.

The scheme was completed in the 1950s. In terms of town planning, EUR has been quite successful and people are still keen to live here. The great marble halls house government offices and museums.

The Museo della Civiltà Romana displays a vast scale model of Rome at the time of Constantine and casts of the reliefs on Trajan's Column. These, and the interesting planetarium, make the museum worth a visit.

To the south is a lake and park, and the huge domed Palazzo dello Sport built for the 1960 Olympics.

⓰ San Paolo fuori le Mura

Via Ostiense 186. **Tel** 06-6988 0800.
🚌 23, 128, 170, 670, 707, 761, 769.
Ⓜ San Paolo. **Open** 7am–6:30pm
daily. Cloister and museum: **Open**
8am–6:15pm daily. 🚻 ♿ 📷

19th-century mosaic on façade of San Paolo fuori le Mura

Today's church is a faithful reconstruction of the great 4th-century basilica destroyed by fire on 15 July 1823. Few fragments of the original church survived. The triumphal arch over the nave is decorated on one side with restored 5th-century mosaics. On the other side are mosaics by Pietro Cavallini, originally on the façade. The splendid Venetian apse mosaics (1220) depict the figures of Christ with St Peter, St Andrew, St Paul and St Luke.

The fine marble canopy over the high altar is signed by the sculptor Arnolfo di Cambio (1285) "together with his partner Pietro", who may have been Pietro Cavallini. Below the altar is the *confessio*, the tomb of St Paul. To the right is an impressive Paschal candlestick by Nicolò di Angelo and Pietro Vassalletto.

The cloister of San Paolo, with its pairs of colourful inlaid columns supporting the arcade, was spared completely by the fire. Completed around 1214, it is considered one of the most beautiful in Rome.

⓱ Centrale Montemartini

Via Ostiense 106. **Tel** 06-0608.
🚌 23, 769. **Open** 9am–7pm Tue–Sun
(last adm: 6:30pm). **Closed** 1 Jan,
1 May, 25 Dec. 📷 🏛 ♿ 🖥 🛍

An enormous old industrial site has been restored to house the ACEA art centre. Originally, the building was used as Rome's first power station and its two huge generators still occupy the central machine room creating quite an intriguing contrast to the exhibitions. On display are Roman statues and artifacts belonging to the Capitoline Museums *(see pp70–73)*. Many of the statues were discovered during excavations in the late 19th and early 20th centuries, including some from the Area Sacra dell'Argentina *(see p152)*.

Casino del Bel Respiro, summer residence in Villa Doria Pamphilj

⓲ Villa Doria Pamphilj

Via di San Pancrazio. 🚌 31, 44, 75, 710, 870. Park: **Open** dawn–dusk daily.

One of Rome's largest public parks, the Villa Doria Pamphilj was laid out in the mid-17th century for Prince Camillo Pamphilj. His uncle, Pope Innocent X, paid for the magnificent summer residence, the Casino del Bel Respiro, and the fountains and summerhouses, some of which still survive.

Statue in Centrale Montemartini, former power plant-turned-art centre

Day Trips Around Rome

Tivoli, a favourite place to escape the heat of the Roman summer

⑲ Tivoli

31 km (20 miles) northeast of Rome.
🚆 from Tiburtina. 🚌 COTRAL from
Ponte Mammolo (on Metro line B).

Tivoli has been a popular
summer resort since the days of
the Roman Republic. Among
the famous men who owned
villas here were the poets
Catullus and Horace, Caesar's
assassins Brutus and Cassius,
and the Emperors Trajan and
Hadrian. Tivoli's main attractions
were its clean air and beautiful
situation on the slopes of the
Tiburtini hills, its healthy sulphur
springs and the waterfalls of the
Aniene – the Emperor Augustus
said these had cured him of
insomnia. The Romans' luxurious
lifestyle was revived in
Renaissance times by the
owners of the Villa d'Este, the
town's most famous sight.

In the Middle Ages Tivoli
suffered frequent invasions as
its position made it an ideal
base for an advance on
Rome. In 1461 Pope
Pius II built a fortress
here, the Rocca Pia,
declaring: "It is easier
to regain Rome
while possessing
Tivoli, than to
regain Tivoli while
possessing Rome."

After suffering
heavy bomb-
damage in 1944,
Tivoli's main
buildings and
churches were
speedily restored.

Detail of Fontana
dell'Organo at Villa d'Este

The town's cobbled streets are
still lined with medieval houses.
The Duomo (cathedral) houses
a beautiful 13th-century life-size
wooden group representing the
Deposition from the Cross.

⑳ Villa d'Este

Piazza Trento 5, Tivoli. **Tel** 0774-332 920.
🚌 COTRAL from Ponte Mammolo (on
Metro line B). **Open** 8:30am–approx
1 hour before sunset Tue–Sun; also
8:30pm–midnight (last adm: 11pm) Fri
& Sat in summer. **Closed** 1 Jan, 25 Dec.
🎫 (free 1st Sun in month). 💻
🌐 villadestetivoli.info

The villa occupies the site of an
old Benedictine convent. In the
16th century the estate was
developed by Cardinal Ippolito
d'Este, son of Lucrezia Borgia. A
palace was designed by Pirro
Ligorio to make the most of its
hilltop situation, but the villa's
fame rests more on the terraced
gardens and fountains laid out by
Ligorio and Giacomo della Porta.
The gardens have suffered
neglect in the past, but
the grottoes and
fountains still give a
vivid impression of the
great luxury which the
princes of the church
enjoyed. From the
great loggia of the
palace you descend
to the Grotto of Diana
and Bernini's Fontana
del Bicchierone.
Below to the right is
the Rometta (little
Rome), a model of

Tiber Island with allegorical
figures and the legendary she-
wolf. The Rometta is at one end
of the Viale delle Cento Fontane,
100 fountains in the shapes of
grotesques, obelisks, ships and
the eagles of the d'Este coat of
arms. Other fountains are now
being restored to their former
glory. The Fontana dell'Organo
is a water-organ, in which the
force of the water pumps air
through the pipes. The garden's
lowest level has flower beds and
fountains and splendid views
out over the plain below.

Terrace of 100 Fountains in the gardens
of Villa d'Este

㉑ Villa Gregoriana

Largo Sant'Angelo, Tivoli. 🚆 🚌 Tivoli,
then short walk. **Tel** 0774-332 650.
Open Mar & mid-Oct–mid-Dec:
10am-4pm Tue–Sun; Apr–mid-Oct:
10am-6:30pm Tue–Sun (last adm:
1 hour before closing) 🎫 📷

The main attractions of this
steeply sloping park are the
waterfalls and grottoes created
by the River Aniene. The park is
named after Pope Gregory XVI,
who in the 1830s ordered the
building of a tunnel to ward
against flooding. This tunnel
created a new waterfall, called
the Grande Cascata, which
plunges 160 m (525 ft) into
the valley behind the town.

The Canopus at Hadrian's Villa, with replicas of its original caryatids lining the canal

㉒ Hadrian's Villa

Villa Adriana, Largo M. Yourcenar 1.
Site is 6 km (4 miles) southwest of
Tivoli. **Tel** 0774-382 733. **FS** Tivoli,
then local bus No. 4. **🚌** COTRAL from
Ponte Mammolo (on Metro line B).
Open 9am–approx 1 hour before
sunset daily (last adm: 90 mins before
closing). **Closed** 1 Jan, 1 May, 25 Dec.
🏛️ 📷 💺 🚻 **W** villaadriana.
beniculturali.it

Built as a private summer
retreat between AD 118 and
134, Hadrian's Villa was a vast
open-air museum of the finest
architecture of the Roman
world. The grounds of the
Imperial Palace were filled
with full-scale reproductions
of the emperor's favourite
buildings from Greece and
Egypt. Although excavations
on this site began in the 16th
century, many of the ruins lying
scattered in the surrounding
fields have yet to be identified
with any certainty. The grounds
of the villa make a very
picturesque site for a picnic,
with scattered fragments of
columns lying among olive
trees and cypresses.

For an idea of how the whole
complex would have looked
in its heyday, study the scale
model in the building beside the
car park. The most notable
buildings are signposted and
several have been partially
restored or reconstructed. One
of the most impressive is the
so-called Maritime Theatre. This
is a round pool with an island
in the middle, surrounded by

Pair of Ionic columns in the vaulted
baths of Hadrian's Villa

columns. The island, reached by
means of a swing bridge, was
probably Hadrian's private studio,
where he withdrew from the
cares of the Empire to indulge
in his two favourite pastimes,
painting and architecture. There
were also theatres, Greek and
Latin libraries, two bathhouses,
extensive housing for guests
and the palace staff, and formal
gardens with fountains, statues
and pools.

Hadrian also loved Greek
philosophy. One part of the
gardens is thought to have been
Hadrian's reproduction of the
Grove of Academe, where Plato
lectured to his students. He also
had a replica made of the Stoà
Poikile, a beautiful painted
colonnade in Athens, from
which the Stoic philosophers
took their name. This copy
enclosed a great piazza with a
central pool. The so-called Hall
of the Philosophers, close to the
Poikile, was probably a library.

The most ambitious of
Hadrian's replicas was the
Canopus, a sanctuary of the god
Serapis near Alexandria. For this
a canal 119 metres (130 yards)
long was dug and Egyptian
statues were imported to
decorate the temple and its
grounds. This impressive piece
of engineering has been
restored and the banks of the
canal are lined with caryatids.

Another picturesque spot in
the grounds is the Vale of Tempe,
the legendary haunt of the
goddess Diana with a stream
representing the river Peneios.
Below ground the emperor even
built a fanciful re-creation of the
underworld, Hades, reached
through underground tunnels, of
which there were many linking
the various parts of the villa.

Plundered by barbarians who
camped here in the 6th and
8th centuries, the villa fell into
disrepair. Its marble was burned
to make lime for cement and
Renaissance antiquarians
contributed even further to its
destruction. Statues unearthed
in the grounds are on show in
museums around Europe. The
Vatican's Egyptian Collection
(see p236) has many fine works
that were found here.

㉓ Ostia Antica

Viale dei Romagnoli 717. Site is 25 km (16 miles) southwest of Rome.
Tel 06-5635 0215. Ⓜ Piramide, then train from nearby Porta San Paolo station. Excavations and museum:
Open 8:30am–1 hour before sunset (last adm: 1 hour before closing).
Closed 1 Jan, 1 May, 25 Dec. 🅿 Free on first Sun of the month. 🅰 📷 ♿
🆆 ostiaantica.beniculturali.it

In Republican times Ostia was Rome's main commercial port and a military base defending the coastline and the mouth of the Tiber. The port continued to flourish under the Empire, despite the development of Portus, a new port slightly to the northwest, in the 2nd century AD. Ostia's decline began in the 4th century, when a reduction in trade was combined with the gradual silting up of the harbour. Then malaria became endemic in the area and the city, whose population may have been nearly 100,000 at its peak, was totally abandoned.

Buried for centuries by sand, the city is remarkably well preserved. The site is less spectacular than Pompeii or Herculaneum because Ostia died a gradual death, but it gives a more complete picture of life under the Roman Empire. People of all social classes and from all over the Mediterranean lived and worked here.

Visitors can understand the layout of Ostia's streets almost at a glance. The main road through the town, the Decumanus Maximus, would have been filled with hurrying slaves and citizens, avoiding the jostling carriages and carts, while tradesmen pursued their

Ruins of shops, offices and houses near Ostia's theatre

business under the porticoes lining the street. The floorplans of the public buildings along the road are very clear. Many were bathhouses, such as the Baths of the Cisiarii (carters) and the grander Baths of Neptune, named after their fine black-and-white floor mosaics.

Beside the theatre, three large masks, originally part of the decoration of the stage, have been mounted on large blocks of tufa. Beneath the great brick arches that supported the semicircular tiers of seats were taverns and shops. Classical plays are put on here in the summer.

The Tiber's course has changed considerably since Ostia was the port of Rome. It once flowed past just to the north of Piazzale delle Corporazioni, the square behind

Mask decorating the theatre

the theatre. The corporations were the guilds of the various trades involved in fitting out and supplying ships: tanners and rope-makers, shipbuilders and timber merchants, ships' chandlers and corn weighers. There were some 60 or 70 offices around the square. Mosaics showing scenes of everyday life in the port and the names and symbols of the corporations can still be seen. There were also offices used by ship-owners and their agents from places as far apart as Tunisia, the south of France, Sardinia and Egypt. In one office, belonging to a merchant from the town of Sabratha in North Africa, there is a delightful mosaic of an elephant.

The main cargo coming into Rome was grain from Africa. Much of this was distributed free to prevent social unrest. Although only men received this *annona* or corn dole, at times over 300,000 were eligible. In the centre of the square was a temple, probably dedicated to Ceres, goddess of the harvest. Among the buildings excavated are many

Mural from Ostia featuring cupid and a woman on a horse

large warehouses in which grain was stored before it was shipped on to Rome.

The Decumanus leads to the Forum and the city's principal temple, erected by Hadrian in the 2nd century AD and dedicated to Jove, Juno and Minerva. In this rather romantic, lonely spot, it is hard to imagine the Forum as a bustling centre, where justice was dispensed and officials met to discuss the city's affairs. In the 18th century it was used as a sheepfold.

Floor mosaic in Ostia of a sea lion monster

Sculpture of Cupid and Psyche kissing at Ostia

Away from the main street are the buildings where Ostia's inhabitants lived. The great majority were housed in rented apartments in blocks three or four storeys high, known as *insulae*. These varied considerably in their comfort and decoration. The House of Diana was one of the smarter ones, with a balcony around the second floor, a private bathhouse and a central courtyard with a cistern where tenants came to collect their water. Around the ground floor of the block were shops, taverns and bars selling snacks and drinks. In the bar at the House of Diana you can see the marble counter used by customers buying their sausages and hot wine sweetened with honey.

For the wealthy there were detached houses (*domus*) such as the House of the Dioscuri, which has fine mosaics, and the House of Cupid and Psyche, named after a statue there. This is now in the site's Museo Ostiense, near the Forum, along with other sculptures and reliefs found in Ostia.

Among the houses and shops there are a number of other fascinating buildings including a laundry and the firemen's barracks.

The religions practised in Ostia reflect the cosmopolitan nature of the port. There are also no fewer than 18 temples dedicated to the Persian god Mithras, as well as a Jewish synagogue dating from the 1st century AD and a Christian basilica.

A plaque records the death of St Augustine's mother in a hotel here in AD 387.

Also Worth Seeing

Anagni FS from Termini (c.60 min), then local bus (infrequent) or long walk.
Picturesque hill-town with papal palace and famous cathedral featuring well-preserved frescoes.

Bracciano FS from Ostiense (c.70 min). from Saxa Rubra, reached by train from Roma Nord (then bus, c.90 min).
Volcanic lake with villages and wooded hills. Nice for walks or a visit to Orsini Castle. Swimming in summer.

Cerveteri FS from Termini or Ostiense to Ladispoli-Cerveteri, then local bus (c.70 min). from Cornelia, on Metro line A (bus c.80 min).
One of the greatest Etruscan cities. Necropolis with complete streets and houses.

Nemi from Anagnina, on Metro line A (bus c.90 min); may need to change at Genzano.
Charming village at volcanic lake in the Castelli Romani. Famous for its wine and strawberries.

Palestrina from Anagnina, on Metro line A (bus c.60 min).
Impressive Roman sanctuary to goddess Fortuna. Museum and the Mosaic of the Nile.

Pompeii FS from Termini to Naples, then change to local train (c.130 min). Special tours from tourist agents.
Excavations of the wealthy and bustling Roman city where the busy daily life was put to a sudden end by the eruption of Vesuvius in AD 79.

Subiaco from Ponte Mammolo, on Metro line B (bus c.80 min).
Birthplace of St Benedict. Two monasteries to visit.

Tarquinia FS from Termini or Ostiense plus local bus (c.100 min). from Lepanto, on Metro line A. Change at Civitavecchia (c.150 min).
Outstanding collection of Etruscan objects and frescoes from Tarquinia's necropolis.

Viterbo FS from Ostiense (c.115 min) or train from Roma Nord, Piazzale Flaminio, on Metro line A (c.150 min). from Saxa Rubra reached by the train above (then bus, c.90 min).
Medieval quarter, papal palace and archaeological museum within 13th-century walls.

NINE GUIDED WALKS

Rome is an excellent city for walking. The distances between major sights in the historic centre are easily covered on foot and many streets are pedestrianized. When you get tired, stop at one of the pavement cafés in lovely settings, such as Piazza Navona and Campo de' Fiori. If you are interested in archaeology, then a walk across the Forum *(see pp78–89)* and over the Palatine *(see pp98–103)* takes you away from the roaring traffic of modern Rome to a different world of scattered ruins and shady pine trees.

The first of the nine suggested walks takes in picturesque quarters on either side of the Tiber. The second walk, along the perfectly straight Via Giulia, gives a vivid impression of the Renaissance city. The next three walks

each follow a particular theme. You can savour the glory of ancient Rome through the triumphal arches of the emperors, tour early Christian churches with well-preserved mosaics, or explore the great contribution of Bernini to the appearance of the city.

The sixth walk is outside the centre along the best-known of all Roman roads, the Via Appia Antica, parts of which are still intact after more than 2,000 years of use. The seventh walk explores some macabre points of interest, including a park said to be haunted by Emperor Nero. The next couples Trastevere's atmospheric backstreets with the romantic viewpoints of the Janiculum. Lastly, there is a tour of churches and ancient ruins on and around the tranquil, leafy Aventine.

Choosing a Walk

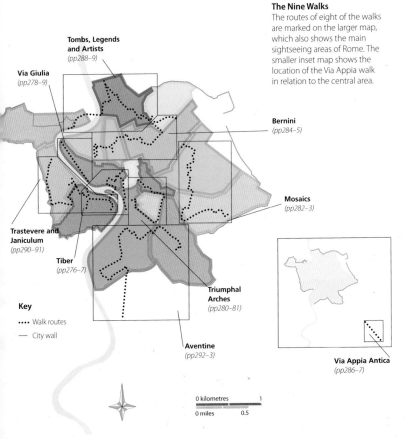

Tombs, Legends and Artists
(pp288–9)

Via Giulia
(pp278–9)

The Nine Walks
The routes of eight of the walks are marked on the larger map, which also shows the main sightseeing areas of Rome. The smaller inset map shows the location of the Via Appia walk in relation to the central area.

Bernini
(pp284–5)

Mosaics
(pp282–3)

Trastevere and Janiculum
(pp290–91)

Tiber
(pp276–7)

Triumphal Arches
(pp280–81)

Key

•••• Walk routes

— City wall

Aventine
(pp292–3)

Via Appia Antica
(pp286–7)

0 kilometres 1

0 miles 0.5

◄ Cobbled street leading to the Pantheon

A Two-Hour Walk by the River Tiber

Rome owes its very existence to the Tiber; the city grew up around an easy fording point where a marketplace developed. The river could also be a hazard; shallow and torrent-like, it flooded the city every winter up to 1870, when work began on the massive Lungotevere embankments that run along both sides of the river. These provide many fine views from points along their avenues of plane trees. The walk also explores the neighbourhoods along the riverside, in particular the Jewish Ghetto and Trastevere, which have preserved much of their character from earlier periods in the colourful history of Rome.

① Santa Maria in Cosmedin

From the old port of Rome to Via dei Funari

Starting from the church of Santa Maria in Cosmedin ① (see p204), cross the piazza to the Temples of the Forum Boarium ② (see p205). This was the cattle market that stood near the city's river port. The river here has preserved two less obvious structures from ancient Rome: the mouth of the Cloaca Maxima ③, the city's great sewer, and one arch of a ruined bridge, known as the Ponte Rotto ④. In Via Petroselli stands the rather extraordinary medieval Casa dei Crescenzi ⑤ (see p205), decorated with fragments of Roman temples. Passing the modern Anagrafe (public records office) ⑥, built on the site of the old Roman port, you come to San Nicola in Carcere ⑦ (see p153).

You are now in the Foro Olitorio, Rome's ancient vegetable market. To the east stand the ruins of a Roman portico and the medieval house of the Pierleoni family. Head for the massive Theatre of Marcellus

⑧ (see p153); go and look at the three Corinthian columns of the Temple of Apollo beside it. Turn into Piazza Campitelli and walk up to Santa Maria in Campitelli ⑨ (see p153). The church honours a miraculous image of the Virgin credited with halting the plague in 1656. The 16th-century piazza was the home of Flaminio Ponzio, its architect, who lived at No. 6. Take Via dei Delfini to Piazza Margana where you should look up at the 14th-century tower of the Margani family ⑩. Retrace your steps, then go up Via dei Funari (Street of the Ropemakers) to the 16th-century façade of Santa Caterina dei Funari ⑪.

The Ghetto

From Piazza Lovatelli take Via Sant'Angelo in Pescheria, which leads to the ruined Portico of Octavia ⑫

(see p154) in the Jewish Ghetto (see p154). The Roman portico, once Rome's fish market, houses the church of Sant'Angelo in Pescheria. Find the marble plaque on the façade: fish longer than this slab were given to the city's *conservatori* (governors).

Turn into the Ghetto: two column stumps belonging to the Portico stand in front of a patched-up doorway made of fragments of Roman sculpture. The cramped buildings and streets around Via del Portico

④ Arch of the Ponte Rotto

⑨ Main altar of Santa Maria in Campitelli

d'Ottavia are typical of old Rome: see the Casa di Lorenzo Manilio ⑬ *(see p154)*, and turn down Via del Progresso, past Palazzo Cenci ⑭ *(see p154)*, towards the river. On Lungotevere walk past the Synagogue ⑮ *(see p154)* to the small church of San Gregorio ⑯. Here stood the Ghetto's gates, which were locked at sundown.

Across the river to Trastevere

Crossing to Tiber Island *(see p155)* by Ponte Fabricio, with its two ancient stone heads on the parapet, you can enjoy a

⑭ Classical relief of Medusa above the doorway of Palazzo Cenci

Piscinula and the surrounding streets retain much of the spirit of old Trastevere. Walk up to the start of Viale di Trastevere at

As you go down Via della Lungaretta to Piazza Santa Maria in Trastevere, do not miss the old-fashioned chemist's shop at No. 7. The piazza itself, in front of the magnificent church of Santa Maria in Trastevere ㉒ *(see pp214–15)*, has a cheerful atmosphere, and the fountain steps are a favourite meeting place. Go back a little way to Via del Moro. This leads to Piazza Trilussa, dominated by the fountain of the Acqua Paola ㉓, where you emerge on to the bank of the river again. Note the lifelike statue, near the fountain, of Roman poet Trilussa, who wrote in the local dialect. From Ponte Sisto ㉔ *(see p212)*, look back to Tiber Island and, beyond it, to the medieval bell tower of Santa Maria in Cosmedin, set against the pine trees on the summit of the Palatine.

㉓ Fountain of the Acqua Paola

0 metres 250
0 yards 250

Key

••• Walk route

good view of the river in both directions. On the island itself, you should not miss the Pierleoni Tower ⑰ or the church of San Bartolomeo all'Isola ⑱.

Trastevere

As you cross into Trastevere, you can see the medieval house of the powerful Mattei family ⑲, with its fragments of ancient sculpture. Beyond it, Piazza in

Piazza Belli. After crossing the road look back at the medieval tower of the Anguillara ⑳ and the statue honouring the poet Gioacchino Belli ㉑ *(see p211)*.

Piazza in Piscinula, old Trastevere

Tips for Walkers

Starting point: Piazza della Bocca della Verità.
Length: 3.5 km (2 miles).
Getting there: The 23, 44, 81, 160, 280, 628, 715 and 716 buses stop near Santa Maria in Cosmedin.
Best time for walk: This walk can be very romantic in the evening but is enjoyable at any time.
Stopping-off points: Piazza Campitelli and Piazza Margana have elegant restaurants, and Via del Portico d'Ottavia has many restaurants and a bakery. Tiber Island has a bar and the famous Sora Lella restaurant *(see p314)*. In Viale Trastevere there are bars and pizzerias. Piazza Santa Maria in Trastevere has lively bars and restaurants with outdoor tables.

A One-Hour Walk Along Via Giulia

Laid out by Bramante for Pope Julius II in the early 16th century, Via Giulia was one of the first Renaissance streets to slice through Rome's jumble of medieval alleys. The original plan included new law courts in a central piazza, but this project was abandoned for lack of cash. The street is dominated now by antiques shops and furniture restorers. On summer evenings, hundreds of oil lamps light the street while cloisters and courtyards provide romantic settings for a special season of concerts.

⑦ Baroque capital on the façade of Sant'Eligio degli Orefici

From Lungotevere to Largo della Moretta

Starting from Lungotevere dei Tebaldi ① at the eastern end of Via Giulia, you will see ahead of you an archway ② spanning the road. This was the start of Michelangelo's unrealized project linking Palazzo Farnese and its gardens (see p149) with the Villa Farnesina (see pp220–21) on the other side of the river.

Just before you reach the archway, you will see to your left the curious Fontana del Mascherone ③, in which an ancient grotesque mask and granite basin were combined to create a Baroque fountain.

Beyond the Farnese archway on the left is the lively Baroque façade of the church of Santa Maria dell'Orazione e Morte ④ (see p149). A bit further along on the same side of the road stands Palazzo Falconieri ⑤, enlarged by Borromini in 1650. Note its two stone falcons glowering at each other across the width of the façade. On the other side of the road you pass the yellowish façade of Santa Caterina da Siena ⑥, church of the Sienese colony in Rome, which has pretty 18th-century reliefs. The figures of Romulus and Remus

⑥ Relief of Romulus and Remus on Santa Caterina da Siena

symbolize Rome and Siena – there is a legend that the city of Siena was founded by the less fortunate of the twins. After passing the short street that leads down to Sant'Eligio degli Orefici ⑦ (see p150) and the façade of Palazzo Ricci ⑧ (see p151), you come to an area of half-demolished buildings around the ruined church of San Filippo Neri ⑨, called Vicolo della Moretta. If you look to the left down to the river, you can see Ponte

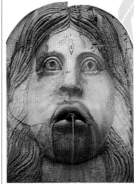

③ Fontana del Mascherone

Mazzini and the huge prison of Regina Coeli on the other side of the Tiber. At this point you may like to make a small detour to the right to the beginning of Via del Pellegrino, where there is an inscription ⑩, defining the pomerium, or boundary, of the city in the time of the Emperor Claudius.

From Largo della Moretta to the Sofas of Via Giulia

Further on, facing the narrow Vicolo del Malpasso are the imposing prisons, the Carceri

Key

••• Walk route

0 metres	250
0 yards	250

Nuove ⑪, built by Pope Innocent X Pamphilj in 1655. When first opened, they were a model of humane treatment of prisoners, but were replaced by the Regina Coeli prison across the river at the end of the 19th century. The buildings now house offices of the Ministry of Justice and a small Museum of Crime.

At the corner of Via del Gonfalone, a small side street running down to the river, you

② Farnese archway across Via Giulia, built to a design by Michelangelo

originates from the traditional distribution of bread to the poor that took place on the saint's feast day.

On the corner there are more travertine blocks belonging to the foundations of Julius II's projected law courts, known because of their curious shape as the "Sofas of Via Giulia".

The Florentine Quarter

Your next stop should be the imposing Palazzo Sacchetti at No. 66 ⑮. Originally this was the house of Antonio da Sangallo the Younger, the architect of Palazzo Farnese, but it was greatly enlarged by later owners. The porticoed courtyard houses a 15th-century Madonna and a striking Roman relief of the 3rd century AD. Just opposite Palazzo Sacchetti, note the beautiful late Renaissance portal of Palazzo Donarelli ⑯. The 16th-century house at No. 93 is richly decorated with stuccoes and coats of arms ⑰. No. 85 is another typical Renaissance palazzo with a heavily rusticated ground floor ⑱. There is a tradition that, like

⑮ Plaque honouring Antonio da Sangallo on Palazzo Sacchetti

many houses of the period, it once belonged to Raphael. Palazzo Clarelli ⑲ was built by Antonio da Sangallo the Younger as his own house. The inscription above the doorway bears the name of Duke Cosimo II de' Medici, whose family later bought the palazzo.

This whole area used to be inhabited by a flourishing Florentine colony, which had its own water-mills built on pontoons along the Tiber. Their national church is San Giovanni dei Fiorentini ⑳ (see p155), the final great landmark at the end of Via Giulia. Many Florentine artists and architects had a hand in its design including Sangallo and Jacopo Sansovino.

⑰ Coat of arms of Pope Paul III Farnese on the façade of Via Giulia No. 93

⑬ Detail on the side of the door of Santa Maria del Suffragio

can see part of the foundations of Julius II's planned law courts. Just down the street stands the small Oratorio di Santa Lucia del Gonfalone ⑫, which is often used for concerts.

The next interesting façade is Carlo Rainaldi's 17th-century Santa Maria del Suffragio ⑬ on the left. On the same side is San Biagio degli Armeni ⑭, the Armenian church in Rome. It is often referred to by local people as San Biagio della Pagnotta (of the loaf of bread). The nickname

Tips for Walkers

Starting point: Lungotevere dei Tebaldi, by Ponte Sisto.
Length: 1 km (1,100 yards).
Getting there: The 116 goes to and along Via Giulia, or you can take 46, 62 or 64 to Corso Vittorio Emanuele II, then walk down Via dei Pettinari, or take a 23 or 280 along Lungotevere.
Best time for walk: On summer evenings oil lamps often light the street. At Christmas, there are cribs on display in some shop windows.
Stopping-off points: There are bars in Via Giulia, at Nos. 18 and 84. Campo de' Fiori has better bars, with outdoor tables, and a wide choice of places to eat. These include a fried fish bar in Piazza Santa Barbara dei Librari (closed Sun).

A 90-Minute Tour of Rome's Triumphal Arches

Rome's greatest gift to architecture was the arch, and the Roman people's highest tribute to its victorious generals was the triumphal arch. In Imperial times, arches were erected to honour an emperor's campaign victories almost as a matter of course, promoting his personal cult and ensuring his subsequent deification. Spectacular processions passed through these arches. Conquering generals, cheered by rapturous crowds, processed in their chariots to the Capitol, accompanied by their legions bearing spoils from their campaigns.

③ Part of the Via Sacra, once spanned by the Arch of Augustus

① Relief of barbarian captives on the Arch of Septimius Severus

Arches of the Forum

This walk through the Forum and around the base of the Palatine takes in Rome's three great surviving triumphal arches and two arches of more humble design that were used simply as places of business. It starts from the Arch of Emperor Septimius Severus ① and his sons Geta and Caracalla *(see p85)* in the Forum. Erected in AD 203, it celebrates a successful campaign in the Middle East. Eight years later, when Caracalla had his brother killed, all mention of Geta was removed from the inscription.

Look up at the reliefs showing phases of the campaigns. Set in tiers, they are probably the sculptural counterparts of the paintings illustrating the general's feats that were borne aloft in the triumphal procession. On the right, the inhabitants of a fortified city surrender to the Romans' siege machines. Below are smaller friezes showing the triumphal procession itself.

Heading east, make your way through the Forum to the ruins

of the Temple of Julius Caesar ②. The temple was built by Augustus in 29 BC, on the site where Caesar's body was cremated after Mark Antony's famous funerary oration. A nearby sign marks the ruins of one of the arches dedicated to Augustus ③, spanning the Via Sacra between the Temple of Castor and Pollux ④ *(see p86)* and the Temple of Caesar. This arch, erected after Augustus had defeated Mark Antony and Cleopatra, was finally demolished in 1545, and its materials were used in the new St Peter's. From here, proceed uphill towards the elegant Arch of Titus ⑤ *(see p89)*. Compared with Septimius Severus's arch, it shows an earlier, simpler style. Look up at the beautiful lettering of the inscription before you examine the inner bas-reliefs. These show Roman legionaries carrying the spoils looted from the conquest of Jerusalem, heralds holding plaques with the names of vanquished peoples and cities, and Titus riding in triumph in his chariot.

The medieval Frangipane family turned the Colosseum into a vast impregnable stronghold and incorporated the Arch of Titus into their fortifications. Notice the wheelmarks

④ Capital from Temple of Castor and Pollux

Key

• • • Walk route

0 metres		250
0 yards		250

scratched on the inside walls of the arch by centuries of cartwheel traffic; they indicate the steady rise in the level of the Forum floor before it was eventually excavated in the 18th and 19th centuries. Many of the carts that passed through the arch would have been

⑬ Four-sided Arch of Janus in the Forum Boarium

hectic battle scenes just above the smaller arches, sculpted in AD 315. In the curious dwarf-like soldiers, you can see the transition from Classicism to a cruder medieval style of sculpture.

Now take Via di San Gregorio, which runs the length of the valley between the Palatine and Celian hills. This was the ancient route taken by most triumphal processions. Passing the entrance to the Palatine ⑧ and the well-preserved arches of the Claudian Aqueduct ⑨ on the right, you come to Piazza di Porta Capena ⑩, named after the gate that stood here to mark the

⑤ Arch of Titus in a 19th-century watercolour by the English artist Thomas Hartley Cromek

⑨ Arches of Domitian's extension to the Claudian Aqueduct

beginning of the Via Appia (see p267). After rounding the back of the Palatine, follow Via dei Cerchi, which runs alongside the grassy area that preserves, in an oval outline, all that remains of the Circus Maximus ⑪ (see p207).

Arches of the Forum Boarium

When you reach the church of Sant'Anastasia ⑫, turn right up Via di San Teodoro, then first left down Via del Velabro. Straddling the street is the four-sided Arch of Janus ⑬ (see p204), erected in the 3rd century AD. This is not a triumphal arch but a covered area where merchants could

take shelter from the sun or rain when discussing business. Like the Arch of Titus, it became part of a fortress built by the Frangipane family during the Middle Ages.

Tucked away beside the nearby church of San Giorgio in Velabro ⑭ (see p204) is what looks like a large rectangular doorway. This is the Arco degli Argentari, or Moneychangers' Arch ⑮. Look up at the inscription, which says that it was erected by local silversmiths in honour of Septimius Severus and his family in AD 204. As in the emperor's triumphal arch, the name of Geta has been obliterated by his brother and murderer, Caracalla. Geta's figure has also been removed from among the portraits on the panels inside the arch. Triumph in Imperial Rome could be very short-lived.

Tips for Walkers

Starting point: The Roman Forum, entrance Largo Romolo e Remo, on Via dei Fori Imperiali.
Length: 2.5 km (1.5 miles).
Getting there: The nearest Metro station is Colosseo on line B. Buses 75, 85, 87, 117, 186 and 810 stop in Via dei Fori Imperiali, near Forum entrance.
Best time: Any time during Forum opening hours (see p85).
Stopping-off points: Several bars and restaurants overlook the Colosseum. There is a marvellous pasticceria on the corner of Via dei Cerchi and Via di San Teodoro, and an organic market (Sun) at the start of Via di San Teodoro. For a meal, try Alvaro al Circo Massimo (closed Mon) in Via di San Teodoro.

carrying building materials quarried from the Forum's many ruined monuments.

Arch of Constantine

Leave the Forum by heading down the hill towards the Colosseum ⑥ (see pp94–7) and the nearby Arch of Constantine ⑦ (see p93). This arch, hastily built to commemorate the emperor's victory over his rival Maxentius in AD 312, is a patchwork of reliefs from different periods. Stand on the Via di San Gregorio side and compare the earlier panels at the top (AD 180–193) with the

A Three-Hour Tour of Rome's Best Mosaics

In imitation of the audience chambers of Imperial palaces, Rome's early Christian churches were decorated with colourful mosaics. These were pieced together from cubes of marble, coloured stone and fragments of glass. To create a golden background, gold leaf was placed between pieces of glass. These were then heated so that they fused. The glorious colours and subjects portrayed gave the faithful a glimpse of the heavenly court of the King of Kings. This walk concentrates on a few of the churches decorated in this wonderful medium.

③ Apse mosaic in the Chapel of Santa Rufina

② Domed baptistry and papal altar inside San Giovanni in Laterno

San Giovanni

Start from Piazza di Porta San Giovanni, where you can visit the heavily restored mosaic of the Triclinio Leoniano ① (see p181). Originally in the banqueting hall of Pope Leo III (795–816), it shows Christ among the Apostles. On the left are Pope Sylvester and the Emperor Constantine, on the right, Pope Leo and Charlemagne just before he was crowned Emperor of the Romans in AD 800. Inside the basilica of San Giovanni in Laterano ② (see pp182–3), the 13th-century apse mosaic shows Christ as he appeared miraculously during the consecration of the church. In the panels by the windows, look for the small figures of two Franciscan friars; these are the artists Jacopo Torriti (left) and

Jacopo de Camerino (right). Leave by the exit on the right near the splendid 16th-century organ and head for the octagonal Baptistry of San Giovanni ③, where the Chapel of Santa Rufina has a beautiful apse mosaic, dating from the 5th century. In the neighbouring Chapel of San Venanzio, there are golden 7th-century mosaics, showing the strong influence of the Eastern Church at this time.

Santo Stefano Rotondo to San Clemente

Leave the piazza by the narrow road that leads to the round church of Santo Stefano Rotondo ④ (see p187). One of its chapels contains a 7th-century Byzantine mosaic honouring two martyrs buried here. Further on, in Piazza della Navicella, is the church of Santa Maria in Domnica ⑤ (see p195). It houses the superb mosaics commissioned by Pope Paschal I, who gave new impetus to Rome's mosaic production in the 9th century. He is represented kneeling beside the Virgin. On leaving the church, notice the façade of San Tommaso in Formis ⑥, which has a charming mosaic of Christ flanked by two freed slaves, one black and one white, dating from the

③ Ceiling mosaic, Baptistry of San Giovanni

③ Interior of Baptistry of San Giovanni

13th century. From here, head up the steep hill, past the forbidding apse of Santi Quattro Coronati ⑦ *(see p187)*, to the fascinating church of San Clemente ⑧ *(see pp188–9)*. Its 12th-century apse mosaic shows the cross set in a swirling pattern of acanthus leaves. San

Clemente also has a fine 12th-century Cosmatesque mosaic floor.

The Colle Oppio

Passing the old entrance to the church, cross Via Labicana and walk up the hill to the small Colle Oppio park ⑨. This has fine views of the Colosseum and contains the ruins of the Domus Aurea ⑩ *(see p177)* and the Baths of Trajan ⑪. Across the park lie San Martino ai Monti ⑫ *(see p172)*, which has a 6th-century mosaic portrait of Pope St Sylvester near the crypt, and Santa Prassede ⑬ *(see p173)*. Here the Chapel of St Zeno contains the most important Byzantine mosaics in Rome, reminiscent of the fabulous mosaics of Ravenna. Pope Paschal I erected the chapel as a mausoleum for his mother Theodora.

in the nave depict Old Testament stories, while the triumphal arch has scenes relating to the birth of Christ, including one of the Magi wearing striped stockings. In the apse there is a *Coronation of the Virgin* by Jacopo Torriti (1295).

On leaving Santa Maria, pass the obelisk ⑮ in the piazza behind the church and go downhill to Via Urbana and Santa Pudenziana ⑯ *(see p173)*. The figures in the apse mosaic, one of the oldest in Rome (AD 390), are remarkable for their naturalism. The two women with crowns are traditionally identified as Santa Prassede and Santa Pudenziana. When you leave the church, you can either retrace your steps to Santa Maria Maggiore or walk down Via Urbana to Via Cavour Metro station.

⑬ Mosaic saint in Santa Prassede

⑯ 11th-century frieze above the doorway of Santa Pudenziana

The apse and triumphal arch of the church itself also have fine mosaics. When you move on to Santa Maria Maggiore ⑭ *(see pp174–5)*, go to the column in the centre of the piazza in front of the church to see the beautiful 14th-century façade mosaics by Filippo Rusuti. Inside, the 5th-century mosaics

Tips for Walkers

Starting point: Piazza di Porta San Giovanni.

Length: 3.5 km (2 miles).

Getting there: The nearest Metro station is San Giovanni, on line A, in Piazzale Appio, just outside Porta San Giovanni. The 16, 81, 85, 87, 218 and 650 buses and the 3 tram stop in front of San Giovanni in Laterano, while 117 stops around the corner on Piazza San Giovanni in Laterano.

Best time for walk: Go in the morning, in order to appreciate the mosaics in the best light.

Stopping-off points: The bars and restaurants in Piazza del Colosseo are popular with tourists. In the Parco del Colle Oppio there is a café kiosk with tables. There are several bars around Santa Maria Maggiore, some with outdoor tables.

Key

••• Walk route

— City Wall

0 metres	250
0 yards	250

A Two-Hour Walk Around Bernini's Rome

Gian Lorenzo Bernini (1598–1680) is the artist who probably left the strongest personal mark on the appearance of the city of Rome. Favourite architect, sculptor and town planner to three successive popes, he turned Rome into a uniquely Baroque city. This walk traces his enormous influence on the development and appearance of the centre of Rome. It starts from the busy Largo di Santa Susanna just northwest of Termini station, at the church of Santa Maria della Vittoria.

② Bernini's Fontana del Tritone

Through Piazza Barberini

Santa Maria della Vittoria ① (see p257) houses the Cornaro Chapel, the setting for one of Bernini's most revolutionary and controversial sculptures, *The Ecstasy of St Teresa* (1646). From here take Via Barberini to Piazza Barberini. In its centre is Bernini's dramatic Fontana del Tritone ② (see p256) and at one side stands the more modest Fontana delle Api ③ (see p256). As you go up Via delle Quattro Fontane, you catch a glimpse of Palazzo Barberini ④ (see p257) built by Bernini and several other artists for Pope Urban VIII. The gateway and cornices are decorated with the bees that made up part of the Barberini family crest. Next make your way to the crossroads, decorated by Le Quattro Fontane ⑤ (see p164), to enjoy the splendid views in all four directions.

Passing the diminutive San Carlo alle Quattro Fontane ⑥ (see p163), built by Bernini's rival

Borromini, take Via del Quirinale. The long wing of the Palazzo del Quirinale ⑦ (see p160), nicknamed the "Manica Lunga" (long sleeve), is by Bernini. On the other side of the road is the façade of Sant'Andrea al Quirinale ⑧ (see p163), one of Bernini's greatest churches. When you reach the Piazza del Quirinale ⑨, note the doorway of the palazzo, attributed to Bernini. From the piazza, go down the stairs to

⑬ Façade of Santa Maria in Via

Leave the piazza along Via delle Muratte where the composer Donizetti lived at No. 77 and turn into Via di Santa Maria in

Via della Dataria, and into Vicolo Scanderbeg which leads to a small piazza with the same name ⑩. Scanderbeg was the nickname of the Albanian prince Giorgio Castriota (1403–68), the "Terror of the Turks". His portrait is preserved on the house where he lived.

The Trevi Fountain

Go along the narrow Vicolo dei Modelli ⑪, where male models waited to be chosen by artists, then turn towards the Trevi Fountain ⑫ (see p161). Its energy is clearly inspired by Bernini's work, a tribute to his lasting influence on Roman taste.

⑱ Neptune Fountain at the north end of Piazza Navona

Via, where the church ⑬ has a fine Baroque façade by Bernini's follower Carlo Rainaldi. At the top of this street, turn left down to Via del Corso. On the other side of the road, you will see the towering Column of Marcus Aurelius ⑭ *(see p117)* in Piazza Colonna. Beyond this is Palazzo di Montecitorio ⑮, begun in 1650 by Bernini and now the home of the Italian parliament *(see p116)*.

⑱ Statue of the River Nile from the Fontana dei Quattro Fiumi, Piazza Navona

Key

• • • Walk route

0 metres   250
0 yards   250

central fountain, the Fontana dei Quattro Fiumi *(see p122)*, was by Bernini, though the figures symbolic of the four rivers were sculpted by other artists. The central figure in the Fontana del Moro, however, is by Bernini himself. Bernini's contemporaries were fascinated by the innovative use of shells, rocks and other natural forms in his fountains, and his expert handling of water to create constant movement.

An extended walk

More energetic walkers may like to head towards the river to see the Ponte Sant'Angelo and its Bernini angels, and then on to St Peter's *(see pp228–31)* where they can admire Bernini's great colonnaded piazza in front of the church, the papal tombs, his altar decorations and the bronze baldacchino.

Angel on Ponte Sant'Angelo

Pantheon to Piazza Navona

Via in Aquiro leads you to the Pantheon ⑯ *(see pp114–15)*. Refusing Pope Urban VIII's request for him to redecorate the dome, Bernini said that although St Peter's had a hundred defects, the Pantheon did not have any. From the Pantheon, make a small detour to Piazza della Minerva where you can see the obelisk, supported by Bernini's small, bizarre elephant, by the church of Santa Maria sopra Minerva ⑰ *(see p112)*. Then retrace your steps and take Salita dei Crescenzi to reach the fabulous Piazza Navona ⑱ *(see p122)* which was remodelled by Bernini for Pope Innocent X Pamphilj. The design for the

Tips for Walkers

Starting point: Largo di Santa Susanna.

Length: 3.5 km (2 miles).

Getting there: Take Metro line A to Repubblica or any bus to Termini, then walk. Buses 61, 62 and 492 stop in Via Barberini.

Best time for walk: Go either between 9am and noon for good lighting conditions in the churches, or between 4 and 7pm.

Stopping-off points: The Piazza Barberini and Fontana di Trevi areas have lots of bars and pizzerias. The many elegant cafés en route include the famous Caffè Giolitti *(see p113)* and outdoor cafés and restaurants are plentiful around Piazza della Rotonda and Piazza Navona.

For keys to symbols *see back flap*

A 90-Minute Walk Along the Via Appia Antica

Lined with cypresses and pines as it was when the ancient Romans came here by torchlight to bury their dead, the Via Appia is wonderfully atmospheric. The fields are strewn with ruined tombs set against the picturesque background of the Alban hills to the south. Although the marble or travertine stone facings of most tombs have been plundered, a few statues and reliefs survive or have been replaced by copies.

⑨ Tomb of Sixtus Pompeus the Righteous

Capo di Bove

Start from the Tomb of Cecilia Metella ① *(see p268)*. In the Middle Ages this area acquired the name Capo di Bove (ox head) from the frieze of festoons and ox heads still visible on the tomb. On the other side of the road you can see the ruined Gothic church of San Nicola ②, which, like the Tomb of Cecilia Metella, was part of the medieval fortress of the Caetani family.

② Gothic windows in the church of San Nicola

Proceed to the crossroads ③, where there are still many original Roman paving slabs, huge blocks of extremely durable volcanic basalt. Just past the next

tombs, some still capped with the remains of the medieval towers that were built over them. On the right, after passing what remains of a thermal complex, you come to a military zone around the Forte Appio ⑤, one of a series of forts built around the city in the 19th century. On the left, a little further on, stand the ruins of the Tomb of Marcus Servilius ⑥, showing fragments of reliefs excavated in 1808 by the Neo-Classical sculptor Antonio Canova. He was one of the first to work on the principle that excavated tombs and their inscriptions and reliefs should be allowed to remain *in situ*. On the other side of the road stands a tomb with a relief of a man, naked except for a short cape,

② The ruined church of San Nicola

turning (Via Capo di Bove), you will see on your left the nucleus of a great mausoleum overgrown with ivy, known as the Torre di Capo di Bove ④. Beyond it, on both sides of the Appia, are other

Key

••• Walk route

0 metres   250
0 yards   250

known as the "Heroic Relief" ⑦. On the left of the road are the ruins of the so-called Tomb of Seneca ⑧. The great moralist Seneca owned a villa near here, where he committed suicide in

Artist's impression of how the mausoleums and tombs lining the Via Appia looked in the 2nd century AD

Section of the Via Appia Antica, showing original Roman paving stones

AD 65 on the orders of Nero. The next major tomb is that of the family of Sixtus Pompeus the Righteous, a freed slave of the 1st century AD ⑨. The verse inscription records the father's sadness at having to bury his own children, who died young.

From Via dei Lugari to Via di Tor Carbone

Just past Via dei Lugari on the right, screened by trees, is the Tomb of Pope St Urban (reigned 222–30) ⑩. Set back from the road on the left stands a large ruined podium, probably part of a Temple of

Jupiter ⑪. The next stretch was excavated by the architect Luigi Canina early in the 19th century. On the right is the Tomb of Caius Licinius ⑫, followed by a smaller Doric tomb ⑬ and the imposing Tomb of Hilarius Fuscus ⑭, with five portrait busts in relief of members of his family. Next comes the Tomb of Tiberius Claudius Secondinus ⑮, where a group of freedmen of the Imperial household were buried in the 2nd century AD.

Passing a large ruined columbarium, you reach the Tomb of Quintus Apuleius ⑯

and the reconstructed Tomb of the Rabirii freed slaves (1st century BC) ⑰. This has a frieze of three half-length figures above an inscription. The figure on the right is a priestess of Isis. Behind her you can see the outline of a *sistrum*, the metal rattle used at ceremonies of the cult.

The majority of the tombs are little more than shapeless stacks of eroded brickwork. Two exceptions in the last stretch of this walk are the Tomb of the Festoons ⑱, with its reconstructed frieze of festive putti, and the Tomb of the Frontispiece ⑲, which has a copy of a relief with four portraits. The two central figures are holding hands.

When you reach Via di Tor Carbone, the Via Appia still stretches out ahead of you in a straight line and, if you wish to extend your walk, there are many more tombs and ruined villas to visit along the way.

⑦ **Figure on the Tomb of the Heroic Relief**

Tips for Walkers

Starting point: Tomb of Cecilia Metella.
Length: 3 km (2 miles).
Getting there: Reach the tomb by taxi, or take the Archeobus (see p384), the 118 from Piazzale Ostiense or the 660 from Colli Albani on Metro Line A.
Best time: On Sunday, when the road is closed to traffic. Go fairly early, before it becomes too hot.
Stopping-off points: There is a bar on the corner of Via Metella and a pleasant picnic area in the grounds of a thermal complex just beyond Vicolo di Tor Carbone. There are also several restaurants on the first stretch of the Appia, including the Cecilia Metella, Via Appia Antica 129, tel 06-512 6769 (closed Mon).

A Two-Hour Tour of Roman Tombs, Legends and Artists

The northern half of central Rome with its air of mystery is a great place for families to explore. Following this trail of creepy places and famous deaths interspersed with glimpses of the city's historic artists' centre, visitors can see Imperial mausoleums, a death mask and a crypt decorated with monks' bones. This is also a Rome where art is not just in the museums – it is everywhere – so you will see working art studios, pass Rome's Gallery of Fine Arts and wander down the famous "artists' row".

① Castel Sant'Angelo, site of Emperor Hadrian's tomb

Imperial Tombs

Begin at Emperor Hadrian's tomb, deep in the heart of the papal Castel Sant'Angelo ① *(see pp250–51)*. From the castle's riverside entrance, turn left then left again along the star-shaped walls, before turning right into Piazza Cavour, dominated on the south by the huge, ostentatious Palazzo di Giustizia ② *(see p249)*, slowly sinking under its own weight since 1910. Turn right down Via Colonna to cross the Tiber on Ponte Cavour. Once across the busy Lungotevere, turn left to go into the church of San Rocco ③ *(see p143)*. Just beyond it lies the Mausoleum of Augustus ④ *(see p143)*, sprouting a miniature grove of cypresses. To its left sits the ancient altar, Ara Pacis ⑤ *(see p142)* showing Augustus' family.

designed in 1845 by Pietro Camporese. On the right, at the corner of Via Canova, is the church of Santa Maria Portae Paradisi ⑦, designed in 1523 by Antonio Sangallo the Younger with a 1509 *Madonna and Child* by the sculptor Sansovino. The octagonal

⑤ Frieze from Ara Pacis

The Tridente

Continue heading north up Via di Ripetta. On your left is the graffiti-covered courtyard of the Accademia di Belle Arti ⑥, Rome's fine art academy,

interior dates to 1645. Turn right down Via Canova (named after the sculptor Antonio Canova), to see the exterior of his studio ⑧ at No. 16, a corner building studded with ancient statues and carvings. Turn left onto Via del Corso ⑨, Rome's High Street. This is 1.5 km (just under a mile) of *palazzi* and shops that has hosted parades, carnivals, races and processions for centuries and still functions as the main drag for Rome's evening stroll, the *passeggiata*. As you pass San Giacomo on your left (once the church of a

⑩ Baroque magnificence inside the Chiesa di Gesù e Maria

| 0 metres | | 200 |
| 0 yards | | 200 |

Key

••• Walk route

⑱ The Piazza di Spagna and the famous Spanish Steps, usually busy with visitors but quiet on rare occasions

Tips for Walkers

Starting point: Castel Sant'Angelo.
Length: 3.6 km (2.2 miles).
Getting there: Take bus 30, 34, 40, 49, 62, 70, 87, 130, 186, 224, 280, 492, 913, 926 or 990.
Best time for walk: Go in the afternoon, when the area starts to come alive.
Stopping-off points: Piazza del Popolo is flanked by two great Roman cafés with clear political affiliations – leftist Rosati (see p321) on the west side, right-wing Canova on the east. The Spanish Steps area has some great eateries (see pp315–17) as well as the usual fast food chains.

hospital founded in 1339 as a hospice for pilgrims), you will see on the right Chiesa di Gesù e Maria ⑩, Carlo Rinaldi's 1675 Baroque masterpiece. Further along, at No. 18, is the Casa di Goethe ⑪ (see p138). The Corso ends in the

dramatic Piazza del Popolo ⑫ (see p139). The square is named after the church on its north end, Santa Maria del Popolo ⑬ (see pp140–41). The church, which is full of art treasures, gets its name "St Mary of the People" and was built to help exorcise the ghost of Nero from a walnut grove on this site, once Nero's family estate where the disgraced emperor was secretly buried. The estate once continued up the slopes of what are now the Pincio Gardens ⑭ (see p138), above the piazza to the east, and locals declare that the ravens' screams are those of the dead emperor. Leave Piazza del Popolo from the southeast corner to stroll down Via del

Babuino ⑮, lined with art galleries hawking everything from Old Master Madonnas to Modernist abstracts. Take the third left, then right onto quiet Via Margutta ⑯, home of artists' studios and galleries for centuries. Turn right again down Via Orto di Napoli to return to Via del Babuino, then left. On your right, reclining on a fountain and surrounded by various graffiti and placards, is one of the ugliest – and most respected – statues in Rome. The Babuino ⑰ (like the famous Pasquino, see p126) has served as a soapbox for political and social dissent for centuries. Via del Babuino ends in Piazza di Spagna ⑱ (see p135), usually thronged with tourists. The pink house to the right of the Spanish Steps is the Keats-Shelley Memorial House ⑲ (see p136). Take a look inside to see Keats' death mask.

The Spanish Steps to the Capuchin Crypt

Go up the famed Spanish Steps ⑳ (see pp136–7) to Trinità dei Monti ㉑ (see p137). Turn

right down Via Gregoriana to No. 28, where painter Federico Zuccari turned the door and window frames of his Palazzetto Zuccari ㉒ into monsters. At the bottom of Via Gregoriana, turn left up to Via F. Crispi, then right down Via Sistina into Piazza Barberini ㉓, noting Bernini's fountains (see p256). Turn left up the square, cross Via V. Veneto, and left again. A few dozen paces up on the right is the staircase to the church of Santa Maria della Concezione. To finish, go into the Capuchin Museum and its creepy crypt ㉔ (see p256), where there are four chapels decorated with mosaics and skeletal displays. When you leave the crypt head for Piazza Barberini and the Metro station.

㉔ Bones and skulls from monks in the Capuchin Crypt

A Two-Hour Walk Around Trastevere and Janiculum Hill

This walk begins in the warren of cobbled, medieval streets of Trastevere, which is becoming ever more popular, and shows you the neighbourhood's hidden gems rather than its major sights. In the morning enjoy the mosaics and frescoes in the local churches before pausing for lunch in central Trastevere. Then go for a gentle climb up the Gianicolo, or Janiculum Hill. This long crest parallels the Tiber, and is blessed with the best panoramic views in Rome. At sunset, couples find it a romantic place to go for a stroll.

③ The high altar of San Benedetto

Southern Trastevere

Start at Santa Cecilia in Trastevere ① *(see p213)*, a church that hides its best – the basement excavations of St Cecilia's house and Pietro Cavallini's sole surviving Roman fresco inside the cloistered convent – hidden among an otherwise bland interior. Turn left out of the church, left again onto Via dei Salumi, then right on Via in Piscinula into Piazza in Piscinula ②, named for the remains of a bathing pool underneath. On the piazza's south side, below an 11th-century belltower, sits the tiny church of San Benedetto in Piscinula ③, (ring the doorbell for entry). It contains parts of a beautiful Cosmati mosaic pavement, 13th-century frescoes, and the saint's cell. Head west along Via della Lungaretta and cross the Viale di Trastevere to visit the excavations of a 5th-century basilica and fragments of its later frescoes below San Crisogono ④ *(see p212)*.

Central Trastevere

Turn left out of the church and left again to continue along Via della Lungaretta to Piazza Santa Maria in Trastevere ⑤,

a communal outdoor parlour, busy with cafés, guitar-strumming backpackers on the fountain steps, and visitors to the gorgeous Santa Maria in Trastevere ⑥ *(see p214–15)*. Exit the square on the south side into tiny Piazza San Callisto, and take the right fork down Via di San Cosimato into the large triangular Piazza di San Cosimato ⑦, bustling (until 2pm) with an open-air food market. Backtrack to Piazza Santa Maria in Trastevere. Along the square's north side you will see a tiny street called Fonte d'Olio, entrance into the twisting maze of alleys and ivy-covered buildings at the heart of Trastevere. The street bends sharply left, then turn right onto Vicolo del Piede to arrive at the diminutive Piazza de' Renzi, lined with medieval houses. Turn left to follow Via della Pelliccia, then left again at the pedestrian intersection. This will bring you into the elongated triangle of Piazza di Sant'Egidio ⑧, alive with cafés and bars. A short

staircase at No. 9 leads to the Museo di Roma in Trastevere ⑨ *(see p212)*, devoted to the history of everyday Roman life. Exit the piazza at the northwest corner and cross Vicolo del Cedro to continue straight on Via della Scala, past shops and

⑥ Piazza Santa Maria in Trastevere and its enchanting church

of frescoing the Villa Farnesina ⑬ *(see pp220–21)*, just up Via della Lungara, he spent so much time with his lover that, unlike the famed *Galatea* in the dining room, the "Raphael" work in the Loggia of Cupid and Psyche was executed largely by his assistants. Across from the Farnesina squats the Palazzo Corsini and the Galleria Nazionale d'Arte Antica ⑭ *(see p222)*. Tucked behind the gallery – accessible by backtracking down Via della Lungara and turning right on Via Corsini – are the Botanical Gardens ⑮ *(see p222)*.

⑬ Raphael's *Galatea* in the Villa Farnesina

The Gianicolo

Continue back south on Via della Lungara through the Porta Settimiana, and turn right up Via G. Garibaldi to climb Janiculum Hill. After the road makes a sharp left turn, veer right up a set of steps to San Pietro in Montorio, home to Bramante's Tempietto ⑯ *(see p223)*.
Go on up Via G.

Tips for Walkers

Starting point: Santa Cecilia in Trastevere.
Length: 4.7 km (2.9 miles).
Getting there: Take bus 23, 44 or 280.
Best time for walk: Weekdays (to see the Cavallini fresco in Santa Cecilia), starting mid-morning while the churches of southern Trastevere are still open.
Stopping-off points: Trastevere is the most restaurant-intensive district in Rome, so it has plenty of eateries and bars *(see pp317–19)*.

Garibaldi to the broad basin of the Fontana dell'Acqua Paola ⑰ *(see p223)*. Continue along Via G. Garibaldi to the 1644 Porta San Pancrazio ⑱, which had to be rebuilt in 1849 due to cannon damage. Turn right onto Passeggiata del Gianicolo to enter the park, where the first wide space with a panoramic vista over Rome is Piazzale Garibaldi with its equestrian

Key

• • • Walk route

bars into Piazza della Scala, where the Carmelite convent of Santa Maria della Scala ⑩ *(see p212)* has an ornate interior.

Northern Trastevere

The far northern part of Trastevere, between the Gianicolo and the river, is where the artist Raphael dallied with a baker's daughter at the Casa della Fornarina ⑪ *(see p212)*, on the right just before the Porta Settimiana ⑫ *(see p222)*. Instead

⑮ The tranquil Botanical Gardens

monument to the general ⑲ *(see p222)*. Here, paths are lined with marble busts of other Risorgimento heroes. When you reach the Lighthouse of Manfredi ⑳ *(see p218)*, the dome of St Peter's appears to the north. Continue down the steps at the Passeggiata's first bend to see the remains of Tasso's Oak planted in the late 16th century ㉑ *(see p218)*. At the foot of the steps, rejoin the Passeggiata. Beyond it, a few steps up, finish at the lovely church of Sant'Onofrio ㉒ *(see p223)*. From Viale Aldo Fabrizi you can catch bus No. 870 back to the city centre.

For keys to symbols *see back flap*

A Two-Hour Walk Around the Aventine

Rising just across the Circus Maximus from the Palatine, the residential Aventine Hill has served as a leafy haven of villas and mansions since Imperial times. This southernmost of Rome's legendary seven hills is still an oasis where traffic noise all but disappears. Yet few visitors walk here – despite the lure of fine old churches, lovely city panoramas, and rarely visited ancient ruins. You will also explore Testaccio, a fine area for authentic local cuisine, and see a Roman pyramid.

① The gymnasium at the northwest side of the Baths of Caracalla

The Aventine

Begin at one of Rome's most magnificent ancient sites, the massive Baths of Caracalla ① (see p199), where plebeian and patrician alike once bathed (and, much later, where the poet Shelley found inspiration for *Prometheus Unbound*). Just outside the Baths' entrance sits the church of SS Nero e Achilleo ② (see p196), with 9th-century mosaics. Across Viale delle Terme di Caracalla lies tiny San Sisto Vecchio ③, first home of the Dominican nuns (see p195). Turning northwest up Viale delle Terme di Caracalla, take the first right onto Via di Valle delle Camene, a tree-lined avenue parallel to the main road. Angle right up Salita di San Gregorio and ascend the imposing staircase of San Gregorio Magno ④ (see p194) for great views of the Palatine. Look for the 3rd-century marble table (in the St Barbara chapel, on the left side of the church) at which St Gregory the Great shared meals with the poor and, once,

an angel in disguise. Turn left down Via di San Gregorio and cross wide Piazza di Porta Capena, keeping the long dusty oval of the Circus Maximus ⑤ (see p207) on your right. At the start of Viale Aventino you will see the modernist bulk of FAO ⑥, originally intended to be the Ministry of Italian Africa when Mussolini was launching his ill-fated conquest of the Horn of Africa. Since its 1952 completion, it has housed the UN's Food and Agriculture Organization.

Across the Aventine

Turn right on Via del Circo Massimo, and immediately left onto Via della Fonte di Fauno to start climbing the Aventine Hill. This leads you to a small piazza before the church of Santa Prisca ⑦, built in the 3rd century atop the house where the martyred saint's parents hosted St Peter.

⑦ The apse of Santa Prisca

The current church dates largely to a Renaissance-era remodelling, and includes a Passignano altarpiece. Continue north up Via di Santa Prisca, angle left through Largo Arrigo VII, turn left on Via Eufemiano, and immediately right onto Via Sant'Alberto Magno. This leads right into Parco Savello ⑧, a garden of orange trees with a panoramic river view over Trastevere. Leaving the park, turn right onto Via di Santa Sabina to the

0 metres 300
0 yards 300

gorgeous basilica of Santa Sabina ⑨ *(see p206)*, where its rare, 5th-century wooden doors incorporate one of the earliest Crucifixion representations. Continue along Via di Santa Sabina to see the fine Cosmati work in SS Bonifacio e Alessio ⑩ *(see p206)*. The street ends in the Piazza dei Cavalieri di Malta ⑪ *(see p206)*, where you get a tiny view of St Peter's dome through the keyhole at number 3. Turn left down Via di Porta Lavernate,

⑮ Keats' gravestone at the Protestant Cemetery on Via Caio Cestio

Tips for Walkers

Starting point: The Baths of Caracalla entrance on Viale delle Terme di Caracalla 52.
Length: 5 km (3 miles).
Getting there: You can walk from the Circo Massimo Metro stop, or take bus 118 or 628.
Best time for walk: Start in the morning, timing your walk so that you can lunch in Testaccio.
Stopping-off points: You're spoilt for choice as fantastic and authentic local eateries abound in and around Piazza Testaccio, from cheap pizza places to traditional Roman restaurants.

have long burrowed into its flanks to take advantage of the terracotta's constant, cool temperature for storing wine. Turn left through Piazza Orazio

Key

••• Walk route

passing the façade of Sant'Anselmo ⑫. Built in 1900, the church houses a 3rd-century mosaic scene of Orpheus found during excavations. From Piazza dei Servili turn right on Via Asinio Pollione to go down off the Aventine.

Testaccio and South

Cross Via Marmorata and continue down Via Galvani. As you cross Via Nicola Zabaglia, you see Testaccio market ahead on your right, while the ground on your left rises to form Monte Testaccio ⑬ *(see p206)*, an ancient rubbish tip made up entirely of potsherds. It is lined with various restaurants that

Giustiniani to continue skirting the hill along Via di Monte Testaccio. Across the street, you will see the blind arcades of the Ex-Mattatoio ⑭, a defunct abattoir whose workers were paid, in part, with the day's offal. They would carry this *quinto quarto* (fifth quarter) of the animal across the street to one of Testaccio's early eateries,

where it would be turned into such (now) classic Roman delicacies as oxtail stew and *pajata* (calf intestines). Continue along Via di Monte Testaccio, which becomes Via Caio Cestio, to the Protestant Cemetery ⑮ *(see p207)* where such luminaries as Keats and Shelley lie in peace. At Via Marmorata, turn right to pass the Porta di San Paolo ⑯, a city gate dating to AD 402. As you walk through the remains of the Aurelian Wall into Piazzale Ostiense, you cannot miss on your right the Pyramid of Caius Cestius ⑰ *(see p207)*. The final leg is a long stroll down Via Ostiense or, alternatively, hop on the bus (Nos. 23, 271, or 769) to see the wonderfully weird Centrale Montemartini ⑱, an early Industrial Age power plant now stuffed with ancient sculptures *(see p269)*. Bus numbers 23 and 769 will take you back to within walking distance of Piramide Metro.

⑱ Ancient sculptures on display in the Centrale Montemartini

For keys to symbols *see back flap*

TRAVELLERS' NEEDS

WHERE TO STAY

Rome has been a major tourist centre since the Middle Ages, when pilgrims from all over Europe came to visit the home of Catholicism and its relic-packed churches. The nostalgic can still sleep in a 15th-century hotel, or stay around the Campo de' Fiori market, where visiting ecclesiastics were entertained by courtesans in the Renaissance era. Those who prefer their history a little less raffish could opt for an ex-monastery or convent, or stay in a still-functioning religious house. Romantics can sleep in the house once occupied by Keats, while star gazers can stay in former palaces graced by celebrities of

the past and present. Rome can offer the full range of accommodation, mostly in historical buildings, very little purpose-built. *Pensione* (guesthouse) no longer refers to a specific type of establishment, but in practice many retain the name and more personal character that has made them so popular with travellers. Other possibilities include hostels, residential hotels and self-catering accommodation.

The hotel listings *(pp300–303)* are organized according to their theme and area, with DK Choice entries highlighted – see Recommended Hotels on pages 298–9 for more information.

Hotel Prices

Prices are set by the state, and hotels should display the official rate on the door of each room. VAT (IVA in Italian) is usually included, and has been taken into account in the price categories on page 300.

Hotels in Rome generally have low and high season rates. April to June, September and October are high season. Double-check tariffs when booking hotels at other times of year as you may initially be quoted the higher rate. Excepting Christmas and New Year, there are some real bargains to be had between November and February, and also in July and August. Many hotels also offer special Internet booking deals, especially if made

far in advance, or at the last minute. Discounts for long-stay visitors and groups are often negotiable. Rooms without a bathroom can cost about 30 per cent less. Single travellers are badly catered for, and though it is possible to find a single room for 60 per cent of the price of a double, on average you'll pay as much as 70 per cent, and occasionally even more.

Hidden Extras

Even if the price of your room includes service, you are frequently expected to tip bellboys and for room service.

Rates are often not inclusive of breakfast, especially at some luxury hotels, where it may cost

up to €50. Hotels usually add hefty surcharges to international phone calls, and may charge for parking and air conditioning. The cost of drinks in minibars can also be high.

All hotels, B&Bs and campsites in Rome must add a city tax *(contributo di soggiorno)* to the final bill. At present this tax is for the first ten days of any stay and is fixed at €1 per day per person for campsites, €2 for establishments up to and including three-star hotels, and €3 for four- and five-star hotels. Children under ten are exempt, as are visitors staying in youth hostels.

Facilities

Internet access, air conditioning and bathrooms with hair dryers are common in most mid-range hotels, and phones in middle- to lower-price rooms, although budget travellers staying in cheaper hotels shouldn't expect much more than a clean room.

Because most hotels occupy historic buildings, room sizes can vary dramatically even within the same establishment (and this is often reflected in the pricing), so do ask to see your room before you check in. Swimming pools are rare, but roof terraces or gardens are common across the range of hotels.

Top-class hotels will usually have some soundproofing; otherwise noise levels can be dreadful, in which case ask for a room facing away from the road.

Spacious suite at the Hotel Majestic Roma *(see p302)*

◀ One of the many charming restaurants in Rome

Entrance to the luxurious Eden hotel, established in 1889 *(see p302)*

Parking in central Rome is a problem, though a few hotels have a limited number of parking spaces of their own.

Business visitors to the capital are well catered for, with practical hotel facilities such as conference rooms.

How to Book

It is best to book through the hotel website, by phone or by email. You should do this at least two months in advance if you want a particular hotel during peak season. If you require any particular features, such as a view, insist on confirmation in writing to ensure that you get what you have been promised.

If a deposit is required you can usually pay by debit or credit card. Under Italian law a booking is valid as soon as the

Elegant bar area at the boutique-style Hotel Art *(see p300)*

deposit is paid, so you could lose money if you pull out. Double-check bookings prior to departure. Many hotels have a fierce cancellation policy and there is every chance that you will be charged for at least one night, even if you don't stay. Another reason for checking bookings is that some hotels deliberately overbook and then offer unsatisfactory alternative accommodation.

If you arrive by train, touts may descend on you at the station with offers of hotels. They can be of some use if you are looking for a budget hotel, but exercise the usual caution. A better bet if you have not booked in advance is to head for one of the Rome City Tourist Board offices, where staff will reserve you a room within the price range you specify.

Checking In and Out

Italian hoteliers are legally obliged to register you with the police, which is the reason they always ask for your passport. Everyone in Italy is supposed to carry with them some sort of identification.

In some of Rome's cheaper *pensioni*, do not be surprised if you are asked to pay on arrival. Mention in advance if you intend to pay by credit card. A common tax dodge by many hotels is to ask for payment in cash; you are entitled to refuse.

Disabled Travellers

Provision for disabled travellers is poor. Hotels that occupy parts of buildings often start their rooms up several flights of stairs, while others can only accommodate disabled guests on the ground floor. Ramps, wide doorways and bathroom handrails are rare.

Contact the hotel featured in the listings directly, before booking, to check whether they are wheelchair accessible and can provide any other specific requirements (for more information *see p368*).

Roma Per Tutti is a useful website dedicated to mobility

Fine view of the Colosseum from the dining room at the Palazzo Manfredi *(see p301)*

within Rome, while the Lazio region provides advice on accessibility further afield (800 27 1027). Public transportation authority **Bus Abile** offers a pick-up service and bus tourism for travellers with disabilities – this must be reserved in advance.

Travelling with Children

Children and are usually welcome across the range of hotels in Rome. Most hotels can provide cots or small beds, but high chairs, children's meals and babysitting services are rare.

Many hotels do not have special rates for children and charge a standard rate if you require an extra bed in a room, whether for a baby or an adult, which can add anything from a few euros to 40 per cent on to the price. For a family with older children, two-room suites are sometimes available.

Contact the hotel in advance of booking for more information on family rates and children's facilities.

Bed & Breakfast

A popular option for visitors to Rome is bed & breakfast accommodation. This can be anything from a spare room in an apartment to something more like a small hotel. The type of breakfast can also vary depending on the owner. Contact the **Bed & Breakfast Association** of Rome for details or visit Rome's tourist board website *(see p299)*.

Residential Hotels

If you want the comfort and privacy of your own apartment coupled with the services of a hotel, you could opt to stay in a residence. Prices range from around €300 to over €3,000 for a week in a two-bedded room, though some residences are only available for fortnightly or monthly lets.

Contact **Adagio Aparthotel, Rome Renting**, or **Vittoria** to book a centrally located apartment. Found in the Flaminio neighbourhood, the elegant **Residence Hotel Parioli** offers various self-catered suites. A full list of residential hotels is available from tourist board offices.

Religious Institutions

If you do not mind an early curfew, quite a few religious institutions take in paying guests. All religions are welcome and you do not have to be a practising Catholic. Book well in advance as all of the following places cater for groups of students and pilgrims. **Casa Il Rosario** convent is located near the Colosseum, while **Nostra Signora di Lourdes** and the **Casa di Santa Brigida** are in the centre of Rome. Prices are in the range of a cheaper hotel.

Budget Accommodation

Even if you are travelling on a shoestring, it is possible to find a decent room in Rome. More and more affordable options are now available, including simple boutique hotels and *pensioni*. Dormitory accommodation can be found at rock-bottom prices in simple establishments such as the **Sandy Hostel**. Youth hostels are also a good option. **AIG Hostels** are part of the International Youth Hostel Federation network of accomodation. At the **Alessandro Palace** bed, breakfast and shower can all be had at a reasonable cost. **Mammarampa** has excellent facilities for the price, including a pretty terrace; like **Stargate**, it is located near Termini station.

Women can get rooms at **Casa Internazionale della Donna** (see p301) or **Foresteria**

The reception area of the Regina Hotel Baglioni *(see p302)*

Orsa Maggiore in Trastevere or at the **YWCA** near Termini (those arriving in Termini at night should take care). There are also several budget hotels in the city centre offering clean rooms and often a free breakfast. See websites like www.venere.com and www.euro cheapo.com for more options.

Self-Catering Apartments

Independent apartments are a good alternative and allow you more freedom. Apartments range from luxury locations with a daily cleaning service to smaller basic facilities. Most come equipped with cooking utensils, towels and bed linens. **RetRome Bed & Breakfast** and **Coach House Rentals** provide apartments at various locations around town. Websites like **Airbnb** and **Cross Pollinate** have further lists of vacation apartments.

Camping

Camping has come a long way since the simple tent and trailer.

Rooftop dining at the regal Hotel Inghilterra *(see p302)*

Camp sites around Rome offer everything from fully equipped cabins (with private bath) to Jacuzzis and on-site discos. Most camp sites are located quite far out of town but offer a shuttle service, as well as airport transport; **Flaminio Village** is one exception, at only 6 km (4 miles) north of the centre. Like many sites it has a pool, coffee bar, restaurant and Internet access.

Tourist Boards

The **Rome City Tourist Board** and provincial tourist boards can provide advice on accommodation. The tourist boards run a booking service with offices at Termini station, as well as both of the city's airports.

Recommended Hotels

The hotels recommended on pages 300–303 are listed under five categories: Boutique, Budget, Historic, Luxury, and Pensions and B&B. Boutique hotels are smaller and designed with an artistic eye, whether it be modern or ancient in style. Budget accommodation, while the least expensive option, is not reserved to hostels and B&Bs. Surprisingly, Rome has some great options for frugal travellers who know where to look. The city is also full of historic accommodation as many Renaissance palaces and villas have been turned into hotels. Antique furniture and exposed architectural elements make them the most romantic choices. Luxury hotels provide

5-star service and facilities, most with stunningly beautiful rooms, panoramic rooftop terraces and award-winning restaurants. Pensions and B&Bs may provide more basic facilities, but are often full of character at an affordable price.

Our hotels are divided into five geographical areas. In Central Rome, from Piazza Navona to the Jewish Ghetto and southward as far as the Tiber, you will find a plethora of hotels for all budgets. Many exclusive boutique hotels can be found here, as well as a number of mid-range options. Ancient Rome, from the Colosseum to the Esquiline Hill, including the Lateran and the Aventine, offers varied accommodation, including a number of budget options, particularly near Termini station. Most of the luxury hotels can be found in the Spanish Steps and Via Veneto neighbourhoods, categorized under Spagna,

Penthouse Villa Medici Suite at the luxurious Hassler Roma *(see p302)*

Veneto and Around, which also includes the Quirinal Hill. Trastevere and Around, including the Vatican and Janiculum areas, offers some great historical choices and many B&Bs. The Further Afield section covers hotels outside the centre and in nearby Tivoli.

Throughout the listings, certain hotels are highlighted as DK Choice. These offer a special experience – superlative service, beautiful interiors, cutting-edge amenities or gadgets, an excellent restaurant, or a combination of these.

DIRECTORY

Disabled Travellers

Bus Abile
Tel 06-6710 5387.
(call between 10am and 1pm Mon–Fri).
w atac.roma.it

Roma per Tutti
w romapertutti.it

Bed & Breakfast

B&B Rome Service
Tel 06-6813 5677.
w bedand-breakfastroma.com

Bed & Breakfast Association of Rome
Via A. Pacinotti 73.
Tel 06-5530 2248.
Open 10am–2pm, 3–7pm Mon–Fri.
w b-b.rm.it

Residential Hotels

Adagio Aparthotel
Via Damiano Chiesa 8, 00136. Tel 06-30198.
w adagio-city.com

Residence Hotel Parioli
Via Mercalli 26. Tel 06-9442 9100. **w** residence hotelparioli.com

Rome Renting
Vicolo Moroni 35–36, 00153. Tel 331-254 2263.
w romerenting.com

Vittoria
Via Vittoria 60–64, 00187.
Tel 06-679 7533.
w residenceugolini.it

Religious Institutions

Casa di Santa Brigida
Piazza Farnese 96, 00186.
Tel 06-6889 2596.

Casa Il Rosario
Via Sant'Agata dei Goti 10, 00184. Tel 06-679 2346.
w casailrosarioroma.it

Nostra Signora di Lourdes
Via Sistina 113, 00187.
Tel 06-474 5324.
w rndlourdes.org

Budget Accommodation

AIG Hostels
Via Nicotera 1. Tel 06-487 1152. **w** aighostels.it

Alessandro Palace
Via Vicenza 42, 00185.
Tel 06-446 1958. **w** hostelsaless andro.com

Foresteria Orsa Maggiore
Via di San Francesco di Sales 1A, 00165.
Tel 06-689 3753.
w foresteriaorsa. altervista.org

Mammarampa
Rampa Brancaleone 12, 00165. Tel 349-841 0800.
w mammarampa.it

Sandy Hostel
Via Cavour 136.
Tel 06-488 4585.
w sandyhostel.com

Stargate
Via Palestro 88, 00185.
Tel 06-445 7164.
w stargatehotels.com

YWCA
Via C. Balbo 4, 00184.
Tel 06-488 3917.
w ywca-ucdg.it

Self-Catering

Airbnb
w airbnb.com

Coach House Rentals
Tel 333-565 8225.
Tel (44) 208 1338 332 (UK).
w chsrentals.com

Cross Pollinate
w cross-pollinate.com

RetRome Bed & Breakfast
Tel 06-7049 5471.
w retrome.net

Camping

Flaminio Village
Via Flaminia Nuova 821, 00189. Tel 06-333 2604.
w campingflaminio.com

Tourist Board

Rome City Tourist Board
Termini Station 00185.
Tel 06-0608.
Open 8am–7:30pm daily.
Terminal 3 (arrivals), Leonardo da Vinci Airport, Fiumicino. **Open** 7:45am–7:30pm daily.
w 060608.it

Where to Stay

Boutique

Ancient Rome

Best Western Canada €
Via Vicenza 58, 00185
Tel 06-445 7770 **Map** 6 E2
W hotelcanadaroma.com
Rooms vary at this above-average three-star hotel; some have canopy beds. Free Wi-Fi.

Domus Aventina €€
Via di Santa Prisca 11b, 00153
Tel 06-574 6135 **Map** 8 E3
W hoteldomusaventina.com
Simple but elegantly decorated rooms open onto a quiet courtyard. A good family option.

DK Choice

Fortyseven €€
Via Luigi Petroselli 47, 00186
Tel 06-678 7816 **Map** 8 E1
W fortysevenhotel.com
Located right in the middle of the ancient city, Fortyseven offers stellar views of the Forum. The modern interior was designed by artists and well-known designers, and the top floor rooms feature luxurious terraces. Free transfers to the airport. Perfect for a romantic weekend.

Hotel Celio €€
Via dei Santi Quattro 35/c, 00184
Tel 06-7049 5333 **Map** 9 A1
W hotelcelio.com
This is an elegant hotel with a touch of whimsy. Reproduction artwork is found in every room.

San Anselmo €€
Piazza Sant'Anselmo 2, 00153
Tel 06-570 057 **Map** 8 D3
W aventinohotels.com
A romantic choice, San Anselmo offers four-poster beds and claw-foot tubs for a memorable stay.

Central Rome

Albergo Santa Chiara €€
Via di Santa Chiara 21, 00186
Tel 06-687 2979 **Map** 12 D3
W albergosantachiara.com
A well-located hotel with an impressive, spacious lobby and simply furnished rooms.

Campo de' Fiori Hotel €€
Via del Biscione 6, 00186
Tel 06-6880 6865 **Map** 11 C4
W hotelcampodefiori.com
This place features romantically decorated rooms with charming details and views of rooftops.

Locanda Cairoli €€
Piazza Benedetto Cairoli 2, 00186
Tel 06-6880 9278 **Map** 12 D5
W hotelcairoliroma.com
Centrally located and comfortable hotel with a cosy family-style breakfast room. Quirky and eclectic furnishings.

Portoghesi €€
Via dei Portoghesi 1, 00186
Tel 06-686 4231 **Map** 11 C2
W hotelportoghesiroma.it
Found in a quiet cobbled alley, this is a good-value central hotel. It has a lovely breakfast terrace.

Sole al Pantheon €€
Piazza della Rotonda 63, 00186
Tel 06-678 0441 **Map** 12 D3
W soleal pantheonrome.com
The nice rooms at this place offer unparalleled views of the Pantheon, but can be noisy.

Teatropace 33 €€
Via del Teatro Pace 33, 00186
Tel 06-687 9075 **Map** 11 C3
W hotelteatropace.com
Charming hotel decorated in ornate Baroque style with an excellent price-quality ratio.

Spagna, Veneto and Around

Parlamento €
Via delle Convertite 5, 00187
Tel 06-6992 1000 **Map** 12 E1
W hotelparlamento.it
Offering romantic rooms with whimsical touches, this hotel has a rooftop terrace with a lovely view.

Deko Rome €€
Via Toscana 1, 00187
Tel 06-4202 0032 **Map** 5 C1
W dekorome.com
This hotel has small but comfortable rooms in minimalist style. Luxurious bathrooms.

The sleek, contemporary interior of the Babuino181 hotel

Hotel Art €€
Via Margutta 56, 00187
Tel 06-328 711 **Map** 4 F1
W hotelartrome.com
While the art-inspired public spaces may be over the top, the rooms at Art are sleek.

Piranesi €€
Via del Babuino 196, 00187
Tel 06-328 041 **Map** 4 F1
W hotelpiranesi.com
This hotel exudes a quiet yet sophisticated elegance. Facilities here include a roof garden and small gym.

Babuino181 €€€
Via del Babuino 181, 00187
Tel 06-3229 5295 **Map** 4 F1
W romeluxurysuites.com
A Renaissance palace remodelled with a sleek, modern look and luxurious details.

Portrait Roma €€€
Via Bocca di Leone 23, 00187
Tel 06-6938 0742 **Map** 5 A2
W lungarnocollection.com
Owned by Salvatore Ferragamo, this stylish hotel's rooms are individually decorated and have marble bathrooms.

Trastevere and Around

Domus Tiberina €
Via in Piscinula 37, 00153
Tel 06-581 3648 **Map** 8 D1
W hoteldomustiberina.it
This is a quaint hotel on a picturesque, vine-covered alleyway. Steps away from the Tiber.

Sant'Anna €
Borgo Pio 134, 00193
Tel 06-6880 1602 **Map** 3 C3
W santannahotel.net
Sant'Anna offers modern convenience with an old-fashioned feel. The exquisite courtyard provides respite from the busy street.

Hotel Ponte Sisto €€
Via dei Pettinari 64, 00186
Tel 06-686 3100 **Map** 11 C5
W hotelpontesisto.it
This hotel has comfortable rooms with panoramic views and a delightful inner garden.

Warm and inviting room at the Due Torri hotel in Central Rome

Palazzo Cardinal Cesi €€
Via della Conciliazione 51, 00193
Tel *06-684 039* **Map** 3 C3
🆆 palazzocesi.it
In a former cardinal's palace, this hotel features classic Italian style, original mouldings, coffered ceilings and a romantic garden.

San Francesco €€
Via Jacopa de' Settesoli 7, 00153
Tel *06-5830 0051* **Map** 7 C2
🆆 hotelsanfrancesco.net
An unassuming entrance hides a gem of a hotel. It has tasteful rooms and a chic rooftop bar.

Budget
Ancient Rome

DK Choice

The Beehive €
Via Marghera 8, 00185
Tel *06-4470 4553* **Map** 6 E3
🆆 the-beehive.com
This gem is owned by an American couple, and has private rooms and small dorms. Basic, yet comfortable. Many extras are on offer – yoga lessons, massage sessions and a café serving freshly baked bread and organic coffee. An excellent choice for frugal travellers. Book early.

Hostel des Artistes €
Via Villafranca 20, 00185
Tel *06-445 4365* **Map** 6 E2
🆆 hostelrome.com
Friendly and clean hostel with dorm accommodation. Simple private rooms are also available.

Blue Hostel €€
Via Carlo Alberto 13, 00185
Tel *340-925 8503* **Map** 6 D4
🆆 bluehostel.it
This impressive, spotless hostel in a heritage-listed building offers excellent value for money.

Central Rome

Mimosa €€
Via di Santa Chiara, 61, 00186
Tel *06-6880 1753* **Map** 12 D3
🆆 hotelmimosa.net
Mimosa has affordable accommodation with basic rooms that are comfortable, clean, and air conditioned.

Palazzo Olivia €€
Via dei Leutari 15, 00186
Tel *06-6821 6986* **Map** 11 C3
🆆 palazzo-olivia.it
The Palazzo Olivia is set in a 17th-century palace. The self-catered apartments are each named after an opera character.

Spagna, Veneto and Around

Hotel Grifo €€
Via del Boschetto 144, 00184
Tel *06-487 1395* **Map** 5 B4
🆆 hotelgrifo.com
The compact, functional rooms are kept immaculately clean at Hotel Grifo. Breakfast is served on a cosy terrace with a charming view.

Trastevere and Around

Casa Internazionale delle Donne €
Via di San Francesco di Sales 1A, 00165
Tel *06-689 3753* **Map** 4 D5
🆆 casainternazionaledelle donne.org
Basic and inexpensive hostel-type accommodation in a quiet but central area is offered here. For women only.

Hotel Trastevere €
Via Luciano Manara 24a, 00153
Tel *06-581 4713* **Map** 7 C1
🆆 hoteltrastevere.net
This hotel is good value for the area, with basic service and large and bright, though unimaginative, rooms.

Maria Rosa Guesthouse €
Via dei Vascellari 55, 00153
Tel *338 770 0067* **Map** 8 D1
🆆 maria-rosa.it
This small, cheerfully furnished guesthouse in a 19th-century building is a good family option.

Villa Riari €
Via dei Riari 44, 00153
Tel *06-6880 6122* **Map** 11 A5
🆆 villariari.it
Rock-bottom prices at this religious centre located on a quiet street. It has a lovely garden.

Historic
Ancient Rome

Hotel Forum €€€
Via Tor de' Conti 25, 00184
Tel *06-679 2446* **Map** 5 B5
🆆 hotelforum.com
Dark wooden floors and rich fabrics evoke an old-world feel at this hotel. There are stunning views of Ancient Rome.

Palazzo Manfredi €€€
Via Labicana 125, 00184
Tel *06-7759 1380* **Map** 9 B1
🆆 palazzomanfredi.com
Located near the Colosseum, this converted Renaissance palace has elegantly decorated rooms.

Central Rome

Casa di Santa Brigida €€
Piazza Farnese 96, 00186
Tel *06-6889 2596* **Map** 11 C4
🆆 brigidine.org
Although it is not the cheapest option, the superb location and rooftop terrace of this convent make a stay here worth while.

Due Torri €€
Vicolo del Leonetto 23, 00186
Tel *06-6880 6956* **Map** 11 C1
🆆 hotelduetorriroma.com
This converted Renaissance palace has small but well-appointed rooms and friendly service.

Teatro di Pompeo €€
Largo del Pallaro 8, 00186
Tel *06-6830 0170* **Map** 11 C4
🆆 hotelteatrodipompeo.it
This simple but evocative hotel, built on the ruins of Pompey's ancient theatre. Attentive staff.

Sole al Biscione €€€
Via del Biscione 76, 00186
Tel *06-6880 6873* **Map** 11 C4
🆆 hotelsoleroma.it
This functional but charming hotel claims to be the oldest in Rome. Fantastic rooftop terrace.

For more information on types of hotels *see pp297–9*

Spagna, Veneto and Around

Locarno €€
Via della Penna 22, 00186
Tel 06-361 0841 **Map** 4 F1
W hotellocarno.com
Many classic films have been shot on the exquisite rooftop terrace of this Art Deco masterpiece.

Trastevere and Around

Bramante €€
Vicolo delle Palline 24, 00193
Tel 06-6880 6426 **Map** 3 C3
W hotelbramante.com
Bramante is situated on a quaint and cobbled back-street in the shadow of St Peter's basilica. Quiet and tasteful rooms.

DK Choice

Donna Camilla Savelli €€
Via Garibaldi 27, 00153
Tel 06-588 861 **Map** 7 B1
W hoteldonnacamillasavelli.com
Built by Baroque architect Borromini, this ex-monastery is now a four-star hotel. All rooms are decorated with period furniture and some have Jacuzzi tubs. The cloister is an oasis in the heart of the city.

Relais Casa della Fornarina €€
Via di Porta Settimiana 7, 00153
Tel 06-6456 2268 **Map** 11 B5
W casadellafornarina.com
This hotel is set in the house where Raphael's muse, the famous baker's daughter, lived. Busy area at night.

Luxury

Ancient Rome

Hotel Mediterraneo €€
Via Cavour 15, 00184
Tel 06-488 4051 **Map** 6 D3
W romehotelmediterraneo.it
This hotel has Art Deco design, comfortable rooms and a terrace with sweeping views.

Kolbe Hotel €€
Via di San Teodoro 48, 00186
Tel 06-679 8866 **Map** 8 E1
W kolbehotelrome.com
The Kolbe Hotel mixes modern furnishings with ancient architectural elements. Some rooms look directly over the Forum.

Radisson Blu es. hotel €€
Via Filippo Turati 171, 00185
Tel 06-444 841 **Map** 6 E4
W radissonblu.com/eshotel-rome
A magnificent rooftop pool, cutting-edge design and breathtaking views make for an unforgettable stay at this Radisson Blu hotel.

Central Rome

Hotel Indigo Rome – St. George €€
Via Giulia 62, 00186
Tel 06-686 611 **Map** 11 B4
W hotelindigorome.com
This discreet, romantic hotel has a rooftop terrace offering chic *aperitivi* and river views. The rooms feature striking details, such as a huge mural of the FIAT 500.

Grand Hotel de la Minerve €€€
Piazza della Minerva 69, 00186
Tel 06-695 201 **Map** 12 D3
W grandhoteldelaminerve.com
There are postcard views from nearly every room at this hotel plus an unbeatable rooftop terrace. Luxurious service and decor.

Nazionale €€€
Piazza di Montecitorio 131, 00186
Tel 06-695 001 **Map** 12 E2
W hotelnazionale.it
Decked with period furniture and rich fabrics, this is an elegant four-star hotel. Ask for the Jacuzzi with a view.

Raphael €€€
Largo Febo 2, 00186
Tel 06-682 831 **Map** 11 C2
W raphaelhotel.com
World-class service, a panoramic terrace and gorgeous decor make for a romantic stay at the Raphael.

Spagna, Veneto and Around

Aleph €€
Via di San Basilio 15, 00185
Tel 06-422 901 **Map** 5 B2
W hotelalephrome.com
Modern opulence reigns at this five-star hotel where facilities include elegant conference rooms and a luxurious spa.

Eden €€
Via Ludovisi 49, 00187
Tel 06-478 121 **Map** 5 B2
W edenroma.com
Outstanding service and an award-winning rooftop terrace restaurant at this elegant hotel.

Boscolo Exedra €€€
Piazza della Repubblica 47, 00185
Tel 06-489 381 **Map** 5 C3
W exedra-roma.boscolo
hotels.com
With an award-winning spa and a rooftop infinity pool, this is a lavish, modern five-star hotel.

De Russie €€€
Via del Babuino 9, 00187
Tel 06-328 881 **Map** 4 F1
W roccofortehotels.com
Spectacular gardens surround this Renaissance villa-turned-hotel. It has a fully-equipped spa.

DK Choice

Hassler Roma €€€
Piazza Trinità dei Monti 6, 00187
Tel 06-699 340 **Map** 5 A2
W hotelhasslerroma.com
Impeccable service, plush furnishings and incomparable views have made this legendary hotel the favourite Roman *pied-à-terre* for many celebrities. Each room is individually styled and every possible comfort is available for a price. Family rooms are available. It is enviably located atop the Spanish Steps.

Hotel d'Inghilterra €€€
Via Bocca di Leone 14, 00187
Tel 06-699 811 **Map** 5 A2
W hoteldinghilterra.com
This hotel offers sumptuous accommodation in a fantastic location. There is a candlelit rooftop terrace.

Hotel Majestic Roma €€€
Via Veneto 50, 00187
Tel 06-421 441 **Map** 5 B2
W hotelmajestic.com
Renovated by architect Gaetano Koch, this hotel is a celebration of Neo-Classical style inside and out.

Impressive lobby of the Grand Hotel de la Minerve

Key to prices *see p300*

Regina Hotel Baglioni €€€
Via Veneto 72, 00187
Tel 06-421 111 **Map** 5 B2
W baglionihotels.com
This gem of Art Deco-style decor
and architecture has opulent
furnishings and every comfort.

St. Regis Hotel €€€
Via Vittorio Emanuele Orlando 3, 00185
Tel 06-47091 **Map** 5 C3
W stregisrome.com
Boasting an on-site spa and
fitness center, this is an
extravagant palace hotel.

Villa Spalletti Trivelli €€€
Via Piacenza 4, 00184
Tel 06-4890 7934 **Map** 5 B3
W villaspalletti.it
Understated elegance and
impeccable taste at this villa
nestled in a lush garden setting.

Westin Excelsior €€€
Via Veneto 125, 00187
Tel 06-47081 **Map** 5 B2
W westinrome.com
This hotel is a favourite with
honeymooners; the perfect spot
to indulge in *la dolce vita*.

Further Afield

Aldrovandi Villa Borghese €€€
*Via Ulisse Aldrovandi 15, 00197,
Villa Borghese*
Tel 06-322 3993 **Map** 2 D4
W aldrovandi.com
With airy rooms and a poolside
restaurant, this spectacular
hotel offers views of the
Borghese gardens.

Pension and B&B

Ancient Rome

La Casa di Amy €
Via Principe Amedeo 85A, 00185
Tel 06-446 0708 **Map** 6 D4
W lacasadiamy.com
This family-run B&B has a friendly
atmosphere, funky decoration
and bright, clean rooms.

Paba €
Via Cavour 266, 00184
Tel 06-4782 4902 **Map** 5 B5
W hotelpaba.com
Proximity to the Forum makes
Paba a convenient budget option.
Rooms are simply furnished.

Piccolo Principe €
Via Giovanni Giolitti 255, 00185
Tel 320-699 3110 **Map** 6 E4
W bebromatermini.it
Brightly painted rooms with basic
furnishings and clean bathrooms
are offered at this place. Located
near the Termini station.

Charming decor at the inviting Pantheon View

Central Rome

Casa Banzo €€
Piazza del Monte di Pietà 30, 00186
Tel 06-683 3909 **Map** 11 C4
W casabanzo.it
Impressive details and period-
style furniture make this low-
priced option quite enjoyable.
There is a lovely courtyard too.

DK Choice

Pantheon View €€
Via del Seminario 87, 00186
Tel 06-699 0294 **Map** 12 D3
W pantheonview.it
This pension offers the
comforts of a hotel, in
addition to details such
as wood-beamed ceilings,
exposed brickwork, chandeliers
and copper taps. Most rooms
have views of the Pantheon.

Spagna, Veneto and Around

Hotel Julia €
Via Rasella 29, 00187
Tel 06-488 1637 **Map** 5 B3
W hoteljulia.it
This is a reasonably priced
three-star hotel with friendly
staff and simple, comfortable
rooms, including three
for families.

Oceania €
Via Firenze 38, 00187
Tel 06-482 4696 **Map** 5 C3
W hoteloceania.it
There is plenty of old-world
charm and quirky details at this
simple but tasteful hotel.

Panda €
Via della Croce 35, 00187
Tel 06-678 0179 **Map** 5 A2
W hotelpanda.it
Elegantly furnished rooms
are warmed by terracotta-tiled
floors and wood-beamed ceilings
at this hotel.

DK Choice

Casa Howard €€
*Via di Capo le Case 18, 00187 and
Via Sistina 149, 00187*
Tel 06-6992 4555 **Map** 12 F1
W casahoward.com
This guesthouse inspired by
E M Forster's novel *Howard's End*
has 10 unique rooms. What it
lacks in round-the-clock service,
it makes up for in style and
character. Some rooms do not
have private baths, but kimonos
are provided for convenience.

Hotel Suisse €€
Via Gregoriana 54, 00187
Tel 06-678 3649 **Map** 5 A2
W hotelsuisserome.com
Located near the Trevi Fountain,
this pension offers great value and
warm service. The rooms feature
the original 1920s parquet flooring.

Residenza Cellini €€
Via Modena 5, 00184
Tel 06-4782 5204 **Map** 5 C3
W residenzacellini.it
This place offers spacious rooms
with basic furnishings. Some of
the bathrooms have Jacuzzi tubs.

Trastevere and Around

Arco del Lauro €€
Via dell'Arco de' Tolomei 27, 00153
Tel 06-9784 0350 **Map** 8 D1
W arcodellauro.it
This is a tiny hotel with simple
but lovely rooms in a picturesque
medieval setting.

Further Afield

Palazzo Maggiore €
*Via Domenico Giuliani 89, 00019,
Tivoli*
Tel 393-104 4937
W palazzomaggiore.com
This sweet family-run B&B with
cosy rooms is the perfect base
to explore Tivoli's incredible villas.
The rooms all have balconies.

For more information on types of hotels see pp297–9

WHERE TO EAT AND DRINK

In Rome, eating out can be both a gastronomic joy and an entertaining experience. On warm summer evenings tables spill out into every conceivable open space and diners dedicate long hours to the popular social activity of people-watching (and of being noticed and admired themselves) in a confusion of passers-by, buskers, rose sellers and traffic. Romans have always loved to linger at the table, but the lavish feasts of ancient Rome have slimmed down and today's cooking is based on simplicity, freshness and good quality local raw ingredients. Fast food is available, but it is fundamentally alien to the Roman temperament and way of life.

The restaurants reviewed in this chapter have been selected from the best that Rome has to offer across all price ranges. Their descriptions, including the highlighted DK Choice entries, will help narrow down your choice and enjoy a variety of cuisine types. The section on *Light Meals and Drinks* on pages 320–25 has details of recommended cafés, pizzerias, wine bars and other places for more casual eating.

Types of Restaurants

In general, a *trattoria* is a family-run establishment with good home cooking, while a *ristorante* is more upmarket, more elegant and thus more expensive.

Some eating places – where paper tablecloths give a clue to low prices – simply have no name. They offer excellent, basic home cooking. A number of them offer a great deal more than that, and your chances of finding authentic Roman cooking are higher in the best of these establishments than in expensive restaurants.

There will probably be times when you do not want a large meal, and Rome offers a huge variety of places for more casual eating (*see pp320–25*). One type of place offering snacks or more substantial dishes is the

enoteca, which doubles as a well-stocked wine shop for browsers and connoisseurs.

Other places for a sit-down, informal lunch or dinner are *birrerie*, which are not only for beer drinkers, but also offer pizzas and even four-course meals.

There is always interesting takeaway food for sale – *pizza rustica* or *pizza al taglio* (pizza by the slice) is available all over the city. For the best full-size pizzas, choose places with wood stoves (*forno a legna*). Other takeaways such as a whole roast chicken, or *pomodori al riso* (tomatoes stuffed with rice), can be had from a *rosticceria*. A self-service *tavola calda* will serve an impressive array of hot food and is ideal for lunchtimes.

Fresh artichokes, a Roman speciality

Vegetarian Food

Purely vegetarian restaurants are few and far between in Rome, but everywhere you will find pasta and rice dishes (*risotto*). Most menus include an extensive list of vegetable-based side dishes (*contorni*) which could be anything from artichokes (stewed – *alla Romana* or fried – alla giudia), grilled or au gratin vegetables, and sautéed spinach, chard or chicory. Vegetables stuffed with rice then baked in the oven are also menu staples. Most menus are adaptable, as dishes are prepared to order. Tell your waiter that you are *vegetariano* (female: *vegetariana*) and he will advise accordingly.

The Price of a Meal

What you pay will depend on your choice of establishment. In a *tavola calda* or Roman pizzeria, for example, you can still eat for as little as €15 a head. A local *trattoria* costs perhaps €25, whereas in a smarter restaurant reckon on around €30 and up. Bottled wine, as opposed to a jug or carafe of house wine (*vino della casa*), will cost more but should offer a more interesting range of tastes (*see pp308-9*). House wine can be hit-or-miss.

Reading the Menu

The waiter will often tell you the day's specialities (*piatti del giorno*), usually not mentioned on the menu but almost always worth ordering. Or, ask for *la lista* (the menu) and then allow yourself to be guided.

A meal could begin with *antipasti* (appetizers) or *primi piatti* – the latter consisting of *pasta asciutta* (pasta with some

Welcoming trattoria *Maccheroni (see p312)*

kind of sauce), *pasta in brodo* (clear broth with pasta in it), *pasta al forno* (baked pasta), risotto or a substantial soup. You then move on to the *secondi*, the main meat or fish course, for which you will usually need to order vegetables (*contorni*) separately. Afterwards you have *formaggi* (cheeses), *frutta* (fruit) or *dolci* (desserts). Romans do not usually eat cheese as well as a sweet dish. Strong espresso coffee, and perhaps a liqueur (*amaro* or *digestivo*) rounds off the meal (*see p309*). You may want to skip the first course, or prefer to choose a salad or vegetable dish. Pasta alone is not seen traditionally as a full meal.

Opening Times

Restaurants are generally open from about noon to 3pm and from 8pm to 11pm or later. The busiest times tend to be 9pm–9:30pm for dinner and 1pm–1:30pm at lunchtime. Dinner is generally the preferred time for dedicated, relaxed eating, particularly in summer. Bars are open all day, often from the early hours, serving all kinds of drinks (alcohol can be sold at any time of day) and snacks. The quietest month is August, when many restaurant owners take their annual holiday (shown by *chiuso per ferie* signs).

Booking a Table

Booking (*prenotazioni*) is generally advisable. Sunday is the main lunch date of the week when you should definitely book; the same usually goes for

A well-stocked wine cellar at Roscioli *(see p314)*

Saturday evening. Check the weekly closing day if you do not book. Many places are closed on Mondays, and Sunday evening can also be difficult.

In summer try to book a shady table outside, since air conditioning is not universal.

Wheelchair Access

Rome is becoming more solicitous towards those in wheelchairs, but a call to the restaurant in advance will help secure the right table.

Children

Children are made very welcome, particularly in family-run places. You can usually order half-portions, or just ask for an extra plate. High chairs (*seggioloni*) may also be available.

Smoking

Smoking is banned in restaurants, bars and cafés.

Recommended Restaurants

Every area of Rome has its own culinary delights (*see Flavours of Rome pp306–7*). Our restaurants are divided into five geograph-ical areas: Ancient Rome; Central Rome; Spagna, Veneto and Around; Trastevere and Around; and Further Afield. Ancient Rome begins near the Forum, stretching past the Colosseum to encompass Testaccio, the Aventine Hill, the Lateran and the Esquiline Hill (where Termini station is found). Central Rome is the very heart of town, from Piazza Navona and the Pantheon down to the river, including

Campo de' Fiori and the Jewish Ghetto. Spagna, Veneto and Around covers the heavily trafficked areas from Piazza del Popolo to Piazza Barberini, as well as the Quirinal Hill and the gastronomically rich neighbour-hood of Monti. Trastevere and Around includes the Vatican and the foothills of the Janiculum as well. Further Afield covers any-thing from areas just outside the centre, like Monteverde and Parioli, to nearby towns like Tivoli and Fiumicino.

Each restaurant listed is given a cuisine category. Traditional Roman cuisine is hearty and meat-based with lots of offal dishes, although vegetarian dishes do exist. Modern Italian restaurants use traditional recipes as a spring-board to create new and exciting dishes using unexpected ingredients. Every Italian region has its own local cuisine and they vary drastically. Opt for a regional Italian restaurant to sample these varieties. Pizzerias abound, but keep in mind some serve a range of other dishes, while others offer nothing but the beloved dough. The *enotecas* and *birrerias* listed offer food to go with drinks, from cheese platters to full meals. For an extraordinary meal, try a fine dining option, but be prepared for a hefty bill. Rome's internat-ional restaurants are great when pasta and pizza begin to get old.

Throughout our listings, we've marked recommended restaurants as DK Choice. We've highlighted these because they offer a special experience – either for the superb cuisine, for enjoying a particularly Italian night out, for the excellent value they offer, or a combination of these.

Tables set out for alfresco dining at Da Giggetto *(see p313)*

The Flavours of Rome

There are few more enduring pleasures than lingering over a leisurely al fresco meal in a piazza in the Eternal City. Roman food is tasty, nutritious, simple and extremely varied. Menus tend to be seasonal and there are even specialities eaten on specific days of the week. Traditionally, Thursday is *gnocchi* day, Friday is for salted cod *(baccalà)* and Saturday for tripe. Food is redolent of aromatic herbs, olive oil, garlic and onion, and there are many signature dishes, including pasta. But much authentic Roman cuisine takes its origins from offal, and slow, inventive cooking transforms these tradtionally "poor" cuts into rich and flavoursome dishes.

Olives and olive oil

Pasta being made by hand in traditional style

Cucina Romana

Traditional Roman cuisine originated in the Testaccio area, near the old slaughter-house whose butchers *(vaccinari)* were paid partly in cash and partly in meat – or rather offal. The "fifth quarter" *(quinto quarto)* included head, trotters, tail, intestines, brain and other unmentionable bits of the beast which, when carefully cooked and richly flavoured with herbs and spices, are transformed into culinary delight. These robust dishes, such as *coda alla vaccinara* (literally, "oxtail cooked in the style of the slaughterhouse butcher"), still feature on the menus of many of Rome's top restaurants.

For more squeamish carnivores, lamb is popular, often served simply roasted. Veal is another speciality, as is piglet seasoned with herbs. Authentic *cucina romana* also has roots in the Jewish cuisine of the Ghetto area. Local globe artichokes are fried whole in olive oil *(carciofi alla giudia)* or served *alla romana*, with oil, garlic and Roman mint. Courgette *(zucchini)* flowers are also deep-fried, as are Jewish-style salt cod fillets *(filetti di baccalà)*.

Seafood and fish restaurants are among the best in Rome, although they can be very

Marinated artichokes   Roast peppers   Sun-blush tomatoes   Sweet baby peppers
Olives   Marinated mushrooms

Selection of delicious, typically Roman *antipasti* (appetizers)

Regional Dishes and Specialities

As an appetizer, *bruschetta* (Roman dialect for "lightly burnt bread") may be served with a selection of delicious toppings. Other *antipasti* include crispy-fried or marinated vegetables. A much-loved pasta dish is *bucatini all'amatriciana* – pasta tubes in a spicy tomato and sausage or bacon sauce, sprinkled with grated tangy pecorino cheese. Veal is a great favourite and delicacies include *rigatoni alla pajata* (pasta with milk-fed veal intestines). Lamb is also very popular, in dishes such as *abbacchio al forno* (roasted milk-fed lamb) or *alla cacciatora* ("huntsman's style" with anchovy sauce). The generic word for offal is *animelle* (or *interiora*) and Roman delicacies include *cervella* (calves' brains), *pajata* (veal intestines) and *trippa* (tripe).

Bruschetta

Supplì These tasty fried rice croquettes are stuffed with mozzarella cheese that oozes out when they are cut.

Selecting fresh vegetables at a market in central Rome

expensive. Everything is available, from sumptuous seafood platters to small fish caught off the Lazio coast and served fried or used in soups, as well as superb sea bass (*spigola*) cooked Roman-style with porcini mushrooms.

Pasta, Pasta

Pasta is the mainstay of the Roman meal, especially spaghetti. *Spaghetti alla carbonara*, made with *pancetta* (cured bacon) or *guanciale* (pig's cheek), egg yolks and cheese, is a classic Roman dish, as is *spaghetti alle vongole*, with clams. Many menus also include *spaghetti cacio e pepe* (with pecorino cheese and pepper) and *bucatini all'amatriciana* (with a spicy tomato and bacon sauce). At a conservative estimate, there is

one type of pasta for every day of the year. Many have wonderfully descriptive or poetic names, such as *capelli d'angelo* (angel's hair), *strozzapreti* (priest chokers) or *ziti* (bridegrooms), whose shape is best left to the imagination.

Huge wheels of pecorino cheese ready to be cut and enjoyed

La Dolce Vita

For those with a taste for "the sweet life", nuts, fruits and versatile ricotta cheese are often combined in mouthwateringly delicious desserts. Ice cream is an art form in Rome, where some parlours offer over 100 flavours of home-made *gelati*. Types vary from the classic *crema* and *frutta* to *grattachecca* (water ice), from *semifreddo* (a half-frozen sponge pudding, similar to French parfait in consistency) to *granita* (ice shavings flavoured with fruit syrups). Glorious *gelato* is one of the great pleasures here, to be enjoyed at any time of the day – or night.

ON THE MENU

Abbacchio alla cacciatora Lamb simmered in Castelli Romani wine with anchovies, garlic, rosemary and olive oil.

Bruschetta Toasted bread rubbed with garlic, drizzled with olive oil, may be served with a variety of toppings.

Gnocchi alla romana Little semolina dumplings served with a tomato or *ragù* (meat) sauce, or just with butter.

Pecorino romano The traditional Roman cheese, made from ewe's milk.

Spigola alla romana Sea bass with *porcini* mushrooms, shallots, garlic, Castelli Romani wine and olive oil.

Spaghetti alla carbonara The creamy sauce thickens as the hot pasta mixes into the egg yolks and cheese.

Saltimbocca alla romana Veal slices are rolled with prosciutto and sage. Saltimbocca means "jump into the mouth".

Crostata di ricotta This rich, baked cheesecake is made using ricotta and flavoured with Marsala and lemon.

What to Drink in Rome

Italy is one of Europe's most significant wine-producing countries, keeping up a tradition started in the hills around Rome over 2,000 years ago. Today, wine is usually drunk with meals as a matter of course, and knowing the difference between *rosso* (red) and *bianco* (white) may be all the vocabulary you need to get by. Beer is widely available too, as well as good ranges of apéritifs and digestifs. Rome's drinking water, another debt to the ancient Romans, is particularly good, fresh and sweet, and in abundant supply.

The vineyards of Frascati, southeast of Rome

White Wine

Vines thrive in the warm climate of Lazio, the region around Rome, producing abundant supplies of inexpensive dry white wine for the city's cafés and restaurants. It is usually sold by the carafe. Of local bottled wines, Frascati is the best known, but Castelli Romani, Marino, Colli Albani and Velletri are very similar in style. All are made from one grape variety, the Trebbiano, though better quality versions contain a dash of Malvasia for perfume and flavour. Other central Italian whites worth trying are Orvieto and Verdicchio. Quality white wines from all over Italy, including fine whites from Friuli in the northeast, are widely available in Rome.

Orvieto   Frascati

Calcaia comes from Barberani, a reliable producer of Orvieto.

Bigi produce good quality Orvieto, especially the single-vineyard Torricella.

Wine Type	Good Vintages	Good Producers
White Wine		
Friuli (Pinot Bianco, Chardonnay, Pinot Grigio, Sauvignon)	The most recent	Gravner, Jermann, Puiatti, Schiopetto, Volpe Pasini
Orvieto/ Orvieto Classico	The most recent	Antinori, Barberani, Bigi, Il Palazzone
Red Wine		
Chianti/ Chianti Classico/ Chianti Rufina	2007, 2006, 2001, 2000, 99, 97, 95, 90, 88, 85	Antinori, Castello di Ama, Castello di Cacchiano, Castello di Volpaia, Felsina Berardenga, Fontodi, Frescobaldi, Isole e Olena, Il Palazzino, Riecine, Rocca delle Macie, Ruffino, Vecchie Terre di Montefili, Villa Cafaggio
Brunello di Montalcino/ Vino Nobile di Montepulciano	2007, 2004, 2001, 99, 97, 95, 90, 88, 85	Altesino, Avignonesi, Biondi Santi, Caparzo, Case Basse, Lisini, Il Poggione, Poliziano, Villa Banfi
Barolo/Barbaresco	2006, 2004, 2000, 99, 98, 97, 95, 90, 89, 88	Aldo Conterno, Altare, Ceretto, Clerico, Gaja, Giacomo Conterno, Giacosa, Mascarello, Ratti, Voerzio

Casal Pilozzo is an easy-drinking white wine from the Frascati producers, Colli di Catone. Choose the youngest vintage.

Colle Gaio, with its rich, fruity flavour, stands out among the dry white Frascatis.

Red Wine

Though some local red wine is made, most of the bottled red wine in Rome comes from other parts of Italy. Regions like Tuscany and Piedmont produce very good everyday drinking as well as top-class wines like Barolo. Price should reflect quality – try Dolcetto, Rosso di Montalcino or Montepulciano for good-value reds.

Tuscan table wine   Barolo

Montepulciano d'Abruzzo, a rich and juicy red wine, is always good value. It is produced in the Abruzzi region east of Rome.

Chianti Classico Riserva is older and stronger than a normal Chianti Classico.

Torre Ercolana is produced in small quantities and is generally regarded as one of Lazio's best red wines. It is made from Cesanese and Cabernet grapes and requires at least five years' ageing.

Reading the Label

Italy has a two-tier system for labelling quality wine. DOC *(denominazione di origine controllata)* means you can be sure the wine is from the region declared on the label and is made from designated grape varieties. A higher classification – DOCG *(denominazione di origine controllata e garantita)* – is given to top wines such as the reds Barolo, Barbaresco, Chianti Classico and Brunello di Montalcino.

Chianti Classico

Apéritifs and Other Drinks

Bitter, herb-flavoured drinks like Martini, Campari or Aperol are the most popular apéritifs. (Ask for an *analcolico* if you prefer a non-alcoholic one.) Italians drink their apéritifs neat or with ice and soda. Strong after-dinner drinks, known as *digestivi* or *amari*, are worth trying, as is aniseed *sambuca*, served with coffee beans. Italian brandy and grappa can be very fiery and Italian beer is made in lager style.

Campari

Drinking Water

Unlike many Mediterranean cities, Rome benefits from a constant supply of fresh drinking water, piped down from the hills through a system of pipes and aqueducts which has changed little from ancient Roman times. Only if there is a sign saying *acqua non potabile* is the water not safe to drink.

One of Rome's many fresh water drinking fountains

Soft Drinks

Italian fruit juices are good and most bars squeeze fresh orange juice *(spremuta di arancia)* on the spot. Iced coffee and fruit-flavoured tea, such as peach, are popular.

Refrigerated storage for wine and beer

Coffee is almost more important to Roman life than wine. Take espresso for neat strong black coffee at any time of day, milky cappuccino for breakfast or mid-afternoon, caffè latte for extra milk.

Espresso

Cappuccino

Caffè latte

Where to Eat and Drink

Ancient Rome

0,75 €
Enoteca **Map** 8 E1
Via dei Cerchi 65, 00186
Tel *06-687 5706*
Named for the size of a bottle
of wine, this friendly *enoteca*
offers a meal at almost any time
of day.

Angelina a Testaccio €
Traditional Roman **Map** 8 D4
Via Galvani 24a, 00153
Tel *06-5728 3840*
The gem of Testaccio, this
shabby-chic bistro offers a
tempting Sunday brunch.

Bibenda €
Enoteca **Map** 9 A1
Via Capo d'Africa 21, 00184
Tel *06-7720 6673*
The official wine bar of Rome's
most renowned sommelier
academy, Bibenda also offers a
wide selection of tasty snacks
to pair with white or red.

I Clementini €
Traditional Roman **Map** 9 B1
*Via di San Giovanni in
Laterano 106, 00184*
Tel *06-4542 6395*
The chefs at this simple, authentic
and traditional restaurant take
pride in using their
grandmothers' recipes.

La Gallina Bianca €
Pizzeria **Map** 6 D4
Via Antonio Rosmini 9, 00184
Tel *06-474 3777*
Excellent pizza and much more at
this casual restaurant with country-
style decor. Do not miss the
tempting homemade desserts.

Hang Zhou €
Chinese **Map** 6 E5
Via Principe Eugenio 82, 00184
Tel *06-487 2732*
This is unanimously touted as
serving the best Chinese food
in town. The all-you-can-eat
buffet is a steal, but generally
prices are higher than average.

Il Nuovo Mondo €
Pizzeria **Map** 8 D3
Via Amerigo Vespucci 15, 00153
Tel *06-574 6004*
Lively, brash and popular with
locals, this family-owned pizzeria
is the place for thin Roman pizzas
with all the usual toppings.

Oasi della Birra €
Birreria **Map** 8 D3
Piazza Testaccio 39, 00153
Tel *06-574 6122*
The name says it all – this beer
oasis starts serving drinks and
food in the early afternoon
and no guest leaves thirsty.

Da Oio a Casa Mia €
Traditional Roman **Map** 8 D3
Via Galvani 43, 00153
Tel *06-578 2680*
Friendly but unrefined service
at this family-style restaurant
serving traditional Roman
recipes. Do not miss the lip-
smacking oxtail stew.

Pecorino €
Traditional Italian **Map** 8 D4
Via Galvani 64, 00153
Tel *06-5725 0539*
The extensive menu at this
impressive eatery features Italian
staples including several varieties
of pasta, eggplant *parmigiana*
and classic summer dishes such
as melon and ham.

Il Pentagrappolo €
Enoteca **Map** 9 A1
Via Celimontana 21b, 00184
Tel *06-709 6301*
A modern wine bar, Il Pentagrappolo
serves both creative snacks and
full meals. There is live jazz and
blues on most weekend nights.

Queen Makeda €
Japanese **Map** 8 D3
Via di San Saba 11, 00153
Tel *06-575 9608*
A Japanese-style kaiten carries
international dishes and lots of
fried delicacies such as squids, fish
and chips, or crunchy tomino
cheese. They also serve great
burgers. Pleasant bamboo garden.

Da Remo €
Pizzeria **Map** 8 D3
*Piazza di Santa Maria
Liberatrice 44, 00153*
Tel *06-574 6270*
Thin, crispy pizzas baked in
a wood-burning oven and
plenty of fried starters are on
offer here. Arrive early to avoid
the long queues.

La Taverna dei Quaranta €
Traditional Roman **Map** 9 A1
Via Claudia 24, 00184
Tel *06-700 0550*
Enjoy classic Roman dishes such
as *cacio e pepe* or *carbonara* and
homemade desserts at this
family-run taverna. Sit outside for
distant views of the Colosseum.

The bar area at 0,75, a trendy *enoteca*

Charly's Saucière
French-Swiss   €€
Map 9 B1
*Via di San Giovanni in
Laterano 270, 00184*
Tel *06-7049 5666*
Nourishing soups, warming au
gratin dishes and fondue are a
few of the specialities available
at this popular restaurant.

Checchino dal 1887
Traditional Roman   €€
Map 8 D4
Via di Monte Testaccio 30, 00153
Tel *06-574 3816*
Hearty Roman dishes, including
offal and great pasta, lovingly
prepared, make Checchino
dal 1887 a favourite spot for
discerning diners.

Cuoco e Camicia
Modern Italian   €€
Map 5 C5
Via di Monte Polacco 2/4, 00184
Tel *06-8892 2987*
A cheerful eatery that uses
only the freshest local ingredients
to revisit old classics. Try the
tortelli filled with *carbonara*
sauce or, if you're feeling
adventurous, try the chef's
tasting menu.

Da Danilo
Traditional Roman   €€
Map 6 E5
Via Petrarca 13, 00185
Tel *06-7720 0111*
Typical Roman dishes are served
at this homely *trattoria* run by
mother and son. Also boasts an
impressive list of artisanal beers
and a good selection of wines.

Felice a Testaccio
Traditional Roman   €€
Map 8 D3
Via Mastro Giorgio 29, 00153
Tel *06-574 6800*
Black-and-white checked floors
and exposed brickwork make a
charming setting. Roman cuisine,
including offal, is on offer.

Flavio al Velavevodetto
Traditional Roman   €€
Map 8 D4
Via di Monte Testaccio 97, 00153
Tel *06-574 4194*
Simple and satisfying Roman
pasta and meat dishes, plus a
few tasty seafood options, all
at reasonable prices. There is
lots of outdoor seating space
in good weather.

Perilli
Traditional Roman   €€
Map 8 D3
Via Marmorata 39, 00153
Tel *06-575 5100*
Generous portions of authentic
Roman favourites are served
here. The *carbonara* is especially
good, as is the oxtail, and
prices are reasonable. If you're
not eating early, reservations
are recommended.

Seating at the well-reviewed Checchino dal 1887

DK Choice

Trattoria Monti
Traditional Roman   €€
Map 6 D4
Via di San Vito 13a, 00185
Tel *06-446 6573*
The daily specials at this *trattoria*
feature seasonal ingredients that
are explained to guests in detail
by the brothers who own the
place. Items on the menu include
a large *antipasti* buffet, *carpaccios*,
homemade pastas and various
meat dishes. Reservation required.

Agata e Romeo
Fine Dining   €€€
Map 6 D4
Via Carlo Alberto 45, 00185
Tel *06-446 6115*
High-end dining with exceptional
tasting menus. Even traditional
recipes have a sophisticated
twist. Cavernous wine cellar.

Aroma
Fine Dining   €€€
Map 9 A1
Via Labicana 125, 00184
Tel *06-7759 1380*
A well-reviewed restaurant with
sleek interiors and unequalled
views of the Colosseum. Seasonal
menu with regional favourites.

Vibrant interior at the extravagant
Agata e Romeo

Enjoy a pre-dinner cocktail on
the lounge bar terrace.

Tempio di Iside
Seafood   €€€
Map 9 B1
Via Pietro Verri 11, 00184
Tel *06-700 4741*
The menu specializes in fish
of all kinds, much of it raw,
including several varieties of
oyster. The romantic, candlelit
interior has exposed brickwork.

Central Rome

Acchiappafantasmi
Pizzeria   €
Map 11 B3
Via dei Cappellari 66, 00186
Tel *06-687 3462*
This pizzeria, whose name means
"Ghostbusters", serves tasty and
crunchy ghost-shaped pizzas, as
well as standard-shaped ones.

Angolo Divino
Enoteca   €
Map 11 C4
Via dei Balestrari 12, 00186
Tel *06-686 4413*
An intimate and romantic wine
bar with a delicious, simple menu
and an excellent selection of
Italian wines. Leave room for one
of the inspired chocolate desserts.

Baffetto
Pizzeria   €
Map 11 C3
Via del Governo Vecchio 114, 00186
Tel *06-686 1617*
The thin, crisp Roman-style pizza
served here is considered by many
as the best in Rome. Be prepared
for a long wait.

CamBio Vita
Vegetarian   €
Map 11 C3
Via del Governo Vecchio 54, 00186
Tel *06-6830 1534*
This bistro epitomizes all the
healthy food trends: the menu
is vegan, organic and has plenty
of gluten-free options. A great
place for a quick lunch, a snack
or a refreshing smoothie.

For more information on types of restaurants *see pp304–5*

Diners at the cosy Nonna Betta, known for its authentic Jewish cuisine

La Campana €
Traditional Roman   **Map** 12 D1
Vicolo della Campana 18, 00186
Tel 06-687 5273
Packed on any night of the week, this quaint, historic eatery dates back nearly 500 years. The menu includes meat classic such as suckling pig with artichokes, and rabbit.

Cantina e Cucina €
Traditional Roman   **Map** 11 B3
Via del Governo Vecchio 87, 00186
Tel 06-689 2574
You can rely on this *trattoria* to provide a selection of all-time favourites, such as *spaghetti alla carbonara* with artichokes accompanied by great wines.

Il Corallo €
Traditional Roman   **Map** 11 B3
Via del Corallo 10, 00186
Tel 06-6830 7703
Located on a charming street, simple yet imaginative dishes are served by friendly staff. The fried artichokes and octopus salad is one of their specials. The wine list is impressive.

Cul de Sac €
Enoteca   **Map** 11 C3
Piazza di Pasquino 73, 00186
Tel 06-6880 1094
This narrow yet cosy wine bar boasts hundreds of labels as well as a wide variety of tasty eats, including pastas, cheeses and cured meats and vegetable pies. Great atmosphere.

Enoteca il Goccetto €
Enoteca   **Map** 11 B3
Via dei Banchi Vecchi 14, 00186
Tel 06-686 4268
A casual wine bar that serves top-quality bottles at fair prices; delicious snacks are also available. Popular with locals.

Maccheroni €
Traditional Roman   **Map** 12 D2
Piazza delle Coppelle 44, 00186
Tel 06-6830 7895
A Roman institution, this large restaurant relies on tried and trusted Roman recipes, served in a rustic atmosphere by jovial staff.

DK Choice

Nonna Betta €
Traditional Roman   **Map** 12 D5
Via Portico d'Ottavia 16, 00186
Tel 06-6880 6263
An authentic Jewish eatery in the heart of the Jewish quarter, the renowned Nonna Betta specializes in delectable Roman-Jewish cuisine. The fried mozzarella balls are highly recommended. The ambience is warm and cosy.

Open Baladin €
Birreria   **Map** 11 C5
Via degli Specchi 6, 00186
Tel 06-683 8989
Over 100 labels of craft beers and 40 draught Italian beers are on offer, as well as a variety of burgers.

Osteria del Gallo €
Traditional Roman   **Map** 11 C2
Vicolo di Montevecchio 27, 00186
Tel 06-687 3781
Classic Roman dishes and tasty seafood options are served at this informal spot with plenty of outdoor seating on a secluded piazza.

Da Pancrazio €
Traditional Roman   **Map** 11 C4
Piazza del Biscione 92, 00186
Tel 06-686 1246
Offering a slice of history, Da Pancrazio is set above the ruins of Pompey's 1st-century BC theatre and serves superb Roman recipes.

Pantha Rei €
Traditional Italian   **Map** 12 D3
Via della Minerva 19, 00186
Tel 06-8902 1922
Traditional culinary flair is combined with a romantic atmosphere at Pantha Rei. The menu includes a selection of *carpaccios* and cooked *scamorza* cheese dishes.

Polese €
Traditional Roman   **Map** 11 B3
Piazza Sforza Cesarini 40, 00186
Tel 06-686 1709
Authentic traditional recipes are served with a smile here. Outdoor seating on a large square ensures a table even on a busy night.

La Pollarola €
Traditional Italian   **Map** 11 C4
Piazza Pollarola 24–25, 00186
Tel 06-6880 1654
Just around the corner from Campo de' Fiori, this gem of a restaurant has simple yet delicious food and good daily specials.

Settimio al Pellegrino €
Traditional Roman   **Map** 11 B3
Via del Pellegrino 117, 00186
Tel 06-6880 1976
Knock if the door is closed at this old-fashioned favourite with locals. Simple Roman food and friendly service.

Sora Margherita €
Traditional Roman   **Map** 12 D5
Piazza delle Cinque Scole 30, 00186
Tel 06-687 4216
This simple and authentic eatery whips up classic Italian fare. If you're not sure what to order the chef will happily serve a selection of dishes for you to try. Do not expect English translations or any space between tables.

Vinando €
Enoteca　　　　　**Map** 12 E4
Piazza Margana 23, 00186
Tel *06-6920 0741*
Great vegetarian options, as well as meat and fish dishes and good pizzas, are served at this chic wine bar located in a pleasant, quiet square. Open all day.

Vitti €
Traditional Roman　　**Map** 12 E1
Piazza di San Lorenzo in Lucina 33, 00186
Tel *06-687 6304*
In fine weather, be sure to snatch a table outside in one of the most stylish piazzas in town. The food is basic but the location makes up for it.

Al Duello €€
Traditional Roman　　**Map** 12 D2
Vicolo della Vaccarella 11, 00186
Tel *06-687 3348*
Hearty Roman fare is served in this *trattoria* named for the infamous duel in which the painter Caravaggio (1571–1610) killed his opponent.

Armando al Pantheon €€
Traditional Roman　　**Map** 12 D3
Salita i Crescenzi 31, 00186
Tel *06-6880 3034*
Established in 1961, this genuine family-run Roman *trattoria* is operated by two brothers. Classic dishes and some interesting appetizers on offer. Very popular, so book ahead.

Il Bacaro €€
Modern Italian　　**Map** 12 D2
Via degli Spagnoli 27, 00186
Tel *06-687 2554*
Specialities at this romantic and centrally-located restaurant include tagliolini with artichoke and octopus. Tasting events are also organized once a month with a menu dedicated to famous figures from the city's past. Dine inside or out on the quiet street.

Ba'Ghetto Milky €€
Traditional Roman　　**Map** 12 D5
Via Portico d'Ottavia 2a, 00186
Tel *06-6830 0077*
Heavenly Jewish-Roman cuisine served strictly kosher; only vegetarian and fish options are available. There's outdoor seating on a bustling pedestrian street when the weather is good.

Casa Bleve €€
Enoteca　　　　　**Map** 12 D3
Via del Teatro Valle 48, 00186
Tel *06-686 5970*
Vaulted ceilings and ceramic-tiled floors add a sense of occasion to any meal at this sophisticated wine bar. Ample buffet lunch.

Clemente alla Maddalena €€
Modern Italian　　**Map** 12 D2
Piazza della Maddalena 4, 00186
Tel *06-683 3633*
The head chef creates imaginative takes on regional dishes from all over Italy. Outdoor seating in a lovely square close to the Pantheon. An extensive wine list highlights wines from the Lazio region.

Enoteca Capranica €€
Enoteca　　　　　**Map** 12 D2
Piazza Capranica 104, 00186
Tel *06-679 0860*
Numerous bottles line the walls of this large yet cosy wine bar. Pair mouthwatering dishes and delicious pizzas with excellent wines. Make sure to save room for dessert.

Da Giggetto €€
Traditional Roman　　**Map** 12 E5
Via Portico d'Ottavia 21/22, 00186
Tel *06-686 1105*
Dine in the shadow of ancient ruins at this famous Jewish-Roman eatery. The deep-fried artichokes are the best in the area, but prices are high.

Spectacular vaulted ceilings add to the atmosphere at Casa Bleve

Hostaria dell'Orso €€
Fine Dining　　**Map** 11 C2
Via dei Soldati 25c, 00186
Tel *06-6830 1192*
Traditional dining raised to an art form and inspired by the flavours of the Mediterranean. Try the *paccheri* with *ragú*. This legendary restaurant and nightclub is housed in a 14th-century building.

The Library €€
Modern Italian　　**Map** 11 C3
Vicolo della Cancelleria 7, 00186
Tel *334-806 1200*
Located on a narrow back street, this minuscule and romantic spot has just a handful of tables. Great wine and main courses. Try the tagliata steak with balsamic vinegar, and end your meal with a home-made dessert such as *tiramisú*.

Mimí e Cocó €€
Enoteca　　　　　**Map** 11 C3
Via del Governo Vecchio 72, 00186
Tel *06-6821 0845*
Fresh ingredients and a friendly atmosphere define this Mediterranean restaurant and wine bar. The pleasant outdoor patio is a great spot to try the delicious *biscotti al limoncello*.

Montevecchio €€
Traditional Roman　　**Map** 11 C2
Piazza Montevecchio 22/a, 00186
Tel *06-686 1319*
This is a tiny, sophisticated restaurant where well-heeled locals converse in hushed tones over delectable pasta and meat dishes from the Roman tradition. Tucked away in a little courtyard this is a lovely place to relax. Don't miss the octopus dish.

Maccheroni combines industrial chic style with traditional Roman cuisine

The bold and interesting dinning area at Il Pagliaccio

Nest Osteria in Roma €€
Modern Italian   Map 12 D5
Via del Leone 23, 00183
Tel *06-6880 4506*
Try innovative Italian food prepared with locally-sourced ingredients. The "easy lunch" menu includes tasty handmade pasta and dessert.

DK Choice

Osteria del Pegno €€
Traditional Roman   Map 11 C2
Vicolo di Montevecchio 8, 00186
Tel *06-6880 7025*
This small and intimate restaurant creates lovingly prepared staples in traditional Roman and Italian style. Raw fish *antipasti* and aubergine *parmigiana* are some of the most popular menu entries. There is an ample wine list.

Osteria del Sostegno €€
Modern Italian   Map 12 D2
Via delle Colonnelle 5, 00186
Tel *06-679 3842*
Tucked away in a tiny alley, this charming little restaurant creates inventive versions of classic Roman recipes. Booking is advisable.

Il Pagliaccio €€
Fine Dining   Map 11 A3
Via dei Banchi Vecchi 129, 00186
Tel *06-6880 9595*
A blend of Italian and other Mediterranean cuisines is offered here. For true gourmands, the tasting menus have up to ten courses.

Piperno €€
Traditional Roman   Map 12 D5
Via Monte de' Cenci 9, 00186
Tel *06-6880 6629*
Set in a pretty piazza, this place serves traditional Roman cuisine, offering a large selection of seafood and excellent fried artichokes. Wine lovers will enjoy the extensive drinks menu.

Roscioli €€
Enoteca   Map 11 C4
Via dei Giubbonari 21, 00186
Tel *06-687 5287*
Roscioli is part wine bar and part *salumeria* (delicatessen and charcuterie). A selection of meats and cheeses accompanies a dizzying range of wine labels.

Sangallo ai Coronari €€
Modern Italian   Map 11 B2
Via dei Coronari 180, 00186
Tel *06-686 5549*
Time-honoured recipes from Rome and the region immediately south of the city. Try a gelato for dessert.

Sora Lella €€
Traditional Roman   Map 8 D1
Via di Ponte Quattro Capi 16, 00186
Tel *06-686 1601*
Sora Lella has the distinction of being the only restaurant on the Isola Tiberina. This historic family-run *trattoria* serves lighter versions of traditional Roman recipes.

Terra di Siena €€
Regional Italian   Map 11 C3
Piazza di Pasquino 77, 00186
Tel *06-6830 7704*
Enjoy hearty Tuscan dishes such as Florentine steak and *ribollita* soup in a cheerful dining room or on the buzzing piazza.

Vino e Camino €€
Regional Italian   Map 11 A2
Piazza dell'Oro 6, 00186
Tel *06-6830 1332*
Wine bottles line the walls and there is a working fireplace. The menu includes delicious grilled meats and excellent wine.

Camponeschi €€€
Fine Dining   Map 11 C4
Piazza Farnese 50/50a, 00186
Tel *06-687 4927*
World-class al fresco dining with a view of Piazza Farnese. Try the tagliolini with black truffles. Wild game is the house speciality. Impressive desserts.

Il Convivio-Troiani €€€
Fine Dining   Map 11 C2
Vicolo dei Soldati 31, 00186
Tel *06-686 9432*
This elegant restaurant takes pride in its handmade products, from bread to pasta. Exquisite wine list.

Pierluigi €€€
Modern Italian   Map 11 B4
Piazza de' Ricci 144, 00186
Tel *06-686 8717*
A sprawling outdoor seating area in a cobbled piazza enhances the imaginative food based on fish.

La Rosetta €€€
Seafood   Map 12 D2
Via della Rosetta 8/9, 00186
Tel *06-686 1002*
Enjoy top-quality seafood right in front of the Pantheon. There's a lunchtime oyster bar too.

Il Sanlorenzo €€€
Seafood   Map 11 C4
Via dei Chiavari 4, 00186
Tel *06-686 5097*
This sleek restaurant with modern art on marble walls is pricey, but worth it for some of the best sea-food in town. Try the tasting menu to make your money go further.

Spagna, Veneto and Around

Abruzzi ai SS Apostoli €
Regional Italian   Map 12 F3
Via del Vaccaro 1, 00187
Tel *06-679 3897*
Cold appetizers make an excellent start to specialities from the Abruzzo region. The Rigatoni alla Carbonara comes highly recommended. Popular place with the locals.

The cool, cavernous interior at Roscioli restaurant

Ai Tre Scalini €
Enoteca   Map 5 B4
Via Panisperna 251, 00184
Tel *06-4890 7495*
One of the hippest wine bars in town. It offers an impressive array of wines, beers and savoury delicacies.

Antica Birreria Peroni €
Birreria   Map 12 F3
Via di San Marcello 19, 00187
Tel *06-679 5310*
A casual spot that has been serving beer since 1906. All-Italian beef and pork dishes prepared on the grill.

L'Asino d'Oro €
Regional Italian   Map 5 B4
Via del Boschetto 73, 00184
Tel *06-4891 3832*
A reincarnation of a famous *trattoria* in Orvieto. Serves Umbrian specialties and Roman classics. Dishes are creative and tasty.

Asmara €
Ethiopian/Eritrean   Map 6 D2
Via Cernaia 36, 00185
Tel *06-481 4409*
A surprising combination of flavours, which enliven the mostly meat-based dishes; many vegetarian options are also available. Asmara has a lively atmosphere.

Canova-Tadolini Museum Atelier €
Traditional Roman   Map 4 F2
Via del Babuino 150/a, 00187
Tel *06-3211 0702*
Dine amid dozens of artworks at the studio of the legendary 18th-century sculptor Canova. Try the pasta with lobster.

La Carbonara €
Traditional Roman   Map 5 B4
Via Panisperna 214, 00184
Tel *06-482 5176*
This welcoming *osteria* serves hearty local fare including the very dish it was named for, a Roman favourite.

Cavour 313 €
Enoteca   Map 5 B5
Via Cavour 313, 00184
Tel *06-678 5496*
This place features a wood-panelled wine bar. Choose tasty dishes from either the varied menu or from the list of daily specials. The staff can help you select a memorable vintage.

'Gusto €
Pizzeria   Map 4 F2
Piazza Augusto Imperatore 9, 00186
Tel *06-322 6273*
Gusto has a unique factory-like setting with exposed brick. Serves thick-crusted and chewy Neapolitan-style pizzas. Great lunch buffet.

Gusto Rotisserie €
Enoteca   Map 4 F2
Piazza Augusto Imperatore 28, 00030
Tel *06-6813 4221*
Chic wine bar that also serves cocktails, tea and coffee, tasty snacks and desserts.

Il Palazzetto Wine Bar €
Enoteca   Map 5 A2
Vicolo del Bottino 8, 00187
Tel *06-6993 41000*
Sip wine and enjoy the fabulous views on the roof terrace at the top of the Spanish Steps. Perfect for early evening drinks, accompanied by pizza and small snacks.

San Marco €
Pizzeria   Map 5 C1
Via Sardegna 38D, 00187
Tel *06-4201 2620*
Also a wine bar and grill, but noted mostly for its pizzas. The day's specials are listed on the chalkboard-covered walls.

Trimani Il Wine Bar €
Enoteca   Map 6 D2
Via Cernaia 37b, 00185
Tel *06-446 9630*
Modern wine bar with a vast selection of labels perfectly paired with cold and hot dishes as well as a range of cheeses. The desserts are good too. Friendly and knowledgeable staff.

Babette €€
Modern Italian   Map 4 F1
Via Margutta 1d, 00187
Tel *06-321 1559*
Inspired by the film *Babette's Feast*, this large restaurant whips up unusual versions of popular dishes from around the country.

Baccano €€
Modern Italian   Map 12 F2
Via delle Muratte 23, 00184
Tel *06-6994 1166*
Retro decor dominates at this restaurant serving classic Italian dishes with alternative ingredients. Gourmet burgers and sandwiches are also on offer.

Brunello Lounge & Restaurant €€
Fine Dining   Map 5 B2
Via Veneto 70/a, 00187
Tel *06-421 111*
This contemporary restaurant serves Mediterranean cuisine. Try the turbot fillet with porcini mushrooms. Good cocktails.

Colline Emiliane €€
Regional Italian   Map 5 B3
Via degli Avignonesi 22, 00187
Tel *06-481 7538*
Elegant *trattoria* serving hearty Bolognese specialities such as handmade tortellini and filling meat dishes.

Doozo €€
Japanese   Map 5 C4
Via Palermo 51, 00184
Tel *06-481 5655*
Courses in origami, a Bonsai exhibit and book presentations, plus mouthwatering sushi, feature at this restaurant and Japanese cultural centre.

Eataly €€
Modern Italian   Map 5 C3
Piazza della Repubblica 41, 00185
Tel *06-4550 9130*
In addition to selling the best Italian food in a sort of luxury supermarket, Eataly also has a few restaurant corners serving high-quality pizzas, pastas and much more.

Exposed brickwork and subtle lighting at 'Gusto

Edoardo   €€
Regional Italian   Map 5 C2
Via Lucullo 2, 00187
Tel *06-486 428*
Taste delicious takes on Italian
regional dishes, from pastas
with seafood to risottos, at this
elegant restaurant. Service is
refined. Live music on weekends.

Hamasei   €€
Japanese   Map 12 F1
Via della Mercede 35/36, 00187
Tel *06-679 2134*
A minimalist black and white
setting with low tables for
authentic Japanese dining.
Ultra-fresh sushi and sashimi.

Osteria Margutta   €€
Modern Italian   Map 5 A2
Via Margutta 82, 00187
Tel *06-323 1025*
Historic restaurant on an idyllic
vine-covered street. Serves
classic Roman and Italian dishes
which change by the season.

Piccolo Buco   €€
Traditional Roman   Map 12 F2
Via del Lavatore 91, 00187
Tel *06-6938 0163*
This small, delightful restaurant
serves delicious, authentic Italian
cuisine. The pizzas are superb
and guests can watch them
being cooked in the wood oven.
The house wines are excellent,
as is the service.

DK Choice

Rhome   €€
Modern Italian   Map 4 F2
*Piazza Augusto Imperatore 46,
00186*
Tel *06-6830 1430*
As its name implies, the
objective of this restaurant is
to make its guests feel at home.
Plush couches and overstuffed
armchairs pull right up to the
table. The dining experience
here gives a whole new
meaning to the term "comfort
food". Carefully prepared classic
dishes mingle with more
daring ones. Good value set
lunch menu.

La Taverna dei Fori Imperiali €€
Traditional Roman   Map 5 B5
*Via della Madonna dei Monti 9,
00184*
Tel *06-679 8643*
The whole family pitches in
to make this inviting *trattoria*
a favourite with locals and
visitors alike. The *burrata* ravioli
is divine. Booking ahead is
highly recommended.

Spectacular city views and romantic interiors at Imàgo

DK Choice

Urbana 47   €€
Modern Italian   Map 5 C4
Via Urbana 47, 00184
Tel *06-4788 4006*
This restaurant offers healthy
and flavourful meals. Vintage
furniture combined with
designer pieces creates an
eclectic setting to enjoy locally
sourced, high-quality food at
reasonable prices. The menu
has been created by Michelin-
starred chefs. The wine list has
a great selection. Live music
on weekends.

Vineria Il Chianti   €€
Modern Italian   Map 12 F2
Via del Lavatore 81, 00187
Tel *06-678 7550*
Elegantly arranged cheese and
salami platters are followed by
creative pan-Italian starters
and mains. There's an outside
patio with shared tables, perfect
for watching the world go by.

Harry's Bar   €€€
Fine Dining   Map 5 B2
Via Veneto 150, 00187
Tel *06-484 643*
Take a bite of la dolce vita at
this iconic bar and café serving
exquisite meals and the famous
Bellini cocktail.

Imàgo   €€€
Fine Dining   Map 5 A1
Piazza Trinità dei Monti 6, 00187
Tel *06-6993 4726*
Stellar dining with an exceptional
view from the top of the
Spanish Steps. Chef Apreda
serves creative Italian cuisine
made with luxury ingredients.
Specialities include lobster bites
and lamb fillet.

Le Jardin de Russie   €€€
Fine Dining   Map 4 F1
Via del Babuino 9, 00187
Tel *06-3288 8870*
Delectable Mediterranean dishes
are served with great flair and
artistry at this restaurant. The
tranquil garden setting is close
to the Piazza del Popolo but feels
like a world apart.

Mirabelle   €€€
Fine Dining   Map 5 B1
Via di Porta Pinciana 14, 00187
Tel *06-4216 8838*
Impeccable service and a
panoramic view at this rooftop
restaurant. Imaginative yet
subtle Mediterranean dishes.

Open Colonna   €€€
Modern Italian   Map 5 B4
Via Milano 9/a, 00184
Tel *06-4782 2641*
Perched above the Palazzo delle
Esposizioni (*see p166*), this modern,
glassed-in open space provides
an airy setting to enjoy tempting,
creative dishes. Great buffet lunch.

Pipero al Rex   €€€
Fine Dining   Map 5 C3
Via Torino 149, 00184
Tel *06-481 5702*
Meticulously prepared dishes
are served at this small but
accomplished restaurant. Try their
creative tasting menus. Book early
to avoid disappointment.

La Terrazza dell'Eden   €€€
Fine Dining   Map 5 B2
Via Ludovisi 49, 00187
Tel *06-4781 2752*
Special culinary events and
sensational tasting menus with
Italian-Mediterranean flavours
make this award-winning rooftop
restaurant a stunning venue.
Ideal for special occasions.

Vivendo...il Mediterraneo €€€
Modern Italian **Map** 5 C3
Via Vittorio Emanuele Orlando 3, 00185
Tel *06-4709 2736*
Luxurious decor and fabulous Mediterranean cuisine. Choose from a three-course menu with the option of a perfectly matched wine pairing. Children are catered for with a special menu.

Trastevere and Around

Bir & Fud €
Birreria **Map** 11 B5
Via Benedetta 23, 00153
Tel *06-589 4016*
Artisanal beers and microbrews from around Italy; perfect for washing down the crusty pizzas and gourmet potato chips. There are a few tables outside.

Dar Poeta €
Pizzeria **Map** 4 E5
Vicolo del Bologna 45, 00153
Tel *06-588 0516*
A justifiably popular pizzeria that prides itself on the quality of the pizza dough as much as the various toppings. Excellent salads too.

Fish Market €
Seafood **Map** 7 C2
Vicolo della Luce 2/3, 00153
Tel *320 391 0934*
Choose the fresh fish you like from the counter, tell the staff exactly how you would like it cooked, and collect it when it's ready. This place has a loud, lively and fun ambience.

Da Gildo €
Traditional Roman **Map** 7 C1
Via della Scala 31, 00153
Tel *06-580 0733*
The quirky decoration of this restaurant gives it a charming feel. An outdoor seating area is also available. Try the simple and divine *gnocchi alla romana.*

In Vino Veritas €
Enoteca **Map** 4 D5
Via Garibaldi 2a, 00153
Tel *06-580 9758*
A cosy and informal wine bar, with chess and other games in the tiny seating area. There's also a well-chosen selection of beer and good cocktails.

Ivo a Trastevere €
Pizzeria **Map** 7 C1
Via di San Francesco a Ripa 158, 00153
Tel *06-581 7082*
Delicious super-thin-crust Roman pizza has this simple eatery bustling with locals and the odd celebrity. Service can be slow.

Da I Sandri €
Regional Italian **Map** 7 C2
Via Roma Libera 19, 00153
Tel *06-581 6469*
Every meal can be served gluten free at this jovial spot known for its traditional Roman cuisine. There are traditional music performances on Fridays.

Meridionale €
Regional Italian **Map** 7 C1
Via dei Fienaroli 30a, 00153
Tel *06-589 7196*
Friendly and bright, this delightful restaurant specializes in fresh cuisine from southern Italy. Seafood options are particularly tempting.

Pizzeria Panattoni (L'Obitorio) €
Pizzeria **Map** 7 C1
Viale di Trastevere 53, 00153
Tel *06-580 0919*
This pizzeria is nicknamed "the morgue" for its long marble-topped tables. Try the *supplì al telefono* (fried rice balls), a favourite with locals.

Roma Sparita €
Traditional Roman **Map** 8 D1
Piazza di Santa Cecilia 24, 00153
Tel *06-580 0757*
Set in an enviable position in front of a gorgeous church, this traditional spot serves the best *cacio e pepe* (cheese and pepper pasta) in town.

Da Teo €
Traditional Roman **Map** 8 D1
Piazza del Ponziani 7a, 00153
Tel *06-581 8355*
Situated in a charming and quiet piazza, this casual yet elegant spot offers classic local recipes and flavourful marinated dishes. Good local wines.

Antico Arco €€
Fine Dining **Map** 7 A1
Piazzale Aurelio 7, 00152
Tel *06-581 5274*
Truffles, wild strawberries, and other such delights fill the exquisite menu at this highly recommended restaurant. The vast wine list is equally tantalizing. Excellent service.

Arlù €€
Traditional Roman **Map** 3 C3
Borgo Pio 135, 00193
Tel *06-686 8936*
The most authentic restaurant in the busy Vatican area. A husband-and-wife team serve up delectable Roman cuisine.

Ivo a Trastevere, famous for its super-thin-crust pizza

Wine cellar at Spirito Divino, located within a 10th-century synagogue

Da Benito e Gilberto €€
Seafood
Via del Falco 19, 00193
Tel *06-686 7769*
This small and friendly restaurant, run by a father and son, prepares classic pasta dishes and elaborate seafood delicacies. Weekends are busy, so book ahead.

Da Cesare €€
Traditional Roman **Map** 4 D2
Via Crescenzio 13, 00193
Tel *06-686 1227*
The owners of this local favourite are dedicated to using only locally sourced products that are in season for their classic Roman dishes.

La Gensola €€
Modern Italian **Map** 8 D1
Piazza della Gensola 15, 00153
Tel *06-581 6312*
This sweet little *osteria* whips up excellent seafood and offers a surprisingly original take on traditional Roman cuisine. Don't miss the desserts.

DK Choice

Isole di Sicilia €€
Regional Italian **Map** 7 B1
Via Garibaldi 68, 00153
Tel *06-5833 4212*
This cheerful restaurant dishes up some of the best Sicilian food in town. Inspired by the native cuisine of the tiny islands surrounding Sicily, the elaborate dishes use aubergine, capers, peppers, almonds, basil and, of course, heaps and heaps of super-fresh fish. A vast *antipasto* spread kicks off a memorable meal. Pavement seating on the tree-lined street in good weather.

Lo Scarpone €€
Traditional Roman **Map** 7 A2
Via di San Pancrazio 15, 00152
Tel *06-581 4094*
Nestled in a lush garden with plenty of outdoor seating plus a cosy interior. Order one of their homemade pastas.

DK Choice

Spirito Divino €€
Modern Italian **Map** 8 D1
Via dei Genovesi 31, 00153
Tel *06-589 6689*
An elegant, family-run establishment, housed in an 11th-century synagogue, but thoroughly modernized inside. The owner delights in describing to guests every exquisite dish on the ever-changing menu, while his wife lovingly prepares each of them in the kitchen. Take a peek into the 2,100-year-old wine cellar.

Taverna Angelica €€
Modern Italian **Map** 3 C2
Piazza Amerigo Capponi 6, 00193
Tel *06-687 4514*
Creative seafood and meat specialities are popular at this cosy restaurant. The choice on the dessert menu goes beyond the usual offerings, and the Sunday lunches are superb.

Taverna Trilussa €€
Traditional Roman **Map** 4 E5
Via del Politeama 23, 00153
Tel *06-581 8918*
This bustling yet elegant spot serves classic Roman recipes, including delicious offal dishes. Some pasta dishes are served in the pan they were cooked in.

Velando €€
Modern Italian **Map** 3 C3
Borgo Vittorio 26, 00193
Tel *06-6880 9955*
This fantastic restaurant presents modern takes on well-loved classic dishes from Lombardy and beyond. The saffron *ravioli* is a favourite. Make sure to save room for dessert.

Veranda €€
Fine Dining **Map** 3 C3
Borgo Santo Spirito 73, 00193
Tel *06-687 2973*
In a stunning setting inside a frescoed palace with vaulted ceilings, this restaurant offers finely tuned pasta, meat and fish dishes.

Antica Pesa €€€
Fine Dining **Map** 7 B1
Via Garibaldi 18, 00153
Tel *06-580 9236*
The walls of this Roman institution are covered with murals by top international artists. Meals are served in a leafy courtyard in warm weather.

Glass €€€
Modern Italian **Map** 4 E5
Vicolo del Cinque 58, 00153
Tel *06-5833 5903*
This Michelin-starred, sleekly modern restaurant offers glorified Mediterranean cuisine with a dash of international flavour.

Further Afield

Brasserie 4:20 €
Birreria **Map** 7 C3
Via Portuense 82, 00153
Tel *06-5831 0737*
Draft craft beers from around the world are served with hamburgers. Knowledgable bar staff are on hand to offer recommendations.

La Gatta Mangiona €
Pizzeria
Via Federico Ozanam 30, 00152
Tel *06-534 6702*
Creative toppings and daily specials make this Monteverde pizzeria popular with locals.

Mò Mò Republic €
Pizzeria
Piazza Forlanini 10, 00151
Tel *06-537 3087*
A 19th-century mansion nestled in a leafy garden is the setting for this modern and trendy pizzeria. In summer, start with *aperitivi* on the lawn. Pasta, meat and fish dishes are also available.

Osteria Flaminio €
Modern Italian **Map** 1 B3
Via Flaminia 297, 00196
Tel *06-323 6900*
This restaurant, just north of the centre, offers a range of innovative and original Italian dishes and a carefully selected wine list. Booking is advisable, particularly for weekends.

Smoke Ring €
American
Via Portuense 86, 00152
Tel *06-5814400*
Come here for grilled meats and American-style barbeque food. Smoke Ring offers all the classics, from chicken wings to ribs and steaks, all seasoned to perfection.

Sukhothai €
Thai
Via Andrea Busiri Vici 48/50, 00152
Tel *06-5526 3993*
At what is one of the very few Thai restaurants in Rome, the Thai chef prepares his dishes with the freshest ingredients, a good balance of spices and skillful decorations. The result is a refined and high-quality experience.

Verde Pistacchio €
Modern Italian
Via Ostiense 181, 00154
Tel *06-4547 5965*
A small bistro that combines local ingredients to create delicious salads, pastas, and sandwiches. The pistachio crème brulee is fabulous.

Vivi Bistrot €
International
Via Vitellia 102, 00152
Tel *06-582 7540*
Nestled in the sprawling grounds of Villa Pamphilj, Vivi Bistrot serves American-style breakfast as well as picnic options and *aperitivi* on the grass in summer.

Ambasciata d'Abruzzo €€
Regional Italian **Map** 2 D3
Via Pietro Tacchini 26, 00197
Tel *06-807 8256*
Traditional Abruzzese dishes, such as *maccheroni* with lamb ragù, mingle with Roman favourites in a convivial setting at this restaurant. Make sure to save room for dessert.

Avec 55 €€
Modern Italian
Via Domenico Giuliani 55, 00019, Tivoli
Tel *07-7431 7243*
A restaurant and culinary workshop combined. Chef Raoul Reperi teaches amateur cooks how to recreate his gastronomic feats. The menu changes regularly but whatever dishes are served you'll be in for a culinary feast.

Osteria Scaloni €€
Traditional Roman
Via Carlo Mirabello 8, 00195
Tel *06-372 1593*
Simple, regional cuisine is taken a step further with unexpected ingredients and creative touches at this restaurant. The wine list is excellent. Relaxed, intimate atmosphere and friendly staff.

Magnificent city skyline, as seen from the dining area of La Pergola

Settembrini €€
Modern Italian
Via Luigi Settembrini 21, 00195
Tel *06-323 2617*
Talented chef Federico Delmonte serves creative Italian cuisine that is both well presented and tasty. The seafood options are particularly delectable. A favourite with locals.

La Sibilla €€
Regional Italian
Via della Sibilla 50, 00019, Tivoli
Tel *07-7433 5281*
Sweeping views of Villa Gregoriana and Roman ruins provide an unforgettable setting for indulging in impressive cuisine, created using the freshest ingredients.

Oliver Glowig €€€
Fine Dining **Map** 2 D4
Via Ulisse Aldrovandi 15, 00197
Tel *06-321 6126*
This impressive poolside restaurant serves rich Mediter-ranean delicacies such as scampi with artichoke and burrata cheese.

DK Choice

La Pergola €€€
Fine Dining
Via Alberto Cadlolo 101, 00136
Tel *06-3509 2152*
Universally recognized as Rome's finest restaurant, La Pergola is also the only one to earn three Michelin stars. Chef Heinz Beck dazzles diners with his exquisite Mediterranean creations. Perched atop Monte Mario hill, there are stunning views of St Peter's and the entire city skyline. The atmosphere is refined, and the award-winning wine cellar boasts over 3,000 labels and more than 53,000 bottles, the oldest dating to 1888. Book well ahead.

Seating in the beautiful gardens at Vivi Bistrot

Light Meals and Drinks

Rome can delight the most demanding gourmet and satisfy the keenest appetite, whatever the hour. An enticing array of *gelaterie, pasticcerie, pizzerie, enoteche, rosticcerie* and *gastronomie* means that good food and drink are, literally, around the corner.

Hotel breakfasts often aren't up to scratch and you would be better off starting the day with a genuine Italian breakfast at your local stand-up bar: a cappuccino or latte with a hot *cornetto* (croissant) or *fagottino* (similar to a *pain au chocolat*). If you are in Italy during late winter, when blood-red oranges from Sicily are in season, order a *spremuta*, a freshly squeezed orange juice.

A heavy morning's sightseeing may leave you ready for a coffee or an apéritif in one of Rome's elegant 19th-century bars, followed by lunch at a wine bar or Roman-style fast food joint. Later, enjoy tea in a tearoom or coffee and cakes at a *pasticceria*. Once the sun starts to set, there are many places to sip a drink, linger over an ice cream and reflect on another wonderful day in the city.

Pizzerias

Roman *pizzerias* are an obvious choice if you feel like an informal meal: they are noisy, convivial and great fun. Many, however, open only in the evening. Look out for the *forno a legna* (wood-burning oven) sign – electric ovens simply don't produce the same results. In the best *pizzerias* you can sit in view of the vast marble slabs where the *pizzaioli* flatten the dough and whip the pizzas in and out of the oven on long-handled pallets. The turnaround is fast and queues are common so you may not be encouraged to linger after you have eaten.

The running order is fairly straightforward: you might have a *bruschetta* (toasted tomato or garlic bread) to start with, some *supplì* (fried rice croquettes) or *fiori di zucca* (courgette flowers in batter, filled with hot mozzarella and a single anchovy). Alternatively, try the *filetti di baccalà* (battered cod fillets) or perhaps a plate of *cannellini* beans in oil. Follow this with a crisp *calzone* (folded-over pizza) or the classic Roman pizza – round, thin and crunchy – with a variety of toppings: the basic *margherita* (tomato, mozzarella), *napoletana* (tomato, anchovies, mozzarella), *capricciosa* (ham, artichokes,

eggs, olives) or anything else the *pizzaiolo* fancies. Draught beer or *birra alla spina* is the classic drink, but wine is always available, even if limited in choice and quality. You should expect to pay around €14 a head for a meal.

The most representative Roman *pizzerias*, from all points of view, are **Da Baffetto** which can be easily found by looking for the queue outside, and its offspring, **La Montecarlo**. **Da Remo** in Testaccio and **Dar Poeta** and **Pizzeria Ivo** in Trastevere, where tables line the road in summer, are also typically Roman. Another place not to be missed is **Panattoni – L'Obitorio**, where a huge variety of customers patiently queue for a pavement seat on Viale Trastevere in summer, or clamour for one of the marble-topped tables (which gives it its nickname "the mortuary") inside. For slick interiors and Neapolitan-style (high-rise) pizza, try **'Gusto**, but once again, be prepared to queue. Over in Testaccio, the take-away **Trapizzino** outlet gives its own totally delicious take on the pizza formula.

Enoteche

Enoteche or wine bars offer a very fine selection of wines, mainly from Italy, but often from around the world. Usually run by experts, keen to share their knowledge and advise on the best combinations of wine and food, many are simply shops for browsing and buying wine. Others, such as **Achilli Enoteca al Parlamento** *(see p343)* and **Angolo Divino** *(see p354)*, offer the traditional *mescita* – wine and champagne tasting by the glass, accompanied by snacks and canapés. Prices are fairly reasonable: about €3 for a glass on tap, €5 upwards for a quality wine or for a *prosecco* or *spumante*, Italian champagne. **Il Nolano** in Campo de' Fiori is a typical spot for *mescita*, especially at night. Nearby, the beautiful **Il Goccetto**, with original painted ceilings, serves excellent wines and delicious food.

Some of the oldest wine bars are inside historic buildings, such as **Caffè Novecento**, which serves excellent food, mainly vegetarian.

For more substantial food for around €20–30 per head, try the bistro- or restaurant-style *enoteche*, open from lunch until late. Particularly recommended are **Verso Sera**, **Trimani** *(see p343)*, **Il Tajut** serving specialities from Friuli, and **Cavour 313**, which boasts hundreds of wines from all over Italy. Nearby is **Al Vino al Vino**, a well-stocked bar with locals taking their glasses out onto the bustling Via dei Serpenti. Food emporium **'Gusto** *(see p343)* has a wine bar with a gourmet cheese selection, while **Cul de Sac** offers cheese and cured meat platters to accompany great wines, as well as pasta dishes. The **Antico Forno Roscioli** is particularly creative, with great dishes such as pasta with *radicchio* and orange peel and pear pastry with coconut.

Enoteche are often tucked away near famous sights or in unlikely places. **Vinando** is extremely convenient for the Capitol, the Tuscan **Vineria Il Chianti** is near the Trevi Fountain, and **Etablì** is behind Piazza Navona. Over in Testaccio, **Divinare** offers fine labels alongside top quality preserves and chocolate. There are a growing number of wine bars across the river. Crowds at **Enoteca Trastevere** spill on to the pavement outside, while **Friends Art Café** is a quieter venue with a reasonable evening menu. When night falls, try the lively **In Vino Veritas Art Bar** at the foot of the Janiculum Hill.

Birrerie

Roman *birrerie* or beer houses had their heyday in the early 1900s, often with sumptuous interiors and abundant stained glass. Although many subsequently closed, thanks to their growing popularity with most Italian teenagers they are today undergoing something of a revival. Many British- and Irish-style pubs have also opened. At German-style beer houses you can still enjoy beer and substantial snacks in traditional wood-panelled rooms. The **Old Bear** pub is a jewel inside a 17th-century convent, with romantic candlelight and excellent food and beer. **Löwenhaus** is bedecked with old oil paintings depicting typical Bavarian scenes, again with low lighting for a mellow evening. The ever crowded **Antica Birreria Peroni**, serving classic beer-drinkers' fare, is also well worth a visit for its local beer and lovely decor. Attracting Italians and foreigners alike is the lively **Ma Che Siete Venuti a Fà** with its excellent range of well-selected ales. Across the river in Testaccio is the equally charming **L'Oasi della Birra**, which also serves good food. Other beer houses with a great atmosphere, food and late closing times are **The Fiddler's Elbow**, often with live music, **La Pace del Cervello** (meaning "peace of mind") or **Trinity College**, a favourite of expats and Romans alike.

Fast Food

The term "fast food" in Rome encompasses a cornucopia of choice. The most prolific establishments are *pizza a taglio*

shops where slices of freshly baked pizza are available for €1 or €2 – these are sold by weight. Many of these places also sell spit-roasted chickens (*pollo allo spiedo*), *supplì* and other fried fare. **Forno La Renella** in Trastevere is one of the finest. Pizza with fig and ham or potato and rosemary are typical toppings. At **La Pratolina**, near the Vatican, pizza with sausage, potato and truffle is a good choice.

Rosticcerie and *gastronomie* also offer roast chicken and potatoes, as well as ready-made pasta dishes, cooked vegetables *sott'olio* (in oil), salads and desserts – useful for takeaway picnics. Many offer stools and narrow bars where you can also devour your purchases on the spot. Near the Vatican are some of the finest, such as **Franchi** (*see p342*) and **Ercoli dal 1928**.

For a sit-down snack, bars with a *tavola calda* (hot table) have a similar selection, especially at lunchtime. One of the best is **Volpetti Più** in Testaccio. For unusual flavour combinations, head to **Pizza, Pere e Gorgonzola** near Piazza del Popolo. In the Galleria Alberto Sordi, opposite the Piazza Colonna, the excellent **Trevi e Tritone** offers hot and cold food until 10pm.

Most *alimentari* (food stores) or *salumerie* (delicatessens) will make you a *panino* (filled roll). Especially delicious are **Lo Zozzone**'s hot plain pizza pockets stuffed with choices from the shop's counters, where you can also sip a glass of wine. Try a typical local speciality if you see the sign *porchetta* – whole aromatic roast pig with crackling, sliced into *rosette* (rolls) or thick country-bread sandwiches. **Made in Sud**, on Via di San Giovanni in Laterano is a great place to try some delicious pizza. Alternatively, go to the hole-in-the-wall **Er Buchetto**, where you can sit down in (relative) comfort with a glass of wine. For a really typical Roman snack, make a late-afternoon detour to **Filetti di Baccalà** serving, as the name suggests, fried cod fillets.

For cheese, go to **Obicá** near the Pantheon. This bar offers a vast choice of fresh buffalo and cow mozzarella; eat it as it should be – unadulterated – or prepared in a variety of creative ways. Nearby is **Ciao Checca**, which serves fresh, tasty salads and pasta dishes with discounts for refills.

Termini now has two good options for those waiting or rushing for trains – the self-service restaurant **Chef Express Gusto** or **Vyta** (*see p342*), which makes up gourmet sandwiches to go.

Bars, Cafés and Tearooms

Roman bars are the city's lifeline: places to meet, eat, drink, buy milk or coffee, make phone calls or find a toilet. Some are small, stand-up, basic one-counter bars for grabbing a quick *cornetto* and cappuccino; some may be more luxurious, doubling as a cake shop, ice-cream parlour, tearoom or *tavola calda*; or a combination of all these. Most open early at about 7:30am and close late, particularly at weekends, at around midnight or 2am. If you sit down you will be served by a waiter and pay for the privilege. At busy times, or at popular bars, the crowds at the counter will be large and you will have to wait your turn. If you choose to stand you pay for your drink at the till beforehand. A small tip (10 or 20 cents per drink) may increase your chances of speedy service. In summer, tables cover all the available outdoor space, and the fight for a place in the shade is never ending.

Traditionally elegant – and expensive – bars for people-watching are the admirably located **Rosati** and **Doney**, as well as **Caffè Greco**, the 19th-century haunt of artists, writers and composers (*see p135*), or the carefully restored **La Caffettiera**, near the Pantheon. Another popular and established café is the **Café Romano**, which is highly recommended for late-night drinks. **Zodiaco** on Monte Mario pulls in the crowds for its panoramic views as does **Oppio Café** near the Domus Aurea. For sheer decadence go to **La Terrazza dell'Eden** at the Hotel Eden or **Stravinskij Bar** at the Hotel de Russie for wonderful martinis or a relaxed cup of coffee.

Tearooms are becoming increasingly popular. **Babington's Tea Rooms** (see p136) on Piazza di Spagna serves an outrageously expensive cup of tea and scones in genteel surroundings, while **Di Qua'** is worth visiting for its desserts alone. Much better value can be found at **Green T** and **Sciascia Caffè**. For serious luxury, you can have a full afternoon tea at the **Grand Bar** in the St. Regis Hotel (see p303).

Coffee fiends should try a *gran caffè speciale* at the counter of **Caffè Sant'Eustachio**, or one of Rome's best espressos at **La Tazza d'Oro** (see p106). Less familiar to tourists, however, are the excellent **Antico Caffè del Brasile** (see p343), **Bar del Cappuccino**, **Ciamei** or **Spinelli**. **Ciampini al Café du Jardin** with its garden setting and roof-top views is unbeatable in summer, particularly at the apéritif hour. Gradually becoming the norm in Rome are bookshop cafés – **Caffè la Feltrinelli** and **Bibliotèq** are two examples – and museum cafés. The **Caffetteria Bistrot al Chiostro del Bramante** is in an art gallery on the upper loggia of a beautiful cloister. The bar at the Capitoline Museums has breathtaking views if average food, whilst the café in the **Palazzo delle Esposizioni** (see p166) is open throughout the day with an attractive selection of snacks and drinks.

Pasticcerie

On Sunday mornings you will often see the Romans emerging from the local pastry shop or *pasticceria* with a beautifully wrapped package. This can contain dainty individual pastries, whole cakes or tarts, traditional Easter *colombe* (doves) or the Christmas *panettoni* – huge cakes with raisins and candied peel – all for consumption by large gatherings of friends or family after lunch. The window displays of cake shops are often fantastic. These, and the aroma of brewing coffee, will tempt even those who claim not to have a sweet tooth. The selection is vast from a hot *cornetto* or *brioche* in the early morning, a midday *pizzetta* or savoury tart at lunch, or a choux pastry or fruit tart in the afternoon. **Cipriani** (see p339), open since 1906, has delicious biscuits, ricotta cake and apple tart. Nearby **Regoli** has wonderful *mille feuilles* and *torta con crema e pinoli* (pine kernels). **Dagnino** prepares hundreds of Sicilian specialities every day while **Boccione** specializes in traditional Roman-Jewish cakes, while for *tiramisù*, locals swear by **Bar Pompi**, which dubs itself "the kingdom of *tiramisù*". As well as cakes, numerous shops offer handmade chocolates. At some, such as **Rivendita Libri Cioccolata e Vino** (see p342), you can pause over a cup of coffee or glass of wine while deciding which you like best.

Gelaterie

Ice cream (*gelato*) is one of summer's main delights and at Rome's ice-cream parlours, you are certainly in for a lavish treat. Look for the word *artigianale*, if you want to savour the best. The choice is endless – water-ices made with a phenomenal variety of fruit; lemon and coffee *granite* (crushed ice); as well as more exotic ice-cream flavours such as rice pudding, *zuppa inglese* (English trifle), *zabaglione* and *tiramisù*. Choose as many varieties as the size of your cone or cup will hold, ask for an optional topping of whipped cream (*panna*) and go for a sensation-filled stroll. Or take a seat and rest awhile – you will be served an obscenely sized creation at the table (at a price). *Gelaterie* are open all day, many until late at night, and are an integral part of Roman socializing. **Tre Scalini** in Piazza Navona is a famous spot for enjoying the pricey, yet so heavenly, chocolate *tartufo* (truffle), while a summer evening in EUR, especially with children, nearly always ends in a trip to **Giolitti**, a historic ice-cream name. The strategically placed, crowded original near the Pantheon deserves at least one visit too. Gourmet fans of *gelato* should not miss **San Crispino**, which offers home-made delicacies crafted with the best ingredients. Its *zabaglione* is made using 20-year-old barrel-aged Marsala. In summer try the mouth-watering *susine* (yellow plum) and in winter, the *arancia selvatica* (wild orange) should not be missed.

Adults may prefer to pick their night-time treat at **Chalet del Lago**, again in EUR, while sitting beside the lake. If you come across a small kiosk with the sign *grattachecche* (most likely in Trastevere and Testaccio), try one of Rome's oldest traditions – ice grated by a gloved hand on the spot and enlivened with a variety of classic flavourings. Try **Sora Mirella**, near the Tiber Island. Equally distinctive are the fresh fruit *cremolati* at **Café du Parc**.

Everyone has their own favourite flavours and preferred *gelateria*, but the quest for perfection is an ongoing pleasure. For top *zabaglione*, try **Fiocco di Neve**, **Giolitti** of Via Vespucci or **Petrini dal 1926**. **Palazzo del Freddo** makes an exceptionally wonderful rice pudding flavour and its own *La Caterinetta* – one of the secret ingredients is honey. **Al Settimo Gelo**, a witty play on words (*settimo* is seventh, *cielo* is heaven and *gelo* is ice), creates exciting chestnut sorbet, chocolate with *peperoncino*, ginger, and ice cream made from Greek yoghurt. For those with dairy allergies, visit the Sicilian *gelateria*, **Gelarmony**, which also uses soya milk and has 14 different flavours on offer. At **Fior di Luna** in Trastevere, all ingredients are organic. Excellent ingredients also distinguish **Fattori**, located in the hip Pigneto neighbourhood, and the more central branches of **GROM**.

DIRECTORY

Capitol

BARS, CAFÉS AND TEAROOMS

Caffè Capitolino
Piazzale Caffarelli 4.
Map 12 F5.

Piazza della Rotonda

PIZZERIAS

Barroccio
Via dei Pastini 13.
Map 12 D2.

Er Faciolaro
Via dei Pastini 123.
Map 12 D2.

La Sagrestia
Via del Seminario 89.
Map 12 E3.

ENOTECHE

Achilli Enoteca al Parlamento
Via dei Prefetti 15.
Map 12 D1.

Enoteca Corsi
Via del Gesù 87/88.
Map 12 E3.

BIRRERIE

Trinity College
Via del Collegio Romano 6.
Map 12 E3.

FAST FOOD

Ciao Checca
Piazza Firenze 25.
Map 12 D1.

Obicá Mozzarella Bar
Piazza Firenze 28.
Map 12 D1.

BARS, CAFÉS AND TEAROOMS

Caffè Sant'Eustachio
Piazza Sant'Eustachio 82.
Map 12 D3.

La Caffettiera
Piazza di Pietra 65.
Map 12 E2.

Ciampini
Piazza S. Lorenzo in Lucina 29. **Map** 12 D1.

La Tazza d'Oro
Via degli Orfani 82/84.
Map 12 D2.

Teichner
Piazza San Lorenzo in Lucina 15–17.
Map 12 D1.

GELATERIE

Fiocco di Neve
Via del Pantheon 51.
Map 12 D2.

Giolitti
Via degli Uffici del Vicario 40. **Map** 12 D2.

GROM
Via della Maddalena 30A.
Map 12 D2.

Piazza Navona

PIZZERIAS

Da Baffetto
Via del Governo Vecchio 114. **Map** 11 B3.

Da Francesco
Piazza del Fico 29.
Map 11 B2.

La Montecarlo
Vicolo Savelli 12/13.
Map 11 C3.

ENOTECHE

Caffè Novecento
Via del Governo Vecchio 12. **Map** 11 B3.

Cul de Sac
Piazza Pasquino 73.
Map 11 C3.

Etablì
Vicolo delle Vacche 9A.
Map 11 B2.

Giulio Passami l'Olio
Via di Monte Giordano 28.
Map 11B2.

Il Piccolo
Via del Governo Vecchio 74–75.
Map 11 C3.

BIRRERIE

Old Bear
Via dei Gigli d'Oro 2.
Map 11 C2.

FAST FOOD

Lo Zozzone
Via del Teatro Pace 32.
Map 11 B3.

BARS, CAFÉS AND TEAROOMS

Caffeteria Bistrot al Chiostro del Bramante
Via della Pace.
Map 11 C2.

PASTICCERIE

La Deliziosa
Vicolo Savelli 50.
Map 11 B3.

GELATERIE

Da Quinto
Via di Tor Millina 15.
Map 11 C3.

GROM
Via Agonale 3 (corner Piazza Navona).
Map 11 C2.

Tre Scalini
Piazza Navona 28.
Map 11 C3.

Piazza di Spagna

PIZZERIAS

'Gusto
Piazza Augusto Imperatore 9. **Map** 4 F2.

PizzaRé
Via di Ripetta 14.
Map 4 F1.

ENOTECHE

Antica Enoteca di Via della Croce
Via della Croce 76B.
Map 5 A2.

Buccone
Via di Ripetta 19.
Map 4 F1.

'Gusto
See Pizzerias.

Il Brillo Parlante
Via della Fontanella 12.
Map 4 F1.

BIRRERIE

Löwenhaus
Via della Fontanella 16B.
Map 4 F1.

FAST FOOD

Difronte A
Via della Croce 38.
Map 4 F2.

Fratelli Fabbi
Via della Croce 27.
Map 4 F2.

Pizza, Pere e Gorgonzola
Via Laurina 7. **Map** 4 F1.

BARS, CAFÉS AND TEAROOMS

Babington's Tea Rooms
Piazza di Spagna 23.
Map 5 A2.

Café Romano
Via Borgognona 4.
Map 12 E1.

Caffè Greco
Via Condotti 86.
Map 5 A2.

Ciampini al Café du Jardin
Viale Trinità dei Monti.
Map 5 A2.

Di Qua'
Via delle Carrozze 85B.
Map 4 F2.

Rosati
Piazza del Popolo 5.
Map 4 F1.

Stravinskij Bar
Hotel de Russie,
Via del Babuino 9.
Map 5 A2.

GELATERIE

Venchi
Via della Croce 25.
Map 5 A2.

Campo de' Fiori

ENOTECHE

Angolo Divino
Via dei Balestrari 12.
Map 11 C4.

Antico Forno Roscioli
Via dei Giubbonari 21.
Map 11 C4.

Il Goccetto
Via dei Banchi Vecchi 14.
Map 11 B3.

Il Nolano
Piazza Campo dei Fiori 11.
Map 11 C4.

Verso Sera
Piazza del Biscione.
Map 11 C4.

Vinando
Piazza Margana 23.
Map 12 E4.

FAST FOOD

Filetti di Baccalà
Largo dei Librari 88.
Map 11 C4.

DIRECTORY

Forno Campo de' Fiori
Piazza Campo de'Fiori 22.
Map 11 C4.

Hostaria Da Benito
Via dei Falegnami 14.
Map 12 D4.

Pizza Florida
Via Florida 25.
Map 12 D4.

BARS, CAFÉS AND TEAROOMS

Alberto Pica
Via della Seggiola 12.
Map 12 D5.

Bar del Cappuccino
Via Arenula 50.
Map 12 D4.

Bibliotèq
Via dei Banchi Vecchi 124.
Map 11 B3.

Caffè la Feltrinelli
Largo Torre Argentina 5.
Map 12 D4.

PASTICCERIE

Boccione
Via del Portico d'Ottavia 1.
Map 12 E5.

La Dolceroma
Via del Portico d'Ottavia 20B. **Map** 12 E5.

Il Mondo di Laura
Via Portico d'Ottavia 6.
Map 12 D5.

GELATERIE

Blue Ice
Via dei Baullari 130 and 141. **Map** 11 C4.

Kosher Gelato
Via del Portico d'Ottavia 3.
Map 12 E5.

Quirinal

PIZZERIAS

Est! Est! Est!
Via Genova 32. **Map** 5 C4.

Grazie a Dio è Venerdí
Via dei Capocci 1.
Map 5 C4.

ENOTECHE

Al Vino al Vino
Via dei Serpenti 19.
Map 5 B4.

Cavour 313
Via Cavour 313.
Map 5 B5.

Monti DOC
Via Giovanni Lanza 93.
Map 5 C5.

Vineria Il Chianti
Via del Lavatore 81.
Map 12 F2.

BIRRERIE

The Albert Pub
Via del Traforo 132.
Map 5 B3.**Antica Birreria Peroni**
Via San Marcello 19.
Map 12 F3.

FAST FOOD

Er Buchetto
Via Viminale 2.
Map 5 C3.

Striscia la Pizza
Via Milano 33.
Map 5 B4.

Trevi e Tritone
Galleria Alberto Sordi.
Map 12 E2.

BARS, CAFÉS AND TEAROOMS

Antico Caffè del Brasile
Via dei Serpenti 23.
Map 5 B4.

La Bottega del Caffè
Piazza della Madonna dei Monti 5.
Map 5 B5.

Green T
Via Pié di Marmo 28.
Map 11 E3.

Palazzo delle Esposizioni
Via Milano 15–17.
Map 5 B4.

Theatre Café
Largo Magnanapoli 157A.
Map 5 B4.

PASTICCERIE

Dagnino
Galleria Esedra, Via Vittorio Emanuele Orlando 75.
Map 5 C2.

GELATERIE

San Crispino
Via della Panetteria 42.
Map 12 F2.

Termini

PIZZERIAS

Formula Uno
Via degli Equi 13.
Map 6 F4.

San Marco
Via Sardegna 38D.
Map 5 B1.

ENOTECHE

Enoteca Chirra
Via Torino 132–133.
Map 5 C3.

Trimani
Via Cernaia 37B.
Map 6 D2.

FAST FOOD

Chef Express Gusto
Galleria Termini – Exit Via Marsala. **Map** 6 D3.

Vyta
Galleria Termini – Exit Via Marsala. **Map** 6 D3.

Wok
Stazione Termini (Lower Level). **Map** 6 D3.

BARS, CAFÉS AND TEAROOMS

Grand Bar
St. Regis Hotel, Via Vittorio Emanuele Orlando 3. **Map** 6 C3.

Spinelli
Via dei Mille 58.
Map 6 E3.

Esquiline

BIRRERIE

Birreria Marconi
Via di Santa Prassede 9C.
Map 6 D4

The Fiddler's Elbow
Via dell'Olmata 43.
Map 6 D4.

FAST FOOD

Panella
Via Merulana 54.
Map 6 D5.

BARS, CAFÉS AND TEAROOMS

Ciamei
Via Emanuele Filiberto 57.
Map 6 E5.

Oppio Café
Via delle Terme di Tito 72.
Map 5 C5.

PASTICCERIE

Cipriani
Via C. Botta 21. **Map** 6 D5.

Regoli
Via dello Statuto 60.
Map 6 D5.

GELATERIE

Palazzo del Freddo
Via Principe Eugenio 65/67. **Map** 6 E5.

Lateran

BIRRERIE

La Pace del Cervello
Via dei SS Quattro 63.
Map 9 A1.

ENOTECHE

Il Tajut
Via di San Giovanni in Laterano 244–246.
Map 9 B1.

FAST FOOD

Made in Sud
Via San Giovanni, Laterano 46. **Map** 9 A1.

PASTICCERIE

Paci
Via dei Marsi 33.
Off Map 6 F4.

Pompi
Via Albalonga 7–11.
Map 10 D3.

GELATERIE

San Crispino
Via Acaia 56. **Map** 9 C4.

Aventine

PIZZERIAS

Da Remo
Piazza Santa Maria Liberatrice 44. **Map** 8 D3.

Trapizzino
Via Branca 90. **Map** 8 D3.

ENOTECHE

Divinare
Via Manuzio 13.
Map 8 D3.

BIRRERIE

L'Oasi della Birra
Piazza Testaccio 40.
Map 8 D3.

DIRECTORY

FAST FOOD

Farinando
Via Luca della Robbia 30.
Map 8 D3.

Volpetti Più
Via Alessandro Volta 8.
Map 8 D3.

GELATERIE

Café du Parc
Piazza di Porta San Paolo.
Map 8 E4.

Giolitti
Via Vespucci 35.
Map 8 D3.

Trastevere

PIZZERIAS

Da Vittorio
Via di S. Cosimato 14A.
Map 7 C1.

Dar Poeta
Vicolo del Bologna 45.
Map 11 B5.

Panattoni – L'Obitorio
Viale Trastevere 53.
Map 7 C1.

Pizzeria Ivo
Via S. Francesco a Ripa
158. **Map** 7 C1.

ENOTECHE

Ferrara
Via del Moro 1A.
Map 7 C1.

Friends Art Café
Piazza Trilussa 41.
Map 11 B5.

Enoteca Trastevere
Via della Lungaretta 86.
Map 7 C1.

BIRRERIE

**Ma Che Siete Venuti
a Fà**
Via Benedetta 25.
Map 11 B5.

FAST FOOD

Forno La Renella
Via del Moro 15.
Map 7 C1.

BARS, CAFÉS AND
TEAROOMS

Ombre Rosse
Piazza Sant'Egidio 12.
Map 7 C1.

PASTICCERIE

Innocenti
Via della Luce 21A.
Map 7 C2.

Pasticceria Trastevere
Via Natale del Grande 49.
Map 7 C1.

**Rivendita Libri
Cioccolata e Vino**
Vicolo del Cinque 11A.
Map 11 B5.

GELATERIE

Fior di Luna
Via della Lungaretta 96.
Map 7 C1.

La Fonte della Salute
Via Cardinale Marmaggi
2–4. **Map** 7 C1.

Sora Mirella
Lungotevere degli
Anguillara (corner of
Ponte Cestio).
Map 8 D1.

Janiculum

ENOTECHE

**In Vino Veritas
Art Bar**
Via Garibaldi 2A.
Map 11 B5.

Vatican

PIZZERIAS

L'Archetto
Via Germanico 105.
Map 3 C2.

Napul'è
Viale Giulio Cesare 91.
Map 3 C1.

ENOTECHE

Costantini
Piazza Cavour 16.
Map 4 E2.

Del Frate
Via degli Scipioni 118.
Map 3 C1.

BIRRERIE

Cantina Tirolese
Via Vitelleschi 23.
Map 3 C2.

Fonclea
Via Crescenzio 82A.
Map 3 C2.

FAST FOOD

Ercoli dal 1928
Via Montello 26.
Off Map 1 A5.

Franchi
Via Cola di Rienzo 200.
Map 4 D2.

La Pratolina
Via degli Scipioni 248.
Map 3 C1.

BARS, CAFÉS AND
TEAROOMS

Sciascia Caffé
Via Fabio Massimo 80A.
Map 3 C1.

PASTICCERIE

Antonini
Via Sabotino 19–29.
Just **off Map** 1 A5.

Gran Caffè Esperia
Lungotevere Mellini 1.
Map 4 E1.

GELATERIE

Al Settimo Gelo
Via Vodice 21A.
Just **off Map** 1 A5.

Gelarmony
Via Marcantonio Colonna
34. **Map** 4 D1.

Via Veneto

PIZZERIAS

San Marco
Via Sardegna 38D.
Map 5 C1.

BARS, CAFÉS AND
TEAROOMS

Doney
Via Veneto 141.
Map 5 B2.

La Terrazza dell'Eden
Via Ludovisi 49.
Map 5 B2.

**VyTa Santa
Margherita**
Largo M. Mastroianni 1.
Map 5 B1.

EUR

ENOTECHE

La Cave des Amis
Piazzale Ardigò 27–29.

BARS, CAFÉS AND
TEAROOMS

Palombini
Piazzale Adenauer 12.

GELATERIE

Chalet del Lago
Lake, EUR.

Giolitti
Casina dei Tre Laghi,
Viale Oceania 90 EUR.

Further Afield

PIZZERIAS

**Al Forno
della Soffitta**
Via Piave 62.
Map 6 D1.

La Pantera Rosa
Piazzale del Verano 84.
Off Map 6 F4.

BARS, CAFÉS AND
TEAROOMS

TreeBar
Via Flaminia 226.
Map 1 B3.

Zodiaco
Viale Parco Mellini 88–92.
Off Map 3 A1.

PASTICCERIE

Bar Pompi
Via Albalonga 7B/9/11.
Map 10 D3.

Mondi
Via Flaminia 468.
Off Map 1 A1.

GELATERIE

Fattori
Via Alberto da Giussano
80. **Map** 10 F1.

Petrini dal 1926
Piazza dell'Alberone 16A.
Map 10 F4.

SHOPS AND MARKETS

Rome has been a thriving centre for design and cosmopolitan shopping since ancient times. In the heyday of the Empire the finest craftsmen were drawn to Rome, and artifacts and produce of all kinds, including gold, furs and wine, were imported from far-flung corners of the Empire to service the needs of the wealthy Roman population. Shopping in Rome today in many ways reflects this diverse tradition. Italian designers have an international reputation for their luxuriously chic style in fashion, knitwear and leather goods (especially shoes and handbags), as well as in interior design, fabrics, ceramics and glass. The artisan tradition is strong and the love of good design filters through into the smallest items. Rome is not a city for bargains (although it often offers better value than Florence or Milan), but the joys of window shopping here will offer plenty of compensation.

Best Buys

Leather goods of all kinds, including shoes and bags, are a strong point. Ready-to-wear Italian designer clothes are not cheap, but they are certainly less expensive than in other countries. Armani jeans are a good example *(see p331)*. You are also likely to find designer lighting fixtures, for example, at lower prices here. Both modern and traditional Italian ceramics and handicrafts can be very beautifully made and, if you have time to wander around the back streets, really unusual and individual gifts can often be found.

Sales

Bargain hunters may like to visit Rome during sale time *(saldi)*, from mid-July to mid-September and the period from just after Christmas to the first week in March. Top designers *(see p330)* can slash prices by half, but their clothes are still very expensive even then. Good bargains can be found in the young designer-wear shops *(see p331)* and good-quality small and large shoe sizes are sold off very cheaply. In general, though, sales in Rome tend to offer moderate rather than huge discounts.

Both the original and the sale price should be quoted on each reduced item. *Liquidazioni* (closing-down sales) are usually genuine and can sometimes be worth investigating. However, other signs in shop windows such as *vendite promozionali* (special introductory prices) and *sconti* (discounts) are often only lures to get you into the shop. The sign on the door saying *entrata libera* means "browsers welcome".

When to Shop

Shops are generally open from 9am to 1pm and from 3:30pm

Antiques at Acanto *(see p340)*

to 7:30pm (4pm to 8pm in the summer months). Most shops in the centre stay open all day from 10am to 7:30pm.

Most shops are closed on Sunday (except just before Christmas). Shops are also closed on Monday morning, apart from most food stores, which close on Thursday afternoons in winter and Saturday afternoons in high summer.

August brings the city to a virtual standstill as Roman families escape the heat to the sea or the mountains, but this is gradually changing, with Romans taking shorter summer holidays. Most shops close for at least two weeks around 15 August, the national holiday.

Shopping Etiquette

Apart from a few department stores, most Roman shops are

Flower stalls in Piazza Campo de' Fiori *(see p344)*

small, specializing in just one field. Browsing at leisure may at first seem daunting if you are used to large shopping centres. Customers will almost always receive better attention if they dress smartly – the emphasis on *fare una bella figura* (making a good impression) is taken seriously.

Sizes are not always uniform, so it is wise to try clothes on if possible before buying, since refunds and exchanges are not often given.

Stylish leather gloves on display

How to Pay

Most shops accept all the major credit cards, whose signs are displayed on the shop window. Some will also accept foreign currency, though the exchange rate may not be good. When you make a purchase you are bound by Italian law to leave the shop with a *scontrino fiscale* (receipt). You can try asking for a discount if paying cash and you may be lucky, though many shops have a *prezzi fissi* (fixed prices) sign.

VAT Exemption

Value Added Tax – VAT (*IVA* in Italy) is 21 per cent of the good's price. Marked or advertised prices normally include the IVA. It is possible for non-European Union residents to obtain an IVA

One of many designer shops around Piazza di Spagna *(see p329)*

refund for individual purchases that exceed €155, but be prepared for a long and bureaucratic process. The simplest method is to shop at a place displaying the "Euro Free Tax" sign. Present your passport when you make your purchase and ask for a tax refund cheque. On leaving Italy, show your new purchases and receipts at customs and get the cheque stamped. You can then collect your refund at Fiumicino airport by presenting the cheque at the **Global Blue** desk, where you will be reimbursed.

If you wish to buy something from a shop which is not part of the "Euro Free Tax" scheme, you must get the Italian customs to stamp the vendor's receipt at your departure, showing them the purchased article, then post the receipt back to the shop, who should then send you a refund.

Mercato delle Stampe *(see p344)*

Department Stores and Shopping Centres

Department stores, known as *grandi magazzini*, are few and far between in Rome, but they tend to have longer opening hours than smaller shops. **La Rinascente** and **Coin** are good for ready-to-wear clothes, both for men and women, household linens and haberdashery, and have well-stocked perfume counters. The **Oviesse** and **Upim** chain stores offer moderately priced medium-quality clothes and a variety of household goods.

Another alternative for the zealous shopper is to head for one of Rome's shopping malls. **Cinecittà Due Centro Commerciale**, built in 1988, offers around 100 shops

Bargains in Via Sannio *(see p345)*

plus bars, banks and restaurants within easy reach of the centre by Metro (line A to Cinecittà).

Rome's Best: Shopping Streets and Markets

The most interesting shops in Rome are in the old centre, so shopping is easy to combine with sightseeing. The shops are often housed in medieval or Renaissance buildings and their window displays can be exquisite. Just like shopkeepers in past centuries, traders tend to specialize in one type of merchandise. Street names often refer to the old tradesmen: locksmiths in Via dei Chiavari, leather jerkin makers in Via dei Giubbonari and chairs in Via dei Sediari. Today, antiques merchants have taken over from the rosary sellers on Via dei Coronari. The top names in fashion and modern design dominate the Via Condotti area, and the artisan tradition is still strong around Campo de' Fiori and Piazza Navona.

Via Cola di Rienzo
Situated close to the Vatican Museums, this long wide street has the finest food shops and is also good for clothes, books and gifts.

Via dei Coronari
Art Nouveau and antiques enthusiasts will love browsing in the shops that line this charming street just northwest of Piazza Navona. But be prepared for high prices as most of the items are imported.

Pia
Sp

Vatican

Pia

R

Piazza
Navona

Janiculum

Ca
de

Trasteve

Via del Pellegrino
Book and art shops abound here next to working artisans in the historic centre. Do not miss the mirror-lined alley near Campo de' Fiori.

Via dei Cappellari
This narrow, medieval street is a great place for watching furniture restorers and other artisans plying their crafts in the open air.

Porta Portese
You can buy anything from antiques to a tin whistle at Trastevere's Sunday morning flea market (see p345).

Via Margutta
Up-market antique shops mix with genteel restaurants on this peaceful, cobbled street.

Via del Babuino
This street is renowned for designer furniture, lighting and glass, as well as interesting antique and fashion shops.

0 metres 500

0 yards 500

Via Veneto

Quirinal

Forum

Palatine

Esquiline

Lateran

Caracalla

VIA DELLA CROCE

VIA

D&G

VIA MARIO

Missoni

Prada

PIAZZA DI SPAGNA

VIA DELLE CARROZZE

BOCCA

Giorgio Armani

Gucci

VIA

DI LEONE

CONDOTTI

Trussardi

Valentino

PIAZZA MIGNANELLI

VIA

DE' FIORI

VIA DI PROPAGANDA

BELSIANA

VIA BORGOGNONA

VIA

FRATTINA

Max Mara

VIA DEL CORSO

VIA DELLA VITE

VIA DELLA MERCEDE

Designer Shopping

All the well-known stars of the Italian fashion scene, plus exclusive jewellers, gift shops, shoe designers and tailors, are concentrated in this cluster of chic and stylish shopping streets by the Spanish Steps (see pp330–35). Romans love to stroll here in the early evening.

Testaccio Market
A visual feast of fruit and vegetables greets the eye in this lively market (see p344).

Via Borgognona
Crowds flock here to buy, or just gaze at, high-fashion clothes, shoes, leather bags and other accessories.

Men's and Women's Fashion

Italy is one of the leading lights in high-class fashion, or *alta moda*. Many of the most famous designers are based in Milan, but Rome is home to a cluster of sophisticated and internationally distinguished fashion houses. There is also a wonderful selection of *alta moda* shops. Boutiques displaying an eclectic mix of designer goods rub shoulders with showrooms devoted to single collections. But even for those of us unable to splash out on genuine designer-wear, much fun can be gained from a stroll down the glittering streets that radiate out from the Piazza di Spagna, as some of the window displays are truly spectacular.

The "atelier" made-to-measure fashions are beyond most pockets, but the designers also offer ready-to-wear alternatives in their boutiques. These are not cheap, but cost far less than a tailor-made garment.

Women's High Fashion

Rome's most famous designer internationally is probably **Valentino**, who retired in 2008 but whose boutique on Piazza di Spagna is still a mecca for the younger fashionista. A few steps away is the showroom of **Krizia**, which showcases the extravagant *alta moda* and ready-to-wear designs of Mariuccia Mandelli.

The equally impressive **Fendi** occupies a 19th-century palazzo in Largo Goldoni. Fendi made its name with high-fashion furs, then branched out into leather goods, accessories and ready-to-wear, collaborating with Karl Lagerfeld who designed the coveted double-F logo which emblazons its very collectable products. Third-generation family members design the younger, less expensive Fendissime line.

For well over a decade, **Laura Biagiotti** has reigned as Rome's queen of discreet, conservative couture. From her headquarters in a castle just outside Rome, she designs a range of time-lessly elegant knitwear and silk separates for women who don't want to sacrifice style for comfort. She is famous for her use of cashmere and white as well as her creative use of fabrics and quality of finish. Her flagship showroom in Via Mario de' Fiori stocks her complete collection, which now includes hosiery, perfumes, swimwear and leather goods. Her scarves

make wonderful presents, and are often reduced in price during sales; other items from previous collections are available in the shop all year round at very good discounts. Meanwhile, in nearby Via Condotti, there is the temple to the creations of **Salvatore Ferragamo**.

Other internationally known Rome-based designers include **Renato Balestra**, who produces tailored suits and glamorous evening wear.

Milan's miraculous fashion house **Prada** has an alluring branch on Via Condotti, selling clothes, shoes and accessories in unmistakable style. The window display is always worth a look. Other luminaries of Italian fashion who have shops in Rome include **Versace** and **Trussardi**. Top designers **Giorgio Armani** and **Dolce & Gabbana** also have stores in the Via Condotti area.

An affirmed star in ready-to-wear is **Roberto Cavalli**, whose design team produces some

coolly imaginative and stylish collections.

In a league of her own is **Soledad Twombly**. Make an appointment to see her original creations mingling fabrics from all over the world.

If you are looking for clothes from more unconventional designers, **Gente** is the place to go – its Roman showrooms have exclusive rights to the original couture collections of avant-garde stylists such as Dolce & Gabbana, Moschino, and Jean-Paul Gaultier.

MaxMara also has a number of branches here. Chic suits and separates are the mainstays of this popular label. The quality of fabric and finish is superb and, with suits available for around €500, its prices are much lower than other *alta moda* couture designers' ready-to-wear lines.

Men's Tailors and Designer Wear

Italian men are every bit as fashion conscious as the women, and there is no shortage of choice in Rome for the well-dressed man. Suits tend to begin at around €620, jackets €415 and trousers €155.

Most of the "star" designers of women's *alta moda* have a shop for men, like **Salvatore Ferragamo**, **Prada** and **Versace**. The designs are generally less dramatic than the women's, with the accent on understated sophistication and casual sportiness. **Valentino**'s distinctive monogrammed accessories are relatively

Valentino

One of the high priests of Italian fashion, **Valentino Garavani** opened the doors of his Roman studio in 1959 to a distinguished clientele that included Sophia Loren, Audrey Hepburn and Jackie Kennedy. Before retiring in 2008, Valentino created some of the most dramatic and flattering evening dresses of the last 50

years. In the 1970s he began designing ready-to-wear lines for both men and women alongside his *alta moda* collections, and you can now find his very distinctive "V" logo on a wide range of accessories. The Valentino brand is still based in a huge palazzo in Piazza Mignanelli, and there are separate ready-to-wear boutiques nearby (see p334).

affordable. **Battistoni** is probably the most prestigious designer concentrating on menswear. Giorgio Battistoni and family's fine custom-made shirts and suits have been in demand with film stars and top society for over 50 years. **Etro** sells classically cut clothes and accessories for men and women in exotic Italian-designed printed fabrics.

Ermenegildo Zegna is housed in a Baroque palazzo setting. It offers elegant ready-to-wear, and the master tailor Gaetano will also make to measure. **Davide Cenci** has been a mecca for those in search of the English country gentleman look since 1926. **Brioni** offers traditional tailor-made and own-label ready-to-wear men's clothing, **Trussardi** sells beautifully tailored classics, and **Cerruti** has impeccably tailored suits that appeal to younger Romans. **Degli Effetti** stocks more avant-garde designers such as Romeo Gigli and Jean-Paul Gaultier.

Young Designer Wear

There is a huge choice for the young. Top designer Giorgio Armani offers his particular styles translated into more affordable lines at **Emporio Armani** (Armani jeans are good value at around €100). **Fendi** has its Fendissime line, and **Ermanno Scervino** has a boutique in Via Borgognona. Targeted at the younger set, these are good places to pick up stylish, sporty numbers.

Timberland is another casual label very popular with young Italians. Average prices are in the region of €52 for a shirt and €210 for raincoats.

Momento stocks unique pieces, as well as items by international designers that you won't find elsewhere in Rome, and also has its own line of dresses and shoes. Trussardi's casual line is found at **Tru Trussardi**, and **Diesel** and **SBU** are also very popular. **Eventi Up** represents the more avant-garde styles – *dark*, as they call it here – fusing Gothic, New Age and punk influences

which can result in some outrageous window creations. For women, Via del Governo Vecchio is the place to head for. **Arsenico 36**, **Luna e L'altra**, **Kokoro** and **Maga Morgana** offer some unconventional designer clothes in a pleasant, friendly atmosphere.

High Street Fashion

Rome is not a good place to look for everyday wear, since there is a distinct lack of mid-price shops bridging the huge gap between the dazzlingly priced *alta moda* designer exclusives and the ultra-cheap goods sold in markets *(see pp344–5)*. Lower-budget shops do exist, but quality is often poor. If you have the stamina, you may find a bargain along Via del Corso, Via del Tritone, Via Nazionale, Via Cavour, Via Cola di Rienzo, Via Ottaviano or the Via dei Giubbonari.

The most convenient places to shop are department stores like La Rinascente, Coin and Upim *(see p327)*. They may not sound exciting, but you can browse at leisure and occasionally find nice things. It is also worth trying shops mentioned under Young Designer Wear – particularly the *alta moda* designers' cheaper lines such as **Emporio Armani**. At the different branches of **Discount dell'Alta Moda** you can find end-of-season designer labels at 50 per cent less than the boutique prices. **List** is a chain selling chic, classic Italian clothes for women. And while you do not need to come all the way to Rome to shop at **Benetton** or **Zara**, there are many branches of both to be found.

Knitwear

Knitwear is a particular strength in Italian design, and in Rome there are plenty of specialist shops. **Laura Biagiotti** is celebrated for her luxurious cashmere separates, and **Missoni** for spectacular kaleidoscopic patterns and colours. Krizia no longer has a shop in Rome but

sophisticated knitwear can be purchased at **Liz**.

Other shops, such as the **Luisa Spagnoli** outlets, offer a wider selection, including lower-priced items, as does **Stefanel**, which has various branches in the city.

Lingerie

This is another Italian speciality excelling in both style and quality, with lines like La Perla exported worldwide. Lingerie is traditionally sold in top household linen shops *(see p337)* – **Cesari**, for example, has its own complete range. There are also boutiques specializing in lingerie and swimwear.

Marisa Padovan has a range of swimwear that is ideal for Italian beaches, as well as light, bright summer dresses. **Brighenti** is said to be where film stars go for their lingerie. **Schostal** has more traditional underwear with a very good men's section. The popular chain **Intimissimi** has stores in most shopping areas and sells classy lingerie.

Second-Hand Clothes

Those who are willing to browse will find a wide variety of second-hand clothes, whether inspired by a collector's interest in vintage clothes or a low budget. Apart from Via Sannio and Porta Portese markets *(see p345)*, which have many second-hand clothes stalls, the mecca is Via del Governo Vecchio. Among the best shops in this ancient street near Piazza Navona is **Tempi Moderni**, which has mostly vintage leather coats, jeans and some hats.

Le Gallinelle offers a marvellous selection of second-hand and vintage clothes, as well as their own line. **Sitenne** in the Piazza Vittorio area has some excellent Italian clothes from the 1920s to the 1980s for both women and men. Via del Pellegrino is also a good street for shops selling second-hand clothes and for independent stores.

Shoes and Accessories

Italy's leather industry is renowned all over the world, and shoes, bags and belts are a good buy in Rome. Accessories in general are not just an afterthought but an integral part of an outfit for the well-dressed Roman. The choice of stylish jewellery, scarves, ties and other accessories is excellent and the shops themselves are often a visual treat.

Shoes

Rome is full of shoe shops, ranging from high-quality stores in the Via Condotti area (where prices tend to start at €170) to the more economical shops around the Trevi Fountain, and every big market has its bargain shoe stalls on its fringes.

Probably the best-known shop is **Ferragamo** – one of the world's top shoe shops. It stocks classic yet fashion-conscious shoes, as well as women's clothing and leather goods. The silk signature scarves are famous.

Fratelli Rossetti is a close contender for the number one position. Founded by brothers Renzo and Renato some 50 years ago, this company produces classic men's shoes and beautiful, dressy low-heeled shoes for women that reflect the most up-to-the-minute trends. Along with shops like **Tod's** in Via Condotti it represents the epitome of elegance. The prices, of course, are sky-high but why not buy something small, and at least you will have the bag!

Boccanera's retail outlets, over in Testaccio, offer the latest men's and women's shoe styles from top Italian and British designers, with prices to match.

Silvano Lattanzi is one of the longer-lived shoe shops in Rome, having been in business for almost two decades, but it can't compete with **Domus**, which opened in 1938. Silvano Lattanzi sells made-to-measure footwear for both men and women, particularly shoes for special occasions and to customers' personal specifications. Domus sells a selection of high-quality footwear, specializing in classic shoes for women. They also stock a limited range of

leather bags and accessories. **De Bach** has colourful shoe styles for women.

Via Frattina has several more great shoe shops such as **Campanile**, which specializes in footwear for both men and women in trendy and imaginative styles. Native designer **Fausto Santini** stocks original, stylish, colourful designs for younger people. Beautiful, bright options for both men and women can also be found at **Baldinini**.

Borini stocks simple and elegant, low-heeled styles. As the name suggests, **Mr Boots** stocks a wide range of trendy boots and casual shoes for men and women, while the **Empresa** chain is known for its almost post-industrial designs. If comfort is your priority, head to the **Geox** flagship store on Via del Corso.

Leather Bags and Accessories

The most famous of Rome's leather shops is the super-trendy **Gucci**, a dandy's paradise selling shoes, suitcases, handbags, wallets, belts and other accessories. It has a fashion boutique for men and women and is well-known for its silk ties and scarves. **Fendi** also has exquisite leather goods as well as some lower-priced lines in synthetic materials and a range of gift items. Although their famous "stripe" line of leather-finished synthetic handbags cost €130 (and their all-leather ones start at €155), they are at least cheaper to buy here than abroad. **Ibiz**, near Campo de' Fiori, makes excellent sturdy bags and wallets in various colours and reasonable prices while nearer the Trevi Fountain is **La Sella**. It sells all

things leather, including a range of shoes, bags, purses and belts.

Mandarina Duck's brightly coloured fabric bags and range of luggage are very much in fashion and make an attractive (and vegetarian) alternative to the more traditional leather styles. For sleek, utterly fashionable handbags check out the latest creations by **Salvatore Ferragamo** or go for one by **Alviero Martini**, such as his famous "map" bags.

For a more unusual men's present, try **La Cravatta Su Misura** in Trastevere. In addition to their selection of classy handmade ties, they also manufacture ties to customers' specifications. You can choose the design, material, length and shape of the tie to create the perfect gift.

Classic Jewellery

What Cartier is to Paris, Tiffany & Co. is to New York and Asprey's is to London, **Bulgari** is to Rome. This internationally revered jeweller's has passers-by glued to the windows gazing at its large gemstones. These "windows" are rather curious small boxes inserted into a wall with one or two pieces of jewellery in each of them, which adds to the feeling of looking at precious items in a case at a museum. Bulgari's watches, especially the men's, are popular and very elegant, as are the famous mesh necklaces. It specializes in large, colourful stones in High Renaissance-style settings but also produces a selection of contemporary designs. This was one of Andy Warhol's favourite shops, and it is definitely the most palatial outfit on Via Condotti. Inside, the shop's atmosphere is one of almost religious awe and contemplation.

Angeletti sells the collections of **Buccellati,** an offshoot of the famous Florentine dynasty, which was begun by Mario Buccellati in the 1920s and patronized by the poet Gabriele

D'Annunzio. Its delicately engraved designs are inspired by the Italian Renaissance, and are real classics, displaying superb craftsmanship.

Ansuini designs are fashionable yet classic with strong, imaginative themes being introduced for each new collection. **Massoni**, founded in 1790, is one of Rome's oldest jewellery houses. Its refined one-offs and brooches are quite outstanding.

At **Moroni Gioielli** you will also find imaginative, unique pieces of the highest-quality workmanship.

Peroso is an old-fashioned shop which has been going since 1891 and specializes in antique jewellery and silver-ware. You have to ring the bell to be admitted, and purchases can be extremely expensive.

Tiffany & Co. sells its classic designs in jewellery, watches, accessories and gifts at an exquisite outlet on elegant Via del Babuino.

Costume Jewellery

For less conventional tastes, there are several shops selling innovative, avant-garde designs, often using semi-precious metals and stones. **Granuzzo**, in Via dei Coronari, is worth trying.

Tempi Moderni has an interesting collection of Art Deco and Liberty (Art Nouveau) period jewellery including Bakelite brooches. There is also a range of designer pieces from the fifties and sixties.

Danae makes interesting pieces using silver and precious stones, inspired by Coco Chanel, while **Massimo Maria Melis** uses antique coins and precious stones to produce his marvellous gold creations.

For a different but equally modern approach, check out the exquisite boutique of **Delfina Delettrez** on Via del Governo Vecchio.

Traditional Goldsmiths and Silversmiths

The mainstay of Rome's jewellery industry is still the traditional artisan goldsmith and silversmith, working to order in tiny studio workshops. These are concentrated in the old Jewish Ghetto area by the Tiber river, Campo de' Fiori, Ponte Sisto near Via Giulia, and in Montepietà (which is also where the city pawnbrokers are situated).

Artisan jewellery can also be found in Via dei Coronari, Via dell'Orso and Via del Pellegrino. The jewellers create individual pieces to their own designs and have often learned their profession from their parents and grandparents. They will also do repair work, or take old gold jewellery, melt it down and make it into something to the customer's order.

Gioie d'Arte produces some traditional artisan jewellery and always works to customers' commissions.

Gloves, Hats and Hosiery

If you are looking for top quality, you will find an expensive line in gloves at **Di Cori** and **Sermoneta**, both of which stock every imaginable kind and hue.

To find smart leather gloves to match your new shoes and handbags, whatever their colour, make a visit to **Settimio Mieli** which is sure to have something suitable, and at a reasonable price.

Catello d'Auria specializes in gloves and hosiery. **Borsalino** is a good place to go for all sorts of hats, including its namesake.

Calzedonia has several branches in the city and will serve you with almost any colour or pattern of tights and stockings that you could wish for.

Size Chart

For Australian sizes follow British and American convention.

Children's clothing

Italian	2-3	4-5	6-7	8-9	10-11	12	14	14+ (years)
British	2-3	4-5	6-7	8-9	10-11	12	14	14+ (years)
American	2-3	4-5	6-6x	7-8	10	12	14	16 (size)

Children's shoes

Italian	24	25½	27	28	29	30	32	33	34
British	7	8	9	10	11	12	13	1	2
American	7½	8½	9½	10½	11½	12½	13½	1½	2½

Women's dresses, coats and skirts

Italian	38	40	42	44	46	48	50
British	8	10	12	14	16	18	20
American	6	8	10	12	14	16	18

Women's blouses and sweaters

Italian	81	84	87	90	93	96	99 (cms)
British	31	32	34	36	38	40	42 (inches)
American	6	8	10	12	14	16	18 (size)

Women's shoes

Italian	36	37	38	39	40	41
British	3	4	5	6	7	8
American	5	6	7	8	9	10

Men's suits

Italian	44	46	48	50	52	54	56	58 (size)
British	34	36	38	40	42	44	46	48 (inches)
American	34	36	38	40	42	44	46	48 (inches)

Men's shirts (collar size)

Italian	36	38	39	41	42	43	44	45 (cms)
British	14	15	15½	16	16½	17	17½	18 (inches)
American	14	15	15½	16	16½	17	17½	18 (inches)

Men's shoes

Italian	39	40	41	42	43	44	45	46
British	6	7	7½	8	9	10	11	12
American	7	7½	8	8½	9½	10½	11	11½

DIRECTORY

Women's High Fashion

Dolce & Gabbana
Via Condotti 51–52.
Map 5 A2.
Tel 06-6992 4999.

Fendi
Largo Goldoni 419.
Map 12 E1.
Tel 06-334 501.

Gente
Via del Babuino 81.
Map 4 F1.
Tel 06-320 7671.
Also: Via Frattina 69.
Map 5 A2.
Tel 06-678 9132.

Giorgio Armani
Via Condotti 77. **Map** 5 A2.
Tel 06-699 1461.

Krizia
Piazza di Spagna 87.
Map 5 A2.
Tel 06-679 3772.

Laura Biagiotti
Via Mario de' Fiori 26.
Map 12 F1.
Tel 06-679 1205.

MaxMara
Via Frattina 28. **Map** 5 A2.
Tel 06-679 3638.

Prada
Via Condotti 88.
Map 5 A2.
Tel 06-679 0897.

Renato Balestra
Via Cola di Rienzo 9–11.
Map 3 C2.
Tel 06-482 1723.

Roberto Cavalli
Via Borgognona 25. **Map** 5
A2. **Tel** 06-6992 5469.

Salvatore Ferragamo
Via Condotti 65.
Map 5 A2.
Tel 06-678 1130.

Soledad Twombly
Via Gregoriana 34.
Map 5 A2.
Tel 06-4565 4157.

Trussardi
V. Frattina 42-43.
Map 5 A2.
Tel 06-6938 0939.

Valentino
Piazza di Spagna 38.
Map 5 A2.
Tel 06-9451 5710.

Versace
Piazza di Spagna 12.
Map 5 A2.
Tel 06-678 0521.

Men's Tailors and Designer Wear

Battistoni
Via Condotti 61A.
Map 5 A2.
Tel 06-697 6111.

Brioni
Via Condotti 21A.
Map 5 A2.
Tel 06-678 3428.

Cerruti
Via Cola di Rienzo 46.
Map 3 C2.
Tel 06-321 6793.

Davide Cenci
Via Campo Marzio 1–7.
Map 4 F3 & 12 D2.
Tel 06-699 0681.

Degli Effetti
Piazza Capranica 79.
Map 4 F3 & 12 D2.
Tel 06-679 1650.

Dolce & Gabbana
Piazza di Spagna 93.
Map 5 A2.
Tel 06-669 1592.

Ermenegildo Zegna
Via Condotti 58.
Map 5 A2.
Tel 06-6994 0678.

Etro
Via del Babuino 102.
Map 5 A2.
Tel 06-678 8257.

Gucci
Via Condotti 8.
Map 5 A2.
Tel 06-679 0405.

Salvatore Ferragamo
See Women's High Fashion.

Trussardi
See Women's High Fashion.

Versace
See Women's High Fashion.

Young Designer Wear

Armani Jeans
Via del Babuino 70A.
Map 4 F1.
Tel 06-3600 1848.

Arsenico 36
Via del Governo
Vecchio 7.
Map 11 B3.
Tel 06-683 3936.

Diesel
Via del Corso 118.
Map 4 F3 & 12 E1.
Tel 06-678 3933.

Emporio Armani
Via del Babuino 140.
Map 4 F1.
Tel 06-322 1581.

Ermanno Scervino
Via del Babuino 97.
Map 5 A2.
Tel 06-679 3173.

Eventi Up
Via dei Serpenti 134.
Map 5 B4.
Tel 06-484 960.

Kokoro
Via del Boschetto 75.
Map 5 B4.
Tel 06-487 0657.

Luna e L'Altra
Piazza Pasquino 76.
Map 4 E4 & 11 C3.
Tel 06-6880 4995.

Maga Morgana
Via del Governo
Vecchio 27.
Map 4 E4 & 11 C3.
Tel 06-687 8095.

Momento
Piazza Benedetto Cairoli 9.
Map 4 F5.
Tel 06-6880 8157.

SBU
Via S. Pantaleo 68.
Map 11 C3.
Tel 06-6880 2547.

Timberland
Via Nazionale 47.
Map 5 C3.
Tel 06-488 1920.

Tru Trussardi
Via Frattina 42.
Map 5 A2.
Tel 06-6938 0939.

High Street Fashion

Benetton
Piazza della Fontana di
Trevi 91–94.
Map 12 F2.
Tel 06-6919 0919.

**Discount dell'Alta
Moda**
Via di Gesù e Maria16A.
Map 4 F2.
Tel 06-322 5006.

Emporio Armani
See Young Designer Wear

List
Via dei Giubbonari 79.
Map 11 C4.
Tel 06-686 9525.

Zara
Via del Corso 189
Map 4 F2.
Tel 06-6979 17210.
Also:
Via del Corso 129–135.
Map 12 E2.
Tel 06-6992 3196.

Knitwear

Laura Biagiotti
See Women's High Fashion.

Liz
Via Appia Nuova 90.
Map 10 D2.
Tel 06-700 3609.

Luisa Spagnoli
Via del Tritone 30.
Map 5 A3–B3 & 12 F1.
Tel 06-6992 2769.
Also:
Via Appia Nuova 63.
Map 10 D2.
Tel 06-7049 3400.

Missoni
Piazza di Spagna 78.
Map 5 A2.
Tel 06-679 3419.

Stefanel
Piazza Venezia 5.
Map 12 F4.
Tel 06-6992 5836.

Lingerie

Brighenti
Via Frattina 7–8.
Map 5 A2.
Tel 06-679 1484.

Cesari
Via Giampaolo della
Chiesa 10.
Off Map 7 A4.
Tel 06-638 1241.

Intimissimi
Via del Corso 203.
Map 4 F2.
Tel 06-6992 4132.

Marisa Padovan
Via delle Carrozze 81–82.
Map 5 A2.
Tel 06-679 3946.

Schostal
Via Fontanella Borghese
29. **Map** 12 D1.
Tel 06-679 1240.

Second-Hand Clothes

Le Gallinelle
Via Panisperna 61.
Map 5 B4.
Tel 06-488 1017.

Sitenne
Via Petrarca 1.
Map 6 E5.
Tel 06-7725 0991.

Tempi Moderni
Via del Governo
Vecchio 108.
Map 4 E4 & 11 B3.
Tel 06-687 7007.

Shoes

Baldinini
Via del Babuino 150.
Map 4 F2.
Tel 06-3601 0347.

Boccanera
Via Luca della Robbia 36.
Map 8 D3.
Tel 06-575 0847.

Borini
Via dei Pettinari 86–87.
Map 4 E5 & 11 C5.
Tel 06-687 5670.

Campanile
Via Frattina 25.
Map 12 E1.
Tel 06-6994 0621.

De Bach
Via del Babuino 123.
Map 4 F1.
Tel 06-678 3384.

Domus
Via Belsiana 52.
Map 4 F2.
Tel 06-678 9083.

Empresa
Largo S. Susanna 102–104.
Map 5 C2.
Tel 06-6930 3284.

Fausto Santini
Via Frattina 120.
Map 5 A2.
Tel 06-678 4114.

Ferragamo
Via Condotti 65.
Map 5 A2.
Tel 06-678 1130.

Fratelli Rossetti
Via Borgognona 5A.
Map 5 A2.
Tel 06-678 2676.

Geox
Via del Corso 443.
Map 4 F2.
Tel 06-6889 2720.

Mr Boots
Via A Brunetti 2.
Map 4 F1.
Tel 06-321 5733.

Silvano Lattanzi
Via Salandra 34.
Map 5 A2.
Tel 06-678 6119.

Tod's
Via Condotti 52–53.
Map 5 A2.
Tel 06-699 1089.

Leather Bags and Accessories

Alviero Martini Prima Classe
Via Frattina 116.
Map 5 A2.
Tel 06-6992 3381.

La Cravatta Su Misura
Via di Santa Cecilia 12.
Map 8 D1.
Tel 06-8901 6941.

Fendi
See Women's High Fashion.

Gucci
Via Borgognona 7D.
Map 5 A2.
Tel 06-6919 0661.
Also: Via Condotti 8.
Map 5 A2.
Tel 06-679 0405.

Ibiz
Via dei Chiavari 39.
Map 11 C4.
Tel 06-6830 7297.

Mandarina Duck
Via Due Macelli 59F/G.
Map 12 F1.
Tel 06-678 6414.

Salvatore Ferragamo
See Women's High Fashion.

La Sella
Via del Lavatore 56.
Map 5 A3 & 12 F2.
Tel 06-679 6654.

Classic Jewellery

Angeletti
Via Condotti 11A.
Map 5 A2.
Tel 06-6994 1207.

Ansuini
Corso Vittorio Emanuele
151. **Map** 4 E4 & 11 C3.
Tel 06-6880 6909.

Bulgari
Via Condotti 10.
Map 5 A2.
Tel 06-696 261.

Massoni
Via Margutta 54A.
Map 4 F1.
Tel 06-321 6916.

Moroni Gioielli
Via Belsiana 32A.
Map 4 F2.
Tel 06-678 0466.

Peroso
Via Sistina 29A.
Map 5 B3.
Tel 06-474 7952.

Tiffany & Co.
Via del Babuino 118.
Map 5 A2.
Tel 06-679 0717.

Costume Jewellery

Danae
Via della Maddalena 40.
Map 12 D2.
Tel 06-679 1881.

Delfina Delettrez
Piazza Euclide 30.
Map 2 D2.
Tel 06-808 6352.

Granuzzo
Via dei Coronari 193.
Map 4 E3 & 11 B2.
Tel 06-6880 1503.

Massimo Maria Melis
Via dell'Orso 57.
Map 4 E3.
Tel 06-686 9188.

Tempi Moderni
Via del Governo
Vecchio 108.
Map 4 E4 & 11 B3.
Tel 06-687 7007.

Traditional Goldsmiths and Silversmiths

Gioie d'Arte
Via de' Gigli d'Oro 10.
Map 4 E3 & 11 C2.
Tel 06-687 7524.

Gloves, Hats and Hosiery

Borsalino
Piazza del Popolo 20.
Map 4 F1.
Tel 06-3265 0838.
Also: Via Sistina 58A.
Map 5 B2.
Tel 06-678 8821.

Calzedonia
Via del Corso 106.
Map 4 F2.
Tel 06-6992 5436.

Catello d'Auria
Via dei Due Macelli 55.
Map 5 A2 & 12 F1.
Tel 06-679 3364.

Di Cori
Piazza di Spagna 53.
Map 5 A2.
Tel 06-678 4439.

Sermoneta
Piazza di Spagna 61.
Map 5 A2.
Tel 06-679 1960.

Settimio Mieli
Via San Claudio 70.
Map 5 A3 & 12 E2.
Tel 06-678 5979.

Interior Design

Italian design belongs to a long-established tradition based on the skills of the master craftsman, and some firms have a history going back hundreds of years. Rome's stylish interior design shops are worth seeking out, even if it is only to look around and enjoy the ambience. You might well pick up some design ideas for your home, or find some interesting or unusual things to buy. They are an excellent place to get souvenirs and presents to take home.

Furniture

Italy is well-known for its stylish, well-made furniture. Although there is no distinct area of Rome that is renowned for its furniture shops, many of the top stores are located to the north of the city centre.

In the heart of the historic centre, on Via della Scrofa, is **Arcon**. This airy outlet is packed with various slick furniture designs, particularly chairs, desks and lighting, though there are some smaller and more affordable household items. Not far from Campo dei Fiori is Nordic **Oggetti & Design**, stocking a handpicked selection of Scandinavian design objects.

Tucked in a side street off Via Giulia, **Sfera** displays a provocative blend of classic and modern well-upholstered chairs and divans matched with more minimalist designs.

For a taste of the renowned Italian design, the **IKONOS**, store in the Parioli neighbourhood showcases architect-designed living spaces and provides perfect examples of sleek Italian style. The large showroom displays well-known icons of design and unique designer furnishings for the home. These include sofas, chairs, tables, lamps and smaller objects, all jumbled together in a fascinating display.

Nearby, on Piazza Cairoli, stands **Confalone**, a furniture shop that specializes in well-upholstered sofas and armchairs, though dining tables and chairs also crowd the display area. The shop's wide range of classical designs suits any interior.

Benedetti, which occupies a line of shops on the Via Marmorata, offers a range of fine modern wood furniture, while **Fattorini**, on Via Arenula, gives a modern Italian take on 1970s retro styling.

Lighting Fixtures

Lighting fixtures are one of the most popular and more easily transportable items, and there are several superb showrooms in Rome that are worth a visit.

Flos is a merger of two design houses whose Roman show-room displays its lights as if they were museum exhibits. The design style is chic and minimalist, with plenty of black and white, chrome and steel.

Nearby **Artemide** is, like Flos, a design house in its own right, and is similarly well known abroad, above all for its classic anglepoise lamps in a variety of colours. Its show-room in Rome is elegant, with expensive, hi-tech lighting design. Best known for its plexiglass creations, **Kartell** has a showroom in Monti, stocking its sleek, colourful lamps, while **Piccola Bottega** is a veritable treasure trove of all kinds of lamps, lighting fixtures and lampshades.

To see examples of light fittings from all of Italy's leading producers, head to **Obor**, where high-tech items are displayed alongside a range of more traditional models.

Italian electrical equipment is designed for 220–240 volts. If you are going to use it in countries with lower voltage always ask the shop whether the product needs a transformer, as this can depend on the model.

Lighting fixtures generally take screw-bulbs, although some designer models can be ordered with fittings for bayonet bulbs.

Kitchens and Bathrooms

It is worth taking a look at the ultra-modern hi-tech kitchen designs in Rome.

For an overview of the latest smart, steel products, visit **Arclinea** for its select display of state-of-the-art kitchens. **IKONOS** offers made-to-measure kitchens that are available to be shipped internationally.

Italian bathroom shops concentrate almost exclusively on modern designs, some of which are luxuriously decadent. **Ravasini** has very decorative floral fixtures with some matching accessories. **Materia** is another bathroom shop that sells all the latest styles.

Tiles

The Italian ceramic tile tradition is an ancient one. A great variety of tiles is displayed in kitchen and bathroom show-rooms, but there are also one or two specialist shops.

Ceramiche Musa specializes in modern tiles incorporating decorative floral and ancient Roman motifs, for those who want to introduce a hint of antiquity into their home.

Glass

Decorative glass objects are a popular buy in Rome. **Murano Più**, just behind Piazza Navona, sells Murano and other glass items at reasonable prices. This shop is one of the few that open on Sundays – which can be useful for visitors on short trips to Rome.

Of slightly larger dimensions are the Murano glass artifacts on display at **La Murrina**. Look out for their modern colourful take on the traditional chandelier theme. **Leone Limentani** in the Jewish quarter sells a range of glass objects with a more traditional flavour.

For a wide selection of more affordable gifts, try **Stilvetro**. It is the ideal place for items such as pasta bowls, glass and ceramics.

An added advantage is that shipment abroad can usually be arranged at any of these glass establishments so you can make your purchase without worrying about transporting it home.

Fabrics

At **Casa del Tessuto** you can find all manner of fabrics, some at bargain discount prices.

If you are looking for further bargains, take a walk round the old Jewish quarter, Il Ghetto, that runs from Largo Argentina down to the Tiber; the area contains numerous fabric shops such as **Paganini**. During sale times *(see p326)*, remnants of fabrics *(scampoli)* are always sold off cheaply, and if you are lucky you could find just the right fabric for just the right price.

Household Goods and Kitchenware

Shops selling household goods abound in Rome. For a selection of lovely sheets and other bed linens head to **Frette**.

If you enjoy designer kitchenware, don't miss **c.u.c.i.n.a.**, which is tucked away in Via Mario de' Fiori. The shop stocks kitchen utensils from all over the world, as well as pots and pans in both rustic and hi-tech styles and countless space-saving kitchen accessories.

Right next to Piazza Venezia, **Sorelle Adamoli** specializes in articles for the table and kitchen, selling every accessory and gadget imaginable.

The Roman pizzeria **'Gusto** *(see p315)* also offers an interesting range of kitchen utensils and essentials in its ground-floor shop.

Finally, there is **Leone Limentani**, whose basement shop in the old Jewish quarter is well stocked with interesting gift ideas. Here, you will find an extraordinary array of household and kitchenware, including silver, china and crystal items.

DIRECTORY

Furniture

Arcon
Via della Scrofa 104.
Map 12 D1.
Tel 06-6833 3728.

Benedetti
Via Marmorata 141.
Map 8 D3.
Tel 06-574 6610.

Confalone
Piazza Cairoli 110.
Map 12 D4.
Tel 06-6880 3684.

Fattorini
Via Arenula 55.
Map 12 D5.
Tel 06-6813 6615.

IKONOS
Via Tagliamento 35.
Tel 06-886 3345.

Nordic
Via del Pellegrino 128.
Map 4 E4.
Tel 06-6476 0312

Sfera Otto
Via delle Carceri 6.
Map 11 B3.
Tel 06-6889 2630.

Lighting Fixtures

Artemide
Via Margutta 107.
Map 4 F1.
Tel 06-3600 1802.

Flos
Via del Babuino 84.
Map 5 A2.
Tel 06-320 7631.

Kartell
Via del Leone 15.
Map 4 F3 & 12 D1.
Tel 06-687 6341.

Obor
Piazza San Lorenzo in Lucina 28.
Map 12 E1.
Tel 06-687 1496.

Piccola Bottega
Via del Leone 9.
Map 12 D1.
Tel 06-687 6401.

Kitchens and Bathrooms

Arclinea
Viale Liegi 46A.
Map 2 F4.
Tel 06-8530 5329.

IKONOS
See Furniture.

Materia
Corso Vittorio Emanuele II 189.
Map 11 C3.
Tel 06-686 1896.

Ravasini
Via di Ripetta 69–71.
Map 4 F2.
Tel 06-322 7096.

Tiles

Ceramiche Musa
Via Campo Marzio 39.
Map 4 F3 & 12 D1.
Tel 06-687 1204.

Glass

Leone Limentani
Via del Portico d'Ottavia 47.
Map 12 E5.
Tel 06-6830 7000.

Murano Più
Corso Rinascimento 43–45.
Map 4 E3 & 11 C3.
Tel 06-6880 8038.

La Murrina
Piazza di Porta S. Paolo 10–11.
Map 8 E4.
Tel 06-574 4936.

Stilvetro
Via Frattina 56.
Map 5 A2.
Tel 06-679 0258.

Fabrics

Casa del Tessuto
Via dello Statuto 64–66.
Map 6 D4.
Tel 06-487 2813.

Paganini
Via Aracoeli 23.
Map 4 F5 & 12 E4.
Tel 06-678 6831.

Household Goods and Kitchenware

c.u.c.i.n.a.
Via Mario de' Fiori 65.
Map 5 A2.
Tel 06-679 1275.
Via di Parione 21.
Map 4 E4 & 11 C3.
Tel 06-324 3723.

Frette
Piazza di Spagna 11.
Map 5 A2.
Tel 06-679 0673.

'Gusto
Piazza Augusto Imperatore 9.
Map 4 F2.
Tel 06-323 6363.

Leone Limentani
See Glass.

Sorelle Adamoli
Via del Plebiscito 103.
Map 12 E3.
Tel 06-679 4208.

Books and Gifts

Rome offers huge scope for gift buying, both in the well-established tourist stores in the *centro storico* (historic centre) and smaller shops in less frequented parts of the city. Seeking out the smaller shops can be an adventure in itself, as many are in attractive parts of the city that you might not otherwise visit.

Unusual artisan ceramics, wonderful books on Italian art and architecture, paper products, vintage Italian film posters, beautiful prints of historic views of Rome and specialist sweets and cakes make ideal souvenirs to take home. While masterpieces by Michelangelo, Raphael and Caravaggio are popular icons for t-shirts, statuettes and postcards, religious souvenirs are also readily available in the city that hosts the papal seat.

Bookshops

Rome is rich in bookshops, from the encyclopaedic to the very specialized. Italian books, both hardback and softback, are generally very attractive but also tend to be expensive.

As Italy's largest and most renowned bookshop chain, **Feltrinelli** dedicates its endless shelf space to both modern and classic Italian literature, and also houses a wide selection of non-fiction titles. **Feltrinelli International** in Via Emanuele Orlando has an excellent range of foreign-language fiction and specialist non-fiction, covering various subjects including art, cookery, travel and history. It also stocks some superb photographic, art and cinema posters. Magazines and stationery are available as well and the notice-board is a lifeline for information on rooms for rent and Italian language courses.

Specialist English bookstores include the **Anglo-American Book Co.**, which is located near Piazza di Spagna. In Trastevere, the **Almost Corner Bookshop**, though small, has probably the most extensive selection of English language fiction in the capital, as well as non-fiction titles – from ancient Rome to modern Italian culture and politics.

Libreria Arion, near Piazza Cavour, has a small English section, as well as interesting gadgets and design objects.

Another Arion branch inside Palazzo delle Esposizioni specializes in art, design and architecture, and has been listed among the 20 most beautiful bookstores in the world. **IBS** boasts two floors of books (also in English), DVDs and computer games. For prospective chefs, fantastic recipe books on Italian and international cuisine can be found at **'Gusto** *(see p343)* in Piazza Augusto Imperatore.

As an alternative to traditional bookstores, there are lots of cut-price deals at the second-hand book stalls in Via delle Terme di Diocleziano and in Largo della Fontanella di Borghese.

Multimedia and Music

The split-level **Feltrinelli** in Galleria Alberto Sordi on Via del Corso and its sister store in Largo Argentina, represent the closest Rome gets to a multimedia mega-store. At both these stores, in addition to their stock of fiction and non-fiction titles, there is a reasonable selection of CDs and DVDs that covers mainstream tastes.

Stationery and Paper Crafts

Near the Pantheon, the Florentine **Il Papiro** sells a great range of illustrious paper-based products that include notebooks, diaries, envelopes and beautiful seal and wax sets that make for an ideal gift. Visit **Cartolerie Internazionali** for a wealth of pretty notebooks, writing instruments, and school supplies. **Pineider**, stationery suppliers to the Roman gentry, will print sets of exquisite visiting cards for you. The more modern **Vertecchi** is filled with original paper gifts, including boxes of every shape and size, while **Fabriano** has its own fabulous line of stationery and notebooks.

Posters and Prints

Near Piazza Navona, **L'Image** has an extensive range of artistic, photographic and film posters on sale, as well as a decent range of stationery, souvenirs and calendars. Geared more towards antiques, **Galleria Trincia** sells good quality and reasonably priced prints of 17th-century panoramic paintings of Rome, as well as watercolours. It also undertakes restoration work.

For superb posters on past exhibitions as well as stylish souvenirs and postcards, visit Rome's museum shops, for example **Il Chiostro del Bramante** near Piazza Navona, or **Complesso del Vittoriano** next to the Forum.

Artisan Handicrafts and Design

The central Via del Pellegrino is a street crammed with small specialist outlets such as **Le Tre Ghinee**, which sells ceramics and glass objects. **La Chiave** is a good choice for gifts, selling all things ethnic with the emphasis on bright furnishings and original jewellery.

If you are more interested in contemporary design, visit the **Palazzo delle Esposizioni** *(see p166)* where a wide range of objects by famous designers is available. For a really original gift, try **Bottega del Marmoraro**, a workshop that reproduces ancient Roman and Pompeian inscriptions on marble. The owner will recreate any design you choose to order.

Souvenirs and Religious Artifacts

Most of the tobacconists in central Rome sell postcards, stamps and a variety of souvenirs. Cheap and sometimes appealingly kitsch souvenirs are also found at the mobile stalls around the major tourist attractions.

Bookshops near the main basilicas, such as **Libreria Belardetti**, sell souvenirs and religious mementos. Other shops specialize in religious articles for both the clergy and the layperson. Facing the Vatican gates in Via di Porta Angelica there are several shops, such as **Al Pellegrino Cattolico**, selling artifacts to visiting pilgrims.

Sweets and Biscuits

In addition to the several bars and cafés that sell cakes and biscuits to take away (da portare via), there are a number of specialist stores in Rome well worth taking the time out to visit.

Near Piazza Navona in the centre, **La Deliziosa**, though small, offers a great range of classic Italian desserts and cakes; the ricotta-based variety deserves a special mention. In the Galleria Esedra, near Piazza della Repubblica, **Dagnino** is renowned throughout the city as one of the best places for sugary Sicilian delicacies, such as cannoli and cassate.

For a wonderful range of fresh and appetizing Italian biscuits to suit all occasions and every whim, head for **Cipriani** (see p322) in Esquilino near Termini station or **Innocenti**, a historic pasticceria famed for its elaborate biscotti of the highest quality, prepared with varied ingredients including almonds, pine kernels and honey. Innocenti is situated in Trastevere, across the Tiber from the centro storico. Right next to the Circus Maximus, the renowned café **San Teo** (previously Cristalli di Zucchero) in Via San Teodoro has a wide range of marvellous mini-pastries.

DIRECTORY

Bookshops

Almost Corner Bookshop
Via del Moro 45.
Map 7 C1.
Tel 06-583 6942.

Anglo-American Book Co.
Via della Vite 102.
Map 12 E1.
Tel 06-679 5222.

Emporio Libreria 'Gusto
Piazza Augusto Imperatore 7.
Map 4 F2.
Tel 06-323 6363.

Feltrinelli
Largo di Torre Argentina 5A.
Map 4 F4.
Tel 199 151 173.
Also: Galleria Alberto Sordi 31–35. **Map** 12 E2.
Tel 199 151 173.
W lafeltrinelli.it

Feltrinelli International
Via E. Orlando 84–86.
Map 5 C3.
Tel 06-482 7878.

IBS
Via Nazionale 254–255.
Map 5 C3.
Tel 06-488 5405.

Libreria Arion
Via Giovanni Pierluigi da Palestrina 1. **Map** 4 E2.
Tel 06-3260 9923.

Also: Palazzo delle Esposizioni, Via Milano 15–17. **Map** 5 C4.
Tel 06-4891 3361.

Multimedia and Music

Feltrinelli
See Bookshops.

Stationery and Paper Crafts

Cartolerie Internazionali
Via Arenula 85.
Map 4 F5.
Tel 06-6880 1050.

Fabriano
Via del Babuino 173.
Map 4 F2.
Tel 06-3260 0361.

Il Papiro
Via del Pantheon 50 (leading to Via Degli Orfani).
Map 12 D2.
Tel 06-679 5597.

Pineider
Via dei Due Macelli 68.
Map 12 F1.
Tel 06-679 5884.

Vertecchi
Via della Croce 70.
Map 4 F2.
Tel 06-332 2821.

Posters and Prints

Il Chiostro del Bramante
Via della Pace 5. **Map** 11 C2. **Tel** 06-6880 9035.

Complesso del Vittoriano
Via San Pietro In Carcere.
Map 5 A5.
Tel 06-678 0664.

Galleria Trincia
Via Laurina 12. **Map** 4 F1.
Tel 06-361 2322.

L'Image
Via della Scrofa 67. **Map** 12 D2. **Tel** 06-686 4050.

Artisan Handicrafts and Design

Bottega del Marmoraro
Via Margutta 53B. **Map** 5 A2. **Tel** 06-320 7660.

La Chiave
Largo delle Stimmate 28.
Map 12 D4.
Tel 06-6830 8848.

Palazzo delle Esposizioni
Via Milano 15–17. **Map** 5 B4. **Tel** 06-3996 7500.

Le Tre Ghinee
Via del Pellegrino 90.
Map 11 B3.
Tel 06-687 2739.

Souvenirs and Religious Artifacts

Al Pellegrino Cattolico
Via di Porta Angelica 83.
Map 3 C2.
Tel 06-6880 2351.

Libreria Belardetti
Via della Conciliazione 4A.
Map 3 C3.
Tel 06-686 5502.

Sweets and Biscuits

Cipriani
Via C. Botta 21.
Map 6 D5.
Tel 06-7045 3930.

Dagnino
Galleria Esedra, Via Vittorio Emanuele Orlando 75.
Map 5 C2.
Tel 06-481 8660.

La Deliziosa
Vicolo Savelli 50.
Map 11 B3.
Tel 06-6880 3155.

Innocenti
Via della Luce 21A.
Map 7 C2.
Tel 06-580 3926.

San Teo
Via di San Teodoro 81.
Map 8 E1.
Tel 06-6992 0945.

Art and Antiques

Rome's art and antique shops range from exclusive establishments to contemporary art galleries. In response to a fashion for collecting early 20th-century artifacts, new dealers and galleries are springing up throughout Rome – Venini's Murano glass is popular, as are lighting and furniture. Many more sell general bric-a-brac and jewellery. Copies of antique prints can be picked up for a fraction of the original's price. Rome is not good for antique bargains, but it is worth looking in shops along Via dei Cappellari and Via del Pellegrino or going to the Porta Portese Sunday market *(see p345)*.

Antiques and Old Master Paintings

There are antique shops dotted all over the centre of Rome, though the cream of the crop tend to be concentrated in distinct areas. Discreet haggling in the shops is accepted practice, but even if you get a reduction in price, make sure the dealer provides you with the relevant export documents.

The famous Via del Babuino, and to a lesser extent Via Margutta, which is better known for its art galleries, are home to around 30 of Rome's grandest showrooms for antique furniture, Old Master paintings and *objets d'art*. **Paolo Antonacci** sells a wide range of beautiful objects, from furniture to works of art. The 19th century pencil and ink drawings are exquisite. If you cannot get hold of an original, **Maurizio Grossi** on nearby Via Margutta sells fine reproduction ancient Roman busts and obelisks. On the same street is **Goffi Carboni**, more Asian in outlook, with Chinese and Japanese ceramics and prints alongside its 17th- to 19th-century European art collection.

Cesare Lampronti is owned by the top dealer of that name. Aided and complemented by his partner Carlo Peruzzi, he sells 16th- to 18th-century European paintings, with an emphasis on Roman and Italian works in general.

Alberto Di Castro, situated in Piazza di Spagna, is a fourth-generation dealer specializing in statues, paintings and other precious objects from the medieval to the Neo-Classical periods. Nearby, **M Simotti-Rocchi** stocks Greek and Roman statuary, as well as more luggage-friendly coins and figurines.

Via Giulia *(see p155)* has many high-quality antique shops to choose from. Definitely worth a visit is **Antiquariato Valligiano**. This is the only place in Rome where you can find 19th-century Italian country furniture, a rustic antidote for those overpowered by the grandiose Baroque.

Via Monserrato, running parallel, is worth scouring for slightly lower-quality pieces at more attainable prices. An exception to this rule is **Alessio Ponte**, specializing in 19th-century Italian paintings and sculpture.

Via dei Coronari is largely devoted to antiques, with over 20 shops lining both sides of the street. Quality is very high – as are the prices. It is a good place for Baroque and Empire elaborate inlaid vases, secretaries and consoles. **Antiqua Domus** is a treasure trove of antique Italian furniture. Pieces dating from ancient Rome through to the 19th century are on sale. **Bruschini Tanca** sells a variety of objects including micro-mosaic pieces and antique paintings, while **Hutong** specializes in art and antiques from China, Vietnam and Myanmar, stocking furniture, statues and *objets d'art*. **Galleria dei Coronari** has a superb collection of tapestries, clocks, paintings and statuary, as well as watches.

Slightly further away is Via della Stelletta, which is home to a handful of unusual and fascinating shops. **Arte Antica Rufini** is an antique dealer selling an eclectic mix of furniture, paintings, jewellery, prints and *objets d'art*.

Bilenchi is yet another specialist, this time in exquisite, early 20th-century lamps.

Another relatively undiscovered area is the one around Via del Boschetto and Via Panisperna. Shops around here tend to specialize in early 20th-century artifacts, with some English Victorian pieces thrown in.

Of course there are many perennial favourites apart from these streets. The best way to discover them is through word of mouth or just by chance as you stroll along. **Antichità Carnovale** is a shop full of interesting 19th- and 20th-century canvases, while **Agostini** is one of the oldest antique shops in Rome, and definitely one of the largest. It offers an impressive collection of European antiques.

Definitely worth a visit if you have a taste for mid-20th-century modern furniture and objects is **Attik**, a stone's throw from the MAXXI gallery *(see p261)* in the north of the city. Ceramics and glass ornaments from the 1950s to the 1970s cover tables and sideboards from similar periods. The shop also has an eclectic range of lamps and lighting fixtures.

Modern Art

Rome is rich in avant-garde galleries exhibiting paintings by recognized Modern Masters through to the up-and-coming generation of young, mainly Italian, artists.

Rome's art galleries are usually open 10am–1pm and 5–8pm Tue–Sat. Some open only in the afternoon; others are also open on Monday afternoon. The best times to visit are afternoons and early evenings.

As with Rome's antique shops, the art galleries tend to be concentrated in a couple of distinct areas. The largest of these covers the triangular area between Via del Babuino and Via di Ripetta and adjoining streets, known locally as the Trident (*Il Tridente*). Via Margutta is also home to several prestigious private galleries.

The **Galleria Valentina Moncada** exhibits contemporary Italian and international art and also showcases 20th-century photography, while **Archeologia Monogramma Arte Contemporanea** deals with promising young artists from Italy and abroad. One of this area's highlights is the Via Margutta art fair (*see p345*), which usually takes place around Christmas and in springtime.

Not far from Piazza Navona, **Z20 Sara Zanin** has a busy exhibition programme presenting international contemporary artists.

Via Giulia and its surroundings is the next area to investigate. Fabio Sargentini at **L'Attico** follows the latest trends in Italian art from Del Giudice to Corsini and Fabiani.

Another innovative venture in the centre is **Galleria Bonomo** (owned by Alessandra Bonomo), which spotlights Italian and foreign painters such as Schifano, Boetti, Twombly, Nunzio, Tremlett, LeWitt and Dokoupil. Nearby, but stepping back a few decades in time, Italian art of the 1920s and 1930s is celebrated at the **Galleria del Laocoonte**. Artists such as Sironi, Funi and Gaudenzi are showcased alongside many others of the so-called Roman School.

Just across from Largo Argentina, the **Galleria Lorcan O'Neill** showcases contemporary Italian and international art. Past exhibitions have included works by Tracey Emin, Martin Creed, Sam Taylor-Johnson, Jeff Wall, Richard Long and Rachel Whiteread. This is definitely an exhibition space to watch.

Antique Prints and Photographs

In a large showroom over in the Via Veneto area, **Eufemi** sells artistic prints from the 16th to the 20th centuries, with themes ranging from geographic maps and landscapes to flowers, hunting scenes, religious art and scientific prints.

Another Roman institution, **Casali**, has been trading for over 100 years. The family now runs two shops specializing in 16th- to 19th-century drawings and engravings of Roman scenes ranging from museum-standard Piranesi down to relatively inexpensive unknown and delightfully decorative floral scenes.

Another place definitely worth heading for in search of that perfect print of old Rome and some enjoyable, relaxing and maybe persuasive browsing is the Mercato delle Stampe (*see p344*).

DIRECTORY

Antiques and Old Master Paintings

Antiqua Domus
Via dei Coronari 41.
Map 4 E3 & 11 B2.
Tel 06-686 1186.

Agostini
Piazza Borghese 1. **Map** 12 D1. **Tel** 06-687 3632.

Alberto Di Castro
Piazza di Spagna 5. **Map** 5 A2. **Tel** 06-679 2269.

Alessio Ponte
Via Monserrato 8. **Map** 11 B4. **Tel** 06-687 1425.

Antichità Carnovale
Via del Governo Vecchio 71. **Map** 11 C3.
Tel 06-686 4850.

Antiquariato Valligiano
Via Giulia 193. **Map** 4 E5 & 11 B5. **Tel** 06-686 9505.

Arte Antica Rufini
Via dei Coronari 79.
Map 4 D3 & 11 B2.
Tel 06-686 5046.

Attik
Via Tiepolo 4B. **Map** 1 B3. **Tel** 06-9761 1053.

Bilenchi
Via della Stelletta 17.
Map 4 F3 & 12 D2.
Tel 06-687 5222.

Bruschini Tanca
Via Arco della Pace 16.
Map 11 C2.
Tel 06-687 5634.

Cesare Lampronti
Via di San Giacomo 22.
Map 4 F2.
Tel 06-321 8624.

Galleria dei Coronari
Via dei Coronari 59.
Map 4 E3 & 11 B2.
Tel 06-686 9252.

Goffi Carboni
Via Margutta 109A.
Map 5 A2. **Tel** 06-322 7184.

Hutong
Via dei Coronari 55. **Map** 11 C2. **Tel** 06-323 3145.

M Simotti-Rocchi
Largo Fontanella Borghese 76. **Map** 12 D1. **Tel** 06-687 6656.

Maurizio Grossi
Via Margutta 109.
Map 5 A2.
Tel 06-3600 1935.

Paolo Antonacci
Via del Babuino 141A.
Map 4 F2.
Tel 06-3265 1679.

Modern Art

Archeologia Monogramma Arte Contemporanea
Via Margutta 102.
Map 5 A2.
Tel 06-3265 0297.

L'Attico
Via del Paradiso 41.
Map 4 E4 & 11 C4.
Tel 06-686 9846.

Galleria Bonomo
Via del Gesù 62. **Map** 12 E3. **Tel** 06-6992 5858.

Galleria del Laocoonte
Via Monterone 13.
Map 12 D3.
Tel Tel 06-6830 8994.

Galleria Lorcan O'Neill
Vicolo dei Catinari 3.
Map 4 D4.
Tel 06-6889 2980.

Galleria Valentina Moncada
Via Margutta 54. **Map** 5 A2. **Tel** 06-320 7956.

Z20 Sara Zanin
Via della Vetrina 21.
Map 11 B2.
Tel 06-7045 2261.

Antique Prints and Photographs

Casali
Piazza della Rotonda 81A/82. **Map** 4 F4 & 12 D3. **Tel** 06-678 3515.
Also: Via dei Coronari 115.
Map 11 B2.
Tel 06-687 3705.

Eufemi
Via Francesco Crispi 93.
Map 5 B2.
Tel 06-3105 9717.

Food and Drink

Having sampled the local cuisine during your stay in Rome, you may be tempted to take home some irresistible delicacies that are typical of Italy. The traditional Italian food stores, *alimentari*, offer an extensive range of goods and are a great place to start. However, specialist shops are also well worth a visit. Shop around and choose from many typically Italian products such as pecorino romano cheese, Parma ham, extra-virgin olive oil, dried porcini mushrooms, sun-dried tomatoes, olives and grappa as well as superb wines from Lazio and elsewhere. If coffee or chocolate feature on your list, then there is plenty of opportunity to satisfy those cravings too.

Do bear in mind, however, that customs restrictions can apply to certain foodstuffs. Also, when on your shopping sprees, a decent pocket-sized dictionary can be very useful in helping you decipher the labels.

Alimentari

The well-stocked **Fratelli Fabbi**, near Piazza di Spagna, has an exceptional selection of delicious cold meats and cheeses from every corner of Italy, as well as carefully chosen quality wines and sparkling wines to accompany them. A few doors down Via della Croce, **Focacci** is a stiff competitor with its wonderful array of Italian delicacies, while nearby **Cambi** caters to its loyal clientele with similarly first-rate fare.

Elsewhere in the centre, near Campo de' Fiori, **Roscioli**, with a reputation for quality and friendly service, is a favourite among locals. In the Campo itself is the **Antica Norcineria Viola**, which is the place to go for an excellent range of sausages and salami.

Further afield, **Franchi** *(see p321)* in Prati is recognized as one of the best delicatessens in the capital for its tempting window display of seafood platters, pâtés, regional cheeses and cold meats that continue to pull in the crowds. The historic but expensive **Volpetti** in Testaccio is synonymous with great service and uncompromising quality. Aside from specializing in unusual cheeses, olive oils, vinegars and a fabulous selection of food hampers it also stocks a variety of Italian lard and caviar – you can even try before you buy. Tiny **Antonaci** prepares

delicious sandwiches made with quality cheeses and preserves, though those who favour organic produce may prefer to head for **Canestro**.

In the vicinity of Via Veneto is **Carlo Gargani**, with its elaborate variety of food items.

A saviour for commuters and tourists is **Vyta** *(see p321)* located inside Termini station; you can choose from a selection of appetizing sandwiches or wines by the glass *(alla mescita)* and enjoy them at the bar. An excellent weekend farmers' market, **Campagna Amica** (closed Aug) is tucked away behind the church of Santa Maria in Cosmedin and is well worth visiting for its stalls of organic, locally produced food and wine.

Rome's most impressive temple of food is next to the Ostiense station: **Eataly** offers four floors of eateries and excellent-quality Italian products – a dizzying experience for any gourmet.

Cheese Specialists

For the ultimate cheese lover, a wider choice of regional and national cheeses, including the best buffalo mozzarella in town, can be found in a select number of specialist shops. In the Pinciano district, the **Casa dei Latticini Micocci** sells a wide range of cheeses from even the most remote regions of Italy. In Trastevere, the family-run store

Antica Caciara Trasteverina also has a vast choice of local and regional products, including sheep's ricotta and the Piemontese *toma del fen*. In the Jewish quarter, **Beppe e I Suoi Formaggi** sells a wide selection of French and Italian cheeses.

Chocolate Specialists

The capital boasts a number of specialist shops designed to fulfil the needs of the ever-expanding luxury food market. In Santa Croce, **La Bottega del Cioccolato** is known for its creativity – try their chocolate Colosseums. Elsewhere, close to the Pantheon, the landmark **Moriondo e Gariglio** has been in operation since 1850, serving up strictly Piedmontese treats. Neapolitan chocolate makers **Gay Odin** sell fine chocolates and have a great selection of pralines made in house, as well as a great chocolate liqueur. In San Lorenzo, **Said**, housed in a 1920s chocolate factory, has a café and shop selling home-made delicacies. **Rivendita Libri Cioccolata e Vino** *(see p322)* is also recommended.

Enoteche

Although most *alimentari* and supermarkets stock a decent selection of reasonably priced Italian wines, Rome's many *enoteche (see p320)* represent a more characteristic alternative. As well as being wine bars and sometimes even restaurants, they also sell carefully selected wines, after-dinner liqueurs, spirits and beers to take away.

In the pretty Celio district, **Bibenda Wineconcept** is a minimalist wine bar created by the Italian sommelier association and serves a hand-picked selection of the finest Italian wine labels, accompanied by tapas-like food. **Il Goccetto** *(see p320)* near Campo de' Fiori, while maintaining its status as an institution for bohemian drinkers, also successfully doubles up as a well-stocked and competitively priced wine shop.

Better known for its Neapolitan pizza parlour, chic restaurant

---

and lively wine bar, 'Gusto (see p320) offers an outstanding assortment of wines for sale too. Don't pass by the shop either, as it is full of designer kitchen accessories and specialist cookbooks with recipes for both Italian and international cuisine.

The central **Achilli Enoteca al Parlamento** (see p320) and **Angolo Divino** both warrant a visit for a refined alternative, especially if you want to relax with an apéritif while you select wines to carry home. **Ferrazza** in San Lorenzo and **Il Vinaietto** near Campo de' Fiori also deserve special mentions for their extensive wine lists and memorable ambience.

In Trastevere, the well-stocked off-licence **Bernabei** is good value for money as is the family-run **Trimani** (see p320) near Termini, which has an astounding variety of wines and spirits.

Others that should not be overlooked include the **Costantini** in Piazza Cavour, the beer-oriented **Ferrara** in Trastevere and **Marchetti** in Pinciano, which is the wine experts' not so closely guarded secret.

Coffee Specialists

Italian brand coffee has been internationally available for many years but if you are looking for something rarer or more exotic then make your way to **Antico Caffè del Brasile** (see p322) in Monti for four mouth-watering blends, from Brazilian gem (the 90 per cent pure variety) to economy and family mixes. In the shadow of the Pantheon, the historic **Tazza d'Oro** (see p106) also offers a fantastic selection of blends, including the Queen of Coffees and Jamaican Blue Mountain.

DIRECTORY

Alimentari

Antica Norcineria Viola
Campo de' Fiori 43.
Map 11 C4.
Tel 06-6880 6114.

Cambi
Via del Leoncino 30.
Map 12 D1.
Tel 06-687 8081.

Campagna Amica
Via di San Teodoro 74.
Map 8 E1. Tel 06-489 931.

Canestro
Via Luca della Robbia 12.
Map 8 D2.
Tel 06-574 6287.

Carlo Gargani
Via Lombardia 15. Map 5 B2. Tel 06-474 0865.

Da Francesco
Via del Boccaccio 17.
Map 5 B3.
Tel 06-488 2529.

Eataly
Piazzale XII Ottobre 1492.
Map 8 F5.
Tel 06-9027 9201.

Focacci
Via della Croce 43.
Map 4 F2.
Tel 06-679 1228.

Franchi
Via Cola di Rienzo 200.
Map 3 C2.
Tel 06-687 4651.

Fratelli Fabbi
Via della Croce 28.
Map 4 F2.
Tel 06-679 0612.

Roscioli
Via dei Giubbonari 21.
Map 11 C4.
Tel 06-687 5287.

Volpetti
Via Marmorata 47.
Map 8 D2.
Tel 06-574 2352.

Vyta
Galleria Termini
(Termini Station).
Map 6 D3.
Tel 06-4201 4301.

Cheese Specialists

Antica Caciara Trasteverina
Via San Francesco a Ripa 140a/b. Map 7 C1.
Tel 06-581 2815.

Beppe e I Suoi Formaggi
Via di Santa Maria del Pianto 9A. Map 12 D5.
Tel 06-6819 2210.

Casa dei Latticini Micocci
Via Collina 14–16.
Map 6 D2.
Tel 06-474 1784.

Chocolate Specialists

La Bottega del Cioccolato
Via Leonina 82. Map 5 C5.
Tel 06-482 1473.

Gay Odin
Via Antonio Stoppani 9.
Map 2 E3.
Tel 06-8069 3023.

Moriondo e Gariglio
Via del Piè di Marmo 21.
Map 12 E3.
Tel 06-699 0856.

Rivendita Libri Cioccolata e Vino
Vicolo del Cinque 11A.
Map 11 B5.
Tel 06-5830 1868.

Said
Via Tiburtina 135.
Map 6 F4.
Tel 06-446 9204.

Enoteche

Achilli Enoteca al Parlamento
Via dei Prefetti 15.
Map 12 D1.
Tel 06-687 3446.

Angolo Divino
Via dei Balestrari 12–14.
Map 11 C4.
Tel 06-686 4413.

Bernabei
Via San Francesco a Ripa 48.
Map 7 C1.
Tel 06-581-2818.

Bibenda Wineconcept
Via Capo d'Africa 21.
Map 12 E1.
Tel 06-7720 6673.

Costantini
Piazza Cavour 16.
Map 11 B1.
Tel 06-321 3210.

Ferrara
Piazza Trilussa 41.
Map 4 E5.
Tel 06-580 3769.

Ferrazza
Via dei Volsci 59.
Map 6 F4.
Tel 06-490 506.

Il Goccetto
Via dei Banchi Vecchi 14.
Map 11 B3.
Tel 06-686 4268.

'Gusto
Piazza Augusto Imperatore 9.
Map 4 F2.
Tel 06-322 6273.

Palombi
Piazza Testaccio 38/41.
Map 8 D3.
Tel 06-574 6122.

Trimani
Via Goito 20.
Map 6 D2.
Tel 06-446 9661.

Il Vinaietto
Via Monte della Farina 38.
Map 12 D4.
Tel 06-6880 6989.

Coffee Specialists

Antico Caffè del Brasile
Via dei Serpenti 23.
Map 5 B4.
Tel 06-488 2319.

Tazza d'Oro
Via degli Orfani 84.
Map 12 D4.
Tel 06-678 9792.

Street Markets

Rome's open-air markets are essential to visit if you are interested in soaking up the bustling atmosphere of Italian market-life. The markets can be incredibly colourful and vivid, as Italian stallholders have raised the display of even the humblest vegetable to an art form.

The city is dotted with popular, small local food markets, and there are several fascinating well-established markets near the centre, along with the famous flea market over in Trastevere.

It is important to keep your wits about you in markets because pickpockets work with lightning speed in the bustling crowds. But this said, Roman markets provide a vibrant source of entertainment and it would be a shame to let such caveats deter you from joining in.

The street fairs that take place throughout the year are fun to go to, if they coincide with your visit, as they normally sell a good variety of local produce, handicrafts and clothes. Seasonal fairs also occur, especially around Christmas, when you can stock up on Italian specialities.

Campo de' Fiori

Piazza Campo de' Fiori. **Map** 4 E4 & 11 C4. 🚌 40, 46, 62, 64, 70, 81, 116, 492, 628. 🚋 8. **Open** 7am–1:30pm Mon–Sat. *See p148.*

Right in the heart of the old city, Rome's most picturesque market is also its most historical. Its name, Campo de' Fiori, which translates as field of flowers, sometimes misleads people into expecting a flower market. In fact the name is said to derive from Campus Florae (Flora's square) – Flora being the lover of the great Roman general Pompey. A market has actually been held in this beautiful piazza for many centuries. Every morning, except Sunday, the piazza is transformed by an array of stalls selling fruit and vegetables, meat, poultry and fish. One or two stalls specialize in pulses, rice, dried fruit and nuts and there are also flower stalls situated near the fountain. But the huge open baskets of broccoli and spinach, chopped vegetables and freshly prepared green salad mixes are the main attraction for visitors. They provide a real visual display as well as an edible feast.

The excellent delicatessen shops on the square, and bread shops nearby, complement the market. They make it a great place to stock up for an impromptu picnic if the weather turns out fine and you are tempted to do some al fresco dining in one of Rome's many parks. The market gets extremely busy on Saturdays, so be prepared to fight your way through the crowds.

Mercato delle Stampe

Largo della Fontanella di Borghese. **Map** 4 F3 & 12 D1. 🚌 81, 116, 117, 492, 628. **Open** 7am–1pm Mon–Sat.

This market is a veritable haven for lovers of old prints, books (both genuine antiquarian and less-exalted second-hand), magazines and other printed ephemera. The quality varies, but it is a good deal more specialized than the *banche* or stalls near Termini station which are a more obvious tourist trap. Italian-speaking collectors can enjoy a field day leafing through back issues of specialist magazines. Other visitors might prefer the wonderful selection of illustrated art books and old prints of Rome. It is a good place to pick up that Piranesi print of your favourite Roman vista, ruin or church – but be prepared to bargain hard.

Mercato dei Fiori

Via Trionfale. **Map** 3 B1. 🇲 Ottaviano S. Pietro. 🚌 23, 51, 70, 490. **Open** 10:30am–1pm Tue.

Essentially a trade market, the Flower Market, just north of Via Andrea Doria, is open to the public only on Tuesdays. Housed in a covered hall, it has two floors brimming with cut flowers upstairs and all kinds of pot plants on the lower floor. Anyone who has an interest in flowers will enjoy this wonderful array of Mediterranean blooms, which are on sale at giveaway prices.

Mercato Andrea Doria

Via Andrea Doria. **Map** 3 B1. 🇲 Ottaviano S. Pietro. 🚌 23, 70, 490. **Open** 7am–1:30pm Mon–Sat.

The market used to stretch the whole length of this wide avenue. It has now been transferred to a modern, covered state-of-the-art building. Apart from the magnificent displays of fruit and vegetables, it has numerous stalls selling meat, poultry, fish and groceries, as well as an interesting clothes and shoe section. Situated northwest of the Vatican Museums, it is a little off the normal beaten track and has remained very much a Roman market that caters for the needs of the large local population.

Nuovo Mercato Esquilino

Via Principe Amedeo. **Map** 6 E5. 🇲 Vittorio Emanuele. 🚌 105. **Open** 7am–2pm Mon–Sat. *See p176.*

In the past, bustling Piazza Vittorio was perhaps the most Roman of the city's larger markets.

Rechristened and housed in covered premises, it is still the place where bargain-hunting *popolari*, Rome's bustling shoppers, buy their food. Stallholders offer cheap prices if you buy by the kilo, but watch out for bad fruit.

This is also one of the city's more international markets and features African and Asian food stalls that cater to the area's diverse groups. Definitely a place to go if you want to capture the atmosphere of a traditional but changing city.

Mercato di Testaccio

Between Via A. Volta and Via Galvani. **Map** 8 D3. 🇲 Piramide. 🚌 23, 75, 280. 🚋 3. **Open** 7:30am–1:30pm Mon–Sat.

Filled with stalls selling fresh produce of every kind, the local market for this most Roman of areas is a theatre-set of seductive colours and textures. Uniquely, it also houses the Roman remains found on the site during the construction of the present building; appropriately enough, archaeologists reckon that the ruins testify to a market that stood here in ancient times. Popular with local residents, who insist on high-quality produce at reasonable prices, the market also appeals to visitors for its cafés and relaxed and friendly atmosphere.

Porta Portese
Via Portuense & Via Ippolito Nievo.
Map 7 C3. ⬛ H, 23, 44, 75.
🚋 3, 8. **Open** 6:30am–2pm Sun.

The *mercato delle pulci* or flea market is a relatively new market in Roman terms. Established shortly after the end of World War II, it is said to have grown out of the thriving black market that operated at Tor di Nona opposite Castel Sant'Angelo during those lean years. Stallholders come from as far away as Naples and set up shop in the early hours of the morning – if you are strolling in that direction after a late night in Trastevere, it is well worth pausing just to watch them.

Anything and everything seems to be for sale, piled high on stalls in carefully arranged disorder – clothes, shoes, bags, luggage, camping equipment, linen, towels, pots, pans, kitchen utensils, plants, pets, spare parts, old cassettes, CDs, LPs and even 78s.

Furniture stalls tend to be concentrated around Piazza Ippolito Nievo along with what they call "antiques", though you may have to sort through an awful lot of junk before finding a real one. And then you will have to bargain for it. The technique is to offer them half the asked price and then walk away. A lot of people go just for the fun of it and always end up buying something.

There are also second-hand clothes – leather or sheepskin coats and jackets go for €20 – with many of the Via Sannio stall-holders relocating here for the Sunday trade. In recent years Porta Portese has become much frequented by customers belonging to the various immigrant groups in the capital. If you have a Sunday morning to spare, a visit to the market is now one of the most cosmopolitan experiences that the city offers.

Mercato di Via Sannio
Via Sannio. **Map** 9 C2. Ⓜ San Giovanni.
⬛ 16, 81, 87. **Open** 8am–1pm Mon–Fri, 8am–6pm Sat.

In the 1960s and 1970s this used to be Italy's answer to Carnaby Street. Today, at first glance, it seems not to have anything very special to offer – random stalls selling inexpensive casual clothes, shoes,

bags, belts, jewellery, toys and kitchen utensils. But towards the end of the street there is a large covered section which extends back to the Aurelian Wall (*see p198*) with many stalls piled high with second-hand clothes at very low prices for those who like to rummage.

There is also a section that sells military-style goods plus some camping and fishing equipment.

Some of these stalls move their wares to Porta Portese on a Sunday morning.

Local Markets
Generally **Open** 7am–1pm Mon–Sat.

Piazza delle Coppelle (**Map** 4 F3 & 12 D2), near the Pantheon, is probably the most picturesque of the food markets sprinkled around the city. A tiny market devoted to food and fruit and flowers, it offers a charming splash of colour in the heart of the city.

Piazza San Cosimato (**Map** 7 C1) in Trastevere hosts another lively local market with some tempting cheeses and salami.

There is a fairly big market on **Via Alessandria** (**Map** 6 D1) in Nomentana, and other smaller ones in **Via della Pace** (**Map** 4 E4 & 11 C3) near Piazza Navona, and in **Via Balbo** (**Map** 5 C4) and **Via Milazzo** (**Map** 6 E3) near Termini station.

All markets usually have at least one stall selling household goods and basic Italian kitchen gadgets.

Street Fairs

A special and interesting feature of shopping in Rome is the street fair.

Neglected and under-exploited for most of the year, the lower banks of the Tiber come into their own in summer during the mid-June–early September **Lungo il Tevere** festival. This takes place daily from 6pm until after midnight on the stretch of river between Ponte Palatino and Ponte Sisto. Stalls sell a wide variety of goods – from regional produce and ethnic bric-a-brac, to books and confectionery. You can also take a break at one of the many bars and eateries lining the route.

There are various open-air antiques markets held in the city throughout the year. One of the most central and best known is **La Soffitta sotto i Portici** (The Attic beneath the Porticoes), which is held 8am–7pm every other Sunday (except August) along the eastern edge of Piazza Augusto Imperatore. Professional and weekend sellers run stalls offering antique (or simply retro) furniture, lamps, jewellery and *objets d'art*.

The **Via Margutta Art Fair** usually takes place around Christmas and in springtime. Set in one of the most charming and exclusive streets of the city, this is an event not to be missed, although it is more for browsing as prices are very high.

The utterly glamorous **Alta Roma Fashion Show** is a must for fashionistas though tickets to the various events are often by invitation only. However, the public can squeeze in to some events to enjoy this display of all-Italian designer fashion. So far it has been held mid to late July.

The traditional **Christmas Fair** held in Piazza Navona from mid-December until 6 January is now rather down-at-heel, but still fascinating for those who have not seen it before or for children. Stalls selling clay statues for nativity scenes and sweets that look like pieces of coal are the main attraction.

Natale Oggi is a well-established event taking place near Christmas at the Fiera di Roma in the Portuense district, and worth visiting to have a look at the Italian Christmas treats.

Via Giulia hosts art fairs now and then, and open evenings when the antique and art galleries stay open late offering food and wine to all visitors.

Every year Trastevere hosts its very own carnival, the **Festa de Noantri**, in late July, when Viale Trastevere is overrun with the typical *porchetta* stalls (*see p347*), party lights, gift stalls and people.

The details given here may change, so check the local listings, the tourist office or ring the tourist call centre (*see p369*).

ENTERTAINMENT IN ROME

There is a particular excitement attached to Roman entertainment. Football and opera, for example, are both worth experiencing for sheer atmosphere alone, whether or not you are a fan. The jazz scene is especially good with international stars appearing alongside local talent. And concerts and films take on an added dimension when performances take place beneath the stars in the many open-air arenas spread across the city. Unexpectedly, given the general shutdown among shops and restaurants, the summer remains Rome's liveliest time for live music and other cultural events. Rome's graceful Renaissance squares, vast parks, villa gardens, Classical ruins and other open spaces host various major arts festivals. For those who prefer sport, or want to try out some Roman nightclubs, there is plenty on offer too.

Saxophonist at Planet Roma *(see p350)*

Practical Information

A good source of information about what's on is *TrovaRoma*, the weekly Thursday supplement to *La Repubblica* newspaper. It has a day-by-day rundown of what's on and where, and covers music, exhibitions, theatre, cinemas, guided tours, restaurants and children's entertainment. Daily newspapers like *Il Messaggero*, *Il Manifesto* and *La Repubblica* usually list that evening's entertainment, but only in Italian.

The magazine *Wanted in Rome*, found at Via Veneto newsagents or English bookshops, provides less detailed listings in English, while the monthly *Where Rome*, available from reception desks of four-and five-star hotels, is a good source of information and up-to-date listings. Also worth getting hold of is *L'Evento*, a free booklet that is available from tourist information offices around the city *(see p369)*. Published every two months, it gives details in English of classical music, festivals, theatre, exhibitions and more in the city and surroundings. Up-to-date information can also be found on various websites.

Punctuality is not what Italians are renowned for, so don't be surprised if events start later than advertised.

Booking Tickets

Booking in advance is not part of Italian lifestyle, though this is slowly changing. Two ticket agencies that will book tickets for some performances for you (for a small fee) are **Orbis** and the Internet-based **TicketOne**. Rome's **Tourist Info Line** also helps visitors book tickets for various events. Many theatres themselves do not accept telephone bookings – you have to visit the box office in person. They will charge you a *prevendita* supplement (about 10 per cent of the normal price) for any tickets sold in advance. The price of a theatre ticket can be anything between €8 and €52.

Tickets for classical concerts are usually sold on the spot, and are sometimes for that night only, an arrangement that

favours the last-minute decision to go. Opera is the exception. Tickets are sold months in advance, with just a few held back until two

Many restaurants and bars have live music

days before the performance. It is usually easier (and also a bit cheaper) to get tickets for the open-air summer performances.

The Teatro dell'Opera box office *(see p349)* handles face-to-face and online sales for both summer and winter seasons.

Tickets for most big rock and jazz events can be bought at Orbis and at large book and music shops such as the Torre Argentina branch of **Feltrinelli**.

If you are trying to get hold of a ticket for a performance that has already sold out, you are unlikely to be able to obtain one from unofficial sources – there are very few ticket touts in Rome, except at major football matches, such as finals.

Member of contemporary dance group Momix *(see p349)*

Reduced-Price Tickets

Theatres and concert venues tend not to offer discounts directly, although there is a centralized service (**Last Minute Teatro**) offering up to 50 per cent off seats on the day of the performance (closed Jun–Aug).

Cinemas occasionally offer people aged over 60 and disabled people a 30 per cent reduction on weekdays. Many cinemas also have cheaper ticket prices for weekday afternoon screenings and for all shows on Wednesdays.

Some clubs offer reductions: look out for *due per uno* coupons in local bars that allow two people entrance for the price of one.

Facilities for the Disabled

Few Roman venues provide easy access for people with restricted mobility, and any disabled visitors and their companions are likely to find the lack of provision for them very frustrating.

The situation does improve a little in summer, however, when a great many performances in the city are held at open-air venues. The classical concerts held in the beautiful gardens of Villa Giulia *(see pp264–5)* have wheelchair access.

For more general information on provision for disabled people visiting Rome, see pages 368–9.

Open-Air Entertainment

Open-air opera, cinema and concerts fill the calendar from late June until the end of

Summer night outdoor performance among Roman ruins

September. These outdoor performances can be wonderful, with spectacular settings and enthusiastic audiences. Some of them are grand affairs, but smaller events may be just as evocative – a recital in the grounds of the Theatre of Marcellus *(see p153)*, for example, or jazz in the gardens of Villa Celimontana *(see p195)*.

Singers performing the *Barber of Seville*

Some cinemas roll back their roofs in summer for open-air screenings, or else move to outdoor arenas, and there are also annual open-air cinema festivals. The Cineporto along the Tiber and the Festival di Massenzio offer films, food and small exhibitions in July and August.

Theatre also moves outside in summer. Greek and Roman plays are staged at Ostia Antica *(see p272)* and other shows take place at the Anfiteatro Quercia del Tasso *(see p353)*.

The Basilica of Constantine and Maxentius in the Forum *(see p88)* hosts the Festa della Letteratura (mid-May–mid-Jun), with major international writers reading from their works. Hadrian's Villa *(see p271)* is the equally stunning setting for the Villa Adriana Festival of music and modern dance (Jun–Jul). Consult listings in newspapers, magazines or websites *(see p346)* or watch for posters around the city for the most

up-to-date information. More traditional is Trastevere's community festival, Festa de' Noantri with music, fireworks and processions. This festival begins on the Saturday after 16 July but celebrations continue into August. The Festa dell'Unità, run by the DS (the former Communist Party), but not limited to politics, is generally held in summer. The programme includes games, stalls, food and drink.

Finally, if you like your entertainment less structured, do as the Romans do and take part in the *passeggiata* (early evening stroll) – the city's favourite spots are Piazza Navona *(see p122)* and along Via del Corso.

DIRECTORY

Ticket Agencies

Feltrinelli
Largo Argentina 11. **Map** 12 D4.
Tel 06-9436 4767. Music concerts and some sporting events.

Last Minute Teatro
Piazza Fiume (at Arion bookshop in underpass). **Map** 6 D1.
Tel 06-4411 7799. **Open** 2–8pm Tue–Sat, 2–4pm Sun.

Orbis
Piazza dell'Esquilino 37.
Map 6 D4. **Tel** 06-482 7403.

Tourist Info Line
Tel 06-0608.

Useful Websites

W listicket.com
W ticketone.it
W turismoroma.it
W vivaticket.it

The Teatro dell'Opera *(see p348)*

Classical Music and Dance

Classical concerts take place in a surprisingly high number of venues; tickets for opera premieres may be hard to get, but soloists, groups or orchestras playing in gardens, churches, villas or ancient ruins are more accessible. World-renowned soloists and orchestras make appearances all year round; past visitors have included Luciano Pavarotti and Placido Domingo, the Berlin Philharmonic and prima ballerina Sylvie Guillem.

Programmes are generally international in scope but sometimes you will find a festival dedicated to one of Italy's own, like Palestrina, the great 16th-century master of polyphonic church music, or Arcangelo Corelli, inventor of the Baroque *concerto grosso*.

Music in Churches

One of Rome's main attractions for classical music is the rich repertoire in the city's churches. Always sacred in theme (by decree of Pope John Paul II), music is mainly performed as concerts rather than during services.

Programmes are posted around the city and outside the churches. You will often find very good musicians playing in the main churches, while the smaller, out-of-the-way churches frequently have young musicians and amateur choirs as well.

St Peter's (see pp228-9) hosts one major RAI (national broadcasting company) concert on 5 December attended by the Pope and free for the general public. It has two established choirs. The Coro della Cappella Giulia sings at the 10:30am mass and 5pm vespers on Sunday. The Coro della Cappella Sistina sing whenever the Pope celebrates mass here, as on 29 June (St Peter and St Paul's Day).

Important choral masses also take place on 25 January in San Paolo fuori le Mura (see p269), when the Pope attends, on 24 June in San Giovanni in Laterano (pp182-3) and on 31 December at the Gesù (see pp110-11) where the *Te Deum* is sung. The church of Sant'Ignazio di Loyola (see p108) is another favourite venue for choral concerts.

Plainsong and Gregorian chant can be heard in **Sant' Anselmo** every Sunday (Oct–Jul) at the 8:30am mass and 7:15pm vespers.

Easter and the Christmas festivities are a great time for atmospheric concerts.

Orchestral, Chamber and Choral Music

Up until the opening of the Renzo Piano-designed **Parco della Musica** on the Via Flaminia in 2002, with its three auditoriums and open-air arena, the **Auditorium Conciliazione** and the **Teatro dell'Opera** had been Rome's two main auditoriums. All venues have their own resident orchestras and choirs and offer varied seasons that include visiting groups and soloists from all over the world. Rome's own Orchestra e Coro dell'Accademia di Santa Cecilia performs at the Parco della Musica throughout the year.

The season at the **Teatro Olimpico** usually offers good chamber music, some orchestral concerts and ballet with at least one concert a week.

Although a variety of classical concerts take place at the **Accademia Filarmonica Romana**, the emphasis is on chamber and choral music, with an internationally renowned series of concerts running from mid-October to mid-May. Performances take place in the Sala Casella, which seats around 180.

Ticket prices for classical concerts depend a lot on performers and venue. The Foro Italico sells tickets for most concerts for under €15; a ticket for the **Teatro Olimpico** costs between €15–€25, but seats for a prestigious concert at **Teatro dell'Opera** may cost more than €80.

The Associazione Musicale Romana, dedicated to Renaissance and Baroque music, organizes three annual festivals in the Palazzo della Cancelleria (see p151): the Festival Internazionale di Cembalo (harpsichord festival) in March; Musica al Palazzo in May; and the Festival Internazionale di Organo in September. Classical music fans should also watch out for performances by the Orchestra di Roma e del Lazio at Teatro Argentina (see p353).

It is always worth checking which musicians are due to be playing at the **Teatro Ghione**, the **Oratorio del Gonfalone** and especially the **Aula Magna dell'Università La Sapienza**, which has one of the most innovative programmes of classical and contemporary music.

Open-Air Summer Concerts

In the summer music lovers can enjoy concerts in cloisters, palazzo courtyards and ancient ruins. Concerts can be one-offs or part of a festival programme, regular fixtures or impromptu. Do as the Romans do, wait until the last moment and keep an eye on the posters and listings pages (see p346).

Open-air opera and dance have their summer home in the Baths of Caracalla (see p199), which provide a splendid backdrop to performances. Classical concerts are often part of festivals like RomaEuropa (see p349) but there are also open-air festivals and concert series dedicated to classical music. Among the more interesting are those that take place in some of the city's historic churches. It is well worth checking out the summer programmes for Sant'Ivo alla Sapienza (see p124) and San Clemente (see pp188–9).

The Associazione Musicale Romana organizes Serenate in Chiostro – a lively and varied programme of concerts during July in the cloisters of Santa Maria della Pace (see p123) with tickets at reasonable prices. The Concerti del Tempietto are a real summer treat with concerts held almost every evening from July to September in the Area Archeologica del Teatro di Marcello (see p153) or in the park of the Villa Torlonia.

Festival Villa Pamphilj in Musica, in July, is a series of concerts in the gardens of Villa Doria Pamphilj (see p269). Programmes range from comic opera to jazz and 20th-century classical music.

Brass bands can be heard in the Pincio Gardens (see p138) on Sunday mornings from the end of April until mid-July – they usually strike up at around 10:30am.

Contemporary Music

The Parco della Musica and the Accademia Filarmonica Romana (usually at the **Teatro Olimpico**) often include contemporary pieces in their programmes but these are less popular than the classical pieces and there is no set venue with a regular contemporary programme.

International names appear on festival programmes and at one-off concerts at the **Aula Magna dell'Università La Sapienza**. The most interesting contemporary music festival is organized by the Nuova Consonanza in the autumn, while electronic and digital music is showcased at the Dissonanze festival, which is generally held in May. Also worth keeping an eye out for are performances by scholars of the French Academy at Villa Medici (see p137).

Opera

Italy and opera are to many people synonymous. Critics will tell you (justifiably) that Rome's opera is not up to the standard of Milan's La Scala or Naples's San Carlo. But that doesn't mean it is not worth visiting – world-class singers do appear here, mainly in premières or solo recitals. However you judge the quality of the performances, the surroundings in which they take place are often incomparable. In summer the visual spectacle of Aida, say, performed in the open air, is quite magnificent.

The season starts late at **Teatro dell'Opera**, between November and January. In recent years programmes have concentrated on the great popular operas, rather than staging experimental productions. Tickets range from €17 to €130.

The Teatro dell'Opera moves outdoors in July and August to stage opera and ballet in the ancient Baths of Caracalla (see p199). Popular works by Verdi and Puccini are performed, and although the acoustics are not perfect, the unique setting makes up for it.

Ballet and Dance

Opportunities to watch ballet or contemporary dance can be limited in Rome. The opera house's resident company Corpo di Ballo del Teatro dell'Opera di Roma performs the great classics as well as Roland Petit-style ballet choreographies. Performances are staged at **Teatro dell'Opera**.

Contemporary dance is best seen during the Parco della Musica's Equilibrio Festival in February or at summer festivals, but foreign companies also perform at **Teatro Olimpico**. American modern dance groups of the Moses Pendleton school – Pilobolus, Momix, ISO and Daniel Ezralow – are popular visitors. **Teatro Vascello** is another venue noted for its experimental dance performances.

In autumn, top visiting companies from all over the world perform during the **RomaEuropa Festival**.

DIRECTORY

For information about festivals and open-air concerts, see Trovaroma or similar listings (see pp346 & 367).

Orchestral, Chamber and Choral Music

Accademia Filarmonica Romana
Via Flaminia 118. **Map** 1 A1. **Tel** 06-320 1752.
W filarmonicaromana.org

Auditorium Conciliazione
Via della Conciliazione 4. **Map** 3 C3. **Tel** 06-684 391.
W auditorium conciliazione.it

Aula Magna dell'Università La Sapienza
Piazzale Aldo Moro 5. **Tel** 06-361 0051.
W concertiiuc.it

Oratorio del Gonfalone
Via del Gonfalone 32A. **Map** 4 D4 & 11 A3. **Tel** 06-687 5952.
W oratoriogonfalone. com

Parco della Musica
Viale de Coubertin 30. **Map** 1 C2. **Tel** 06-8024 1281 (for information); **Tel** 892 982 (for credit card sales).
W auditorium.com

Sant'Anselmo
Piazza Cavalieri di Malta 3. **Map** 8 D2. **Tel** 06-579 11.

Teatro Ghione
Via delle Fornaci 37. **Map** 3 B4. **Tel** 06-637 2294.
W teatroghione.it

Teatro Olimpico
Piazza Gentile da Fabriano 17. **Tel** 06-326 5991.
W teatroolimpico.it

Opera

Teatro dell'Opera
Piazza Beniamino Gigli 1. **Map** 5 C3. **Tel** 06-481 601.
W operaroma.it

Ballet & Dance

RomaEuropa Festival
Via dei Magazzini Generali 20A. **Tel** 06-4555 3050.
W romaeuropa.net

Teatro Olimpico
Piazza Gentile da Fabriano 17. **Tel** 06-326 5991.
W teatroolimpico.it

Teatro dell'Opera
Piazza Beniamino Gigli 1. **Map** 5 C3. **Tel** 06-481 7003. W operaroma.it

Teatro Vascello
Via G Carini 78. **Map** 7 A2. **Tel** 06-588 1021.
W teatrovascello.it

Rock, Jazz, Folk and World Music

Rome's non-classical music scene is unpredictable and subject to vast seasonal changes, but there is a huge variety of music to be enjoyed at the many clubs and stadiums, with visiting foreign and home-grown stars. Summer months bring excellent open-air rock, jazz and world music festivals.

The music sections of the listing magazines *TrovaRoma* (see p346) gives a good idea of what's on, and ticket agencies at Orbis and Feltrinelli *(see p347)* will have details of the latest tours. For smaller venues you might need to buy a *tessera* (monthly or annual membership card) costing anything from €2 to €11, which often includes the entrance fee for smaller bands.

Rock Music

Big-name rock concerts are held in sports venues at the **Palalottomatica** and the legendary **Stadio Olimpico**, though it is also a good idea to keep an eye on who is performing at the **Atlantico**. The *centro sociale* **CSOA Ex Snia Viscosa**, on the edge of the Pigneto district, is an alternative space that puts on concerts and other events, while the **Parco della Musica** also hosts top acts. Entrance can cost above €25, but there are plenty of opportunities for smaller pockets. If you are in Rome for 1 May, join the crowds at the massive open-air concert which is usually held at Piazza San Giovanni. Bands also play for free during the European Festival of Music celebrations on and around 21 June. For all mega-concerts it is always a good idea to turn up an hour or so before the act gets under way to be sure of a good place.

Not far from the Vatican, **Fonclea** and **The Place** are also worth checking out.

One of the city's most interesting venues is **Forte Prenestino**, a former prison taken over by squatters and turned into a social centre with a characteristically alternative feel. It now hosts rock concerts, debates and art exhibitions. Meanwhile, **Locanda Atlantide**, with its low entrance fee and central location, is a place where many up-and-coming Roman bands and soloists cut their teeth. **Init** is also worth checking out, as is **ConTestaccio**, whose live evenings focus on emerging talent.

Discos often double as live music venues too, so check to see if there are any mid-week surprises at the **Piper Club** or weekend concerts at the more alternative **Brancaleone**, a nightclub and arts venue where films, theatre, performance and visual arts also feature on the programme.

Jazz

Rome's taste for jazz has developed over the years as a result of visits from American and other foreign musicians. Miles Davis played one of his last concerts here and other jazz gurus such as Pat Metheny, Michael Brecker, Sonny Rollins and Joe Zawinul's Syndicate were all frequent visitors. On no account should aficionados miss a visit to the excellent **Casa del Jazz**. Top musicians also play at **Alexanderplatz** and Trastevere's **Big Mama** club, one of the city's legendary addresses for important names. For over 30 years it has been offering punters everything from trad r'n'b to progressive jazz and rock. It is also worth checking out what's on at **Gregory's**, **Boogie Club** and Be Bop jazz and blues club. **Planet Roma** is unique in offering separate concert halls and interesting festivals featuring high-quality ensembles. Other-wise check local listings to see what's on at **28 Divino Jazz** or **Caruso – Café de Orient**. Some of Rome's smaller venues, like **Charity Cafè**, also showcase formidable new talent.

If you want to mix music with your meal, then try **'Gusto**, a slick pizzeria / restaurant in the city centre with live jazz performances on most nights. If Creole cuisine is more to your taste, then book a table in advance at Alexanderplatz.

Local names to look out for include pianist Antonio Salis, who mingles jazz and Caribbean rhythms, and respected soul-singer Fulvio Tomaino. Other leading lights on the blues scene are Roberto Gatto and Maurizio Gianmarco, frequent visitors at Big Mama.

The Roman summer abounds with jazz. Check out who's performing in the gardens of the Casa del Jazz or catch one of the bigger acts out at the **Ippodromo delle Cappanelle** race track. Another important fixture is the yearly Autumn Roma Jazz Festival with big names from the Italian and international jazz scene visiting the **Parco della Musica**.

Folk Music

Since the sad demise of Rome's historic Folkstudio, there is no single venue for folk *aficionados* in the city, though those prepared to scour the listings may uncover a country evening at **Four Green Fields**.

Traditional Roman folk music has been more or less reduced to tourist-diluted serenades at outdoor restaurants; besides, young locals tend to favour the folk music of other regions and countries. Many bands from various parts of Italy, such as Mau Mau and Agricantus, have found success by drawing on regional rhythms and singing in dialect. Italians' love of all things Irish also means that strains of the fiddle and drum can be heard in many of the Irish pubs dotted throughout the city. If you have to choose one, then make it the Guinness-enriched **Fiddler's Elbow** near Santa Maria Maggiore.

World Music

As the capital of a Latin country which has strong links with other Mediterranean cultures, Rome is a city where world music flourishes. Whether you are looking for South American salsa, African rhythms or Arab cadences, you are unlikely to be disappointed.

Latin American music is no passing fad, as the well-established festivals, dance-schools and sell-out tours by the likes of Brazilian mega-star Caetano Veloso testify. Many venues offer opportunities to enjoy Latin American music throughout the year. **Arriba Arriba** serves up a choice menu of strictly spicy Latin rhythms. Check too what's on at **Caruso – Café de Oriente** in Testaccio, where you can enjoy a cocktail or two along with the predominantly Cuban music.

But it is summer when Latin American music really comes into its own. The two-month Fiesta festival at the **Ippodromo delle Capannelle** has become by far the most popular feature of the long list of Roman summer events, clocking up in excess of one million ticket sales.

If your tastes are more eclectic, there's also the excellent Roma Incontra Il Mondo. This summer festival of world music takes place at **Villa Ada**, a large park north of the city centre, from mid-June to early August. Fans gather each evening to appreciate the talents of names like Angelique Kidjo, hip-hop legend Afrika Bambaataa and South African pianist Abdullah Ibrahim. These concerts are always democratically priced makes their appeal to the young (and not-so-young) even greater.

World music is served up at the **Palladium**, which hosts regular concerts. For a rather more eclectic experience, head to the Piramide district's **Caffé Letterario**, a library, literary café and restaurant that hosts book readings and conferences on various themes, as well as tango nights and concerts.

DIRECTORY

28 Divino Jazz
Via Mirandola 21.
Map 10 F2.
Tel 340 824 9718.

Alexanderplatz
Via Ostia 9.
Map 3 B1.
Tel 06-8377 5604.

Arriba Arriba
Via Celsa 6.
Map 12 E4.
Tel 06-678 0501.

Atlantico
Viale dell'Oceano
Atlantico 271D, EUR.
Tel 06-591 5727.

Be Bop
Via Giulietti 14.
Map 8 E4.
Tel 345 717 9871.

Big Mama
Vicolo San Francesco a Ripa 18.
Map 7 C2.
Tel 06-581 2551.

Boogie Club
Via Gaetano Astolfi 63–65 (southeast of Stazione Trastevere).
Tel 06-6066 4283.

Brancaleone
Via Levanna 13 (in Monte Sacro). **Tel** 06-8200 4382.

Caffé Letterario
Via Ostiense 95.
Map 8 E4.
Tel 06-5730 2842.

Caruso – Café de Orient
Via di Monte Testaccio 36.
Map 8 D4.
Tel 06-574 5019.

Casa del Jazz
Viale di Porta Ardeatina 55.
Map 9 A4.
Tel 06-704 731
W casajazz.it

Charity Cafè
Via Panisperna 68.
Map 5 C4.
Tel 06-4782 5881.

ConTestaccio
Via di Monte Testaccio 65b. **Map** 8 D4.
Tel 06-5728 9712.

CSOA Ex Snia Viscosa
Via Prenestina 173.
Tel 06-2780 0816.

Fiddler's Elbow
Via dell'Olmata 43.
Map 6 D4.
Tel 06-487 2110.

Fonclea
Via Crescenzio 82A.
Map 3 C2.
Tel 06-689 6302.

Forte Prenestino
Via F. Delpino (east of city, along Via Prenestina).
Tel 06-2180 7855.

Four Green Fields
Via Morin 38.
Map 3 B1.
Tel 06-372 5091.

Gregory's
Via Gregoriana 54D.
Map 5 A2.
Tel 06-679 6386
or 327 826 3770.

'Gusto
Via della Frezza 23.
Map 4 F2.
Tel 06-322 6273.

Init
Via della Stazione
Tuscolana 133.
Map 10 F3.
Tel 06-3107 4253.

Ippodromo delle Capannelle
Via Appia Nuova 1245 (km 12). **Tel** 06-718 2139 or 06-5422 0870 (Roma Rock).

Locanda Atlantide
Via dei Lucani 22B (San Lorenzo district).
Tel 06-9604 5875.

Palalottomatica
Piazzale dello Sport, EUR.
Tel 06-540 901.

Palladium
Piazza B. Romano 8 (to the south of Stazione Ostiense).
Tel 06-5733 2772.

Parco della Musica
Viale de Coubertin 15.
Map 1 C2.
Tel 06-8024 1281.
W auditorium.com

Piper Club
Via Tagliamento 9 (north of the city centre)
Tel 06-855 5398
W piperclub.it

Planet Roma
Via del Commercio 36–38. **Map** 8 D5.
Tel 06-574 7826.

Stadio Olimpico
Viale dei Gladiatori (north-west of city centre, across the Tiber by Monte Mario).

Villa Ada
Via Salaria 197 (north of the city centre).
Tel 06-4173 4712.
W villaada.org

Cinema and Theatre

Cinema-going is very popular in Rome. The excellent Casa del Cinema and high profile International Festival of Cinema reflect the city's enduring love of the big screen.

The great majority of Roman cinemas are *prima visione* (first run) and show the latest international films in dubbed versions. The smaller art cinemas are more likely to show subtitled versions of foreign films.

Theatre productions are performed in Italian whether the plays are national classics or by foreign playwrights. The main theatres offer a selection by great Italian playwrights. There are also performances of traditional cabaret, avant-garde theatre and dance theatre. Theatre tickets cost between €8 and €50 and can be booked in advance by visiting the theatre box office, or through the last-minute booking service *(see p346)*.

Prima Visione

There are over 80 *prima visione* cinemas in the city. The best cinemas for decor and comfort are the **Fiamma** (two screens) and **Roma** (three screens).

Foreign films are usually dubbed. Films in the original language are shown at the **Nuovo Olimpia** (daily) and occasionally at the **Greenwich**.

Tickets for new films cost around €7, but a few cinemas listed as *prima visione* charge less, namely **Farnese** and **Reale**. Over 60s and disabled people are normally entitled to a 30 per cent reduction on weekdays. Tickets are reduced in many cinemas on weekday afternoons and on Wednesdays. Check the newspaper or listings such as *TrovaRoma* for details *(see p346)*.

Art Cinemas

True film buffs flock to Rome in October for the International Festival of Cinema (www. romacinemafest.it) with events centring on the **Parco della Musica**.

There are two main types of art cinema in Rome: the *cine-clubs* and the *cinema d'essai*. Both are good if you're interested in catching older classics and new foreign films as well as films by contemporary Italian directors.

The *d'essai* cinemas now and then show films in the original language (indicated by *v.o.* for *versione originale* in the listings). Try the **Azzurro Scipioni** (one of the few to be open throughout summer), **Filmstudio** or Nanni Moretti's **Nuovo Sacher**. Some of the smaller cinemas are called *cine-clubs* and require membership.

The **Palazzo delle Esposizioni** shows interesting series of international films, but head for the **Casa del Cinema** for the real art-house experience.

Cartoons and children's favourites are shown at **Dei Piccoli**, in the leafy surrounds of the Villa Borghese.

English-Language Films

In addition to occasional undubbed showings of British, American and Australasian films in art cinemas and at the **Nuovo Olimpia** and **The Space Cinema Moderno**, the excellent **Casa del Cinema** has a policy of screening all films in their original language.

Summer Cinema

Some Roman cinemas have roll-back s which are in use during the summer, while the others close down. The **Nuovo Sacher** has an outdoor arena. Rome also has various summer cinema festivals, the most central being L'Isola del Cinema on the Tiber Island. Several themed films are screened each night from 9pm until the small hours, with food and drinks on sale and often live music during the intervals.

The Venezia a Roma event in September gives film buffs the chance to see movies from the summer Venice Film Festival.

The listings pages *(see p346)* have details on retrospectives and avant-garde film seasons at the **Azzurro Scipioni** and the open-air arts festivals like RomaEuropa *(see p349)* and Festa dell'Unità *(see p347)*. Finally, aficionados of Italian cinema should consider taking the **Cinecittà Shows Off** tour at the famous studios. This is the chance to see where block-busters such as *Cleopatra* and *Gangs of New York* were made and perhaps sense the spirit of Federico Fellini (tours are in English at 11:30am and 4pm from Wed–Mon).

Mainstream Theatre

The backbone of Rome's theatrical repertoire are Luigi Pirandello's dramas and comedies by 18th-century Venetian Carlo Goldoni, 20th-century Neapolitan Eduardo de Filippo and Nobel Prize winner Dario Fo. Major foreign playwrights are also performed from time to time.

The best classic productions are staged at the **Teatro Argentina**, **Teatro Quirino**, **Teatro Eliseo** and **Teatro Piccolo Eliseo**. Teatro Argentina is state-owned and home of Rome's permanent theatre company. Its sister theatre, **Teatro India**, stages more innovative works. The historic **Teatro Ambra Jovinelli**, near Termini station, is the best place to go for comedy acts. Plays at the Quirino often feature famous Italian actors. The Eliseo and Piccolo Eliseo are among the city's best private theatres.

At **Teatro Sistina** and **Teatro Brancaccio** you can see hit musicals by visiting foreign companies and shows by popular Italian actors, while **Teatro Vittoria** goes in for plays by Noël Coward or Neil Simon.

Contemporary Theatre

Contemporary theatre is performed at the ever-dynamic **Teatro Vascello**, the **Teatro** dell'Orologio and in a host of small theatres in cellars, garages, apartments or even tents.

The **Palladium** and the Vascello tend to stage works by contemporary authors and occasional avant-garde productions. Some of them, like **Teatro India** and Orologio, also put on foreign-language productions.

Folk, Cabaret and Puppet Theatre

Roman and Neapolitan folk songs and cabaret can be enjoyed in Trastevere's tourist-trade restaurants, like **Meo Patacca**, while La. Vi. (see p357) offers more sophisticated evenings.

Puppet theatre is another Roman tradition. Shows take place early in the evening at weekends, and sometimes during the week, at **Teatro Verde** and **Teatro Mongiovino**. In the Villa Borghese, the **Teatro San Carlino** also presents plays with the younger audience in mind.

Open-Air Theatre

The open-air summer theatre season usually features Greek and Roman plays at **Ostia Antica** (see pp272–3) and at Rome's own **Globe Theatre** in Villa Borghese.

The **Anfiteatro Quercia del Tasso** on the Janiculum stages

comedy shows from July to September. In winter the company performs at the **Teatro Anfitrione**.

Nearby is a street puppet theatre booth. Shows are usually in the afternoons, with morning shows on Sundays.

English Theatre

The **English Theatre of Rome** brings English-language productions to the Teatro Arciliuto, while the **Miracle Players** perform comic adaptations of classics in various historical locations including the Roman Forum in summer.

DIRECTORY

Prima Visione

Farnese
Piazza Campo de' Fiori 56.
Map 4 E5. **Tel** 06-686 4395.

Fiamma
Via Bissolati 47. **Map** 5 C2.
Tel 06-8880 1284.

Greenwich
Via Bodoni 59. **Map** 7 C3.
Tel 06-574 5825.

Nuovo Olimpia
Via in Lucina 16. **Map** 12
E1. **Tel** 06-8880 1283.

Reale
Piazza Sonnino 7.
Map 7 C1. **Tel** 06-5810 234.

Roma
Piazza Barberini 24. **Map** 5
B3. **Tel** 06-8639 1361.

The Space Cinema Moderno
Piazza della Repubblica 45.
Map 5 C3. **Tel** 892 111.

Art Cinemas

Azzurro Scipioni
Via degli Scipioni 82.
Map 3 C2.
Tel 06-3973 7161.

Casa del Cinema
Largo M. Mastroianni 1.
Map 5 B1. **Tel** 06-423 601.
W casadelcinema.it

Dei Piccoli
Viale della Pineta 15.
Map 5 B1. **Tel** 06-855 3485.

Filmstudio
Via degli Orti d'Alibert 1C.
Map 4 D4.
Tel 06-4543 9775.

Nuovo Sacher
Largo Ascianghi 1. **Map** 7
C2. **Tel** 06-581 8116.

Palazzo delle Esposizioni
Via Nazionale 194. **Map** 5
B4. **Tel** 06-3996 7500.
W palazzoesposizioni.it

Parco della Musica
Viale de Coubertin 30.
Map 1 C2.
Tel 06-8024 1281.
W romacinemafest.it

Studio Tours

Cinecittà Shows Off
Via Tuscolana 1055.
Tel 06-722 931.
W cinecitta studios.it

Mainstream Theatre

Teatro Ambra Jovinelli
Piazza G. Pepe 43. **Map** 6
E4. **Tel** 06-8308 2884.

Teatro Argentina
Largo Argentina 52. **Map**
4 F4. **Tel** 06-684 0001.
W teatrodiroma.net

Teatro Brancaccio
Via Merulana 244. **Map** 6
D5. **Tel** 06-8068 7231.
W teatrobrancaccio.it

Teatro Eliseo
Via Nazionale 183. **Map** 5
B4. **Tel** 06-488 721.
W teatroeliseo.it

Teatro India
Lungotevere Vittorio
Gassman 1. **Map** 7 C5.
Tel 06-684 0001.

Teatro Piccolo Eliseo
Via Nazionale 183. **Map** 5
B4. **Tel** 06-488 2114.

Teatro Quirino
Via delle Vergini 7.
Map 5 A4 & 12 F2.
Tel 06-679 4585.
W teatroquirino.it

Teatro Sistina
Via Sistina 129. **Map** 5 B2.
Tel 06-420 0711.

Teatro Vittoria
Piazza S. Maria Liberatrice
8. **Map** 8 D3.
Tel 06-574 0598.

Contemporary Theatre

Palladium
Piazza B. Romano 8 (south
of Stazione Ostiense).
Tel 06-5733 2768.

Teatro dell'Orologio
Via dei Filippini 17A. **Map**
11 B3. **Tel** 06-687 5550.
W teatroorologio.com

Teatro Vascello
Via G. Carini 72. **Map** 7 A2.
Tel 06-588 1021.
W teatrovascello.it

Folk, Cabaret, Puppet Theatre

Meo Patacca
P. dei Mercanti 30. **Map** 8
D1. **Tel** 06-581 6198.

Teatro Mongiovino
Via Genocchi 15.
Tel 06-513 9405.
W accettellateatro.it

Teatro San Carlino
Viale dei Bambini (Pincio).
Map 4 F1. **Tel** 06-6992
2117. W sancarlino.it

Teatro Verde
Circonvall. Gianicolense
10. **Map** 7 B4. **Tel** 06-588
2034. W teatroverde.it

Open-Air Theatre

Anfiteatro Quercia del Tasso
Passeggiata del Gianicolo.
Map 3 C5. **Tel** 06-575 0827.

Globe Theatre
Largo Aqua Felix.
Map 2 E5. **Tel** 06-0608.

Teatro Anfitrione
Via di San Saba 24. **Map** 8
E3. **Tel** 06-575 0827.

English Theatre

English Theatre of Rome
Teatro Arciliuto,
Piazza Montevecchio 5.
Map 3 C5. **Tel** 06-575 0827.

Miracle Players
W miracleplayers.it

Nightlife

Rome's nightlife has never been as diverse or vibrant as it is today. The city has witnessed a sharp rise in the number of bar and club openings that cater for an ever more demanding clientele. Where once the choice was limited to the Irish theme bars near Termini, the few well-established but crowded bars in the historic centre and the hugely popular clubs in Testaccio, the capital now offers a wide range of options to satisfy all tastes and budgets. Depending on your mood, head first for a stylish pre-clubbing bar and then on to one of the centre's exclusive clubs, or simply relax with friends and a bottle of good wine in an earthy wine bar in one of the city's breathtaking piazzas. For a memorable first stop, enjoy spectacular views with an apéritif from a rooftop terrace bar.

On the downside, despite the greater number of bars and clubs, prices have soared in Rome since the euro was introduced – today you can be charged up to €10 for a cocktail! For cheaper alternative nights out, away from the tourist traps, visit a bar in San Lorenzo.

What's On

As in any major city, Rome's nightlife is constantly evolving. Roman club-goers are an extremely varied group and most clubs arrange different nights to appeal to the diverse range of tastes – so it is essential to keep up-to-date on what's happening by checking listings magazines (see p346) that hit the newsstands every Thursday.

Flyers for many nightclubs are handed out in some of the busier piazzas in and around the centre, such as Campo de' Fiori and Piazza del Fico. They are also distributed inside the many pre-clubbing bars dotted around Testaccio such as **33 Testaccio Lounge Bar**.

Practicalities

Preferred clubbing nights are Friday and Saturday, when the cars and scooters of revellers block the streets of the city centre. Queues at the most popular venues can be very long at peak entrance time (around midnight), so it is advisable to get there an hour or so earlier. However, if you are unable to do so, and don't feel like waiting, try ringing up in advance and charming your way onto the guestlist.

Instead of an entrance fee, some smaller clubs require a tessera, a monthly or yearly membership card, which you can buy and fill out on the spot. If you're paying just to get through the door that night, hold on to your entrance ticket as it usually entitles you to a free first drink (la consumazione); your second could be expensive and cost as much as €15.

As a general rule, remember that all-male groups are rarely welcome, and in some exclusive clubs neither are unaccompanied men. Also, to enter any of the more select venues you'll need both an introduction from one of the regulars and clothes that aim to impress.

Bars

Riding the crest of the popularity wave is **Bar del Fico**, a stone's throw from Piazza Navona, while the number of bars is ever-growing in Campo de' Fiori. One of the best of the bunch is **Il Nolano** (see p320), while just around the corner **Angolo Divino** (see p320) is less well-known, and consequently not as bustling. It nonetheless remains a perfect spot for socializing over great wines and heart-warming food.

The Pigneto neighbourhood is known for its bars and vibrant nightlife, with **Necci** standing out for its great drinks, rich aperitivos, and intellectual crowd. **Fluid**, on Via del Governo Vecchio, is much livelier and has made its mark in the capital as the perfect venue to get you in the mood for late-night clubbing. A few doors down but really a world away, the comfortable and candlelit **Mimì e Cocò** is a great place to relax (al fresco or inside) and linger over subtle wines, served with a smile. Just off the top end of the same street, moving away from Corso Vittorio Emanuele II, is **Giulio Passami l'Olio**, a warm, welcoming and animated enoteca, tucked away from the usual passaggiate (promenade) routes. Closer to Piazza di Spagna, the striking interior and extensive choice of wines by the glass make the **Antica Enoteca di Via della Croce** a favourite spot for wine connoisseurs. Although it's definitely not cheap, the impressive bar buffet is well worth sampling.

In Trastevere, too, the romantic streets are full of tiny bars aimed at diverse crowds. Find a table if you can outside **Ombre Rosse** in the wonderful Piazza Sant'Egidio and watch the world go by. If Ombre Rosse is too crowded, **Caffè della Scala**, just a few minutes' walk away, is a good alternative. Other bars in the area include the hip **Freni e Frizioni** and **Friends Art Café**, which is a perfect spot to enjoy a refreshing, though expensive apéritif with complimentary but elaborate snacks – a growing trend in the Eternal City. The simple, but vintage, **Bar San Callisto**, located just off Piazza Santa Maria, draws strictly non-conventional patrons, while across the river, **Rec 23** is perfectly positioned for drinks before going clubbing in Testaccio.

Elsewhere in the city, the sophisticated **Ferrazza** (see p343), in San Lorenzo, serves up exceptional wines for more sophisticated customers, while the ancient wine bar **Il Vinaietto** has a dizzying selection of wine bottles which they also serve by the glass. The slick surf-bar **Duke's** in Parioli is slightly away from the centre, but is worth it for star-spotting. Duke's has tried to curb its soaring popularity by closing on Saturday nights, but to no avail. It remains the number one place to be seen in north Rome.

Finally, and not just for hopeless romantics, breath-taking views of Rome can be enjoyed at the lavish rooftop terrace bars at hotel **Eden** *(see p302)*, near Via Veneto, and **Bar Zest** in the Radisson Blu es. hotel *(see p302)* near Termini. At dusk, particularly after a sunny day, these stunning venues offer a great place to start an unforgettable evening out. Not far from the Colosseum, **Caffè Propaganda** is a chic café whose interior is reminiscent of an early 20th-century Parisian bistro while **Porto Fluviale** in the up-and-coming nightlife hub of Ostiense is the place to go for aperitivo and beyond.

Clubs

To brush shoulders with TV starlets and parliamentary under-secretaries, head for **Gilda**. Its glitzy dance-floor and restaurant have made it a favourite with the Roman jet set and hangers-on. The famous Sixties nightclub, **Jackie O**, revamped in lavish style, with a lush interior, a piano bar and an expensive eatery, draws an international, thirty-something crowd.

Also in the Via Veneto area is **Elegance Café** with its live jazz music, while further north the traditional disco is at its best at **Piper**, which changes look each season and organizes imaginative floor shows and other events. Smack in the centre of town is **Micca Club**, which relocated here from its Esquilino location. This quirky club has a unique programme of selected oldies and also

specializes in burlesque evenings, with stars from all over the world as well as local ones trained in the club's own burlesque academy. **The Nag's Head** is a disco-pub that is especially worth noting.

In and around Testaccio, the undisputed clubbing heart of Rome, you'll find it difficult to decide which club to visit. The lavish and sophisticated **La Cabala** attracts celebrities and Rome's up-market clientèle with its Lungotevere location, while the multi-functional **Shari Vari** is the place for eating, drinking, relaxing and dancing. **Radio Londra** can always be counted on to offer a good DJ set, while nearby is the ever-popular, Mexican-infused **Charro Café**. Just off the Via Ostiense is the trendy **La Saponeria** and at the alternative **Planet Roma**, you can drift between three rooms offering three completely different DJ sets. Last but by no means least, the legendary **Goa** remains the champion of Roman clubs, attracting the best of Italian as well as international DJs.

The wine bar at **'Gusto** offers live music and the chance to explore the venue's various restaurant areas while enjoying a glass of wine from the vast selection available. A similar multi-purpose venue is the nearby **La.Vi.** with its terrace and late night lounge music. However, if you're in the mood for a mainstream alternative that is free of charge and easier to gain entry to, then head to the upbeat **Habana Café** for a continuous programme of live music and DJ sets every evening.

For something a little different, the **Radio Café** is a multi-functional venue with a lounge, café, disco and meeting spaces frequented by a trendy media set.

Gay Scene

While the city's gay scene is not as well renowned as Europe's larger capitals, there has been a steady rise in the number of gay

bars and clubs here. While some are exclusively gay, others attract a mixed clientèle.

For lively social drinking, head for **Anfiteatro My Bar** and **Coming Out**, between San Giovanni and the Colosseum, to mingle with a mixed crowd that usually spills out onto the street. Nearby, the men-only bar **Hangar** continues to pack them in.

When it comes to clubbing, the ever-growing number of gay one-nighters in both alternative and mainstream clubs in many ways present the best venues for drinking and dancing until the early hours. **Goa**, just off Via Ostiense, occasionally hosts gay nights such as the women-only Venus Rising once a month; Mucca Assassina (quite literally "homicidal cow") pulls in the crowds every Friday at the monumental **Qube** in Tiburtino, while **Planet Roma** hosts the Gorgeous I Am one-nighters every Saturday. These clubs are in addition to the justly famous gay-friendly disco **Alibi** in Testaccio with its explosive mix of house music and retro classics.

Pride Week, a yearly event held at the end of June/early July, is a time when gay Romans hit the streets for seven days of non-stop partying. The programme and date change from year to year, so it is wise to consult listing magazines for full details.

In summer, as with most clubs, Rome's gay venues move outdoors in an attempt to beat the stifling heat. Often the outdoor club nights are hosted at **Gay Village**, a summer-long outdoor beanfeast. This is yet another important indication that gay culture is finally beginning to be accepted on the main-stream entertainment scene.

Centri Sociali

Centri sociali, or illegally occupied buildings that have been converted into centres for the arts and entertainment, give an alternative edge to

Rome's vivacious nightlife and cultural scene. While some centres are run on a professional basis and are able to successfully compete with many of the capital's swankier and established venues, others have continued to maintain a staunch anti-establishment stance.

Top billing must go to **Brancaleone** in north Rome, which regularly features progressive Italian and international DJs for the very best in electronic and house tunes. This well-run establishment is also home to an organic café and shop, superb art exhibitions and a cinema club. Near the Baths of Caracalla, the **Angelo Mai Centre** regularly

organizes a multitude of cultural events, including exhibitions and showings of art house films – sometimes even in their original non-dubbed version. At weekends, the venue dedicates its space primarily to club nights, covering a spectrum of tastes from underground and ethnic live bands to wild DJ sets. They also boast their own eatery.

Further away from the centre, the abandoned fort, **Forte Prenestino**, is a magical maze of spooky rooms and endless corridors and represents the most bizarre of Rome's social centre venues. Famous for its anti-establishment Labour Day concert – the official and free rock concert is held in Piazza

San Giovanni in Laterano – it also holds theatre productions, film festivals and club nights throughout the year for a young but alternative crowd. Slightly closer to the centre, **CSOA Ex Snia Viscosa**, situated in a disused factory on the edge of the edgy Pigneto district, offers a range of services. It regularly hosts concerts, and is extremely proud of its green credentials: no cars, or even *motorini*, are allowed near the premises.

Jazz, Salsa and African Sounds

Rome offers countless venues for jazz, from trad and swing to modern fusion (*see p350*). Several jazz and Latin American

DIRECTORY

Bars

33 Testaccio Lounge Bar
Via di Monte Testaccio 33.
Map 8 D4.
Tel 06-575 5142.

Angolo Divino
Via dei Balestrari 12–14.
Map 11 C4.
Tel 06-686 4413.

Antica Enoteca di Via della Croce
Via della Croce 76B.
Map 4 F2.
Tel 06-679 0896.

Bar del Fico
Piazza del Fico 26.
Map 11 C2.
Tel 06-6821 0425.

Bar Necci
Via Fanfulla da Lodi 68.
Map 10 F1.
Tel 06-9760 1552.

Bar San Callisto
Piazza San Callisto 3–4.
Map 7 C1.
Tel 06-583 5869.

Bar Zest
Radisson Blu es. hotel,
Via Filippo Turati 171.
Map 6 D4.
Tel 06-444 841.

Caffè Propaganda
Via Claudia 15.
Map 9 A1.
Tel 06-9543 4255.

Caffè della Scala
Via della Scala 4.
Map 7 C1.
Tel 06-580 3610.

Duke's
Viale Parioli 200.
Map 2 D1.
Tel 06-8066 2455.

Eden
Via Ludovisi 49.
Map 5 B2.
Tel 06-478 121.

Ferrazza
Via dei Volsci 59.
Map 6 F4.
Tel 06-490 506.

Fluid
Via del Governo
Vecchio 46/47.
Map 11 C3.
Tel 06-683 2361.

Freni e Frizioni
Via del Politeama 4–6.
Map 4 E4.
Tel 06-4549 7499.

Friends Art Café
Piazza Trilussa 34.
Map 4 E5.
Tel 06-581 6111.

Giulio Passami l'Olio
Via di Monte Giordano 28.
Map 11 B2.
Tel 06-6880 3288.

Mimì e Cocò
Via del Governo
Vecchio 72.
Map 11 C3.
Tel 06-6821 0845.

Il Nolano
Campo de' Fiori 11/12.
Map 11 C4.
Tel 06-687 9344.

Ombre Rosse
Piazza Sant'Egidio 12.
Map 7 C1.
Tel 06-588 4155.

Porto Fluviale
Via del Porto Fluviale, 22.
Map 8 D5.
Tel 06-574 3199.

Rec 23
Map 8 D2.
Tel 06-8746 2147.

Vinaietto
Via Monte della Farina 37.
Map 6 F4.
Tel 06-6880 6989.

Clubs

La Cabala
Via dei Soldati 25.
Map 8 D4.
Tel 06-6830 1192.

Charro Café
Via di Monte Testaccio 73.
Map 8 D4.
Tel 06-578 3064.

Elegance Café
Via Veneto 93.
Map 5 B2.
Tel 06-4201 6745.

Gilda
Via Mario de' Fiori 97.
Map 12 F1.
Tel 06-678 4838.

Goa
Via Libetta 13.
Tel 06-574 8277.

'Gusto
Via delle Frezza 23.
Map 4 F2.
Tel 06-322 6273.

Habana Café
Via dei Pastini 120.
Map 12 D2.
Tel 06-678 1983.

Jackie O
Via Boncompagni 11.
Map 5 B2.
Tel 06-4288 5457.

La. Vi.
Via Tomacelli 23.
Map 12 D1.
Tel 06-4542 7760.

Micca Club
Via degli Avignonesi 73.
Map 5 B3.
Tel 392 22 43 672.

clubs combine live music with dancing, eating and drinking. For South American style music, **Fonclea** or occasionally one of the various sections at the multi-venue **Planet Roma** all pay homage to Latin American and world music. For jazz and blues, **Big Mama** in Trastevere and **Caffè Latino** in Testaccio are by far and away the best places to check out at the weekend, or any other day of the week for that matter.

Clubbing in Summer

At the height of the sweltering summer, when virtually every-thing closes down in the capital, **Art Cafè** in Villa Borghese stands out as the supreme club venue for the fun-loving, young and hip. From June through to August, a number of smaller venues open up on the Tiber too, with wining and dining accompanied by live music as the river surges past just metres below. Some of the bigger clubs also move further afield, hitting the coast from July through to December – most notably in Ostia and in Fregene, where the sophisticated **Singita** beach club holds a special sunset ceremony accompanied by a DJ set. Back in town, the rooftop of the 1940s-built Palazzo dei Congressi in EUR hosts **Le Terraazze Roma**, a summer-only club featuring great views of the city, an upmarket crowd, and alternating house and commercial music.

After Hours

Most Roman clubs stay open until 2am or 3am. However, night-owls may find one or two dance havens that see in the dawn, especially during the beach-party season. Before heading off to bed, you could join the other die-hard clubbers for a final drink at one of the city's 24-hour watering holes, or else make for one of the early-morning bakers. Many a long night of Roman revels ends with a feast on early breakfast *cornetti* straight from the oven, enjoyed while most of the city is still sleeping.

DIRECTORY

The Nag's Head
Via IV Novembre 138B.
Map 5 A4.
Tel 06-679 4620.

Piper
Via Tagliamento 9
(north of the city centre).
Tel 06-855 5398.

Planet Roma
Via del Commercio 36/8.
Map 8 D5.
Tel 06-574 7826.

Radio Café
Via Principe Umberto 67.
Map 6 E5.
Tel 06-4436 1110.

Radio Londra
Via di Monte
Testaccio 67.
Map 8 D4.
Tel 06-575 0044.

Salotto 42
Piazza di Pietra 42.
Map 12 E2.
Tel 06-678 5804.

La Saponeria
Via degli Argonauti 20
(to the south of
Stazione Ostiense,
off Via Ostiense).
Tel 06-574 6999.

Shari Vari
Via de' Nari 14.
Map 12 D3.
Tel 06-6880 6936.

Gay Scene

Alibi
Via di Monte
Testaccio 39–44.
Map 8 D4.
Tel 06-574 3448.

Anfiteatro My Bar
Via San Giovanni in
Laterano 12.
Map 9 A1.
Tel 06-700 4425.

Coming Out
Via San Giovanni
in Laterano 8.
Map 9 A1.
Tel 06-700 9871.

Gay Village
Phone or check website
for venue.
Tel 393-004 6560.
W **gayvillage.it**

Goa
See Clubs.

Hangar
Via in Selci 69.
Map 5 C5.
Tel 06-488 1397.

Planet Roma
See Clubs.

Qube
Via di Portonaccio 212
(east of the city centre).
Tel 06-438 5445.

Centri Sociali

Angelo Mai
Viale delle Terme di
Caracalla 55A.
Map 9 A2.
Tel 329 448 1358.

Brancaleone
Via Levanna 11
(in Monte Sacro).
Tel 06-8200 4382.

CSOA Ex Snia Viscosa
Via Prenestina 173 (east of
city). **Tel** 06-2780 0816.

Forte Prenestino
Via F. Delpino
Tel 06-2180 7855.

Jazz, Salsa and African Sounds

Big Mama
Vicolo San Francesco a
Ripa 18. **Map** 7 C2.
Tel 06-581 2551.

Caffè Latino
Via di Monte
Testaccio 96. **Map** 8 D4.
Tel 06-578 2411.

Fonclea
Via Crescenzio 82A.
Map 3 C2.
Tel 06-689 6302.
W **fonclea.it**

Planet Roma
See Clubs.

Clubbing in Summer

Art Cafè
Viale del Galoppatoio 33
(Villa Borghese).
Map 5 A1.
Tel 06-322 0994.

Singita
Via Slvi Marina.
Tel 06-6196 4921.

Le Terrazze Roma
Piazza John F. Kennedy 1.
Tel 339 611 9070.

Sport

Do not be surprised if the peace of a Sunday afternoon in Rome is interrupted by the honking of cars and people shouting. It simply means that one of the home football teams has won at the stadium and the whole city appears to be celebrating the result.

Football is Italy's national sport but other sports also attract a large following and sports fans have a varied choice of events and activities to watch or participate in.

You will find times and venues for most spectator sports listed in *TrovaRoma* (see p346), as well as the local sections of *La Gazzetta dello Sport* or *Corriere dello Sport*.

Football

An Italian football match is an experience not to be missed for the quality of the play and the fun atmosphere, though hooliganism has begun to raise its ugly head.

Rome has two teams, Roma and Lazio, and they take it in turns to play at the **Stadio Olimpico (CONI)** on a Sunday afternoon at 3pm, in the Campionato Italiano (Italian championship league).

Seats can be scarce, so get tickets in advance from the stadium (€20 to €100) from noon onwards on the day itself, or through club websites (www.sslazio.it and www.asroma.it). The cheapest seats are in the Curve and Distinti stands; the middle-range and most expensive are in the various Tribuna sections of the stadium.

On Wednesday evenings there may be international competitions – the UEFA Cup or the Coppa dei Campioni (European Championship Cup). In between these, teams battle it out for the national Coppa Italia.

Tennis

A major event, the International Championships go on at **Foro Italico** for two weeks in May. The world's top tennis stars thrash it out on clay courts at 1pm and 8:30pm from Tuesday to Friday, and at 1pm only at weekends. Buy tickets in advance either directly from the Foro Italico or from a ticket agency.

If you wish to play, there are now more than 350 tennis clubs in Rome. It's essential to book at least a week in advance and there is usually a court fee.

Clubs where membership is not required include **Tennis Club Nomentano** and the **Circolo Tennis della Stampa** in northern Rome and the **Oasi di Pace**, just off the Via Appia Antica. Large hotels offer tennis for a reasonable price. The **Crowne Plaza** requires a small annual membership fee on top of the court price, which includes the gym and the pool (in summer).

Horse-Racing and Riding

Important races include the Derby in May and the Premio Roma in November. There are both flat races and steeplechases at the **Ippodromo delle Capannelle**.

The International Horse Show is held in May in Piazza di Siena, Villa Borghese *(see p260)*. It is organized by the Federazione Italiana Sport Equestri (**FISE**) and is one of the most important social and sporting events in the calendar, and has a great setting.

Through the FISE, it may be possible to find a riding club that will take you on a hack in the countryside around Rome, but most do not accept short-term members.

Golf

Even the most elite golf clubs will accept a touring golfer with a home membership and handicap. Many clubs close on Mondays and at the weekend when they host competitions and guests cannot play. Prices range from €60 to over €100. The **Olgiata Golf Club** is open to everybody, though it is best to phone first if you want to play at the weekend, when demand and fees are much higher. **Country Club Castel Gandolfo** is the newest club and **Circolo del Golf di Roma Acquasanta** the oldest and most prestigious. Within the city ring road is the course at the **Sheraton Golf Hotel** (closed Tuesdays) which offers special play and stay deals.

One of the many important competitions on the various golf courses around Rome is the Circolo Golf Roma Coppa d'Oro (Gold Cup) in April.

Car and Motorbike Racing

Motorbike racing takes place on various Sundays throughout the year at **Vallelunga**; be prepared for some expensive entrance fees. Every November the track also hosts the Six Hours of Vallelunga Race for sports cars.

Rugby

With the formation of **Federazione Italiana Rugby** and, since 2000, Italy's participation in the Six Nations tournament, rugby has been increasing in popularity. In winter (usually Feb–Mar) there are a couple of international matches in Rome. The home team is drawn against two other member "nations" each year: France, England, Scotland, Ireland or Wales.

Rowing

In mid-June an Oxbridge crew challenges the historic Aniene crew to a race taking place alternately on the Thames and the Tiber. The best place to view this from is between the Marg-herita and the Sant'Angelo bridges. The race usually starts at around 6pm. Another event is the battle between the Roma and Lazio crews, from Ponte Duca d'Aosta to Ponte Risorgimento, on the same variable date as the Roma-Lazio football derby.

Swimming

Swimming pools are few and definitely not geared to the short-term visitor. It is often necessary to pay an expensive membership plus a monthly tariff. Most pools also require you to produce a medical certificate assuring your good health, and have lane-only swimming. The state-owned pools can be slightly cheaper, but you still have to pay an initial membership fee.

The **Shangri-La Hotel** opens its pool to non-residents in the summer, as does the **Cavalieri Rome Hotel**, for an entry fee. The best deal for families in summer is probably to be found in the EUR district in the south of the city: the **Piscina delle Rose** is an Olympic-sized pool open from June to September 9am–5:30pm daily (to 7pm at weekends). For a swim with a view, book a chaise longue by the rooftop pool of the **Radisson Blu es. Hotel,** located on the Esquiline Hill.

Health Clubs

Like the swimming pools, Roman health clubs usually require both a membership fee and monthly payments. For a short stay in Rome, it is more sensible to try the facilities in your hotel, or, if you are willing to pay, head for one of the private clubs. Use of club facilities may well be negotiable.

Open in summer only, **Mondofitness Village** is a large outdoor sports complex with a swimming pool and gym space. It offers a variety of activities including cycling, rowing and martial arts. The entry fee for the swimming pool starts at €7 for a half day and €9 for a full day.

Jogging and Cycling

Rome's perfect climate and stunning scenery attract thousands of well-dressed joggers and cyclists into the city's many parks. Early on weekday mornings or at any time on a Sunday you'll find the more popular locations looking more like a high-speed fashion show than sweat tracks. Each March, however, serious runners take part in the **Maratona di Roma** (Rome Marathon).

Villa Doria Pamphilj *(see p269)* is an extensive park situated above the Janiculum, where you can choose from various tracks, plenty of open spaces and a network of paths. Villa Borghese *(see p260)* is another vast, popular place with a running track.

Alternatively, jog under the acacia trees and palms at **Villa Torlonia**, on the spot-lit track at Villa Glori, or combine sport with culture by running the Via Appia Antica *(see p267)* branching off into Parco Caffarella. Other favourite places are Viale delle Terme di Caracalla, Circo Massimo, Parco degli Aquedotti and Parco di Colle Oppio.

All of the above are also ideal for cyclists, and you can hire bikes from many places including **Collalti** and **Treno e Scooter Rent** *(see also p386)*.

DIRECTORY

Football

Stadio Olimpico (CONI)
Via Foro Italico.
Tel 06-36851.

Tennis

Circolo Tennis della Stampa
Piazza Mancini 19.
Map 1 A2.
Tel 06-323 2452.

Crowne Plaza
Via Aurelia Antica 415.
Tel 06-66420.

Foro Italico
Viale dei Gladiatori 31.
Tel 06-3272 3301.
W ctforoitalico.coni.it

Oasi di Pace
Via degli Eugenii 2.
Tel 06-718 4550.
W oasidipaceroma.it

Tennis Club Nomentano
Viale Rousseau 124.
Tel 06-8680 1888.
W clubnomentano.it

Horse-Racing and Riding

FISE
Tel 06-8366 8416.
W fise.it

Ippodromo delle Capannelle
Via Appia Nuova 1255.
Tel 06-71 67 71.

Golf

Circolo del Golf di Roma Acquasanta
Via Appia Nuova 716A.
Tel 06-780 3407.
W golfroma.it

Country Club Castel Gandolfo
Via di Santo Spirito 13,
Castelgandolfo.
Tel 06-931 2301.

Olgiata Golf Club
Largo dell'Olgiata 15.
Tel 06-3088 9141.
W olgiatagolfclub.com

Sheraton Golf Hotel
Viale Salvatore Rebecchini 39. **Tel** 06-65288.

Motor Racing

Vallelunga
Autodromo di Roma,
Via Cassia km 34.5.
Tel 06-901 5501.
W vallelunga.it

Rugby

Federazione Italiana Rugby
Tel 06-4521 3117.
W federugby.it

Swimming

Cavalieri Rome Hotel
Via Cadlolo 101.
Tel 06-350 91.
W romecavalieri.com

Piscina delle Rose
Viale America 20.
Tel 06-5422 0333.
W piscinadellerose.com

Radisson Blu es. Hotel
Via Filippo Turati 171.
Map 6 D4.
Tel 06-444 841.

Shangri-La Hotel
Viale Algeria 141.
Tel 06-591 6441.

Health Clubs

Mondofitness Village
Viale di Tor di Quinto 55–57. **Tel** 342 694 4959.
W mondofitness-roma.com

Jogging and Cycling

Collalti
Via del Pellegrino 82.
Map 4 E4.
Tel 06-6880 1084.

Maratona di Roma
Tel 06-406 5064.
W maratonadiroma.it

Treno e Scooter Rent
Termini Station.
Map 6 D3.
Tel 06-4890 5823.

Villa Torlonia
Villa Nomentana 70.
Tel 06-0608
W museivillatorlonia.it

CHILDREN'S ROME

Italians love having children around, and you can be sure yours will be made welcome wherever they go. But there are few special facilities for children, and the heat, crowds and lack of clean public toilets mean that Rome is not an ideal city for a holiday with babies or under-sevens. It does, however, have plenty to offer slightly older children, especially those who are keen on history or art. The temptation may be to wear yourself and your children out by packing too many sights into one day. Plan in advance and leave plenty of time to wander around the city: looking at the quirkier fountains and monuments, watching knife-grinders at work in the markets, and spending hours agonizing over the choice of ice-cream flavours and special pizza toppings.

Practical Advice

If you are planning to bring your children to Rome, try to come in early spring or late autumn, when the weather is good, but not too hot. Easter is best avoided, as the city is more crowded than usual, and you're constantly jostled on packed buses and streets.

Where you stay is crucial. A hotel near the Villa Borghese park will give your children plenty of chance to relax and let off steam, though you may end up spending a lot of time and money to get to and from the town centre. A hotel in the old centre is ideal, as you can easily pop back during the day for a rest and a clean bathroom.

As hygienic toilets and changing facilities are rare within the city, it is really not advisable to bring a baby to Rome unless you are visiting friends or family.

As with many historic cities, Rome may not instantly appeal to all children, but there is plenty to inspire their imaginations. Use this book to make the buildings and history come alive. Children might also enjoy learning a few Italian words and phrases so they can greet locals, order food and buy things by themselves. If lingering over drinks on the café terraces is what you enjoy best, bring something to keep your children busy once they have finished with their treat. You are unlikely, however, to see Italian children playing with their phones at the table. Alternatively, most other adults are very tolerant of children running around and making

Fairground ride in the Villa Borghese park

a noise while they relax and, if yours are reasonably outgoing, they could join in with the local children playing spontaneous ball games in early evenings on piazzas like Campo de' Fiori.

If you feel the need for a total break, most hotels will be able to provide a babysitter or help you to contact a qualified childminding agency.

In the event of an accident, see pages 370–71 for information on what to do and a list of emergency numbers.

A selection of bicycles for hire in the Villa Borghese park

Getting Around

Bumpy cobbles, narrow streets without pavements and overcrowded buses make pushing children around in pushchairs tiring work. Mothers with young children are, however, usually allowed to jump queues. Outside rush hours, the Metro is often less busy. Kids under 1 m (3 ft 3 in) tall travel free on public transport.

Although the city is not good for cyclists, families with older children could hire bikes to ride along the Tiber on the cycle tracks to the north of the city, or to take on a regional train into the country. The bikes, tandems and rickshaws for hire in Villa Borghese are good fun, and the bike hire hut in the Pincio gardens has free baby seats.

Eating Out

Children are normally warmly welcomed in neighbourhood pizzerias

Families enjoying a sunny day in the Villa Borghese Gardens

and trattorias, and high chairs are often available for toddlers and babies. If there is no high chair, be prepared for the waiters to improvise for you with armloads of cushions or telephone directories. Most places are perfectly happy to serve half portions (*mezzo piatto*), or to let children share meals.

In trattorias it can sometimes be difficult to be exactly certain what a certain dish contains (especially when there is no menu and the dishes of the day are reeled off, usually at top speed, by the waiter), so faddy eaters are likely to be happier in pizzerias (*see pp320–21*).

Here they can choose their own topping (remember that *prosciutto,* which is usually translated in menus as ham, is cured). The most entertaining pizzerias for kids are the old-fashioned ones where they can watch the chefs pound, stretch and flip the pizza dough before the toppings are added.

Restaurants open in the evening at or soon after 7pm and the best places get busy from around 8:30pm, so it is wise to go early to avoid having to queue.

Picnics

Picnics in the parks are ideal, and shopping for the food is often half the fun. There is no problem finding cartons of fruit juice and branded canned drinks, but these are expensive unless you go to a supermarket – various outlets are dotted around the city centre.

Water from the drinking fountains is potable, so it is worth carrying plastic cups or small bottles around with you.

As well as picnic food from bakeries and markets, there are lots of scrumptious takeaway foods. Many of them are appealingly messy, so it is wise to take paper tissues or wet wipes along. Try deep-fried fruit and vegetables from Antico Forno Roscioli on Via dei Giubbonari (*see p323*) and *supplì al telefono*, rice croquettes with a gooey string of mozzarella inside, from *pizza al taglio* or *pizza rustica* outlets. A *tramezzino* comes quite close to an English sandwich and if your kids are miserable without Marmite, you can find it (and other foreign foods) at Castroni on Via Cola di Rienzo.

Ice Cream

Rome, of course, is famous for ice cream; you and your children are likely to be tempted at every turn by the vast range of flavours on offer. Real ice-cream fans may even want to plan their day's sightseeing to be sure to take in one of the best *gelaterie* (*see pp322–5*).

It is far cheaper to buy either a cone or tub of ice cream to eat in the street, but in some of the more traditional places it is worth paying to sit down, as the interiors can be fun and attractive to children.

At Fassi, they have an old-fashioned ice cream-making machine on display and at Giolitti, you can enjoy gargantuan sundaes in the elegant parlour (*see p113*).

If you are worried that your kids might have too much ice cream, look for places that sell the smaller *cono baby*.

Rome's oldest ice-cream parlour Giolitti, in operation since 1890

Sightseeing with Children

Entrance to the Villa Borghese Zoo

General Tips

Rome does not have many museums with child-friendly, hands-on exhibits. Instead, look for fun or unusual details while exploring streets and squares. Bernini's marble elephant *(see p112)* and the fat *facchino*, or porter *(p109)*, tend to appeal to kids. The Capuchin crypt at Santa Maria della Concezione *(p256)*, the catacombs *(pp266–8)* and the Mamertine Prison *(p93)* will grab the more ghoulish imaginations, and children will also enjoy putting their hands into the Bocca della Verità *(p204)*.

Keep your children's interest alive by looking for details like the dirty toenails on figures in Caravaggio's paintings, the Etruscan votives, which were offered to the gods, at the Villa Giulia *(pp264–5)*, and the illusory collapsing ceiling in the Chiesa Nuova, *(see p126)* as well as the fake dome of Sant'Ignazio di Loyola *(see p108)*.

Museums your children will enjoy include **Museo Explora**, full of interesting hands-on exhibits for children, and the Museo delle Mura, which explores a short length of the Aurelian Wall *(p198)*. Among the churches, St Peter's *(see pp228–9)* and San Clemente *(see pp188–9)* are the most fun.

At the Vatican children will like the animal statues and mosaics in the Animal Gallery and also the Sistine Ceiling *(pp244–5)*, especially once they know that Michelangelo had to paint it hunched up on a scaffolding platform. Remember that Vatican dress etiquette *(see p229)* applies to kids too.

Ancient Ruins

The ancient ruins best appreciated by children are the Colosseum *(see pp94–7)*, and Trajan's Market *(see pp90–91)*. You can still make out what both these

buildings looked like from their remains. The scant ruins of the Forum and Palatine, on the other hand, may not appeal so strongly. Ostia Antica, where the remains include a theatre, shop and 20-seater public toilet, is much more likely to interest them *(see pp272–3)*.

Mosaics

There are scores of vivid, sometimes quirky, mosaics in buildings all over Rome.

Mosaic from the Vatican

Many of these are particularly appealing to children. Details in the mosaics range from brilliantly coloured flowers, leaves, animals and buildings (in the churches of San Clemente, Santa Prassede and Santa Maria in Trastevere, *see pp188–9, p173* and *pp214–15*) to the debris of a banquet (in the Vatican's Museo Gregorio Profano, *see pp232–3*).

Entertainment

To find out what's on for children in Rome, scour the cinema pages of newspapers and the listings in *TrovaRoma* and *Wanted in Rome* and entertainment websites *(see pp346–7)*. Most theatres and cinemas have reduced entry fees for children, but shows are often only in Italian.

There are cartoons shown at Villa Borghese's Cinema dei Piccoli and traditional puppet shows every afternoon, except Wednesday, on Janiculum Hill. Located inside Villa Borghese, the **Casina di Raffaello** is a playhouse and mini-library with

Miniature train in Villa Borghese

Christmas market stalls on Piazza Navona

toys and reading areas.
It also organizes activities.

An appealing time for kids to be in Rome is over Christmas, when Piazza Navona hosts a Christmas toy fair, with stalls selling toys and sweets.

Parks

Villa Borghese (see p260) has rowing boats to hire; pony-cart rides; bikes to rent; a mini cinema; a small funfair; and a zoo. Villa Celimontana (see p195) has bike trails, and open-air theatre performances in the summer. Technotown, a multimedia playhouse, in the grounds of Villa Torlonia (see p359) is fun. At EUR (see p268) is the Piscina delle Rose, a swimming pool open in the summer (see p359). The Bomarzo Monster Park, 95 km (60 miles) north of Rome, was built in the 16th century for a mad duke. Children can clamber over its giant stone monsters.

Toys

A visit to a Roman toyshop can be a lot of fun. **Città del Sole** sells educational toys and games, while the window display at **Al Sogno** is a delight for kids who love cuddly toys.

Children enjoying pony-cart rides at Villa Borghese

DIRECTORY

General Tips

Museo Explora
Via Flamino 82.
Map 1 C5.
Tel 06-361 3776 (book ahead).
w mdbr.it

Entertainment

Casina di Raffaello
Piazza di Siena, Villa Borghese.
Map 2 E5.
Tel 06-0608.
w casinadiraffaello.it

Toys

Al Sogno
Piazza Navona 53.
Map 4 E4 & 11 C3.
Tel 06-686 4198.

Città del Sole
Via della Scrofa 65.
Map 4 F3 & 12 D2.
Tel 06-6880 3805.

Children's Clothes

Benetton
Piazza della Fontana
di Trevi 91–94.
Map 12 F2.
Tel 06-6919 0919.

Lavori Artigianali Femminili
Via Capo le Case 6.
Map 5 A3 & 12 F1.
Tel 06-679 2992.

Rachele
Vicolo del Bollo 6–7
(off Via del Pellegrino).
Map 11 C4.
Tel 06-686 4975.

Children's Clothes

Italians adore dressing their children up, especially on Sunday afternoons. Many shops sell beautifully hand-crafted children's shoes and clothes – the downside is that they can often be expensive and impractical: dry-clean-only clothes are common and shoes are not made for mud.

Lavori Artigianali Femminili sells handmade silk and wool clothes for children up to the age of eight. **Rachele** offers top-quality handmade clothes for children, while **Benetton** has more wallet-friendly smart casuals.

SURVIVAL GUIDE

PRACTICAL INFORMATION

Romans often seem unconcerned by the priceless art treasures and ancient ruins which lie casually among the buildings and workings of their hectic 21st-century city. However, it's not always easy for visitors to make the most of these wonders; relaxed local attitudes make for dozens of variations in opening hours, and many places – including shops, banks and offices – close for 2 or 3 hours over lunch, reopening in the late afternoon. On a more positive note, most of the main sights are within easy walking distance of one another. Start your day early and wear comfortable shoes. Rome can be a delightfully informal city to visit, but remember to observe dress rules and cover up in churches, since this is one area where regulations are strictly enforced.

Steps leading to Michelangelo's Piazza del Campidoglio

When to Go

Rome enjoys a Mediterranean climate, with hot, dry summers and mild-to-cold, rainy winters. From late March to June and from September to October, the pleasant, sunny weather allows for plenty of time outdoors. Visitors can expect to pay more to stay during the high season, between March and November. In hot August, most Romans are on holiday and the smaller shops and restaurants are closed, but all tourist sights stay open, the city is quieter, and you can find good hotel deals.

Visas and Passports

Italy is part of the Schengen agreement, which means travellers moving from one Shengen country to another are not subject to border controls, although there are occasional spot checks.

All visitors to Italy must register with the police within eight working days of arrival. If you

are staying in a hotel, this will be done for you. Otherwise, you should contact the local *questura* (police station). European Union nationals and citizens of the US, Canada, Australia and New Zealand do not need visas for stays of up to three months.

Anyone wishing to stay for more than three months (eight working days for citizens from countries other than those mentioned above) will have to obtain a *permesso di soggiorno* (permit to stay). European Union citizens can apply for a permit at any main police station. Non-EU citizens must apply in advance in their home country for a permit to stay; it is very difficult for non-EU citizens to obtain a work permit. If you lose your passport contact your embassy (*see p369*).

Travel Safety Advice

Visitors can get up-to-date travel safety information from the **Foreign and Commonwealth**

Office in the UK, the **State Department** in the US and the **Department of Foreign Affairs and Trade** in Australia.

Customs Information

Duty-free allowances are as follows: non-EU citizens can bring into Italy 200 cigarettes or 50 cigars or 100 cigarillos or 250 grams of tobacco, 1 litre of spirits or 4 litres of wine and 50 grams of perfume. EU residents do not need to declare goods, but random checks are often made to guard against any drugs traffickers. To find out what you can take back from Italy to a non-EU country, contact that country's customs department. The refund system for Value Added Tax (*IVA* in Italy) for non-EU residents is very complex (*see p327*).

Tourist Information

Information kiosks run by the Comune di Roma are dotted around the city centre and have English-speaking staff who provide free maps, leaflets and advice. Alternatively ring their **Rome City Tourist Office** for information in English. Rome Council's two useful websites have information on all the sights as well as on current exhibitions, events and hotels in the city. A privately run company called **Enjoy Rome** has an informative website and offices close to the Termini railway station. Note that admission prices and opening times change often, and sights can be closed for long periods for restoration (*chiuso per restauro*) or because of a strike (*sciopero*).

◄ Visitors exploring Rome by bicycle taxi

Opening Hours and Admission Prices

Museums are generally open all day, although most close on Mondays and on some public holidays. Open-air sights such as the Forum are open daily year-round, closing one hour before sunset.

The two-day or three-day **Roma Pass** (€28 and €36 respectively) allows free transport within Rome, free entrance to two museums or archaeological sites, and discounts for various exhibitions, events and services. Many national and city museums offer entrance free of charge to people under 18 – sometimes limited to EU citizens. Those aged between 18 and 25 get discounted entry with a valid student ID card.

Entrance to churches is free and many contain extraordinary works of art: keep in mind that you may be charged a small fee to see a certain area, such as chapel, cloister or underground ruins.

Some of Rome's sights, such as Nero's Aqueduct and the Vatican Gardens, are accessible only on personal application or by written appointment *(see below)*. The *Area by Area* section of this guide gives opening times for each sight and tells you whether there is an admission charge.

During the Beni Culturali (Ministry for Culture and Heritage) week in April, admission to all state-run sites is free.

The weekly supplement of the daily paper *La Repubblica*, *TrovaRoma (see p375)* has a small English section with details of current exhibitions.

Sightseeing Permits

To visit certain sights in Rome, you need to obtain a written permit and/or book your visit in advance, particularly for some archaeological sites, which may sometimes be open only for groups with an authorized guide. Call the **Rome City Tourist Office** number on page 369, giving your name, the number of people in your party (individual visits are generally not possible) and when you would like to visit. You may then be asked to send written confirmation by email or fax.

Social Customs and Etiquette

Romans are generally courteous and friendly to foreign visitors. Italians are delighted at any effort to speak their language, so it is worth learning a few phrases *(see p439)*. Italians tend to drink only with meals and are unlikely to be seen drunk – obvious drunkenness is frowned upon. Smoking is banned on public transport and in restaurants, bars and cafés.

Visiting Churches

Many of Italy's churches are very dark, but they usually have electric, coin-operated light meters to illuminate chapels and works of art. Recorded information in several languages is also often available. Dress codes *(see below)* are firmly upheld in churches and should be respected; St Peter's *(see pp228–31)* is especially strict – you cannot wear shorts.

Catholic Services

For many Catholics, a visit to Rome means an audience with the pope. General audiences are usually held every Wednesday at 10:30am either in St Peter's Square, indoors at the Sala Paolo VI or at Castel Gandolfo. To attend an audience, ring the **Prefettura**

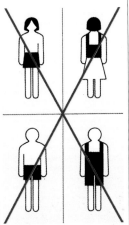

Unacceptable dress in church: both sexes should cover torsos, upper arms and legs

The altar of Santa Maria Maggiore

della Casa Pontificia *(see p229)* or go in person to the office through the bronze doors on the right of the colonnade in St Peter's Square (9am–1pm). Travel agencies can also arrange an audience as part of a coach tour.

Mass is held daily in the main churches of Rome (High Mass is on Sunday). Confession is heard in St Peter's *(see pp228– 31)*, San Giovanni in Laterano *(pp182–3)*, San Paolo fuori le Mura *(p269)*, Santa Maria Maggiore *(pp174–5)*, the Gesù *(pp110–11)*, Santa Sabina *(p206)* and Sant'Ignazio *(p108)*. English-speaking Catholic churches include San Clemente *(see pp188–9)* and Santa Susanna *(see p257)*.

For details of non-Catholic services *see p369*.

Tipping

Service is sometimes included in the bill at restaurants, bars and cafés. Italians usually tip a few euros if the service was good. It is not necessary to tip taxi drivers – rounding up to the next euro is enough. Keep small change handy for sacristans, cleaners, doormen and porters.

Accessibility to Public Toilets

Public toilets are few and far between. There are clean ones by the Colosseum (with facilities for the disabled) and at St Peter's. Most cafés will let you use theirs, but some will ask you to buy something.

Disabled access sign at the Vatican

Disabled Travellers

Rome is not particularly well-equipped for disabled visitors (*see also p297 and p299*). The **Disabled Customer Assistance (Sala Blu)** centre at Termini station offers help and advice on train travel. Disabled travellers needing assistance getting on and off the train should book a special lift service 12 hours in advance, clearly stating the names of all the stations at which they require help. A limited number of buses and trams have wheelchair access and not all metro stations have working lifts. Ramps, lifts and modified WCs are available in an increasing number of places, including Termini station, although you may find a lift is broken down indefinitely, or a ramp is blocked by an illegally parked car. Some restaurants have wheelchair access to the dining area, but not to the WC.

If you are travelling without an escort, consider a specially designed tour, or contact an organization for disabled travellers before you set off.

The Vatican Museums, Sistine Chapel and St Peter's are all accessible by wheelchair.

Senior Travellers

Discounts for *anziani* (elderly citizens) are available at some museums and sights and on some Trenitalia tickets (*see p379*). This offer is only available to those that have a Carta Argento card. The card costs €30 for over 60s and is free for those aged 75 and above.

Student Information

If you are an EU passport holder, it is worth having an International Student Identity Card (ISIC) or a Youth International Educational Exchange Card (YIEE) because you will receive reduced admission prices to national museums. Non-EU members with an ISIC or a YIEE card can also benefit from discounts at some private museums.

Contact the **Centro Turistico Studentesco** for general student information. The **Associazione Italiana Alberghi per la Gioventù** (the Italian YHA) operates four hostels across the city.

International Student Identity Card

Gay and Lesbian Travellers

The main venue for Rome's gay community is the gay-friendly bar **Coming Out** (*see p355*), near the Colosseum. The Gay Pride parade takes place in June. The two-month-long **Gay Village** event (one of Europe's largest gay festivals) begins in July. In Rome, displays of public affection between same sex individuals are not common, and some violence against homosexuals has been reported in the past.

Rome Time

Rome is 1 hour ahead of Greenwich Mean Time (GMT). Examples of the time difference with Rome for other major cities are as follows: London: -1 hour; New York: -6 hours; Dallas: -7 hours; Los Angeles: -9 hours; Perth: +7 hours; Sydney: +9 hours; Auckland: +11 hours; Tokyo: +8 hours. These figures can vary for brief periods during local changes in summertime. For all official purposes, Italians use the 24-hour clock.

Conversion Table

Imperial to Metric
1 inch = 2.54 centimetres
1 foot = 30 centimetres
1 mile = 1.6 kilometres
1 ounce = 28 grams
1 pound = 454 grams
1 pint = 0.57 litres
1 gallon = 4.6 litres

Metric to Imperial
1 centimetre = 0.4 inches
1 metre = 3 feet 3 inches
1 kilometre = 0.6 miles
1 gram = 0.04 ounces
1 kilogram = 2.2 pounds
1 litre = 1.8 pints

Electrical Adaptors

Electric current in Italy is 220V AC, with two- or three-pin round-pronged plugs. Adaptors can be bought in most countries. Most hotels of three or more stars have hair dryers and shaving points in all bedrooms.

A Gay Pride march passing the Colosseum

Responsible Tourism

Rome is aware of the need to become more "green", and environmental initiatives are taking place across the city. Italian cookery has always placed an emphasis on local seasonal food, but Italians are also starting to understand the importance of reducing carbon emissions. Eating local is a good way to support the area's economy, as well as helping the environment.

Organic shops and restaurants are springing up across Rome. Buy regional food at **Spazio Bio**, inside the Città dell'Altra Economia, a large expo space dedicated to the promotion of an organic and sustainable lifestyle, fair trade, ethical tourism and recycling (which

Shady terrace at Rome's Bed & Breakfast Bio

is gradually being introduced in Rome). Shops can also no longer use non-biodegradable plastic bags. Those dreaming of greener nights can book a room in one of the mini-boutique hotels and B&Bs offering an eco-friendly stay.

Two such establishments are **EcoHotel** and **Bed & Breakfast Bio**, both of which guarantee energy- and water-saving rooms, serve organic breakfasts and offer free bicycles for rides in the surrounding parks and natural reserves.

DIRECTORY

Travel Safety Advice

Australia Department of Foreign Affairs and Trade
 dfat.gov.au
 smartraveller.gov.au

UK Foreign and Commonwealth Office
 gov.uk/foreign-travel-advice

US Department of State
 travel.state.gov

Embassies

Australia
Via A. Bosio 5.
Tel 06-852 721.
 italy.embassy.gov.au

Canada
Via Zara 30. **Tel** 06-8544 441.  canada international.gc.ca

United Kingdom
Via XX Settembre 80A.
Map 6 D2.
Tel 06-4220 0001.
 ukinitaly.fco.gov.uk

United States
Via Veneto 119A/121.
Map 5 B2. **Tel** 06-46741.
 italy.usembassy.gov

Tourist Information

Enjoy Rome
Via Marghera 8A. **Map** 6 E3.
Tel 06-445 1843.
 enjoyrome.com

Rome City Tourist Office
Termini Station (Platform 24).
Map 6 D3. **Tel** 06-0608.
 turismoroma.it and
 060608.it

Opening Hours and Admission Prices

Roma Pass
Tel 06-0608.
 romapass.it

Religious Services

American Episcopal
St Paul's, Via Napoli 58.
Map 5 C3.
Tel 06-488 3339.

Anglican
All Saints, Via del Babuino 153. **Map** 4 F2.
Tel 06-3600 1881.

Jewish
Sinagoga (Tempio Maggiore), Lungotevere Cenci. **Map** 4 F5 & 12 D5.
Tel 06-684 0061.

Methodist
Via del Banco di Santo Spirito 3.
Map 4 E3 & 11 A2.
Tel 06-686 8314.

Muslim
The Mosque (Grande Moschea). Viale della Moschea 85 (Parioli district). **Map** 2 F1.
Tel 06-808 2258.

Prefettura della Casa Pontificia
Città del Vaticano.
Map 3 B3.
Tel 06-6988 5863.

Presbyterian
St Andrew's, Via XX Settembre 7.
Map 5 C3.
Tel 06-482 7627.

Disabled Travellers

Disabled Customer Assistance (Sala Blu)
Termini Station (Platform 1). **Map** 6 D3.
Tel 800-906 060.

Student Information

Associazione Italiana Alberghi per la Gioventù
Via Settembrini 4.
Map 1 A5. **Tel** 06-487 1152.  aighostels.it

Centro Turistico Studentesco
Piazza Sforza Cesarini 26.
Map 11 B3. **Tel** 06-6880 3290.  cts.it

Gay and Lesbian Travellers

Coming Out
Via San Giovanni, Laterano 8. **Map** 9 A1.
Tel 06-700 9871.
 comingout.it

Gay Village
Parco del Ninfeo (EUR).
 gayvillage.it

Responsible Tourism

Bed & Breakfast Bio
Via Cavalese 28.
Tel 335-715 1749.
 bedandbreakfastbio.com

EcoHotel
Via di Bravetta 91.
Tel 06-6615 6920.
 ecohotelroma.com

Spazio Bio
Città dell'Altra Economia, Largo Dino Frisullo.
Map 8 D4. **Tel** 06-575 9272.  cittadellaltra economia.org

Personal Security and Health

On the whole, Rome is a safe, unthreatening place for visitors, but petty street crime is a problem. Do not carry more money than needed for the day and leave other valuables or documents in a hotel safe. Cameras are less likely to be snatched if they are in a carrier bag rather than an obvious case. Take particular care in crowded places, such as stations, or on full buses, and steer clear of bands of innocent-looking children – they may be skilful professional pickpockets.

Carabinieri in dress uniform

Police

There are several different police forces in Rome. The *polizia* (state police) wear blue uniforms with white belts and berets. They deal with all kinds of criminal offences and are the ones who issue *permessi di soggiorno* (residence permits) to foreigners and passports to Italian citizens (*see p366*).

The *vigili urbani* (municipal police) wear blue uniforms in winter and white in summer, and can issue heavy fines for traffic and parking offences. They can usually be seen patrolling the streets, enforcing laws or regulating traffic.

The *carabinieri* (military police) wear red striped trousers. They deal with everything from fine-art thefts to speeding offences.

The *guardia di finanza* are the tax police and wear grey uniforms. They deal with tax evasion and with customs; you will see them at the airport, behind the "goods to declare" counter.

To report stolen or lost items, go to the nearest police station (*questura*) or *carabinieri* office. If you believe your car may have been towed away, you should find a member of the *vigili urbani* on the streets or have the Comune put you through to them by calling 06-0606.

What to Be Aware of

Be wary of bag-snatchers on mopeds who operate in quiet streets. Carry your bag at your side away from the road, or carry a discreet money belt or a securely fastened, long-strapped shoulder bag across your body. Equipment like video cameras should be disguised. Pickpockets (sometimes children) adopt highly sophisticated distraction techniques with pieces of card or newspaper while they sever you from your possessions in seconds. Take extra care of your valuables in market places or on public transport. Bus routes 40 and 64, which run between Termini station and the Vatican, are notorious for pickpockets.

Thefts from cars are also rife. Jackets or bags should never be left visible inside a car parked on Rome's streets, and do not carry luggage on a roof rack. The streets to the east and south of Termini station are well-known for prostitution and drug-peddling, and are unsavoury at night.

Women travelling alone (or even in small groups) may need to take extra care. Women without male escorts attract more attention than they do in much of the rest of Europe and North America.

Beware of unauthorized minicab drivers who are probably not insured and frequently overcharge. They operate in particular at the airport and Termini station, waiting to profit from new arrivals. Hotel touts and unofficial tour guides are also best avoided; instead stick to the official tourist agencies (*see p297 and p369*).

In an Emergency

For emergency phone numbers see the Directory. For other medical attention, contact the First Aid (*Pronto Soccorso*) department of a main hospital such as **Policlinico Umberto I**, or **Ospedale di Santo Spirito**, or check the Yellow Pages (*Pagine Gialle*) for a doctor (*medico*) or dentist (*dentista*). For children, the **Ospedale Pediatrico Bambino Gesù** is renowned. Emergency care in public hospitals is free, even for foreigners.

Municipal policeman directing traffic

Poliziotto – a member of the state police

Carabiniere – a member of the military police

Police car

Ambulance

Fire engine

Lost Property

For items lost on a bus or on the Metro, contact the numbers in the Directory. Otherwise, ask at a police station. To make an insurance claim, report your loss to a police station and get a signed form. For lost passports, contact your embassy or consulate (see p369); for lost credit cards or traveller's cheques, contact the issuing company's office (see p372).

Hospitals and Pharmacies

English-speaking doctors can be found at **Rome American Hospital** or by looking in the English Yellow Pages, which is available at some hotel receptions and international bookshops. For access to paediatricians, visit the **Ospedale Pediatrico Bambino Gesù**. The **Ospedale Odontoiatrico G Eastman** can help with serious dental problems.

Pharmacists display late-opening rosters (several stay open all night), and can usually supply the local equivalent of foreign medicines. The **Vatican Pharmacy** stocks some American and British pharmaceutical products. For minor problems, pharmacists can give advice and recommend over-the-counter medications.

Minor Hazards

No inoculations are needed for Rome, but take mosquito repellent and sun screen in the summer. Be sure to wash your hands frequently if you use public transport, especially in winter when colds and flu are passed around easily. The Tiber is polluted but water from taps and potable street fountains is piped straight from the hills, and is fresh and palatable.

Travel and Health Insurance

EU residents are officially entitled to reciprocal medical care, but the bureaucracy involved can be daunting. Before you travel, make sure you obtain the European Health Insurance Card (EHIC) from the UK Department of Health (www. dh.gov.uk) or a post office. The card comes with a booklet of advice and information on the procedure for claiming free medical treatment. All visitors should take out insurance to cover everything. When booking air travel, ask if there are any waivers included in your particular ticket for medical problems, death in the family or other emergencies.

Take out adequate property insurance before you travel (it is difficult to arrange once you are in Italy), and look after your belongings while you are in Rome. Be particularly careful when using public transport and when visiting crowded tourist sights, where pick-pocketing is common. If possible, leave valuables at your hotel instead of carrying them around with you. Some hotels provide personal safes in the bedrooms. You can set these with your own memorable number. (Do not use your date of birth; it is on your passport and registration slip.) To be prepared for all eventualities, it is advisable to keep a separate

photocopy of vital documents, such as your passport and air tickets, to minimize the problem of replacing them if they are lost or stolen. It is also useful to take a spare passport-sized photograph or two.

DIRECTORY

In an Emergency

Ambulance
Tel 118 (free from any telephone).

Fire
Tel 115 (free from any telephone).

General SOS
Tel 113 (free from any telephone).

Police
Tel 112 (carabinieri); 113 (police) (free from any telephone).

Samaritans
Tel 800-860 022. **Open** 1–10pm daily. w samaritansonlus.org

Traffic Police
Tel 06-67691.

Lost Property

Buses and Trams
Tel 06-4695 2400.

Metro
Line A Tel 06-4695 7068.
Open 9:30am–12:30pm Mon, Wed, Fri. **Line B Tel** 06-4695 8165.
Open 8am–1pm Mon–Fri.
After 10–15 days:
Tel 06-6769 3214.

Hospitals and Pharmacies

Ospedale Odontoiatrico G Eastman
Viale Regina Elena 287B.
Map 6 F2. **Tel** 06-77301.

Ospedale Pediatrico Bambino Gesù
Piazza S. Onofrio 4.
Map 3 C4. **Tel** 06-68591.

Ospedale di Santo Spirito
Lungotevere in Sassia 1.
Map 3 C3. **Tel** 06-68351.

Policlinico Umberto I
Viale del Policlinico 155. **Map** 6 F2. **Tel** 06-49971, 800-283 110.

Rome American Hospital
Via E Longoni 69. **Tel** 06-22551.

Vatican Pharmacy
Porta Sant'Anna, Via di Porta Angelica. **Map** 3 C2.
Tel 06-6988 9806.

Banking and Local Currency

ATMs are easily found across Rome. Many businesses will accept credit cards, but some smaller family-run establishments still only accept cash. Exchanging money and traveller's cheques can involve a lot of paperwork. Bank and post office exchange rates are generally more favourable than those offered in travel agents. Carry some small change, since coins are needed for tips and illuminating works of art and chapels in churches *(see p367)*.

The Banca d'Italia, Italy's central bank

Banks and Bureaux de Change

It is best to have a few euros when you arrive to avoid having to change money immediately. However, ATMs are found everywhere, including at Fiumicino and Ciampino airports.

For the best exchange rates, change money at a bank (look for the sign *Cambio*). Exchange offices and hotels tend to give poor rates, even if they charge modest commissions.

Queues in banks can be long and the form-filling involved in changing money can take up a lot of time. Take some form of identification with you, such as a passport. You may be asked to leave handbags, shopping bags and metal objects in the small lockers outside the bank.

Post offices also give good exchange rates, but queues can be long here as well. Currency can also be changed at the main post offices, such as the one near Piramide Metro station.

Banks are usually open 8:30am–1:20pm and 3–4:30pm Mon–Fri, but opening times vary. They are always closed on public holidays.

Bureaux de change have more generous opening times, similar to shop hours. The two exchange offices at Termini station *(see p378)* are also open on Sundays.

ATMs

ATM machines (*Bancomat*) can be found throughout the city and accept a wide range of credit and debit cards. The daily limit for withdrawals is usually €250. A fee is charged for each withdrawal. ATM crime (mainly related to card cloning rather than to theft) has been reported in the past. Always use caution at an ATM: cover the hand that is entering the code with the other hand, and avoid withdrawing cash from any machine you are unsure about.

Credit Cards and Traveller's Cheques

Credit cards are widely accepted in hotels, restaurants and shops. All major credit and charge cards (American Express, MasterCard, Visa, Diners Club) are well known. Banks and cash dispensers are more likely to accept Visa cards for cash advances, but MasterCard is accepted by many retail outlets in Italy. Take both if you have them. Paying for anything in foreign currency will almost always be expensive.

Some restaurants and shops set a minimum expenditure level, below which they will not accept credit card payment. Ask first or check you have some cash just in case.

Traveller's cheques are not as popular as they used to be and tourists are finding it increasingly hard to cash or spend them. If you decide to use them, choose a well-known name such as American Express. Record the traveller's cheque numbers and refund addresses separately from the cheques themselves in case they are stolen.

DIRECTORY

Banks and Bureaux de Change

Banca Intesa San Paolo
Via del Corso 226. **Map** 12 E3.
Tel 06-67121. **Open** 8:05am–8pm Mon–Fri.

Banca Nazionale del Lavoro BNL
Piazza Venezia 6. **Map** 12 F4.
Tel 06-678 2979. **Open** 8:35am–1:35pm Mon–Fri.

Lost and Stolen Credit Cards

American Express
Tel 06-7290 0347.

Diners Club
Tel 800-393 939 (toll free).

Visa and MasterCard
Tel 800-819 014 (toll free).

The Euro

The euro (€) is the common currency of the European Union. It went into general circulation on 1 January 2002, initially for 12 participating countries. Italy was one of those original countries.

The area comprising the EU member states using the euro as sole official currency is known as the eurozone. Several EU members have opted out of joining this common currency.

Euro notes are identical throughout the eurozone, each one including designs of fictional architectural structures. The coins, however, have one side identical (the value side), and one side with an image unique to each country. Notes and coins are exchangeable in all participating euro countries.

Euro Bank Notes

Euro bank notes have seven denominations. The €5 note (grey in colour) is the smallest, followed by the €10 note (pink), €20 note (blue), €50 note (orange), €100 note (green), €200 note (yellow) and €500 note (purple). All notes show the stars of the European Union.

€5 note

€10 note

€20 note

€50 note

€100 note

€200 note

€500 note

€2 coin

€1 coin

50 cents

20 cents

10 cents

Coins

The euro has eight coin denominations: €1 and €2; 50 cents, 20 cents, 10 cents, 5 cents, 2 cents and 1 cent. The €2 and €1 coins are both silver and gold in colour. The 50-, 20- and 10-cent coins are gold. The 5-, 2- and 1-cent coins are bronze.

5 cents

2 cents

1 cent

Communications and Media

With the most recent advances in technology, it is easier and cheaper than ever to stay in touch with family and friends while abroad. Even if you don't have a mobile with Internet capabilities, you'll find that Wi-Fi and Internet cafés are everywhere in Rome, and phone cards offering very reasonable call rates abound. You can stay abreast of the news at home through BBC World (most likely available in your hotel) or the English-language publications available at many newsagents in the centre of Rome.

Telephone company logo

International and Local Telephone Calls

The mobile phone revolution led the Italian national telephone company, Telecom Italia, to dismantle the last remaining public telephone booths in 2014. However, privately owned "call centres" offer a convenient way of making private long-distance calls for travellers who are not using their own mobile phones. They are equipped with several metered telephones in sound-proofed booths. An assistant will assign you a booth and meter your call. You pay at the desk when you have finished so coins are not needed. Call centres tend to be open from early morning until late night and many also offer fax, Internet and photocopying facilities.

Public telephone sign

International phone cards, such as the Europa card, are by far the cheapest option if phoning abroad from Italy. They come in either €5 or €10 cards, which give 120 (or more) minutes of calling time. When using, dial the main number on the card, key in the pin code and then dial the number required.

Any Italian landline telephone number dialled needs to have the full relevant local code (including the zero) dialled in front of it, even if you are calling within the same city. Mobile phone number prefixes begin with a 3 and do not require a 0.

Keep in mind that telephone calls from hotel rooms are usually very expensive, sometimes marked up by as much as several hundred per cent.

Mobile Phones

If you are staying in Rome for a longer period of time, it is probably worth setting up a roaming agreement with your mobile phone provider at home or buying an Italian SIM card, with its own unique telephone number, to use with your mobile. You must show an official ID (such as a passport) when buying a SIM card. There are five main mobile providers: Vodafone, TIM, Tre, PosteMobile and Wind. The SIM cards cost around €15 and usually come with €5 of free credit. They can be purchased, and topped up, from various mobile phone outlets throughout the city.

Once you have the SIM, you can also top up your credit with a scratch-off card (*ricarica*) bought at tobacconist's shops or some newsagents. Some tobacconist's shops have a computerized system where they insert your mobile number and put the credit on your phone for you, which is easier and quicker than following the instructions on the scratch-off card. You can also top up at ATM machines.

Smart phone applications such as WhatsApp and Viber can be used to make free calls. The services can only be used if the person you are calling is using the same application and your phone is connected to the Internet.

Internet café sign

Internet Access

Many hotels offer an Internet connection or Wi-Fi so you can access the Internet and email with your own laptop (sometimes for an extra fee). There are some Internet cafés (Italians call them "Internet point") where you can go online, such as **Yex Change** in the city centre. Those travelling without their

Reaching the Right Number

- The code for Rome is 06 (obligatory also within the city and after dialing +39 when calling from abroad).
- Multilingual directory enquiries is on 1254 (press 2).
- Operator assistance is on 170. Reverse charge and credit card calls are also accepted.
- Italian directory enquiries is on 1254 (press 1).
- To reach the operator in your own country to place a collect or credit card call dial 800 172 then: 441 for the UK; 444 for AT&T, US; 401 for Verizon, US; 405 for US Sprint; 610 for Telstra, Australia; and 611 for Optus, Australia.

own laptop or smart-phone can also use the Internet at one of the phone centres around Termini station.

Some Internet cafés offer headphones and webcams so customers can use Skype or other chat programmes. Many Internet points have Wi-Fi so you can access the Internet through your own laptop with a password provided by the assistant. An anti-terrorism law requires Internet café staff to take customers' information from an official ID (such as a passport), so staff may want to take a photocopy before allowing use of the Internet on their computers. This does not apply to customers using their own laptops.

Many cafés and bars have wireless hotspots. You can also sign up to access free Wi-Fi for a couple of hours a day in select public spaces throughout Rome by registering at www.romawireless.com.

Postal Services

Post offices are multi-functional in Italy, used not only for postal services, but also for paying bills, managing certain bank accounts and more. Lines can be long and disorganized, so if you are just sending a regular letter or postcard, save yourself the exasperation and buy a stamp at a tobacconist's shop. Then drop your letter in the post boxes on walls around the city; most are red, with a slot for mail within Rome (Roma e provincia di Roma) and one for mail outside Rome (per tutte le altre destinazioni). There are also some blue post boxes exclusively for foreign destinations (marked estero).

Vatican post office sign

Vatican postage stamps

The post itself is quite reliable and efficient, though it tends to be slower around Christmas time. For urgent items, use the post office's express or registered service.

The Italian post office offers a poste restante service, where letters and parcels addressed to you can be picked up directly at the post office. Post should be sent care of (c/o) Fermo Posta and the name of the relevant post office. Print the surname clearly in block capitals and underline it to make sure it is filed correctly. To collect your post, you have to show your passport and pay a small charge.

Regular post office hours are generally from around 8:30am to 2pm (8:30am to noon on Saturdays and on holiday eves), but main offices stay open until well into the evening for some services (such as registered post).

Post box with two slots

Newspapers, TV and Radio

Rome's main newspapers are La Repubblica and Il Messaggero. British and American newspapers are readily available, with the International Herald Tribune and the Guardian on sale on the day of issue. The TrovaRoma supplement, in the Thursday edition of La Repubblica is generally considered the main guide to what's on in the capital. There is a useful section in English at

Vatican Post

The Vatican postal service costs the same as the state post, but is faster. Buy cards and stamps at the post office near the Vatican Museums entrance, or in Piazza San Pietro. Letters bearing Vatican stamps can only be posted within Vatican city.

Foreign papers at a newsstand

the back providing the week's top listings. The magazines Wanted in Rome (www.wantedinrome.com) and Where Rome (www.whererome.it) also have English listings. Some of these publications also have websites full of information.

The state TV channels are RAI Uno, Due and Tre, matched by four private channels. Analogue TV has been replaced by digital across the country, so as well as picking up Italian state and private networks, most televisions give access to various channels in English.

Vatican Radio transmits on 93.3MHz and 105MHz (FM) and also broadcasts news in English.

GETTING TO ROME

Many national airlines, including Italy's Alitalia, fly direct to Rome from most European cities and several in North America. Fiumicino airport now has a high-security terminal, Terminal 5, for flights to the US and Israel. Ciampino airport is smaller and mainly caters to low-cost airlines flying in from other European cities. Rome also has train and coach links with the rest of Europe. These take a lot longer than flights (about 24 hours from London, for example, compared with about 2½ hours by air), but tend to cost about the same, so are only really worthwhile if you want to travel overland. The trains are often crowded during the summer.

Arriving by Air

If you are flying from the United States, **Delta**, **American Airlines**, and **Alitalia** operate regular direct scheduled flights to Rome, with services from New York. Flying time is about 8½ hours. **Air Canada** and **Qantas** operate from Canada and Australia respectively. There are also direct flights from Boston, Atlanta, Miami, Philadelphia and Toronto. However, it may be considerably cheaper for intercontinental travellers to take a budget flight to London, Paris, Athens, Frankfurt or Amsterdam and continue the journey to Rome from there. **British Airways** and **Alitalia** both operate direct scheduled flights from London Heathrow to Rome (Fiumicino), and you can also fly **BA** and **Norwegian** from Gatwick. **Swiss** and **KLM** also fly to Rome from London and other British cities, including Manchester, Bristol, Edinburgh and Cardiff. A change in Zurich or Amsterdam is usually involved.

Part of the extension to Fiumicino airport

Excursion fares generally offer the best value in scheduled flights, but you must purchase them well in advance. They are subject to penalty clauses if you cancel, so it is advisable to take out insurance as soon as you buy your ticket.

In addition to BA and Alitalia, you can book low-cost tickets direct from airlines **easyJet** and **Ryanair**, which have daily flights from London and other locations to Rome. Hotels and car rental can also be booked via these airlines' websites, and both offer their own privately chartered bus to transport incoming passengers from Ciampino airport to Termini.

Regular charter flights for Rome's Ciampino airport run all year round. Most leave from Stansted, Gatwick and Luton, but there are also a few flights that leave from Manchester, Glasgow and Birmingham. The price of fares varies, peaking in summer and in Holy Week for the Pope's Easter blessing. In Rome, the American Express travel office (see p369) will also book flights.

Fiumicino Airport

Rome has two international airports. Leonardo da Vinci – known as Fiumicino – is the largest one and handles most scheduled flights, as well as several easyJet routes. It is located about 30 km (18 miles) southwest of the city and has four terminals: 1 for domestic flights, 2 for EU flights, 3 for international flights and 5 for flights to the US or Israel. The vast shopping area inside the airport offers a variety of stores, selling the most important Italian brands.

From Fiumicino there are two types of train to Rome: one (€8) runs every 15–30 minutes (5:57am–11:27pm) to

Check-in area at Fiumicino, Rome's main international airport

Fara Sabina station, stopping at Trastevere, Ostiense, Tuscolana and Tiburtina, but not Termini. The other train, known as the "Leonardo Express", is faster and more expensive (€14), running non-stop to Termini every half-hour (6:23am–11:23pm). If the ticket office is not open, try the automatic ticket machine (you can choose to see the instructions in English). Remember to specify which train you want when buying your ticket.

Ostiense station is linked with Piramide Metro (Line B) where you can catch an underground train to the city centre from 5:30am until 11:30pm daily (to 1:30am Fri and Sat). It can be hard to find a taxi at Ostiense after 9pm, but there are buses (Nos. 80, 83 and 30) to Piazza Venezia. At night there is a coach service from Fiumicino to Tiburtina station (see also p380–81). Car rental is available from offices at the airport (see p387).

Check-in area at Rome's Ciampino airport

Train linking Fiumicino airport to Stazione Termini

Ciampino Airport

The other airport that serves Rome is Giovanni Battista Pastine Airport, known as Ciampino. It is located approximately 20 km (12½ miles) southeast of the city and used by the majority of charter flights and low-cost airlines. Ciampino airport is always busy and sometimes chaotic, so it is advisable to arrive there well in advance of your departure time.

Major car hire firms have a rental office at the airport (see p387), though you may find it less harrowing to travel into the city centre on public transport or by taxi.

The swiftest way to get to the centre of Rome is by the private **Terravision**, **Atral/Schiaffini** or **SITBusShuttle** coach services. Coaches go direct to Termini station and tickets cost between €4 and €6 one way. You can buy them on board the bus or online (often with a discount). A cheaper option is by **COTRAL** bus to Anagnina Metro station, then by underground train to Termini. Tickets (€1.50, plus €1.50 for each large bag) can be bought on the bus. A local bus service also links the airport to Ciampino mainline station.

Airport Taxis

Always use the official white taxis with a "taxi" sign on the roof. They usually line up in the yellow TAXI lanes in front of the airports and stations. The Rome Comune has established a flat fee for taxi rides from and to the airports: €48 to/from Fiumicino from/to anywhere in the centre (inside the Aurelian walls) and €30 to/from Ciampino from/to the centre. The fare covers a maximum of four people with baggage included. If a taxi refuses to apply the flat fee, you should report the driver by calling 06-6710 70721 and stating the cab number (or code name, which usually includes the name of a city, eg Firenze 8), that is found on both the inside and the outside of the car.

DIRECTORY

Arriving by Air

Air Canada
w aircanada.com

Alitalia
w alitalia.com

American Airlines
w aa.com

British Airways
Tel 02-6963 3602.
w britishairways.com

Delta
w delta.com

easyJet
w easyjet.com

KLM
w klm.com

Norwegian
w norwegian.com

Qantas
w qantas.com

Ryanair
w ryanair.com

Swiss
w swiss.com

Fiumicino and Ciampino Airports

Atral (Ciampino)
w atral-lazio.com

COTRAL (both airports)
w cotralspa.it

SITBusShuttle (both airports)
Tel 06-5916 826.
w sitbusshuttle.it

Terravision (Ciampino)
w terravision.eu

Arriving in Rome by Train, Coach or Car

Any overland journey to Rome is fastest by train, though there are coach connections to most major European cities. Within Italy, journeys between large cities are usually also best done by train, but when travelling from towns which are not on the main Intercity rail routes, coaches can be quicker. For drivers, the Italian Automobile Club provides free assistance and excellent maps to members of affiliated automobile clubs from all over the world.

A Frecciarossa train

The concourse at Stazione Termini

Stazione Termini

Stazione Termini, Rome's main train station, is also the hub of the urban transport system. Beneath it is the interchange between Metro lines A and B, and outside, on Piazza dei Cinquecento, is the central bus terminus. Though it is one of Rome's most stunning 20th-century buildings, it also has some unsavoury aspects, so do not linger longer than necessary at night.

If you do arrive here late, there are usually taxis available (go to the official queue) even in the small hours, and many of the city's night buses start at Termini.

In summer the station gets crowded, and you can expect long queues. Termini has a left luggage office, a police station, a bureau de change, and tourist and travel information offices. Other facilities include many tobacconists and newsagents (where you can buy bus and Metro tickets), as well as various bars and restaurants on the mezzanine floor, with more eateries and shops, including a bookstore, on the lower Termini Forum level. A post office is adjacent to platform 24, as are desks for car-hire firms. There is only one waiting room, located next to platform 1.

Of Rome's other stations, four are most likely to be useful for tourists. They are Ostiense and Trastevere, for trains to Fiumicino airport and Viterbo *(see p273)*; Tiburtina, for some of the late-night and high-speed trains on the north-south line through Italy; and Roma Nord, for trains to Prima Porta.

Travelling by Train

Trenitalia, the Italian State Railway, has several levels of service, including the Regionale trains. These stop at almost every station, often have no air conditioning and are much cheaper than the other trains. In Regionale and InterRegionale trains, sometimes first-class seats are "declassed" so second-class ticket holders can sit there. The Eurostar, a cleaner, faster train, offers a first- and second-class service. It runs between Rome and Milan, Turin, Genoa, Bari, Naples and Venice, with an extra fast *(alta velocità)* Frecciarossa service operating on the Naples-Rome-Milan and Venice-Rome lines, although it now faces stiff competition from the private high-speed **Italo** trains (book in advance for the best deals). You have to reserve a seat and you are charged hefty supplements for the privileges of speed and hostess service. Intercity trains, which are for fast long-distance journeys, also charge a supplement. First- and second-class tickets are available to the larger cities. From Rome you can also take international or Eurocity (EC) trains to destinations all over Europe.

Trenitalia logo

Termini, the heart of Italy's rail network and Rome's transport system

Reservations are compulsory on all trains except those on Regionale and InterRegionale routes. Tickets for immediate travel can be bought at the station, but you should allow plenty of time to queue.

The Trenitalia website *(see below)* is useful for planning trips, checking train times and buying tickets. If you book in advance or are a family with a child, you may be able to get a cheaper rate. However, it is easiest to go to a travel agency for a discounted ticket because Trenitalia's offers and fares change all the time.

An Intercity train

Travelling by Coach

Long-distance coaches terminate at Tiburtina, which is the city's main coach station. Information and tickets for coaches to European cities are available from the **Eurolines**, **Baltour** or **Italybus** websites. The latter usefully brings together various regional, inter-regional and international coach routes and companies. Local buses, serving villages and towns within the Lazio region, are run by **COTRAL**. All bus stations used by COTRAL in Rome are linked to Metro stations. Tickets are purchased on the spot and cannot be booked in advance. Some day trips from Rome by bus are described on pages 270–73.

Machines for Trenitalia Rail Tickets

These machines are easy to use, and most have instructions on screen in a choice of six languages. They accept coins, notes and credit cards.

1 Touch screen: choose destination, train and ticket type, make seat reservations and choose payment method.

2 Insert coins here.

3 Payment with credit card: touchpad with slot for card below.

4 Receive train tickets, seat reservations and change here.

5 Insert banknotes here.

Travelling by Car

To drive your own car in Italy you need your driving licence, an international Green Card (for insurance purposes) and the vehicle registration document. A translation of your driving licence, available at Italian tourist offices abroad, is useful. Wearing seatbelts is compulsory in Italy. Headlights must be turned on even during the day on motorways and outside of built-up areas. Heavy fines are levied for using a mobile phone while driving. You must also carry a warning triangle and a reflective orange or yellow vest to wear if you leave your car in case of breakdown. Main routes to Rome connect with the Grande Raccordo Anulare (GRA), Rome's ring-road. Tolls are charged on most Italian motorways. You take a ticket when you enter a toll road, and pay on exit. Tolls can be paid with cash, credit cards or a prepaid ViaCard. The latter is widely available (even at motorway services), and the toll is docked from the card on leaving the motorway. Prices vary according to road type.

The official speed limits are 30–70 km/h (18–40 mph) in town, 80–110 km/h (50–70 mph) on two-lane roads outside town, and 130 km/h (80 mph) on motorways.

Directory

Travelling by Train

Italo
w italotreno.it

Stazione Termini
w romatermini.com

Trenitalia
Tel 89 20 21. w trenitalia.com

Travelling by Coach

Baltour
w baltour.it

COTRAL
w cotralspa.it

Eurolines
w eurolines.com

Italybus
w italybus.it

Eurolines coach connecting Rome with the rest of Europe

Arriving in Rome

This map shows the main bus, rail and Metro links used by travellers arriving in Rome. The connections between Rome's two airports and the city centre are shown, as well as links between Rome and the rest of Italy and international rail routes from neighbouring European countries. Travel information, including details of journey times and service frequency, is listed separately in each box.

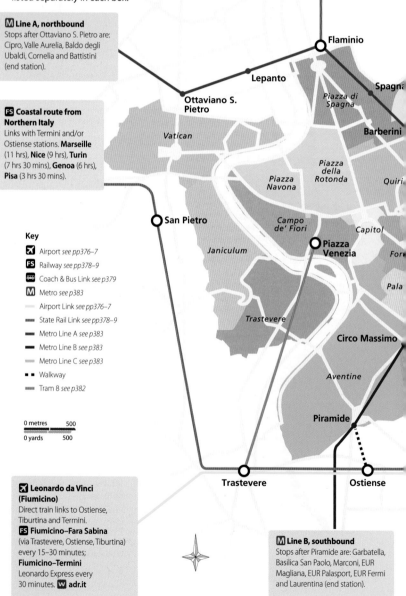

FS Local train connections
Links to Flaminio (Roma Nord station) from **Viterbo** (2 hrs 30 mins).

M Line A, northbound
Stops after Ottaviano S. Pietro are: Cipro, Valle Aurelia, Baldo degli Ubaldi, Cornelia and Battistini (end station).

FS Coastal route from Northern Italy
Links with Termini and/or Ostiense stations. **Marseille** (11 hrs), **Nice** (9 hrs), **Turin** (7 hrs 30 mins), **Genoa** (6 hrs), **Pisa** (3 hrs 30 mins).

Key

- 🛪 Airport *see pp376–7*
- FS Railway *see pp378–9*
- 🚌 Coach & Bus Link *see p379*
- M Metro *see p383*
- — Airport Link *see pp376–7*
- — State Rail Link *see pp378–9*
- — Metro Line A *see p383*
- — Metro Line B *see p383*
- — Metro Line C *see p383*
- ▪ ▪ Walkway
- — Tram 8 *see p382*

0 metres   500
0 yards   500

Flaminio
Lepanto
Ottaviano S. Pietro
Spagna
Piazza di Spagna
Barberini
Vatican
Piazza della Rotonda
Quiri
Piazza Navona
San Pietro
Campo de' Fiori
Capitol
Janiculum
Piazza Venezia
For
Pala
Trastevere
Circo Massimo
Aventine
Piramide
Ostiense
Trastevere

🛪 Leonardo da Vinci (Fiumicino)
Direct train links to Ostiense, Tiburtina and Termini.
FS Fiumicino–Fara Sabina
(via Trastevere, Ostiense, Tiburtina) every 15–30 minutes;
Fiumicino–Termini
Leonardo Express every 30 minutes. **W adr.it**

M Line B, southbound
Stops after Piramide are: Garbatella, Basilica San Paolo, Marconi, EUR Magliana, EUR Palasport, EUR Fermi and Laurentina (end station).

For keys to symbols *see back flap*

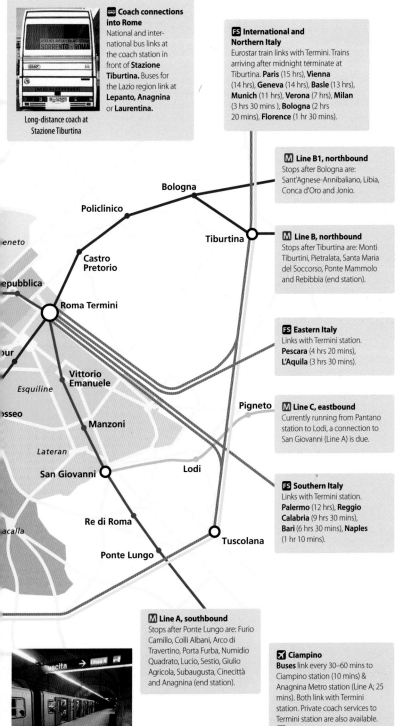

Coach connections into Rome
National and international bus links at the coach station in front of **Stazione Tiburtina.** Buses for the Lazio region link at **Lepanto, Anagnina** or **Laurentina.**

Long-distance coach at Stazione Tiburtina

FS International and Northern Italy
Eurostar train links with Termini. Trains arriving after midnight terminate at Tiburtina. **Paris** (15 hrs), **Vienna** (14 hrs), **Geneva** (14 hrs), **Basle** (13 hrs), **Munich** (11 hrs), **Verona** (7 hrs), **Milan** (3 hrs 30 mins), **Bologna** (2 hrs 20 mins), **Florence** (1 hr 30 mins).

M Line B1, northbound
Stops after Bologna are: Sant'Agnese-Annibaliano, Libia, Conca d'Oro and Jonio.

M Line B, northbound
Stops after Tiburtina are: Monti Tiburtini, Pietralata, Santa Maria del Soccorso, Ponte Mammolo and Rebibbia (end station).

FS Eastern Italy
Links with Termini station. **Pescara** (4 hrs 20 mins), **L'Aquila** (3 hrs 30 mins).

M Line C, eastbound
Currently running from Pantano station to Lodi, a connection to San Giovanni (Line A) is due.

FS Southern Italy
Links with Termini station. **Palermo** (12 hrs), **Reggio Calabria** (9 hrs 30 mins), **Bari** (6 hrs 30 mins), **Naples** (1 hr 10 mins).

M Line A, southbound
Stops after Ponte Lungo are: Furio Camillo, Colli Albani, Arco di Travertino, Porta Furba, Numidio Quadrato, Lucio, Sestio, Giulio Agricola, Subaugusta, Cinecittà and Anagnina (end station).

Ciampino
Buses link every 30–60 mins to Ciampino station (10 mins) & Anagnina Metro station (Line A; 25 mins). Both link with Termini station. Private coach services to Termini station are also available.
W adr.it

Bologna
Policlinico
eneto
Castro Pretorio
epubblica
Roma Termini
Tiburtina
our
Vittorio Emanuele
Esquiline
osseo
Manzoni
Pigneto
Lateran
San Giovanni
Lodi
Re di Roma
acalla
Tuscolana
Ponte Lungo

Termini Metro station

GETTING AROUND ROME

Rome's centre is compact and, even though walking absolutely everywhere would be over-ambitious, it is a city in which you can spend much of your time on foot. As the main streets in the centre are usually clogged with traffic, driving and cycling cannot be recommended, but courageous motorbike or scooter riders can have great fun buzzing around on a rented Vespa. Travelling by bus and tram can be very slow, so use overland public transport only when you have a long way to go. The Metro, designed to connect the suburbs with the centre, has no stops in the historic city centre near the Pantheon or Piazza Navona, though it is certainly the swiftest way of crossing the city.

Green Travel

As the largest and most advanced city of the ancient world, Rome was the first to face (and combat) air pollution from burning wood. The fight against smog continues today, as many Romans rely exclusively on their cars. Car-sharing schemes, city-owned bicycles and some (but not enough) bike lanes, **electric-car charging stations**, and car-free Sundays (in the springtime) are among the initiatives. Video cameras prevent unauthorized cars from entering the *centro storico*, where many bus lines (three of which are electric) cover almost everything there is to see. Though often busy and chaotic, public transportation is always a better option than driving, and some used bus tickets will buy you discounted entry to selected exhibitions

Bus stop listing details of routes served

(see instructions on the ticket itself). Walking around the centre is pleasant, so if you want to enjoy the warm sunshine and avoid public transport, make sure you wear sturdy, comfortable shoes. It is a good idea to find accommodation in a pedestrian-friendly area if you want to cover the centre on foot. Areas such as Trastevere, Celio, or around the Piazza Navona and Via del Corso are packed with sights, restaurants and boutiques.

Buses and Trams

Rome's public transport company is called **ATAC** (Azienda Tramvie e Autobus del Comune di Roma). Scores of buses and a few trams cover most parts of the city. Most run from early morning until midnight, meaning the last bus leaves from the end of the line at midnight. There are also a few night buses.

Apart from some small electric minibuses (like the 116 and 119), no buses can run through the narrow streets of the historic centre. But there are plenty of bus routes to take you within a short walk of the main sights *(see inside back cover)*.

Bus stops list the details of routes taken by all buses using that stop. Night buses are indicated by an "N" before the number.

There are several trams in the city but the only main line of tourist interest is the 8, which runs from Piazza Venezia to Casaletto, going through Trastevere and Monteverde. The **Muoversi a Roma** website and app is useful for calculating waiting times.

Using Buses and Trams

The main terminus is on Piazza dei Cinquecento outside Termini station, but there are other major route hubs throughout the city, most usefully those at Piazza del Risorgimento and Piazza Venezia. Information on public transport can be obtained from ATAC kiosks, the customer service office or the ATAC website. You should board the bus at the front or the back; the central door is reserved for people getting off. You must stamp your ticket in the yellow machine once you get on the bus. Timed tickets, *biglietto integrato a tempo* (BIT), can be used on all means of transport. Buses and trams are often overcrowded, and you may have to stand for all of your journey. Beware of pickpockets,

A modern tram taking passengers through the city

One of Rome's red and grey ATAC buses

especially on the more central lines, and when standing in front of the exit door.

Tickets

Tickets for buses, trams and Metros should be bought in advance and stamped in the appropriate machine as soon as you start your journey. You can buy tickets at bars, some newsagents and tobacconists, as well as in Metro stations and at bus termini. There are automatic ticket machines at main bus stops and Metro stations that take coins. Some buses have a machine on board for buying tickets, but there is no way of knowing which

buses have one, so purchase a ticket before you board.

BIT tickets are valid for 100 minutes, during which time you can take one Metro ride and as many buses and trams as you like. If you are going to make four or more journeys in one day, buy a daily (BIG) ticket. There are also three-day, seven-day and monthly passes. To travel farther afield in Lazio, consider a regional BIRG ticket. Fare-dodging incurs a hefty fine.

Metro

Rome's underground system, the Metro (Metropolitana), has three

lines. A and B cross the city in a rough X-shape, converging at Termini station (*see inside back cover*). Line A (red) leads from Battistini in the west to Anagnina in the southeast of the city, from where buses go to Ciampino airport. Line B (blue) runs from Rebibbia in the northeast, branches off at Bologna station, then goes down to EUR in the southwest, where buses leave for the coast. Line C (green) currently runs from Pantano station to Luni and construction is underway

Metro logo

to link it up with Line A at San Giovanni by the end of 2017. Stations are clearly marked by the Metro logo, a white M on a red background. Among the most useful stations are Colosseo, Spagna, San Giovanni, Ottaviano S. Pietro and Piramide (for trains to Fiumicino). Lines run from 5:30am until 11:30pm every day (to 1:30am Friday and Saturday). For more details, visit www.atac.roma.it.

Useful Bus Routes

This map shows some of the buses that go through interesting parts of Rome with good views of major sights. The 40 Express is always full of tourists, since it goes from Termini to St Peter's and the Vatican. The other routes are likely to be less crowded.

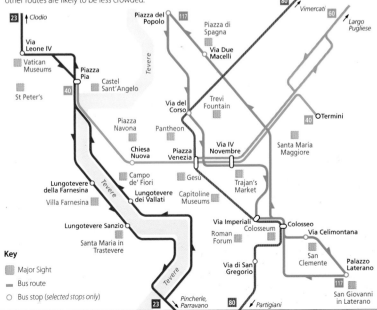

Walking

Wandering through Rome's old centre is one of the most enjoyable aspects of the city. You can take in the architectural details, absorb the streetlife, make diversions at will, and peek into any church, shop or bar that catches your interest. You can easily visit several of the main tourist sights in a few hours.

Explore the city area by area, using public transport when distances are too far. Although some parts of the historic centre are now pedestrianized, a street which is closed to cars may still be used by cyclists and, illegally, by scooter riders. There have been many plans to create more traffic-free zones, but imposing such measures on a population as insubordinate as Rome's is not easily done.

During the height of summer, you'll have a more enjoyable time if you follow the example of the Italians. Walk slowly on the shady side of the street; have a long lunch followed by a siesta in the hottest part of the day. Continue exploring in the late afternoon, when churches and shops reopen and the streets are at their liveliest. Wandering at night is delightful, as the streets are cool and many façades floodlit.

Crossing Roads

First impressions suggest there can be only two sorts of pedestrian in Rome: the quick and the dead. Even if you cross

Passengers sightseeing on an open-top tour bus

roads by traffic lights and pedestrian crossings strictly in your favour, there is sure to be some van or Vespa hurtling toward you with apparently homicidal intent. Fortunately, Roman drivers have quick reactions and accidents are relatively rare. The best tactic is to be as alert and confident as Romans. The roads are very busy. When crossing, you should try to leave as large a gap as possible between yourself and oncoming traffic. Step purposefully into the road, making eye contact with approaching motorists, and do not hesitate or change your course. Once a driver sees that you are determined to cross, he will stop, or at least swerve. Pedestrians must take particular care at night, when the traffic lights are switched to a constantly flashing amber, turning the crossings into free-for-alls.

Street Signs

Theoretically, although it may not always seem to be the case, pedestrians have right of way at crossings when the green *avanti* sign is lit up. The red sign *alt* means you must wait. Underground crossings are indicated by a sign reading *sottopassaggio*.

It is easy to get lost in the maze of streets and piazzas of the historic centre. Until you know your way around you can follow the yellow signs marking routes

between the sights and piazzas of particular interest to tourists. Routes leading to other landmarks are indicated by signs on a brown or grey background.

Guided Tours

Several companies offer guided tours in English; these include the excellent **Walks of Italy**, **Green Line Tours**, **Context** and **Carrani Tours**. Full-day city tours with lunch cost around €100; half-day tours around €40. Alternatively **City Sightseeing Roma** offers hop-on, hop-off tours aboard double decker buses with audio guides in eight languages. Tours run every 15–20 minutes daily between 9am and 7pm and last 1 hour and 40 minutes. Buses can be boarded at any of the eight stops, which

Nuns walking in Rome's city centre

Avanti: go! Pedestrians have right of way

Alt: stop! Traffic has right of way

Directions for walkers

Watch out for children

Pedestrian crossing

include the Colosseum, Santa Maria Maggiore and the Vatican. Tour guides can be hired at major sights, such as the Roman Forum (see pp78–89). Use only official guides and establish the fee in advance; they usually charge at least €50 for a half-day tour.

Driving

Driving in Rome can be an extremely intimidating experience for visitors. The flamboyant aggression of Italian drivers is notorious, pedestrians step out into the roads without warning, and the one-way system operating in much of the centre makes retaining a sense of direction impossible. You'll also find motorists overtaking on the wrong side, while scooters and Vespas zoom among the lanes of traffic and go the wrong way down one-way streets. One rule to remember is to give way to the right. Additionally, non-resident drivers cannot enter the city centre's ZTL (Limited Traffic Zone) during the day and on some weekend nights. There are cameras at the entrance of the ZTL, and cars without a permit will receive a fine each time they pass in front of the camera. The cameras are very visible, and there is always an electronic sign saying whether access is open to everyone (varco aperto or varco non attivo) or restricted (varco chiuso or varco attivo). You

No stopping

No parking

One-way street

No through road

can call 06-57003 or check www. atacmobile.it for ZTL times. Unless you are accustomed to driving in Italian cities and fully aware of the ZTL regulations and zones, leave your car at home – or, failing that, in a guarded car park.

Thefts from cars are rife in Rome, so never leave anything of value in your vehicle, even out of sight: areas such as Campo de' Fiori are patrolled by gangs on the lookout for anyone leaving cameras and other costly items in the car. You should also

remove the car radio and Sat Nav if you can – you will not be the only person carrying these with you.

Take extra care if driving late at night. Not only do traffic lights switch to flashing amber, but some drivers are astonishingly cavalier about driving under the influence of drink or drugs. In the case of a breakdown, call the **ACI** (see pp386–7).

Parking

The most convenient car park is below the Villa Borghese. Much of the city centre is reserved for residents with permits but there are around 2,000 metered parking spaces marked with a blue line (from 8am–8pm or 8am–11pm, depending on the area). If you do find a legal place to park, however, you may return and find that you have been hemmed in by double-parked cars. Locations of some of the most useful car parks are listed on page 387.

Beware of illegal parking attendants, found especially at night in busy areas where parking is free, who direct you to a space (sometimes even an unauthorized one) in exchange for some change. This practice is against the law, but Italians often pay, for fear the attendant will damage their car if they do not.

Petrol

Petrol is very expensive. It can be bought from roadside petrol pumps (many of which are self-service, which is cheaper, operated by banknotes or debit/credit cards), as well as from regular garages. Check whether your car uses lead-free petrol (benzina senza piombo or benzina verde) or not. Late-night petrol stations are listed on page 387. At night, most self-service stations are attended by illegal petrol station attendants, who will put the petrol in for you in exchange for a tip.

The state petrol company logo

Illegal Parking

Rome's traffic police are vigilant. If you've parked illegally, your car may be clamped or (if it is causing an obstruction) towed away, so phone 06-67691 or 06-0606 before reporting it stolen. No-parking zones should be clearly marked, but check in case the sign is hidden by a tree.

zona rimozione fermata consentita per salita e discesa con conducente a bordo

Signpost for a tow-away area (zona rimozione)

A tow truck at work

Car Hire

Major international firms (**Avis, Hertz, Europcar**) and **Sixt** have rental offices at the airports, Termini station and in the city. However, you may get a better deal by booking a car before you arrive through a travel agent or online, or by using a local firm (such as **Maggiore**). Check that breakdown service and collision damage waiver are included. Prospective renters usually need to be at least 25 years old and have held a driving licence for at least a year. You will also need to leave a deposit – a credit card number is usually enough. Some firms also ask for an international licence (available from your national automobile association).

The most popular car hire option for short hops in the city is through **car2go**, the Europe-wide car-sharing scheme whereby users obtain the whereabouts of hundreds of Smart cars through a smartphone app. These can be booked and used immediately.

Accident rates on Italian roads are high, so make sure you are fully insured against all eventualities. It is a good idea to join an internationally affiliated automobile association (such as the AA in Britain or the AAA in the US) so that if you do break down, the **ACI** (Italian Auto-mobile Club) will tow your car without charging.

Details of road and traffic conditions (in Italian) are available from a special **Road Conditions** number. For more information on driving and parking in the city, as well as understanding road signs and buying fuel, see page 385.

Moped and Bicycle Hire

Rome's narrow streets and heavy traffic, combined with the seven steep hills on which it was built, make it a challenging place for even the most serious of cyclists. However, there are a few areas, such as the Villa Borghese, the banks of the Tiber and some pockets in the historic centre (around the Pantheon and Piazza Navona), where bike lanes make for a relaxing way to see the city.

Mopeds (*motorini*) and scooters – like the classic Piaggio Vespa, meaning "wasp" – are good for getting through the traffic. You may want to stick to quiet streets to begin with, though.

Bikes and scooters can be hired from **Collalti, Bici & Baci** and **Barberini Scooters for Rent**. There are also **Bike Rental** spots dotted around the city. Motorcyclists, scooter drivers and their passengers must wear helmets by law; these can be rented from most hire shops. You may be asked to leave a credit card number or cash as a deposit when you pick up the vehicle (*see also p359*).

Taxi on a busy street in Rome's city centre

Taxis

Official taxis in Rome are white, say "Comune di Roma" on the side and bear a "taxi" sign on the roof. Do not use the taxis offered by touts at stations and tourist spots; official taxi drivers do not tout for customers. Official taxis can be hailed at specially marked taxi ranks or on the street (drivers are not meant to stop in the street but many of them do). You can nearly always find them at the main tourist sights, at airports and at stations (including Termini and Ostiense). Roman taxi drivers are not renowned for their friendliness and may even refuse to take you if you're going too far from the lucrative city centre or, conversely, if the ride is too short.

Taxis are not particularly cheap, so, unless you have heavy luggage or screaming toddlers, public transport is usually a better option. Taxi drivers charge supplements for more than one bag, night journeys (10pm–6am), and journeys on Sundays or public holidays.

Customers should ensure the meter is turned on and visible. The meter continues running while you are at a standstill, so traffic jams can become expensive. Drivers may take suspiciously circuitous routes. Italians don't tip taxi drivers; they simply round up to the nearest euro. You can phone for a taxi (but you will pay from the time the driver gets the call from the switchboard) from **Mondo Taxi, Radiotaxi 3570** or **Chiama Taxi Numero Unico,** the

Motorbikes and scooters, a popular means of transport in Rome

central number. Taxi rides to and from the city's airports incur a flat fee for up to four passengers and their luggage *(see p377)*.

River Tour

The summer service offered by **Battelli di Roma** runs from embarkation points near the Ponte Sant'Angelo and Tiber Island on the hour between 10am and 7pm; bear in mind that bad weather can interrupt the service.

Horse-Drawn Carriages

You can hire horse-drawn caleches *(carrozzelle)* for a gentle tour of the historic centre. Carriages carry up to five people

Horse-drawn carriage offering tours from St Peter's Square

and can be hired from many points: Piazza di Spagna, the Colosseum, Trevi Fountain, St Peter's, Via Veneto, Villa Borghese, Piazza Venezia and Piazza Navona. Trips last half an hour, an hour, half a day or a

day. They tend to be expensive, but prices for longer rides are negotiable; establish the price before you set off and make sure you understand whether the rate is per person, or for the whole carriage.

DIRECTORY

Electric-Car Charging Stations

Via Cola di Rienzo.
Map 4 D2.

Piazza Mastai. **Map** 7 C1.
W colonnineelettriche.it.

Buses and Trams

ATAC
Piazza dei Cinquecento.
Map 6 D3. **Tel** 06-46951.
W atac.roma.it

Traffic Info
Piazzale degli Archivi 40.
Tel 06-57003. W agenzia mobilita.roma.it
W muoversia roma.it

Guided Tours

Carrani Tours
Via V. E. Orlando 95.
Map 5 C3. **Tel** 06-432 181.
W carrani.com

City Sightseeing Roma
Tel 06-6979 7554.
W roma.city-sightseeing.it

Context
Tel 06-9672 7371.
W contexttravel.com/city/rome

Green Line Tours
Via Amendola 32.
Map 6 D3. **Tel** 06-482 7480.
W greenlinetours.com

Walks of Italy
Tel 06-9480 4888.
W walksofitaly.com

Parking

Acqua Acetosa station.
Map 2 E1.
Also: Lepanto Metro station. **Map** 4 D1.
Also: Villa Borghese.
Map 5 A1.
Also: Piazzale dei Partigiani. **Map** 8 E4.

Useful 24-Hour Petrol Stations

Portuense
Piazzale della Radio.
Map 7 B5.

Trastevere
Lungotevere Ripa.
Map 8 D1.

Car Breakdown Services

ACI Breakdown
Tel 803 116.

Road Conditions
Tel 1518.

Car Hire

Avis
Tel 199-100 133
(centralized booking).
Also: Ciampino airport.
Tel 06-7934 0195.

Also: Fiumicino airport.
Tel 06-6501 1531.
Also: Via Sardegna 38A.
Map 5 C1.
Tel 06-4282 4728.
W avisautonoleggio.it

Car2Go
W car2go.com/en/roma

Europcar
Tel 199 307 030
(centralized free booking).

Also: Fiumicino airport.
Tel 06-6576 1211.

Also: Stazione Termini.
Map 6 D3.
Tel 06-488 2854.
W europcar.it

Hertz
Via Gregorio VII 207.
Tel 06-3937 8808.

Also: Stazione Termini.
Map 6 D3. **Tel** 06-488 3967.

Also: Fiumicino airport.
Tel 06-6501 1553.
W hertz.it

Maggiore
Stazione Termini. **Map** 6
D3. **Tel** 199 151 120.
Also: Via Po 8A. **Map** 5 C1.
Tel 199 151 120.
W maggiore.it

Sixt
Tel 06-652 111.
W sixt.it

Moped and Bicycle Hire

Barberini Scooters for Rent
Via della Purificazione 84.
Tel 06-488 5485.

Bici & Baci
Via del Viminale 5.
Map 5 C3.
Tel 06-482 8443.
W bicibaci.com

Bike Rental
Piazza del Popolo.
Map 4 F1.
Also: Piazza di Spagna.
Map 5 A2.

Collalti
Via del Pellegrino 82.
Map 4 E4 & 11 C4.
Tel 06-6880 1084 (bikes).

Taxis

Chiama Taxi Numero Unico
Tel 06-0609.

Mondo Taxi
Tel 06-8822.

Radiotaxi 3570
Tel 06-3570.

River Tour

Battelli di Roma
W battellidiroma.it
(or email: info@battellidiroma.it)

STREET FINDER

Map references given with sights, hotels, restaurants, shops and entertainment venues refer to the maps in this section (*see How the Map References Work opposite*). A complete index of the street names and places of interest marked on the maps follows on pages 390–99. The key map below shows the area of Rome covered by the *Street Finder*. This includes the sight-seeing areas (which are colour-coded) as well as the whole of central Rome with all the districts important for restaurants, hotels and entertainment venues. Because the historic centre is so packed with sights, there is a large-scale map of this area on maps 11 and 12.

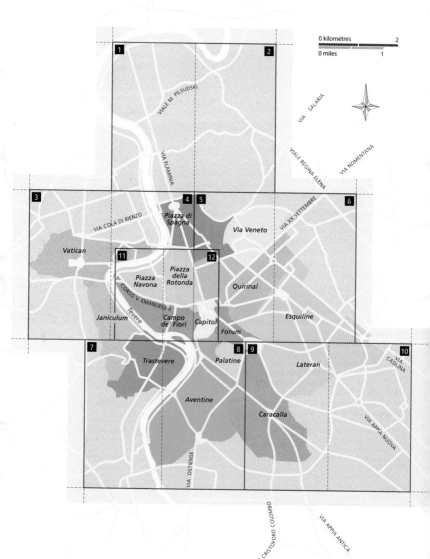

How the Map References Work

The first figure tells you which *Street Finder* map to turn to.

❼ Trevi Fountain

Fontana di Trevi. **Map 5** **A3** & **12 F2**. 🚌 52, 53, 61, 62, 63, 71, 80, 116, 119.

The letter and number give the grid reference. Letters go across the map's top and bottom; figures on its sides.

The second reference refers to the large-scale maps of central Rome (11 & 12). It is read in exactly the same way as the first.

The map continues on map 8 of the *Street Finder.*

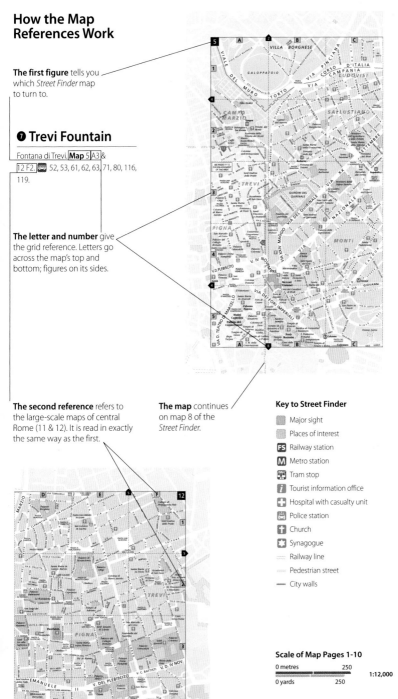

Key to Street Finder

- 🟫 Major sight
- 🟨 Places of interest
- 🄵🅂 Railway station
- Ⓜ Metro station
- 🚋 Tram stop
- ℹ️ Tourist information office
- ➕ Hospital with casualty unit
- 🚓 Police station
- ✝️ Church
- ✡️ Synagogue
- ⎓ Railway line
- ⋯ Pedestrian street
- — City walls

Scale of Map Pages 1-10

| 0 metres | 250 |
| 0 yards | 250 |

1:12,000

Scale of Map Pages 11 & 12

| 0 metres | 150 |
| 0 yards | 150 |

1:7,600

The key to the abbreviations used in the *Street Finder* is on page 390.

Street Finder Index

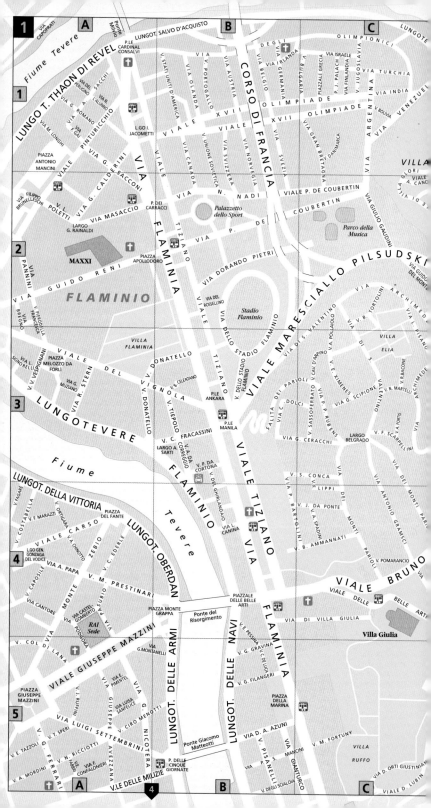

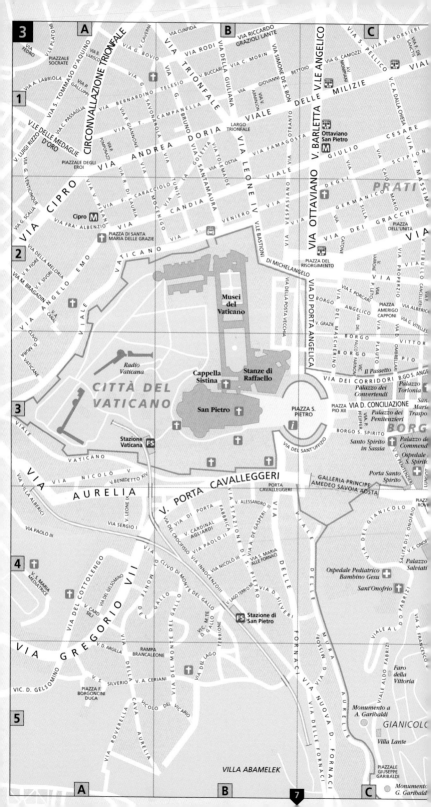

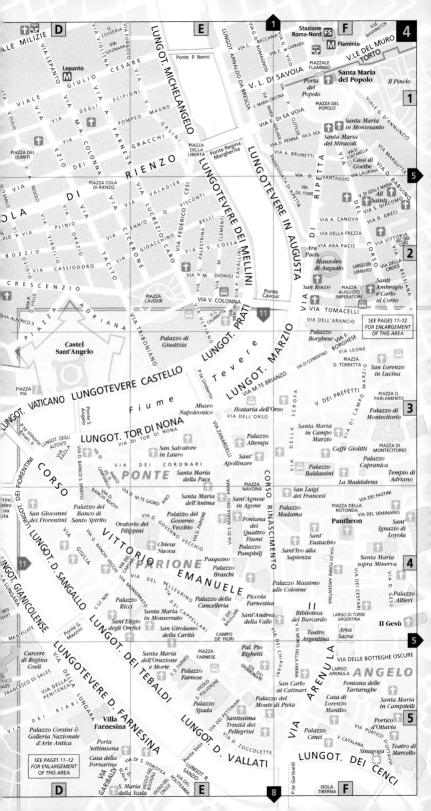

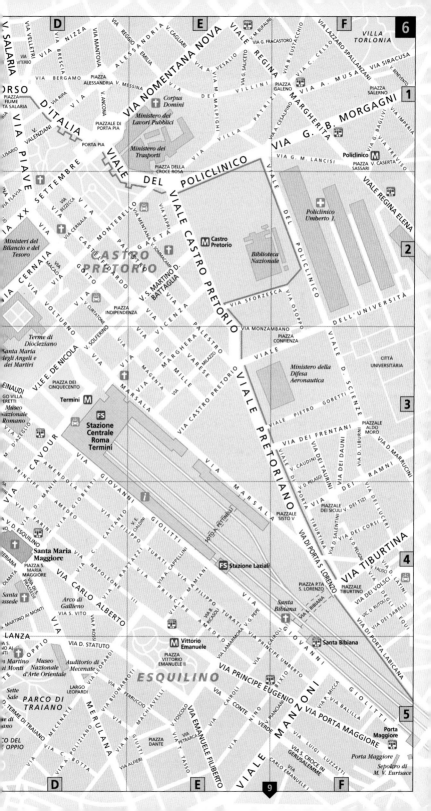

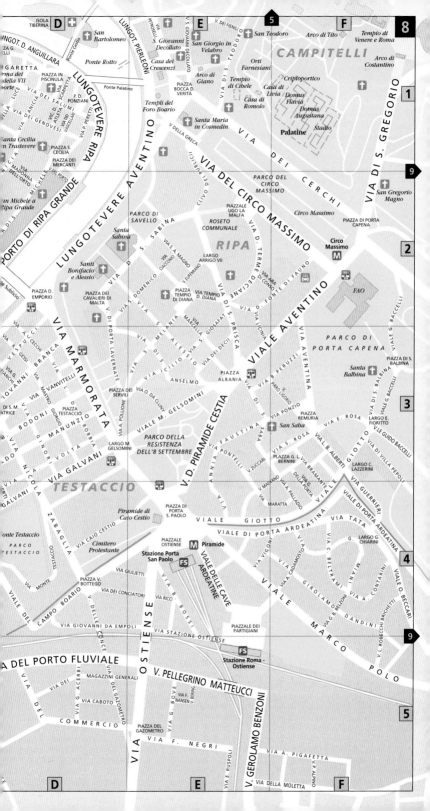

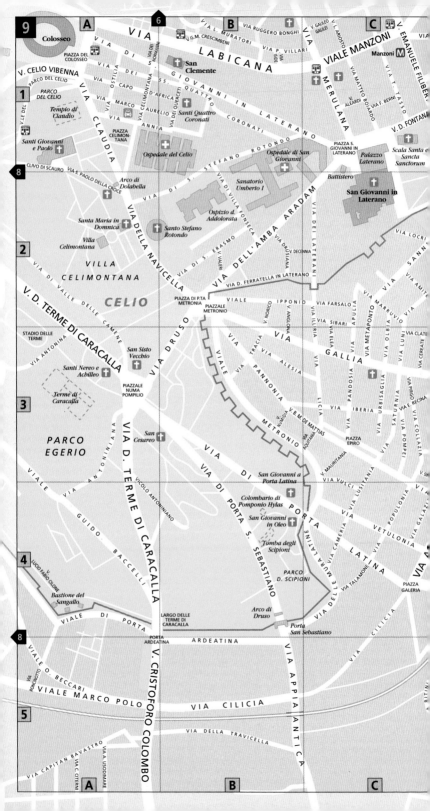

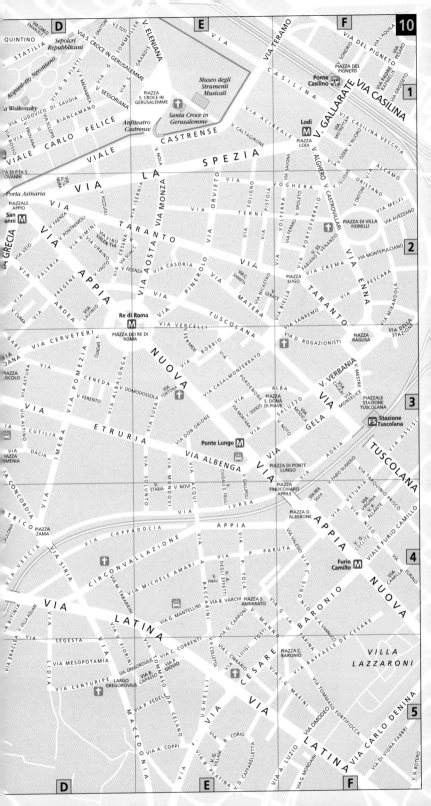

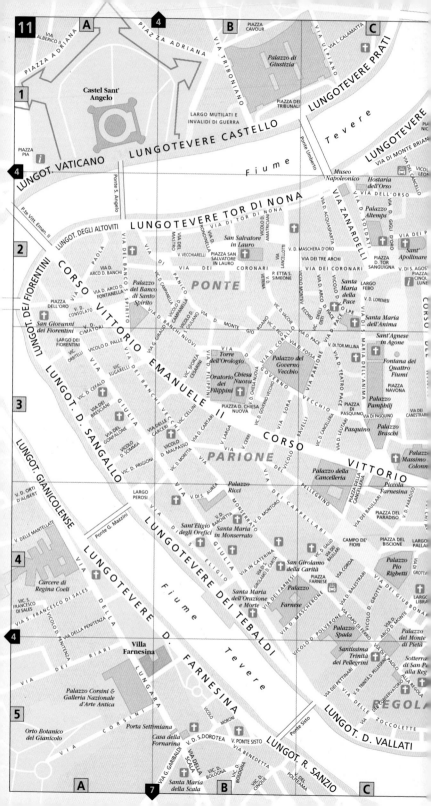

General Index

Page number in **bold** refer to main entries.

Acknowledgments

Dorling Kindersley would like to thank the many people whose help and assistance contributed to the preparation of this book.

Main Contributors

Olivia Ercoli is an art historian and tour guide, who has lived all her life in Rome. Bilingual in English and Italian, she lectures on art history and writes on a range of subjects for English and Italian publications.
Travel writer **Ros Belford** conceived the idea of the Virago Woman's Guides, of which she is now series editor, and wrote the *Virago Woman's Guide to Rome*. She has travelled widely in Europe and as well as writing guide books contributes to a variety of publications including *The Guardian*.
Roberta Mitchell heads the editorial section of the UN's Publishing Division in Rome, where she has lived for many years. An experienced writer and editor with extensive knowledge of the city, she has contributed to a number of guides to Rome including the *American Express Guide to Rome*.

Contributors

Reid Bramblett, Sam Cole, Mary Jane Cryan Pancani, Daphne Wilson Ercoli, Laura Ercoli, Lindsay Hunt, Adrian James, Leonie Loudon, Christopher McDowall, Davina Palmer, Rodney Palmer, Pardeep Sandhu, Debra Shipley. Dorling Kindersley wishes to thank the following editors and researchers at Websters International Publishers: Sandy Carr, Matthew Barrell, Siobhan Bremner, Serena Cross, Valeria Fabbri, Annie Galpin, Gemma Hancock, Celia Woolfrey.

Additional Photography

Max Alexander, Marta Bescos, Giuseppe Carfagna, Demetrio Carrasco, Andy Crawford, Peter Douglas, Mike Dunning, Philip Enticknap, Steve Gorton, John Heseltine, Nigel Hicks, Britta Jaschinski, Neil Mersh, Ian O'Leary, Poppy, Rough Guides/James McConnachie, Alessandra Santarelli, David Sutherland, Martin Woodward.

Additional Illustrations

Anne Bowes, Robin Carter, Pramod Negi, Gillie Newman, Chris D Orr.

Additional Picture Research

Sharon Buckley.

Cartography

Advanced Illustration (Cheshire), Contour Publishing (Derby), Euromap Limited (Berkshire), Alok Pathak, Kunal Singh. Street Finder maps: ERA Maptec Ltd (Dublin) adapted with permission from original survey and mapping from Shobunsha (Japan).

Cartographic Research

James Anderson, Donna Rispoli, Joan Russell.

Research Assistance

Janet Abbott, Flaminia Allvin, Fabrizio Ardito, Licia Bronzin, Lupus Sabene.

Revisions Team

Namrata Adhwaryu, Beverley Ager, Emma Anacootee, Jasneet Arora, Rupanki Arora Kaushik, Hansa Babra, Shruti Bahl, Claire Baranowski, Meghna Baruah, Sreemoyee Basu, Marta Bescos Sanchez, Tessa Bindloss, Peter Bently, Vandana Bhagra, Subhashree Bharati, Hilary Bird, Subhadeep Biswas, Divya Chowfin, Lucinda Cooke, Michelle Crane, Vanessa Courtier, Kristin Dolina-Adamczyk, Peter Douglas, Vidushi Duggal, Claire Edwards, Jon Eldan, Simon Farbrother, Emer FitzGerald, Karen Fitzpatrick, Anna Freiberger, Vanessa Hamilton, Marcus Hardy, Kaberi Hazarika, Sasha Heseltine, Sally Ann Hibbard, Paul Hines, Stephanie Jackson, Claire Jones, Sumita Khatwani, Steve Knowlden, Priya Kukadia, Rahul Kumar, Rakesh Kumar Pal, Mary Lambert, Kathryn Lane, Maite Lantaron, Janette Leung, Carly Madden, Shahid Mahmood, Nicola Malone, Alison McGill, Jane Middleton, Ian Midson, Casper Morris, Fiona Morgan, Daniel Mosseri, George Nimmo, Jane Oliver-Jedrzejak, Helen Partington, Catherine Palmi, Naomi Peck, Helen Peters, Marianne Petrou, Adrian Potts, Pure Content, Carolyn Pyrah, Pete Quinlan, Salim Qurashi, Rada Radojicic, Pamposh Raina, Marisa Renzullo, Lucy Richards, Ellen Root, Collette Sadler, Alice Saggers, Sands Publishing Solutions, Mathew Baishakhee Sengupta, Ankita Sharma, Jane Shaw, Azeem Siddiqui, Rituraj Singh, Akanksha Siwach, Susana Smith, Solveig Steinhart, Clare Sullivan, Avantika Sukhia, Rachel Symons, Andrew Szudek, Alka Thakur, Stuti Tiwari, Daphne Trotter, Ajay Verma, Karen Villabona, Diana Vowles, Penny Walker, Lynda Warrington, Stewart J. Wild.

Special Assistance

Dottore Riccardo Baldini, Mario di Bartolomeo of the Soprintendenza dei Beni Artistici e Storici di Roma, Belloni, Dorling Kindersley picture department, David Gleave MW, Debbie Harris, Emma Hutton and Cooling Brown Partnership, Marina Tavolato, Dottoressa Todaro and Signora Camimiti at the Ministero dell'Interno, Trestini.

Photography Permissions

Dorling Kindersley would like to thank the following for their kind permission to photograph at their establishments: Bathsheba Abse at the Keats-Shelley Memorial House, Accademia dei Lincei, Accanto, Aeroporti di Roma, Aldrovandi Palace, Alpheus, Banco di Santo Spirito at Palazzo del Monte di Pietà, Rory Bruck at Babington's, Caffè Giolitti, Caffè Latino, Comune di Roma (Ripartizione X), Comunità Ebraica di Roma, Guido Cornini at Monumenti Musei e Gallerie Pontificie, Direzione Sanitaria Ospedale di Santo Spirito, Dottoressa Laura Falsini at the Soprintendenza Archeologica di Etruria Meridionale, Hotel Gregoriana, Hotel Majestic, Hotel Regina Baglioni, Marco Marchetti at Ente EUR, Dottoressa Mercalli at the Museo Nazionale di Castel Sant'Angelo, Ministero dell'

Interno, Plaza Minerva, Ristorante Alberto Ciarla, Ristorante Filetti di Baccalà, Ristorante Romolo, Signor Rulli and Signor Angeli at the Soprintendenza Archeologica di Roma, Soprintendenza Archeologica per il Lazio, Soprintendenza per i Beni Ambientali e Architettonici, Soprintendenza per i Beni Artistici e Storici di Roma, Daniela Tabo at the Musei Capitolini, Villa d'Este, Villa San Pio, Mrs Marjorie Weeke at St Peter's.

Picture Credits

a - above; b - below/bottom; c - centre; f - far; l - left; r - right; t - top..

Works of art have been reproduced with the permission of the following copyright holders: *Town with Gothic Cathedral*, Paul Klee © DACS, London 2011 239br.

The publishers are grateful to the following individuals, companies and picture libraries for permission to reproduce their photographs:

123RF.com: Wiesław Jarek 132clb; **4Corners:** SIME/Sandra Raccanello 279tl.

Accademia Nazionale di San Luca, Rome: 162br; **AFE:** 59bc, 63cra; Sandro Battaglia 61c, 63bl, 63br, 328br; **Aeroporti di Roma:** 376bl, 377tr; **Agenzia Sintesi:** 370bl, 370br, 370cla; Marco Marcotulli 370bc; **AKG-Images:** Andrea Jemolo 10br; **Alamy Images:** Vito Arcomano 163tl; Caro 151tr; CuboImages srl/Gimmi 387tr; Kathy DeWitt 307tl; Michele Flazone 44; Antonio J Galante - VWPics 261tl; Eddie Gerald 360bc; Hemis 319bl; Lautaro 194c; Prisma Archivo 241tl; Travel Division Images 310b; Travel Ink/Jim Gibson 374crb; Jozef Sedmak 200; Kumar Sriskandan 364–5; Sklifas Steven 216; Superstock 64–5; Vito Arcomano 176tr; John G. Wilbanks 274; Robin Wilkinson 371tl; Wilmar Topshots 252; **AGF foto:** 42–3c; **Alitalia:** 376cr; **Ancient Art and Architecture:** 20bl, 25tl,29bc, 38crb, 39c, 48clb; **Art:** 297bl; **Artothek,** Städelsches Kunstinstitut Frankfurt, Goethe in the Roman Campagna by JHW Tischbein 138tr.

Babuino 181, Rome: 300tc; **Baglioni hotels SPA:** 298tr; **Banca d'Italia:** 372cla; **Bed and Breakfast Bio:** 369tr; **Biblioteca Reale, Torino:** 32–3c **Bridgeman Art Library, London/New York:** 22br, 41tr, 164crb; Agnew & Sons, London 55tr; Antikenmuseum Staatliches Museum, Berlin 23bc; Bibliothèque da la Sorbonne 32c, British Museum, London 31cra; Christie's, London 97tr; The Fine Art Society, London 153tr, 281tl; Galleria degli Uffizi, Florence 35bl; Giraudon/Château de Versailles, France 37tr; Greek Museum, University of Newcastle-upon-Tyne 20br; Index/Biblioteca Publica Episcopal, Barcelona 110bl, /Piacenza Town Hall, Italy/31br; King Street Galleries, London 37bc; Lauros-Giraudon/Louvre 30br, 58br; Roy Miles Gallery, 29 Bruton St, London 248t; Musée des Beaux-Arts, Nantes 57tr; Museo e Gallerie Nazionali di Capodimonte, Naples, Detail from the predella of San Ludovico by Simone Martini 30tr; Musée Condé, Chantilly f.71v Très Riches Heures, 30tc; Museum of Fine Arts, Budapest 114br; Museo

Archeologico di Villa Giulia 52cl; Palazzo Doria Pamphilj, Rome 109br; Private Collection 23br, 26bc, 28bc, 31tr, 181tl; Pushkin Museum, Moscow 115tc; Sotheby's, London 22bl; Vatican Museums & Galleries 45c, 235tr.

Capitoline Museums, Rome: 73cr; **Casa Bleve:** 313tr; **Cephas Picture Library:** Mick Rock 308tr; **Corbis:** Art on File 12bl; Alessandra Benedetti 367tr; Bettmann 8–9; epa/Ettore Ferrari 100cla; Owen Franken 306cla; JAI/Francesco Lacobelli 363tl; Ken Kaminesky 156; Bob Krist 307c; Araldo de Luca 21bc, 70tr; Robert Harding World Imagery/Bruno Morandi 258; **Checchino dal 1887, Rome:** 311tr; **Corpo Nazionale dei Vigili del Fuoco:** 371cl; **Croce Bianca Italiana:** 371cla.

Da Giggetto: 305bl; **Il Dagherrotipo:** 147tc, 327bl, 378cla; Stefano Chieppa 291bc, 292bc; Andrea Getuli 289tl; Stephano Occhibelli 290cla, 290br; Paolo Priori 206tr; Giovanni Rinaldi 198tr, 288cla, 288br, 289br, 292cla, 293br, 293tc, 383tl; **Dorling Kindersley:** Courtesy of Basilica San Clemente 178; Courtesy of the Ministero della Pubblica Instruzione 263bc; **Dreamstime.com:** Sergey Aleluhin 136br; Avorym 13br; Bramble100 66; Sorin Colac 5c; Danileon 12tr, 190; Dennis_dolkens 107br; Ioana Grecu 384tr; Kasto80 229tl; Elvira Kolomiytseva 5cr; Krylon80 98; Sergiu Marian Leustean 361cr; Lornet 73crb; Luis007 294–5; Marinv 229ca; Maui01 144; Mawerix 273tr; Sander Moerman 4crb; Monick79 167bl; Konstantinos Papaioannou 135clb; William Perry 272bl; Marek Poplawski 28c, 360cra; Rinofelino 60cra; Sailorr 4ca; Scaliger 228cl; Thejipen 57cl; Dave Tonkin 273cl; Trevoux 175br.

Ecole Nationale Superieure des Beaux-Arts: 25cb, 26–7, 250tr; **Eden:** 297tl; **ET Archive:** 18, 21tc, 21clb, 23tl, 23tc, 27t, 31clb, 35crb, 36br, 41bc; **Eurolines:** 379bl; **Mary Evans Picture Library:** 22cla, 27cb, 28cl, 33br, 34clb, 34bc, 35tl, 38tc, 38bl, 69br, 76tr, 83b, 93tc, 95br, 97tl, 137tr, 215bc.

Coraldo Falsini: 43tl, 346b, 347t, 347c; **Ferrovie dello stato:** 379cl, 379tr; **Werner Forman Archive:** 21cr, 24bc, 27crb, 27bl, 27br, 51ca, 177br; **Folklore Museum, Rome:** 212cra.

Getty Images: 42cb; AFP 61br; AFP/Andreas Olaro 368br; Sylvain Grandadam 171tc; Andre Thijssen 368tl; Stone/Richard Passmore 1c; Visions of our land 78; **Giolitti:** 361bl; **Giraudon:** 19b, 32br, 40bc; **Grandi Stazioni S.p.A:** 378b; **Grand Hotel de la Minerve, Rome:** 302br; **Ronald Grant:** 56br.

Sonia Halliday: 23ca, 26br, 29cb; Laura Lushington 28bl; **Hotel Due Torri, Rome:** 301tl; **Hotel Majestic Roma:** 296bl; Tono Labra 184tl; G White 61bl; **Hotel Hassler Roma:** 299tr; **Hotel d'Inghilterra:** 298bc; **Hulton Deutsch:** 59cr, 365c.

Imago, Hassler Roma: 316t.

Keats-Shelley Memorial House: 133bl.

Maccheroni: 304bl, 313bl; **Magnum:** Erich Lessing 21tl, 91crb; **Mansell:** 23tr, 29bl, 30cb, 35ca, 58cl, 59cl, 77cla, 77c, 80cra, 94cb, 116c, 127tr, 134br, 135cr, 138bl, 141bl, 141bc, 174bl, 174bc, 176cl, 183crb, 198c, 212bl, 220bl, 247cb;

Alinari 143bl, 256bc; Anderson 141crb, 165tl, 248crb; **Marka**: V Arcomano 37cr; D. Donadoni 11br; Lorenzo Sechi 10cla, 226bc; **MAXXI**: Roberto Galasso 261br; **Moro Roma**: 40cl, 41cl, 42bc, 43tr, 42br; **Museo Nazionale Romano**: Fabio Ratti 129cr, 129br, 165br.

National Portrait Gallery, London: 58tr, 59tr; **Grazia Neri**: Vision/Giorgio Casulich 116br, 158bc, Vision/Roberta Krasnig 126tr, 285tr; © **Nippon Television Network Corporation, Tokyo 1999**: 242bl and all pictures on 244–5; **Nonna Betta, Rome**: 312t.

Il Pagliaccio: Aromicreativi 314tl; **Palazzo Manfredi**: 297tr; **Pantheon View, Rome:** Gantcho Beltchev Photography 303tl.
La Pergola: Courtesy of Rome Cavalieri 319tr

Rex Features: Steve Wood 43crb; **Robert Harding Picture Library**: 27cra, 36bl, 81cr, 272c; Mario Carrieri 39tr; 347bl; **Roscioli**: 305tr.

Scala Group S.p.A: 51tr, 96tr, 127tl, 231tl, 280cl; Chiesa del Gesù 111tl, Galleria Borghese 36cla, 262tr, Galleria Colonna 159crb, Galleria Doria Pamphilj 50br, 107cr, Galleria Spada 50cl, Galleria degli Uffizi 20–21, 31bl, Museo d'Arte Orientale 177cl, Musei Capitolini 51br, Museo della Civiltà Romana 52tr, 52b, Museo delle Terme 25tr, Museo Napoleonico 53cr, Museo Nazionale, Napoli 25cl, Museo Nazionale, Ravenna 26cl, Museo del Risorgimento, Milano 40cb, 40–1c, Museo del Risorgimento, Roma 41tl, Palazzo Barberini 254bl, Palazzo Ducale 23cla, 25tr, Palazzo della Farnesina 220clb, Palazzo Madama 24cr, Palazzo Venezia 51cr, 68bl, San Carlo alle Quattro Fontane 37c, San Clemente 39clb, Santa Costanza 28–9c, Santa Maria dell'Anima 123tr, Santa Maria Maggiore 47tr, Santa Maria del Popolo 141tc, 141cra, Santa Prassede 30bl, 32clb, Santa Sabina 29ca, 33cb, Vatican Museums 23crb, 29tl, 29cr, 29cra, 31crb, 33tl, 33cr, 34cla, 35cr, 35br, 36c, 36clb, 45cra, 50cla, 52cr, 53bl, 226clb, 227cra, 233tl, 236 all, 238–9 all, 240–41 all except 241tl, 243 all, 291tl; **Lourens Smak**: 11tl; **Spirito Divino, Rome**: 318t; **STA Travel Group**: 368c; **Superstock**: Tips images 208.

Thanks also to Dottoressa Giulia De Marchi of **L'accademia Nazionale di San Luca**, Rome for 162br, Rettore Padre Libianchi of **La Chiesa di Sant'ignazio di Loyola** for 108t, **Ente Nazionale per il Turismo**, and to **La Repubblica Trovaroma**.

Front Endpapers
Alamy Images: Jozef Sedmak Lfbr, Sklifas Steven Lfbl, Wilmar Topshotes Rtl; **Corbis**: Ken Kaminesky Rftl; **Dorling Kindersley**: Courtesy of Basilica San Clemente Rfbr; **Dreamstime.com**: Bramble100 Rtr, Danileon Rbc, Krylon80 Rfcrb, Maui01 Lfclb; **Getty Images**: Visions of our land Rfcr; **Superstock**: Tips Images Lbr.

Map Cover
Getty Images: Andrea Pistolesi.

Cover

Front: **Getty Images**: Andrea Pistolesi.

Back: **Dreamstime.com**: Roland Nagy t.

Spine: **Getty Images**: Andrea Pistolesi.

All other images © Dorling Kindersley.
For further information see: www.dkimages.com

Special Editions of DK Travel Guides
DK Travel Guides can be purchased in bulk quantities at discounted prices for use in promotions or as premiums. We are also able to offer special editions and personalized jackets, corporate imprints, and excerpts from all of our books, tailored specifically to meet your own needs.

To find out more, please contact:
in the United States **specialsales@dk.com**
in the UK **travelguides@uk.dk.com**
in Canada DK Special Sales at **specialmarkets@dk.com**
in Australia **penguincorporatesales@penguinrandomhouse.com.au**

Phrase Book

In Emergency

Help!	Aiuto!	eye-**yoo**-toh
Stop!	Ferma!	fair-**mah**
Call a doctor	Chiama un medico	kee-**ah**-mah oon **meh**-dee-coh
Call an ambulance	Chiama un' ambulanza	kee-**ah**-mah oon am-boo-**lan**-tsa
Call the police	Chiama la polizia	kee-**ah**-mah lah pol-ee-**tsee**-ah
Call the fire brigade	Chiama i pompieri	kee-**ah**-mah ee pom-pee-**air**-ee
Where is the telephone?	Dov'è il telefono?	dov-eh el teh-**leh**-foh-noh?
The nearest hospital?	L'ospedale più vicino?	loss-peh-**dah**-leh pee-**oo**vee-**chee**-noh?

Communication Essentials

Yes/No	Sì/No	see/noh
Please	Per favore	pair fah-**vor**-eh
Thank you	Grazie	**grah**-tsee-eh
Excuse me	Mi scusi	mee **skoo**-zee
Hello	Buon giorno	bwon **jor**-noh
Goodbye	Arrivederci	ah-ree-veh-**dair**-chee
Good evening	Buona sera	**bwon**-ah **sair**-ah
morning	la mattina	lah mah-**tee**-nah
afternoon	il pomeriggio	eel poh-meh-**ree**-joh
evening	la sera	lah **sair**-ah
yesterday	ieri	ee-**air**-ee
today	oggi	**oh**-jee
tomorrow	domani	doh-**mah**-nee
here	qui	kwee
there	la	lah
What?	Quale?	**kwah**-leh?
When?	Quando?	**kwan**-doh?
Why?	Perchè?	pair-**keh**?
Where?	Dove?	**doh**-veh

Useful Phrases

How are you?	Come sta?	**koh**-meh stah?
Very well, thank you.	Molto bene, grazie	**moll**-toh **beh**-neh **grah**-tsee-eh
Pleased to meet you.	Piacere di conoscerla.	pee-ah-**chair**-eh dee coh-**noh**-shair-lah
See you soon.	A più tardi.	ah pee-**oo** tar-dee
That's fine.	Va bene.	va **beh**-neh
Where is/are …?	Dov'è/Dove sono…?	dov-**eh**/doveh **soh** noh?
How long does it take to get to …?	Quanto tempo ci vuole per andare a …?	**kwan**-toh **tem**-poh chee voo-**oh**-leh pair an-**dar**-eh ah…?
How do I get to …?	Come faccio per arrivare a …?	koh-meh **fah**-choh pair arri-**var**-eh ah…?
Do you speak English?	Parla inglese?	par-lah een-**gleh**-zeh?
I don't understand.	Non capisco.	non ka-**pee**-skoh
Could you speak more slowly, please?	Può parlare più lentamente, per favore?	pwoh par-**lah**-reh pee-**oo** len-ta-**men**-teh pair fah-**vor**-eh?
I'm sorry.	Mi dispiace.	mee dee-spee-**ah**-cheh

Useful Words

big	grande	**gran**-deh
small	piccolo	**pee**-koh-loh
hot	caldo	**kal**-doh
cold	freddo	**fred**-doh
good	buono	**bwoh**-noh
bad	cattivo	kat-**tee**-voh
enough	basta	**bas**-tah
well	bene	**beh**-neh
open	aperto	ah-**pair**-toh
closed	chiuso	kee-**oo**-zoh
left	a sinistra	ah see-**nee**-strah
right	a destra	ah **dess**-trah
straight on	sempre dritto	**sem**-preh **dree**-toh
near	vicino	vee-**chee**-noh
far	lontano	lon-**tah**-noh
up	su	soo
down	giù	joo
early	presto	**press**-toh
late	tardi	**tar**-dee
entrance	entrata	en-**trah**-tah
exit	uscita	oo-**shee**-ta
toilet	il gabinetto	eel gah-bee-**net**-toh

free, unoccupied	libero	**lee**-bair-oh
free, no charge	gratuito	grah-**too**-ee-toh

Making a Telephone Call

I'd like to place a long-distance call.	Vorrei fare una interurbana.	vor-**ray far**-eh oona in-tair-oor-**bah**-nah.
I'd like to make a reverse-charge call.	Vorrei fare una telefonata a carico del destinatario.	vor-**ray far**-eh oona teh-leh-fon-**ah**-tah ah **kar**-ee-koh dell dess-tee-nah-**tar**-ree-oh.
I'll try again later.	Ritelefono più tardi.	ree-teh-**leh**-foh-noh pee-oo **tar**-dee.
Can I leave a message?	Posso lasciare un messaggio?	**poss**-oh lash-**ah**-reh oon mess-**sah**-joh?
Hold on	Un attimo, per favore	oon **ah**-tee-moh, pair fah-**vor**-eh
Could you speak up a little please?	Può parlare più forte, per favore?	pwoh par-**lah**-reh pee-**oo** for-teh, pair fah-**vor**-eh?
local call	la telefonata locale	lah teh-leh-fon-**ah**-ta loh-**kah**-leh

Shopping

How much does this cost?	Quant'è, per favore?	kwan-**teh**, pair fah-**vor**-eh?
I would like …	Vorrei …	vor-**ray**…
Do you have …?	Avete …?	ah-**veh**-teh…?
I'm just looking.	Sto soltanto guardando	stoh sol-**tan**-toh gwar-**dan**-doh
Do you take credit cards?	Accettate carte di credito?	ah-chet-**tah**-teh **kar**-teh dee **creh**-dee-toh?
What time do you open/close?	A che ora apre/ chiude?	ah keh or-ah **ah**-preh/kee-**oo**-deh?
this one	questo	**kweh**-stoh
that one	quello	**kwell**-oh
expensive	caro	**kar**-oh
cheap	a buon prezzo	ah bwon **pret**-soh
size, clothes	la taglia	lah **tah**-lee-ah
size, shoes	il numero	eel **noo**-mair-oh
white	bianco	bee-**ang**-koh
black	nero	**neh**-roh
red	rosso	**ross**-oh
yellow	giallo	**jal**-loh
green	verde	**vair**-deh
blue	blu	bloo
brown	marrone	mar-**roh**-neh

Types of Shop

antique dealer	l'antiquario	lan-tee-**kwah**-ree-oh
bakery	la panetteria	lah pah-net-tair-**ree**-ah
bank	la banca	lah **bang**-kah
bookshop	la libreria	lah lee-breh-**ree**-ah
butcher's	la macelleria	lah mah-chell-eh-**ree**-ah
cake shop	la pasticceria	lah pas-tee-chair-**ee**-ah
chemist's	la farmacia	lah far-mah-**chee**-ah
department store	il grande magazzino	eel **gran**-deh mag-gad-**zee**-noh
delicatessen	la salumeria	lah sah-loo-meh-**ree**-ah
fishmonger's	la pescheria	lah pess-keh-**ree**-ah
florist	il fioraio	eel fee-or-**eye**-oh
greengrocer	il fruttivendolo	eel froo-tee-**ven**-doh-loh
grocery	alimentari	ah-lee-men-**tah**-ree
hairdresser	il parrucchiere	eel par-oo-kee-**air**-eh
ice cream parlour	la gelateria	lah jel-lah-tair-**ee**-ah
market	il mercato	eel mair-**kah**-toh
news-stand	l'edicola	leh-dee-koh-lah
post office	l'ufficio postale	loo-**fee**-choh pos-**tah**-leh
shoe shop	il negozio di scarpe	eel neh-**goh**-tsioh dee **skar**-peh
supermarket	il supermercato	eel su-pair-mair-**kah**-toh
tobacconist	il tabaccaio	eel tah-bak-**eye**-oh
travel agency	l'agenzia di viaggi	lah-jen-**tsee**-ah dee vee-**ad**-jee

Sightseeing

art gallery	la pinacoteca	lah peena-koh-**teh**-kah
bus stop	la fermata dell'autobus	lah fair-**mah**-tah dell **ow**-toh-booss
church	la chiesa	lah kee-**eh**-zah
	la basilica	lah bah-**seel**-i-kah
garden	il giardino	eel jar-**dee**-no
library	la biblioteca	lah beeb-lee-oh-**teh**-kah
museum	il museo	eel moo-**zeh**-oh
railway station	la stazione	lah stah-tsee-**oh**-neh
tourist information	l'ufficio turistico	loo-**fee**-choh too-**ree**-stee-koh

Staying in a Hotel

closed for the public holiday	**chiuso per la festa**	*kee-oo-zoh pair lah fess-tah*
Do you have any vacant rooms?	**Avete camere libere?**	*ah-veh-teh kah-mair-eh lee-bair-eh?*
double room	**una camera doppia**	*oona kah-mair-ah doh-pee-ah*
with double bed	**con letto matrimoniale**	*kon let-toh mah-tree-moh-nee-ah-leh*
twin room	**una camera con due letti**	*oona kah-mair-ah kon doo-eh let-tee*
single room	**una camera singola**	*oona kah-mair-ah sing-goh-lah*
room with a bath, shower	**una camera con bagno, con doccia**	*oona kah-mair-ah kon ban-yoh, kon dot-chah*
porter	**il facchino**	*eel fak-kee-noh*
key	**la chiave**	*lah kee-ah-veh*
I have a reservation.	**Ho fatto una prenotazione.**	*oh fat-toh oona preh-noh-tah-tsee-oh-neh*

Eating Out

Have you got a table for …?	**Avete un tavolo per … ?**	*ah-veh-teh oon tah-voh-loh pair …?*
I'd like to reserve a table.	**Vorrei riservare un tavolo.**	*vor-ray ree-sair-vah-reh oon tah-voh-loh*
breakfast	**colazione**	*koh-lah-tsee-oh-neh*
lunch	**pranzo**	*pran-tsoh*
dinner	**cena**	*cheh-nah*
The bill, please.	**Il conto, per favore.**	*eel kon-toh pair fah-vor-eh*
I am a vegetarian.	**Sono vegetariano/a.**	*soh-noh veh-jeh-tar-ee-ah-noh/nah*
waitress	**cameriera**	*kah-mair-ee-air-ah*
waiter	**cameriere**	*kah-mair-ee-air-eh*
fixed price menu	**il menù a prezzo fisso**	*eel men-noo ah pret-soh fee-soh*
dish of the day	**piatto del giorno**	*pee-ah-toh dell jor-no*
starter	**antipasto**	*an-tee-pass-toh*
first course	**il primo**	*eel pree-moh*
main course	**il secondo**	*eel seh-kon-doh*
vegetables	**il contorno**	*eel kon-tor-noh*
dessert	**il dolce**	*eel doll-che*
cover charge	**il coperto**	*eel koh-pair-toh*
wine list	**la lista dei vini**	*lah lee-stah day vee-nee*
rare	**al sangue**	*al sang-gweh*
medium	**a puntino**	*a poon-tee-noh*
well done	**ben cotto**	*ben kot-toh*
glass	**il bicchiere**	*eel bee-kee-air-eh*
bottle	**la bottiglia**	*lah bot-teel-yah*
knife	**il coltello**	*eel kol-tell-oh*
fork	**la forchetta**	*lah for-ket-tah*
spoon	**il cucchiaio**	*eel koo-kee-eye-oh*

Menu Decoder

apple	**la mela**	*lah meh-lah*
artichoke	**il carciofo**	*eel kar-choff-oh*
aubergine	**la melanzana**	*lah meh-lan-tsah-nah*
baked	**al forno**	*al for-noh*
beans	**i fagioli**	*ee fah-joh-lee*
beef	**il manzo**	*eel man-tsoh*
beer	**la birra**	*lah beer-rah*
boiled	**lesso**	*less-oh*
bread	**il pane**	*eel pah-neh*
broth	**il brodo**	*eel broh-doh*
butter	**il burro**	*eel boor-oh*
cake	**la torta**	*lah tor-tah*
cheese	**il formaggio**	*eel for-mad-joh*
chicken	**il pollo**	*eel poll-oh*
chips	**patatine fritte**	*pah-tah-teen-eh free-teh*
baby clams	**le vongole**	*leh von-goh-leh*
coffee	**il caffè**	*eel kah-feh*
courgettes	**gli zucchini**	*lyee dzoo-kee-nee*
dry	**secco**	*sek-koh*
duck	**l'anatra**	*lah-nah-trah*
egg	**l'uovo**	*loo-oh-voh*
fish	**il pesce**	*eel pesh-eh*
fresh fruit	**frutta fresca**	*froo-tah fress-kah*
garlic	**l'aglio**	*lahl-yoh*
grapes	**l'uva**	*loo-vah*
grilled	**alla griglia**	*ah-lah greel-yah*
ham	**il prosciutto**	*eel pro-shoo-toh*
cooked/cured	**cotto/crudo**	*kot-toh/kroo-doh*
ice cream	**il gelato**	*eel jel-lah-toh*
lamb	**l'abbacchio**	*lah-back-kee-oh*

lobster	**l'aragosta**	*lah-rah-goss-tah*
meat	**la carne**	*la kar-neh*
milk	**il latte**	*eel laht-teh*
mineral water	**l'acqua minerale**	*lah-kwah mee-nair-ah-leh*
fizzy/still	**gasata/naturale**	*gah-zah-tah/nah-too-rah-leh*
mushrooms	**i funghi**	*ee foon-gee*
oil	**l'olio**	*loll-yoh*
olive	**l'oliva**	*loh-lee-vah*
onion	**la cipolla**	*lah chee-poll-ah*
orange	**l'arancia**	*lah-ran-chah*
orange/lemon juice	**succo d'arancia/ di limone**	*soo-koh dah-ran-chah/ dee lee-moh-neh*
peach	**la pesca**	*lah pess-kah*
pepper	**il pepe**	*eel peh-peh*
pork	**carne di maiale**	*kar-neh dee mah-yah-leh*
potatoes	**le patate**	*leh pah-tah-teh*
prawns	**i gamberi**	*ee gam-bair-ee*
rice	**il riso**	*eel ree-zoh*
roast	**arrosto**	*ar-ross-toh*
roll	**il panino**	*eel pah-nee-noh*
salad	**l'insalata**	*leen-sah-lah-tah*
salt	**il sale**	*eel sah-leh*
sausage	**la salsiccia**	*lah sal-see-chah*
seafood	**frutti di mare**	*froo-tee dee mah-reh*
soup	**la zuppa, la minestra**	*lah tsoo-pah, lah mee-ness-trah*
steak	**la bistecca**	*lah bee-stek-kah*
strawberries	**le fragole**	*leh frah-goh-leh*
sugar	**lo zucchero**	*loh zoo-kair-oh*
tea	**il tè**	*eel teh*
herb tea	**la tisana**	*lah tee-zah-nah*
tomato	**il pomodoro**	*eel poh-moh-dor-oh*
tuna	**il tonno**	*eel ton-noh*
veal	**il vitello**	*eel vee-tell-oh*
vegetables	**i legumi**	*ee leh-goo-mee*
vinegar	**l'aceto**	*lah-cheh-toh*
water	**l'acqua**	*lah-kwah*
red wine	**vino rosso**	*vee-noh ross-oh*
white wine	**vino bianco**	*vee-noh bee-ang-koh*

Numbers

1	**uno**	*oo-noh*
2	**due**	*doo-eh*
3	**tre**	*treh*
4	**quattro**	*kwat-roh*
5	**cinque**	*ching-kweh*
6	**sei**	*say-ee*
7	**sette**	*set-teh*
8	**otto**	*ot-toh*
9	**nove**	*noh-veh*
10	**dieci**	*dee-eh-chee*
11	**undici**	*oon-dee-chee*
12	**dodici**	*doh-dee-chee*
13	**tredici**	*treh-dee-chee*
14	**quattordici**	*kwat-tor-dee-chee*
15	**quindici**	*kwin-dee-chee*
16	**sedici**	*say-dee-chee*
17	**diciassette**	*dee-chah-set-teh*
18	**diciotto**	*dee-chot-toh*
19	**diciannove**	*dee-chah-noh-veh*
20	**venti**	*ven-tee*
30	**trenta**	*tren-tah*
40	**quaranta**	*kwah-ran-tah*
50	**cinquanta**	*ching-kwan-tah*
60	**sessanta**	*sess-an-tah*
70	**settanta**	*set-tan-tah*
80	**ottanta**	*ot-tan-tah*
90	**novanta**	*noh-van-tah*
100	**cento**	*chen-toh*
1,000	**mille**	*mee-leh*
2,000	**duemila**	*doo-eh mee-lah*
5,000	**cinquemila**	*ching-kweh mee-lah*
1,000,000	**un milione**	*oon meel-yoh-neh*

Time

one minute	**un minuto**	*oon mee-noo-toh*
one hour	**un'ora**	*oon or-ah*
half an hour	**mezz'ora**	*medz-or-ah*
a day	**un giorno**	*oon jor-noh*
a week	**una settimana**	*oona set-tee-mah-nah*
Monday	**lunedì**	*loo-neh-dee*
Tuesday	**martedì**	*mar-teh-dee*
Wednesday	**mercoledì**	*mair-koh-leh-dee*
Thursday	**giovedì**	*joh-veh-dee*
Friday	**venerdì**	*ven-air-dee*
Saturday	**sabato**	*sah-bah-toh*
Sunday	**domenica**	*doh-meh-nee-kah*